MATERIALIZED VIEWS

MATERIALIZED VIEWS

Techniques, Implementations, and Applications

Edited by

Ashish Gupta

Inderpal Singh Mumick

Foreword by Jeffrey D. Ullman

The MIT Press
Cambridge, Massachusetts
London, England

All source notes can be found on pp. 578–579.

This book was set in Computer Modern by the authors and Windfall Software using LaTeX and was printed and bound in the United States of America.

Library of Congress Cataloging-in-Publication Data

Materialized views: techniques, implementations, and applications / edited by Ashish Gupta and Inderpal Singh Mumick. Foreword by Jeffrey D. Ullman.
   p. cm.
  Includes bibliographical references and index.
  ISBN 0-262-57122-6 (pbk.: alk. paper)
  1. Database management. 2. Data warehousing. 3. Materialized views (Computer science) I. Gupta, Ashish, 1968– . II. Mumick, Inderpal Singh.
QA76.9.D3M3853   1998
005.74′068—dc21

98-17338
CIP

To my father Dharam Paul, my mother Urmila, my sister Shikha, and my wife Nita, who have all unconditionally supported me.

—Ashish

To my father Ichhpal, my mother Narinder, my brother Barinderpal, my wife Ravneet, my sons Kieraj and Saran, and my daughter Ruhani.

—Inderpal

Contents

Foreword

Jeffrey D. Ullman

At first glance the term "materialized views" is an oxymoron. However, the concept has grown in importance along with the development of new kinds of database systems: data warehouses, data-cube systems, billing systems, and information integrators.

In essence, any index on, or summary of, a database is a materialized view. Thus, the creation and maintenance of materialized views can be a major performance enhancement. Because of these and many other applications, a book covering the technology of materialized views is timely indeed.

It is therefore no surprise that many of the papers in this collection deal with the incremental maintenance of views. Conventional data warehouses are reconstructed from scratch, perhaps every night, every week, or every month.

However, a fundamental research question is the development of algorithms that take changes in the underlying data and turn them into changes to the materialized view that reflect the underlying changes exactly. This improvement offers orders of magnitude improvement in maintenance time, as well as allowing warehouses to be far closer to real-time than is possible with previous approaches.

Another very interesting outgrowth of the study of materialized views is the concept of "answering queries using views." Here, the integrated data is virtual rather than materialized, but the existing sources of data are conceived to be materialized views of some abstract, global database. The idea has led to a number of experimental "mediator" systems, such as AT&T's Information Manifold and the Tsimmis system at Stanford. In this book are several of the papers that, although possibly intended for a different application, are ancestral to these important developments.

I have a personal pleasure in seeing this work published. Not only are both authors former students of mine, but I counted among the authors of the contained articles eight other former students, along with a number of other colleagues and friends. Nevertheless, I can claim no influence in this process; in almost all cases, the authors arrived at their interest in one or another aspect of materialized views quite independently and after they left the university.

Finally, the existence of this book and the importance of the work it contains reminds me of something that I, for one, often forget: theoretical work that is well judged and natural often has a way of proving its worth decades or generations downstream, even when cynics have pronounced it worthless.

In the matter at hand, the late '70s and '80s saw a lot of work on "deductive databases" and the theory of relational queries. The applications that I and others had in mind—a new generation of database systems based on logic and recursion—went largely unrealized except for some small commercial attempts and some influence on the SQL3 standard.

However, as natural concepts often do, these theories turned out to have applications far outside what was envisioned initially. As you will see from reading many of the articles in this book, both of the major uses for materialized view technology—maintenance of warehouses and integration by mediators—draw heavily on concepts such as conjunctive queries that by now form part of the traditional core of database theory.

I hope you enjoy reading and using this book. I share the wishes and beliefs of the authors that the material will serve well the needs of a growing technology and industry centered around the materialized view concept.

Stanford CA

Preface

Materialized views have recently seen a renewed interest in the research and commercial communities because of their applications in warehousing, retailing, billing, visualization, integrity constraints, query optimization, and decision support. All leading database vendors are currently implementing materialized views, in some form, in their systems. Several database research groups in academia are also studying materialized views. A workshop on materialized views was held in conjunction with the SIGMOD 1996 conference in June 1996.

The purpose of the book is to collect together important work that has been done on views and to provide a reference for students and implementors on which to base their work. The book will also encourage further research and will make it easier to implement materialized views in commercial systems.

Ashish Gupta
Inderpal Singh Mumick

MATERIALIZED VIEWS

PART I

REJUVENATION OF MATERIALIZED VIEWS

1

INTRODUCTION TO VIEWS
Ashish Gupta, Inderpal Singh Mumick

1 Introduction

What is a view?   A view is a derived relation defined in terms of base (stored) relations. A view thus defines a function from a set of base tables to a derived table; this function is typically recomputed every time the view is referenced.

Why are views interesting?   Views are needed because usually the actual schema of the database is normalized for implementation reasons and the queries are more intuitive using one or more denormalized relations that better represent the real world. Then defining a new relation as a view allows queries to be intuitively specified. The increasing demand for nonrecord interfaces, such as object-oriented and multi-dimensional interfaces, is increasing the demand for multiple non-normalized views of record-oriented base data. Just as indexes supplemented simple access methods to cope with demand for increased efficiency, views supplement basic query constructs to cope with the demand for "higher-level" views of data.

What is a materialized view?   A view can be materialized by storing the tuples of the view in the database. Index structures can be built on the materialized view. Consequently, database accesses to the materialized view can be much faster than recomputing the view. A materialized view is thus like a cache—a copy of the data that can be accessed quickly. Materialized views eliminate the need to expand and recompute the view definition each time the view is used.

Why use materialized views?   Like a cache, a materialized view provides fast access to data; the speed difference may be critical in applications where the query rate is high and the views are complex so that it is not feasible to recompute the view for every query, for example, on-line analytical processing (OLAP). Further, a view may underlie many higher-level interfaces that are collectively queried at a high enough frequency that the view needs to be materialized.

What is view maintenance?   Just as a cache gets dirty when the data from which it is copied are updated, a materialized view gets dirty whenever the underlying base relations are modified. The process of updating a materialized view in response to changes to the underlying data is called *view maintenance.*

What is incremental view maintenance?   In most cases it is wasteful to maintain a view by recomputing it from scratch. That is, the heuristic of inertia often applies (only a part of the view changes in response to changes in the base relations). Thus, it is cheaper to compute only the changes in the view to update its materialization. Algorithms that compute changes to a view in response to changes to the base relations are called *incremental view maintenance* algorithms.

Views are strongly related to, and can form the basis of, integrity constraints and triggers. In this chapter we also explore these similarities and discuss the relationships between materialized views, integrity constraints, and triggers.

2   Example

Consider a retailer that has multiple stores across the United States, and the country is divided into multiple regions for administrative and accounting purposes. Each retailer carries many items and has an elaborate relational database/warehouse for analysis, marketing, and promotion purposes. Consider some of the tables in such a database and their cardinality:

pos(storeID, itemID, date, qty, price) – $1,000,000,000$.
stores(storeID, city, region) – 100.
items(itemID, name, category, cost) – $50,000$.

The pos table represents point-of-sale transactions, with one tuple for every item sold in a transaction. The tuple has the ID of the item sold, the ID of the store selling it, the date of sale, the quantity of the item sold, and its selling price. The stores table has location information about each store—namely its ID, city, and geographical region. The items table describes each item—namely its ID, name, product category, and cost price per unit.

The above data can be used in many different ways.

For example, the regional marketing manager might query the database to find out the names and product categories of the items bought from stores in that particular region. The query for region "Pacific NW" can be written as

```
SELECT  DISTINCT (name, category)
FROM    items, pos, stores
WHERE   stores.region = "Pacific NW" AND
        stores.storeID = pos.storeID AND
        pos.itemID = items.itemID.
```

The above query will be posed by every regional manager to enable a routine inventory analysis. Each query requires that the tables items and pos be joined on the attribute "itemID." Materializing this join as a view will enable the managers' queries to be efficiently answered by avoiding joining the pos table with a table of $50,000$ rows (cardinality of items table). In particular, the materialized view would be

```
CREATE  VIEW items_sold(name, category, storeID) AS
        SELECT DISTINCT (name, category, storeID)
        FROM    items, pos
        WHERE   pos.itemID = items.itemID.
```

Note that the view includes the attribute "storeID" to enable its use in the target query. When either the table pos or the table items changes, the above view can easily be incrementally maintained.

Consider the business development division of this store chain that wants to know the total revenue generated for each store by each category of items. Further, the division is also interested in monitoring the total sales for each region. The two queries are as follows:

($Q1$):   SELECT storeID, category, SUM(qty*price) FROM pos, items
           WHERE pos.itemID = items.itemID GROUPBY storeID, category.

($Q2$): SELECT region, SUM(qty*price) FROM pos, stores
WHERE pos.storeID = stores.storeID GROUPBY region.

Both these queries require that the `pos` table be joined with another table and then aggregated. The `pos` table will typically be millions of rows because it records each transaction. In our example, it has $1,000,000,000$ rows. Thus, it is expensive to repeatedly aggregate the `pos` table. An alternative is to first partially aggregate the `pos` table as follows:

DEFINE VIEW total_sales(itemID, storeID, total) AS
SELECT itemID, storeID, SUM(qty*price) FROM pos GROUPBY itemID, storeID.

The above view will have far fewer rows than the table `pos`. In particular, if we assume that every store sells about $1/2$ the items that the chain carries, then we will get $(100*50,000)/2$ rows in the view `total_sales`, which is a factor of 40 smaller than the table `pos`. The above view can be used in place of the table `pos` to compute queries $Q1$ and $Q2$ as follows:

($Q1$): SELECT storeID, category, SUM(total) FROM total_sales, items
WHERE total_sales.itemID = items.itemID GROUPBY itemID, name.

($Q2$): SELECT region, SUM(total) FROM total_sales, stores
WHERE total_sales.storeID = stores.storeID GROUPBY region.

In addition to avoiding a join with a table that is 40 times larger, the join can be made efficient by building indexes on the itemID and storeID columns of view `total_sales`. The view can then be efficiently joined with the tables `items` and `stores` to answer queries $Q1$ and $Q2$. Materialized views make the above optimizations possible. Note, nonindexed joins are orders of magnitude slower than indexed joins. When rows are added to the table `pos`, the materialized view `total_sales` can be incrementally maintained by simply incrementing the column "total" for the correct row in the view or by adding a new row into the view.

3 Views and Integrity Constraints

Integrity constraints are a way of enforcing conditions on the data inside a database. They are required to ensure consistency in the data contained in a repository. For example, an integrity constraint might require that the age of a person be a positive number. Constraints can also relate multiple tables. For example, integrity constraint $IC1$ might require that every itemID in the `pos` table necessarily occur in the `items` table. This would be a "referential integrity" constraint. Constraints can be more general, corresponding to arbitrarily complex conditions. Commercial database systems such as Oracle provide constraints and thereby enable much cleaner application development wherein the constraints need not be embedded into the code of applications that manipulate data.

Constraints are closely related to views, as explained below. Consider the referential integrity constraint $IC1$ specified above, namely, that each itemID in the table `pos` also occur in the table `items`. Now consider the view `bad_itemID`:

(ICV): DEFINE VIEW bad_itemID AS
SELECT itemID FROM pos
WHERE itemID NOT IN (SELECT itemID FROM items).

Constraint $IC1$ is violated whenever the view `bad_itemID` is non-empty. In general, an integrity constraint can be expressed using a view such that the view is non-empty whenever the constraint is violated [Gup94]. Realizing the constraint as a materialized view then translates to materializing an empty view. Checking the constraint when the underlying relations change corresponds to maintaining the view and indicating a violated integrity constraint whenever the view becomes non-empty.

In fact, some of the early work on checking integrity constraints [KSS87] uses algorithms as the underlying basis for incremental maintenance of materialized views. The work on incremental maintenance of materialized views applies to constraint checking, as explained above. The algorithms may have to be implemented differently because views and constraints are often used differently and are also considered at different times in the life cycle of a database (for example, constraints often are enforced within a transaction, whereas view updates are propagated after a transaction commits).

4   Relationship to Rules and Triggers in Active Databases

Another related area that has been studied in some detail is that of rules and triggers in active databases [WC96]. Rules have associated trigger conditions that when satisfied by the database cause an action to be executed. For example, a trigger condition may check whether more than 250 units of an item are sold at a store in one day, and the action may be to alert the manager of that store. The semantics of rules and how they are implemented is well researched and is not a topic we will cover here. Please refer to [WC96] for a comprehensive treatment of active databases.

Materialized views relate to triggers and rules in many ways. The first is the use of materialized views to capture the conditions associated with rules in the same way as with integrity constraints. However, the mapping is not as simple as in the case of constraints because rules require the notion of state change. For example, a rule may fire whenever the associated condition changes from false to true but not if the condition stays true. Thus, if a view were used to represent the condition part of a rule, then updates to the view matter but not its contents. Thus, techniques for incremental view maintenance are clearly applicable for efficiently checking trigger conditions.

Materialized views are important in one other aspect in this scenario. They enable trigger conditions to be specified on derived relations and not only on base relations, as is assumed in most cases. For example, consider a rule that monitors all those regions whose total sales are below average. This rule can be specified on the following derived relation (the same as that defined by the second query $Q2$ in Section 2):

```
DEFINE  VIEW regional_sales AS
SELECT  region, SUM(total) FROM  total_sales, stores
WHERE  total_sales.storeID = stores.storeID GROUPBY  region.
```

The above view definition itself uses a materialized view. The violation condition that determines when to fire the required rule can be expressed as the following view:

```
DEFINE  VIEW rule_violated AS
SELECT  region FROM regional_sale
WHERE   total < (SELECT AVG(total) FROM  regional_sale).
```

When view `rule_violated` is non-empty, the required rule is violated and the appropriate action can be taken.

Conversely, the use of trigger-driven rules in maintaining materialized views is also well acknowledged. Thus, incremental view maintenance algorithms can be implemented using rules that fire whenever the base relations are updated. Further, many of the optimizations that identify irrelevant updates can be made a part of the trigger conditions. For example, the rules that update the view `total_sales` may have a condition that if the quantity column of a new `pos` tuple is 0 then the rule need not fire (if the item is already in the view). This condition avoids updating materialized view `total_sales` when the view is unaffected. Note, a 0 quantity update may capture inquiries as opposed to purchases—an important market research tool. [CW91] discuss the implementation of a view maintenance algorithm using the Starburst rule system.

5   Active Elements in Databases

Materialized views, integrity constraints, rules, triggers, and Standing orders are different types of active elements in databases and are strongly correlated. Thus, it is not surprising that some of them can be implemented in terms of others—that is, they do not all provide mutually orthogonal functionality. Further, they all require going out of the domain of the database query language in implementing them. Many issues arise in implementing active elements in a database. Below we mention some of the issues, though the book does not cover all of them.

Interaction with Transactions   Theoretically, a transaction indicates a unit of work. However, transactions are rarely simple and often are composed of many smaller units of work (such as nested transactions). Further, "unit of work" was defined keeping in mind when changes to the database must be committed. This unit may not be the same when some other actions need to be taken. Thus, it is not possible to always associate the consummation of an active element with traditional transactional boundaries. For example, an integrity constraint may be such that it need not be checked after each SQL statement but only after the entire transaction. However, some integrity constraints might indeed be so crucial that they always hold and thus require checking after each operation. Thus, when should an integrity constraint be checked? Similarly, one materialized view may need updating only after a transaction is complete, whereas another view that is used inside the same transaction that affects it may require that it be kept current at all times.

Scalability   Active elements add significant computational power to relational databases and do not always fall within the expressivity of SQL. For example, active elements are inherently recursive in nature. Thus, they are not easy to implement in conjunction with relational constructs such as indexes, query optimizers, replicated data, transactions, etc. The execution engine of an RDBMS needs to be enhanced to accommodate active elements and consequently poses demands on the RDBMS and hampers scalability in more ways than one. First, the ability to add more features is hampered given that the execution semantics are no longer those of only SQL but are more involved. Second, it is more difficult to distribute data and to connect disparate databases because many active elements force centralized decision making. Third, the recursive nature of active elements increases the possibility of potentially fatal feedback loops and again hampers their unrestricted (and autonomous) specification.

6   Historical Work

Materialized views were investigated in the 1980s as a tool to speed up queries on views and to provide access to old copies of data [AL80]. Several view maintenance algorithms were proposed [NY83, Pai84, SI84, BLT86, LHM+86, BCL89, SP89b, QW91], analytical models for the cost of view maintenance were developed [Han87, SR88, SF90], and the impact of materialized views on the performance of queries was studied [Han87, BM90a]. The use of view maintenance algorithms in maintaining integrity constraints was also recognized [BC79, KSS87]. A classification and survey of several view maintenance algorithms appears in [GM95] and is reproduced here in Chapter 11. However, implementations of materialized views in research prototypes and commercial systems were missing (with the sole exception of the ADMS system [Rou91]). The benefit of materialized views to applications was never proven, and no killer application came up to force the implementation of materialized views.

Now materialized views are witnessing a resurgence due to a variety of new applications, as discussed in the following section of the book.

2

MAINTENANCE POLICIES
Ashish Gupta, Inderpal Singh Mumick

1 Maintenance Steps

The use of materialized views in any scenario hinges on the views being "consistent" with the underlying data they capture. Thus, views have to be maintained just as constraints have to be checked, rules have to be fired, or any other active element has to be responded to. Maintenance of a view involves two main steps:

- A step to compute the changes to the view that result from the changes to the base data. We call this step *propagate*.

- A second step to apply the changes (computed by the *propagate* step) to bring the materialized view table up-to-date. We call this step *refresh*.

2 Maintenance Policies

A view maintenance policy is a decision on *when* a view is refreshed. As in these other areas, the implementation and semantics of applications change radically depending on when the maintenance is done. Note, the question of "how" is also important but often is an efficiency issue. We discuss the "when" issue further in this chapter because it helps the reader to better understand the applications and challenges discussed in the following chapters. A view can be refreshed within the transaction that updates the base tables, or the refresh can be delayed. The former case is referred to as *immediate* view maintenance, while the latter is called *deferred* view maintenance. When a refresh is delayed to occur outside the transaction that updates the base tables, there are several possibilities for when the refresh actually occurs—just before a query on the view (lazily), after a certain number of changes have occurred (forced delay), or at pre-established time intervals (periodically). A view maintenance policy does not specify when changes are propagated, other than the fact that the propagate step must occur before the refresh step.

We now list the various maintenance policies:

Immediate Views: The view is refreshed immediately upon an update to a base table used to derive the view, as a part of the transaction that updates the base table. Immediate maintenance allows fast querying, at the expense of slowing down update transactions.

Immediate views have to be consistent with the tables they are defined over, as they exist in the current state.

Deferred Views: The view is refreshed in a separate transaction T_1, outside the transaction T_0 that updates a base table used to derive the view. Further, the refreshing transaction T_1 must be serialized *after* the updating transaction T_0. Deferred maintenance does not significantly slow down update transactions.

Several different deferred maintenance policies can be defined:

Lazy Deferred: The view is refreshed as late as is possible to delay the refresh, while guaranteeing that all queries on the materialized view generate the same answers as if the view were virtual. Lazy deferred views need not be consistent with the tables they are defined over, but queries over lazy deferred views have to be answered as if views are consistent, and consistency is achieved by making the lazy deferred view consistent at query time, thereby slowing down queries. Often, the term *deferred maintenance* is loosely used to mean lazy deferred maintenance.

Periodic Deferred (Snapshot): The view is refreshed periodically at pre-established times (e.g., every six hours, every day, etc.) in a special refresh transaction. Periodic deferred maintenance allows fast querying and does not slow down updates, but queries can read data that are not up-to-date with base tables.

The term *snapshot maintenance* is synonymous with periodic deferred maintenance. A view that is maintained in a periodic deferred manner is called a *snapshot*.

Snapshots are required to be consistent with the state of the deriving tables that existed at the time of the last refresh.

Forced Delay: The view is refreshed after a pre-established number of changes have occurred on the base tables used to derive the view (e.g., five tuples have been inserted into the base table).

Forced delay views are also required to be consistent with the state of the deriving tables that existed at the time of the last refresh.

Immediate View Maintenance: The immediate maintenance approach has the disadvantage that each update transaction incurs the overhead of propagating the changes to the base tables and refreshing each view that is derived from the changed base tables. The overhead increases with the number of views, and the approach is not scalable with respect to the number of immediate views.

Further, in some applications, immediate view maintenance simply is not possible. For example, consider a data warehouse that integrates data from several component databases into materialized views at the warehouse. Under immediate view maintenance policy a component database cannot delay committing the local transactions until materialized views are refreshed at the remote data warehouse.

Deferred View Maintenance: Deferring view maintenance removes the propagate and refresh overhead on update transactions. However, deferred maintenance imposes different overhead on the update transactions—the changes to the base tables must be recorded in a log so that they are available for a later maintenance operation. Deferred maintenance also allows changes from several update transactions to be batched together into a single propagate and refresh operation.

However, lazy deferred maintenance imposes significant overhead on all query transactions because a query may have to wait for a materialized view to be refreshed. When applications can tolerate stale data, the query performance can be improved by using forced delay or snapshot maintenance. When applications need a stable data store that is insulated from all changes to the base tables (e.g., a data warehouse that needs to run long decision-support queries), snapshot maintenance can give excellent performance.

3 Choice of Maintenance Policies

An application has to make a view immediate if it expects a very high query rate and/or real-time response requirements. For example, consider a cellular billing application, wherein the balance due is defined as a view on cellular call data and is used to block future cellular calls. Clearly, this view must be immediately maintained. However, immediate maintenance is not scalable with respect to the number of views, so a system cannot define many immediate views. Deferred and snapshot maintenance are scalable with respect to the number of views, so it is desirable to define most views as deferred or snapshot. The following example illustrates how different view maintenance policies may be chosen.

EXAMPLE 3.1 Consider the previous retail database of point-of-sale (pos) information from several stores, extended with information about suppliers, supplies, and customer information. The pos table is itself extended to contain information about returns made by customers. Tables pos, customers, supplier, and supplies are maintained in the database. The pos table contains the detailed transaction data. The customers and supplier tables contain information about customers and suppliers, respectively. The supplies table contains information about items supplied to a store by each supplier. The following materialized views are built:

- CustReturns: Defined as the join between customers and pos transactions that are marked as returns. This table may be queried by stores when processing a return, and it needs to be current.

- TotalItemReturns: Total amount and number of returns for each item (aggregate over CustReturns). This view is used for decision support.

- LargeSales: Customers who have made single purchases of more than $1,000 (join between customers and pos). This view is used for decision support, marketing, and promotions.

- ItemStoreStock: For each item and store, the total number of items in stock in the store (join over aggregates over pos and supplies). This is used to trigger restocking decisions and is queried frequently.

- ItemSuppSales: Total sales for each item, by supplier pair (aggregate over join of pos, supplies, and supplier). The view is used for decision support.

- ItemProfits: Contains the total profits for each item category (aggregate over join of ItemSuppSales and supplies). This view is also used for decision support.

Let us consider the desired maintenance policies for each view. CustReturns should provide up-to-date results because it is used for making return decisions. However, queries to this view are likely to be relatively infrequent, and the view could be maintained only when it is queried (deferred maintenance). TotalItemReturns and LargeSales are used for decision support and marketing, need a stable version of data, and can be maintained periodically (snapshot maintenance). ItemStoreStock is monitored frequently and is used to trigger restocking decisions. It thus needs to be maintained using an immediate maintenance policy. ItemSuppSales and ItemProfits are used for decision support and can be maintained periodically—say, once a day.

■

3

APPLICATIONS OF MATERIALIZED VIEWS

Ashish Gupta, Inderpal Singh Mumick

1 Introduction

While database vendors consider supporting some form of materialized views, application developers are already building materialized views into application code. In this chapter we illustrate some of the applications of materialized views. Most of the applications use materialized views or materialized view maintenance techniques to obtain fast access to derived data, lower CPU and disk loads, reduce communication requirements, reduce code complexity, and sometimes even reduce storage requirements. After discussing the applications of materialized views here, we will describe some of the problems the applications present in Chapter 4.

Materialized views are finding a number of applications, spurred on by increasing computing power and falling disk prices. As table 1 shows, some of these are new and novel applications, while others arise from a fresh look at traditional applications.

We will show that several existing applications can be managed more efficiently and with fewer errors, using materialized views. Some of these applications represent a new way of modeling existing functions, some appear far-fetched until you see exactly how materialized views can be applied, and still others illustrate new concepts and thinking.

We are sure that more applications remain to be discovered!

Traditional Applications	New Applications
Banking	Data Warehousing
Billing	Data Mining
Network Management	Data Replication
Query Optimization	Situation Monitoring
Integrity Constraints	Data Visualization
Switching Software	Mobile Systems
	Distributed CD-ROM Services
	Advanced Messaging Services
	Data Pumping

Table 1 Applications of Materialized Views

13

2 Fast Access, Lower CPU and Disk Load

Materialized views find applications in any problem domain that needs quick access to derived data, or where recomputing the view from base data may be expensive or infeasible, or where queries impose very high disk and CPU loads. This theme underlies most of the applications discussed in this chapter.

For example, consider a retailing database that stores several terabytes of point-of-sale transactions representing several months of sales data, and supports queries giving the total number of items sold in each store for each item the company carries. These queries are made several times a day, by vendors, store managers, and marketing people. By defining and materializing the result, each query can be reduced to a simple lookup on the materialized view; consequently, it can be answered faster, and the CPU and disk loads on the system are reduced. View maintenance algorithms keep the materialized result current as new sale transactions are posted.

As another example, consider a transactional system with `orders` and `items` relations, where a large number of queries take a join between the `orders` and `items` relations. We can precompute this join and store it as a materialized view. Each query can now use the materialized view and can be answered quicker. At the same time, the CPU and disk loads on the system are reduced, as the time and I/O required to compute the join for every query are no longer needed.

3 Data Warehousing

Data warehouses [Kim96, Poe96] are an active area of research and development. All major database vendors, including Informix (MetaCube), Oracle (IRI Express), and Sybase (IQ), have announced data warehousing products. Red Brick Systems and NCR/Teradata are marketing purely warehousing systems. Almost every major corporation is investing heavily in building corporate warehouses.

Despite all of the warehousing activity, there is no universal agreement on what a data warehouse means. To some people, a data warehouse is the database of record—the central data repository of a corporation. These people believe that a data warehouse must be able to store a very large amount of detailed information and be able to combine or integrate data stored in different systems within the corporation. To other people, a data warehouse is a system that stores summary tables and supports OLAP queries. To yet others, a data warehouse is any system that stores data snapshots [AL80]—stable copies of data that do not change in sync with the operational data stores and hence can be used for complex and long decision-support queries.

These three functions are not mutually exclusive, and can be provided in the same system. For our purpose, a system that provides one or more of the functions listed in table 2 will be called a data warehouse.

1.	Collects and stores data from several databases into a database of record (data integration).
2.	Stores summary tables and answers OLAP queries.
3.	Provides a stable copy of the data for decision-support queries.

Table 2 What is a data warehouse?

Materialized views can be useful in each of these three functions. In fact, it is clear that materialized views technology is critical for building good warehouse systems [GM96]. We illustrate how materialized views can be applied for each of these functions.

3.1 Data Integration in Data Warehouses

A database that collects and stores integrated data from several databases is often described as a data warehouse. The warehouse usually integrates data from multiple sources and provides a different way of looking at the data than do the databases being integrated.

Data about related entities—such as customer data in a corporation, or available jobs data on the internet—are often scattered into several data sources. Some of the data sources keep the data in databases, while others may keep the data in file systems. It can be very useful to provide an integrated view over all the data sources of interest and to provide a uniform interface to access all of these data. For example, it is critical for a corporation to have a complete understanding of its customers. As another example, it is much easier for each person looking for a job to look at one place for job listings, rather than find and go out to each and every source of job listings.

Data integration requires one to resolve modeling differences, semantic differences, query capability differences, and inconsistencies between data sources. These are immense problems. One way to do so is to define wrappers on each data source that are responsible for doing the translation of data into a common data model and into a common schema.

Assuming we have taken care of the above problem, there are two architectures for doing the integration: the virtual view model and the materialized view model. In either model, an integrated view, or a set of views, is defined over the different data sources. The view describes how the data are going to be combined together. Common ways to combine data include taking a union, taking an outer join [GJM97], or using complex matching [ZHKF95].

Virtual View Model: In the virtual view model, the integrated database consists purely of the (virtual) view definitions, a querying interface, and a querying engine. No data are stored in the integrated database. Users ask queries over the virtual views, and the query engine translates these into queries over the remote data sources. Each data source, possibly through its wrapper, answers the query and sends results back to the integrated database. The query engine is responsible for combining these results into an answer to the original query.

Materialized View Model: In the materialized view model, the data from remote data sources are brought into the integrated database. The integrated views are computed using these data sets, materialized, and stored in the integrated database. User queries are answered by the query engine by looking up data in the local materialized views.

An integrated database using the materialized view model is known as a data warehouse. The materialized view model requires a lot of initial set-up work. All of the relevant data from the remote data sources have to be extracted and translated through the wrappers. The full integrated views then need to be computed and written out into materialized views. In contrast, the virtual view model requires almost no initial data movement and translation. However, the query response time in the materialized view model is much better than in the virtual view model. Further, queries can be answered even if some of the remote data sources are unavailable. On the flip side, the materialized view model requires more storage than the virtual view model.

The remote data sources stay active and continue to support current applications. This means that updates continue to occur on the remote data sources. The problem of keeping the integrated database synchronized with the remote databases is now the same as the problem of maintaining materialized views in a distributed setting.

To be able to maintain materialized views in the integrated database, we assume that each data source can log the changes that occur at the source, and that the wrapper picks up these logs of changes and sends them to the integrated database whenever they need to be applied to the materialized views. It is possible that the data sources do not have the ability to log the changes, in which case the wrapper needs to provide a way to extract the changes from the data source. In general, extracting the changes from a data source can be expensive and could require that the entire database be cached at the wrapper.

Once the log of changes comes to the integrated database, view maintenance techniques (Part III) are used to apply the changes to the materialized views. Chapters 5 and 19 are specially devoted to maintaining views in an integrated database warehouse.

[LMSS95b] presents another model of data integration. They consider views defined using some remote and some local relations. They materialize the view partially, without accessing the remote relation, by retaining a reference to the remote relation as a constraint in the view tuples. The model needs access to the remote databases during queries and thus differs from a typical warehousing model.

EXAMPLE 3.1 As an example of a data warehouse that stores integrated data, consider a university where the library, registrar's office, and computer science department each keeps a database of student information. The computer science department maintains a relation cs_phd containing, for each student in the department, his student identifier (StuID), the name of his advisor, the number of years he has spent in the Ph.D. program, whether he has finished his course requirements, and the qualifying exam taken, if any. The registrar's office maintains the relation registrar that contains, for each student, her name, address, and phone extension, the number of units she is registered for, and the tuition paid. We assume that if a student is not registered then registrar does not have a tuple for that student. The relation library states the borrowing privilege for each student. The three relations reside in three different databases, as illustrated in figure 1. Each relation has a key, which we underline in the schema below.

cs_phd($\underline{StuID}, Advisor, Year, Courses, Qual$).
registrar($\underline{StuID}, Name, Address, Phone, Units, Tuition$).
library($\underline{StuID}, Borrowing\_Privilege$).

The university graduate office may want to look at all attributes of all students, regardless of what databases these appear in. For this purpose, the university defines an integrated view by joining the three relations on the attribute $StuID$ as follows (we use a syntactic variant of SQL, and we use a subset of attributes from each relation to make the view definition easy to read):

(B):   CREATE VIEW univ_student AS
        SELECT $StuID, Name, Address, Phone, Borrowing\_Privilege, Year$
        FROM cs_phd($StuID, Year$) |&| registrar($StuID, Name, Address, Phone$) |&|
                library($StuID, Borrowing\_Privilege$).

The symbol $|\&|$ is used as shorthand for the keyword "full outer join." Repeated variable names are used to represent equi-joins. Intuitively, the above outer join view contains the tuples in the (inner) join of the three base relations on the attribute $StuID$ and also contains all the tuples of the three relations that do

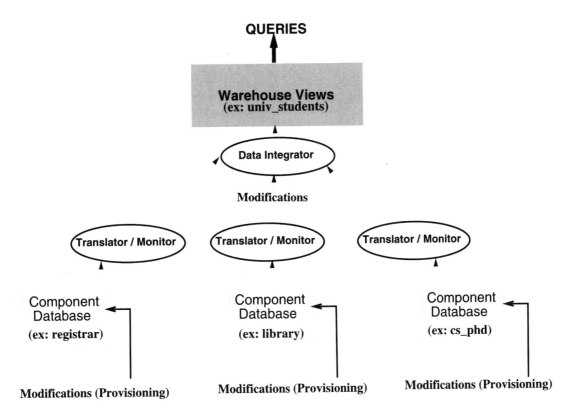

Figure 1 Integrated database as a warehouse.

not contribute to the inner join. The latter tuples have NULL values for the attributes of the relation that did not contribute a joining tuple. As an example, consider the following database (considering only the relevant attributes) in which `cs_phd` $= \{(s1, \text{first}), (s2, \text{second})\}$, `registrar` $= \{(s1, john, holly\ ave, 1234)\}$, `library` $= \{(s1, yes), (s3, no)\}$. The integrated view `univ_student` is

StuID	Name	Address	Phone	Borrowing_Privilege	Year
s1	john	holly ave	1234	yes	first
s2	NULL	NULL	NULL	NULL	second
s3	NULL	NULL	NULL	no	NULL

∎

3.2 On-Line Analytical Processing in Warehousing

A data warehouse often collects detailed data, from one or multiple sources, so that marketing, financial, and business analysis can be done on the data. The analysis can be used to detect trends and anomalies, make projections, make business decisions. When such analysis involves asking a large number of aggregate queries on the detailed data, the analysis is called *on-line analytical processing*, or OLAP.

OLAP warehouses use a special star join or snowflake data model [Kim96]. The aggregate queries asked in OLAP can be related to each other using a lattice, and a data cube operator [GBLP96] is available to compute all related aggregates with one query. Given that the detailed data (called the `fact` table) in an OLAP warehouse can be several hundred gigabytes, it is infeasible to answer a lot of aggregate queries by scanning the detailed data. Materialized views must be used to precompute and store a lot of *summary tables* for the warehouse to have acceptable performance. We illustrate these concepts through an example.

Star Schemas

Consider the warehouse of retail information from Chapter 1, Section 2, with point-of-sale (`pos`) data from hundreds of stores. The point-of-sale data are stored in the warehouse in a large `pos` table, called a *fact table*, that contains a tuple for each item sold in a sales transaction. Each tuple has the following format:

> pos(storeID, itemID, date, qty, price).

The attributes of the tuple are the ID of the store selling the item, the ID of the item sold, the date of the sale, the quantity of the item sold, and the selling price of the item. The `pos` table is allowed to contain duplicates, for example, when an item is sold in different transactions in the same store on the same date.

In addition, the warehouse also has *dimension tables*, which contain information related to the fact table. Let the `stores` and `items` tables contain store information and item information, respectively, as in the following example. The key of each relation is underlined.

> stores(<u>storeID</u>, city, region).
> items(<u>itemID</u>, name, category, cost).

Data in dimension tables often represent *dimension hierarchies*. A dimension hierarchy is essentially a set of functional dependencies among the attributes of the dimension table. For our example we will assume that in the stores dimension hierarchy, storeID functionally determines city, and city functionally determines region. In the items dimension hierarchy, itemID functionally determines name, category, and cost.

In general, an OLAP warehouse will have one or two large fact tables and a number of smaller dimension tables. Aggregate queries in the warehouse have the following common form: They take a join of a fact table with one or more dimension tables, group by some of the dimension attributes, and compute aggregation functions. Figure 2 gives examples of four such queries.

The joins in the queries $Q1 - Q4$ of Figure 2 are in the shape of a star, in that all dimension tables join into the fact table that is at the center of the star. The dimension tables do not join with each other. For example, in our scenario, the dimension tables `stores` and `items` will join into the fact table `pos`, which is at the center of the star. Such joins are called *star joins*, and the OLAP database schemas are called *star schemas*.

Data Cube

The data cube [GBLP96] is a convenient way of thinking about multiple aggregate views, all derived from a fact table using different subsets of group-by attributes. For example, given the `pos` table, one can think of grouping it by (storeID, itemID, date), or by (storeID, itemID), or by (storeID, date), or by (itemID, date), or by (storeID), or by (itemID), or by (date), or just treating it as one group (no `GROUPBY` clause). The query

(C1):   `SELECT` storeID, itemID, date, `COUNT`(*), `SUM`(qty), `MIN`(date)

(Q1): SELECT storeID, itemID, date, COUNT(*) AS TotalCount, SUM(qty) AS TotalQuantity
    FROM pos
    GROUPBY storeID, itemID, date

(Q2): SELECT city, date, COUNT(*) AS TotalCount, SUM(qty) AS TotalQuantity
    FROM pos, stores
    WHERE pos.storeID = stores.storeID
    GROUPBY city, date

(Q3): SELECT storeID, category, COUNT(*) AS TotalCount, MIN(date) AS EarliestSale, SUM(qty) AS TotalQuantity
    FROM pos, items
    WHERE pos.itemID = items.itemID
    GROUPBY storeID, category

(Q4): SELECT region, COUNT(*) AS TotalCount, SUM(qty) AS TotalQuantity
    FROM pos, stores
    WHERE pos.storeID = stores.storeID
    GROUPBY region

Figure 2 Example OLAP queries.

```
    FROM pos
    CUBEBY storeID, itemID, date .
```

computes each of the eight group-by queries that can be obtained by grouping on a subset of (storeID, itemID, date).

Data cubes are popular in OLAP because they provide an easy and intuitive way for data analysts to navigate various levels of summary information in the database. In a data cube, attributes are categorized into *dimension attributes*, on which grouping may be performed, and *measures*, which are the results of aggregate functions. A data cube with k dimension attributes is a shorthand for 2^k aggregate queries, each one defined by a single SELECT-FROM-WHERE-GROUPBY block, having identical aggregation functions, identical FROM and WHERE clauses, no HAVING clause, and one of the 2^k subsets of the dimension attributes as the group-by columns.

Lattices The aggregate queries represented by a data cube can be organized into a lattice. For example, the data cube for the pos table (query $C1$) can be represented by the lattice in figure 3.

Construction of the lattice corresponding to a data cube was first introduced in [HRU96]. The dimension attributes of the data cube are storeID, itemID, and date, and the measures are COUNT(*) and SUM(qty). Because the measures computed are assumed to be the same, each point in the figure is annotated simply by the group-by attributes. Thus, the point (storeID, itemID) represents the cube view corresponding to the query

(SI):   SELECT storeID, itemID, COUNT(*), SUM(qty)
    FROM pos
    GROUPBY storeID, itemID .

Another example of a cube query, defined below,

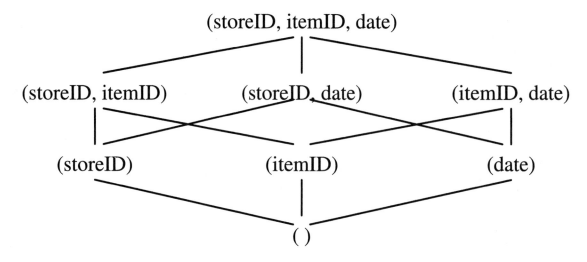

Figure 3 Data cube lattice.

$(C2)$:   SELECT storeID, itemID, date, COUNT(*), SUM(qty), MIN(date)
          FROM pos, stores, items
          CUBEBY storeID, city, region, itemID, category, date .

computes each of the 64 group-by queries that can be obtained by grouping on a subset of (storeID, city, region, itemID, category, date). However, because of the functional dependencies between the dimension attributes, some of these 64 queries are redundant. A group-by on (storeID, city) gives the same results as the group-by on (storeID).

Such redundant computations can be avoided by noticing that the various dimensions represented by the group-by attributes of a fact table often are organized into dimension hierarchies. For example, in the stores dimension, stores can be grouped into cities, and cities can be grouped into regions. In the items dimension, items can be grouped into categories. A dimension hierarchy can also be represented by a lattice, similar to a data cube lattice. For example, figure 4 shows the lattices for the store and item dimension hierarchies. Note that the bottom element of each lattice is "none," meaning there is no grouping by that dimension. Furthermore, although the store and item dimensions depicted here are total orders, partial orders where some elements in the hierarchy are incomparable are also possible—such as in the time dimension, where weeks and months do not strictly contain each other.

We can construct a lattice representing the set of views that can be obtained by grouping on each combination of elements from the set of dimension hierarchies. It turns out that a direct product of the lattice for the fact table along with the lattices for the dimension hierarchies yields the desired result [HRU96]. For example, figure 5 shows the lattice combining the fact table lattice of Figure 4 with the dimension hierarchy lattices of figure 4.

The Role of Materialized Views in OLAP

As should be clear from the above discussion, OLAP involves computing a lot of aggregate queries. If each of these queries were computed from the fact and dimension tables, the system would spend all its time

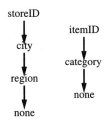

Figure 4   Dimension hierarchy lattices.

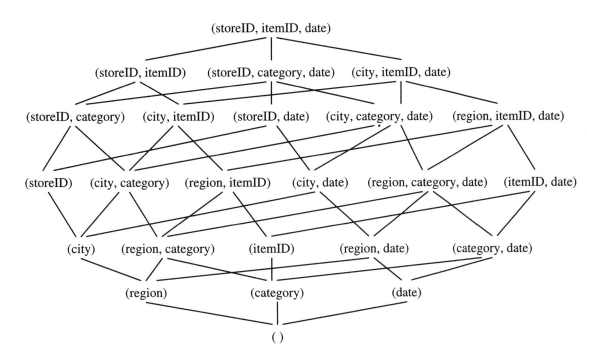

Figure 5   Combined lattice.

```
CREATE VIEW SID_sales(storeID, itemID, date, TotalCount, TotalQuantity) AS
SELECT storeID, itemID, date, COUNT(*) AS TotalCount, SUM(qty) AS TotalQuantity
FROM pos
GROUPBY storeID, itemID, date

CREATE VIEW sCD_sales(city, date, TotalCount, TotalQuantity) AS
SELECT city, date, COUNT(*) AS TotalCount, SUM(qty) AS TotalQuantity
FROM pos, stores
WHERE pos.storeID = stores.storeID
GROUPBY city, date

CREATE VIEW SiC_sales(storeID, category, TotalCount, EarliestSale, TotalQuantity) AS
SELECT storeID, category, COUNT(*) AS TotalCount, MIN(date) AS EarliestSale, SUM(qty) AS TotalQuantity
FROM pos, items
WHERE pos.itemID = items.itemID
GROUPBY storeID, category

CREATE VIEW sR_sales(region, TotalCount, TotalQuantity) AS
SELECT region, COUNT(*) AS TotalCount, SUM(qty) AS TotalQuantity
FROM pos, stores
WHERE pos.storeID = stores.storeID
GROUPBY region
```

Figure 6 Example summary tables.

scanning large fact tables and would be able to support only very limited querying. Further, it would not be possible to have the interactive response times needed by data analysts.

OLAP warehouses speed up querying and system throughput by materializing a large number of summary tables. A summary table is a materializing aggregate view. Figure 6 shows four summary tables corresponding to the queries of figure 2, each defined as a materialized SQL view. Note that the names of the views have been chosen to reflect the group-by attributes. The character S represents storeID, I represents itemID, and D represents date. The notation sC represents the city for a store, sR represents the region for a store, and iC represents the category for an item. For example, the name SiC_sales implies that storeID and category are the group-by attributes in the view definition.

As sales are made in the stores, changes representing the new point-of-sale data come into the OLAP warehouse. The OLAP warehouse then has the task of applying these changes to the summary tables. Using the incremental maintenance approach, either the warehouse can be updated *immediately* as soon as a change is received, or the update can be *deferred* until a time when a large batch of updates is applied to the warehouse. For example, the Wal-Mart decision-support system stores all changes in separate files and applies them in a nightly batch window.

In Part IV of this book, we review several papers that discuss the role of materialized views for OLAP warehouses.

3.3 Stable Copy for Warehousing

Consider a small retailing company selling toys, with a database storing all sales transactions, product information, and shipping information. Each sale is recorded in the database as the sale is made at the cash register during the day. Similarly, information about new products is entered into the system as they arrive, and shipping details are recorded as packages are shipped out.

The company has sales analysts who ask decision-support queries, some of which are similar to the OLAP queries of Section 3.2, and some of which need to look at detailed sales and shipping transactions.

Suppose the performance of the database system permits the analysts to work on the same copy of the data that is being modified by the new sales and shipping transactions. However, it is not acceptable to the analysts that the data they look at should change while they are analyzing the data, in between several queries made to the system during an analysis session. For example, an analyst may be looking at the sales for each toy. Having found that sales for Sesame Street toys are running very high, the analyst might want to compare the morning sales against the afternoon sales for the toys. To obtain meaningful results, and to be able to follow chains of exploration similar to this example, the analyst does not want the data to change between his queries.

The application thus requires a materialized view over the detailed data to be made available to the analysts, with the maintenance of the materialized view being done at periodic intervals, say every eight hours. A materialized view that is maintained periodically is called a snapshot. The snapshot could be in the same database where the operational data are kept (provided the performance of the system can support the operational and decision-support needs), or more commonly, the snapshot could be in a separate database.

4 Data Replication

Every major database vendor provides replication servers to help replicate data from one database into another database. The replication servers allow one to control exactly what data gets replicated and how often it gets replicated.

There are numerous applications of replication servers. Customer and account data in a bank needs to be replicated into a remote site for disaster recovery. A mobile sales force needs copies of a part of the central inventory database for day-to-day operations. To build an integrated warehouse, selected data from the remote data sources needs to be replicated into the warehouse, as a way to obtain the log of changes occurring at the remote data sources. Selected data from the data warehouse needs to be replicated into data marts. A data mart is a copy of a selected portion of the data warehouse meant for local processing. For example, while the sales data for the entire retailing corporation is kept in one warehouse, each regional office may want a copy of the summary data that pertains to that region. Each product manager may want a copy of the summary data that pertains to her product. Such smaller subsets of the warehouse are called data marts.

The data replica managed by replication servers can be defined as a view over the database that is the source for the replica. Most replication servers recognise the need for replicas that correspond to general SQL queries stored as materialized views. The techniques to support join and aggregate materialized views can be used to support such replicas. The techniques for determining updates relevant to a view can help in reducing the changes that must be propagated by the replication server from the source site to the replica site.

5 Data Visualization

Data visualization is the art of creating visual images from large sets of data, so that the viewer may develop an understanding of the data. Data visualization tools typically give the user control over the data set being viewed and the visual images being shown. Graphs, maps, and perspective walls are common examples of visual images. Use of a visualization tool is an interactive experience—the user selects a data set and a visual image, develops some understanding of the data, and then tries to explore parts or neighbors of the data set that look interesting. The user may also choose to change the type of visual tool used to display the data sets.

Data visualization applications thus broadly consist of two components—a data querying module and a graphical display module. The data querying module identifies and computes the data to be visualized, and the graphical display module displays the computed data. As the user learns about the data by looking at the display, she modifies the queries to select a slightly different data set, and the display module then displays the modified data set. For the application to be interactive, it is important that the computation of the new query, and its display, occurs in seconds.

Materialized views fit naturally in the above framework. The querying module defines a view, computes it, and materializes the view. The materialized view is then sent to the display module for an on-screen display. The materialized view may be stored into a table or into an in-memory data structure desired by the display module. When the user wants to look at slightly different data, she changes the view definition, and the display has to be updated accordingly. Materialized view adaptation technology (Chapter 9 [GMR95a]) can be used to incrementally compute the changes to the materialized view in response to changes to the view definition. Assume that the display module is incremental. This means that a currently active display can be changed in response to some changes to the data set, without recomputing the entire display from the new data set. For example, when displaying a set of restaurants on a map, a new restaurant can be shown by adding a point. A restaurant can be removed by deleting its point, without redisplaying the map and all other restaurants on the map. The changes to the materialized view can thus be given to the incremental display module, and the display can be quickly changed to reflect the new query by the user.

EXAMPLE 5.1 Consider the following relations E (employees), W (works), and P (projects):

$E(\underline{Emp\#}, Name, Address, Age, Salary)$.
$W(\underline{Emp\#, Proj\#}, Hours)$.
$P(\underline{Proj\#}, Projname, Leader\#, Location, Budget)$.

The key of each relation is underlined. A graphical interface can be used to pose queries on the above relations using SELECT-FROM-WHERE-GROUPBY and other SQL constructs. For instance, consider the following view defined by query Q_1.

```
(Q1):   CREATE VIEW V AS
SELECT       Emp#, Proj#, Salary
FROM         E & W
WHERE        Salary > 20000 AND Hours > 20 AND E.Emp# = W.Emp#.
```

Query Q_1 might be specified graphically using a slider for the *Salary* attribute and another slider for the *Hours* attribute. As the position of these sliders is changed, the display is updated to reflect the new answer.

Say the user shifts the slider for the *Salary* attribute, making the first condition *Salary* > 25000. The answer to this new query can be computed easily from the answer already displayed on the screen. All those tuples for which *Salary* is more than 20000 but not more than 25000 are removed from the display. This incremental computation is much more efficient than recomputing the view from scratch.

Other changes to the view definition may require more work. For instance, if the slider for the *Salary* attribute is moved to lower the threshold of interest to *Salary* > 15000, then (a) the old tuples still need to be displayed and (b) some more tuples need to be added, namely, those tuples for which *Salary* is more than 15000 but not more than 20000. Thus, even though the new query is not entirely computable using the answer to the old query, it is possible to substantially reduce the amount of recomputation that is needed, and just give a few extra data points to the display module for visualization. Further, the user starts seeing results for her query with a minimal wait time.

A more detailed discussion of this example as well as techniques to adapt a materialized view in response to changes in the view definition are presented in Chapter 9. ∎

An interface for such queries in a real estate system is reported in Chapter 10 [WS92], where they are called *dynamic queries*. Data archaeology [BST+93] is a similar application, wherein an archaeologist discovers rules about data by formulating queries, examining the results, and then changing the query iteratively as her understanding improves. By materializing a view and incrementally recomputing it as its definition changes, the system keeps such applications interactive.

6 Mobile Systems

Palmtop computers, also known as Personal Digital Assistants (PDA), are commonplace. Currently, these are used mostly for managing addresses, calendars, notes, and to-do lists. It is envisioned that the PDAs will be combined with Geo-Positioning Systems (GPS) and Personal Communication Services (PCS) offered over wireless cellular systems to offer a wide range of data services to mobile customers. For the sake of discussion, let the envisioned device be called a Personal Data Communicator (PDC).

For instance, one would like to support queries of the following form from mobile users, including when they might be traveling in a car.

"Which police stations are within a 5-mile radius?"
"Which is the nearest Pizza Hut?"
"What is the traffic status on the various routes to my destination?"

One way of providing (a subset of) such services is to include all the data needed to answer such queries in the PDC. However, as the nature of the above queries illustrates, the data sets will be large, and these queries will impose significant processing loads on the PDC. Even if we could support the data and processing requirements, the data sets would need to change as one travels from one area to another. Further, within one area itself, data such as traffic status, or restaurant locations, change with time.

A second way of providing such services is for the PDC to communicate with a server, very much like the PDC has to connect with a wireless network. A different server could be used for different types of mobile services. The PDC then does not maintain the data needed to answer the queries and does not do the query computation. Assume that the connection is mostly over a wireless network, such as a cellular network. Such a connection has limited bandwidth and is expensive, and it is paramount to minimize the data transferred between the server and the PDC.

EXAMPLE 6.1 Consider a scenario where a mobile PDC user, traveling in her car, asks for restaurants within a 5-mile radius. The PDC first connects to the yellow pages server over a cellular network. The

PDC then transmits the user ID, the query, and the user's own geographical position (using the GPS subsystem). The server opens a profile for the user, computes the query over its database, and sends a map with the location of restaurants marked on the map, along with information about each restaurant.

The user travels for a mile and repeats the query. How should this query be answered?

The naive implementation is for the server to recompute the query and send the new answer back to the PDC. In other words, the new query is treated as being totally independent of the old query.

A better way to implement the second query is to utilize the answers to the earlier query already available at the PDC. The server gets the new query and computes the change in the answer resulting from the movement of the user. For example, the server may now include three new restaurants and remove two of the restaurants that had qualified earlier. The server now transmits only the changes to the PDC. The PDC applies these changes to the cache, maintained as a materialized view, and presents the new materialized view to the user.

∎

There are a number of different ways to use materialized views to optimize the data communication between the server and the PDC. For example, the PDC could compute the differential query needed to compute the changes between the old and new queries, so that the server does not need to remember the last query asked by each user.

7 Switching Software

Network switches, such as the Lucent 5ESS (5th Electronic Switching System), are massive computers responsible for routing and completion of telephone calls, and for providing options such as call forwarding, call waiting, and answering services. The switches have large databases to control their operations. We consider two such data sets here.

EXAMPLE 7.1 The first data set we consider is for terminating calls into subscriber homes. A switch has a number of physical ports, each with its portID. Subscribers to telephone service have telephone lines running from a physical port in the switch to their home. Subscriber lines are identified by telephone numbers (telNum), which are different from physical ports. Internally, the switch maintains a mapping table that maps each telephone number onto a physical port:

portMap(telNum, portID)

The **portMap** table is updated when a new subscriber comes in, or when an existing customer changes her number, or when a physical port becomes defective. The switch also stores a **customer** table of service options selected by each subscriber:

customer(telNum, forwardingNum, callWaiting, answeringPort)

The telephone number is the key. If call forwarding has been activated, *forwardingNum* gives the number to which calls must be forwarded; otherwise, *forwardingNum* = 0. *callWaiting* is a flag to indicate whether call waiting is active. If an answering service has been selected, the port number of the voice mailbox is given by the *answeringPort* field.

In order to complete a call, the switch needs to join these tables, as it needs to know the physical port number to which the incoming call must be routed, as well as the features to be activated on that physical port number. While the above tables are disk resident, the high volume of calls and the real-time call-completion needs require that the switch keep the join precomputed in memory as a materialized view. Further, the materialized view must be maintained incrementally in response to selection of options by customers and changes in the physical port mappings. ∎

EXAMPLE 7.2 The second data set we consider is for routing outbound calls. A switch has a number of trunk routes, each one leading to another switch. Every long-distance call has to be routed by the switch where the call originates onto one of the outgoing trunks, based upon the current traffic conditions on the trunk and the switch at the other end of the trunk. There exist tables giving (1) the traffic on each trunk, (2) the traffic on remote switches, (3) the mapping from outbound trunks to the switch at the other end of the trunk, and (4) the area code(s) terminating in each switch. Routing of all long-distance calls in the United States is done based upon the three-digit area code. The preferred outbound trunk or trunks for each area code can be defined as a complex view upon all these data tables using joins and aggregations:

`routing`(areaCode, trunkNum)

The routing of an outbound call can thus be accomplished by computing the `routing` tuple for the area code of the destination of the call.

However, the switch is required to complete a call very quickly, in seconds, and cannot afford to do the joins and aggregations for each call. The switch must define a materialized view that computes and stores the routing information in memory and must incrementally maintain the materialized view in response to changes to any of the tables that derive the view. ∎

The above two examples are indicative of the fact that most of the switch functions are driven by complex mapping of data sets. The performance requirements for the switch are such that all the complex mappings must be precomputed and stored in memory. Consequently, there are many derived data sets in the switch. In fact, a significant fraction of the very large code base of a switch is devoted to the maintenance of these views and the preservation of integrity constraints to ensure that the derived data sets are consistent with each other.

The derived data sets and integrity constraints in a switch should be treated as materialized views, and appropriate view maintenance techniques should be used. The task is complex because the data sets are kept as C++ data structures in memory. A formal model of defining and maintaining such views is needed. However, doing so could help reduce the complexity of the switch software.

8 Network Management

Consider a computer network consisting of a number of nodes, arranged hierarchically as shown in figure 7. Each node represents a router in the network. A node n gets a request to transmit packets to another node m in the network. The node n can send the incoming packets to its parent, or to one of its children, with a request that the packet be sent further to node m.

Management of such a network requires monitoring the traffic flowing through the network and taking steps to avoid congestion and loss of packets. Routing and buffering algorithms are built into the nodes to do so, and human intervention is also permissible.

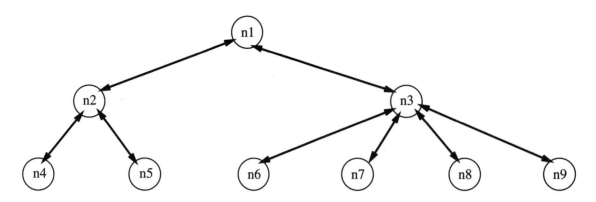

Figure 7   Hierarchical organization of nodes in a network.

Each node keeps statistics of the number of packets entering or leaving the node over the last 1 minute, 5 minutes, and 10 minutes. The number of packets that are dropped, the average waiting time for a packet, and the average size of a packet are also tracked for the same time periods. To manage the network, we require that these statistics be aggregated at each hierarchical level, so that the statistics at each node n represent the aggregate of the statistics of all nodes that are descendants of n in the network. We can define the aggregates at each node as views over the aggregates at its children nodes. However, computing these views as virtual views on every query is infeasible.

For effective network management, the views at each node must be materialized. The views need to be maintained at short periodic intervals. View maintenance technology is needed to define the changes that must be propagated from a node to its parents, so that the views at the parents can be maintained efficiently without looking at any remote data.

9   Chronicle Systems in Banking and Billing

Banking and billing systems deal with a continuous stream of transactional data. This ordered sequence of transactional tuples has been called a chronicle (Chapter 18 [JMS95]). Debit/credit transactions in a banking system and telephone call records in a telecommunications billing system are examples of chronicles. One characteristic of a chronicle is that it can get very large, and it can be beyond the capacity of any database system to even store the chronicle, far less access the entire chronicle, for answering queries. Consequently, the data are stored for only a specific period of time (this can vary from a few weeks, to a few months, to a few years), and even then these data typically form the largest data set in the system.

The banking and billing systems, however, need to answer queries over the entire chronicle to support their operations. In order to validate debit transactions, the banking system needs to check whether the balance in a customer's account, which is an aggregate over all her transactions in the past, is sufficient to cover the debit. A cellular billing system needs to query the total usage and charges accumulated by a customer to ensure that the customer is within the credit limit before completing a new cellular call.

The banking and billing systems therefore must define, build, and maintain summaries in their applications to enable them to answer the queries needed to support their operations. Materialized views provide a way to automate the building and maintenance of the summaries that allow the system to answer queries over the chronicle without accessing the chronicle. At the same time, the application is simpler and less prone to damaging financial errors, and it is easier and faster to add new types of summaries.

EXAMPLE 9.1 (Banking Example)

Consider a large bank with millions of customers and millions of transactions every month. The bank keeps two main tables:

customer(accountNum, name, address).
ledger(accountNum, transactionType, date, location, amount).

The customer table stores the account number, name, and address of each customer. The ledger table stores one record for each transaction between a customer and the bank, giving the account number as well as the type, date, location, and amount of the transaction. The amount field is positive for deposits into the account and negative for withdrawals from the account.

The balance amount in an account can be defined using the following query:

(Qb):   SELECT accountNum, SUM(amount) AS balance
        FROM ledger
        GROUPBY accountNum;

The balance query is of paramount importance to the bank. Every withdrawal transaction must first query the balance to ensure that there is enough money in the account to support the withdrawal. Further, these balance queries must be completed within 1–2 seconds. A customer can also call and check her balance. In addition, the monthly account statement must list the starting and ending balance at the end of the month.

The number and performance requirements of the balance query are such that it is not feasible to compute the balance from the ledger table on each query. The bank thus adds an extra attribute to the customer table:

customer(accountNum, name, address, balance)

and requires that the balance attribute always reflect the result of the query *Qb*. The burden of maintaining the balance attribute is upon the application code. For example, all transactions that update the ledger table must also update the balance attribute of a customer. For banking transactions, which must be optimized for performance and must replicate data for perfect accounting and journaling, the added complexity of application code is significant enough to cause publicly embarrassing errors.

In a well-publicized incident on February 18, 1994, every ATM withdrawal by customers of Chemical Bank (since renamed Chase Manhattan Bank) was posted to their account twice [Tim94]. In other words, if you withdrew $100 from a Chemical Bank ATM on that day, your balance was decreased by $200. If you had $300 in your account to start with, and had written a check for $150 that came in for payment on February 19, the check was returned unpaid. The mistake affected thousands of customers and caused thousands of bounced checks before it was discovered.

The fault was found to be an extra line of code in a new version of ATM software released the previous night. The extra line caused an extra debit in the balance field!

If we were to model the balance field as a materialized view, we could achieve the performance requirements of the bank and avoid the application complexity of maintaining the balance. Let the materialized view be defined as

(*Vb*):   CREATE VIEW balanceView(accountNum, balance) AS
           SELECT accountNum, SUM(amount) AS balance
           FROM ledger
           GROUPBY accountNum;

The maintenance of the balance is now the responsibility of the database system. The application code for transactions that update the `ledger` table do not need to compute the new balance. Further, the database system does not have to maintain the balance within the transactions that update the `ledger` table. The database can use a deferred approach to do the maintenance later, as long as it can guarantee that queries read the correctly updated balance value.   ■

Telecommunication billing systems need to query and maintain several summary fields similar to the balance field in a banking system. Usage and charges of various types accumulated from a phone number are examples of such fields. Materialized views can be defined to compute and store the summaries of interest over the chronicle of telephone records. View maintenance techniques are needed to maintain these summaries as new transactions are added to the chronicle, but without accessing the old entries in the chronicle (Chapter 18 [JMS95]).

10   Distributed CD-ROM Services

Several large reference data sets are distributed by CD-ROMs. Common data sets include geographical maps, road maps, telephone directories, encyclopedias, product catalogs, and help manuals. However, these data sets change frequently, and the users either need to get updated CD-ROMs (usually for a fee), or they need to live with outdated information. In fact, the characteristics of some of these data sets (e.g., telephone directories) are such that any published CD-ROM is guaranteed to be out of date before it even reaches the first user.

We propose a new type of information service, enabled by materialized views technology, that provides current information to users of CD-ROMs. The premise of the service is that while data changes frequently, the changes are small compared to the full data set. We illustrate the concept using the telephone directory data.

Let a version of the telephone directory that is current as of January 1, 1997, be distributed to subscribers of the service. Any changes since January 1, 1997, are stored in an incremental database on a central server managed by the provider of the directory service. The incremental database is small, may be assumed to fit in memory, and can be queried very quickly. The user of the directory service asks directory queries using the software that came on the CD-ROM. A user query Q is handled as follows:

- The query Q is computed locally on the data in the CD-ROM. A local answer A is generated.

- If the user is connected to the network, the query Q is also shipped to the directory server.

  - The server evaluates the query against the incremental database of changes since January 1, 1997, and computes an incremental answer ΔA.

  - The incremental answer is shipped to the user.

- The directory software combines the local answer A with the incremental answer ΔA, if any, to compute the complete answer to the user query.

Several variations and enhancements of the basic service described here are possible. For example, there can be several versions of the CD-ROM data that have been distributed among users. As another variation, the service provider may choose to distribute changes up to a certain date over the network, so that they can be stored on the user's hard disk, and the incremental queries can be executed on the user's machine.

The computation of the incremental answer ΔA, and the combination of the incremental answer with the local answer to compute the final answer, is very similar to doing view maintenance. The local answer corresponds to a materialized view over the base data in the local CD-ROM. The set of changes at the server represents the changes to base data. The computation of the incremental answer corresponds to computing the changes to the materialized view. The combination of the incremental answer with the local answer corresponds to refreshing the materialized view.

11 Advanced Messaging Services

Electronic messages, such as email or voicemail, are common means of communications. A message is typically sent from one user to another by naming the other user, or from one user to a set of other users either by explicitly naming the recipient users or by using mailing lists. For example, a user "John" can send an email message to every student in Stanford University's computer science department, provided such an email list has been defined earlier. The recipient of messages has a mailbox to receive incoming messages. The recipient typically has little or no control on what gets into her mailbox.

One can envision advanced messaging systems where a sender can specify the recipients of a message through views, and a recipient can specify her mailboxes as materialized views over a large conceptual message store. We illustrate the concepts through examples.

11.1 Views for the Sender

Consider three mailing lists:

1. csStudents: A list of all students in the computer science department at Stanford University.

2. undergradStudents: A list of all undergraduate students at Stanford University.

3. aiStudents: A list of all students doing work in artificial intelligence at Stanford University.

A professor of artificial intelligence wishes to send an email to all undergraduate students in order to encourage them to do artificial intelligence. The professor desires that the email not be sent to any student who is already working in artificial intelligence. The professor must define a new mailing list as a view:

```
CREATE VIEW aiTargets(name) AS
  SELECT name FROM csStudents, undergradStudents
  WHERE csStudents.name = undergradStudents.name
      EXCEPT
  SELECT name FROM aiStudents ;
```

Assuming that each mailing list is a unary relation of names, the above view definition defines a new mailing list, which should be the target of the mailing by the professor. If we have a separate relation giving additional information about the students, such as the courses taken by the students, we can use that information as well in defining the new mailing list views. Depending upon how frequently these new lists will be used, they could be materialized and maintained by the system.

11.2   Materialized Views for the Recipient

Imagine that all the messages sent from a user to another user of an email service are available in the following relation:

`emailStore`(messageID, from, to, date, subject, body)

A message sent to multiple users is represented by multiple tuples with the same messageID, one tuple for each recipient. The `emailStore` relation can be viewed as a chronicle, as defined in Section 9, because new messages can be inserted, but old messages cannot typically be removed.

A user of the email service can now specify the contents of her mailbox as a view over all the messages that were sent to her or that she has the authority to read. For example, for a user "Mary," the statement $V1$ below defines a view `InMailbox` that contains the messages that were sent to "Mary" but were not sent to anyone else. The view `junkMailbox` defined by statement $V2$ contains messages that had 11 or more recipients.

```
(V1):   CREATE VIEW InMailbox(messageID) AS
            SELECT  messageID
            FROM  emailstore e1
            WHERE e1.to = "Mary" AND
                1 = (SELECT  COUNT(e2.to)
                    FROM  emailstore e2
                    WHERE  e2.messageID = e1.messageID) ;
```

```
(V2):   CREATE VIEW junkMailbox(messageID) AS
            SELECT  messageID
            FROM  emailstore e1
            WHERE e1.to = "Mary" AND
                10 < (SELECT  COUNT(e2.to)
                    FROM  emailstore e2
                    WHERE  e2.messageID = e1.messageID) ;
```

Using a special function that understands the semantics of the message fields, we can define mailboxes for work-related messages (statement $V3$), for messages about conference announcements (statement $V4$), or for messages about current talks (statement $V5$).

```
(V3):   CREATE VIEW workMailbox(messageID) AS
            SELECT  messageID
            FROM  emailstore e
            WHERE e.to = "Mary" AND
                domain(e.from) = "stanford.edu" ;
```

```
(V4):   CREATE VIEW conferenceMailbox(messageID) AS
            SELECT  messageID
            FROM  emailstore e
            WHERE e.to = "Mary" AND
                keyword("conference") IN e.subject ;
```

```
(V5):   CREATE VIEW talksMailbox(messageID) AS
```

```
SELECT messageID
FROM emailstore e
WHERE e.to = "Mary" AND
      keyword("talk") IN e.subject AND
      e.date = today() ;
```

The definition of the last view uses a special function *today()* that returns the current date. Thus, the `talksMailbox` always shows messages about the talks on the day when the mailbox is viewed.

Mailboxes can even be defined as pairs or triples of messages. Each of the mailboxes defined by a user can then be materialized as a set of message identifiers and the associated messages. An appropriate language may be defined for the mailboxes so that each mailbox can be incrementally maintained as a new message enters the system.

12 Data Pumping

A data pumping service pumps data into several users' machines that are distributed over a network, giving each user the ability to view only that portion of the data that is of interest to the user. Further, the user has the ability to see the data in the format and layout she prefers. *Push* and *broadcast* technologies also refer to similar concepts.

Data pumping services are becoming very common over the internet. Pointcast is perhaps the best known example of such a service. Pointcast lets each user define a profile specifying the data sets of interest and the frequency at which the data should be refreshed. For example, the user can specify that she wants to look at stock prices and business news stories on Apple and Microsoft, and that she should be informed of the new stock prices and the newly released business stories every 30 minutes. Pointcast pumps the data by broadcasting data and having a client process at each user site listen in to the broadcast data and capture the data that are of interest to the user.

Materialized views provide a framework within which to study several of the performance problems faced by data pumping services such as Pointcast. The analogy of user profiles to materialized views is straightforward. Each user of a data pumping service defines a view, or several views, over the data that are to be pumped to the users. The user then requires the views to be materialized locally to the user, which happens to be remote from the data server that contains the data to be pumped.

We thus have a situation where hundreds, thousands, or even millions of materialized views have been defined remotely from a data source. Each materialized view could be in a separate remote machine.

Now, as the data in the source change, we need to maintain the materialized views at the user machines. A good solution to the problem of maintaining a large number of materialized views over a common set of data sources would give us a scalable data pumping service.

13 Query Optimization

One of the primary problems in database applications is that of quick response time to user queries. Query optimization has been gaining in importance, especially with the advent of decision-support systems that require support for efficient ad-hoc querying. Further, new applications warrant more sophisticated optimization that was not required in OLTP systems. A frequently used optimization technique in code optimization, assembly line design, and even day-to-day living is to identify shared work in different tasks and to do the shared work only once for all the tasks. Materialized views offer the same opportunity. Thus, if a database system maintains several materialized views, the query optimizer can use these materialized views to answer queries even when the queries do not mention the views.

EXAMPLE 13.1 Consider the university database of Example 3.1 and in it a materialized view maintained by the computer science department to keep track of the students enrolled in the Ph.D. program:

```
CREATE VIEW cs_phd AS
      SELECT StuID, Name, Address, Phone, Year
      FROM  cs_phd(StuID, Year) ⋈ registrar(StuID, Name, Address, Phone);
```

Now consider a query that finds the addresses of all first-year students to mail them an orientation package:

```
(Q):  SELECT  Name, Address, Phone
      FROM     cs_phd(StuID, Year) ⋈ registrar(StuID, Name, Address, Phone)
      WHERE    Year = "first";
```

Query Q can be answered using view cs_phd as follows:

```
SELECT  Name, Address, Phone
FROM     cs_phd WHERE Year = "first";
```

The above rewrite avoids a join when view cs_phd is a materialized view.   ■

Note, the user need not be aware of what views are materialized because the optimizer makes the choice of whether to use the view; users build their applications in terms of the base tables. The use of the optimizer is critical because blind reuse of materialized views is not always the best strategy (due to missing indexes, tertiary storage, etc.).

The determination of when a query can be answered using one or more existing views is especially useful in OLAP applications where people routinely roll-up to higher levels of aggregation, thereby enabling a direct reuse of the underlying detailed views. For example, consider the data cube lattice of Figure 3. An analyst might first want to see the total sales for each item and store, and cache this aggregate as a materialized view V. Subsequently, when the analyst wants to roll-up the view to see the total sales for each item, the new query can be computed by aggregating the materialized view V, thereby avoiding access to a much larger sales-transactions table. The following example illustrates a more complicated reuse of a materialized view.

EXAMPLE 13.2 Consider a data warehouse with historical sales data for a large chain of department stores with the following relations:

item(<u>itemID</u>, item_name, category, manufacturer);
store(<u>storeID</u>, street_addr, city, state);
sales(<u>salesID</u>, itemID, storeID, month, year, sale_amt);

The item relation contains information about each stocked item. The store relation contains the address of each store. The sales relation contains one tuple for every sale that is made. Consider a typical decision-support application that computes the toy sales made by stores in the state of California during each of the past six years:

```
SELECT  year, SUM(sale_amt)
FROM sales, store, item
WHERE  sales.storeID = store.storeID AND
       sales.itemID = item.itemID AND
       sales.year >= 1991 AND
       item.category = "toy" AND
       store.state = "California"
GROUPBY  year;
```

Now suppose a `yearly_sales` view is materialized, listing the total yearly sales by both item and store for all stores in the state of California.

```
CREATE VIEW  yearly_sales AS
     SELECT  sales.storeID, sales.itemID, sales.year, SUM(sale_amt) AS total
     FROM    sales, store
     WHERE   sales.storeID = store.storeID AND
             store.state = "California"
     GROUPBY  sales.storeID, sales.itemID, sales.year;
```

Notice that the materialized view involves the relations `sales` and `store`, while the query involves the relations `sales`, `store`, and `item`. Using algorithms in [GHQ95] for answering aggregate queries using materialized aggregate views, we can transform the query into one that uses the `yearly_sales` materialized view.

```
SELECT yearly_sales.year, SUM(total)
FROM    item, yearly_sales
WHERE   item.itemID = yearly_sales.itemID AND
        item.category = "toy" AND
        yearly_sales.year >= 1991
GROUPBY  year;
```

The view `yearly_sales` has several orders of magnitude fewer tuples than the relation `sales` because the view has information about only one state and makes no distinction between months and different transactions. Thus, the query using the materialized view is likely to be much more efficient than the query over the base relations. ∎

[RSU95, LMSS95a] discuss the problem of answering a conjunctive query (SPJ query) given a set of conjunctive view definitions. Optimization of aggregation queries using materialized views is discussed in [CKPS95, GHQ95, SDJL96]. The view adaptation results of [GMR95a] can be used to optimize a query using only one materialized view. Materialized views are being used to optimize queries in commercial systems such as the Informix Universal Server and the Red Brick DBMS. The Red Brick solution is more ambitious and includes the ability to dynamically alter the set of materialized views in response to a changing query load.

14 Integrity Constraint Checking

As discussed in Chapter 1, most static integrity constraints can be represented as a set of views such that if any of the views is non-empty then the corresponding constraint is violated. If the system satisfies all the constraints then the initial set of views is empty. Subsequently, when the underlying database changes, then checking constraints translates to maintaining the corresponding views. Thus, view maintenance techniques can be used to efficiently check integrity constraints. Further, materialized views yield a powerful way to implement integrity constraints in real systems because not all constraints are always satisfied in a system and views are useful to capture the exceptions that should not repeatedly surface.

EXAMPLE 14.1 Consider an inventory system that requires the quantity of each stocked item to be less than 100 unless approved by the store manager. For the constraint to hold, the query that selects items with " quantity > 100" should yield an empty result set. If the query results are non-empty then the constraint is violated for all those items that have not been approved by the manager. This same query provides a list of the errant items for the manager's approval. The results of the query can be materialized to keep a record of the approved items. Subsequently, the constraint is checked by ensuring that the materialized view does not grow in size. If the materialized view does grow, then the insertions yield a new list for the manager's approval.   ■

Chapter 27 describes in detail the EKS system developed at ECRC that implements a common framework for maintaining views and checking constraints. Often, the expression to check integrity constraints can be simplified when the constraint holds before the modification, i.e., the corresponding views initially are empty [BB82, BC79, BMM91, CW90, LST87, Gup94, NY83]. This intuition is similar to using the contents of a view to maintain the view.

EXAMPLE 14.2 For the constraint from Example 14.1 let the materialized view contain a single approved item—namely, "toys" with quantity "200." If the underlying database is updated to add another "toy" it is possible to incrementally maintain the view to reflect that "toy" now has quantity "201" by using only the contents of the view and the update (without looking at the underlying database). The corresponding constraint is checked equivalently—the update does not cause any new constraint violation because "toy" would have to be an approved item to be in the materialized view to begin with. By keeping materialized the view corresponding to the constraint, the checking process becomes more efficient.   ■

15   Distributed Situation Monitoring

Distributed situation monitoring applications[1] [SSMR96] have four common characteristics: a *situation*, *data sources*, a *decision maker*, and *standing requests for information*.

A *situation* is the state of a large progressing plan, or a sequence of events, that must be monitored. The current situation is represented piecewise in a set of distributed, heterogeneous, and autonomous *data sources*. Each data source maintains some information relevant to the "big picture," but none represents the global situation in its entirety.

The *decision maker* is a human being responsible for steering the state of the situation toward goal states and away from undesirable or unrecoverable states. The decision maker must therefore be able to rapidly predict the approach of desirable and undesirable global states. However, predicting the states can be difficult, because (1) the decision maker deals in terms of the "big picture" and is not necessarily aware of the location or contribution of the various data sources; and (2) the decision maker is interested only in key decision-relevant indicators, not in the entirety of available information.

The solution is to define and automatically monitor the key indicators, or *standing requests for information* (SRIs). SRIs are predicates expressed in terms of a federated schema defined over data in the remote data

---

[1]We thank Len Seligman and Ken Smith for contributing to this section.

sources. When the SRI is satisfied, an *alert* is sent to the decision maker. SRIs make it possible for the decision maker to focus on his job and not deal with large-scale data transformation and filtering problems.

EXAMPLE 15.1 Consider an airlift of relief supplies to a disaster area. The relief plan must coordinate many activities in parallel, including loading flights from supply warehouses, refueling aircraft and feeding relief personnel en route, and unloading aircraft. Highly constrained schedules must be produced that ensure refueling without overburdening the refueling stations. Status information maintained at both civilian and military airbases along the entire route is needed to monitor the relief plan, as are warehouse inventory information, local weather reports, flight plans, and aircraft characteristics.

An SRI can be used to determine an airbase's capacity to receive incoming refueling flights. MOG ("maximum on ground") is a complex function of many factors at an airbase, including physical runway space, fuel levels, and warehouse capacity. By monitoring the MOG level of airbases on the flights route in an SRI, the decision maker can focus on decision-critical information, and head off an impending crisis by redirecting planes when necessary. ∎

Materialized views are a necessary component of distributed situation monitoring. In the traditional federated database architecture described in [SL90], queries against the federated schema (such as SRIs) are decomposed and executed at relevant data sources, and the answers are returned and combined at the site of origin. Due to many impeding factors—such as intermittently connected mobile data sources, the need to possibly contact *all* data sources when only one relevant change has occurred, and the computational overhead of reconciling data source heterogeneity, computing views, and computing SRIs from base data— this approach is too time-costly to be feasible.

Instead, anywhere a decision maker can issue queries, a custom set of materialized views is maintained such that all SRIs can be answered based solely on information in these local views. As illustrated in figure 8, as remote changes occur at the data sources, they are propagated and used to maintain the materialized views. Changes in the views trigger the re-evaluation of SRIs, possibly resulting in issuing an alert to the decision maker.

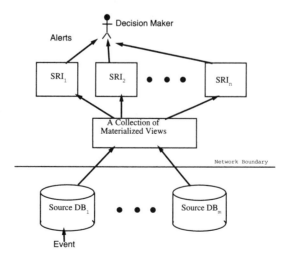

Figure 8 Situation monitoring.

CHALLENGES IN SUPPORTING MATERIALIZED VIEWS

Ashish Gupta, Inderpal Singh Mumick

1 Introduction

We discuss the technical and implementation problems that exist in the field of materialized views. Solutions to these problems will increase the benefit from materialized views to several of the applications discussed in the previous chapter. The problems are presented in three categories:

- General problems, relevant to using materialized views in any application domain.

- Application-specific problems, relevant to using materialized views in a specific application domain.

- Database integration problems, relevant to integrating materialized views into commercial database products.

While some of these problems have been partially solved, this chapter provides a number of open problems for the research community. Further, this chapter can be used by the database vendors or application developers to focus on problems that are relevant to the application at hand. Citations to the recent work addressing these problems are included.

2 General Problems

This section discusses some of the challenges in materialized views independent of the application in which they are being used. The problems span the spectrum of issues such as how to efficiently maintain views, how to use them, how to implement materialized views, and the performance tradeoffs in using views.

View Maintenance Algorithms:

- How to maintain views that use aggregation and/or foreign functions? The problem of aggregate views has been only partially addressed in [GMS93, GL95, Qua96, MQM97]. OLAP and warehousing applications make it important to deal with aggregate views that are more general than SUM, MIN, etc. The need for foreign function views is made important by data integration applications and more general data types as used by Illustra and other object relational systems.

- How to maintain sets of views? The view maintenance process is a series of steps many of which may be shared between different views that are being maintained together. For example, consider two views V

and W, where view V is the join of three relations R, S, and T and view W is a join of relations R and S. Thus, V can be computed from W, making preferable a maintenance expression that first maintains W and then V. A different maintenance strategy would result if W were not a subcomponent of V because then it might not be advantageous to first maintain the join of R, S (depending on size of deltas, possible join orders, etc.). Thus, the interrelationship between the views in the set determines how information flows from one view to another, making preferable some maintenance paths over others. A very important example of such views is that of the aggregation lattice in a roll-up hierarchy of a multidimensional data source.

- How to treat different kinds of updates? It is not always advantageous to model updates of existing tuples using deletions and insertions. For one reason, the model causes information loss because an update of an existing tuple implies the continuing existence of a tuple, whereas a deletion does not. For example, updating an attribute A in a table T can be translated into an update on an existing tuple in a view V if V has the key of T. However, if the update were modeled as a deletion followed by an insertion, then maintaining V might involve joining T with some other relation. Thus, it is useful to have maintenance algorithms that model updates of existing tuples as first-class operations. Updates can be further classified as increments, decrements, non-key, etc., and yield special cases that may be more easily maintainable.

  Further, how do maintenance algorithms change when the granularity of change may be captured by a function that specifies how an atomic value changed? For example, if one of the attributes of a relation is a document and changes to the document are captured by an application then how are those changes applied to a view that has copied the document?

- How to maintain views in the presence of incomplete information? Most view maintenance algorithms assume that the underlying relation and often the old contents of the view are available. However, that assumption is not always true (for example, in a data warehousing environment where the underlying relations are not always available). The work on self-maintenance [BCL89, GJM96] explores some scenarios where the underlying relations are not present. The work on local-checking [Gup94] considers the case where only the updated relation is present. What algorithms are needed to exploit the availability of an arbitrary subset of the underlying relations?

- How to use auxiliary data? If the database system has available the results of other queries then these results can be used to incrementally maintain the view. This problem becomes especially important because it feeds back into maintenance with incomplete information [QGMW96, MQM97].

- How to use semantic information? Often, a database system has available integrity constraints, functional dependencies, and constraints on the possible values for attributes. This information is useful in view maintenance because it helps identify irrelevant updates and optimize computations. For example, primary key information is used to efficiently handle updates and also to propagate deletions to views.

- How to maintain selected parts of views? Often, queries over a view select only a single tuple or a small subset of tuples. When using deferred maintenance, would we like to maintain only those view tuples that are selected by the query? What algorithms and data structures are needed for *partial maintenance* of views?

- What is the complexity of view maintenance? How do we identify query languages that can be maintained in a given space and time? For example, the dynamic complexity classes of [PI94] and the incremental maintenance complexity of [JMS95] characterize the computational complexity of maintaining a materialized copy of the view. [PI94] show that several recursive views have a first-order dynamic complexity, while [JMS95] define languages with constant, logarithmic, and polynomial incremental maintenance complexity.

Using Materialized Views:

- How to determine whether a given query can be answered using one or more of the available views? For example, the result of the query "name and age of people with age>10" can be used to answer the query "name and age of people with age>15." Some work on the problem has been done by [YL87, CKPS95, GHQ95, LMSS95a, SDJL96], but many unexplored angles remain. The problem is especially interesting in the context of aggregate views and OLAP queries.

- What are the benefits of reusing a view? [CKPS95] discusses how a system-R style query optimizer may make this determination. What are the general cost metrics associated with materializing and reusing views? How does one factor in the cost of maintenance? [BM90a] also studies this problem in the context of single join queries. A more detailed study will be useful for determining dynamically whether to use a view and, further, to identify which views to materialize and when to drop a view.

Implementation of View Maintenance:

- How to keep track of the validity of a view? If a query can use a table and a view, how does the optimizer know that the states of the two are consistent? It is important to "expire" views as the underlying relations are updated. Just as in locking, different granularities for expiry make sense because the whole view need not be invalidated at once. What are the ways of tombstoning and maintaining views in part in order to use only the valid portions?

- When are materialized views maintained—before the transaction that updates the base relation commits (immediate maintenance), or after the transaction commits (deferred maintenance)? When doing deferred maintenance, how do we choose between lazy, periodic, and forced delay strategies?

- Can different maintenance policies be used for different views in a system? How would we define consistency in such a case? Are there interactions between different maintenance policies? Preliminary work in this area is presented in [CKL+97].

- What transaction consistency guarantees are possible when the view maintenance is deferred? How do we develop and implement concurrency control algorithms to guarantee serializability in the presence of deferred views? When can we do maintenance outside the querying transaction? Preliminary work in this area is presented in [KLM+97].

- How to minimize the down time for a system while maintenance is done? Shadowing and versioning schemes, batching updates, and computing net effects of updates before refreshing the views are ways to minimize down time during maintenance.

- What data structures are needed to store updates? Even though the views may be relational, keeping updates as a table may not be the most efficient representation. Some updates are best kept as an index structure, thereby making the update process that of an index merge. Further, updates may be annotated with counts to represent insertions and deletions both as mathematical operations and avoiding multiple iterations (one iteration to handle deletions and a second one for insertions), thereby reducing the number of scans.

3   Application-Specific Problems

This section discusses the problems posed by some of the applications discussed in Chapter 3.

3.1   Data Warehousing

Data warehousing is one of the most attractive applications of materialized views and also presents some of the most interesting problems in this area. As we did in the applications chapter, we will first discuss the problems in using materialized views for data integration, and then we will discuss the problems in using materialized views for OLAP.

Data Integration: Using materialized views for data integration leads to the following challenging problems:

- What operations should the view definition language provide to enable an integration of data from different sources? Outer joins [GJM94] and general matching [ZHKF95] have been proposed.

- While the materialized views are available for view maintenance in a data warehouse, access to the remote databases may be restricted or expensive. It is thus beneficial if the view maintenance can proceed without accessing the remote databases. Such a maintenance property is called self-maintainability. How do we make the views self-maintainable? When does it help to make a warehouse view self-maintainable? What are the self-maintenance algorithms? [BCL89, GJM96, QGMW96] represent initial work on self-maintainability.

- When a view is not self-maintainable, what are the other views that can be materialized at the warehouse so that the collection of views can be self-maintained?

- The remote databases need to communicate their updates to the warehouse. Depending on the capabilities of the remote databases, they may send the actual changes, the SQL insert/delete/update statements, or database snapshots. Can data replication facilities in database products be used to send a log of changes? How does one run view maintenance in each scenario?

- When a view is not self-maintainable, and a remote database needs to be accessed to maintain it, how do we guarantee consistency of the materialized view? One such algorithm is given by [ZGMHW95], who also show how a modification to a remote database can be counted twice during view maintenance if one is not careful.

- A materialized view in a warehouse may be modified directly at the warehouse, either to make annotations or to clean up erroneous data. Thus, the materialization is no longer derived exactly according to the definition of the view. What types of changes should be permitted at the warehouse? How does one maintain such views without losing the warehouse-specific modifications? How does one propagate such changes back to the data sources?

OLAP: OLAP queries involve many aggregates, and multiple materialized views (called summary tables in the OLAP domain) must be materialized to support the aggregate queries. The number and nature of summary tables has a significant impact on OLAP query performance, database size, and update times, so that choosing the appropriate summary tables and maintaining the summary tables efficiently are crucial to the performance of the OLAP warehouse. Consequently, we are presented with the following problems.

■ What algorithms should be used to maintain aggregate views? OLAP queries can involve joins of one or more fact tables with several dimension tables, with group-by and aggregation. Multiple levels of aggregations may be taken, as when computing the minimum total quantity sold by a store in each state. Joins between aggregated tables may be taken, as when comparing the sales at each store for the last three quarters. Algorithms to maintain such views efficiently need to be developed. For example, [MQM97] shows how single block `SELECT-FROM-WHERE-GROUPBY` views may be maintained.

■ An OLAP warehouse will have multiple materialized summary tables. These are often related in that there may be several summary tables defined over the same fact table but with different combinations of dimension tables, groupings, and aggregations. Is it possible to take advantage of their interrelationships when maintaining them in a batch process? For example, when the summary tables are all a part of the same data cube, they can be arranged in a lattice and maintained together using lattice relationships [MQM97]. What about the cases when the summary tables are not a part of the data cube? Can such summary tables still be arranged in an (extended) lattice? What are the algorithms to arrange an arbitrary set of summary tables into a lattice? Is it profitable to modify a given set of summary tables so that they do fit into a lattice?

■ It is desirable, especially as companies go international and the nightly batch windows disappear, to be able to update the warehouse and summary tables while allowing the database to be read for queries. How can we do so without slowing down the updates? How can we guarantee stability and consistency to the queries that execute while the update process is running? Versioning has been proposed as one way to achieve concurrent updates and queries [QW97].

■ The performance of OLAP queries can be improved by storing more and more summary tables. However, each summary table causes two overheads. First, the summary table consumes extra space, and we may not have large amounts of extra space in a warehouse. Note that a warehouse has large amounts of base data to start with. Second, each summary table needs to be maintained after the base tables are updated. The OLAP warehouses are typically updated in batches during a nightly batch window. The nightly batch window involves updating the base tables (if any) stored at the warehouse and maintaining all the materialized summary tables. The warehouse is usually unavailable to readers while the summary tables are being maintained, due to the large number of updates that need to be applied. Because the warehouse must be made available to readers again by the next morning, the time available for doing all the updates and the maintenance is limited. Further, the length of the nightly batch window itself shrinks when a company goes nationwide, and again when it goes international. In short, the total time available for maintenance can be a limiting factor in the number of summary tables that can be made available in the warehouse.

Given hundreds of possible summary tables in a warehouse, how should we choose the summary tables that should be materialized while satisfying the storage space and maintenance time constraints? What about a situation when the space and maintenance times are not hard constraints but represent costs in the system? How do we optimize a combination of query performance, space cost, and maintenance time cost when choosing the summary tables to materialize? Most of these problems are NP complete. A framework to think about the problem of choosing materialized views is presented in [Gup97]. A greedy heuristic solution for choice of data cube views under space constraints is discussed in [HRU96].

■ Warehouses have very few, if any, deletions and updates of existing tuples in the fact tables. Most of the changes involve insertion of new tuples into the fact table. How do we optimize the maintenance of the summary tables given that all updates are insertions into base tables? For example, suppose that in a retailing warehouse, the newly inserted sales transactions are always for a new date. Consider a summary table for which date is a group-by field. The newly inserted sales transactions can only cause insertions into the summary table. How can we optimize maintenance and availability of such views?

3.2   Data Replication

Data replication is currently supported by database vendors as a way to replicate individual relations or entire databases in a distributed system. Data replication works by capturing the changes occurring at the source site using triggers, or by looking at the log. The changes are then shipped to the destination site, where they are applied on the replica.

We would like to replicate generic views, including join and aggregate views, over base tables that may reside at multiple sites. This requires that we develop maintenance algorithms that work with change logs coming from distributed sites. Further, we would like to minimize the amount of information that is shipped from the source sites to the destination site (*data subscription problem*). One issue is whether some of the computation needed to maintain the view should occur at the source site. For example, consider a site A that needs to maintain an aggregate of a table R at site B. Site B can ship all changes to table R on to site A, or site B can do partial aggregation of the changes to table R locally and ship only the aggregated result on to site A. The latter scheme has the advantage that the amount of data being shipped is reduced. However, it also has the disadvantage that site B must be aware of exactly what views are being maintained at site A. A mechanism to translate materialized view definitions at site A into the aggregations that must be done and shipped from site B is needed. A similar issue arises when the views at site A are selections, projections, or joins over tables at site B. When the views are over tables from multiple sites, we may want to set up semi-join style reducer programs for doing maintenance.

Maintaining the logs that capture the updates to base tables poses interesting problems when multiple replicas are maintained because each delta in the log now applies to a subset of the replicas and has to be phased out when it has been propagated to all the replicas.

3.3   Data Visualization

Data visualization applications present problems of two types for materialized views.

The first issue is that views need to be maintained in response to changes in the view definition, rather than in response to changes in the base data. For instance, in Chapter 5, Example 5.1, we consider an environment where a user changed the selection conditions in the view definition and wanted the system to respond to such changes. The problem of updating a view in response to changes in the view definition is called view adaptation [GMR95a].

The second issue is that data visualization tools often store data in memory, in specialized data structures. In such a scenario, we need view adaptation techniques that directly maintain views stored in the specialized data structures. When designing the internal data structures, one should write interfaces that permit individual data points to be inserted, deleted, or updated. The refresh step of view maintenance must then directly use this interface to change the in-memory data structures. How should the database support materialized views so that such extensions to the refresh step can be easily defined as user functions?

3.4 Mobile Systems

Users of mobile systems typically ask spatial queries, related to the location of the user and the queried objects.

How do we maintain the spatial queries as a user moves? The movement of a user can be modeled in two ways. The first model considers the user's position to be a data point. A movement by the user then corresponds to a change in the base data, and the view must be maintained in response to such a data change. The second model considers the user's position to be a part of the query defining the view. A movement by the user then corresponds to a change in the view definition itself, and the view must be adapted in response to such a definition change.

3.5 Switching Software

The problems in using materialized views in switching software are very similar to the second issue for data visualization, in that switches also keep data in main memory, in special data structures. The view data need to be modified upon changes to data in the underlying relational system or upon direct changes in the main memory system. A main memory implementation of the maintenance algorithms is needed. How should views be defined over data in main memory that is not tabular? When can maintenance algorithms for such views be derived automatically?

3.6 Chronicle Systems in Banking and Billing

Chronicle systems in banking and billing store a number of aggregate views or derived columns that can be defined as aggregate views. These views and/or derived columns often need to be updated after every insertion to the chronicle. Such an update can impose a significant overhead in high-transaction environments such as billing and banking. It is thus important to allow only those aggregate views that can be maintained very efficiently. For example, we may choose aggregate views for which the complexity of maintenance is very low [JMS95]. How should we choose the storage structures so that all the aggregate views that must be updated after a transaction can be updated with a minimal number of I/Os? How do we ensure that the different views affected by a single transaction do not duplicate maintenance computations?

The amount of transactional data in a chronicle system can be very large, and it is often not possible to store the transactional data beyond a certain period of time (typically a few months). However, suppose we are given a set of interesting aggregate queries we would like to answer as if the entire transactional data set was stored in the system. Can we identify aggregate views that we can materialize, so that the queries can be answered even after most of the transactional data have been discarded? Such views must also be maintainable after the transactional data have been discarded.

3.7 Distributed CD-ROM Services

Consider a distributed CD-ROM telephone directory service with thousands of subscribers, each having a certain version of the directory CD-ROM. The central server needs to run incremental queries for a subscriber over the data set that has changed (log) since the version used by the subscriber. How should the changed data set be maintained as the number of versions increases? When the number of versions is small (say, 1–10), the server may be able to store a separate log for each version. However, as the number of versions becomes larger, we must share the logs between different versions. How should the sharing be done? How can we efficiently extract the logs relevant to a particular subscriber?

Now consider a situation where the service provider distributes two or more data sets on a CD-ROM, and the user can ask queries involving joins of these data sets. The incremental queries at the server now involve joins between the logs and the main data sets. Thus, the server must also maintain different versions of the main data sets, one for each version of the data set with any user. How should we share the data sets between different versions? Can we define the log and data set versions as views over a common data store?

3.8   Advanced Messaging Systems

Use of views to define mailing lists and incoming mailboxes represents a new and novel application of views. Mailing lists are unary tables of email addresses, and mailboxes are unary tables of messages. What are the languages in which these views should be defined? The self-maintainability issue is important for mailbox views, because we would like to maintain a mailbox without accessing all past email messages that have been sent through the system. The language design should take self-maintainability into consideration. The maintenance policy of the mailboxes is another issue. Should the mailboxes be maintained immediately, as soon as a message enters the system, or should they be maintained in a deferred manner, when the messages are read? It appears that a two-tiered approach may be necessary, wherein some mailboxes are maintained immediately, and others are maintained in a deferred manner. For example, a mailbox that shows messages about talks being delivered "today" should be maintained in a lazy or periodic deferred manner.

3.9   Data Pumping

The data pumping paradigm presents the obvious problem of maintaining thousands of materialized views in a distributed framework. A naive solution is to broadcast all changes to the data sets to each client that stores materialized views and to let each client maintain its views locally. This solution requires that the views at each client be self-maintainable, and that each client be willing to receive and process changes to all data sets, even those data sets that are irrelevant to the interests of the node. Although the self-maintainability assumption is reasonable, we believe that the second requirement presents significant overhead upon client resources, especially when the clients are PCs and the data sets are huge. Thus, we need a solution wherein each client receives only the changes relevant to the views at the client. For example, is it possible to cluster views into "equivalence" classes where the views in each class have the same set of relevant updates? All the views may not be strictly equivalent with respect to relevant updates: in which case, how should they be grouped approximately? What are the algorithms for clustering views into a manageable number of classes whose maintenance can be optimized at the data server?

3.10   Distributed Situation Monitoring

Recall that a distributed situation monitoring system has a three-layered architecture—data sources, a federated cache, and the SRI monitors. Each of these levels defines a view over the data in the lower level. The first problem is choosing what views should be materialized, and at what level. One would like to avoid materializing the same information multiple times in the federated cache and in several of the SRIs. However, the SRIs actually trigger events, so a trigger must be definable when a change occurs at an SRI.

The data subscription problem discussed in Section 3.2 on data replication and in Section 3.9 on data pumping is also one of the major problems in distributed situation monitoring. Delivering data from the sources to the federated cache involves four big steps:

- Extraction of data from the data source;

- Transfer of data to the federated system;

- Cleansing of data;

- Maintenance of views using the cleansed data.

Each of these steps is expensive. For example, transfer from mobile data sources is not guaranteed, because connections are intermittent. Some data cleansing must be done by hand (resolving inconsistencies, filling in missing values). Therefore, it is important to minimize the amount of data delivery by filtering out the irrelevant data, because data irrelevant to the cached views must go through all the four steps. A technique where the data sources are given relevance tests to apply on all updates before transmitting them to the federated cache would be very useful.

Different materialized views at the federated cache may be refreshed at different times, depending upon the availability of the data sources from which the data are derived. One needs to understand the relative consistency of different views and the impact on queries that access materialized views that are mutually inconsistent. For example, consider an SRI for tracking the movement of a ship using two separate data sensors. The first data sensor tracks the latitude of the ship and transmits the latitude every minute to the federated cache. The second sensor tracks the longitude of the ship and transmits the longitude every hour to the federated cache. The SRI uses a query over these two data sets and observes that the ship is moving in a zigzag manner through the ocean, when the ship is actually sailing in a straight line. Can we provide a way to understand such mutual inconsistencies between materialized views consisting of data having mixed levels of currency? Should we disallow queries over mutually inconsistent data? Can we provide a way to specify "currency requirements" for materialized view data and then infer how often the underlying data sets must be refreshed? Alternatively, given the refresh specifications of underlying data sets, can we infer whether the currency requirements can be achieved or not?

4   Database Systems

This section discusses some of the issues that are relevant for supporting materialized views in commercial database systems.

- How should SQL be extended to support materialized views? Is there a need for a language construct for the user to specify that a view should be materialized and the maintenance policy that should be used to maintain materialized views? Should a user be able to give an SQL command to ask for a view to be maintained? Or should view materialization be treated purely as an optimization technique hidden from the user? The ANSI SQL standard currently does not support materialized views, and there is an attempt not to include optimization-level commands in SQL. However, snapshots and forced delay materialized views result in observable differences in query answers, and so at least these should be supported in the ANSI SQL standard.

- Should the materialization of a view have a separate name from the view itself? For example, one may ask that a view V be materialized into a table M. Then, queries over V would conceptually lead to evaluation of V as a virtual view. Queries over M would look up the materialized table, whether or not it has been maintained since the last updates to the base tables.

- How should the existing query optimizers be extended with knowledge of materialized views? The query optimizers should be capable of optimizing queries by using materialized views, as well as optimizing the maintenance expressions for all the views in the system.

- Should the system be able to maintain deferred views at any time there is spare capacity in the system? Lazy deferred maintenance imposes extra overhead on query transactions. Perhaps by doing the maintenance asynchronously, sometime between the update and the query, the maintenance overhead can be borne at a time when the database system is not busy. However, if the maintenance delay is built into the semantics of snapshot view, we may require that snapshots be maintained only at scheduled intervals.

- When a system has multiple materialized views, with different maintenance policies, it becomes difficult for the user to understand exactly the mutual consistency of the data in these materialized views. Can we somehow group the views together so that the mutual consistency is easy to understand? Is the viewgroup model of [CKL+97] an appropriate model for doing the grouping?

- What is the impact of materialized views on the concurrency control algorithms in the system? What special data structures are needed to ensure that view maintenance activities do not cause extra conflicts with queries and update transactions?

- If materialized views were to be supported as a layer on top of a database system, what minimal features might we require from the core database system so that the implementation would be efficient? For example, it is evident that the system would need to provide a mechanism to track changes and store them in an internal table where they could be accessed by the maintenance algorithms. Further, such change tables should be managed by the database system so as to minimize conflicts between maintenance operations and user queries and updates.

- How does a system dynamically decide the set of materialized views? The queries posed to the system should determine this set. Further, which indexes should be built on the materialized set? How should this set be decided dynamically? Should the index maintenance itself be incremental if the view is maintained incrementally?

- Some class of views are updateable—especially those needed in many replication systems: for example, a sales database that is horizontally partitioned and replicated by many sales agents who deal with mutually exclusive geographic areas. How does the underlying system support updateability? How does it resolve resulting conflicts?

- Metadata management is an important issue. How should materialized views be tracked to allow Database Administrators to effectively manage the system?

PART II

APPLICATIONS OF MATERIALIZED VIEWS

Applications of Materialized Views

This part of the book contains six chapters about of the applications that are driving the work on materialized views.

Chapters 5 and 6 address data integration and data warehousing. The next two chapters focus on reuse of views to answer queries in a variety of contexts; in particular query optimization. Chapter 10 discusses the use of materialized views in the context of a real estate application. Chapter 9 describes techniques for supporting interactive modification of user queries to enable applications like visualization, mining, and decision support. Each chapter contains other specific applications as targeted by their authors. The perspective of each author with regard to the target application is different than our perspective in characterizing applications in Chapter 3. Hence the reader will notice that the techniques in individual chapters apply to multiple application areas from Chapter 3.

Chapter 5 defines the concept of self-maintainable views - namely views that can be maintained using only the contents of the view and the database modifications without accessing any of the underlying databases. Self-maintainability is a desirable property for efficiently maintaining large views in applications that require fast response and high availability. For example, Data Warehousing wherein views integrate data from multiple databases. In addition to warehousing, self-maintainable views are useful in data visualization (where a view captures a rendition that can be quickly updated in response to a stimulus without accessing all of the underlying data), in mobile systems (where precious bandwidth is saved by transmitting only updates), in integrity constraint checking, in chronicle systems, and others.

Chapter 6 uses materialized views for data integration wherein objects in different databases together constitute a larger object in the real world - *i.e.* one object in the integrated system is obtained by combining objects from multiple different databases. This problem is central to information integration in Cooperative Information Systems. Materialized Views are used to model the combined object. The chapter describes a framework for data integration that captures the choices available for building a data integration system using materialized views. (1) The "matching" criterion used to combine component objects. For example, objects may be combined using "look-up" tables, user-defined functions, boolean conditions, historical conditions, and intricate heuristics. (2) The proportions of the integrated data that is materialized, (3) The rate at which the underlying data objects may change, (4) the maintenance strategy for the materialized integrated object, and (5) the frequency with which changes are propagated from the underlying data to the integrated objects. The authors have built a data integration system that allows users to chose different points in the above solution space. Different points in this solution space better suit different applications described in Chapter 3. For example, a chronicle system needs simple matching criterion, high rate of change of underlying sources, full materialization of views, and incremental maintenance. In contrast a warehousing system needs lower update frequency but complex matching criterion. The chapter lays the foundations for analyzing the tradeoffs for different applications.

Chapters 7, 8, and 9 discuss how to use materialized views to answer queries. The question has two components - (1) can the given query be reformulated to use the available views, and (2) does the reuse of views save resources like computation time. A solution to problem (1) is useful by itself because it can be used to answer queries when materialized views are available but the underlying data is not available. The results are useful in applications like query optimization, visualization, mobile systems, mining, replication, warehousing, switching software, decision support etc.

Chapter 7 considers problems (1) and (2) when the views and queries are Select-Project-Join queries. The chapter solves problem (2) by addressing how a relational query optimizer should choose one of the possible alternatives for reusing views. Note, always using a materialized view can result in significantly worse executions than if no views were used to answer a query. The chapter presents a simple, readily implementable extension to the widely used system-R style dynamic programming algorithm to enable a cost-based decision for deciding whether or not to use materialized views to answer a query. Chapter 8 considers problem (1) for SPJ views and queries that may also use disjunction and comparison operators. The chapter gives algorithms and complexity analysis of the solutions for the problem.

Chapter 9 considers a variant of problem (1) - namely when the query is a variant of the view. Such scenarios are common when users interactively and dynamically change their queries and expect to see results quickly. The chapter considers all possible redefinitions of SQL Select-From-Where-Groupby-Union-Except views and shows how the new view can be "adapted" from the old materialized view; sometimes using extra stored information. Data archaeology, data visualization, decision support are some applications considered in the chapter.

5

DATA INTEGRATION USING
SELF-MAINTAINABLE VIEWS

Ashish Gupta, H. V. Jagadish, Inderpal Singh Mumick

ABSTRACT

In this chapter we define the concept of *self-maintainable* views – these are views that can be maintained using only the contents of the view and the database modifications, but without accessing any of the underlying databases. We derive tight conditions under which a view is self-maintainable, and we give algorithms to self-maintain several types of select-project-join views upon insertions, deletions and updates. Self-maintainability is a desirable property for efficiently maintaining large views in applications where fast response and high availability are important. One example of such an environment is Data warehousing wherein views are used for integrating data from multiple databases.

1 Introduction

Most large organizations have related data in distinct databases. Many of these databases may be legacy systems, or systems separated for organizational reasons like funding and ownership. Integrating data from such distinct databases is a pressing business need. A common approach for integration is to define an integrated view and then map queries on the integrated view onto queries on the individual systems. This model is not good for applications where response time is critical, or for decision support applications with complex queries. Further, in this model, the availability of the integrated view is the lowest denominator of the availabilities of all databases touched by a query. Finally, such query translation can become almost impossible when some of the underlying "databases" are actually flat files, or other non-relational systems.

We propose an alternative model, good for applications where fast response to queries and high availability are important: The integrated view is materialized and stored in a database. Queries on the view are then answered directly from the stored view. This approach involves the additional storage expense for the materialized integrated view. Also, we need to maintain the integrated view current as the underlying databases change. Maintaining the integrated database current requires efficient incremental view maintenance techniques.

It may be expensive or impractical to obtain much more than just a periodic report of local updates from each underlying database. Even if an underlying database does not provide relational query support, one can require it to provide a log of changes it makes. Under such circumstances, it becomes crucial that the integrated view be *self-maintainable* (Self-M), meaning that view maintenance should be possible without requiring access to any underlying database, and without access to any information beyond the view itself and the log of the changes. Self-M can be used in data warehousing environments not only to

53

efficiently maintain views but also to avoid concurrency control problems faced by generic view maintenance strategies [ZGMHW95].

We study the syntactic restrictions for SPJ view to be self-M, and gives the corresponding maintenance algorithms. Using the syntactic restrictions it is possible for a data integrator to write self-M views that are efficiently maintainable. Thus, even if a view itself is not self-M, a super-set of the view may often be self-M. The full version of this chapter appears as [GJM94].

Results

- We define the self-maintenance problem as the problem of maintaining a view in response to insertions, deletions, or update (collectively referred to as modifications) using only the view and the set of changes to the referenced relations (without access to the full referenced relations). We obtain complete conditions and syntactic restrictions under which SPJ views (which are views defined using the select-from-where clause of SQL) are self-M with respect to insertions, deletions, and updates and present algorithms for their self-maintenance.

- We model updates directly for the purpose of view maintenance. We show that view maintenance is easier when updates are modeled directly rather than as a set of deletions and insertions; in particular updates can often be self-maintained even when insertions cannot be self-maintained.

2   Background and Notation

We consider SPJ views, *i.e.*, SELECT -Π-JOIN views written using SELECT -FROM -WHERE clauses. A SP (SELECT -Π) view is a SPJ view with only one relation occurrence in the FROM clause.

Definition 2.1 (Distinguished Attribute): An attribute A of a relation R is said to be distinguished in a view V if attribute A appears in the SELECT clause defining view V.   ■

We use keys to define updates and to derive self-maintenance algorithms. A relation may have several keys, and any one of these could be used for any of the results we derive (key(R) refers to the key attributes of R).

Definition 2.2 (Updates): For a relation R that has a key, a tuple in R is said to be updated if one or more attributes of the tuple are assigned a value different from its original value. An update to tuple r that results in tuple r' is represented as $\mu(r, r')$.   ■

For each of the three types of modifications (inserts, deletes, and updates) we identify classes of views that are self-M with respect to the modified relation R. We omit mentioning "with respect to modified relation R" when the context makes it clear that relation R is modified. Also, henceforth the phrase "with respect to R" implicitly assumes that R is used in the view under consideration.

Definition 2.3 (Self Maintainability with respect to a Modification): A view V is said to be self-M with respect to a modification type (insertion, deletion, or update) if for all database states, the view can be self-maintained in response to a modification of that type to the base relations.   ■

Definition 2.4 (Local and Join Predicates): Consider a predicate $p(\bar{X})$ in the WHERE clause of a view. $p(\bar{X})$ is said to be a local predicate if all variables in $\bar{X}$ appear in a single relation in the FROM clause. Otherwise, $p(\bar{X})$ is said to be a join predicate .   ■

Definition 2.5 (Derivation tree [RSUV89]):(Informal) A derivation tree for a tuple t is a tree representation of the manner in which the tuple is derived from base relations. For a tuple t in a base relation, the derivation tree consists of a single node labeled with tuple t. For a tuple t in a view defined as a join between relations $R_1, \ldots, R_k$, a derivation tree consists of a root node labeled with the tuple t, and one child node for each of the tuples $(r_1 \in R_1, r_2 \in R_2, \ldots, r_k \in R_k)$ that join to derive tuple t. ∎

Definition 2.6 (Tuple Derivation): Consider view V defined using relation R, and possibly other relations. A tuple r in R derives a tuple v in V if r appears in some derivation tree for tuple v. ∎

In the chapter we consider SP and SPJ views that are satisfiable [Shm87]. That is, there exists a database for which the view is non-empty. Unsatisfiable views are always empty and hence trivially self-M. Also, we assume that the views do not include valid predicates (like $(X > 10 \text{ OR } X < 20)$).

3 Self-Maintenance for SPJ Views

Whether a view is self-M depends on both the definition of the view and on the type of modification, and also on other finer distinctions such as which attribute of a relation is updated, or the actual value of the modified attribute, or the presence of functional dependencies and other integrity constraints. In this chapter we restrict ourselves to classifying self-maintainability with respect to the relation being modified, the type of modification, and key information. We do not consider the other finer granularity distinctions in this chapter.

Insertions Views are self-M for insertions only under very limited circumstances. We prove that it is not possible to self-maintain an SPJ (select-project-join) view joining at least two distinct relations upon an insertion into a component relation. Even a view involving a self-join of a relation with itself may not be self-M.

Theorem 3.1 *The self-maintainability of an SPJ view in response to insertions is decidable, and can be tested in time exponential in the number of self joins in the SPJ view.* ∎

Proposition 3.1 *An SPJ view that takes the join of two or more distinct relations is not self-M with respect to insertions.* ∎

Proposition 3.2 *All SP views are self-M with respect to insertions. An SPJ view defined using self-joins over a single relation R is self-M if every join is based on* key(R). ∎

Algorithm Outline: For SP views self-maintenance can be done by a selection and a projection on the newly inserted tuples. For an SPJ view with self-joins on a key each newly inserted tuple joins only with itself, so the view definition is evaluated on only the set of inserted tuples.

Deletions

Theorem 3.2 *An SPJ view V that takes the join of one or more relations $R_1, \ldots, R_n$ is self-M with respect to deletions to R_1 if and only if, for every database instance, and for every occurrence of relation R_1 in the view definition, the following holds: Given a tuple t in view V, let a derivation tree for the tuple t use the tuple r in R_1 for the stated occurrence of R_1 in the view definition. Then, it is possible to identify the key of such a tuple r of R_1 from the tuple t and the view definition, without referring to the contents of any of the relations R_i.* ■

A sufficient condition for the conditions of Thm 3.2 to be true is when, for some key of relation R_1, each key attribute is either retained in the view, or is equated to a constant in the view definition. Then, given a tuple t in the view, we can identify the tuple r of R_1 from the key attributes.

Algorithm outline for views satisfying Theorem 3.2: For deleted tuple r in relation R_1, check key(r) satisfies any predicates that equate key attributes to constants in the view definition. Then, look for tuples in the view that have the same values on the remaining key attributes as the deleted tuple. Delete all such tuples from the view.

Updates Updates have been modeled as deletions followed by insertions in previous view maintenance work. This model may lose information that could be useful for incremental view maintenance. Also, such a representation of an update means that a view is self-M with respect to updates only if the view is self-M with respect to both inserts and deletes. In fact, the following lemma may suggest that indeed the above conclusion holds for self-maintenance in response to updates.

Lemma 3.3 *Let V be an SPJ view, and R one of the relations in the* FROM *clause, such that there is at least one predicate on R. Then, the view maintenance problem for V in response to any insertion or a deletion into R can be reduced to the view maintenance problem for V in response to an update to R.* ■

However, a view may be self-M with respect to updates even if it is not self-M with respect to both insertions and deletions because by modeling an update directly, not as a delete plus an insert, we retain the link between the deleted and inserted tuples. Thus, often most of the attributes of the new tuple that needs to be inserted into the view can be obtained from the deleted tuple, enabling self-maintenance.

The information about the "deleted" view tuple that is retained by directly modeling updates facilitates self-maintenance in two respects: the conditions for self-maintenance becomes less onerous than in the case of simple insertions, so that many views that are not self-M with respect to insertions can be self-M with respect to updates; and the computational effort required to perform the insertion is decreased, whether or not the view is self-M.

Whether a view is self-M depends upon the attributes being updated. The following definition captures the property that enables self-maintenance.

Definition 3.1 (Exposed Variable): Given a view definition V, a variable, or equivalently, an attribute, A, of a relation used in the view definition is said to be exposed if it is involved in some predicate. A variable that is not exposed is called a non-exposed variable. ■

A non-exposed attribute does not affect the combinations of tuples that contribute to the view.

Theorem 3.3 *A SPJ view V that joins two or more distinct relations is self-M with respect to updates to relation R_1 if and only if either:*

- *The updated attributes are non-exposed and are not distinguished with respect to view V, or*

- *The updated attributes are non-exposed with respect to view V and V is self-M with respect to deletions to the relation R_1.*

■

Algorithm Outline: The algorithm involves joining the modified tupels with the view on the key attributes to obtain the new value for the modified view tuple.

4 Related Work

Autonomously Computable Views of [BCL89] Blakeley *et al.* [BCL89] defined a view to be *Autonomously computable* with respect to a given update if the view can be maintained using only the materialized view for all database instances for only the given instance of the update. Autonomously Computability thus differs from self-M in that it considers a specific instance of the update, while self-M is defined over all possible updates. The update language of [BCL89] is more powerful – it permits deletions and updates to be specified using arbitrary conditions. In contrast, they do not consider views with self joins and do not use key information for deriving self-M conditions.

View Maintenance: View maintenance [BLT86, CW91, GMS93, HD92, Kuc91, UO92] has been generally studied as a problem to compute the changes to the view given the changes to the underlying relations, while having access to the view and the underlying relations. [TB88, GB95] deduce instance specific conditions for maintaining views without accessing base relations. Also, the above work models updates as deletions + insertions and not directly as updates that may be more easily maintainable.

Self-M is also indirectly related to work in data integration and updatable views.

5 Conclusions and Future Work

We propose materialized views as a way to provide fast access to integrated data in a data warehouse. We define self-maintainability as a desirable property for such views that allows the integrated data to be updated in response to modifications to the base relations without accessing the base relations and thereby avoiding remote accesses and concurrency control. We discuss syntactic restrictions that ensure self-maintainability of SPJ views. We find that SPJ views are self-M with respect to deletions and updates to non-exposed attributes if the keys of the joined relations are included in the view. Also, SPJ views are usually not self-M with respect to insertions. Modeling updates directly, and not as deletions + insertions, facilitates view maintenance and can make some views self-M with respect to updates.

An important application of the results is that they provide guidance to a designer on how to define views in the integrated database so that they may be maintained efficiently. Many times simply keeping an extra attribute can make a view self-M, and greatly reduce the maintenance work. We recommend that integrated views be defined so as to be self-M for as large a class of modifications as possible.

Future Work This chapter opens up a new area of work on view maintenance issues for data warehousing. How can functional dependencies, more general than keys, be used for for self-maintenance? How to self-maintain a *set* of views? How to self-maintain aggregate views?

USING OBJECT MATCHING AND MATERIALIZATION TO INTEGRATE HETEROGENEOUS DATABASES[1]

Gang Zhou, Richard Hull, Roger King, Jean-Claude Franchitti

ABSTRACT

This chapter addresses the problem of object *matching*, that is, determining when object representations (e.g., OIDs) in different databases correspond to the same object-in-the-world. Traditional approaches to data integration based on query pre-processing and query shipping typically use universal keys to perform object matching, and cannot efficiently support more intricate object matching criteria.

We present a framework for data integration that is based on partial or full materialization of integrated views, that can efficiently handle very intricate object matching criteria, e.g., involving boolean conditions and user-defined heuristics. Materialized data is maintained using techniques generalized from active databases.

To establish a context for our research, this chapter presents a taxonomy of the solution space for supporting and maintaining integrated views. The chapter also describes a prototype that we are implementing for data integration, that supports intricate object matching, and incremental maintenance of materialized information.

1 Introduction

One of the most important computer science problems today is to develop flexible mechanisms for effectively integrating information from heterogeneous and geographically distributed databases. A wide range of techniques have been developed to help resolve this problem, including approaches based on creating virtual integrated views and query pre-processing and shipping (e.g., [BLN86, SL90, DH84, SBG+81, ACHK93]), creating materialized integrated views (e.g., [WHW89, WHW90, KAAK93]), foundational work on languages and conceptual models for data integration (e.g., [HM93, Wie92]), maintaining consistency between multiple databases (e.g., [SRK92]), and supporting transactions against multiple databases (e.g., InterSQL [ME93]).

A fundamental issue that has not been resolved concerns the problem of object *matching*, that is, determining when object representations (e.g., object identifiers in the object-oriented paradigm, or keys in the relational paradigm) in different databases refer to the same object in the world[2]. This problem is central to integrating information in the context of Cooperative Information Systems (CIS), because data integration so often involves combining information about the same object from different sources. Most previous approaches to integrating data from heterogeneous databases assume that for each type of object-

---

[1]This research was supported in part by NSF grant IRI-931832, and ARPA grants BAA-92-1092 and 33825-RT-AAS.

[2]In [KAAK93], the term 'proxy object' is used to refer to an object representation, and the term 'entity object' is used to refer to an object in the world.

in-the-world there is some form of (possibly derived) universal key [DH84, ACHK93, WHW89, WHW90]. Indeed, the traditional approach of virtual integrated views and query-shipping is essentially limited to this paradigm: if more intricate object matching criteria are used, then correlating data from different databases about the same set of objects is quite expensive, and this expense is borne with each query. An important discussion of object matching is presented in [KAAK93], which describes an approach to data integration being developed as part of the Pegasus prototype multidatabase system [ADD+91]. In addition to providing a philosophical discussion on the problem *matching*, that paper presents an approach based partially on materialization that can be used to store and access information about matching object representations.

In the present chapter, we describe a framework and prototype tool that can support object matching based on criteria which are much richer than universal keys and that go beyond the options discussed in [KAAK93]. In particular, the framework can accommodate a variety of complex criteria, including "look-up tables", user-defined functions, boolean conditions, historical conditions, and intricate heuristics. Our framework supports rich object matching criteria through the controlled use of data materialization. The primary advantage of materialization is that expensive matching information need be computed only once. In this sense, our approach can be viewed as an extension of research reported in [WHW89, WHW90, KAAK93]. Unlike that work, our approach places major emphasis on the issue of incremental maintenance of the materialized match information.

In our framework, incremental maintenance is provided by using *active modules* [Dal95, BDD+95] – these are software modules that include a rule base, an execution model for rule application, and optionally a local persistent store. Active modules incorporate features of active databases [HW92], without necessarily being tied to a DBMS. In our framework, an active module might operate on the same machine as one of the source databases, or might operate on a separate machine. As used here, active modules can be viewed as a specific approach for implementing mediators in the sense of [Wie92]. Our framework can support a variety of incremental update mechanisms that can work with legacy as well as state-of-the-art DBMSs.

The new approach developed here for object matching can be integrated with previously developed techniques to provide rich support for integrating data from automonous and heterogeneous databases. In our framework, special *match* classes are materialized, that hold correspondences between matching object (representation)s from two or more databases (possibly along with related information about these objects). The match classes can be queried directly, or used in conjunction with data from source databases to create other, more intricate derived classes. These other derived classes might be virtual or materialized. If materialized, they can be maintained incrementally using activeness; and if virtual, they can be accessed using traditional query pre-processing and shipping techniques. It is also straightforward to incorporate constraint monitoring into our framework. Importantly, the constraints might refer to the integrated view, and hence to data that spans two or more databases.

This chapter makes four specific contributions towards database interoperation. To provide context for the research presented here, we (a) present a taxonomy of the solution space for supporting and maintaining integrated views, with an emphasis on situations where part or all of the integrated view is materialized. At a more concrete level, we (b) provide a detailed framework for supporting intricate OID match criteria. We are currently developing a prototype implementation of this approach. From an architectural perspective, our prototype uses a specialized class of active modules, called here *integration mediators*. We also (c) describe how the framework can be extended to support and maintain rich integrated views, where all or part of the view is materialized. Finally, we (d) develop a preliminary version of a high-level Integration Specification Language (ISL), along with a description of how to translate ISL specifications into integration mediators. The focus of the present chapter is on supporting a stand-alone integrated view of portions of two heterogeneous databases; we plan to extend this framework to handle multiple databases, and to extend it for integrating imported data into a local data set (as arises when using a federated architecture [SL90]).

Supporting rich object matching criteria is not the only motivation for materializing integrated views. Two other motivations are: (a) if access time to remote data is substantial (e.g., due to network delay) but response time is critical; and (b) if the computer holding the integrated view is not continuously connected to the source databases, as might occur if the integrated view is stored in a portable computer used in the field. Thus, our work on using activeness to perform incremental maintenance of materialized data is useful even if the object matching criteria in use are straightforward.

The issue of maintaining materialized information in our framework is closely related to the materialized view update problem. We follow here the general spirit of [CW91, Cha94], where active database rules can be used to capture relevant updates against the source databases, and appropriate (possibly restructured) updates can be transmitted to the processor maintaining the materialized copy. That work assumes that the source databases have full active database capabilities (as will probably be true in the future). The taxonomy presented in this chapter offers a broader perspective on how materialized information might be maintained. This is used to generalize work such as [CW91, Cha94], by supporting a variety of incremental update mechanisms that can work with legacy as well as state-of-the-art DBMSs.

Section 2 reviews concepts and technology that our framework builds on. Section 3 gives a motivating example that illustrates our approach to data integration, and then describes an integration mediator that supports an integrated view of the example data. Section 4 presents the taxonomy of the space of approaches to data integration. Section 5 presents the details of our current prototype for data integration, including a description of ISL and how ISL specifications can be translated into integration mediators. The status of our prototype and future directions are discussed in Section 6. Due to space limitations, the presentation in this chapter is somewhat abbreviated.

2 Preliminaries

This section briefly describes three technologies that are used in the development of our framework for data integration, namely *active modules*, *immutable OIDs for export*, and *KQML Agent-Communication Language*.

2.1 Active modules

In its broadest sense, an *active module* [Dal95, BDD$^+$95] is a software module that incorporates:

- a rule base, that specifies the bulk of the behavior of the module in a relatively declarative fashion;

- an execution model for applying the rules (in the spirit of active databases);

- (optionally) a local persistent store

An active module can be viewed as capturing some of the spirit and functionality of active databases, without necessarily being tied to a DBMS. In particular, the separation of rules (logic/policy) from execution model (implementation/mechanism) allows a more declarative style of program specification, and facilitates maintenance of the active module as the underlying environment evolves. Reference [Dal95] describes an implemented prototype system that uses several active modules with different execution models to support complex interoperation of software and database systems.

A key enabling technology in the development of active modules has been the Heraclitus DBPL [HJ91, GHJ96]. This implemented language incorporates syntactic constructs that permit the flexible specification of a wide range of execution models for rule application, and for specifying different kinds of rules (having a range of expressive powers). Heraclitus is based in the relational paradigm; a team at CU Boulder is currently developing H2O [BDD+95], an extension and generalization of Heraclitus for the object-oriented database paradigm. The current experimentation with the framework described in this chapter is based on Heraclitus, and we expect the port to H2O to be relatively straightforward.

As noted in the Introduction, we develop in this chapter a specialized class of active modules, called here *integration mediators*, which are focused on supporting integrated views of data from multiple heterogeneous databases.

2.2   Immutable OIDs for export

If an integration mediator materializes matches between object representations from different databases, then it may be necessary for the mediator to refer to objects from the source databases. If a source database is relational, then a printable key will typically be available for referring to the objects. In contrast, in the object-oriented paradigm, concrete and conceptual objects-in-the-world are typically referred to by object identifiers (OIDs). In some cases a printable key may be associated with objects represented in an object-oriented database, but this is not guaranteed.

While the notion of object identifier (OID) is central to the object-oriented database paradigm, there is no broad consensus as to exactly what an OID is. A common assumption at the formal level is that the particular value of an OID is irrelevant, and only the relationship of the OID to values and other OIDs in a database instance is important [Bee89]. Indeed, in some practical systems (e.g., AP5 [Coh86]) the actual physical value of an OID may change over time even though it continues to refer to the same object-in-the-world. This might arise, for example, as a result of an automatic background garbage collection or other physical re-organization. In other systems (e.g., Exodus [CDRS86]) physical OIDs are in fact addresses on disk and are essentially immutable,

We are interested in the general problem of integrating data from multiple object-oriented databases operated by essentially different groups, and we wish to disrupt their paradigm for physical OIDs as little as possible. However, if an integration mediator materializes matches between object representations from different databases, then it may be necessary for the mediator to refer to specific OIDs from the source databases. Significant disruption may occur if the OIDs of source databases are mutable as a result of background operations.

In our framework we generally assume that the physical OIDs associated with a given entity class in a source database are immutable. If a source database does not use immutable OIDs, then we follow the technique of [EK91], and assume that these source databases have been extended to support immutable OIDs for export. (Reference [EK91] uses the phrase 'global OIDs' for this.) A simple approach for a source database to support immutable OIDs for export is to maintain a binary relation with first coordinate holding internal, physical OIDs, and second coordinate holding symbolic "export" OIDs. The essential requirement is that the "export" OIDs are immutable – they remain constant even if their associated physical OIDs change, e.g., as the result of garbage collection. The binary relation need not give a translation for all of the physical OIDs, but only for the ones that need to be exported to the integration mediator.

```
interface Student {                    interface Employee {
    extent      students;                  extent      employees;
    string      studName;                  string      empName;
    integer[7]  studID;                    integer[9]  SSN;
    string      major;                     Division    division;
    string      local_address;            string      address;
    string      permanent_address;    };
    Set<Course> courses_taken;
};                                    interface Division {
                                          extent      divisions;
interface Course {                        string      divName;
    extent      courses;                 ... ...
    string      courseName;          };
    ... ...
};
```

Subschema of *StudentDB*   Subschema of *EmployeeDB*

Figure 1   Subschemas of `StudentDB` and `EmployeeDB` in ODL syntax

2.3   KQML

In our framework the underlying databases and the active module performing data integration may reside on a single or on different computers. While the choice of communication protocol between the various systems is largely irrelevant, in our prototype implementation we are using the Knowledge Query and Manipulation Language (KQML) [FLM97]. This was developed by the DARPA External Interfaces Working Group as part of a larger effort to develop a standard technology for communication between software agents. KQML is a protocol that defines a conversation model within which autonomous and asynchronous programs can exchange messages. Within this protocol, each message is assumed to have a certain purpose or "attitude", such as that it is *tell*-ing the recipient a new fact, *ask*-ing the recipient a question, or *reply*-ing to a previous message. KQML provides a standard format for packaging messages, so that their purpose and other information is easily obtained. The message contents might be a query in a standard or *ad hoc* query language, or might be a data set formatted according to some protocol. Various implementations of the KQML Application Program Interface (API) are available, which support the protocol and communication between applications in contexts of both local and wide area networks.

3   An Example Problem and Its Solution

This section gives an informal overview of our framework for data integration. A simple example of data integration is presented, with primary focus on the object matching problem. An approach to supporting an integrated view using an "integration mediator" is then presented. The integration mediator materializes the integrated view and also other data from the source databases that is needed for incrementally maintaining the view.

In the example we assume that there are two databases, `StudentDB` and `EmployeeDB`, that hold information about students at a university and employees in a large nearby corporation, respectively. The relevant subschemas of the two databases are shown in Figure 1. An integration mediator, called here `S_E_Mediator`, will maintain correspondence information about persons who are both students and employees. This information can be used to construct integrated view of data from both source databases.

A host of issues are raised when attempting to perform this kind of data integration in practical contexts. The primary emphasis of the present chapter is on three fundamental issues:

(a) Mechanisms to support rich object matching criteria.

(b) Mechanisms to maintain replicated (possibly derived) data.

(c) (Since our solution to (b) involves rule bases), mechanisms to automatically generate rules for a given data integration application.

We are also developing

(d) mechanisms for using the object correspondence information in the construction of rich integrated views, and

(e) mechanisms to monitor constraints concerning the integration of multiple data sets.

In this section we consider each of these issues with respect to the example problem.

With regards to issue (a), we assume in the example that a student object s *matches* an employee object e (i.e., they refer to the same person in the real world) if (1) either $s.\texttt{local\_address} = e.\texttt{address}$ or $s.\texttt{permanent\_address} = e.\texttt{address}$, and (2) their names are "close" to each other according to some metric, for instance, where different conventions about middle names and nick names might be permitted. The "closeness" of names is determined by a function, called here $\texttt{close\_names()}$, that takes two names as arguments and returns a boolean value. It should be noted that no universal key is assumed for the class of student employees, and that the traditional approach based on a virtual integrated view and query shipping would be prohibitively expensive. We now propose an efficient mechanism to provide an integrated view for the example.

To support the object matching criteria between students and employees, we propose that the local persistent store of S_E_Mediator holds three classes: a class called Stud_match_Emp and two *auxiliary* classes that are used to facilitate incremental updates of the objects in Stud_match_Emp class. Speaking intuitively, Stud_match_Emp will hold pairs of matching Student and Employee objects. For this example, the two auxiliary classes are Stud_minus_Emp and Emp_minus_Stud. Stud_minus_Emp will hold one object for each student in Student who is not an employee; and analogously for Emp_minus_Stud.

Figure 2 shows the interfaces of the three classes in more detail. (Subsection 5.2 below develops a mechanism for automatically generating class specifications of an integration mediator from the matching criteria and other input.) Here the Stud_minus_Emp and Emp_minus_Stud classes include the attributes needed to perform matches. The Stud_match_Emp class holds all of the attributes from both Stud_minus_Emp and Emp_minus_Stud.

We now turn to issue (b), that of incrementally maintaining the three classes just described. Two basic issues arise: (i) importing information from the two source databases and (ii) correctly modifying the contents of the three classes to reflect changes to the source databases. With regards to (i), we assume for the present that both source databases can actively report the net effects of updates (i.e., insertions, deletions, and modifications) to S_E_Mediator. (Other possibilities are considered in Section 4.) The net effects are wrapped in KQML messages. Upon arriving at S_E_Mediator, the messages are placed in the

```
interface Stud_minus_Emp {          interface Stud_match_Emp {
  extent      stud_minus_emps;        extent      matchs;
  string      studName;               string      studName;
  integer[7] studID;                  integer[7] studID;
  string      local_address;          string      local_address;
  string      permanent_address;      string      permanent_address;
};                                    string      empName;
                                      integer[9] SSN;
interface Emp_minus_Stud {            string      address;
  extent      emp_minus_studs;      };
  string      empName;
  integer[9] SSN;
  string      address;
```

Figure 2 Class interfaces of S_E_Mediator

```
R1:
on message_from_Student_database
if create Student( x: sn, sid, maj, ladd, padd, ct)
then [create Stud_minus_Emp( new: x.sn, x.sid, x.ladd, x.padd);
      pop Student_database_queue];

R2:
on create Stud_minus_Emp( x: sn, sid, ladd, padd)
if (exists Emp_minus_Stud(y: en, ssn, addr) and
    close_names(x.sn, y.en) and
    (x.ladd = y.addr or x.padd = y.addr))
then [delete Stud_minus_Emp(x); delete Emp_minus_Stud(y);
      create Stud_match_Emp(new: x.sn, x.sid, x.ladd, x.padd,
 y.en, y.ssn, y.addr)];
```

Figure 3 Sample rules for maintaining local store of the integration mediator

queues assigned to the corresponding source databases. A rule base can be developed to perform (ii). Two representative rules responding to the creation of new **Student** objects in the source database **StudentDB**, written in a pidgin H2O [BDD⁺95] rule language, are shown in Figure 3. Intuitively, the two rules state:

Rule R1: If an object of class **Student** is created, create a new object of class **Stud_minus_Emp**.

Rule R2: Upon the creation of a **Stud_minus_Emp** object x, if there is a corresponding object y of class **Emp_minus_Stud** that matches x, then delete x and y, and create a **Stud_match_Emp** object that represents the matching pair.

The complete rule base would include rules dealing with creation, deletion, and modification of objects in both source databases.

```
DEFINE VIEW Expertise
SELECT d.divName, c.courseName
FROM c IN StudentDB:Course, s IN StudentDB:Student,
     e IN EmployeeDB:Employee, d IN EmployeeDB:Division,
     m IN Stud_match_Emp
WHERE s.studID = m.studID and c IN s.courses_taken and
      e.SSN = m.SSN and d IN e.division;
```

(a) Definition of view `Expertise` expressed in extended OQL

```
DEFINE VIEW Expertise_internal
SELECT m.divName, c.courseName
FROM c IN StudentDB:Course, s IN StudentDB:Student,
     m IN Stud_match_Emp
WHERE s.studID = m.studID and c IN s.courses_taken;
```

(b) Query that implements this view under one solution based on partial materialization

Figure 4   Constructing a rich integrated view

With regards to the issue of (c) automatically generating rule bases for data integration applications, we shall introduce a high level integration specification language (ISL) in Subsection 5.1. With the help of the set of rule templates described in Subsection 5.3, an ISL specification can be translated automatically into a rule base that maintains object correspondence information.

We now consider (d) the issue of constructing rich integrated views based on the object correspondence information. As mentioned in the Introduction, match classes can be used along with data from the source databases to include intricate derived classes in an integrated view. Intuitively, a match class can be used as a kind of "glue" to form a "join" between information about objects in different databases. We illustrate this with a simple example. Suppose we want to define a derived class `Expertise` that includes a pair **(dn, cn)** whenever there is a student working in the division with name **dn** that has taken a course with name **cn**. The definition of this class, expressed as a view in extended OQL, is given in Figure 4(a). The notation `EmployeeDB:Employee` indicates class `Employee` of the `EmployeeDB` database, i.e. part of the query defining the view is from `EmployeeDB` database. The class `Stud_match_Emp` is used to specify the correspondences between objects from the `StudentDB` and `EmployeeDB` databases.

The class `Expertise` defined in Figure 4(a) might be supported in S_E_Mediator as virtual, fully materialized, or partially materialized. If a virtual approach is used, then queries against the class would be broken into three pieces, one each for `StudentDB`, for `EmployeeDB`, and for the `Stud_match_Emp` class. (The particular execution plan used would depend on the query.) Suppose now that the cost of query shipping to `EmployeeDB` is considered to be very high. A solution based on partial materialization is as follows. An attribute `divName` (division name) is included in both the `Stud_match_Emp` and `Emp_minus_Stud` classes, and is maintained by S_E_Mediator in a materialized fashion. In this case, the integration mediator could internally use the query of Figure 4(b) to support the derived class `Expertise`.

Finally, we consider (e) the issue of constraints that apply to the integrated view. As a simple example, suppose that the employer wants to enforce the constraint that it employs no more than 100 students.

No	Spectra	Range
1	Matching Criteria	key ↔ lookup-table ↔ compar. ↔ history
2	Materialization	fully materialized ↔ hybrid ↔ fully virtual
3	Activeness of Source	sufficient activ. ↔ restricted ↔ none
4	Maintenance Strategies	incremental update ↔ refresh
5	Maintenance Timing	event triggered ↔ periodic

Table 1   Solution space for object matching when integrating data

This cannot be enforced in either of the source databases independently of the other. On the other hand, it is easy to specify a rule in `S_E_Mediator` that monitors the size of `Stud_match_Emp`, and takes corrective action if this size becomes larger than 100. Importantly, the rules that monitor constraints can be quite independent from the rules for identifying corresponding objects and for maintaining replicated data.

4   A Taxonomy of the Solution Space for Data Integration

The solution presented in the previous section for the Student/Employee example represents just one point in the space of possible approaches to solving data integration problems based on object matching. This section attempts to identify the major spectra of this solution space.

Our taxonomy is based on five spectra (see Table 1). The first two spectra are relevant to all solutions for object matching when integrating data, and the latter three are relevant to solutions that involve some materialization. We feel that these spectra cover the most important design choices that must be addressed when solving a data integration problem. Within each spectra we have identified what we believe to be the most important points, relative to the kinds of data integration problems and environments that arise in practice. Of course, much of our discussion of the latter three spectra is also relevant to the use of materialization in contexts other than object matching.

Before discussing the spectra individually, we indicate where the solution of the previous section fits in the taxonomy. With regards to Matching Criteria (Spectrum 1), there is only one pair of corresponding classes in the Student/Employee example, with matching based on comparison of attribute values. The solution assumed full materialization (Spectrum 2) and that the source databases were sufficiently active (Spectrum 3). The Maintenance Strategy (Spectrum 4) used was incremental update, and Maintenance Timing (Spectrum 5) was event triggering by the source databases.

4.1   Matching Criteria

In some cases the problem of identifying corresponding pairs of objects from different databases can be straightforward; in other cases this can be quite intricate or even impossible. We mention some key points from the spectrum, combinations and variations of these can also arise:

Key-based matching is the most straightforward one; it relies on the equality of keys of two objects to match them. WorldBase [WHW90] and SIMS [ACHK93] are two examples using this approach. A generalization of this is to permit keys that involve derived attributes, as in [DH84].

Lookup-table-based matching uses a lookup-table that holds pairs of immutable OIDs or keys of corresponding objects.

Comparison-based matching provides in addition the possibility of comparing (possibly derived) attributes of two objects, either with arithmetic and logic comparisons or user-defined functions that take the attributes as arguments and return a boolean value, such as the function `close_names()` in the rule `R2` of the Student/Employee example.

Historical-based matching can be used to supplement other matching methods. For instance, an application can specify that two already matching objects stay matched, even if they cease to satisfy the other matching conditions.

The approaches based on keys and lookup-tables are well suited for specifying straightforward object correspondences. The comparison-based approach is much more powerful, because (i) attributes other than keys can be also considered in the matching criteria, and (ii) arbitrary boolean functions can be used to specify complex criteria between object attributes. The next subsection will show that when using the more powerful matching criteria, materialization of the correspondence information has advantages over the traditional virtual approaches to data integration. Neither comparison-based or historical-based match are considered in [DH84, ACHK93, WHW90, KAAK93].

In the Student/Employee example, the `Student` class and the `Employee` class refer to the same kinds of objects in the world, namely, people. In the terminology of [Cha94, CH95], two entity classes from different databases that refer to the same or overlapping domains of underlying objects are called *congruent* classes. In some cases objects from non-congruent classes may be closely related. For example, one database might hold an entity class for individual flights of an airline, while another database might hold an entity class for "routes" or "edges" (connecting one city to another) for which service is available. In the current chapter, we focus exclusively on matching objects from congruent entity classes.

4.2   Materialization

This spectrum concerns the approach taken by an integration mediator for physically implementing the data held in its integrated view. The choices include

fully materialized approach, as in [WHW89] and in the Student/Employee example of Section 3, which materializes all relevant information in the local store of the mediator;

hybrid approach that materializes only part of the relevant information; and

fully virtual approach, as in [DH84, ACHK93], that uses query pre-processing and query shipping to retrieve and compute the correspondence information whenever queries are made against the integrated view.

The fully virtual approach saves storage space and offers acceptable response time for queries if the object matching is straightforward, for example, key-based matching, and network delay is minimal, e.g. the source databases and the mediator are located on a local area network. In many other cases, the fully materialized approach is much more effective, for primarily two reasons. First, if more sophisticated matching criteria, e.g., comparison-based matching using a function, are used, then the fully virtual approach may be very inefficient. This is because under the fully virtual approach the function might have to be evaluated for every possible pair of objects of two classes, for *every* query against the integrated view. In the other approaches, the full set of comparisons will haven to be performed at most once, when the integrated view is materialized; after that incremental maintenance of the view will require a smaller set of comparisons based on inserted or modified objects. Second, if the mediator and the source databases are geographically distributed, local materialization avoids the repeated, typically expensive remote data accesses required by the virtual approach.

A compromise between the fully virtual and fully materialized approaches is the hybrid approach, which materializes only the data that is most critical to the response time and leaves other data virtual to conserve storage space of the mediator. Several variations are possible. A typical case that arises when it is costly to determine corresponding pairs of objects is to materialize the match class and the two auxiliary classes needed to maintain it, but to leave all other export information virtual. When queries involving the non-materialized attributes arise, the attribute values can be retrieved from the source databases. A rather extreme case arises if the mediator is severely space-restricted, as might arise if it resides on a laptop. A possible solution is to materialize only the match class, but not the auxiliary classes. Incremental maintenance of the match class may be difficult if not impossible, and so a refresh maintenance strategy might be be used to maintain the match class (see Subsection 4.4.)

An integration mediator can support more than one of the above approaches for different pairs of corresponding classes.

In this discussion, we do not address the issue of how methods against objects in the mediator will be handled. One approach is to use remote procedure calls, as in [FHMS91].

It is well-known that data from multiple information sources cannot be accessed at precisely the same time. As a result, the answer to a query against an integrated view may not correspond to the state of the world at any given time, and inconsistent data may be retrieved. This problem is exacerbated if some of the data is replicated, as is the case in our approach. Very good approximations to simultaneous access can be obtained by using a scheme based on global transactions, e.g., using time-stamping. However, this can be very costly in terms of throughput, and is not feasible in cases where there is not a continuous connection between some data source and the mediator. At the other extreme, data obtained from different sources and the mediator might be combined without regard for the exact time at which the data was retrieved, in spite of possible errors and/or inconsistencies that might arise. Two basic issues are: (a) what kinds of errors can arise when global transactions are not used, and (b) what are the major points along the spectrum ranging from using global transactions to completely ignoring issues of access time. We plan to address these issues in our future research.

4.3   Activeness of Source Databases

This spectrum concerns the active capabilities of source databases, and is relevant only if some materialization occurs. This spectrum allows for both new and legacy databases. The three most important points along this spectrum are:

sufficient activeness: able to periodically send deltas corresponding to the net effect of all updates since the previous transmission, with triggering based either on physical events or state changes. This approach has two major advantages: First, it could significantly reduce the network traffic by transferring deltas rather than full snapshots of the membership of a class. Second, most algorithms [BLT86, QW91, GMS93] for maintaining materialized views compute the incremental updates on derived data based on the net effects of the updates of the source data.

restricted activeness: the source database has triggering based on some physical events (e.g., method executions or transaction commits), and the ability to send (possibly very simple) messages to the integration mediator. Perhaps the most useful possibility here is that on a physical event the source database can execute a query and send the results to the integration mediator. Even if the source database can send only more limited messages, such as method calls that were executed, then the mediator may be still able to interpret this information (assuming that encapsulation can be violated). At an extreme is the case where the source database provides trigger monitoring but no other support; even in this case it may be possible to incorporate software into the source database to send appropriate messages to the mediator.

no activeness: the source database has no triggering capabilities. In this case the mediator can periodically poll the source databases and completely refresh the replicated information.

4.4   Maintenance Strategies

Maintenance strategies are meaningful only if some materialization occurs in the mediator. We consider two alternative maintenance strategies:

incremental update of the out-of-date objects, and

refresh of the out-of-date classes in the mediator by re-generating all their objects.

In general, refreshing is more straightforward in terms of implementation and can be applied under all circumstances. In contrast, incremental updating is generally more efficient, especially when the updates in the source databases affect only a small portion of the objects, as is true in most cases.

4.5   Maintenance Timing

Maintenance timing concerns when the maintenance process is initiated; this is relevant only if some materialization occurs. The most important points in this spectrum are:

event triggered: the maintenance is triggered by certain predefined events, and

periodic: the maintenance is performed periodically.

There are many kinds of events for the event triggered approaches. We mention here some typical kinds of events: (i) transaction commits in a source database, (ii) net change to a source databases exceeds a certain threshold, for instance, 5% of the source data, (iii) the mediator explicitly requests update propagation, and (iv) the computer holding the mediator is reconnected via a network to the source databases.

With the periodic approach, the user can balance the tradeoff between out-of-date data and maintenance costs, by setting the appropriate length of maintenance cycles. In general, longer time periods between maintenance cycles is more efficient in terms of the update propagation, because it accumulates updates of the source databases propagate the updates together. However, with longer time periods more data is likely to be out-of-date.

5   Towards a General Tool for Building Integration Mediators

Section 4 presented a broad taxonomy of the solution space for supporting data integration. We are currently developing a general tool for building integration mediators that can accommodate many of the points in that solution space. This section describes some of the key components of this tool.

The current focus of our work is to provide substantial support for the full range of object matching criteria, i.e., Spectrum 1 of the taxonomy of Section 4. With regards to the other spectra, we are focused on the left-most positions in Table 1, i.e., on full materialization, sufficiently active source databases, incremental update, and maintenance timing based on event triggering from the source databases. In this presentation we focus on the case where information from two databases is to be integrated; the generalization to multiple databases is a subject of future research.

The tool we are developing will be used to construct integration mediators for specific integration applications. Users can invoke the tool by specifying an integration problem using a high level Integration Specification Language (ISL) (Subsection 5.1). Based on this, our tool uses a simple mechanism (Subsection 5.2) to construct the schema for the local persistent store of the integration mediator, and uses a set of rule templates (Subsection 5.3) to construct the actual rules for data maintenance. Different execution models for rule application in the integration mediator are available (Subsection 5.4).

A final component of our solution is to automatically generate rules to be incorporated into the rulebases of the source databases, so that relevant updates will be propagated to the mediator. We do not address the generation of those rules here.

5.1 Integration Specification Language (ISL)

The Integration Specification Language (ISL) allows users to specify their data integration applications in a largely declarative fashion. The primary focus of ISL is on the specification of matching criteria and of integrated views. (Issues such as specifying transactions against multiple databases, as handled by, e.g., InterSQL [ME93], are not addressed here.) In the current version of ISL, users can specify (1) (relevant portions of) source database schemas, (2) the criteria to be used when matching objects from corresponding pairs of classes in the source databases, (3) derived classes to be exported from the integration mediator, and (4) constraints to be monitored by the integration mediator.

A BNF grammar for ISL is given in Figure 5, and the ISL specification of the Student/Employee example is shown in Figure 6. The ISL is based on the ODL and OQL of the ODMG [Cat93] standard.

We now consider the four parts of an ISL specification in more detail.

(1) Source DB subschemas: These describe relevant subschemas of the source databases using the Object Definition Language (ODL) of the ODMG standard [Cat93]. A key may optionally be specified for each class.

(2) Correspondence specifications: These describe correspondences between objects of corresponding pairs of classes. A correspondence specification for a given pair of classes has two parts:

    Match criteria: We use the query part (this is <query> as defined in p. 79 of [Cat93]) of OQL to specify conditions that must be satisfied by two matching objects. The conditions can be based on, among other things, boolean relations or user-defined functions (that may in turn refer to "look-up tables" or intricate heuristics). Although not shown here, we are developing extensions so that heuristics that are expressed as rules can be incorporated directly into ISL specifications. We are also developing mechanisms to support historical conditions.

    Match object files (optional): specifies the path of the object file(s) containing the implementation of user-defined comparison function(s).

1.	<ISL>	::=	<Source-Subschema> <More-Corresp> <Export> <Constraint>
2.	<Source-Subschema>	::=	<Subschema> <Source-Subschema> | ε
3.	<Subschema>	::=	`Source:` <string> <ODMG-ODL> [<Key-Spec> ;]
4.	<Key-Spec>	::=	<string> [, <Key-Spec>]
5.	<More-Corresp>	::=	<Corresp> <More-Corresp> | ε
6.	<Corresp>	::=	`Corresp #`<number> <Match>
7.	<Match>	::=	`Match criteria:` <ODMG-OQL-Query-Part> <Match-Object-File>
8.	<Export>	::=	`Export classes:` <ODMG-OQL>
9.	<Match-Object-File>	::=	`Match object files:` <string>
10.	<Constraint>	::=	`Constraints:` <ODMG-OQL-Query-Part> <Action> <Action-Object-File>
11.	<Action>	::=	`Actions:` <string>
12.	<Action-Object-File>	::=	`Action object files:` <string>

Figure 5 Grammar for Integration Specification Language (ISL)

(3) Export classes: This part of the ISL defines the export classes, i.e., the classes of the integrated view for export, that are derived from the source databases and the match classes. The export classes are specified using (extended) OQL queries, and may refer to both the source databases and the match classes of the correspondence specifications. If an attribute name is unique within the two classes, it can be used without the class name attached to it, otherwise it takes the form of `class_name.attr_name`.

When we extend the ISL to support hybrid materialized/virtual integrated views, we will incorporate the capability for specifying whether an export class or specific attributes of it are to be supported in a virtual or materialized fashion.

(4) Constraints: Finally, rules are included for monitoring constraints and taking corrective action when they are violated. The constraints are specified as boolean queries using OQL, where a value `True` indicates that the constraint is satisfied.

5.2   Building class definitions for integration mediators

This subsection describes how the class definitions for the local store of an integration mediator are automatically constructed.

As noted before, in the current version of the prototype we are assuming full materialization of both the match classes and of export classes. When constructing the classes to support the matching information we incorporate three kinds of attributes (these sets may overlap):

identification attributes: These are used to identify objects from the source databases. These might be printable attributes known to be keys (e.g., `StudID` and `SSN` in the running example), or might be immutable OIDs from the source databases (see Subsection 2.2). Although OIDs are not technically attributes, we view them as such here.

```
Source-DB: StudentDB                 Correspondence #1:
  interface Student {                  Match criteria:
      extent      students;              close_names(studName, empName)
      string      studName;              AND (address = local_address
      ... ...                              OR address = permanent_address)
  };                                   Match object files:
  key: studName;                         $home/demo/close_names.o

  interface Course {                   Export classes:
      extent      courses;            DEFINE VIEW Expertise
      string      courseName;         SELECT d.divName, c.courseName
      ... ...                           FROM c IN StudentDB:Course,
  };                                         s IN StudentDB:Student,
                                             e IN EmployeeDB:Employee,
                                             d IN EmployeeDB:Division,
Source-DB: EmployeeDB                         m IN Stud_match_Emp
  interface Employee {               WHERE s.studID = m.studID and
      extent      employees;               c IN s.courses_taken and
      string      empName;                 e.SSN = m.SSN and
      ... ...                              d IN e.division;
  };
  key: empName;                       Constraints:
                                        count(Stud_match_Emp) <= 100
  interface Division {                 Action:
      extent      divisions;             send_warning('count exceeded')
      string      divName;             Action object files:
      ... ...                            $home/demo/send_warning.o
  };
```

Figure 6 An example of ISL specification

match attributes: These are the (possibly derived) attributes referred to in the match criteria. In the Student/Employee example, the match attributes of the class `Student` are `studName`, `local_address`, and `permanent_address`; and the match attributes of `Employee` are `empName` and `address`.

export attributes: These are (possibly derived) attributes used in the construction of the export classes. In the example (assuming full materialization), the export attribute of `Student` is the derived attribute `courseName`, and the export attribute of `Employee` is the derived attribute `divName`.

As mentioned in the Student/Employee example, we use three classes in our approach to maintaining match information. Supposing that `R` and `S` are corresponding classes from the two databases, the three classes are defined as:

Auxiliary class I: `R_minus_S` with attribute set equal to the union of the identifying, matching and export attributes of class `R`. Class `R_minus_S` holds one object for each object in `R` which does not correspond to any object of `S`.

Auxiliary class II: `S_minus_R` with attribute set equal to the union of the identifying, matching and export attributes of class `S`. Analogous to `R_minus_S`, `S_minus_R` holds one object for each object in `S` which does not correspond to an object of `R`.

Match class: R_match_S with attribute set the union of those of the two auxiliary classes. Class R_match_S contains an object $\hat{m}_0$ for each pair $(\hat{r}_0, \hat{s}_0)$ of objects from R and S, respectively, that correspond according to the matching conditions.

In this example, we are assuming that the derived attributes courseNames and divName are materialized in the integration mediator. This is possible, given the assumption that the activeness capabilities of the source databases are sufficiently rich to inform the mediator when changes to these derived attributes have occurred. When we generalize our tool to permit source databases with restricted activeness, it may be necessary to replicate more of the source database information in the mediator. (In the example, this might entail replicating portions of the Course and Division classes.)

5.3   Building rule bases for integration mediators

As suggested in the Student/Employee example of Section 3, a rule base is used to maintain the materialized information held by an integration mediator. We consider now mechanisms for automatically generating rule bases that incrementally maintain such information.

The basic approach is to translate ISL specifications into rules. We follow the general spirit of [CW91, Cha94], that describe how view definitions can be translated into rules for performing incremental maintenance, and of [CW91], that describes how constraints can be mapped into rules.

We focus here on the novel aspect of our tool, which is the maintenance of the classes for matching. The primary mechanism used is a family of *rule templates*. These are used to generate the specific rules of an integration mediator.

In the context of sufficient activeness of the source databases and of event-based maintenance timing, a relatively straightforward set of rule templates can be used. This includes templates handling creates, deletes and modifies arising from either source database, and propagating these through the auxiliary and match classes. Due to space limitations, we describe here only rule templates concerning creation of objects for a class R that forms one half of a corresponding pair of classes. The two rule templates presented here were used to generate the two representative rules presented for the running example in Section 3.

rule template #1: R_Create_1
```
    on message_from_R
    if (create R(x: r_1, ..., r_n))
    then [create R_minus_S(new:r_a_1,...,r_a_v);
        pop R_database_queue];
```
Description: on event message_from_R, if a new object x of class R is create, then create a corresponding object of class R_minus_S and pop the message out of the message queue for database R.

rule template #2: R_Create_2
```
    on create R_minus_S(x: r_a_1,...,r_a_v)
    if (exists S_minus_R(y:s_a_1,...,s_a_w) && x match y)
    then [delete R_minus_S(x); delete S_minus_R(y);
        create R_match_S(new: m_1,...,m_u)];
```
Description: on the event that a new R_minus_S object x is created, if an object y of class S_minus_R matches x, then delete x and y and create a R_match_S object.

Translation of these templates into actual rules uses information about the source database classes, the auxiliary and match classes of the integration mediator, and possibly user-defined functions.

Although the rules generated from the above templates refer to individual objects, the execution model might apply the rules in a set-at-a-time fashion.

If the match criteria or export classes use derived attributes from the source databases, then we must also generate rules to be used by the source databases, so that the integration mediator receives appropriate messages about source database updates. If the source databases are sufficiently active, then these rules can be generated in using the spirit of [CW91, Cha94]. When we extend our framework to support source databases with restricted activeness, then the issue of automatically generating rules and/or code to be incorporated into the source databases may become more challenging.

5.4 A note on execution models

The Heraclitus and H2O languages support the specification of a wide variety of execution models. It is not yet clear what execution models are most appropriate for integration mediators, and we are experimenting with several at present. We give a sampling of three possible execution models here.

The simplest execution model that we are considering is the one that nondeterministically selects an applicable rule and fires it as a separate transaction. The primary advantage of this execution model is its conceptual simplicity. If rule firings can be concurrent, then this execution model would have considerable efficiency if there were many small messages coming from the source databases.

A richer execution model is the one that attempts to fire as many rules as possible within one transaction. The impact of each fired rule is accumulated in a delta, and rule conditions are tested in the hypothetical state that corresponds to this delta being applied to the original state. This may reduce accesses to the local store of the integration mediator, and thus yield an efficiency gain.

Finally, we are considering an execution model that enforces a modularization of the rules, with individual modules focused on propagating information out of the queues and into the auxiliary classes, on propagating information into the match classes, on propagating information into the export classes, and for checking constraints. We are experimenting with different maintenance timing for the different modules, to understand trade-offs between efficiency and keeping the export information reasonably up-to-date.

6 Current Status and Future Research

This chapter presents a broad framework for attacking the problem of supporting rich matching criteria when integrating heterogeneous data. As discussed in Section 5, we are now experimenting with prototype implementations of integration mediators. Our current focus is on the full range of object matching criteria, full materialization, and sufficient activeness in the source databases. The prototypes are implemented using the Heraclitus DBPL, but as the H2O DBPL becomes available we shall port our prototypes to H2O. For communication between source databases and the integration mediators we are using KQML, although experiments have also been performed [Dal95, BDD+95] using the Amalgame toolkit [FK93b, FK93a].

As indicated by our taxonomy, a wide variety of issues remain to be explored. In the near future, we plan to extend this research primarily in the directions of source databases that support only restricted activeness, and the hybrid materialized/virtual approach. As a testbed for restricted activeness, we plan to use databases developed on the Texas Instruments Open OODB [WTB92], which provides support for triggers based on physical events and the ability to attach procedures to those triggers. For the hybrid approach, we plan to use the SIMS [ACHK93] query processing engine to execute queries where matching information is materialized but all other export data is virtual. We shall also explore broader applications of the integration mediator in the context of Cooperative Information Systems, for instance, using the mediator to integrate data imported from one database into another database.

Another issue to be explored is the problem of potential inconsistencies between the source databases and the mediator resulting from different access times, as discussed in Subsection 4.2. Finally, we plan to expand our framework to support object matching between any number of databases, instead of just two databases.

Acknowledgments

We are grateful to Omar Boucelma, Ti-Pin Chang, Jim Dalrymple, and Mike Doherty for many interesting discussions on topics related to this research.

7

OPTIMIZING QUERIES WITH MATERIALIZED VIEWS

Surajit Chaudhuri,
Ravi Krishnamurthy,
Spyros Potamianos,
Kyuseok Shim

ABSTRACT

While much work has addressed the problem of maintaining materialized views, the important problem of optimizing queries in the presence of materialized views has not been resolved. In this chapter, we analyze the optimization problem and provide a comprehensive and efficient solution. Our solution has the desirable property that it is a simple generalization of the traditional query optimization algorithm used by commercial database management systems.

1 Introduction

The idea of using materialized views for the benefit of improved query processing has been proposed in the literature more than a decade ago. In this context, problems such as definition of views, composition of views, maintenance of views [BC79, KP81, SI84, BLT86, CW91, Rou91, GMS93] have been researched but one topic has been conspicuous by its absence. This concerns the problem of the judicious use of materialized views in answering a query.

It may seem that materialized views should be used to evaluate a query whenever they are applicable. In fact, blind applications of materialized views may result in significantly *worse* plans compared to alternative plans that *do not* use any materialized views. Whether the use of materialized views will result in a better or a worse plan depends on the query and the statistical properties of the database. Since queries are often generated using tools and since the statistical property of databases are time-varying, it should be the responsibility of the optimizer to consider the alternative execution plans and to make a *cost-based* decision whether or not to use materialized views to answer a given query on a given database. Such enumeration of the possible alternatives by the optimizer must be *syntax independent* and *efficient*. By syntax independent, we mean that the set of alternatives enumerated by the optimizer (and hence the choice of the optimal execution plan) should not depend on whether or not the query explicitly references materialized views. Thus, the optimizer must be capable of considering the alternatives implied by materialized views. In particular, a materialized view may need to be considered even if the view is not directly applicable (i.e., there is no subexpression in the query that *syntactically* matches the view). Also, *more than one* materialized views may be relevant for the given query. In such cases, the optimizer must avoid incorrect alternatives where mutually exclusive views are used together while considering use of mutually compatible views.

The following examples illustrate the issues in optimizing queries with materialized views. The first example emphasizes the importance of syntax independence and also shows that sometimes use of materialized views may result in worse plans. The second example illustrates the subtleties in syntax independent enumeration discussed above. The examples use a database containing an employee relation Emp(name, dno, sal, age) and a department relation Dept(dno, size, loc).

Example 1.1: Let Executive(name, dno, sal) be a materialized view that contains all employees whose salary is greater than 200k. Consider the query that asks for employees (and their department number) whose salary is greater than 200k and who are in the department with dno = 419. If the relation Emp has no index on dno, then it is better to access the materialized view Executive even though the user presents a query which does not refer to the materialized view Executive. This example illustrates that the use of a materialized view can be beneficial even if a query does not refer to the materialized view explicitly. On the other hand, it may be possible to obtain a cheaper plan by *not* using a materialized view even if the query *does* reference the view explicitly. Consider the query that asks for all executives in dno = 419. This query *explicitly* refers to the materialized view Executive. However, if there is an index on the dno attribute of the relation Emp, then it may be better to expand the view definition in order to use the index on dno attribute of the relation Emp. Thus, the choice between a materialized view and a view expansion must be cost-based and syntax-independent. ∎

Example 1.2: The purpose of this example is to illustrate the nature of enumeration of alternatives that arise when materialized views are present. Consider the query which asks for employees who earn more than 220k. Although the materialized view for Executive does not syntactically match any subexpression of the query, it could still be used to answer the above query by retaining the selection condition on salary. Next, we illustrate a case of mutually compatible use of materialized views. Consider the query that asks for employees who earn more than 200k and who have been working in departments of size > 30 employees. If there is a materialized view Large_Dept(dno,loc) containing all departments (with their location) where number of employees exceed 30, then the latter may be used along with Executive to answer the query. Finally, there are cases where uses of two materialized views are incompatible. Assume that a materialized view Loc_Emp(name,size,loc) is maintained that records for each employee the location of her work. If the query asks for all employees who work in large departments located in San Francisco, then each of Loc_Emp and Large_Dept materialized views help generate alternative executions. But, uses of these two materialized views are mutually exclusive, i.e., they cannot be used together to answer a query. ∎

The presence of materialized views and the requirement of syntax-independent optimization has the effect of increasing the space of alternative executions available to the optimizer since the latter must consider use and non-use of the materialized views. Since the query optimization algorithms take time exponential in the size of the queries, we must also ensure that the above enumeration of alternatives is done *efficiently* so as to minimize the increase in optimization time. Furthermore, we must also recognize the reality that for our proposal to be practical and immediately useful, it is imperative that our proposal be a generalization of the widely accepted optimization algorithm [SALP79].

In this chapter, we show how syntax-independent enumeration of alternative executions can be done efficiently. Our proposal constitutes a simple extension to the cost-based dynamic programming algorithm of [SALP79] and ensures the optimality of the chosen plan over the extended execution space. The simplicity of our extension makes our solution practically acceptable. Yet, our approach proves to be significantly better than any simple-minded solution to the problem that may be adopted (See Section 4).

The rest of the chapter is organized as follows. We begin with an overview of our approach. In Section 3, we show how the equivalent queries may be formulated from the given query and the materialized views.

In Section 4, we present the algorithm for join enumeration. We also contrast the efficiency of our algorithm with the existing approaches and present an experimental study. In Section 5, we discuss further generalizations of our approach. Section 6 mentions related work.

2 Overview of Our Approach

In traditional query processing systems, references to views in a query are expanded by their definitions, resulting in a query that has only base tables. Relational systems that support views can do such *unfolding*. However, the presence of materialized views provide the opportunity to *fold* one or more of the subexpressions in the query into references to materialized views, thus generating additional alternatives to the unfolded query. Therefore, we must convey to the optimizer the information that enables it to fold the subexpressions corresponding to the materialized views.

For every materialized view V, we will define a *one-level rule* as follows. The left-hand side of the one-level rule is a conjunctive query (body of the view definition) L and the right-hand side of the rule is a single literal (name of the view). We represent the rule as:

$$L(\mathbf{x}, \mathbf{y}) \rightarrow V(\mathbf{x})$$

where the variables $\mathbf{x}$ correspond to *projection variables* for the view. The variables $\mathbf{y}$ are variables in the body of the view definition that do not occur among projection variables. We call these rules *one-level rules* since a literal that occurs in the right side of any of the rules (view-name) does not occur in any left-hand side since the left-hand side may have references to only base tables. Thus, given a set of views that are conjunctive queries, we can generate the corresponding set of one level rules from the SQL view definitions.

Our approach to optimization in the presence of materialized views has three main steps. First, the query is translated in the canonical unfolded form, as is done in today's relational systems that support views. Second, for the given query, using the one-level rules, we identify possible ways in which one or more materialized views may be used to generate alternative formulations of the query. These two steps together ensure syntax independence. Finally, an efficient join enumeration algorithm, that retrofits the System R style join enumeration algorithm [SALP79], is used to ensure that the costs of alternative formulations are determined and the execution plan with the least cost is selected.

Since the first step is routinely done in many commercial relational systems, in the rest of the chapter, we will focus only on the second and the third steps. In the next two sections, we discuss each of these steps:

- Encode in a data-structure (*MapTable*) the information about queries equivalent to the given one (Section 3).

- Generalize the traditional join enumeration algorithm so that it takes into account the additional execution space implied by the equivalent queries (Section 4). This is the heart of the chapter.

For the rest of the chapter, we assume that the query as well as the materialized views are *conjunctive queries*, i.e., the Select-Project-Join expressions such that the `Where` clause consists of a conjunction of simple predicates (e.g., $=$, $<$, $\geq$) only. Thus, the query has no aggregates or group-by clause. We will use the domain-calculus notation [Ull89] to express conjunctive queries. Generalization of our results for queries that are not necessarily conjunctive are also discussed in this chapter.

3   Equivalent Queries: Generation of MapTable

In this section, we discuss how we can use one-level rewrite rules to derive queries that are *equivalent* to the given query in the presence of materialized views.

Our notion of equivalence of queries is as in SQL standard [ISO92], i.e., two queries are *equivalent* if they result in the *same bag of tuples* over every database. However, we need to define the notion of equivalence of queries *with respect to a set of rewrite rules*. In the following definition, we say that a database is a *valid database* with respect to a set of rules if the left-hand side and the right-hand sides of each rule returns the same bag of tuples over that database.

Definition 3.1: Two queries Q and Q' are *equivalent* with respect to a set of rewrite rule $\mathcal{R}$ if they result in the same bag of tuples over any valid database for $\mathcal{R}$. ∎

We will denote such an equivalence by $Q \equiv_{\mathcal{R}} Q'$. In case Q and Q' are unconditionally equivalent (i.e, equivalent independent of any rewrite rules), we denote that by $Q \equiv Q'$. This problem of generating equivalent queries in the presence of views has been studied before (See Section 6). In addition to a simplified exposition of the problem for conjunctive queries, the novelty here is in generating an *implicit* representation of equivalent queries in such a way that the join enumeration phase can exploit it.

Intuitively, we expect to generate an equivalent query by identifying a subexpression in the query that corresponds to the left-hand side of one-level rewrite rule. The subexpression is then replaced by the literal in the right-hand side of the rule (i.e., the view name). However, it turns out, that a straight-forward substitution could be *incorrect*.

Example 3.2: Consider Example 1.2. The materialized view *Loc_Emp* is represented by the following rule:

$$Emp(name, dno, sal, age), Dept(dno, size, loc)$$
$$\rightarrow Loc\_Emp(name, size, loc)$$

Consider the following query that obtains all employees of age less than 35 who work in San Francisco (SF).

$$Q(name) \quad :- \quad Emp(name, dno, sal, age), age < 35$$
$$Dept(dno, size, \text{SF})$$

Observe that it is possible to obtain the query Q' through a naive substitution using the rewrite rule for *Loc_Emp*.

$$Q'(name) : -Loc\_Emp(name, size, \text{SF}), age < 35$$

However, clearly, Q and Q' are not equivalent queries. In particular, Q' is unsafe. ∎

Example 3.2 makes the point that a syntactic substitution of the body of a materialized view need not result in an equivalent query. The crux of the problem in Example 3.2 is that the naive approach of replacing a matching subexpression resulted in a query with a "dangling" selection condition that refers to a variable in the subexpression that has been replaced. Besides the fact that a straightforward substitution may be incorrect, additional substitutions may be applicable as seen in the following example.

Example 3.3: The presence of the materialized view *Executive* is represented by the following one-level rule.

$$Emp(name, dno, sal, age), sal > 200\text{k}$$
$$\rightarrow Executive(name, dno, sal)$$

Consider the following query which asks for employees who work in a department of size at least 30 and who earn more than 220k.

$$Q(name) : -Emp(name, dno, sal, age), sal > 220\text{k}$$
$$Dept(dno, size, loc), size > 30$$

Observe that there is no syntactic substitution for the rule for *Executive*, since there is no renaming such that the literal $sal > 200\text{k}$ in the one-level rule for the materialized view *Executive* maps to a literal in Q. However, the following query Q' is clearly equivalent to Q.

$$Q'(name) : -Executive(name, dno, sal), sal > 220\text{k},$$
$$Dept(dno, size, loc), size > 30$$

∎

Example 3.3 illustrates a case where although there is no subexpression that syntactically matches the body of the view definition, the materialized view can be applied. This example is specially significant since it illustrates that to be able to use materialized views, we may have to reason with *implication* (subsumption) between sets of inequality (and may be arithmetic) constraints.

In Section 3.1, we define *safe substitution* that identifies equivalent queries that result due to applications of one-level rules. In Section 3.2, we explain how safe substitutions are used to construct *MapTable*, that implicitly stores the queries that are equivalent to the given query. This MapTable is subsequently used in the join enumeration step.

3.1   Safe Substitution

Every safe substitution identifies a subexpression in the given query that may be substituted by a materialized view to generate an equivalent query. Example 3.3 illustrates that presence of inequality constraints needs to be considered in identifying equivalent queries. Accordingly, we adopt the following somewhat more detailed representation of one-level rules that recognizes existence of inequality constraints.

$$L(\mathbf{x}, \mathbf{y}), \mathcal{I}(\mathbf{x}) \rightarrow V(\mathbf{x})$$

where $\mathcal{I}(\mathbf{x})$ represents a conjunction of inequality (and may be arithmetic) constraints that involve *only* the projection variables $\mathbf{x}$ of the rule. However, $L(\mathbf{x}, \mathbf{y})$ may contain variables $\mathbf{y}$ that are not projection variables.

Example 3.4: Consider the one-level rewrite rule for *Executive* in Example 3.3. We note that $\mathcal{I}(name, dno, sal) \equiv sal > 200\text{k}$ and $L(name, dno, sal, age) \equiv Emp(name, dno, sal, age)$. Since $\mathcal{I}$ depends only on sal, we will abbreviate reference to it as $\mathcal{I}(sal)$. ∎

The task of finding a suitable subexpression for substitution begins with renaming of variables in a rule to identify occurrences of the left-hand side of the rule in the query. Let r be a rule with variables V_r and Q be a query with variables V_Q and constants C_Q.

Definition 3.5: A *valid renaming* σ of r with respect to a query Q is a symbol mapping from V_r to V_Q subject to the following two constraints: (a) If $v \in V_r$ is a projection variable, then $\sigma(v) \in V_Q \cup C_Q$. (b) If $v \in V_r$ is *not* a projection variable, then $\sigma(v) \in V_Q$ and $\sigma(v) \neq \sigma(v')$ where v' is any other variable in V_r. ∎

Valid renaming is related to and is derived from *containment mapping* [CM77] (cf. [Ull89]). Specifically, only projection variables may map to constants. Also, no two variables in the rule may map to the same variable in the query unless these two variables are both projection variables. Such renaming results in a query expression that corresponds to a selection over the materialized view. Consider the one-level rule $A(x,y), B(y,z) \rightarrow V(x,z)$. If we map both x and z to r, and y to s, then we obtain the renamed rule $A(r,s), B(s,r) \rightarrow V(r,r)$. Observe that $V(r,r)$ corresponds to a selection over V that equates two columns of the view V.

We will show that if valid renaming of body of a one-level rule matches a set of literals in the query, then those literals may be replaced by the materialized view to obtain an equivalent query. Towards that end, we now define the notions of *safe occurrence* and *safe substitution*. In the following definitions, the symbol $\Rightarrow$ stands for logical implication.

Definition 3.6: Given a set of one-level rules $\mathcal{R}$, a query Q has a *safe occurrence* of $\mathcal{R}$, if for a rewrite rule $r \in \mathcal{R}$ there is a valid renaming of the rule r with respect to Q such that the renamed rule has the form $L(\mathbf{x},\mathbf{y}), \mathcal{I}(\mathbf{x}) \rightarrow V(\mathbf{x})$. Furthermore, the following two conditions must hold:
(1) The query Q has the form:

$$Q(\mathbf{u}) \equiv L(\mathbf{x},\mathbf{y}), \mathcal{I}'(\mathbf{x}), G(\mathbf{v})$$

where each of $\mathbf{x}, \mathbf{y}, \mathbf{u}$ and $\mathbf{v}$ is a set of variables. These sets may share variables except that $\mathbf{y}$ must be disjoint from $\mathbf{x}, \mathbf{u}$ and $\mathbf{v}$.

(2) $\mathcal{I}'(\mathbf{x}) \Rightarrow \mathcal{I}(\mathbf{x})$.

The *safe substitution* corresponding to the above safe occurrence is:

$$Q'(\mathbf{u}) \equiv V(\mathbf{x}), \mathcal{I}'(\mathbf{x}), G(\mathbf{v})$$

∎

Condition (1) ensures that there can be no dangling selection condition (unlike Example 3.2) when the view replaces its matching subexpression in the query. Valid renaming plays an important role in the above definition, making it possible to identify not only subexpressions in the query that match the materialized view, but also subexpressions that match selections over the materialized view. Such selections can be equality to a constant ($x = c$) or equality of column values. For example, assume $A(x,y), B(y,z) \rightarrow V(x,z)$ and the given query is $A(i,j), B(j,i)$ then $V(i,i)$ will be a safe substitution, which corresponds to a selection of the latter kind over the materialized view V.

Testing condition (2) entails checking implication between two sets of inequality constraints. Many efficient algorithms have been proposed that can test such implication (See [Ull89] for an algorithm). In reality, we retain only a subset of inequality constraints in $\mathcal{I}'$, i.e., those constraints that are not subsumed by $\mathcal{I}$. It is possible to have safe substitutions even if there is no syntactic match between left-hand side of a rule and the query (as in Example 3.3)

Example 3.7: Let us revisit Example 3.3 which illustrated the need for reasoning with inequality constraints. In this example, there is a safe occurrence of the one-level rule for *Executive*. This is true since

$\mathcal{I}'(sal) \equiv sal > 220\text{k}$ and $L(name, dno, sal, age) \equiv Emp(name, dno, sal, age)$. Furthermore, the following is true:

$$G(dno, size, loc) \equiv Dept(dno, size, loc), size > 30$$

From Example 3.4, we note that $\mathcal{I}'(sal) \Rightarrow \mathcal{I}(sal)$. Hence, the condition for safe occurrence is satisfied and we obtain the following equivalent query

$$Q'(name) : -Executive(name, dno, sal), sal > 220\text{k},$$
$$Dept(dno, size, loc), size > 30$$

∎

The following lemma states that queries obtained by safe substitution are equivalent to the original query over any database that stores the materialized view, consistent with its view definition. The lemma is true not only for queries with bag semantics, but also for queries with set semantics (Select Distinct).

Lemma 3.8: *If Q' is obtained from Q by a sequence of safe substitutions with respect to a set of rewrite rules $\mathcal{R}$, then Q and Q' are equivalent with respect to $\mathcal{R}$.*

Proof: We sketch the proof that every safe substitution results in an equivalent query. We will use the notation of Definition 3.6. Observe that $\forall\mathbf{x}(L(\mathbf{x}, \mathbf{y}) \wedge \mathcal{I}'(\mathbf{x}) \equiv V(\mathbf{x}) \wedge \mathcal{I}'(\mathbf{x})$. The equivalence is true for bag equivalence as well since $\mathcal{I}'(\mathbf{x})$ acts as a filter and condition (2) holds [CV93]. Since $\mathbf{v}$ and $\mathbf{u}$ in $Q(\mathbf{u})$ are connected to $L(\mathbf{x}, \mathbf{y}) \wedge \mathcal{I}'(\mathbf{x})$ only through $\mathbf{x}$, it follows that $Q(\mathbf{u}) \equiv Q'(\mathbf{u})$. ∎

For queries with set semantics (i.e., Select Distinct), it is not necessary that all equivalent queries are obtained by one or more safe substitutions. For example, if $A(x), B(x) \to V_1(x)$ and $B(x), C(x) \to V_2(x)$ are two rewrite rules, then the query $Q(x) : -A(x), B(x), C(x)$ is equivalent to $Q'(x) : -V_1(x), V_2(x)$, but the latter cannot be obtained from $Q(x)$ by a sequence of safe substitutions. For equi-join queries with bag semantics, the converse of Lemma 3.8 is true as well. The proof exploits unique properties of bag equivalence.

Lemma 3.9: *Let Q and Q' be conjunctive queries without inequalities. If $Q \equiv_{\mathcal{R}} Q'$ up to isomorphism, then Q' must have been obtained from Q by one or more safe substitutions.*

Proof: If there are no occurrences of view symbols in Q', then it follows from [CV93] that Q' and Q are isomorphic. Let us now assume that there is one view literal V in Q' and the rewrite rule corresponding to V be $l \to r$. We assume σ to be a renaming of the rewrite rule above such that $\sigma(r) = V$ and that all existential variables of l are mapped to variables that do not occur in Q'. Let us consider the query Q'' that results from replacing the literal V in Q' with the set of literals in $\sigma(l)$. Observe that Q'' is a query independent of V and $Q'' \equiv Q$. Therefore, Q and Q'' must be isomorphic and let g be the mapping so that $g(Q) = Q''$. It can be seen that $g \circ \sigma$ is a valid renaming of $l \to r$ that results in the safe substitution Q'. The proof extends to the case where there are multiple occurrences of materialized view in Q''. ∎

Generalizations

When the given query and the materialized views are arbitrary relational expressions and *not* restricted to be conjunctive queries, it may not be possible to enumerate *all* safe substitutions by any finite computation.

The above is a consequence of the undecidability of first-order logic. However, we can extend Definition 3.6 such that generalized safe substitutions for arbitrary SQL queries result in equivalent queries. In the following definition, $L(\mathbf{x}, \mathbf{y})$ and $Q(\mathbf{u})$ are arbitrary SQL expressions.

Definition 3.10: Given a set of one-level rules $\mathcal{R}$, a query Q has a *safe occurrence* of $\mathcal{R}$, if for a rewrite rule $r \in \mathcal{R}$ there is a valid renaming of the rule r with respect to Q such that the renamed rule has the form $L(\mathbf{x}, \mathbf{y}) \rightarrow V(\mathbf{x})$. Furthermore, the expression tree for Q has a subexpression $L(\mathbf{x}, \mathbf{y})$ such that it shares only the variables in $\mathbf{x}$ with $\mathbf{u}$ and the rest of the expression for Q, i.e., variables among $\mathbf{y}$ do not occur in among $\mathbf{u}$ or the rest of Q. Then, a *generalized safe substitution* corresponding to the above safe occurrence is obtained by replacing the subexpression $L(\mathbf{x}, \mathbf{y})$ with $V(\mathbf{x})$. ∎

It can be shown that generalized safe substitutions result in equivalent queries. However, for the rest of the chapter, we will continue to focus on conjunctive queries.

We have modeled views using one-level rules where the view is expressed in terms of base tables. Nonrecursive *nested views* can be flattened and are expressed as one-level rules as well. However, we also note that the nested representation of views may be used to identify safe substitutions efficiently. For example, let V' be a nested view defined in terms of another view V: $A(x), B(x) \rightarrow V(x)$ and $V(x), C(x) \rightarrow V'(x)$. Observe that if there is no safe substitution for view V in a query Q, then there can be no safe substitution for V' in Q as well. However, since building MapTable is not a bottleneck (see discussion below), such optimization plays a limited role in performance improvement.

3.2   Representation and Enumeration of Safe Substitutions

Intuitively, each safe substitution results in a new query, equivalent to the given one. We encode the equivalent queries by storing the information about safe substitutions in the *MapTable)* data structure.

From the definition of safe substitution, it follows that every safe substitution of a query Q with respect to a rule $L(\mathbf{x}, \mathbf{y}) \rightarrow V(\mathbf{x})$ corresponds to a renaming σ for the rule. Therefore, we can encode the information about a safe substitution by the doublet $[\sigma(L), \sigma(V)]$. The first component in the doublet is called the *deletelist* and the second component in the doublet is called the *addliteral*. The *deletelist* denotes the subexpression in the query that is replaced due to the safe substitution σ and the *addliteral* denotes the literal that replaces *deletelist*. Since L may have more than one literals, the *deletelist* is a *set* of literals. However, *addliteral* is a *single* literal. The algorithm to construct the MapTable for a given query is shown in Figure 1. The last **for** loop iterates over all literals in the query. Its purpose is best explained in the context of the join enumeration algorithm, described in the next section.

Example 3.11: In addition to the rules for *Executive* and *Loc_Emp*, consider the following one-level rewrite rule for *Large_Dept*

$$Dept(dno, size, loc), size > 30 \rightarrow Large\_Dept(dno, loc)$$

We illustrate the enumeration of safe substitutions using the above three materialized views.

(i) Consider the following query which asks for employees who work at a department in SF.

$$Query(name) : -Emp(name, dno, sal, age), size > 30$$
$$Dept(dno, size, \mathsf{SF})$$

Procedure MakeMapTable($Q, \mathcal{R}$)
begin
    Initialize MapTable
    for each rewrite rule $r : L \to V$ in $\mathcal{R}$ **do**
        for each safe substitution σ from r to Q
        do
            MapTable := MapTable $\cup\ [\sigma(L), \sigma(V)]$
        endfor
    endfor
    for each literal $q \in Q$ **do**
        MapTable := MapTable $\cup\ [\{q\}, q]$
    endfor
end

Figure 1   Algorithm for Creating the MapTable

It can be seen that the MapTable will have the following two doublets.

$$(\{Dept(dno, size, \mathsf{SF}), size > 30\},$$
$$Large\_Dept(dno, \mathsf{SF})$$

$$(\{Emp(name, dno, sal, age), Dept(dno, size, \mathsf{SF})\},$$
$$Loc\_Emp(name, size, \mathsf{SF}))$$

Observe that the doublets correspond to materialized views that are *mutually exclusive*.

(ii) Consider the query to find employees who earn more than 200k and work in departments with more than 30 employees.

$$Q'(name) : -Emp(name, dno, sal, age), sal > 200\mathsf{k},$$
$$Dept(dno, size, loc), size > 30$$

It can be seen that the MapTable will have the following two doublets which correspond to applications of *mutually compatible* materialized views.

$$(\{Emp(name, dno, sal, age), sal > 200\mathsf{k}\},$$
$$Executive(name, dno, sal))$$

$$(\{Dept(dno, size, loc), size > 30\},$$
$$Large\_Dept(dno, loc))$$

Notice that these two doublets implicitly represent three alternatives to the given query. ∎

In our implementation of the optimizer, literals of the query are stored in a *literal-table* and are referenced by unique *literal-ids*. There is one entry in the literal table for each table variable in SQL. For example, a query with four literals may be represented as $\{1, 2, 3, 4\}$. A MapTable entry would be of the form $(\{1, 2\}, 7)$ which indicates that the occurrence of the literal that replaces the subexpression corresponding to $\{1, 2\}$ is stored in position 7 of the literal table. For efficiency of access, *MapTable* is indexed by literal-ids that occur in the *deletelist*.

The running time of the algorithm *MakeMapTable* is linear in the number of safe substitutions. The number of safe substitutions depend on the structure of the query. If the query has at most one literal for every table name, there can be at most one safe substitution for every rule. For such queries, a safe substitution can be found in time *linear* in the size of the query. For example, in Example 3.3, the literal *Emp* in the body of the rule can only map to the literal for *Emp* in the body of the query. As in the case of containment mapping, determining safe substitutions can have exponential running time in the size of the query in the worst case. However, our experience with the *Papyrus* project [CS93] at HP Labs indicates that such is rarely the case since queries tend to have few or no repeated predicates (i.e., few or no "self-joins") and are often connected (i.e., no cartesian products). Furthermore, for a given query, only few rules are applicable. Thus, finding safe substitution is a relatively inexpensive step in optimization.

4   Join Enumeration

In the previous section, we have seen how the information about equivalent queries is *implicitly* stored in MapTable. The equivalent queries provide the optimizer with an extended execution space since the optimizer can pick a plan from the union of execution spaces of these equivalent queries. Therefore, the challenge is to extend the traditional join enumeration algorithm such that optimality over the extended execution space is ensured.

An obvious solution is to invoke the traditional optimizer repeatedly for each equivalent query. Indeed, this technique was adopted in [CGM90]. Unfortunately, the above approach leads to rederivation of many shared subplans among the equivalent queries, thus leading to significant inefficiency in optimization (See Section 4.3). In contrast, our approach guarantees that *no* subplan is rederived. We show that while the worst case complexity of other enumeration algorithms could be an exponential function of the number of safe substitutions, our algorithm takes time only *linear* in the number of safe substitutions. Thus, not only is the enumeration algorithm a simple extension of the traditional approach, it also is an efficient algorithm.

In the first part of this section, we will review the traditional join enumeration algorithm which is widely used in relational systems. Next, we propose our extension to the existing algorithm to enumerate the expanded execution space. We present a result that shows that the algorithm achieves complete enumeration and discuss its time complexity. We contrast our enumeration algorithm with known approaches.

4.1   Traditional Algorithm

The execution of a query is traditionally represented syntactically as *annotated join trees* where the internal node is a join operation and each leaf node is a base table. The annotations provide details such as selection conditions, choice of access paths and join algorithms. The set of all annotated join trees for a query that are considered by the optimizer, is traditionally called the *execution space* of the query. Like many relational optimizers, we will restrict the execution space for each alternative to be its *left-deep trees* only. Note that in such a case, every execution is a total ordering of joins.

Procedure OptPlan(Q) :
begin
    if existOptimal(Q) **then**
        return(plantable[Q]);
    bestPlan := a dummy plan with infinite cost
    for each $q_i \in Q$ **do**
        Let $S_i = Q - \{q_i\}$;
        Temp := OptPlan(S_i);
        p := Plan for Q from Temp and q_i
        if cost(p) < cost(bestPlan) **then**
            bestPlan := p
    endfor
    plantable[Q] := bestPlan
    return(bestPlan)
end

Procedure ExOptPlan(Q) :
begin
    if existOptimal(Q) **then**
        return(plantable[Q]);
    bestPlan := a dummy plan with infinite cost
    for each $((D_i, a_i)$ in MapTable such that $D_i \subseteq Q)$ **do**
        Let $P_i := Q - D_i$
        Temp := ExOptPlan(P_i);
        p := Plan for Q from Temp and a_i
        if cost(p) < cost(bestplan) **then**
            bestPlan := p
    endfor
    plantable[Q] := bestPlan
    return(bestPlan)
end

Figure 2   Traditional and Extended Join Enumeration Algorithm

The optimality of a plan is with respect to a cost model. So far as the cost model is concerned, we assume that the cost model assigns a real number to any given plan in the execution space and satisfies the *principle of optimality* [CLR90].

In this part, we briefly explain the join enumeration algorithm OptPlan (See Figure 2), which is a simplification and abstraction of the algorithm in [SALP79] (cf. [GHK92]). Let us assume that the query is a join among n literals where $n > 2$. The optimal plan for join of n relations can be obtained by enumerating n choices for the last relation to join and for each choice joining the chosen relation with the optimal plan for the remaining $(n-1)$ relations. The optimal plan is the least expensive plan of these n plans, so constructed. We omitted the details of the actual join methods and other annotations of the actual execution since they are not germane to our discussion here. Note that every subset S of the above set of all n relations in a query corresponds to a unique subquery (say, Q_S). Thus, the optimal plan for every subexpression Q_S of Q (referred to as a *subplan*) is constructed *exactly* once and it is stored in the data structure *plantable*. All subsequent calls to *OptPlan* for the same Q_S looks up the cost of the optimal plan from the table. Since looking up the plantable helps avoid repeated recomputation of the optimal plan, the complexity of the algorithm is $O(n2^{n-1})$ (instead of $O(n!)$).

4.2   Extended Algorithm

In this section, we discuss the optimization algorithm in the presence of equivalent queries (implicitly) represented in the MapTable. The *execution space* over which the optimal plan for the query Q (with respect to a set $\mathcal{R}$ of one-level rewrite rules) is being sought is the set of all left-deep trees over the queries that are obtained from Q by safe substitution with respect to $\mathcal{R}$. The *optimization problem* is to pick an optimal plan from the above execution space with respect to a cost model that respects the principle of optimality.

We have presented the enumeration algorithm ExOptPlan in Figure 2. The test $D_i \subseteq Q$ tests whether all the literals that occur in D_i (a deletelist) also occurs in Q. As explained in Section 4.1, in the traditional algorithm, complete enumeration of the search space is achieved by repeating the following step for each literal q_i in the query Q. We construct a plan for the rest of the literals in the query, i.e., the optimal plan for $Q - q_i$. Putting together the optimal plan for $(Q - q_i)$ with q_i results in the optimal plan for Q subject to the restriction that q_i is the last literal being joined. The algorithm ExOptplan follows the above technique for enumeration closely. Recall that MapTable contains the doublets $(\{q_i\}, q_i)$ for each literal q_i that is in the query Q. It can be seen immediately that if these are the only doublets stored in MapTable, the algorithms OptPlan and ExOptPlan in Figure 2 behave identically since P_i in ExOptPlan will be no different from S_i in OptPlan. Let us now consider any other doublet that corresponds to a safe substitution. A key observation is that we can ensure exhaustive enumeration if for each such safe substitution (D_i, a_i), we consider all plans where a_i is the last literal to be joined. However, in the unfolded query, there is no occurrence of the materialized view a_i. Therefore, instead of constructing the plan $(Q - a_i) \bowtie a_i$, we must construct the optimal plan for $(Q - D_i) \bowtie a_i$, since D_i is the set of literals (i.e., subexpression) in the unfolded query which when replaced by a_i results in an *equivalent* query. As can be seen, our algorithm does precisely the above. Therefore, the following theorem follows:

Theorem 4.1: *Algorithm ExOptPlan produces the optimal plan with respect to a given MapTable.*

Complexity

Observe that a step which we need to perform efficiently in $ExOptPlan(Q)$ is to check if deletelist $\subseteq Q$. In order to do so, we use bit maskings to represent the literals in deletelist and the subquery Q. Then, the subset relationship can be checked with bit-wise logical operators in $O(1)$ in most cases.

In the absence of any equivalent queries, the time complexity of ExOptPlan is no different from OptPlan, the traditional join enumeration algorithm used by commercial optimizers. Therefore, the interesting complexity question is the dependence of the time complexity of ExOptPlan on the number of safe substitutions in MapTable (say, l) for the query Q. It can be shown that the time complexity of ExOptPlan is bounded by $O(l2^n)$ (when computed in a generous matter). In contrast, the time complexity for OptPlan is $O(n2^{n-1})$. Thus, the worst case complexity degrades by at most $2l/n$. As argued in Section 3.2, the number of safe substitutions (l) is likely to be small and so the relative increase in optimization time is very modest.

The following theorem establishes the "goodness" of algorithm ExOptPlan, i.e., shows that ExOptPlan avoids generation of redundant plans.

Theorem 4.2: *For every set of equivalent subqueries of the given query with respect to a given MapTable, ExOptPlan stores a unique optimal subplan.*

Proof: Assume that $Q = \{R_1, .., R_n\}$ is the given query over base tables. Observe that every view is equivalent to a join among a subset of relations in Q. Therefore, every subquery is equivalent to some subset of relations in Q. Hence, it suffices to prove that for every subset of relations on Q, a unique plan is stored. As Figure 2 shows, ExOptPlan represents every plan P_i in terms of base relations in Q. Thus, a new plan is compared against its stored *bestplan* and the cheaper is retained. Therefore, the theorem follows. ∎

Comparison to Other Approaches

The simplest alternative to ExOptPlan is to invoke the optimizer for each equivalent query. This approach turns out to be *very* inefficient. Let us assume that a query is of size n and the MapTable has l entries. Then, the worst case time complexity of the simple approach is $O(l^n n 2^{n-1})$, which is significantly worse than the upper bound for ExOptPlan, which is $O(l 2^n)$. Intuitively, the shortcoming of the naive approach is that *no* subplans are reused and all shared plans are rederived. The need for sharing plans for the subqueries was observed in [CS93, CR94]. In that approach, optimal plans of the shared subqueries are maintained and reused. However, while this approach maintains a unique optimal subplan for each *shared* subquery, it does not maintain a unique optimal plan for each set of *equivalent* subqueries. The following example illustrates this point.

Example 4.3: Let us assume that the query Q is represented by the set of literals $\{1, 2, 3, 4\}$ where each integer number represents a literal in the query expression. Let us also assume that the subexpression $\{3, 4\}$ can be replaced by the literal $\{5\}$ by application of a one-level rule. Then, we have two equivalent queries: $\{1, 2, 3, 4\}$ and $\{1, 2, 5\}$. During the optimization, we first build optimal plans for the subqueries in the plan table for $\{1, 2, 3, 4\}$ (e.g., $\{1, 2\}$, $\{1, 3\}$, $\{1, 2, 3\}$). Next, we optimize the query $\{1, 2, 5\}$. During this step, we don't rederive a plan for the entry $\{1, 2\}$ since it was generated while optimizing the first query $\{1, 2, 3, 4\}$. However, we do construct the plan for $\{1, 5\} \bowtie 2$ as well as $\{1, 3, 4\} \bowtie 2$ in [CS93, CR94]. The *principle of optimality* tells us that we would have done as well if we constructed only the plan for $cheaper(\{1, 5\}, \{1, 3, 4\}) \bowtie 2$. In other words, equivalence of subqueries is not fully exploited. ExOptPlan avoids generating such redundant plans by ensuring the above. ∎

4.3   An Experimental Study

Our complexity analysis shows that the increase in optimization cost is modest compared to traditional optimization. To strengthen our confidence, we used our implementation of the optimizer for experimenting, which seems to point to the computational efficiency of our algorithm as well.

Our optimization algorithm was executed on ten queries consisting of seven relations and six equality joins. Among all relations participating in the query, 50% of relations were chosen and an attribute of each selected relation was assigned to have selection predicate with equality predicate. These attributes for selection condition were chosen among those who did not participate in join predicates. For each query, six views were generated as the same as joins in the query and projection attributes of views were selected so that the materialized views can be used to generate equivalent queries. We tested each query varying the number of materialized views available ranging from 0 to 6. Note that due to the presence of indexes, the decision of using (and selecting) materialized views had to be based on cost estimates.

We have used an experimental framework similar to that in [IK90, INSS92, Kan91, Shi93]. The machine used for the experiments was a DECstation 3100. The queries were tested with a randomly generated relation catalog where relation cardinalities ranged from 1000 to 100000 tuples, and the numbers of unique

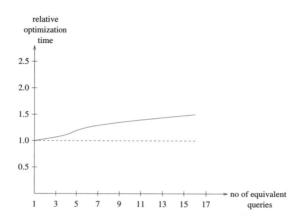

Figure 3   Relative Cost of Optimization

values in join columns varied from 10% to 100% of the corresponding relation cardinality[1]. Each page of a relation was assumed to contain 32 tuples. Each relation had four attributes, and was clustered on one of them. If a relation was not physically sorted on the clustered attribute, there was a B^+-tree or hashing primary index on that attribute. These three alternatives were equally likely. For each of the other attributes, the probability that it had a secondary index was $1/2$, and the choice between a B^+-tree and hashing secondary index were again uniformly random. As for join methods, we used block nested-loops, merge-scan, and simple and hybrid hash-join [Sha86]. In our experiment, only the cost for number of I/O (page) accesses [IK90, Kan91, CS94] was accounted.

The experimental result is shown in Figure 3. The cost of optimization is normalized with respect to the cost of optimizing a single query, as in the traditional optimizer. The effect of saving redundant work by our enumeration algorithm has resulted in a rather slow growth in optimization cost. In particular, for the case where there are 16 equivalent queries, the additional optimization cost on the average was less than 50%.

5   Discussion

In the introduction, we stated that we would like the optimization to be syntax independent and efficient. Let us revisit those desiderata to see whether our optimization algorithm ensures that these requirements are satisfied.

Observe that syntax independent optimization is achieved because we unfold all the queries in terms of base tables to provide a canonical representation of the query. Opportunities for using materialized views are then discovered by enumerating safe substitutions using one-level rules. Furthermore, our enumeration algorithm is also capable of deciding amongst the use of multiple materialized views when their uses are mutually exclusive (i.e., use of one view excludes the use of another).

Example 5.1: Let us assume that the query Q is $\{1, 2, 3, 4, 5, 6\}$. Let the entries in the MapTable be the following three doublets:

$$(\{1, 2\}, 7), (\{2, 3\}, 8), (\{4, 5\}, 9)$$

---

[1]This was the most varied catalog (catalog 'relcat3') that was used in previous experiments [IK90, INSS92, Kan91, Shi93, CS94].

Observe that because of the enumeration strategy in ExOptPlan, any candidate plan P that uses the literal 7 (an occurrence of a materialized view), ensures that in the (unfolded) query corresponding to the rest of the plan, subexpression $\{1, 2\}$ is absent, since they occurred in the deletelist of 7 in the MapTable. Therefore, the rest of the plan P can not have an occurrence of the other "overlapping" materialized view 8 since the subexpression for 2 will be missing. On the other hand, the cost of a plan which uses both the views 7 and 9 will be considered. For simplicity, consider a plan where the literal 7 occurs as the last literal to be joined. The remainder of the plan (i.e., excluding the literal 7) represents the subexpression $\{3, 4, 5, 6\}$. Therefore, while optimizing recursively, the plan for $\{3, 6, 9\}$ will be considered. ∎

Last but not the least, our objective was to ensure that the extensions to the optimizer are simple. A comparison of OptPlan and ExOptPlan in Figure 2 confirms that this goal has been met.

Generalizations

The enumeration algorithm ExOptPlan is robust in that it is completely *independent* of the algorithm used to generate MapTable. This would make it possible to pick an algorithm for generating equivalent queries using other algorithms [Fin82, YL87, CR94] (see discussion in the following section).

The optimization algorithm presented in this chapter extends to the case where the query and the materialized views are single block Select-Project-Join queries (i.e., not necessarily conjunctive queries). Most commercial optimizers optimize multi-block SQL queries by optimizing each block locally. Therefore, we can use ExOptPlan also for multi-block queries.

Finally, note that our algorithm can be used to exploit cached results. Caching results of a query to speed up query processing has been suggested in advanced database management systems such as Postgres. We observe that the cached results of queries differ from materialized views in that there may not be any degree of permanence to the cache. For optimizing an *interactive* query, it may be profitable to exploit the results that are currently cached. However, as in the case of materialized views, such choices need to be cost-based. Therefore, we maintain a system table which records the queries (in unfolded form) that are cached and their corresponding one-level rules. This table is updated by the cache manager to reflect the contents of the current cache.

6 Related Work

To the best of our knowledge, no work has previously been done on extending the dynamic-programming based join enumeration algorithm to optimize queries in a cost-based fashion when the database contains one or more materialized views. For example, although Postgres [SJGP90] provides the ability to implement a view either through materialization or by view expansion, the choice between the approaches has to be predetermined. Thus, the optimizer can not explore both the options depending on the query and cost estimations.

The task of generating equivalent queries based on existing query fragments or semantic knowledge has been studied in several different contexts [Fin82, LY85, YL87, Sel88, CGM90, CS93, CR94]. However, all these techniques generate equivalent queries *explicitly*. In contrast, much of our efficiency in optimization stems from the *implicit* encoding of the set of equivalent queries in MapTable and a join enumeration algorithm that exploits the encoding.

7   Summary

We have presented a comprehensive approach to solving the problem of optimization in the presence of materialized views. Our solution is not only efficient but is also syntax independent and cost-based. Every materialized view corresponds to a one-level rule. The set of equivalent queries due to applications of the above rules are encoded compactly in the MapTable data structure. This data structure is used by the enumeration algorithm to efficiently enumerate the the space of additional execution alternatives generated due to one-level rules (i.e., due to presence of materialized views). Our proposal requires few extensions to the traditional optimization algorithm that is used by commercial systems. Our approach also extends to architectures where results of queries are cached.

8

ANSWERING QUERIES USING VIEWS

Alon Y. Levy, Alberto O. Mendelzon,
Yehoshua Sagiv, Divesh Srivastava

1 Introduction

We consider the problem of using materialized views to answer queries. Aside from its potential of improving performance of query evaluation [LY85, YL87, KB94, CKPS95], the ability to use views is important in other applications. For example, in applications such as Global Information Systems [LSK95], Mobile Computing [DB94, HSW94], view adaptation [GMR95a], maintaining physical data independence [TSI94], the relations mentioned in the query may either not actually be physically stored (e.g., they may be only conceptual relations), or be impossible to consult (e.g. they are stored in a remote server that is temporarily unavailable to a mobile computing device), or be very costly to access.

We consider the complexity of this problem and its variants and describe algorithms for solving them for conjunctive queries involving built-in comparison predicates and for unions of conjunctive queries. Specifically, we consider the problem of finding a rewriting of a query that uses a set of views, the problem of finding a *minimal* such rewriting, and the problem of *completely* solving a query using views, that is, finding rewritings that use nothing but the views and built-in predicates.

The observation underlying our solution of the problem is a general characterization of the usability of views in terms of the problem of query containment. As a consequence, we show that *all* possible rewritings of a query can be obtained by considering *containment mappings* [CM77] from the bodies of the views to the body of the query. Given this characterization, we show that the problem of finding rewritings that mention as few of the database relations as possible is NP-complete for conjunctive queries with no built-in predicates. In fact, we show that these problems have two *independent* sources of complexity. The first comes from the number of possible mappings from the views to the query, and the second source of complexity is determining which literals of the query can be removed when the view literals are added to the query. We describe a polynomial time algorithm for finding literals of the query that can be removed. This algorithm is guaranteed to remove only literals that are necessarily redundant in the rewriting, and we show that under certain conditions (which are likely to cover many practical cases), it is guaranteed to remove the unique maximal set of redundant literals. This algorithm, together with an algorithm for enumerating containment mappings from the views to the query, provides a practical method for finding rewritings of a query. Finally, we show how the presence of built-in predicates in the queries and in the views affect the algorithms and the complexity of the problems.

2 Preliminaries

In our discussion we refer to the relations used in the query as the *database relations*. We consider mostly conjunctive queries, which may in addition contain built-in comparison predicates ($=, \neq, <$ and $\leq$). We briefly describe how our results can be extended to queries that involve unions of conjunctive queries (i.e., Datalog without recursion). We use $V, V_1, \ldots, V_m$ to denote views that are defined on the database relations. Views are also defined by conjunctive queries.

2.1   Rewritings

Given a query Q, our goal is to find an equivalent rewriting Q' of the query that uses one or more of the views:

Definition 2.1: *Conjunctive query Q' is a rewriting of Q that uses the views $V = V_1, \ldots, V_m$ if*

- *Q and Q' are equivalent (i.e., produce the same answer for any given database), and*

- *Q' contains one or more occurrences of literals of V.*

Note that we consider the case in which the rewriting is also a conjunctive query. When queries involve built-in predicates we will see that it may be worthwhile to consider rewritings involving unions.

We say that a rewriting Q' is *locally minimal* if we cannot remove any literals from Q' and still retain equivalence to Q. A rewriting is *globally minimal* if there is no other rewriting with fewer literals.[1]

Example 2.2: Consider the following query Q and view V:

$$Q : q(X, U) \quad :- \quad p(X, Y), p_0(Y, Z), p_1(X, W), p_2(W, U).$$
$$V : v(A, B) \quad :- \quad p(A, C), p_0(C, B), p_1(A, D).$$

The query can be rewritten using V as follows:

$$Q' : q(X, U) \quad :- \quad v(X, Z), p_1(X, W), p_2(W, U).$$

Substituting the view enabled us to remove the first two literals of the query. Note, however, that although the third literal in the query is guaranteed to be satisfied by the view, we could not remove it from the query. This is because the variable D is projected out in the head of V, and therefore, if the literal of p_1 were removed from the query, the join condition between p_1 and p_2 would not be enforced. □

Clearly, we would like to find rewritings that are cheaper to evaluate than the original query. The cost of evaluation depends on many factors that differ from one application to another. In this chapter we consider rewritings that reduce the number of literals in the query, and in particular, reduce the number of database relation literals in the rewritten query. In fact, we show that any rewriting of Q that contains a minimal number of literals is isomorphic to a query that contains a subset of the literals of Q and a set of view literals. Although we focus on reducing the number of literals, it should be noted that rewritings can yield optimizations even if we do not remove literals from the query, as illustrated by the following example.

Example 2.3: Using the same query as in Example 2.2, suppose we have the following view:

$$v_1(A) \quad :- \quad p(A, C), p_1(A, D).$$

---

[1] Note that in counting the number of literals in the query, we ignore the literals of the built-in predicates.

We can add the view literal to the query to obtain the following rewritten query.

$$q(X,U) \quad :- \quad v_1(X), p(X,Y), p_0(Y,Z), p_1(X,W),$$
$$p_2(W,U).$$

The view literal acts as a filter on the values of X that are considered in the query. It restricts the set of values of X to those that appear in the join of p and p_1. $\square$

In some applications we may not have access to any of the database relations. For example, in Global Information Systems [LSK95], the relations used in a query are only *virtual*, and the actual data is all stored in views defined over these relations. Therefore, it is important to consider the problem of whether the query can be rewritten using *only* the views. We call such rewritings *complete rewritings*:

Definition 2.4: *A rewriting Q' of Q, using $\mathcal{V} = V_1, \ldots, V_m$ is a complete rewriting if Q' contains only literals of $\mathcal{V}$ and built-in predicates.*

Example 2.5: Suppose that in addition to the query and the view of Example 2.2 we also have the following view:

$$V_2 : v_2(A,B) \quad :- \quad p_1(A,C), p_2(C,B), p_0(D,E).$$

The following is a complete rewriting of Q that uses V and V_2:

$$Q'' : q(X,U) \quad :- \quad v(X,Z), v_2(X,U).$$

It is important to note that this rewriting cannot be achieved in a stepwise fashion by first rewriting Q using V and then trying to incorporate V_2 (or the other way around). This is because the relation p_0, which appears in V_2 does not even appear in Q' which is the intermediate result of using V in Q. Finding the complete rewriting requires that we consider the usages of both views in *parallel*. $\square$

2.2 Containment Mappings

In the next section we show that the problem of finding a rewriting is closely related to the query containment problem. *Containment mappings* [CM77] have been used to show containment among conjunctive queries. In this chapter we show that they also provide the core of the solution to the problem of finding the possible usages of a view. Formally, a containment mapping from a query Q_1 to a query Q_2 is a mapping from the variables of Q_1 into the variables of Q_2, such that every literal in the body of Q_1 is mapped to a literal in Q_2. (Note that to show that Q_1 contains Q_2, the containment mapping must also map the head of Q_1 to the head of Q_2; however, in this chapter we use the term containment mapping to refer only to mappings on the bodies of the queries). In Example 2.2, the correctness of the rewriting can be established by considering the containment mapping $\{A \rightarrow X, B \rightarrow Z, C \rightarrow Y, D \rightarrow W\}$.

When neither Q_1 nor Q_2 contain built-in predicates, finding a containment mapping is a necessary and sufficient condition for deciding that Q_1 contains Q_2, and is an NP-complete problem [CM77]. This remains true also when Q_2 contains built-in predicates. However, when Q_1 contains built-in predicates, finding a containment mapping provides only a sufficient condition, and the containment problem in this case is Π_2^p-complete [vdM92]. In order to generalize our results to queries containing built-in predicates it is useful to note how containment mappings are also used to show containment of such queries. In particular, it follows from [LS93] that if Q_1 contains Q_2, then there exist queries $Q_2^1, \ldots, Q_2^n$ such that:

- $Q_2^1, \ldots, Q_2^n$ differ only in their built-in literals, and

- Q_2 is equivalent to the union of $Q_2^1, \ldots, Q_2^n$, and

- For every i, $1 \leq i \leq n$, there is a containment mapping ϕ_i from Q_1 to Q_2^i, such that $bi(Q_2^i)$ entails $\phi_i(bi(Q_1))$, where $bi(Q)$ is the conjunction of built-in atoms in the query Q.

For example, consider the following queries, where Q_1 contains Q_2:

$$Q_1 : q(Y) \quad :- \quad e(Y), r(U_1, V_1), U_1 \leq V_1.$$
$$Q_2 : q(X) \quad :- \quad e(X), r(U, V), r(V, U).$$

The query Q_2 can be represented by the union:

$$Q_2^1 : q(X) \quad :- \quad e(X), r(U, V), r(V, U), U \leq V.$$
$$Q_2^2 : q(X) \quad :- \quad e(X), r(U, V), r(V, U), U \geq V.$$

The containment mappings would be

$$\phi_1 : \{Y \to X, U_1 \to U, V_1 \to V\}.$$
$$\phi_2 : \{Y \to X, U_1 \to V, V_1 \to U\}.$$

In the next section we consider the complexity of finding rewritings, minimal rewritings and complete rewritings.

3   Complexity of Finding Rewritings

Previous solutions to the problem of using views to answer queries were based on either finding syntactic or 1-1 mappings from the view to the query. The first observation underlying our solution is that the problem of using views is closely related to the problem of query containment. In fact, the proposition below gives a necessary and sufficient condition for the existence of a rewriting of Q that includes a view V.

Proposition 3.1: *Let Q and V be conjunctive queries with built-in predicates. There is a rewriting of Q using V if and only if $\pi_\phi(Q) \subseteq \pi_\phi(V)$, i.e., the projection of Q onto the empty set of columns is contained in the projection of V onto the empty set of columns.*

Note that the containment $\pi_\phi(Q) \subseteq \pi_\phi(V)$ is equivalent to the following statement: If V is empty for a given database, then so is Q.

The importance of this proposition is in the fact that it provides a *complete* characterization of the problem of using views, thereby enabling us to explore the different aspects of the problem.

Proposition 3.1 and earlier results on the complexity of containment [CM77, vdM92] entail the following complexity results on the problem of finding a rewriting of Q that uses a set of views $\mathcal{V}$:

Proposition 3.2: *Let Q be a query and $\mathcal{V}$ be a set of views.*

   1. *If Q is a conjunctive query with built-in predicates and $\mathcal{V}$ are conjunctive views without built-in predicates, then the problem of determining whether there exists a rewriting of Q that uses $\mathcal{V}$ is NP-complete.*

2. *If both Q and $\mathcal{V}$ are conjunctive and have built-in predicates, then the problem of deciding whether there exists a rewriting of Q that uses $\mathcal{V}$ is Π_2^p-complete.*

Remark: Proposition 3.1 holds for a broader class of queries and rewritings. In particular, suppose $q(\bar{X})$ is any relational calculus query, (or, equivalently, in nonrecursive datalog with negation) as is the view $v(\bar{W})$, and suppose we are considering *conjunctive rewritings*, which are formulas of the form

$$q(\bar{X}) \wedge (\exists \bar{Z}) v(\bar{Y})$$

such that the following equivalence holds:

$$q(\bar{X}) \equiv q(\bar{X}) \wedge (\exists \bar{Z}) v(\bar{Y})$$

Note that $\bar{X}$, $\bar{Y}$ and $\bar{Z}$ are tuples of variables, such that $\bar{Z}$ includes exactly those variables of $\bar{Y}$ that do not appear in $\bar{X}$. Then such a rewriting exists if and only if $\pi_\phi(Q) \subseteq \pi_\phi(V)$. □

The proof of Proposition 3.1 constructs a rewriting of Q using V in which the literal of V contains *new* variables that did not occur originally in Q. The following lemma shows that we can always find a rewriting that does not introduce new variables. The lemma also shows that we do not need to consider rewritings that include database-relation literals that do not appear in the original query, i.e., that it is enough to consider rewritings that include view literals and a *subset* of the original literals in the query. These results enable us to significantly prune the search for a minimal rewriting of Q.

Lemma 3.3: *Let Q be a conjunctive query without built-in predicates*

$$q(\bar{X}) \quad :- \quad p_1(\bar{U}_1), \ldots, p_n(\bar{U}_n).$$

and $\mathcal{V}$ be a set of views without built-in predicates.

1. *If Q' is a locally minimal rewriting of Q using $\mathcal{V}$, then the set of database-relation literals in Q' is isomorphic to a subset of the literals of Q.*

2. *If*

$$q(\bar{X}) \quad :- \quad p_1(\bar{U}_1), \ldots, p_n(\bar{U}_n), v_1(\bar{Y}_1), \ldots, v_k(\bar{Y}_k).$$

   is a rewriting of the query using the views, then there exists a rewriting of the form

$$q(\bar{X}) \quad :- \quad p_1(\bar{U}_1), \ldots, p_n(\bar{U}_n), v_1(\bar{Y}'_1), \ldots, v_k(\bar{Y}'_k).$$

   where $\{\bar{Y}'_1 \cup \ldots \cup \bar{Y}'_k\} \subseteq \{\bar{U}_1 \cup \ldots \cup \bar{U}_n\}$, i.e., a rewriting that does not introduce new variables.

3. *If Q and $\mathcal{V}$ include built-in predicates, then a rewriting as specified in Part 2 exists, with the only difference that the rewriting may be a union of conjunctive queries.*

Note that even though in part 2 of the lemma the rewriting includes all the literals of the query, the set of variables will not increase as a result of removing redundant literals. Therefore, the lemma implies that we can find a minimal rewriting that does not introduce new variables.

Proof: To prove the first part of the lemma, let Q' be a locally minimal rewriting of Q using a set of views $\mathcal{V}$. Let Q'' be the expansion of Q' obtained by replacing every occurrence of a view $V \in \mathcal{V}$ by the body of V, with suitable variable renamings. For any conjunctive query R, let $L(R)$ denote the set of literals database-relation literals in the body of R. Since Q'' and Q are equivalent, there are containment mappings ϕ from Q to Q'' and κ from Q'' to Q. Let C be a *core* of Q, that is, a minimal subset of $L(Q)$ such that there exists a containment mapping from $L(Q)$ to C. Let $S = \phi(C)$, the image of C in the body of Q'' under ϕ. Note that $C' = \kappa(S)$ is also a core of Q, since the composition of ϕ and κ is a containment mapping from $L(Q)$ to C'. It follows from uniqueness of the core up to isomorphism ([CM77]) that C and C' are isomorphic. We claim that ϕ is an isomorphism from C to S. By definition of S, every literal in S is in the image of ϕ, hence every variable in S is in the image of ϕ. Now suppose ϕ mapped two variables of C to the same variable in S. Since containment mappings cannot increase the number of variables, C' would have fewer variables than C, a contradiction. So ϕ is a bijection on the variables of C and S. By minimality of C and the existence of κ, S cannot have fewer literals than C, and by definition of S, S has no more literals than C. Hence S and C are isomorphic. To finish the proof we need to show that every database-relation literal in the body of Q' is in S. Suppose there is some database-relation literal in the body of Q' that is not in S; this literal can be removed from Q' while retaining equivalence to Q, contradicting the minimality of the rewriting. So S contains every database-relation literal in the body of Q', and since S is isomorphic to C, the database-relation literals in S are isomorphic to a subset of C.

To prove the second part, suppose that

$$Q' : q(\bar{X}) \quad :- \quad p_1(\bar{U}_1), \ldots, p_n(\bar{U}_n), v_1(\bar{Y}_1), \ldots, v_k(\bar{Y}_k).$$

is a rewriting of Q. By Proposition 3.1, $\pi_{\bar{\phi}}(q) \subseteq \pi_{\bar{\phi}}(v_i)$ $(i = 1, \ldots, k)$. Therefore, there is a containment mapping h_i from the body of the rule defining v_i into the body of the original rule for q. Let $h_i(\bar{Y}_i) = \bar{Y}'_i$ $(i = 1, \ldots, k)$. Consider the query

$$Q'' : q(\bar{X}) \quad :- \quad p_1(\bar{U}_1), \ldots, p_n(\bar{U}_n), v_1(\bar{Y}'_1), \ldots, v_k(\bar{Y}'_k).$$

It is easy to see that Q' contains Q'' (by using the mappings h_i), and clearly Q'' contains Q. Therefore, Q'' is equivalent to Q, and so it is a rewriting of Q using $\mathcal{V}$. Furthermore, Q'' does not introduce any new variables than those that appeared originally in Q.

The third part is proved in a similar fashion to the second except for one difference. Proposition 3.1 guarantees that for every v_i, there is a union of conjunctive queries $Q_i^1, \ldots, Q_i^{m_i}$ that is equivalent to Q, and there is a containment mapping h_i^j from v_i to every Q_i^j. The rewriting will be a disjunction of conjunctive queries. In every conjunct we choose one of the h_i^j's for every v_i, and construct the conjunct as in the previous case. $\square$

The following example shows that the second part of the above lemma does not hold when the view contains built-in predicates.

Example 3.4:   Consider the query:
$$Q : q(X, Y, U, W) \quad :- \quad p(X, Y), r(U, W), r(W, U).$$

and the view

$$V : v(A, B, C, D) \quad :- \quad p(A, B), r(C, D), C \leq D.$$

There exists no conjunctive query rewriting of Q that uses V and does not introduce new variables. However, the following is a rewriting of Q:

$$Q' : q(X, Y, U, W) \quad :- \quad v(X, Y, C, D), r(U, W), r(W, U).$$

Furthermore, the disjunctive rewriting that does not introduce new variables is:

$$Q' : q(X, Y, U, W) \quad :- \quad v(X, Y, U, W), r(W, U).$$
$$Q' : q(X, Y, U, W) \quad :- \quad v(X, Y, W, U), r(U, W).$$

□

3.1 Finding Minimal Rewritings

In general, we are interested in using views to answer queries in order to reduce the cost of evaluating the query. In this section we consider the complexity of the problems of reducing the total number of literals in the rewriting, reducing the number of database-relations in the rewriting, and finding rewritings that use only the views. Finally, we show that the problem of finding minimal rewritings has two independent sources of complexity.

The following lemma is the basis for several results. It shows that a minimal rewriting of a query Q, using a set of views $\mathcal{V}$, does not *increase* the number of literals in the query.

Lemma 3.5: *Let Q be a conjunctive query and $\mathcal{V}$ be a set of views, both Q and $\mathcal{V}$ without built-in predicates. If the body of Q has p literals and Q' is a locally minimal and complete rewriting of Q using $\mathcal{V}$, then Q' has at most p literals.*

Note that we can always assume that there are views in $\mathcal{V}$ that are identical to the database-relations, and therefore this lemma entails that any locally minimal rewriting of Q will have at most p literals.

Proof: As before, let Q'' be the expansion of a rewriting Q' of Q, in which the view literals in Q' are replaced by their definitions. Consider the containment mapping ϕ from Q to Q''. Each literal $l_1, \ldots, l_p$ in the body of Q is mapped to the expansion of at most one view literal in the body of Q''. If there are more than p view literals in Q', the expansion of some view literal in the body of Q'' must be disjoint with the image of ϕ; but then this view literal can be removed from Q' while preserving equivalence with Q. Hence there is a rewriting with at most p view literals. □

It can be shown that the size of the rewriting is bounded even if the database relations may have functional dependencies, or if the query and views have built-in predicates. The following example shows that the bound of Proposition 3.5 does not hold when the database relations have functional dependencies.

Example 3.6: Consider the query
$$q(X, Y, Z) \quad :- \quad e(X, Y, Z).$$

and the views

$$v_1(X, Y) \quad :- \quad e(X, Y, Z).$$
$$v_2(X, Z) \quad :- \quad e(X, Y, Z).$$

and suppose that in the relation e, the first argument functionally determines the other two. The following is the only complete rewriting of Q using v_1 and v_2:
$$q(X, Y, Z) \quad :- \quad v_1(X, Y), v_2(X, Z). \quad □$$

Using Lemma 3.5, we obtain the following complexity results on finding minimal rewritings.

Theorem 3.7: *Let Q be a conjunctive query without built-in predicates and $\mathcal{V}$ be conjunctive views without built-in predicates.*

1. *The problem of whether there exists a rewriting Q' of Q using $\mathcal{V}$ such that Q' contains no more than k literals, where k is less than or equal to the number of literals in the body of Q, is NP-complete.*

2. *The problem of whether there exists a rewriting Q' of Q using $\mathcal{V}$ such that Q' contains no more than k literals of database relations, where k is less than or equal to the number of literals in the body of Q, is NP-complete.*

3. *The problem of whether there exists a complete rewriting of Q using $\mathcal{V}$ is NP-complete.*

4. *If the query Q and views $\mathcal{V}$ have built-in predicates, then Problem 1 is in Σ_3^p.*

Proof: The proof of the first part is as follows. The problem is in NP because, by the Lemmas 3.5 and 3.3, we need only consider rewritings that have no more literals than the query, have a subset of the literals of the query, and do not introduce new variables. We can guess such a rewritten query, verify that it contains less than k literals, and guess containment mappings from the original query to the rewritten one and vice-versa. For the NP-hardness, reduce the problem of existence of a usage to it as follows. Given a query Q and a view V, let V' be the rule whose head is the same as the head of V and whose body is the conjunction of the bodies of Q and V. Now there is a usage of V' in Q with 1 literal in it if and only if there is a usage of V in Q. The other parts of the theorem are proved in a similar fashion. $\square$

Corollary 3.8: *The problem of finding a globally minimal rewriting of a conjunctive query without built-in predicates, using conjunctive views with no built-in predicates is in Σ_2^P.*

Using the results of [SY80] for unions of conjunctive queries we can generalize the above theorem as follows:

Theorem 3.9: *Let Q and $\mathcal{V}$ be disjunctions of conjunctive queries. When neither Q nor $\mathcal{V}$ have built-in predicates, the problem of whether there exists a complete rewriting of Q using $\mathcal{V}$ is NP-complete.*

The results described up to now suggest a two step algorithm for finding rewritings of a query Q. In the first step, we find some containment mapping from the views to the query and add to the query the appropriate view atoms, resulting in a query Q'. In the second step, we minimize Q' by removing literals from Q that are redundant. These two steps also emphasize the *two* sources of complexity involved in the problem. The first source is the exponential number of possible containment mappings from the views to the query. The second source is determining which literals of Q' are redundant given the mappings from the views to the query. The following theorem shows that these are two *independent* sources of complexity, i.e., that the problem is NP-complete even if there is a single mapping from each view to the query. In the next section we describe a polynomial time algorithm for determining which literals can be removed from the query, and we show that under certain conditions, it is guaranteed to find the unique maximal set of such literals.

Theorem 3.10: *The complete rewriting problem is NP-complete for conjunctive queries and views without built-in predicates even when both the query and the views are defined by rules that do not contain repeated predicates in their body.*

Note that when the query and the views are defined by such rules, then each rule is already non-redundant and, moreover, there is at most one mapping from each view into the query and finding those mappings is easy.

Proof: We use a reduction from the problem of exact cover by 3-sets. Given an instance of this problem, we create a predicate p_i for each element i and use a special variable S_j for each set j. For each p_i, we create an atom as follows. If element i is in set j, then the jth argument position of p_i has the variable S_j; if element i is not in set j, then the jth argument position of p_i has a distinct nondistinguished variable. The query is a conjunction of these atoms (i.e., one atom for each p_i). We may assume that the head of the query has no variables, i.e., it is of the form

$$q() \quad :- \quad p_1(\bar{U}_1), \ldots, p_n(\bar{U}_n).$$

We also create views as follows. For each set j, we create a view v_j. The three subgoals of v_j are the atoms created for the elements that appear in set j. The variables in the head of v_j are all the S_k variables that appear in the body of v_j, except for S_j.

There is exactly one containment mapping from the body of each view into the body of the query. Hence, a minimal rewriting that uses the views will have a subset of the literals in the following query:

$$q() \quad :- \quad p_1(\bar{U}_1), \ldots, p_n(\bar{U}_n), v_1(\bar{Y}_1), \ldots, v_m(\bar{Y}_m).$$

We have to show that there is a containment mapping that eliminates all the $p_i(\bar{U}_i)$ if and only if there is an exact cover. So, suppose that there is an exact cover. We will map each $p_i(\bar{U}_i)$ to the set that covers it. We have to show that the variables $S_1, \ldots, S_n$ are mapped consistently. So, suppose that two atoms $p_i(\bar{U}_i)$ and $p_j(\bar{U}_j)$ share the variable S_k. There are two cases to be considered. First, suppose that in the exact cover, the elements i and j are covered by the same set l. In this case, both of these atoms are mapped to the same view v_l, and clearly, the two occurrences of S_k in these atoms are mapped to the same variable in v_l. The second case is that elements i and j are covered by different sets, say h and l, respectively. Therefore, set k cannot be in the exact cover and, so, $k \neq h$ and $k \neq l$. It thus follows that S_k is a distinguished variable of both v_h and v_l, and hence, the two occurrences of S_k in $p_i(\bar{U}_i)$ and $p_j(\bar{U}_j)$ are mapped to S_k.

Now consider the other direction; that is, suppose that there is a containment mapping that eliminates all the $p_i(\bar{U}_i)$. Hence each $p_i(\bar{U}_i)$ is mapped to a view v_j, such that set j contains i. Since the variable S_j is not distinguished in v_j, it follows that if one $p_i(\bar{U}_i)$ is mapped to v_j, then so are the other two atoms for the elements of set j. Therefore, this mapping provides an exact cover. $\square$

4 Finding Redundant Literals in the Rewritten Query

In the previous section we have shown that finding rewritings for a query using views can be done in two steps. In the first, we consider containment mappings from the bodies of the views to the body of the query, and add the appropriate view literals to the query. In the second step, we remove literals of the original query that are redundant. We have also shown that in general, both steps provide independent sources of exponential complexity.

In this section we describe a polynomial time algorithm for the second step. In particular, given a set of mappings from the views to the query, the algorithm determines which set of literals from the query can be removed. We show that under certain conditions there is a *unique* maximal set of such literals and that the algorithm is guaranteed to find them. In other cases, the algorithm may find only a subset of the redundant literals, but all the literals it removes are guaranteed to be redundant, and therefore the algorithm is always applicable. Note that in such cases, the rest of the query can still be minimized using known, more computationally expensive techniques. Together with an algorithm for enumerating mappings from the views to the query, our algorithm provides a practical method for finding rewritings. For simplicity, we describe the algorithm for the case of rewritings using a single occurrence of a view, and we begin with the case that does not include built-in predicates.

Formally, suppose our query is of the form

$$Q : q(\bar{X}) \quad :- \quad p_1(\bar{U}_1), \ldots, p_n(\bar{U}_n). \tag{8.1}$$

and we have the following view:

$$V : v(\bar{Z}) \quad :- \quad r_1(\bar{W}_1), \ldots, r_m(\bar{W}_m). \tag{8.2}$$

Let h be a containment mapping from the body of v into the body of q, and let the following be the result of adding the view literal to the query:

$$q(\bar{X}) \quad :- \quad p_1(\bar{U}_1), \ldots, p_n(\bar{U}_n), v(\bar{Y}). \tag{8.3}$$

where $\bar{Y} = h(\bar{Z})$. Note that we can restrict ourselves to mappings where the variables of $\bar{Y}$ already appear in the $p_i(\bar{U}_i)$ (by Lemma 3.3). To obtain a minimal rewriting, our goal is to remove as many of the redundant p_i literals as possible.

To determine the set of redundant literals, consider the rule resulting from substituting the definition of Rule (8.2) instead of the view literal in Rule (8.3). That is, we rename the variables of Rule (8.2) as follows. Each variable T that appears in $\bar{Z}$ is renamed to $h(T)$, and each variable of Rule (8.2) that does not appear in $\bar{Z}$ is renamed to a new variable (that is not already among the $p_i(\bar{U}_i)$). Let the following be the result of this substitution.

$$q(\bar{X}) \quad :- \quad p_1(\bar{U}_1), \ldots, p_n(\bar{U}_n), r_1(\bar{V}_1), \ldots, r_m(\bar{V}_m). \tag{8.4}$$

Note that the variables of $\bar{Y}$ are the only ones that may appear in both the $p_i(\bar{U}_i)$ and the $r_j(\bar{V}_j)$.

Given the mapping h, there is a natural containment mapping from Rule (8.4) into the original rule for q (i.e., Rule (8.1)) that is defined as follows. Each literal $p_i(\bar{U}_i)$ is mapped to itself and each literal $r_j(\bar{V}_j)$ is mapped to the same literal of Rule (8.1) as in the containment mapping h (from Rule (8.2) to Rule (8.1)). We denote this containment mapping as ϕ. Note that the containment mapping ϕ maps each variable of $\bar{Y}$ to itself.

Each literal $p_i(\bar{U}_i)$ of Rule (8.1) is the image (under ϕ) of itself, and maybe a few of the $r_j(\bar{V}_j)$ literals. We say that the literals $r_j(\bar{V}_j)$ that map to $p_i(\bar{U}_i)$ under ϕ are the *associates* of $p_i(\bar{U}_i)$. For the rest of the discussion, we choose arbitrarily one of the associates of $p_i(\bar{U}_i)$ and refer to it as *the* associate of $p_i(\bar{U}_i)$. Note that if h does not map two literals $r_j(\bar{V}_j)$ to the same literal in Rule (8.1), then each $p_i(\bar{U}_i)$ will have at most one associate.

Before we show how to find the set of redundant literals, we need the following definition:

Definition 4.1: *A literal $r_j(\bar{V}_j)$ covers a literal $p_i(\bar{U}_i)$ that has the same predicate if the following two conditions hold:*

- *If $p_i(\bar{U}_i)$ has a distinguished variable (i.e., a variable in $\bar{X}$) or a constant in some argument position a, then $r_j(\bar{V}_j)$ also has that variable (or the constant) in argument position a.*

- *If argument positions a_1 and a_2 of $p_i(\bar{U}_i)$ are equal, then so are the argument positions a_1 and a_2 of $r_j(\bar{V}_j)$.*

Intuitively, if $r_j(\bar{V}_j)$ is the associate of $p_i(\bar{U}_i)$ and does not cover $p_i(\bar{U}_i)$, then we cannot remove $p_i(\bar{U}_i)$, because $p_i(\bar{U}_i)$ enforces quality constraints that are not enforced by $r_j(\bar{V}_j)$.

The set of *needed* literals $\mathcal{N}$ of the query Q is defined below. The set of redundant literals is the complement of the set of needed literals.

Definition 4.2: *The set $\mathcal{N}$ is the minimal subset of literals in Q satisfying the following four conditions.*

1. *Literals that have no associate.*

2. *Literals that are not covered by their associates.*

3. *If all the following conditions hold, then $p_i(\bar{U}_i)$ is in $\mathcal{N}$:*

   - *Literal $p_i(\bar{U}_i)$ has the variable T in argument position a_1.*
   - *The associate of $p_i(\bar{U}_i)$ has the variable[2] H in argument position a_1.*
   - *The variable H is not in $\bar{Y}$ (hence, H appears only among the $r_j(\bar{V}_j)$).*
   - *The variable T also appears in argument position a_2 of $p_l(\bar{U}_l)$.*
   - *The associate of $p_l(\bar{U}_l)$ does not have H in argument position a_2.*

4. *Suppose that $p_i(\bar{U}_i)$ is in $\mathcal{N}$ and that variable T appears in $p_i(\bar{U}_i)$. If $p_l(\bar{U}_l)$ has variable T in argument position a and its associate does not have T in argument position a, then $p_l(\bar{U}_l)$ is also in $\mathcal{N}$.*

The third condition in the definition adds to $\mathcal{N}$ those literals in Q whose associates do not enforce the same join constraints. The fourth condition iteratively adds to $\mathcal{N}$ literals that are *connected* to a literal in $\mathcal{N}$ via a common variable. It is important to note that the set of needed variables can be found in polynomial time in the size of the query.

Example 4.3: Consider the query and the view of Example 2.2. The result of substituting the view in the query would be the following:

$$q(X, U) \quad :- \quad p(X, Y), p_0(Y, Z), p_1(X, W), p_2(W, U),$$
$$p(X, C), p_0(C, Z), p_1(X, D).$$

The literal $p_2(W, U)$ is needed because it does not have an associate. The literal $p_1(X, W)$ is needed by the fourth condition of the definition, because its associate $p_1(X, D)$ does not contain the variable W (which appears in $p_2(W, U)$). Consequently, these two literals need to be retained to obtain the minimal rewriting. $\square$

---

[2]Note that the associate of $p_i(\bar{U}_i)$ cannot have a constant in argument position a_1 if $p_i(\bar{U}_i)$ has a variable in that argument position.

Theorem 4.4:

1. *The query*

$$q(\bar{X}) \quad :- \quad \mathcal{N}, v(\bar{Y}). \tag{8.5}$$

   is a rewriting of Q using V.

2. *Suppose that h does not map two literals $r_j(\bar{V}_j)$ to the same literal in Rule (8.1), and Rule (8.1) is minimal. Then the maximal set of redundant $p_i(\bar{U}_i)$ in Rule (8.4) is unique and is exactly the complement of the set $\mathcal{N}$.*

Proof: We will use ψ to denote a containment mapping from the original rule for q (i.e., Rule (8.1)) into the rewritten rule (i.e., Rule (8.4)).

Recall that the composition $\phi\psi$ is a containment mapping from Rule (8.1) to itself. Since Rule (8.1) is minimal, there is a k, such that $(\phi\psi)^k$ is the identity mapping on Rule (8.1). Let $\tau = \psi(\phi\psi)^{k-1}$. Note that τ is a containment mapping from Rule (8.1) into Rule (8.4), and $\phi\tau$ is the identity mapping on Rule (8.1).

The containment mapping ϕ (restricted to the image of τ) is the inverse of τ, since $\phi\tau$ is the identity mapping on Rule (8.1). Therefore, τ maps a literal $p_i(\bar{U}_i)$ of Rule (8.1) either to the literal $p_i(\bar{U}_i)$ or to the associate of $p_i(\bar{U}_i)$ in Rule (8.4).

We will now show that every $p_i(\bar{U}_i)$ in $\mathcal{N}$ must be mapped to itself by τ and, hence, all the $p_i(\bar{U}_i)$ of $\mathcal{N}$ are in the image of ψ. Recall that we already know that τ maps each $p_i(\bar{U}_i)$ either to itself or to its associate. If $p_i(\bar{U}_i)$ satisfies either Condition 1 or 2 (in the definition of $\mathcal{N}$), then clearly $p_i(\bar{U}_i)$ must be mapped to itself.

Suppose that $p_i(\bar{U}_i)$ and $p_l(\bar{U}_l)$ satisfy Condition 3. If $p_i(\bar{U}_i)$ is mapped to its associate, then $p_l(\bar{U}_l)$ must also be mapped to its associate, because variable H appears only among the $r_j(\bar{V}_j)$. But $p_i(\bar{U}_i)$ and $p_l(\bar{U}_l)$ cannot both be mapped to their associates, because $p_i(\bar{U}_i)$ and $p_l(\bar{U}_l)$ have the same variable T in argument positions a_1 and a_2, respectively, while their associates have different variables in these argument positions. Therefore, $p_i(\bar{U}_i)$ must be mapped to itself.

Now suppose that $p_i(\bar{U}_i)$ and $p_l(\bar{U}_l)$ satisfy Condition 4. Since $p_i(\bar{U}_i)$ is in $\mathcal{N}$, we may assume inductively that it must be mapped to itself. Therefore, variable T is mapped to itself and, hence, $p_l(\bar{U}_l)$ must also be mapped to itself. Thus, we have shown that all the literals of $\mathcal{N}$ must be mapped to themselves by τ.

We now define the mapping ψ' from Rule (8.1) into Rule (8.4) as follows. If $p_i(\bar{U}_i)$ is in $\mathcal{N}$, then it is mapped to itself; otherwise, it is mapped to its associate. We will show that ψ' is a containment mapping.

Clearly, every $p_i(\bar{U}_i)$ is mapped to a literal that covers it. So, it remains to show that if $p_i(\bar{U}_i)$ and $p_l(\bar{U}_l)$ have the same variable T in argument positions a_1 and a_2, respectively, then their images under ψ' also have the same symbol in these argument positions. There are three cases to be considered in order to prove this claim. In the first case, both $p_i(\bar{U}_i)$ and $p_l(\bar{U}_l)$ are mapped to themselves and the claim is clearly true.

In the second case, $p_i(\bar{U}_i)$ is mapped to itself (because it is in $\mathcal{N}$) while $p_l(\bar{U}_l)$ is mapped to its associate. By Condition 4 in the definition of $\mathcal{N}$, the associate of $p_l(\bar{U}_l)$ must also have variable T in argument position a_2 (or else $p_l(\bar{U}_l)$ would be in $\mathcal{N}$ and, hence, would be mapped to itself). So, the claim is proved also in this case.

In the third case, both $p_i(\bar{U}_i)$ and $p_l(\bar{U}_l)$ are mapped to their associates. Suppose that the associates have distinct variables, C and D, in argument positions a_1 and a_2, respectively. It is impossible that both C and D are in $\bar{Y}$, because ϕ is one-to-one on the variables of $\bar{Y}$ (because ϕ is the identity on $\bar{Y}$). So, one of them, say C, is not in $\bar{Y}$. But in this case, $p_i(\bar{U}_i)$ and $p_l(\bar{U}_l)$ satisfy Condition 3 in the definition of $\mathcal{N}$ and, hence, $p_i(\bar{U}_i)$ is in $\mathcal{N}$ and is mapped by ψ' to itself—a contradiction. Thus, we have shown that ψ' is a containment mapping.

In conclusion, we have shown that $\mathcal{N}$ is in the image of every containment mapping ψ from the original rule for q (i.e., Rule (8.1)) into the rewritten rule (i.e., Rule (8.4)). We have also shown that there is a mapping ψ', such that the $p_i(\bar{U}_i)$ in the image of ψ' are exactly those of $\mathcal{N}$. Therefore, the set of $p_i(\bar{U}_i)$ not in $\mathcal{N}$ is the unique maximal set of redundant $p_i(\bar{U}_i)$ in Rule (8.4). $\square$

It is well known that a containment mapping can be found in polynomial time if each literal has at most two potential destinations; the exact algorithm is based on a reduction to the 2-SAT problem [SY80]. In some sense, this is the case in the minimization algorithm presented in Theorem 4.4, since each $p_i(\bar{U}_i)$ can be mapped either to itself or to its associate. However, the contribution of Theorem 4.4 is twofold. First, it shows that each $p_i(\bar{U}_i)$ has at most two destinations. This fact is not obvious (indeed, when ordinarily using the reduction to 2-SAT, each literal that covers $p_i(\bar{U}_i)$ is considered a potential destination of $p_i(\bar{U}_i)$). The second contribution of Theorem 4.4 is in providing a more direct (and, hence, likely to be more efficient) way of computing the redundant $p_i(\bar{U}_i)$, as compared to the algorithm that uses the reduction to 2-SAT.

Adding Built-in Predicates

When the views may have built-in predicates, we need to repeat a similar process of finding needed literals for several containment mappings, and we can remove only literals that are not deemed needed for *any* of the mappings. Formally, suppose the result of adding the view literal to the query is

$$Q' : q(\bar{X}) \quad :- \quad p_1(\bar{U}_1), \ldots, p_n(\bar{U}_n), v(\bar{Y}). \tag{8.6}$$

As before, we can expand the definition of v in Q', obtaining the conjunction Q'' (as in Rule 8.4). By Proposition 3.1, there are a set of queries $Q_1, \ldots, Q_m$, that differ only on the built-in predicates, such that:

- Q is equivalent to the union of $Q_1, \ldots, Q_m$, and

- For every i, $1 \le i \le m$, there is a containment mapping ϕ_i from the body of Q'' into the body of Q_i, such that $bi(Q_i)$ entails $\phi_i(bi(Q''))$.

For each one of the ϕ_i mappings we compute the set of needed literals $\mathcal{N}_i$, and we define

$$\mathcal{N} \quad = \quad \mathcal{N}_1 \cup \ldots \cup \mathcal{N}_m.$$

Only the literals in $\mathcal{N}$ from Q remain in the rewritten query.

Example 4.5: Consider the query from Example 3.4:

$$Q : q(X, Y, U, W) \quad :- \quad p(X, Y), r(U, W), r(W, U).$$

and the view

$$V : v(A, B, C, D) \quad :- \quad p(A, B), r(C, D), C \le D.$$

The result of substituting the view in the query would be:

$$
\begin{aligned}
Q' : q(X, Y, U, W) \quad :- \quad & p(X, Y), r(U, W), r(W, U), \\
& v(X, Y, C, D).
\end{aligned}
\tag{8.7}
$$

The query Q can be written as the union

$$
\begin{aligned}
Q_1 : q(X,Y,U,W) \quad &:- \quad p(X,Y), r(U,W), r(W,U), \\
&\qquad U \leq W. \\
Q_2 : q(X,Y,U,W) \quad &:- \quad p(X,Y), r(U,W), r(W,U), \\
&\qquad U \geq W.
\end{aligned}
$$

and the mappings from the expansion of (8.6) to Q_1 and Q_2 are the identity on X, Y, U and W, and

$$
\begin{aligned}
\phi_1 &: \{C \rightarrow U, D \rightarrow W\}. \\
\phi_2 &: \{C \rightarrow W, D \rightarrow U\}.
\end{aligned}
$$

For the mapping ϕ_1, we will deem only the literal $r(W, U)$ as needed, because it does not have an associate, and for ϕ_2, $r(U, W)$ will be deemed needed. Therefore, since the only literal that is not needed for either of the mappings is $p(X, Y)$, it can be removed, resulting in the following rewriting:

$$
q(X,Y,U,W) \quad :- \quad r(U,W), r(W,U), v(X,Y,C,D).
$$

$\square$

5   Related Work

Several authors have considered the problem of implementing a query processor that uses the results of materialized views (e.g., [YL87, Sel88, SJGP90, CR94, TSI94, CKPS95]), but the formal aspects of finding the equivalent (and minimal) rewritings have received little attention.

Yang and Larson [YL87] considered the problem of finding rewritings for select-project-join queries and views. In their analysis they considered what amounts to one-to-one mappings from the views to query, and do not search the entire space of rewritings (and therefore may not always find all the possible rewritings of the query).

Chaudhuri et al. [CKPS95] considered the problem of finding rewritings for select-project-join queries and views, such that the rewritten query preserves the *bag* semantics. They show that in this case all the usages of views are obtained by 1-1 mappings from the views to the query, and therefore their algorithm would not find all the usages in the case where the relations are sets. Chaudhuri et al. [CKPS95] also considered the question of how to extend a query processor to chose between the different rewritings, a question that was not addressed in this paper. Srivastave *et al.* [SDJL96] extended the work in [CKPS95] to consider queries that involve aggregation. Finally, Rajaraman et al. [RSU95] built on our results and considered the problem of finding rewritings when the views may only be queried using specific binding patterns.

9

ADAPTING MATERIALIZED VIEWS
AFTER REDEFINITIONS

Ashish Gupta, Inderpal Singh Mumick,

Kenneth A. Ross

ABSTRACT

We consider a variant of the view maintenance problem: How does one keep a materialized view up-to-date when the view definition itself changes? Can one do better than recomputing the view from the base relations? Traditional view maintenance tries to maintain the materialized view in response to modifications to the base relations; we try to "adapt" the view in response to changes in the view definition.

Such techniques are needed for applications where the user can change queries dynamically and see the changes in the results fast. Data archaeology, data visualization, and dynamic queries are examples of such applications.

We consider all possible redefinitions of SQL `SELECT-FROM-WHERE-GROUPBY`, `UNION`, and `EXCEPT` views, and show how these views can be adapted using the old materialization for the cases where it is possible to do so. We identify extra information that can be kept with a materialization to facilitate redefinition. Multiple simultaneous changes to a view can be handled without necessarily materializing intermediate results. We identify guidelines for users and database administrators that can be used to facilitate efficient view adaptation.

1 Introduction

Visualization applications try to visualize views over the data stored in a database. The view is materialized, and a graphical display program may present the data in the view visually. If the user changes the view definition, the system must be able to recompute the view fast in order to keep the application interactive. An interface for such queries in a real estate system is reported in [WS92], where they are called *dynamic queries* [AWS93].

Data archaeology [BST+92, BST+93] is another application where an archaeologist tries to discover rules about data by formulating queries, looking at the results of the query, and then changing the query iteratively as the archaeologist's understanding improves.

We consider the problem of recomputing a materialized view in response to changes made to the view definition, that is, in response to redefinition of the view. We call this problem the "view adaptation problem."

1.1 Motivating Example

EXAMPLE 1.1 Consider the following relations E (employees), W (works), and P (projects):

$E(\underline{Emp\#}, Name, Address, Age, Salary)$.
$W(\underline{Emp\#, Proj\#}, Hours)$.
$P(\underline{Proj\#}, Projname, Leader\#, Location, Budget)$.

The key of each relation is underlined. Consider a graphical interface used to pose queries on the above relations using **SELECT, FROM, WHERE, GROUPBY**, and other SQL constructs. For instance, consider the following view defined by query Q_1.

```
CREATE VIEW V AS
SELECT  Emp#, Proj#, Salary
FROM    E & W
WHERE   Salary > 20000 AND Hours > 20
```

The natural join between relations E and W on attribute $Emp\#$ is specified as a part of the **FROM** clause using the "&" sign. Query Q_1 might be specified graphically using a slider for the *Salary* attribute and another slider for the *Hours* attribute. As the position of these sliders is changed, the display is updated to reflect the new answer.

Say the user shifts the slider for the *Salary* attribute making the first condition *Salary* > 25000. The answer to this new query can be computed easily from the answer already displayed on the screen. All those tuples that have *Salary* more than 20000 but not more than 25000, are removed from the display. This incremental computation is much more efficient than recomputing the view from scratch.

Not all changes to the view definition are so easily computable. For instance, if the slider for *Salary* is moved to lower the threshold of interest to *Salary* > 15000, then the above computation is not possible. However, we can still infer that (a) the old tuples still need to be displayed and (b) some more tuples need to be added, namely, those tuples that have *salary* more than 15000 but not more than 20000. Thus, even though the new query is not entirely computable using the answer to the old query, it is possible to substantially reduce the amount of recomputation.

Now, say the user decides to change Q_1 by joining it with relation P and then computing an aggregate. That is view V now is defined by a new query Q_2:

```
CREATE  VIEW V AS
SELECT  Proj#, Location, SUM(Salary)
FROM    E & W & P
WHERE   Salary > 20000 AND Hours > 20
GROUPBY Proj#, Location
```

Thus Q_2 requires that Q_1 be joined with relation P on attribute $Proj\#$ and the resulting view be grouped by $Proj\#$ and *Location*. Note that the key for relation P is $Proj\#$ and $Proj\#$ is already in the answer to query Q_1. Thus, to compute Q_2 we need only look up the *Location* attribute from the relation P using the value of $Proj\#$ for each tuple in the current answer set. (To avoid having to materialize Q_2 separately from Q_1, we could reserve in advance free space in each record of Q_1 so that answering Q_2 consists of a simple in place append of an extra attribute to each existing tuple.) The resulting set of tuples is aggregated over the required attributes to compute the answer to query Q_2.

Finally, say the user changes view V to compute the sum of salaries for each *Location* that appears in Q_2. The answer to this query (call it Q_3) is computable using only the result of Q_2. Because the grouping attributes of Q_2 are a superset of the grouping attributes of Q_3, each group of Q_2 is a subgroup of a group in Q_3. Thus, multiple tuples in the result of Q_2 are combined together to compute the answer to Q_3. ∎

We focus on changing a single materialized view, and on recomputing the new materialization using the old materialization and the base relations. In this chapter we do not consider how multiple materialized views may be used to further assist the adaptation process.

1.2 Results

We define the process of redefining a view as a sequence of local changes in the view definition. The adaptation is expressed as an additional query or update upon the old view and the base relations that needs to be executed to adapt the view in response to the redefinition. We identify a basic set of local changes so that a sequence of local changes can be maintained by concatenating the maintenance process for each local change. In almost all cases, this concatenation can be performed without materializing the intermediate results, yielding a single adaptation method for arbitrary changes to a view definition.

We present a *comprehensive* study of different types of local changes that can be made to a view, and present algorithms to maintain the views in response to these changes. These algorithms integrate smoothly with a cost-based query optimizer. The optimizer considers the additional plans provided by the algorithms and uses one of them if its cost is lower than the cost of rematerializing the view.

We show that the maintenance in response to a redefinition is facilitated by keeping a small amount of extra information (beyond the view definition's attributes themselves). We only consider information that can be maintained efficiently, and show how the adaptation process can be made far more efficient with this information.

Our work shows that (a) it is often significantly better to use previously materialized views, and (b) if you know in advance that you might change the views in certain ways, then you can include appropriate kinds of additional information in the views.

1.3 Related Work

The problem of redefining materialized views is related to the problem of optimizing an arbitrary query given that the database has materialized a view V. The query can be considered to be a redefinition of the view V and one may compute the query by changing the materialization of V. However, there is an important difference. Consider a query that returns all the tuples in the view except one. When framed as a query optimization problem, the complexity of using the view is $O(|V|)$, where $|V|$ is the cardinality of the materialization of V. When framed as a view maintenance problem, the complexity of the maintenance process is $O(\log(|V|))$. This will impact the choice of the strategies for query answering and view maintenance differently. Further, the view adaptation approach loses the old materialized view, while the querying approach keeps the old view in storage.

View adaptation differs from the problem of using materialized views to answer queries also in that adaptation assumes the new view definition is "close" to the old view definition, in the sense that the view changes via a small set of local changes. There is no such assumption in the query-answering problem, which means that a query compiler/optimizer would have to spend a considerable time determining how to use the existing views to *correctly* answer a given query. Thus, adaptation considers a smaller search space and yields a smaller but more efficient set of standard techniques that are easily incorporated in relational systems.

Classic [BBMR89] is a system developed at AT&T Bell Laboratories that allows users to define new concepts and optimizes the evaluation of their extents by classifying the concepts in a concept hierarchy, and then computing them starting with the parent concepts. This corresponds to evaluating a new Classic query (the new concept), using information in several materialized views (the old concepts). Classic has been used for data archaeology.

[LY85, YL87] look at the question of answering queries using cached results or materialized views. [LY85, YL87] show how to transform an SPJ (select-project-join) query so that it is expressed completely using a given set of views, without any reference to the base relations. They also have the idea of augmented views where each view is extended with keys of the underlying base relations.

[CKPS95] tackle the broader problem of trying to answer any query given any set of view definitions. Because they look at this more general problem, they have a much larger search space (exponential size) in their optimization algorithm. We have a simple small set of extra plans to check. For the less general problem we can do more, and do it more efficiently.

[RSU95, LMSS95a] also tackle the problem of answering a query given any set of view definitions. They do not consider aggregate queries.

[TSI94] focuses on the broader issue of enhancing physical data independence using "gmaps." They use a logical schema and then specify the underlying physical storage structures as results of "gmap" queries on the logical schema. User queries on the logical schema are rewritten using one or more gmap queries that each correspond an to access to a physical structures. The gmap and user queries are SPJ expressions. Query translation is similar to using only existing views (gmaps) to compute new views (user queries).

2 The System Model

2.1 Notation

We consider simple SQL SELECT-FROM-WHERE views, in addition to views definable using UNION, difference (EXCEPT) and aggregation (GROUPBY). We use a syntactic shorthand to avoid having to write down all the equality conditions in a natural join.

$$
\begin{aligned}
&\text{SELECT} \quad A_1, \ldots, A_n \\
&\text{FROM} \quad\quad R_1 \ \& \cdots \& \ R_m \\
&\text{WHERE} \quad\; C_1 \text{ AND} \cdots \text{ AND } C_k.
\end{aligned}
$$

When the relations in the FROM clause are separated by ampersands rather than commas, we mean that the relations $R_1, \ldots, R_n$ are combined by a natural join over all attributes that are mentioned in more than one relation. If we want an equijoin that is not a natural join, we shall specify the equijoin condition in the FROM clause rather than in the WHERE clause, inside square brackets. Join conditions that are not equijoins or natural joins will be specified in the WHERE clause. The conditions $C_1, \ldots, C_k$ are basic, i.e., non-conjunctive conditions.

When we perform schema changes, we use a shorthand of the form

$$
\begin{aligned}
&\text{UPDATE } v \text{ IN } V \text{ SET } A_i = \ldots \\
&\text{UPDATE } v \text{ IN } V \text{ DROP } A_i
\end{aligned}
$$

The second of these can be expressed alternatively as an SQL2 "ALTER TABLE" statement. The first of these can be expressed as a combination of an SQL2 ALTER TABLE statement and UPDATE statement.

Relations will be of two types – base relations and view relations. Base relations are physically stored by the system, and are updated directly. The view relations are defined as views (i.e, queries) over base relations and other view relations. A *materialized* view relation has its extension physically stored by the system. Materialized views are not updated directly; updates on the base relations and other view relations are translated by a view maintenance algorithm into updates to the materialized view.

Adaptation and Recomputation When view V is redefined, let the new definition be called V'. When the extent of V' is obtained utilizing the previously materialized extent of view V, the process will be called *adapting* view V. When the extent of V' is obtained by evaluating the view definition, without utilizing the previously materialized extent of view V, the process will be called *recomputing* view V. We can look upon a recomputation as a special case of adaptation where the previously materialized extent of view V is not used profitably.

2.2 View Adaptation Issues

We make the minimalistic assumption that the redefinition is expressed as a sequence of primitive local changes. Each local change is a small change to the view definition. For example, dropping or changing a selection predicate, adding an attribute to the result, changing the grouping list, and adding a join relation are all examples of local changes. We shall consider sequences of local changes (without necessarily materializing intermediate results) in Section 6.

Given a redefinable view, the system and/or the database administrator has to first determine (a) whether the view should be augmented with some extra information to help with later adaptation, (b) how the materialized view should be stored (maybe keep some free space for each tuple to grow), and (c) whether the materialized view should be indexed.

A view can be augmented only by adding more attributes and/or more tuples. Thus, the original view has to be a selection and/or projection of the augmented view. The additional attributes may be useful to adapt the view in response to changing selections, projections, grouping, and unions.

Next, as the user redefines a view, the redefinition is translated into the sequence of primitive changes, and the system must analyze the augmented view and the redefinition changes to determine (1) whether the augmented view can be adapted, and (2) the various algorithms for adapting the augmented view. The adaptation algorithms can also be expressed in SQL; For example, the redefined view can be materialized as an SQL query over the old view and the base relations. Alternatively, the redefined view can be defined by one or more SQL inserts, deletes and updates into the old materialization of the view, or even by simply recomputing the view from base relations.. The system can use an optimizer to choose the most cost-effective alternative for adapting the view.

2.3 Primitive changes

We support the following changes as primitive local changes to a view definition.

- Addition or deletion of an attribute in the SELECT clause.
- Addition, deletion, or modification of a predicate in the WHERE clause.
- Addition or deletion of a join operand (in the FROM clause), with associated equijoin predicates and attributes in the SELECT clause.
- Addition or deletion of an attribute from the groupby list.
- Addition or deletion of an aggregation function to a groupby view.
- Addition or deletion of an operand to the UNION and EXCEPT operators.
- Addition or deletion of the DISTINCT operator.

We will discuss each of these primitive changes, and outline an algorithm to adapt the view upon redefinition with the primitive change. As we consider each primitive change, we will build a table of alternative techniques to do the adaptation.

2.4 In-place Adaptation

When view V is redefined to yield V', the new view must be materialized, the old materialization for V must be deleted, and the new materialization must be labeled V. The maintenance process can try to use the old materialization of V as much as possible to avoid copying tuples. Thus, the adaptation method should try to change the materialization of V in place. In place adaptation is done using SQL INSERT, DELETE, and UPDATE commands. We use the following extended syntax for updates:

```
UPDATE   v IN V
SET      A =   (SELECT   B
               FROM     R_1 & ... & R_m
               WHERE    C_1 AND ... AND C_k).
```

The conditions in the WHERE clause of the subquery can refer to the tuple variable v being updated. The subquery is required to return only one value. It is possible that attribute A does not appear in the old definition of view V, and may be added to V by the redefinition. In that case, an in place update may not be possible due to physical space restrictions. On the other hand, systems may choose to keep some free space in each tuple to accommodate frequent adaptation, or use space created by deleted attributes.

3 SELECT-FROM-WHERE Views

In this section we consider views defined by a basic SELECT-FROM-WHERE query and redefinitions that may change the SELECT, the FROM, and/or the WHERE clauses. For each type of possible redefinition, we show: (a) How to maintain the redefinition, and (b) What extra information may be kept to facilitate maintenance.

A generic materialized view V may be defined as

```
CREATE   VIEW V AS
SELECT   A_1, ..., A_n
FROM     R_1 & ... & R_m
WHERE    C_1 AND ... AND C_k
```

As discussed in Section 2.1, an equijoin is written in the FROM clause of a query. Thus, changes to the equijoin predicates are considered in the subsection on the FROM clause, while changes to other predicates are considered in the subsection on the WHERE clause.

3.1 Changing the SELECT Clause

Reducing the set of attributes that define a view V is straightforward: In one pass of the old view we can project out the unneeded attributes to get the new view. Alternatively, one could simply keep the old view V, and make sure that accesses to the new view V' are obtained by pipelining a projection at the end of an access to V.

Adding attributes to a view is more difficult. One solution, is to keep more attributes than those needed for V in an augmented relation W, and to perform the projection only when references to V occur. In that case, we can add attributes to the view easily if they are attributes of W.

The solution mentioned above may be appropriate for a small number of attributes. However, when there are several base relations and many attributes, keeping a copy of all of the attributes may not be feasible. In such cases, we shall prefer where possible to keep *foreign keys* into the base relations.

EXAMPLE 3.1 Suppose our database consists of three relations E, W, and P as in Example 1.1. Define a view V as

```
CREATE VIEW V AS
SELECT Name,Projname
FROM    E  &  W  &  P
WHERE   Location=New-York
```

Keeping all of the attributes in an augmented relation would require maintaining eleven additional attributes. Alternatively, we could just keep *Emp#* and *Proj#* in addition to *Name* and *Projname* in an augmented relation, say *G*.

Suppose we wished to add the *Address* attribute to the view. We could do this addition incrementally by scanning once through relation G, and doing an indexed lookup on the E relation based on *Emp#*. This can be expressed as:

```
UPDATE   g IN G
SET Address = (SELECT Address
               FROM    E
               WHERE   E.Emp# = g.Emp#).
```

The update could be done in place, or it could be done by copying the result into a new version of G. A query optimizer could also rewrite the update statement into a join between E and G and modify the tuples of G as they participate in the join. In either case, the cost of updating G is easily estimated using standard cost-based optimization techniques, and is likely to be far less than recomputing the entire three-way join. ∎

Often the original view itself keeps the key columns for one of the base relations. Thus, if view V includes the key for a base relation R, or the key of R is equated to a constant in the view definition, and a redefinition requires additional columns of R, then the view can be adapted by using the keys present in the old materialization of the view to pick the appropriate tuples from relation R. Sometimes, adaptation can be done even in the absence of a key for R in the view. A sound and complete test for adaptation can be constructed using conjunctive query containment [Ull89, GSUW94], and is discussed in the full version of this chapter.

Changing the DISTINCT Qualifier. Suppose that a user adds a DISTINCT qualifier to the definition of a view that did not previously have one. Thus we have to delete duplicate entries from the old view to obtain the new view. This adaptation is fairly simply expressed as a SELECT DISTINCT over the old view to obtain the new view. Deleting a DISTINCT qualifier is more difficult, since it is not clear how many duplicates of each tuple should be in the new view. Techniques to do so are discussed in the full version of this chapter [GMR95b].

An alternative is to augment the view so as to always keep a count of the number of derivations for each tuple in the view. In this case, changes to the DISTINCT qualifier can be handled easily by either presenting the count to the user, or by hiding the count.

3.2   Changes in the WHERE Clause

In this section we discuss changes to a condition in the WHERE clause. We do not distinguish between conditions on a single relation and conditions on multiple relations (i.e., "join conditions") in the WHERE clause.

Let C_1' be a new condition. (Without loss of generality, we assume we are changing C_1 to C_1' in our generic view.) We want to efficiently materialize V', which could be defined as

```
CREATE  VIEW V' AS
SELECT  A_1,...,A_n
FROM    R_1 & ... & R_m
WHERE   C_1' AND ... AND C_k
```

by taking advantage of the fact that V has already been materialized.

Algebraically, $V' = V \cup V^+ - V^-$ where

$$V^+ = \begin{array}{l} \text{SELECT } A_1,\ldots,A_n \\ \text{FROM} \quad R_1 \& \cdots \& R_m \\ \text{WHERE} \quad C_1' \text{ AND NOT } C_1 \text{ AND} \cdots \text{ AND } C_k \end{array}$$

$$V^- = \begin{array}{l} \text{SELECT } A_1,\ldots,A_n \\ \text{FROM} \quad R_1 \& \cdots \& R_m \\ \text{WHERE} \quad \text{NOT } C_1' \text{ AND } C_1 \text{ AND} \cdots \text{ AND } C_k \end{array}$$

If the attributes mentioned by C_1' are a subset of $\{A_1,\ldots,A_n\}$, then
$$V^- = \text{ SELECT } A_1,\ldots,A_n \text{ FROM } V \text{ WHERE NOT } C_1'$$

or
$$V - V^- = \text{ SELECT } A_1,\ldots,A_n \text{ FROM } V \text{ WHERE } C_1'$$

V can thus be adapted as follows:

```
DELETE FROM V WHERE NOT C_1'

INSERT INTO V
(SELECT  A_1,...,A_n
FROM    R_1 & ... & R_m
WHERE   C_1' AND NOT C_1 AND ... AND C_k)
```

Alternatively, if the attributes of C_1' are not available in the view, the view adaptation algorithm for the SELECT clause could have materialized some extra attributes in an augmented relation W, or obtained these attributes using joins with the relation containing the attribute, as discussed in Section 3.1. In this case, even if C_1' mentioned an attribute not in $\{A_1,\ldots,A_n\}$, we could write V^- as above as long as all the attributes mentioned by C_1' were obtainable using the techniques of the previous section.

Thus we can see that the cost of adapting V in either of the cases above is (at most) one selection on V (or on the augmentation G) to adapt V into $V - V^-$, plus the cost of computing V^+ for insertion into V. As we shall see, in many examples the cost of computing V^+ will be small compared with the cost of recomputing V.

EXAMPLE 3.2 Let E and W be as defined in Example 1.1. Consider a view V defined by

> CREATE VIEW V AS
> SELECT * FROM E & W WHERE $Salary > 50000$

Suppose that we wish to adapt V to

> SELECT * FROM E & W WHERE $Salary > 60000$

Let us refer to the new expression as V'. Using the terminology above, we see that C_1 is "$Salary > 50000$" and C_1' is "$Salary > 60000$." Hence V^- and V^+ can be defined as

$V^- =$ SELECT * FROM V WHERE $Salary \leq 60000$ AND $Salary > 50000$

$V^+ =$ SELECT * FROM E & W WHERE $Salary > 60000$ AND $Salary \leq 50000$

V^+ is empty, since its conditions in the WHERE clause are inconsistent with each other. Hence, the cost of recomputing the view is (at most) one pass over V. Now suppose that V' is defined by

> SELECT * FROM E & W WHERE $Salary > 49000$.

Then V^- is empty, and V^+ is given by

> SELECT * FROM E & W WHERE $Salary > 49000$ AND $Salary \leq 50000$.

If there is an index on salary in E, then (with a reasonable distribution of salary values) $V \cup V^+$ might be computed much more efficiently than recomputing V' from scratch. The query optimizer would have enough information to decide which is the better strategy. ∎

Most queries that involve multiple relations use either equijoins or use single table selection conditions. For example, in one of our application environments, making efficient visual tools for browsing data, users are known to refine queries by changing the selection conditions on a relation interactively. Thus, it is likely that both the old condition C_1 and the new condition C_1' are single table selection conditions on the same attributes. Thus, the condition NOT C_1 AND C_1' can be pushed down to a single base relation, making the computation of V^+ more efficient.

Adding or Deleting a Condition

We can express the addition of a condition C' in the WHERE clause as a change of condition by adding some tautologically true selection to the old view definition V, then changing it to C'. The analysis above then means that V^+ is empty, and the new view can be computed as $V - V^-$, i.e., as a filter on the extension of V.

Similarly, the deletion of a condition is equivalent to replacing that condition by a tautologically true condition. In this case, V^- is empty, and the optimizer needs to compare the cost of computing V^+ with the cost of computing the view from scratch.

3.3   Changing the FROM Clause

If we change an equijoin condition, then it is not clear that V^+ is efficiently evaluable. This corresponds to our intuition, which states that if an equijoin condition changes then there will be a dramatic change in the result of the join, and so the old view definition will not be much help in computing the new join result. We note that it is unlikely that the users will change the equijoin predicates [G. Lohman, personal communication].

Nevertheless, there are situations where we can make use of the old view to efficiently compute a new view in which we have either added or deleted relations from the FROM clause.

Adding a join relation Suppose that we add a new relation R_{m+1} to the FROM clause, with an equijoin condition equating some attribute A of R_{m+1} to another attribute B in R_i for some $1 \leq i \leq m$. Suppose also that we want to add some attributes $D_1, \ldots, D_j$ from R_{m+1} to the view.

If B is part of the view, then the new view can be computed as

$$\text{SELECT } A_1, \ldots, A_n, D_1, \ldots, D_j \text{ FROM } V, R_{m+1} \text{ WHERE } A = B.$$

If the joining attribute A is a key for relation R_{m+1}, or we can otherwise guarantee that A values are all distinct, then we can express the adaptation as an update (we generalize SQL syntax to assign values to a list of attributes from the result of a subquery that returns exactly one tuple):

```
UPDATE v IN V
SET     D_1, ..., D_j = (SELECT  D_1, ..., D_j
                         FROM    R_{m+1}
                         WHERE   R_{m+1}.A = v.B).
```

If B is not part of the view, then it still may be possible to obtain B by joining V with R_i (assuming that V contains a key K for R_i) and hence compute the new view either as

```
UPDATE v IN V
SET     D_1, ..., D_j = (SELECT  D_1, ..., D_j
                         FROM    R_{m+1}, R_i
                         WHERE   R_{m+1}.A = R_i.B AND v.K = R_i.K).
```

if A is a key in R_{m+1}, or as

$$\text{SELECT } A_1, \ldots, A_n, D_1, \ldots, D_j \text{ FROM } V, R_i, R_{m+1} \text{ WHERE } A = B \text{ AND } V.K = R_i.K.$$

if A is not guaranteed to be distinct in R_{m+1}.

EXAMPLE 3.3 For example, suppose we have a materialized view of customers with their customer data, including their zip-codes. If we want to also know their cities, we can take the old materialized view and join it with our zip-code/city relation to get the city information as an extra attribute. ∎

Deleting a join relation When deleting a join operand, one has to make sure that the number of duplicates is maintained correctly, and also allow for dangling tuples. For $R \bowtie S \bowtie T$, when the join with T is dropped, the system (1) needs to go back and find $R \bowtie S$ tuples that did not join with T, and (2) figure out the exact multiplicity of tuples in the new view. The former can be avoided if the join with T is lossless, a condition that might be observed by the database system if the join is on a key of T and if the system enforces referential integrity. The latter can be avoided if the view does not care about duplicates (SELECT DISTINCT), or if T is being joined on its key attributes, and the key of T is in the old view.

3.4 Summary: SELECT-FROM-WHERE Views

Tables 2 and 3 summarizes our adaptation techniques for SELECT-FROM-WHERE queries. We assume that the initial view definition is as stated at the beginning of Section 3. For each possible redefinition, we give the possible adaptations along with the assumptions needed for the adaptation to work. The assumptions

1. Attribute A is from relation S and the key K for S is in view V.

2. An augmented view that keeps a count of number of derivations of each tuple is used.

3. Attribute of condition is either an attribute of the view, or of a wider augmented stored view.

4. $D_1, \ldots, D_j$ and A are attributes of R_{m+1}, and the join condition is $A = B$.

5. B is an attribute of V.

6. A is a key for relation R_{m+1}.

7. B is an attribute of R_i, K is a key of R_i, and K is an attribute of V.

8. Join with R_m is known to be lossless.

9. Either V contains a `SELECT DISTINCT`, or the join of R_m is on a key attribute that is also present in V.

Table 1   Assumptions for the Adaptation Techniques in Table 3

are listed separately in Table 1. In the full version of this chapter [GMR95b] we also discuss adaptation of `SELECT-FROM-WHERE` queries that originally use the `DISTINCT` qualifier.

Tables 2 and 3 can be used in three ways. Firstly, the query optimizer would use this table to find the adaptation technique (and compute its cost estimate) given the properties of the current schema vis-a-vis the assumptions stated in the table. Secondly, a database administrator or user would use this table to see what assumptions need to hold in order to make incremental view adaptation possible at the most efficient level. Given this information, the views can be defined with enough extra information so that view changes can be computed most efficiently. Note that different collections of assumptions make different types of incremental computation possible, so that different "menus" of extra information stored should be considered. Thirdly, the database administrator could interact with the query optimizer to see which access methods and indexes should be built, on the base relations and on the materialized views, in order to facilitate efficient adaptation.

Recommendations for Augmentation.   Keep the keys of referenced relations from which attributes may be added. Store the view with padding in each tuple for future in-place expansion. Keep attributes referenced by the selection conditions in the view definition, or at least keep the keys of referenced relations from which these attributes may be added. Keep the count of the number of derivations for each tuple.

4   Aggregation Views

In this section, we show how to adapt views when grouping columns and the aggregate functions used in a materialized SQL aggregation view change.

EXAMPLE 4.1   Consider again the relations of Example 1.1. We could express the total salaries charged to a project with the following materialized view: We assume that an employee is nominally employed for 40 hours per week, and that if an employee works more or less, a proportional salary is paid. Thus the charge to a project for an employee is obtained by multiplying the salary by the fraction of the 40 hour week the employee works on the project.

```
CREATE  VIEW V(Proj#, Location, Proj_Sal) AS
SELECT  Proj#, Location, SUM((Sal × Hours)/40)
FROM    E & W & P
GROUPBY Proj#, Location
```

Redefined View	Adaptation Technique	Assumptions

SELECT $A, A_1, \ldots, A_n$
FROM R_1 & $\cdots$ & R_m
WHERE C_1 AND $\cdots$ AND C_k
	UPDATE v IN V
	SET $A =$ (SELECT A
	        FROM S
	        WHERE $S.K = v.K$)
		(1)

SELECT $A_2, \ldots, A_n$ FROM R_1 & $\cdots$ & R_m WHERE C_1 AND $\cdots$ AND C_k	UPDATE v IN V DROP A_1	
SELECT DISTINCT $A_1, \ldots, A_n$ FROM R_1 & $\cdots$ & R_m WHERE C_1 AND $\cdots$ AND C_k	INSERT INTO New_V SELECT DISTINCT* FROM V	
SELECT DISTINCT $A_1, \ldots, A_n$ FROM R_1 & $\cdots$ & R_m WHERE C_1 AND $\cdots$ AND C_k	Mark view as being distinct.	(2)
SELECT $A_1, \ldots, A_n$ FROM R_1 & $\cdots$ & R_m WHERE C'_1 AND $\cdots$ AND C_k	DELETE FROM V WHERE NOT C'_1	$C'_1 \Rightarrow C_1$ (3)
SELECT $A_1, \ldots, A_n$ FROM R_1 & $\cdots$ & R_m WHERE C'_1 AND $\cdots$ AND C_k	DELETE INSERT INTO V FROM V SELECT $A_1, \ldots, A_n$ WHERE NOT C'_1 FROM R_1 & $\cdots$ & R_m WHERE C'_1 AND NOT C_1 AND $\cdots$ AND C_k	$C'_1 \not\Rightarrow C_1$ (3)
SELECT $A_1, \ldots, A_n$ FROM R_1 & $\cdots$ & R_m WHERE C_0 AND C_1 AND $\cdots$ AND C_k	DELETE FROM V WHERE NOT C_0	(3)
SELECT $A_1, \ldots, A_n$ FROM R_1 & $\cdots$ & R_m WHERE C_2 AND $\cdots$ AND C_k	INSERT INTO V SELECT $A_1, \ldots, A_n$ FROM R_1 & $\cdots$ & R_m WHERE NOT C_1 AND C_2 AND $\cdots$ AND C_k	(3)

SELECT $A_1, \ldots, A_n, D_1, \ldots, D_j$
FROM R_1 & $\cdots$ & R_m & R_{m+1}
WHERE C_1 AND $\cdots$ AND C_k
	UPDATE v IN V
	SET $D_1, \ldots, D_j =$
	    (SELECT $D_1, \ldots, D_j$
	    FROM R_{m+1}
	    WHERE $R_{m+1}.A = v.B$).
		(4,5,6)

SELECT $A_1, \ldots, A_n, D_1, \ldots, D_j$ FROM R_1 & $\cdots$ & R_m & R_{m+1} WHERE C_1 AND $\cdots$ AND C_k	INSERT INTO New_V SELECT $A_1, \ldots, A_n, D_1, \ldots, D_j$ FROM V, R_{m+1} WHERE $A = B$	(4,5)

Table 2   Adaptation Techniques for SELECT-FROM-WHERE Views (contd. in Table 3)

Suppose we want to modify V so that it gives a location-by-location sum of charged salaries. This modification corresponds to removing the *Proj#* attribute from the list of grouping variables and output variables, to give the following view definition:

CREATE   VIEW V'(*Location, Proj_Sal*) AS
SELECT   *Location, SUM((Salary × Hours)/40)*
FROM   *E & W & P*
GROUPBY   *Location*

Using the commutativity properties of *SUM*, the query optimizer can observe that V' can be materialized as

SELECT   *Location, SUM(Proj-Sal)*
FROM V
GROUPBY   *Location*

Redefined View	Adaptation Technique		Assump-tions
SELECT $A_1, \ldots, A_n, D_1, \ldots, D_j$ FROM R_1 & $\cdots$ & R_m & R_{m+1} WHERE C_1 AND$\cdots$ AND C_k	UPDATE v IN V SET $D_1, \ldots, D_j =$ (SELECT $D_1, \ldots, D_j$ FROM R_{m+1}, R_i WHERE $R_{m+1}.A = R_i.B$ AND $v.K = R_i.K$).		(4,6,7)
SELECT $A_1, \ldots, A_n, D_1, \ldots, D_j$ FROM R_1 & $\cdots$ & R_m & R_{m+1} WHERE C_1 AND$\cdots$ AND C_k	INSERT INTO New_V SELECT $A_1, \ldots, A_n, D_1, \ldots, D_j$ FROM V, R_i, R_{m+1} WHERE $A = B$ AND $V.K = R_i.K$		(4,7)
SELECT $A_1, \ldots, A_n$ FROM R_1 & $\cdots$ & R_{m-1} WHERE C_1 AND$\cdots$ AND C_k	No adaptation needed.		(8,9)
SELECT $A_1, \ldots, A_j$ FROM R_1 & $\cdots$ & R_{m-1} WHERE C_1 AND$\cdots$ AND C_k	UPDATE v IN V DROP $A_{j+1}, \ldots, A_n$		$j < n$, (8,9)

Table 3 Adaptation Techniques for SELECT-FROM-WHERE Views (contd. from Table 2)

In this way we can use the original view to redefine the materialized view more efficiently.

Next, suppose we want to modify V to compute the sum of charged salaries for each *Proj#*. We can adapt V simply by dropping the *Location* attribute because *Proj#* is the key for relation P and functionally determines *Location*. The redefined groups are the same as before. ∎

4.1 Dropping GROUPBY Columns

Given an aggregation view, the set of tuples in the grouped relation that have the same values for all the grouping attributes is called a *group*. Thus, for the original view in Example 4.1, there is one group of tuples for each pair of (*Proj#*, *Location*) values. For the redefined view, there is one group of tuples for each (*Location*) value.

When a grouping attribute is dropped, each redefined group can be obtained by combining one or more original groups, so we can try to get the aggregation function over the redefined groups by combining the aggregation values from the combined groups. For instance, in Example 4.1, after dropping the *Proj#* attribute, the sum for the group for a particular (*Location*) value was obtained from the sum *Proj-Sal* of all the groups with this *Location*. When we dropped the *Location* attribute, we inferred that each redefined group was obtained from a single original group. So no new aggregation was needed

A materialized view can be adapted when grouping columns are dropped if:

- The dropped column is functionally determined by the remaining grouping columns, or
- The aggregate functions in the redefined view are expressible as a computation over one or more of the original aggregation functions and grouping attributes. Table 4 lists a few aggregation functions that can be computed in such a manner.

Table 4 is meant to be illustrative, and not exhaustive. Several other aggregation functions may be decomposed in this manner.

Redefined Aggregation	Adaptation using Original View
$MIN(X)$	$MIN(M)$ where $M = MIN(X)$ was an original aggregation column.
$MAX(X)$	$MAX(M)$ where $M = MAX(X)$ was an original aggregation column.
$MIN(X)$	$MIN(X)$, where X was an original grouping column.
$MAX(X)$	$MAX(X)$, where X was an original grouping column.
$SUM(X)$	$SUM(S)$ where $S = SUM(X)$ was an original aggregation column
$SUM(X)$	$SUM(X \times C)$, where $C = COUNT(*)$ was an original aggregation column, and X was an original grouping column.
$COUNT(*)$	$SUM(C)$ where $C = COUNT(*)$ was an original aggregation column.
$AVG(X)$	$SUM(A \times C)/SUM(C)$ where $C = COUNT(*)$ and $A = AVG(X)$ were original aggregation columns.
$AVG(X)$	$SUM(X \times C)/SUM(C)$ where $C = COUNT(*)$ was an original aggregation columns, and X was an original grouping column.

Table 4   Aggregate functions for a group defined as functions of subgroup aggregates.

4.2   Adding GROUPBY Columns

In general, when adding a groupby column, we would need to go back to the base relations since we are looking to aggregate data at a finer level of granularity. However, in case the added attribute is functionally determined by the original grouping attributes, we can add it just like we add a new projection column (Section 3.1).

Another situation where we can add GROUPBY columns is when there was no grouping or aggregation before. In that case, the new view is formed simply by applying the grouping and aggregation over the old view, assuming that the attributes needed for the grouping and aggregation are present in the old view. Even if the needed attributes are not present, they can be added in many cases, as discussed previously.

4.3   Dropping/Adding Aggregation Functions

Adapting a view to drop an aggregation function is straightforward, similar to the case where a column is projected out (Section 3.1). However, it is not possible to adapt to most additions of aggregation functions, unless the new function can be expressed in terms of existing functions, or unless the aggregation view is significantly augmented. One type of augmentation requires storing the key values of all tuples in a group in the view. This augmentation is, discussed in the full version of this chapter.

4.4   Summary: GROUPBY Views

In this section we have seen several techniques for adapting views with aggregation. A more complete list is available in the full version of this chapter [GMR95b].

Recommendations for Augmentation.   Table 4 illustrates that redefinition can be helped tremendously if the views are augmented with a $COUNT(*)$ aggregation function.

5 Union and Difference Views

5.1 UNION

A view V may be defined as the union of subqueries, say V_1 and V_2. If the definition of V changes by a local change in either V_1 or V_2 but not both, then it would be advantageous to apply the techniques developed in the previous sections to incrementally update either the materialization of V_1 or V_2 while leaving the other unchanged.

In order to do this, we need to know which tuples in V came from V_1 and which from V_2. With this knowledge, we can simply keep the tuples from the unchanged part of the view, and update the changed part of the view. Thus it would be beneficial to store with each tuple an indication of whether it came from V_1 or V_2. Alternatively, one could store V_1 and V_2 separately, and form the union only when the whole view V is accessed.

EXAMPLE 5.1 Consider the schema from Example 1.1. Suppose we want the names of employees who either work on a project located in New York, or who manage a project located in New York. We can write this view V as V_1 UNION V_2 where V_1 and V_2 are as follows.

$V_1 =$ SELECT $Name,SubQ=$"V_1"
  FROM E & W & P
  WHERE $Location=New\text{-}York$

$V_2 =$ SELECT $Name,SubQ=$"V_2"
  FROM E, P $[E.Emp\# = P.Leader\#]$
  WHERE $Location=New\text{-}York$

(We would probably choose not to display the $SubQ$ field to the user, but to keep it as an attribute of a larger augmented relation.) If we wanted to change V_1 so that we get only employees working more than 20 hours per week, then we could do so using techniques developed in the previous sections for tuples in V with $SubQ=$"V_1", and leave the other tuples unchanged. ∎

It is easy to delete a UNION operand if we keep track of which tuples came from which subqueries. We simply remove from V all tuples with the $SubQ$ attribute matching that of the subquery being deleted.

Adding a union operand is also straightforward: The old union is unchanged, and the new operand is evaluated to generate the new tuples.

5.2 EXCEPT

EXAMPLE 5.2 Consider again the schema from Example 1.1. Suppose we want the names of employees who work on a project located in New York, but who are not managers. We can write this view as V_1 EXCEPT V_2 where V_1 and V_2 are defined as follows.

CREATE VIEW V_1 AS	CREATE VIEW V_2 AS
SELECT $Name$	SELECT $Name$
FROM E & W & P	FROM E, P $[E.Emp\# = P.Leader\#]$
WHERE $Location=New\text{-}York$	WHERE $Location=New\text{-}York$

∎

Unlike the case for unions, the extension of V could conceivably be much smaller than the extensions of either V_1 or V_2. Thus, we cannot argue that in general we should keep all of the V_1 and V_2 tuples with an identification of whether they came from V_1 or V_2.

However, in two cases we can still use information in the old view to compute the new view more efficiently.

1. If V_2 is replaced by a view V_2' that is strictly weaker (i.e., contains more tuples) than V_2, then we can observe that V_2^- is empty, and $V' = V$ EXCEPT V_2^+.

2. If V_1 is replaced by a view V_1' that is strictly stronger (i.e., contains fewer tuples) than V_1, then we can observe that V_1^+ is empty, and $V' = V$ EXCEPT V_1^-.

If we want to subtract a new subquery V_2 from an existing materialized view V, then we can do so efficiently using the first observation above. In that case, the new view V' is V EXCEPT V_2 and we can make use of the old extension of V.

In the general case, there is another possibility that the optimizer can consider for computing V'. Suppose that V_2 changes with both V_2^+ and V_2^- nonempty. The new answer is V EXCEPT V_2^+ UNION U where U is $V_1 \cap V_2^-$. While we probably have not materialized V_1, we can still evaluate U by considering each tuple in V_2^- and *checking* that it satisfies the conditions defining V_1. If V_2^+ and V_2^- are small, then this strategy will still be better than recomputing V' from scratch. A symmetric case holds if V_1 changes rather than V_2. In order for this strategy to be effective, the query optimizer needs to estimate the sizes of V_2^+ and V_2^-. For simple views V_2 this may be achieved using selectivity information and information about the domains of the attributes. For complicated queries, it may be hard to estimate these sizes.

5.3   Summary: Views with Union and Difference

In this section we have seen several techniques for adapting views with union and difference. A more complete list is available in the full version of this chapter [GMR95b].

Recommendations for Augmentation.   Keep an attribute identifying which subquery in a union each tuple came from.

6   Multiple Changes to a View Definition

So far we have considered single local changes to a view definition. However, a user might make several simultaneous local changes to a view definition. The new view may easily be obtained by concatenating the adaptations from each local change, but this approach would materialize all of the intermediate results, which may not be necessary.

For example, if more than one condition in the WHERE clause is simultaneously changed, then the analysis of Section 3.2 still applies by thinking of C_1 and C_1' as *conjunctions* of conditions. Similarly, multiple attributes may be added or deleted from a view simultaneously using the techniques of Section 3.1 without materializing intermediate results. Several relations may be added to the FROM clause using the techniques of Section 3.3 without materializing the intermediate results.

If the new view is obtained by making changes of different types, then we can avoid materializing intermediate results by pipelining the results of applying one change into the computation of the next change. Pipelining is possible if each of the basic adaptation techniques can be applied in a single pass over the materialized view. It turns out that, with one exception, all techniques described in this chapter *can* be done in a single pass. The exception is the use of a previously materialized view V within an aggregation that is grouped on an attribute that is not the (physical) ordering attribute of V. Thus, for changes other than this one exception, it is possible in principle to cascade multiple local changes without materializing intermediate results. Note, if updates are done in-place, then there is little choice but to perform the individual adaptations sequentially.

Thus the optimizer can choose the best of the following three choices for adaptation: (a) applying successive in-place updates, (b) cascading the adaptations as above, or (c) recomputing the view from base relations.

7   Conclusions

When the definition of a materialized view changes we need to bring the materialization up-to-date. In this chapter we focus on *adapting* a materialized view, i.e., using the old materialization to help in the materialization of the new view. The alternative to adaptation is to *recompute* the view from scratch, making no use of the old materialization. Often, it is more efficient to adapt a view rather than recompute it, sometimes by an order of magnitude; a number of examples have been described in this chapter.

A number of applications, like data-archaeology and visualization, require *interactive*, and thus quick, response to changes in the definition of a materialized view.

We have provided a *comprehensive list* of view adaptation techniques that can be applied for basic view definition changes. Each of these adaptation techniques is itself expressed as an SQL query or update that makes use of the old materialization. Because the adaptation is itself expressed in SQL, it is possible for the query optimizer to estimate the cost of these techniques using standard cost-based optimization. In some cases there may be several adaptation alternatives, and each of the alternatives would be considered in turn.

Our basic adaptation techniques correspond to local changes in the view definition. We also describe how multiple local changes can be combined to give an adaptation technique for changes to several parts of a view definition. All, but one, techniques for adapting a view in response to a local change can be *pipelined* thereby eliminating the need to store intermediate adapted views when multiple local changes are combined.

Often it is easier to adapt a view if certain additional information is kept in the view. Such additional information includes keys of base relations, attributes involved in selection conditions, counts of the number of derivations of each tuple, additional aggregate functions beyond those requested, and identifiers indicating which subquery in a union each tuple came from. Depending on the type of anticipated change, the view can be defined to contain the appropriate additional information. Additionally, it can be beneficial to reserve some physical space in each record to allow in-place adaptation involving addition of attributes.

We have derived tables of adaptation techniques (see [GMR95b] for a complete list) that can be used in three important ways. Firstly, the query optimizer can use the tables to find the adaptation technique (and compute its cost estimate) given the properties of the current schema vis-a-vis the assumptions stated in the table. Secondly, a database administrator or user can use the tables to see what assumptions would need to be satisfied in order to make view adaptation possible at the most efficient level, and define the view accordingly. Thirdly, the database administrator can interact with the query optimizer to build appropriate access methods and indexes on the base relations and on the materialized views, in order to facilitate efficient adaptation.

The main contributions of this chapter are (a) the derivation of a comprehensive set of view adaptation techniques, (b) the smooth integration of such techniques into the framework of current relational database systems using existing optimization technology, and (c) the identification of guidelines that can be provided to users and database administrators in order to facilitate view adaptation.

Acknowledgments

We thank Arun Netravali for pointing out the importance of redefinition to data visualization, and Shaul Dar and Tom Funkhouser for discussions of the relationship between view maintenance and data visualization.

10

THE DYNAMIC HOMEFINDER: EVALUATING DYNAMIC QUERIES IN A REAL-ESTATE INFORMATION EXPLORATION SYSTEM

Christopher Williamson, Ben Shneiderman

1 Introduction and Background

Most database systems require the user to create and formulate a complex query, which presumes that the user is familiar with the logical structure of the database [Lar86]. The queries on a database are usually expressed in high level query languages such as SQL. This works well for many applications, but it is not a fully satisfying way of finding data. For naive users these systems are difficult to use and understand, and they require a long training period [KKS88].

Clearly there is a need for easy to use, quick and powerful query methods for database and information retrieval. Direct manipulation has proved to be successful for other applications such as display editors, spreadsheets, computer aided design/manufacturing systems, computer games and graphical environments for operating systems such as the Apple Macintosh [Shn83]. Direct manipulation interfaces support:

- Continuous visual representation of objects and actions of interest.

- Physical actions or labeled button presses instead of complex query syntax.

- Rapid, incremental, reversible operations whose results are immediately visible.

- Layered or spiral approaches to learning that permit usage with minimal knowledge.

One of the great advantages of direct manipulation is that it places the task in the center of what users do. Rutkowski (1982) describes it as: "The user is able to apply intellect directly to the task; the tool itself seems to disappear." The success of direct manipulation can be understood in the context of the syntactic/semantic model which describes the different levels of understanding that users have. Objects of interest are displayed so that actions are directly in the high level semantic domain. Users do not need to decompose tasks into syntactically complex sequences. Thus each command is a comprehensible action in the problem domain whose effect is immediately visible. The closeness of the command action to the problem domain reduces user problem-solving load and stress.

For information retrieval and database exploration, there have been several attempts to use direct manipulation and escape some of the pitfalls of contemporary boolean systems [Zlo75, KKS88, Wil84]. The first two systems do not provide any visual display of actions. Zloof's Query-by-Example relies on users entering values with a keyboard. Even though Kim, et al.'s PICASSO supports input through mouse and menus, it requires users to perform a number of operations in each step. The combination of graphical input/output is not applied in any of these systems.

Figure 1   A slider from the Dynamic HomeFinder.

Other solutions have come about with the invention of natural-language query systems. Some of these systems [Sal83, HC90], usually using statistical ranking and/or relevance feedback, do a fine job retrieving textual information. They are, however, very awkward to apply to graphical information systems and they have other well-documented problems [Hel88]. An alternative database interface utilizing dynamic queries [AWS92] would:

- represent the query graphically,

- provide visible limits on the query range,

- provide a graphical representation of the database and the query result,

- give immediate feedback of the result during every query adjustment, and

- allow novice users to begin working with little training, but still provide expert users with powerful features.

With dynamic queries, the query is represented by a number of sliders (figure 1). Each slider consists of a label, a field indicating its current value, a slider bar with a drag box and a value at each end of the slider bar indicating minimum and maximum values. Sliding the drag box with the mouse changes the value of the slider. Clicking with the mouse on the slider bar increases or decreases the value one step at a time. The database is represented on the screen in graphical form. This paper describes a program dealing with real-estate and, accordingly, the map of the area was chosen as the representation. The result of the query can then be highlighted by coloring, changing points of light, marking of regions, or blinking.

The combination of a graphical query and graphical output fits well into the principles of direct manipulation. The slider serves as a metaphor for the operation of entering a value for a field in the query. Norman (1988) promotes the use of sliders since they also provide a mental model of the range. Changing the value is done by a physical action—sliding the drag box with a mouse—instead of entering the value by keyboard. By sliding the drag box back and forth and getting real-time updates of the query results, it is possible to do dozens of queries in just a few seconds. The operation is incremental and, if the query result is not what users expected, the operation is reversible by just sliding the drag box in the opposite direction. Error messages are needed—there is no such thing as an "illegal" operation or a syntax error.

The interaction between the database visualization and the query mechanism is important. The sliders have to be placed close to the visual presentation to reduce eye movement. The highlighting of elements should be in harmony with the coloring scheme of the slider. For example the color of the area to the left of the drag box on the slider bar is the same as the highlighted elements in the visualization, because the values to the left of the drag box are the values that satisfy the query.

2 Dynamic Queries Interface to Real-Estate

The program used for the experiment applied dynamic queries to real-estate. Finding a home is a laborious task for those that have experienced it. The two most common methods currently used are paper and SQL-like database systems. Newspaper and printed listings have survived to still be the most common means for finding a home. These provide little organization, short of being sorted by one field, but are easy-to-use for the novice. In the last few decades, SQL-like systems have appeared to support more complex queries.

Unfortunately, SQL-like systems require training and/or an intermediary; almost none allow the actual homebuyer to perform the search. Further, these systems suffer the problems of most command-line query systems: slow, difficult to use, little feedback, nonreversible, and too many boolean logic errors. In addition, these systems offer no easy way to specify locations. The homebuyer must know neighborhood names, and attempt to figure out if a given neighborhood is near where they wish to live. Finally, these systems suffer from the classic all-or-nothing phenomenon. This commonly occurs when the searcher does not know the contents of the database (as is usually the case in real-estate) and therefore attempts a query that is too general or too restrictive. As a result, the homebuyer alternates between too many and too few results—frantically and laboriously guessing towards the middle to produce a reasonable set of homes. Recently, good natural-language query systems, such as Q&A by Symantec, have been developed in response to complaints about SQL that instead allow queries to be stated in English. This should reduce training with syntax and help novice users, but it does little to correct the other faults of previous query systems.

The dynamic queries interface (figure 2) provides a visualization of both the query formulation and corresponding results. This application was built using the C programming language. A map of the District of Columbia area is displayed on the left. The homes that fulfill the criteria set by the user's current query are shown as yellow dots on the map. Users perform queries, using the mouse, by setting the values of the sliders and buttons in the control panel to the right. The query result is determined by ANDing all sliders and buttons.

The dynamic homefinder interface is best explained through an example. Take a hypothetical situation where a new professor, Dr. Jones, has just been hired by the University of Maryland. She might encounter this tool in a touchscreen kiosk at a real-estate office or at the student union. She selects the location where whe will be working by dragging the "A" on the map. Next, she selects where her husband will be working, downtown, near the capitol, by dragging the "B." Figure 2 shows the interface after Dr. Jones has dragged the "A" and "B" indicators to her desired locations (the indicators are more visible in figure 4).

Dr. Jones would like to ride her bicycle to work, if possible, so she sets the "Distance to A" slider on the right to 5 miles or less. This is indicated by the highlighted region of the slider now indicating from 0–5 miles. Her husband is taking the Metro, so the distance to his office is not very important. Figure 3 shows how the screen looks after she has adjusted the "Distance to A" slider. Note that this is done instantaneously in a fluid-like manner as she moves which cannot be captured with snapshots, but which enables her to quickly see how homes are eliminated as she narrows the distance requirement.

Dr. Jones is only interested in houses, not in apartments or condominiums so she toggles those buttons off. Finally, she drags the bedrooms slider down to 4, since she needs at least four bedrooms, she could have more (for a guest room or study for example), again indicated by the highlighting in figure 4 showing that houses with 4–7 bedrooms are now being displayed. In figure 4, she also drags the cost slider to $140,000, a modestly-priced home where she used to live. Here we encounter the all-or-nothing phenomenon as Dr. Jones has eliminated too many houses with her query. This is easily solved as she realizes that houses must be more expensive in this area. Dr. Jones drags the cost slider up to $220,000 in figure 5, a price that many more houses in the area fulfill.

Finally, just out of curiosity, Dr. Jones clicks on the "Garage" button in figure 6 only to find that few houses have a garage in the price range and area she is looking at. Once she has narrowed her query, it is easy for Dr. Jones to experiment, seeing what services the homes offer, or what is available if she was willing to pay a little more, and so on. In this way the interface encourages exploration and bolsters user confidence.

Although there is no figure depicting it, a mouse click on any of the homes (represented by the yellow dots) brought up a pop-up window with detailed information on that specific home.

3   User Experiment

This experiment compared three different interfaces for database query and visualization: a dynamic queries interface, a natural language query system known as "Q&A," and a traditional paper listing sorted by several fields. The alternative interfaces were chosen to find out how dynamic queries would fare against the two most common methods currently used to search real-estate databases. Using a within-subjects counter-balanced design, subjects answered a series of five types of questions for each of the three interfaces were presented in random order. The independent variable in the experiment was the type of interface with three different treatments: dynamic queries (DQ), natural language retrieval (QA), and paper listings (Paper). The observed dependent variables were time to find correct answer for each of five questions and the subjective satisfaction with each interface.

The primary hypothesis was that the dynamic queries interface, providing both a graphical query input and a graphical visualization of the search result, would give the best user performance results and would be rated highest in user satisfaction. Performance results were measured as the time until correct answer for each question.

Eighteen undergraduate psychology students, 9 females and 9 males from the University of Maryland subject pool, participated voluntarily in the experiment. Only one subject had previous knowledge of real-estate in the area. Both computer interfaces were run on an IBM PS/2 model 70 (16 MHz 80386) with a 12-inch VGA color monitor and mechanical two-button mouse. All interfaces involved querying information on 944 imaginary homes with varying criteria from real-estate in the Washington D.C. Metropolitan area. Although using real home-seekers would be ideal, a reasonable compromise was made by using novices with varying backgrounds.

3.1   Dynamic Queries Interface (DQ)

This interface was already described in detail under section 1.2. As shown previously in figure 4, it is possible to drag the "A" icon to a certain location where the homebuyer might work, for example. When the distance slider is moved to 5, all houses within 5 miles of that location are then highlighted. However, these distance sliders and the "A" and "B" icons on the map were not used in the experiment, since the other two interfaces could not provide this service.

3.2   Natural Language Query Interface (QA)

The natural language query interface (figure 7) used was the "Intelligent Assistant" of a popular commercial package from Symantec, Inc. known as "Q&A." This software allows users to pose queries using English. The user types the English query, the system converts it into a logical database query (figure 7), and then displays the information requested (figure 8). A 386 machine with hard disk was used so the search time was only a few seconds, fast enough that computation speed was not a significant factor. No graphical output was provided, a textual listing of the homes that satisfied the query were displayed as shown in figure 8.

3.3 Paper Interface

There were three sets of laser-printed paper listings in approximately 11-point Courier font, one sorted by cost, one by the number of bedrooms, and one alphabetically by the neighborhood name. Each 10-page listing contained all the information on each of the 944 homes, one-per-line, as shown in figure 9.

3.4 Experiment Procedure and Tasks

A counter-balanced within-subjects design was used. The question sets were always given in the same order, and the interface order was random. The subjects were given a brief description of the tasks and were asked to sign a consent form. Each session lasted an hour and consisted of four phases for each interface condition:

1. Introduction and training: The experimenter set up the appropriate interface and briefly explained the interface to the subject. The subject was invited to try-out the system and get comfortable with it. Subjects were permitted unlimited time to try-out using the system and were free to ask any questions to the experimenter about the interface. Actual training time varied from two to ten minutes for each subject. The QA interface required significantly more training due to its less obvious querying mechanism. Subjects were informed on the more complex sorting and set operations available in the QA interface.

2. Practice task: A practice task (similar to the complex query question used) was given. During this task, subjects were free to ask questions about both the task and the interface.

3. Timed tasks: Five questions were given on paper. Subjects read each question and were asked if they fully understood it. This was done so as to eliminate variations in subject comprehension speed. When the subject was ready, the experimenter started timing. When subjects found the answer, they verbally expressed it. If it was correct, the experimenter recorded the elapsed time; if not, the experimenter asked the subject to try again. The interface was returned to its initial state between each question. In deciding the tasks, an informal task analysis was done by asking a local realtor and a few clients what types of questions they would ask a database. The first two are very general, while the final three are probably more representative of "typical" home-searches:

   - Simple fact—Find a certain element fulfilling a simple criteria. An actual question of this type is "What is the cost of the cheapest apartment in the database?"

   - Simple neighborhood fact search—Find the neighborhood (city) fulfilling a simple criteria. An actual question of this type is "What neighborhood has the most expensive houses?"

   - Complex search—Find one or more elements meeting several criteria. This is the typical type of question a prospective homebuyer would likely ask. An actual question of this type is "What is the address of the cheapest house that has 5 or more bedrooms AND has both a garage and central air conditioning?"

   - Find a trend—Find the trend for some field. This task requires subjects to create a mental picture of how a field changes through the database. An actual question of this type is "Is there a general trend (and if so what is it) of house prices from cheapest to most expensive? (i.e., where

	QA	DQ	Paper	ANOVA
1	93.0	46.3	30.6	$F(2,51) = 9.72$
	(76.0) $\longrightarrow$	(46.2)	(17.8)	(p < .005)
2	92.8	72.5	98.4	$F(2,51) = 0.66$
	(83.2)	(78.0)	(75.3)	(p > .005)
3	144.8	57.6	125.1	$F(2,51) = 11.6$
	(71.1) $\longrightarrow$	(28.4) $\longleftarrow$	(72.4)	(p < .005)
4	227.9	125.3	193.4	$F(2,51) = 17.4$
	(27.0) $\longrightarrow$	(72.4) $\longleftarrow$	(68.5)	(p < .005)
5	189.9	58.8	135.8	$F(2,51) = 29.4$
	(67.2) $\longrightarrow$	(16.3) $\longleftarrow$	(77.0)	(p < .005)
QUIS	68	110	84	$F(2,51) = 19.6$
	(42.3) $\longrightarrow$	(21.5) $\longleftarrow$	(12.5)	(p < .005)

$\longrightarrow$ Scheffe .005 post-hoc showed significant
difference favoring indicated interface

Table 1 Means and standard deviations in seconds for each interface and condition for five tasks and subjective satisfaction (out of a maximum of 140).

are the more expensive houses, and where are the cheapest houses, do they seem to follow any general pattern?) Don't guess, you must find some examples to support your answer."

- Find exception to trend/Complex search—Find the exception to a trend in the database. This is, in fact, often what homebuyers are looking for. An actual question of this type is "There is a trend of houses to increase in cost with the number of bedrooms. Find the two bargain homes with the most bedrooms but are still inexpensive."

4. Subjective evaluation: Subjects were asked to fill-out a shortened QUIS [CDN88] after having completed each interface. Although results for each of the 20 questions (scored on a 7-point scale) were computed, the sum score for each interface (out of a maximum possible of 140) is what is presented in the results section.

4   Experiment Results

The results show a statistically significant difference for the dynamic queries interface over both the other two for all but one task. Analysis of the timed tasks was done using a factorial analysis of variance. An ANOVA showed no significant order or questionnaire difficulty effect (these two were compounded to one factor) with $F(2,51)=1.17$ (p>.05). This, therefore, also shows that there was no significant difference between the three question sets used. Observing the mean times to complete each task shows a significant effect. The mean and standard deviations (in seconds) for each question and interface are shown in table 1 along with the ANOVA and post-hoc analysis. The results for the QUIS are ratings out of a maximum possible of 140. These means, along with 95% error bars are graphed for comparison in figure 10.

5 Discussion and Conclusions

The primary hypothesis that the dynamic queries interface would give the best user performance results is supported in the results with a significant difference ($p<.005$) in speed, favoring dynamic queries, for all but one task. The dynamic queries interface also scored significantly higher on the satisfaction questionnaire. Surprisingly, for all but one task, paper was also better than the QA interface, although often not by a significant amount. The remarks given by the subjects and comments noted by the experimenter suggest several reasons why the dynamic queries interface faired better.

First, the dynamic queries interface was clearly the most "fun," most likely due to its animated graphical nature, and this may have produced a motivational factor. The QUIS clearly indicated a preference for DQ (110) over QA (68) and Paper (84), with subjects rating DQ an average of 6.1 on a range from 1 to 7. Many subjects became very frustrated with the QA interface, attempting to figure out how to form a query (this is discussed more later). One subject remarked: "What the hell does this thing want, anyway?" Subjects seemed very comfortable with paper and usually attacked the question in a logical fashion, utilizing the sorted paper listings to their maximum benefit. The DQ interface was clearly preferred by the sighs of relief and the relaxed manner with which they formed queries. One subject said, "I don't want to stop, this is fun!"

Second, the well-known issue of text readability may partially explain the success of both the DQ and paper interfaces. Although a VGA monitor was used, several subjects noted that it was easier to search the laser-printed listings than a listing on-screen using the QA interface. Subjects using the DQ interface rarely actually looked at the textual information on a specific home. One subject noted on their evaluation of QA that it "takes a while for your eyes to adjust to the small print."

Third, the subjects clearly had semantic difficulties with the QA interface. Grammatical, spelling, and typographical errors were made in query formulation. The QA's processor often resulted in unexpected queries. One common error was asking: "What is the cheaper house?" when the user meant "cheapest house." QA did not see the singular house and figure out that cheapest was actually what was desired, instead producing a listing of all houses with cost less than the average price. This is even more surprising since 9 out of the 15 task questions could actually be typed in literally, word for word, and QA would produce the correct answer. Clearly subjects spent a lot of mental effort trying to formulate the query, probably more than was necessary.

Fourth, the subjects clearly had problems with the classic boolean query problems. Specifically, they asked for ANDs which QA interpreted as a literal AND when OR was actually what the user wanted. Further, subjects often had problems with inclusion, such as specifying "more than 5 bedrooms" when they actually wanted "5 or more bedrooms."

Fifth, the number of ordinary typos was tremendous. Further, the editor in QA was quite poor, not allowing the user to edit the previous query without retyping it in. This led to much of the time spent typing in queries, which for most non-computer people is a slow process. Occasionally QA would not even report a typo, resulting in a query that failed, not due to the logic, but due to a typo. The subject would therefore think their query had failed and would consequently try another approach to the question.

Sixth, the QA interface often produced the correct answer but the subject missed it. Subjects expressed they were unsure if they had asked the right query to get the result and were unsure if it was therefore the correct answer. A few subjects tried multiple approaches and only answered when they got the same answer using each approach. A possible explanation may be that the subjects get so caught up in the query formulation they forget exactly what they were originally looking for. This frustrating feeling of being lost and unsure was not expressed with either of the other two interfaces.

Finally, the DQ interface's use of highlighting and display on one single screen was clearly a benefit for users. They were able to easily input the query with the sliders. Not one of the subjects showed any difficulty in using the sliders effectively. One subject explained the feeling well: "You can see them right up front...they're right there." The display of the results on a map made task 4 (finding a trend) clearly easier since the relative location could be viewed directly on the map, instead of having to refer to it from the city, state information.

The clear benefit of dynamic queries, particularly for trend and exception to trend questions is clear. The significant differences (F=29.4 and 19.5 respectively) for task 4 and 5 are dramatic. The fact that a time limit was placed at four minutes, probably reduced the effect somewhat, since over half the subjects could not answer task 4 using the QA interface in the time alloted. With the DQ interface, however, all but one subject was able to discern the trend in the time allotted.

The scores for task 5 showed dramatic differences, with the DQ interface averaging 58.8 seconds with a standard deviation of only 16.3 seconds, while the QA interface averaged 189.9 seconds, with a standard deviation of 67.2 seconds. In fact, all but one subject answered the question in less than a minute using the DQ interface. The exception to the trend (or multiple search) question required combining the results of two or more searches or finding the outlying point in a set. In this case, the exception was a home that was cheap for what it offered. These types of questions are often what people are searching for in a database. They often wish to find the most stressed part of an airplane, the cheapest car which provides all the options desired, or the deaths that seem to occur not due to cancer or other common environmental factors. Since dynamic queries excel in searching for these outliers, other applications involving this type of search could clearly benefit from its use.

In all fairness, it is difficult to honestly compare the QA, DQ, and paper interfaces since the ways users use each one are so different. QA requires typing with little guidance, while the DQ interface must be "custom-made" for the fields the user will search on. Therefore, it is difficult to specifically identify the advantages or disadvantages; however, from a usability standpoint, it does seem that the DQ interface does perform better, overall, than QA for some types of questions.

This study and others [AWS92] have shown dynamic queries to have several benefits over current systems:

- Queries can be made much faster by sliding the sliders and seeing rapid feedback directly on the display.

- Novices can learn to use the system quickly with both query-formulation and result displayed in task domain.

- Intermittent users do not have to remember any syntax. Repeat users quickly remember how to form a query.

- No error messages are needed since sliders restrict ranges. Also encourages user to explore.

- Users can fine-tune their search easily. Simply restricting one field allows tuning until desired number of hits.

- Actions are incremental and reversible.

- Trends and content of the database are easily inferred.

- Well-suited for geographical information systems and public access using a touchscreen.

- Display in task-domain is more useful, less intimidating, and speeds training time.

Although dynamic queries show promise, they are far from perfect. Many drawbacks limit the range of its applicability or pose other problems:

- Data must be ordered in some way, in particular textual fields don't benefit from the dynamic nature of sliders.

- Limited screen real-estate makes it difficult to keep both tools and display on-screen.

- Difficult to use when a large number of fields are searchable due to limited screen space and computational issues.

- Data structures to permit more rapid querying (especially for large databases) are clearly necessary.

- Work best with data which can be displayed in some graphical fashion.

- Difficult for dynamic queries to offer more complex boolean queries such as unions and negations.

Recently we have developed a range slider with draggable ends, partially solving some of these limitations.

Smarter ways to utilize the limited screen space without sacrificing simplicity are clearly needed.

Perhaps the most major drawback, as of now, they require custom programming to create an interface. Even adding additional criteria (such as crime rate or some such) for querying requires significant adjustment. We are currently designing a DQ toolkit to minimize this difficulty.

This initial study needs to be replicated with other subjects, database domains, queries, and with more experienced users to assess the full range of strengths and weaknesses of dynamic queries. Despite the drawbacks, dynamic queries clearly have application in a range of areas. For geographic information systems they show clear promise. For textual purposes, however, the problems outweigh the benefits. Since the results of this study suggest users find dynamic queries more enjoyable to work with and can complete typical tasks in equal or less time than a traditional natural-language query system, it seems clear these principles have a place in the design of future information retrieval systems.

6 Acknowledgments

We appreciate the support of NCR Corporation and Johnson Controls; as well as the comments from Ben Harper, Christopher Ahlberg, Donna Harman, Kent Norman and other members of the Human-Computer Interaction Laboratory at the University of Maryland.

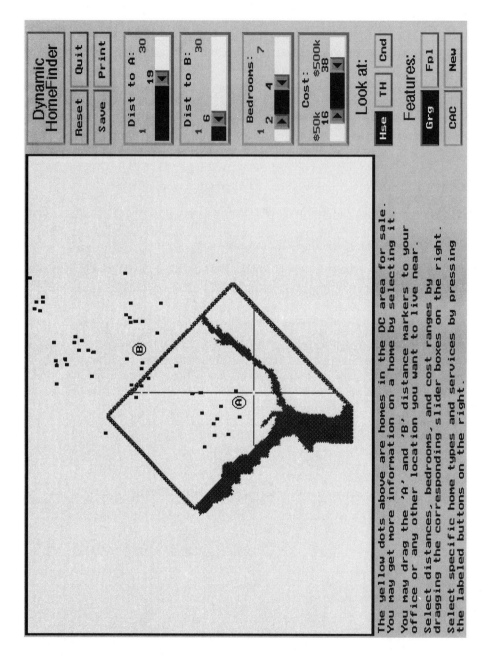

Figure 2   Dynamic HomeFinder (DQ interface) with all homes displayed and A&B markers set. In order to make these shapshots more readable in print, the pallette has been altered; the actual color scheme used was considerably more readable and pleasing than these shapshots depict.

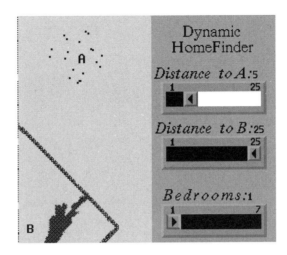

Figure 3 HomeFinder with all homes within a 5-mile radius of the "A" marker displayed.

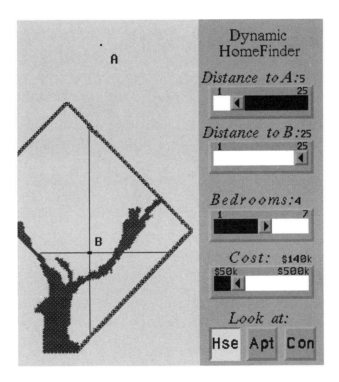

Figure 4 HomeFinder with all houses within a 5-mile radius of the "A" marker AND have 4 or more bedrooms AND cost less than or equal to $140,000.

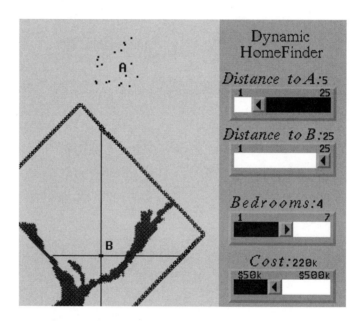

Figure 5   Closeup of Dynamic HomeFinder with all houses within a 5-mile radius of the "A" marker
AND have 4 or more bedrooms and cost less than or equal to $220,000.

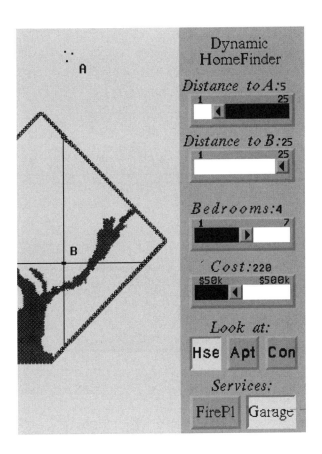

Figure 6 Dynamic HomeFinder with all houses within a 5-mile radius of the "A" marker AND have 4 or more bedrooms AND cost less than or equal to $220,000 AND have a garage.

```
┌──────────────────────────────────────────────────────────────┐
│  WHERE ARE THE 3 MOST EXPENSIVE HOUSES WITH A FIREPLACE?       │
│                                                                │
│                                                                │
│                                                                │
└──────────────────────────────────────────────────────────────┘
```

```
┌──────────────────────────────────────────────────────────────┐
│                    Shall I do the following?                   │
│                                                                │
│         Create a report showing                                │
│            the Address and                                     │
│            the Neighborhood and                                │
│            the Cost and                                        │
│            the Home Type                                       │
│         from the forms on which                                │
│            the Home Type includes "HOUSE" and                  │
│            the Fireplace is YES and                            │
│            the Cost is maximum                                 │
│                                                                │
│         Yes - Continue              No - Cancel Request         │
│                                                                │
└──────────────────────────────────────────────────────────────┘
```
DQ. DTF
Esc-Cancel   F10-Continue

Figure 7   Natural language system (QA interface) processing and converting English query.

```
┌──────────────────────────────────────────────────────────────┐
│  WHERE ARE THE 3 MOST EXPENSIVE HOUSES WITH A FIREPLACE?       │
│                                                                │
│                                                                │
│                                                                │
└──────────────────────────────────────────────────────────────┘
```

```
┌──────────────────────────────────────────────────────────────┐
│      Address          Neighborhood        Cost      Home Type  │
│   ─────────────       ──────────────     ──────    ──────────  │
│   7924 Jones Street   Chevy Chase, MD    $411,950   House      │
│   4719 Dorset Ave.    Chevy Chase, MD    $678,235   House      │
│   1287 Highland Ct.    Potomac, MD        $782,125  House      │
│                                                                │
│                                                                │
│                                                                │
│                                                                │
└──────────────────────────────────────────────────────────────┘
```
DQ. DTF
Esc-Cancel   F10-Continue

Figure 8   Q&A displaying results of converted English query.

```
[Key:  Bed=bedrooms, Fp=fireplace, Gr=garage, Ac=central air, Nw=new]

ID    Type   Address              Neighborhood     Cost       Bed  Fp  Gr  Ac  Nw
39    Apt    3792 Campus Drive    Beltsville, MD   $80,950    3    N   N   N   N
54    Apt    4634 Baltimore Blvd. College Park, MD $90,250    2    N   Y   N   N
230   House  2352 Glass Road      Bladensburg, MD  $100,230   3    Y   Y   N   N
```

Figure 9 Sample lines from paper listing.

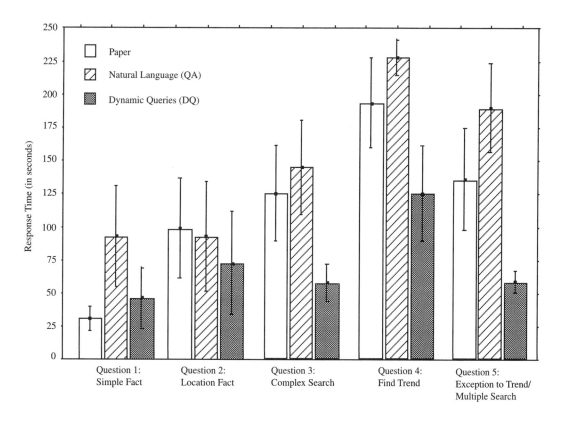

Figure 10 Response times for five questions when tasks were accomplished using paper, natural language, and dynamic queries. Means and 95% error bars are shown.

PART III

MAINTENANCE OF MATERIALIZED VIEWS

Maintenance of Materialized Views

This part of the book contains twelve chapters on maintaining materialized views.

The problem of efficiently maintaining materialized views is the most extensively studied problem in this field. The problem is appealing because the heuristic of intertia - *i.e.* it is cheaper to compute the changes to a view in response to changes to the underlying database than to recompute the view from scratch - makes "incremental" computation of the materialized view attractive. Chapters 11 and 12 define the metrics for measuring the generality and efficiency of incremental maintenance algorithms thereby outlining the framework for studying different view maintenance algorithms proposed in the literature. Nearly all the other chapters in this section consider incremental view maintenance algorithm. Chapters 13, 14, 15, and 17 study different incremental maintenance algorithms for relational views. Chapters 18 and 20 consider view maintenance in semi-relational scanarios. The last two chapters, 21 and 22 study how to identify "irrelevant" updates, *i.e.,* updates that do not affect the view and therefore do not require any recomputation of the view.

Chapter 11 presents a taxonomy of the view maintenance problems based upon the language used to express a view, the resources used to maintain the view, the type of modification to the base data, and whether the algorithm applies to all instances of the view and modifications. The chapter overviews many view maintenance algorithms in terms of the above framework. Chapter 12 extends this framework by specifying additional parameters of the view maintenance problem. (1) The language in which the *view maintenance algorithms* are expressed. Usually it is advantageous if the maintenance algorithms are expressible in a sub-language of the view definition language. (2) The cost of the maintenance process compared to the cost of reevaluating the view - expressed in terms of inherent complexity of the algorithms - given that efficiency is the main reason for incremental maintenance in the first place. (3) The auxilliary information needed for incremental maintenance and the space it occupies. The chapter surveys view maintenance algorithms for recursive views in this extended framework.

Chapter 13 contains one of the earliest studies of view maintenance that led to a lot of further work. The chapter gives necessary and sufficient conditions to detect irrelevant insertions and deletions and for those updates that do affect the view, it gives a differential algorithm to re-evaluate SPJ views using "full information" *i.e.* the view, base tables, and modifications.

Chapter 14 considers views that may use Union, negation, Aggregation (*e.g.* Sum, Min), linear recursion and general recursion. The chapter presents two algorithms - the counting algorithm that is like the algorithm of chapter 13 extended to handle a larger class of queries; and an algorithm to handle recursive views. Both algorithms handle insertions and deletions using full information.

Chapter 15 introduces an algebraic approach to view maintenance instead of the algorithmic approaches used in most other solutions. The algebraic approach has a number of advantages: it is robust and easily extensible to new language constructs, it produces output that can be used by query optimizers, and it simplifies correctness proofs. The authors extend relational algebra operations to bags (multisets) and present an algorithm for efficient maintenance of materialized views that may contain duplicates, thereby handling aggregate views. The chapter also validates the heuristic of inertia by proving that under normal circumstances the change propagation process is significantly faster and more space efficient than completely recomputing the view.

Chapter 16 considers a similar problem wherein view maintenance is deferred to a transaction different from the change transaction. The chapter addresses (1) how to maintain views after the base tables have already been modified, and (2) how to minimize the time for which the view is inaccessible during maintenance.

The chapter also studies the performance and cost effect of maintaining auxiallary information recorded between view refreshes that is needed for deferred maintenance algorithm.

Chapter 17 also considers the maintenance of recursive queries - in particular it gives an algorithm for incrementally maintaining arbitrary datalog queries. However, the chapter's primary focus is to derive non-recursive incremental maintenance expressions for a class of recursive views that can be expressed as regular chain queries (for example, transitive closure of a graph). The algorithm is motivated by the need to have maintenance algorithms in a sub-language of the language used to express a view.

Chapter 18 introduces a new data model, the chronicle model. Chronicles are implementable on a RDBMS but make more efficient the computation and maintenance of views, especially aggregations, in transactional data recording systems - database systems used to record streams of transactional information. Examples of such transactional information are credit card transactions, telephone calls, stock trades, sensor outputs in a control system, *etc.* These systems maintain aggregated data like account balances, total charges to a credit card. The chronicle model allows aggregate computation and maintenance to be moved from the application code to the DBMS thereby making the process simpler and more efficient.

Chapter 19 considers the issue of incremental maintenance of materialized views in a warehousing environment where the view is decoupled from the base data resulting in anomalies if traditional maintenance algorithms are applied. The anomalies result mainly because traditional incremental view maintenance algorithms assume some form of transactional behaviour between the view and the data sources - that is not present in a warehousing scenario where the warehouse and sources are completely independent. The chapter describes how to avoid the anomalies by using compensating queries. The algorithms in effect implement "concurrency control" mechanisms that guarantee correct maintenance of views in multidatabase systems. The results are useful in any materialized view scenario that involves distributed data sources and destinations - like network management applications, chronicle systems, advanced message systems, and replication systems.

Chapter 20 considers the problem of data integration from multiple heterogeneous sources - like databases, knowledge bases or data in software packages accessible only through specific function calls. The authors have built a data integration framework using a rule based language that allows function calls. The model extends relational views not only in the language used to define the view but also by supporting non-ground constrained atoms (like "$X > 5$"). The chapter gives maintenance algorithms for such integrated and "mediated" views. Further, it also considers the "view update" problem wherein the view is updated and the changes are propagated to the underlying data sources.

Chapter 21 and 22 consider how to detect irrelevant updates that do not affect the view. Chapter 21 gives necessary and sufficient conditions for detecting when insertions, deletions, and modifications are irrelevant with respect to a SPJ view. Chapter 22 considers more expressive views - namely views with stratified negation and order constraints. The chapter relates the problem of detecting irrelevant updates to equivalence of datalog programs and using this abstraction generalizes the results of chapter 21. Chapter 21 also considers the self-maintainability problem of how to update a view using only the view and the update (akin to chapter 5).

MAINTENANCE OF MATERIALIZED VIEWS: PROBLEMS, TECHNIQUES, AND APPLICATIONS

Ashish Gupta, Inderpal Singh Mumick

1 Introduction

What is a view? A view is a derived relation defined in terms of base (stored) relations. A view thus defines a function from a set of base tables to a derived table; this function is typically recomputed every time the view is referenced.

What is a materialized view? A view can be materialized by storing the tuples of the view in the database. Index structures can be built on the materialized view. Consequently, database accesses to the materialized view can be much faster than recomputing the view. A materialized view is thus like a cache – a copy of the data that can be accessed quickly.

Why use materialized views? Like a cache, a materialized view provides fast access to data; the speed difference may be critical in applications where the query rate is high and the views are complex so that it is not possible to recompute the view for every query. Materialized views are useful in new applications such as data warehousing, replication servers, chronicle or data recording systems [JMS95], data visualization, and mobile systems. Integrity constraint checking and query optimization can also benefit from materialized views.

What is view maintenance? Just as a cache gets *dirty* when the data from which it is copied is updated, a materialized view gets dirty whenever the underlying base relations are modified. The process of updating a materialized view in response to changes to the underlying data is called view maintenance.

What is incremental view maintenance? In most cases it is wasteful to maintain a view by recomputing it from scratch. Often it is cheaper to use the heuristic of inertia (only a part of the view changes in response to changes in the base relations) and thus compute only the changes in the view to update its materialization. We stress that the above is only a heuristic. For example, if an entire base relation is deleted, it may be cheaper to recompute a view that depends on the deleted relation (if the new view will quickly evaluate to an empty relation) than to compute the changes to the view. Algorithms that compute changes to a view in response to changes to the base relations are called *incremental view maintenance* algorithms, and are the focus of this chapter.

Classification of the View Maintenance Problem There are four dimensions along which the view maintenance problem can be studied:

- Information Dimension: The amount of information available for view maintenance. Do you have access to all/some the base relations while doing the maintenance? Do you have access to the materialized view? Do you know about integrity constraints and keys? We note that the amount of information used is orthogonal to the incrementality of view maintenance. Incrementality refers to a computation that only computes that part of the view that has changed; the information dimension looks at the data used to compute the change to the view.

- Modification Dimension: What modifications can the view maintenance algorithm handle? Insertion and deletion of tuples to base relations? Are updates to tuples handled directly or are they modeled as deletions followed by insertions? What about changes to the view definition? Or sets of modifications?

- Language Dimension: Is the view expressed as a select-project-join query (also known as a SPJ views or as a conjunctive query), or in some other subset of relational algebra? SQL or a subset of SQL? Can it have duplicates? Can it use aggregation? Recursion? General recursions, or only transitive closure?

- Instance Dimension: Does the view maintenance algorithm work for all instances of the database, or only for some instances of the database? Does it work for all instances of the modification, or only for some instances of the modification? Instance information is thus of two types - *database instance*, and *modification instance*.

We motivate a classification of the view maintenance problem along the above dimensions through examples. The first example illustrates the information and modification dimensions.

EXAMPLE 1.1 (Information and Modification Dimensions) Consider relation

$$\text{part}(\text{part\_no}, \text{part\_cost}, \text{contract})$$

listing the cost negotiated under each contract for a part. Note that a part may have a different price under each contract. Consider also the view expensive_parts defined as:

$$\text{expensive\_parts}(\text{part\_no}) = \Pi_{\text{part\_no}} \, \sigma_{\text{part\_cost}>1000}(\text{part})$$

The view contains the **distinct** part numbers for parts that cost more than $1000 under at least one contract (the projection discards duplicates). Consider maintaining the view when a tuple is inserted into relation **part**. If the inserted tuple has $\text{part\_cost} \leq 1000$ then the view is unchanged.

However, say $\text{part}(p1, 5000, c15)$ is inserted that does have cost > 1000. Different view maintenance algorithms can be designed depending upon the information available for determining if $p1$ should be inserted into the view.

- The materialized view alone is available: Use the old materialized view to determine if **part_no** already is present in the view. If so, there is no change to the materialization, else insert part $p1$ into the materialization.

- The base relation **part** alone is available: Use relation **part** to check if an existing tuple in the relation has the same **part_no** but greater or equal cost. If such a tuple exists then the inserted tuple does not contribute to the view.

- It is known that **part_no** is the key: Infer that **part_no** cannot already be in the view, so it must be inserted.

Another view maintenance problem is to respond to deletions using only the materialized view. Let tuple **part**($p1, 2000, c12$) be deleted. Clearly part $p1$ must be in the materialization, but we cannot delete $p1$ from the view because some other tuple, like **part**($p1, 3000, c13$), may contribute $p1$ to the view. The existence of this tuple cannot be (dis)proved using only the view. Thus there is no algorithm to solve the view maintenance problem for deletions using only the materialized view. Note, if the relation **part** was also available, or if the key constraint was known, or if the counts of number of view tuple derivations were available, then the view could be maintained. □

With respect to the information dimension, note that the view definition and the actual modification always have to be available for maintenance. With respect to the modification dimension, updates typically are not treated as an independent type of modification. Instead, they are modeled as a deletion followed by an insertion. This model loses information thereby requiring more work and more information for maintaining a view than if updates were treated independently within a view maintenance algorithm [BCL89, UO92, GJM96].

The following example illustrates the other two dimensions used to characterize view maintenance.

EXAMPLE 1.2 (Language and Instance Dimensions) Example 1.1 considered a view definition language consisting of selection and projection operations. Now let us extend the view definition language with the join operation, and define the view **supp_parts** as the equijoin between relations **supp**(**supp_no**, **part_no**, **price**) and **part** ($\bowtie_{\text{part\_no}}$ represents an equijoin on attribute **part_no**):

$$\text{supp\_parts}(\text{part\_no}) = \Pi_{\text{part\_no}}(\text{supp} \bowtie_{\text{part\_no}} \text{part})$$

The view contains the **distinct** part numbers that are supplied by at least one supplier (the projection discards duplicates). Consider using only the old contents of **supp_parts** for maintenance in response to insertion of **part**($p1, 5000, c15$). If **supp_parts** already contains **part_no** $p1$ then the insertion does not affect the view. However, if **supp_parts** does not contain $p1$, then the effect of the insertion cannot be determined using only the view.

Recall that the view **expensive_parts** was maintainable in response to insertions to **part** using only the view. In contrast, the use of a join makes it impossible to maintain **supp_parts** in response to insertions to **part** when using only the view.

Note, view **supp_parts** is maintainable if the view contains **part_no** $p1$ but not otherwise. Thus, the maintainability of a view depends also on the particular instances of the database and the modification. □

Figure 1 shows the problem space defined by three of the four dimensions; namely the information, modification, and language dimensions. The instance dimension is not shown here so as to keep the figure manageable. There is no relative ordering between the points on each dimension; they are listed in arbitrary order. Along the language dimension, *chronicle algebra* [JMS95] refers to languages that operate over ordered sequences that may not be stored in the database (see Section 4.3). Along the modification dimension, *group updates* [GJM94] refers to insertion of several tuples using information derived from a single deleted tuple.

We study maintenance techniques for different points in the shown problem space. For each point in this 3-D space we may get algorithms that apply to all database and modification instances or that may work only for some instances of each (the fourth dimension).

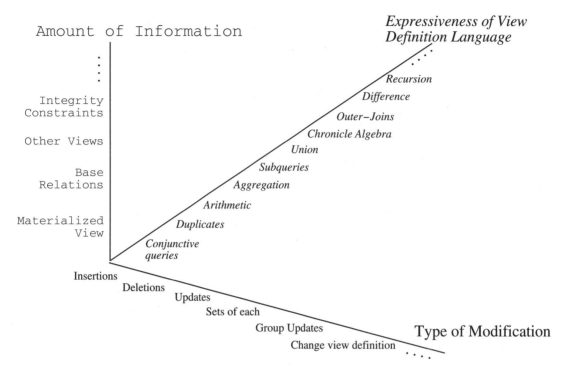

Figure 1 The problem space

Chapter Outline

We study the view maintenance problem with respect to the space of Figure 1 using the "amount of information" as the first discriminator. For each point considered on the information dimension, we consider the languages for which view maintenance algorithms have been developed, and present selected algorithms in some detail. Where appropriate, we mention how different types of modifications are handled differently. The algorithms we describe in some detail address the following points in the problem space.

■ (Section 3:) Information dimension: Use *Full Information* (all the underlying base relations and the materialized view). Instance dimension: Apply to all instances of the database and all instances of modifications. Modification dimension: Apply to all types of modifications. Language dimension: Consider the following languages —

  – SQL views with duplicates, UNION, negation, and aggregation (*e.g.* SUM, MIN).
  – Outer-join views.
  – Recursive Datalog or SQL views with UNION, stratified aggregation and negation, but no duplicates.

■ (Section 4:) Information dimension: Use *partial information* (materialized view and key constraints – views that can be maintained without accessing the base relations are said to be *self-maintainable*). Instance dimension: Apply to all instances of the database and all instances of modifications. Language dimension: Apply to SPJ views. Modification dimension: Consider the following types of modifications —

– Insertions and Deletions of tuples.

– Updates and group updates to tuples.

We also discuss maintaining SPJ views using the view and some underlying base relations.

2   The Idea Behind View Maintenance

Incremental maintenance requires that the change to the base relations be used to compute the change to the view. Thus, most view maintenance techniques treat the view definition as a mathematical formula and apply a differentiation step to obtain an expression for the change in the view. We illustrate through an example:

EXAMPLE 2.1 (Intuition) Consider the base relation $\texttt{link}(S, D)$ such that $\texttt{link}(a, b)$ is true if there is a link from source node a to destination node b. Define view $\texttt{hop}$ such that $\texttt{hop}(c, d)$ is true if c is connected to d using two links, via an intermediate node:

$$\mathcal{D}: \quad \texttt{hop}(X, Y) = \Pi_{X,Y}(\texttt{link}(X, V) \bowtie_{V=W} \texttt{link}(W, Y))$$

Let a set of tuples $\Delta(\texttt{link})$ be inserted into relation $\texttt{link}$. The corresponding insertions $\Delta(\texttt{hop})$ that need to be made into view $\texttt{hop}$ can be computed by mathematically differentiating definition $\mathcal{D}$ to obtain the following expression:

$$\begin{aligned}
\Delta(\texttt{hop}) = \Pi_{X,Y}((\Delta(\texttt{link})(X, V) &\bowtie_{V=W} \texttt{link}(W, Y)) \cup \\
(\texttt{link}(X, V) &\bowtie_{V=W} \Delta(\texttt{link})(W, Y)) \cup \\
(\Delta(\texttt{link})(X, V) &\bowtie_{V=W} \Delta(\texttt{link})(W, Y)))
\end{aligned}$$

The second and third terms can be combined to yield the term $\texttt{link}^{\nu}(X, V) \bowtie_{V=W} \Delta(\texttt{link})(W, Y)$ where $\texttt{link}^{\nu}$ represents relation $\texttt{link}$ with the insertions, *i.e.*, $\texttt{link} \cup \Delta(\texttt{link})$. $\qquad\square$

In the above example, if tuples are deleted from $\texttt{link}$ then too the same expression computes the deletions from view $\texttt{hop}$. If tuples are inserted into and deleted from relation $\texttt{link}$, then $\Delta(\texttt{hop})$ is often computed by separately computing the set of deletions $\Delta^{-}(\texttt{hop})$ and the set of insertions $\Delta^{+}(\texttt{hop})$ [QW91, HD92]. Alternatively, by differently tagging insertions and deletions they can be handled in one pass as in [GMS93].

3   Using Full Information

Most work on view maintenance has assumed that all the base relations and the materialized view are available during the maintenance process, and the focus has been on efficient techniques to maintain views expressed in different languages – starting from select-project-join views and moving to relational algebra, SQL, and Datalog, considering features like aggregations, duplicates, recursion, and outer-joins. The techniques typically differ in the expressiveness of the view definition language, in their use of key and integrity constraints, and whether they handle insertions and deletions separately or in one pass (Updates are modeled as a deletion followed by an insertion). The techniques all work on all database instances for both insertions and deletions. We will classify these techniques broadly along the language dimension into those applicable to nonrecursive views, those applicable to outer-join views, and those applicable to recursive views.

3.1   Nonrecursive Views

We describe the counting algorithm for view maintenance, and then discuss several other view maintenance techniques that have been proposed in the literature.

The counting Algorithm [GMS93]:   applies to SQL views that may or may not have duplicates, and that may be defined using UNION, negation, and aggregation. The basic idea in the counting algorithm is to keep a count of the number of derivations for each view tuple as extra information in the view. We illustrate the counting algorithm using an example.

EXAMPLE 3.1 Consider view hop from Example 2.1 now written in SQL.

CREATE VIEW hop(S, D) **as**
         (**select distinct** $11.S, 12.D$ **from** link 11, link 12 **where** $11.D = 12.S$)

Given link $= \{(a, b), (b, c), (b, e), (a, d), (d, c)\}$, the view hop evaluates to $\{(a, c), (a, e)\}$. The tuple hop(a, e) has a unique derivation. hop(a, c) on the other hand has two derivations. If the view had duplicate semantics (did not have the **distinct** operator) then hop(a, e) would have a count of 1 and hop(a, c) would have a count of 2. The counting algorithm pretends that the view has duplicate semantics, and stores these counts.

Suppose the tuple link(a, b) is deleted. Then we can see that hop can be recomputed as $\{(a, c)\}$. The counting algorithm infers that one derivation of each of the tuples hop(a, c) and hop(a, e) is deleted. The algorithm uses the stored counts to infer that hop(a, c) has one remaining derivation and therefore only deletes hop(a, e), which has no remaining derivation. □

The counting algorithm thus works by storing the number of alternative derivations, count(t), of each tuple t in the materialized view. This number is derived from the multiplicity of tuple t under duplicate semantics [Mum91, MS93b]. Given a program T defining a set of views $V_1, \ldots, V_k$, the counting algorithm uses the differentiation technique of Section 2 to derive a program T_Δ. The program T_Δ uses the changes made to base relations and the old values of the base and view relations to produce as output the set of changes, $\Delta(V_1), \ldots, \Delta(V_k)$, that need to be made to the view relations. In the set of changes, insertions are represented with positive counts, and deletions by negative counts. The count value for each tuple is stored in the materialized view, and the new materialized view is obtained by combining the changes $\Delta(V_1), \ldots, \Delta(V_k)$ with the stored views $V_1, \ldots, V_k$. Positive counts are added in, and negative counts are subtracted. A tuple with a count of zero is deleted. The count algorithm is optimal in that it computes exactly those view tuples that are inserted or deleted. For SQL views counts can be computed at little or no cost above the cost of evaluating the view for both set and duplicate semantics. The counting algorithm works for both set and duplicate semantics, and can be made to work for outer-join views (Section 3.2).

Other Counting Algorithms: [SI84] maintain select, project, and equijoin views using counts of the number of derivations of a tuple. They build data structures with pointers from a tuple τ to other tuples derived using the tuple τ.   [BLT86] use counts just like the counting algorithm, but only to maintain SPJ views. Also, they compute insertions and deletions separately, without combining them into a single set with positive and negative counts. [Rou91] describes "ViewCaches," materialized views defined using selections and one join, that store only the TIDs of the tuples that join to produce view tuples.

Algebraic Differencing: introduced in [Pai84] and used subsequently in [QW91] for view maintenance differentiates algebraic expressions to derive the relational expression that computes the change to an

SPJ view without doing redundant computation. [GLT97] provide a correction to the minimality result of [QW91], and [GL95] extend the algebraic differencing approach to multiset algebra with aggregations and multiset difference. They derive two expressions for each view; one to compute the insertions into the view, and another to compute the deletions into the view.

The Ceri-Widom algorithm [CW91]: derives production rules to maintain selected SQL views - those without duplicates, aggregation, and negation, and those where the view attributes functionally determine the key of the base relation that is updated. The algorithm determines the SQL query needed to maintain the view, and invokes the query from within a production rule.

Recursive Algorithms: The algorithms described in Section 3.3 for recursive views also apply to nonrecursive views.

3.2 Outer-Join Views

Outer joins are important in domains like data integration and extended relational systems [MPP+93]. View maintenance on outer-join views using the materialized view and all base relations has been discussed in [GJM94].

In this section we outline the algorithm of [GJM94] to maintain incrementally full outer-join views. We use the following SQL syntax to define a view V as a full outer-join of relations R and S:

create view V as select $X_1, \ldots, X_n$ **from** R **full outer join** S **on** $g(Y_1, \ldots, Y_m)$

where $X_1, \ldots, X_n$ and $Y_1, \ldots, Y_m$ are lists of attributes from relations R and S. $g(Y_1, \ldots, Y_m)$ is a conjunction of predicates that represent the outer-join condition. The set of modifications to relation R is denoted as $\Delta(R)$, which consists of insertions $\Delta^+(R)$ and deletions $\Delta^-(R)$. Similarly, the set of modifications to relation S is denoted as $\Delta(S)$. The view maintenance algorithm rewrites the view definition to obtain the following two queries to compute $\Delta(V)$.

$((a))$:	**select** $X_1, \ldots, X_n$	(b):	**select** $X_1, \ldots, X_n$
	from $\Delta(R)$ **left outer join** S		**from** R^ν **right outer join** $\Delta(S)$
	on $g(Y_1, \ldots, Y_m)$		**on** $g(Y_1, \ldots, Y_m)$;

R^ν represents relation R after modification. All other references in queries (a) and (b) refer either to the pre-modified extents or to the modifications themselves. Unlike with SPJ views queries (a) and (b) do not compute the entire change to the view, as explained below.

Query (a) computes the effect on V of changes to relation R. Consider a tuple r^+ inserted into R and its effect on the view. If r^+ does not join with any tuple in s, then r^+.NULL (r^+ padded with nulls) has to be inserted into view V. If instead, r^+ does join with some tuple s in S, then $r^+.s$ (r^+ joined with tuple s) is inserted into the view. Both these consequences are captured in Query (a) by using the left-outer-join. However, query (a) does not compute a possible side effect if r^+ does join with some tuple s. The tuple NULL.s (s padded with nulls) may have to be deleted from the view V if NULL.s is in the view. This will be the case if previously tuple s did not join with any tuple in R.

Similarly, a deletion r^- from R not only removes a tuple from the view, as captured by Query (a), but may also precipitate the insertion of a tuple NULL.s if before deletion r^- is the only tuple that joined with s. Query (b) handles the modifications to table S similar to the manner in which query (a) handles the modifications to table R, with similar possible side-effects. The algorithm of [GJM94] handles these side effects.

3.3   Recursive Views

Recursive queries or views often are expressed using rules in Datalog [Ull89], and all the work on maintaining recursive views has been done in the context of Datalog. We describe the DRed **(Deletion and Rederivation)** algorithm for view maintenance, and then discuss several other recursive view maintenance techniques that have been proposed in the literature.

The DRed Algorithm [GMS93]:   applies to Datalog or SQL views, including views defined using recursion, UNION, and stratified negation and aggregation. However, SQL views with duplicate semantics cannot be maintained by this algorithm.   The DRed algorithm computes changes to the view relations in three steps. First, the algorithm computes an overestimate of the deleted derived tuples: a tuple t is in this overestimate if the changes made to the base relations invalidate *any* derivation of t. Second, this overestimate is pruned by removing (from the overestimate) those tuples that have alternative derivations in the new database. A version of the original view restricted to compute only the tuples in the overestimated set is used to do the pruning. Finally, the new tuples that need to be inserted are computed using the partially updated materialized view and the insertions made to the base relations. The algorithm can also maintain materialized views incrementally when rules defining derived relations are inserted or deleted. We illustrate the DRed algorithm using an example.

EXAMPLE 3.2 Consider the view hop defined in Example 3.1. The DRed algorithm first deletes tuples $hop(a, c)$ and $hop(a, e)$ since they both depend upon the deleted tuple. The DRed algorithm then looks for alternative derivations for each of the deleted tuples. $hop(a, c)$ is rederived and reinserted into the materialized view in the second step. The third step of the DRed algorithm is empty since no tuples are inserted into the link table.   □

None of the other algorithms discussed in this section handle the same class of views as the DRed algorithm; the most notable differentiating feature being aggregations. However, some algorithms derive more efficient solutions for special subclasses.

The PF (Propagation/Filtration) algorithm [HD92]:   is very similar to the DRed algorithm, except that it propagates the changes made to the base relations on a relation by relation basis. It computes changes in *one* derived relation due to changes in *one* base relation, looping over all derived and base relations to complete the view maintenance. In each loop, an algorithm similar to the delete/prune/insert steps in DRed is executed. However, rather than running the deletion step to completion before starting the pruning step, the deletion and the pruning steps are alternated after each iteration of the semi-naive evaluation. Thus, in each semi-naive iteration, an overestimate for deletions is computed and then pruned. This allows the PF algorithm to avoid propagating some tuples that occur in the over estimate after the first iteration but do not actually change. However, the alternation of the steps after each semi-naive iteration also causes some tuples to be rederived several times. In addition, the PF algorithm ends up fragmenting computation and rederiving changed and deleted tuples again and again. [GM93] presents improvements to the PF algorithm that reduce rederivation of facts by using memoing and by exploiting the stratification in the program. Each of DRed and the PF algorithms can do better than the other by a factor of n depending on the view definition (where n is the number of base tuples in the database). For nonrecursive views, the DRed algorithm always works better than the PF algorithm.

The Kuchenhoff algorithm [Kuc91]:   derives rules to compute the difference between consecutive database states for a stratified recursive program. The rules generated are similar in spirit to those of [GMS93]. However, some of the generated rules (for the *depends* predicates) are not safe, and the delete/prune/insert three step technique of [GMS93, HD92] is not used. Further, when dealing with positive rules, the Kuchenhoff algorithm does not discard duplicate derivations that are guaranteed not to generate any change in the view as early as the DRed algorithm discards the duplicate derivations.

The Urpi-Olive algorithm [UO92]: for stratified Datalog views derives transition rules showing how each modification to a relation translates into a modification to each derived relation, using existentially quantified subexpressions in Datalog rules. The quantified subexpressions may go through negation, and can be eliminated under certain conditions. Updates are modeled directly; however since keys need to be derived for such a modeling, the update model is useful mainly for nonrecursive views.

Counting based algorithms can sometimes be used for recursive views. The counting algorithm of [GKM92] can be used effectively only if every tuple is guaranteed to have a finite number of derivations[1], and even then the computation of counts can significantly increase the cost of computation. The BDGEN system [NY83] uses counts to reflect not all derivations but only certain types of derivations. Their algorithm gives finite even counts to all tuples, even those in a recursive view, and can be used even if tuples have infinitely many derivations.

Transitive Closures [DT92] derive nonrecursive programs to update right-linear recursive views in response to insertions into the base relation. [DS95a] give nonrecursive programs to update the transitive closure of specific kinds of graphs in response to insertions and deletions. The algorithm does not apply to all graphs or to general recursive programs. In fact, there does not exist a nonrecursive program to maintain the transitive closure of an arbitrary graph in response to deletions from the graph [DLW95].

Nontraditional Views [LMSS95a] extends the DRed algorithm to views that can have nonground tuples. [WDSY91] give a maintenance algorithm for a rule language with negation in the head and body of rules, using auxiliary information about the number of certain derivations of each tuple. They do not consider aggregation, and do not discuss how to handle recursively defined relations that may have an infinite number of derivations.

4   Using Partial Information

As illustrated in the introduction, views may be maintainable using only a subset of the underlying relations involved in the view. We refer to this information as *partial information*. Unlike view maintenance using full information, a view is not always maintainable for a modification using only partial information. Whether the view can be maintained may also depend upon whether the modification is an insertion, deletion, or update. So the algorithms focus on checking whether the view can be maintained, and then on how to maintain the view.

We will show that treating updates as a distinct type of modification lets us derive view maintenance algorithms for updates where no algorithms exist for deletions+insertions.

4.1   Using no Information: Query Independent of Update

There is a lot of work on optimizing view maintenance by determining when a modification leaves a view unchanged [BLT86, BCL89, Elk90, LS93]. This is known as the "query independent of update", or the "irrelevant update" problem. All these algorithms provide checks to determine whether a particular modification will be irrelevant. If the test succeeds, then the view stays unaffected by the modification. However, if the test fails, then some other algorithm has to be used for maintenance.

---

[1]An algorithm to check finiteness appears in [MS93b, MS94].

[BLT86, BCL89] determine irrelevant updates for SPJ views while [Elk90] considers irrelevant updates for Datalog. Further, [LS93] can determine irrelevant updates for Datalog with negated base relations and arithmetic inequalities.

4.2 Using the Materialized View: Self-Maintenance

Views that can be maintained using only the materialized view and key constraints are called *self-maintainable* views in [GJM96]. Several results on self-maintainability of SPJ and outer-join views in response to insertions, deletions, and updates are also presented in [GJM96]. Following [GJM96], we define:

Definition 4.1 (Self Maintainability With Respect to a Modification Type): A view V is said to be self-maintainable with respect to a modification type (insertion, deletion, or update) to a base relation R if for all database states, the view can be self-maintained in response to all instances of a modification of the indicated type to the base relation R. ∎

EXAMPLE 4.1 Consider view supp_parts from Example 1.2 that contains all **distinct** part_no supplied by at least one supplier. Also, let part_no be the key for relation part (so there can be at most one contract and one part_cost for a given part).

If a tuple is deleted from relation part then it is straightforward to update the view using only the materialized view (simply delete the corresponding part_no if it is present). Thus, the view is self-maintainable with respect to deletions from the part relation.

By contrast, let tuple supp($s1, p1, 100$) be deleted when the view contains tuple $p1$. The tuple $p1$ cannot be deleted from the view because supp may also contain a tuple supp($s2, p1, 200$) that contributes $p1$ to the view. Thus, the view is not self-maintainable with respect to deletions from supp. In fact, the view is not self-maintainable for insertions into either supp or part. ☐

Some results from [GJM96] are stated after the following definitions.

Definition 4.2 (Distinguished Attribute): An attribute A of a relation R is said to be distinguished in a view V if attribute A appears in the **select** clause defining view V. ∎

Definition 4.3 (Exposed Attribute): An attribute A of a relation R is said to be exposed in a view V if A is used in a predicate. An attribute that is not exposed is referred to as being non-exposed. ∎

Self-Maintainability With Respect to Insertions and Deletions [GJM96] shows that most SPJ views are not self-maintainable with respect to insertions, but they are often self-maintainable with respect to deletions and updates. For example:

- An SPJ view that takes the join of two or more distinct relations is not self-maintainable with respect to insertions.

- An SPJ view is self-maintainable with respect to deletions to R_1 if the key attributes from each occurrence of R_1 in the join are either included in the view, or are equated to a constant in the view definition.

- A left or full outer-join view V defined using two relations R and S, such that:

    - All exposed attributes of R are distinguished.

  is self-maintainable with respect to all types of modifications to relation S.

Self-Maintainability With Respect to Updates By modeling an update independently and not as a deletion+insertion we retain information about the deleted tuple that allows the insertion to be handled more easily.

EXAMPLE 4.2 Consider again relation $\texttt{part}(\texttt{part\_no}, \texttt{part\_cost}, \texttt{contract})$ where $\texttt{part\_no}$ is the key. Consider an extension of view $\texttt{supp\_parts}$:

$$\texttt{supp\_parts}(\texttt{supp\_no}, \texttt{part\_no}, \texttt{part\_cost}) = \Pi_{\texttt{part\_no}}(\texttt{supp} \bowtie_{\texttt{part\_no}} \texttt{part})$$

The view contains the $\texttt{part\_no}$ and $\texttt{part\_cost}$ for the parts supplied by each supplier. If the $\texttt{part\_cost}$ of a part $p1$ is updated then the view is updated by identifying the tuples in the view that have $\texttt{part\_no} = p1$ and updating their $\texttt{part\_cost}$ attribute. $\square$

The ability to self-maintain a view depends upon the attributes being updated. In particular, updates to non-exposed attributes are self-maintainable when the key attributes are distinguished. The complete algorithm for self-maintenance of a view in response to updates to non-exposed attributes is described in [GJM96] and relies on (a) identifying the tuples in the current view that are potentially affected by the update, and (b) computing the effect of the update on these tuples.

The idea of self-maintenance is not new — Autonomously computable views were defined by [BCL89] as the views that can be maintained using only the materialized view for all database instances, but for a given modification instance. They characterize a subset of SPJ views that are autonomously computable for insertions, deletions, and updates, where the deletions and updates are specified using conditions. They do not consider views with self-joins or outer-joins, do not use key information, and they do not consider self-maintenance with respect to all instances of modifications. The characterization of autonomously computable views in [BCL89] for updates is inaccurate — For instance, [BCL89] determines, incorrectly, that the view "**select** X **from** r(X)" is not autonomously computable for the modification "Update(R(3) to R(4))".

Instance Specific Self-Maintenance For insertions and deletions only, a database instance specific self-maintenance algorithm for SPJ views was discussed first in [TB88]. Subsequently this algorithm has been corrected and extended in [GB95].

4.3 Using Materialized View and Some Base Relations: Partial-reference

The partial-reference maintenance problem is to maintain a view given only a subset of the base relations and the materialized view. Two interesting subproblems here are when the view and all the relations except the modified relation are available, and when the view and modified relation are available.

Modified Relation is not Available (Chronicle Views) A chronicle is an ordered sequence of tuples with insertion being the only permissible modification [JMS95]. A view over a chronicle, treating the chronicle as a relation, is called a chronicle view. The chronicle may not be stored in its entirety in a database because it can get very large, so the chronicle view maintenance problem is to maintain the chronicle view in response to insertions into the chronicle, but without accessing the chronicle. Techniques to specify and maintain such views efficiently are presented in [JMS95].

Only Modified Relation is Available (Change-reference Maintainable) Sometimes a view may be maintainable using only the modified base relation and the view, but without accessing other base relations. Different modifications need to be treated differently.

EXAMPLE 4.3 Consider maintaining view supp_parts using relation supp and the old view in response to deletion of a tuple t from relation supp. If t.part_no is the same as the part_no of some other tuple in supp then the view is unchanged. If no remaining tuple has the same part_no as tuple t then we can deduce that no supplier supplies t.part_no and thus the part number has to be deleted from the view. Thus, the view is change-reference-maintainable.

A similar claim holds for deletions from part but not for insertions into either relation.   □

Instance Specific Partial-reference Maintenance [GB95, Gup94] give algorithms that successfully maintain a view for some instances of the database and modification, but not for others. Their algorithms derive conditions to be tested against the view and/or the given relations to check if the information is adequate to maintain the view.

5   Open Problems

This section describes some open problems in view maintenance, in the context of Figure 1. Many points on each of the three dimensions remain unconsidered, or even unrepresented. It is useful to extend each dimension to unconsidered points and to develop algorithms that cover entirely the resulting space because each point in the space corresponds to a scenario of potential interest.

View maintenance techniques that use all the underlying relations, *i.e.* full-information, have been studied in great detail for large classes of query languages. We emphasize the importance of developing comprehensive view maintenance techniques that use different types of partial information. For instance:

- Use information on functional dependencies, multiple materialized views, general integrity constraints, horizontal/vertical fragments of base relations (*i.e.*, simple views).

- Extend the view definition language to include aggregation, negation, outer-join for all instances of the other dimensions. The extensions are especially important for using partial information.

- Identify *subclasses* of SQL views that are maintainable in an instance independent fashion.

The converse of the view maintenance problem under partial information, as presented in Section 4 is to identify the information required for efficient view maintenance of a given view (or a set of views). We refer to this problem as the "information identification (II)" problem. Solutions for view maintenance with partial information indirectly apply to the II problem by checking if the given view falls into one of the classes for which partial-information based techniques exist. However, direct and more complete techniques for solving the II problem are needed.

An important problem is to implement and incorporate views in a database system. Many questions arise in this context. When are materialized views maintained – before the transaction that updates the base relation commits, or after the transaction commits? Is view maintenance a part of the transaction or not? Should the view be maintained before the update is applied to the base relations, or afterwards? Should the view be maintained after each update within the transaction, or after all the updates? Should active rules (or some other mechanism) be used to initiate view maintenance automatically or should a user start the process? Should alternative algorithms be tried, based on a cost based model to choose between the options? Some existing work in this context is in [NY83, CW91, GHJ96, RCK+95]. [CW91] considers using production rules for doing view maintenance and [NY83] presents algorithms in the context of a deductive DB system. [GHJ96] does not discuss view maintenance but discusses efficient implementation of deltas in a system that can be used to implement materialized views. [RCK+95] describes the ADMS system that implements and maintains simple materialized views, "ViewCaches," in a multi-database environment. The ADMS system uses materialized views in query optimization and addresses questions of caching, buffering, access paths, *etc.*.

The complexity of view maintenance also needs to be explored. The dynamic complexity classes of [PI94] and the incremental maintenance complexity of [JMS95] characterize the computational complexity of maintaining a materialized copy of the view. [PI94] show that several recursive views have a first order dynamic complexity, while [JMS95] define languages with constant, logarithmic, and polynomial incremental maintenance complexity.

Acknowledgments

We thank H. V. Jagadish, Leonid Libkin, Dallan Quass, and Jennifer Widom for their insightful comments on the technical and presentation aspects of this chapter.

INCREMENTAL MAINTENANCE OF RECURSIVE VIEWS: A SURVEY

Guozhu Dong

ABSTRACT

Database views can be divided into relational views and recursive views. The former are defined by relational algebra or SQL, whereas the latter are defined by Datalog, stratified Datalog¬, or polynomial time mappings over databases. In this article we give a short survey on previous results on the maintenance of recursive views.

We discuss the view maintenance algorithms mainly along three dimensions, which are designed to measure how usable and how efficient the view maintenance algorithms are. These dimensions are orthogonal to the four dimensions of [GM95].

1 Dimensions of View Maintenance Methods

Before presenting the three dimensions for measuring how usable and how efficient view maintenance methods are, we first review the following four dimensions given in [GM95] for classifying view maintenance problems:

- The available information dimension: Does the algorithm have access to all/some base relations while doing the maintenance? To materialized views? Does it use knowledge about integrity constraints or keys?

- The allowable modification dimension: What modifications can the view maintenance algorithm handle? Insertions of tuples to base relations? Deletions of tuples? Or sets of tuples?

- The view language dimension: What is the language of the views that can be maintained by the view maintenance algorithm? Is the view expressed as a select-project-join (or conjunctive) query? Relational algebra or SQL? Can it allow duplicates? Transitive closure? General recursion? Datalog or stratified Datalog¬? Or polynomial time mappings?

- The database instance dimension: Does the view maintenance algorithm work for all instances of the database or only some instances of the database?

These above four dimensions basically measure how general a view maintenance algorithm is. We enhance these four dimensions by adding three extra dimensions, which are designed to measure how usable and how efficient a view maintenance algorithm is. Roughly, the three extra dimensions measure the complexity of the view maintenance language, the view maintenance algorithms, and the auxiliary information. Although we concentrate in this survey on recursive views, the efficiency issue (measured by computational complexity or language complexity) is obviously important for nonrecursive views as well.

- The maintenance language dimension: What is the language in which the view maintenance algorithms are expressed? Is it the same as the view language? Is it a sub-language of relational algebra or SQL? Is it using a host programming language (such as C)?

  Usually it is advantageous when the language is a sub-language of the relational algebra, since maintenance algorithms in this language can be used in any relational database system, and since they are in AC_0 (computable by circuits of polynomial number of processors with constant depth, or "computable in theoretical constant parallel time").

- The complexity improvement dimension: Is the view maintenance algorithm demonstrably more efficient than the recomputing from scratch approach, by analysis or by experiment? For example, is there a sequential-complexity speed up from n^3 to n^2, or a parallel complexity speed up from $\log n$ to constant? Can the view maintenance algorithm be written in a more efficient language so that speed up can be argued at a language level?

  Observe that efficiency is the reason why users choose view maintenance over recomputing from scratch.

- The auxiliary information dimension: How much space is required by the auxiliary information to help maintain the view?

  In addition to the obvious issue of space efficiency, it is instructive to know what kind of auxiliary information is needed. Ideally we would like to see that this auxiliary information can be expressed as relations over the constants in the base relations. However, some algorithms use integers or nested relations, which might require extra operators to handle.

There is usually a tradeoff between different dimensions: If we consider a large class of views/updates, then we may need to use less desirable view maintenance algorithms. On the other hand, if we consider restricted views/updates, then we may be able to design better view maintenance algorithms. There is also a space-time trade-off between auxiliary information and computation time.

2   Using Relational Queries as Maintenance Algorithms

There has been considerable work on the maintenance of recursive views using relational queries as maintenance algorithms. In addition to the practical implications to view maintenance, study in this direction is also addressing the interesting theoretical question of whether first-order can define recursion dynamically. It is now known that first-order can define some recursion dynamically; it is open if it can define all recursion expressible by Datalog.

In this framework, we usually consider updates bounded in size in order to have a relational-query (or first-order) maintenance algorithm. (For most algorithms the ability to handle sets of tuples of fixed sizes is identical to the ability to handle single tuples. For this reason we will only refer to their ability to handle single tuples.) There are special cases where certain kind of sets of inserted/deleted tuples can be handled.

Advantages of such maintenance algorithms include the fact that they are easily usable within all relational database systems and they are in AC_0. However, associated with these advantages are the tradeoffs that there might not be such maintenance algorithms for all queries in interesting classes such as Datalog.

To maintain recursive views using first-order queries, some auxiliary relations over constants in the base relations are used (and maintained by first-order queries as well). Auxiliary information allows us to trade space for time.

The following list summarizes many of the views maintainable in first-order.

- In [DT92] (also reprinted in this volume) first-order maintenance algorithms were given for all views defined by right-linear chain Datalog programs. The updates allowed are single tuple insertions. Auxiliary relations over constants in the base relations are necessary when the program is more than a single transitive closure.

  In [DS93] the above result is extended to right-linear chain Datalog programs whose base relations are not necessarily binary. That paper also gave a further extension to the situation where base relations p in right-linear chain Datalog programs P can have initializations: p can be defined by other programs P' where P' does not depend on the relations occurring in P and P' has the so-called Cartesian-product increment property. This Cartesian-product increment property is decidable when P' is a conjunctive (select-project-join) query. This generalized result implies that we can maintain views defined by right-linear chain Datalog programs using first-order queries after the insertions of sets of tuples which are cross-products.

  Extended discussions of these results can be found in [DSR95].

- In [DS95a] a first-order algorithm was given to maintain the transitive closure of acyclic directed graphs, after insertions and deletions of edges.

  In [DP95] a different first-order algorithm was given, and the new algorithm was generalized to maintain transitive closure of general directed graphs, after the deletions of certain kind of sets of edges and nodes.

  The algorithms in [DS95a, DP95] do not use auxiliary relations.

- In [PI94] a first-order query maintenance algorithm was given to maintain the transitive closure of undirected graphs, using ternary auxiliary relations over constants in the base relations. (That paper also discusses maintaining answers to general computational problems in first-order.)

  In [DS95b] a first-order maintenance algorithm for transitive closure of undirected graphs was given, which uses binary auxiliary relations. It was shown there that no such algorithms exist if only unary relations are used. The paper also established that many other queries over undirected graphs, including bipartiteness and "minimum spanning forests" can be maintained using binary auxiliary relations but not unary ones.

- In [DK94] first-order maintenance algorithms were given for the constrained transitive closure in the presence of inequality constraints.

Using auxiliary relations of different arities gives us different abilities to maintain different recursive views. In [DS95b] a strict hierarchy was established for arities up to 2. It is still open if the hierarchy is strict for arities > 2. (See also [DS96].)

As an extension to first-order maintenance algorithms, [DLW95] considered the maintenance of recursive views using SQL queries as maintenance algorithms. It was shown that, if no auxiliary relation is used, SQL still cannot maintain transitive closure of directed graphs, although SQL is more powerful than first-order queries as maintenance algorithms.

Many interesting open problems remain, including the following:

- Can the transitive closure of general directed graphs be maintained using first-order queries after deletions of edges? Using SQL queries?

- Can the same-generation query (over two arbitrary relations) be maintained using first-order queries if only insertions of tuples are considered?

- It is easy to see that all views maintainable using first-order queries must be definable by polynomial time queries. Can all views defined by polynomial queries be maintained using first-order queries? Views defined by Datalog?

It is also interesting to have an analysis showing how much efficiency gain can be achieved if these maintenance algorithms are translated to sequential algorithms, compared to the recomputing from scratch approach.

3   Recursive Maintenance Methods

At least five methods [Kuc91, CW91, UO92, HD92, GMS93] have been given to maintain views defined by stratified Datalog¬ programs. These algorithms were similar in the following aspects: They rewrite rules in the given stratified Datalog¬ program; some of these rules are then applied iteratively (to fixpoint) to derive some estimate of the changes to the view caused by the base relation update; some other rules are then applied to prune the false estimate; this yields the proper change to the view.

Some of the algorithms may differ in some fine details such as how often the pruning steps are applied. For example, in [HD92] the estimate/pruning cycle is applied for each step of the semi-naive iterations.

These algorithms need to use auxiliary relations to store the intermediate derived relations (defined by IDB predicates which are not the view predicate).

These algorithms can be used if the underlying database system can handle stratified Datalog¬ evaluation, but cannot be used within a pure relational database system.

Intuitively these algorithms seem more efficient than recomputing the view from scratch, mainly due to the observation that "small changes in base relations should lead to small changes in views." Formal verification of such gain of efficiency has been lacking in the literature. In particular, the efficiency gain cannot be justified at a language level, since the view maintenance language is usually the same as the view definition language.

In [GKM92] some counting based algorithms are proposed to maintain views, where associated with each derived fact we record the number of times this fact is derived. The algorithms are applicable mostly to acyclic databases, in order to ensure finite counts. The computation is recursive, and additionally stores integers and uses integer arithmetics.

In [AP87] algorithms for maintaining models of stratified Datalog¬ programs are given. These algorithms use the iterative fixpoint evaluation method. They use different kinds of auxiliary information, ranging from sets of facts to sets of sets (or nested sets) of facts, for each fact currently in the model. Again these methods are not usable within normal relational database systems.

Research about on-line algorithms and their complexity from the graph algorithms community (see [Yan90] for references) and the complexity theory community [MSVT94] are also related to view maintenance.

Acknowledgments

I thank my co-authors of [3-11], especially J. Su and R. Topor, for exploring the theme of maintaining recursive views using relational queries with me, L. Libkin, I. S. Mumick, D. Srivastava and J. Su for discussions which helped me bring out some of the ideas in this survey, and J. Su for comments on an earlier draft.

13

EFFICIENTLY UPDATING MATERIALIZED VIEWS

José A. Blakeley,
Per-Åke Larson, Frank Wm. Tompa

ABSTRACT

Query processing can be sped up by keeping frequently accessed users' views materialized. However, the need to access base relations in response to queries can be avoided only if the materialized view is adequately maintained. We propose a method in which all database updates to base relations are first filtered to remove from consideration those that cannot possibly affect the view. The conditions given for the detection of updates of this type, called *irrelevant updates*, are necessary and sufficient and are independent of the database state. For the remaining database updates, a *differential* algorithm can be applied to re-evaluate the view expression. The algorithm proposed exploits the knowledge provided by both the view definition expression and the database update operations.

1 Introduction

In a relational database system, a database may be composed of both *base* and *derived relations*. A derived relation–or *view*–is defined by a relational expression (i.e., a query evaluated over the base relations). A derived relation may be *virtual*, which corresponds to the traditional concept of a view; or *materialized*, which means that the resulting relation is actually stored. As the database changes because of updates applied to the base relations, the materialized views may also require change. A materialized view can always be brought up to date by re-evaluating the relational expression that defines it. However, complete re-evaluation is often wasteful, and the cost involved may be unacceptable.

The need for a mechanism to update materialized views efficiently has been expressed by several authors. Gardarin et al. [GSV84] consider *concrete views* (i.e., materialized views) as a candidate approach for the support of real time queries. However, they discard this approach because of the lack of an efficient algorithm to keep the concrete views up to date with the base relations. Horwitz and Teitelbaum [HT85] propose a model for the generation of language-based environments which uses a relational database along with attribute grammars, and they suggest algorithms for incrementally updating views, motivated by the efficiency requirements of interactive editing. Buneman and Clemons [BC79] propose views for the support of *alerters*, which monitor a database and report to some user or application whether a state of the database, described by the view definition, has been reached.

It must be stressed that the problem analyzed in this chapter is different from the traditional *view update* problem. In the traditional view update problem, a user is allowed to pose updates directly to a view, and the difficulty is in determining how to translate updates expressed against a view into updates to the base relations. In the model proposed in this chapter, the user can only update base relations; direct updates to views are not considered. Therefore, rather than analyzing the traditional problem of deriving appropriate update translations, this chapter is concerned with finding efficient ways of keeping materialized views up to date with the base relations.

The purpose of this chapter is to present a framework for the efficient update of materialized views when base relations are subject to updates. Section 2 presents some previous related work; Section 3 presents the notation and terminology used throughout the chapter; Section 4 describes how to detect updates that have no effect on a view; Section 5 describes a method for differentially updating materialized views; finally, Section 6 contains some conclusions and suggestions for further research.

2   Previous Work

Work directly related to the maintenance of materialized views has been reported by Koenig and Paige [KP81] and by Shmueli and Itai [SI84]. Koenig and Paige [KP81] investigate the support of derived data in the context of a functional binary-association data model. This data model puts together ideas borrowed from binary-association models, functional models, and the entity-relationship model, within a programming language suitable for data definition and manipulation. In their model, views can be explicitly stored and then maintained. For each possible change to the operands of the view, there exists a procedure associated with this change that incrementally updates the view. This procedure is called the *derivative* of the view definition with respect to the change. Their approach relies on the availability of such derivatives for various view definition/change statement combinations.

Shmueli and Itai's approach consists of continuously maintaining an acyclic database, together with information that may be useful for future insertions and deletions. Their definition of views is limited to the projection of a set of attributes over the natural join of all the relations in the database scheme. This is a restricted class of views, since views based on the join of some, but not all, of the relations in the database scheme cannot be handled by this mechanism. Another restriction on the views is the omission of selection conditions.

In related work, Hammer and Sarin [HS77] present a method for efficiently detecting violations of integrity constraints, called *integrity assertions*, as a result of database updates. For each integrity assertion, there exists an *error-predicate* which corresponds to the logical complement of the assertion. If the error-predicate is true for some instance of the database, then the instance violates the assertion. Their approach to the problem of efficiently checking database assertions is based on analyzing the potential effects that an update operation may have on the assertions. This analysis is performed by a compile-time *assertion processor*. The result is a set of candidate tests that will be executed at run-time to determine if the update causes the assertion to be violated. The selection of the least expensive test from the set of candidate tests requires a procedure similar to the one required in query optimization.

Buneman and Clemons [BC79] propose a procedure for the efficient implementation of alerters. In general, the condition that triggers an alerter is expressed in terms of a query—called the *target relation*—over several base relations; in our terminology, a target relation corresponds to a virtual view. One aspect that is emphasized in their work is the efficient detection of base relation updates that are of no interest to an alerter, thus determining when re-evaluation of the associated query is unnecessary.

3 Notation and Terminology

We assume that the reader is familiar with the basic ideas and notation concerning relational databases, as described in [Mai83]. A *view definition* V corresponds to a relational algebra expression on the database scheme. A *view materialization* v is a stored relation resulting from the evaluation of this relational algebra expression against an instance of the database. In this chapter, we consider only relational algebra expressions formed from the combination of selections, projections, and joins, called *SPJ expressions*.

A *transaction* is an *indivisible* sequence of update operations to base relations. Indivisible means that either all the update operations are successfully performed or none are performed. Furthermore, updates within a transaction may update several base relations.

Considering that base relations are updated before the views, it is reasonable to assume that the complete affected tuples from the base relations are available at the time the view is to be updated. The *net* effect of a transaction on a base relation can be represented by a set of tuples that have been inserted and a set of tuples that have been deleted. Formally, given a base relation r and a transaction $\mathcal{T}$, there exist sets of tuples i_r and d_r such that r, i_r, and d_r are disjoint and $\mathcal{T}(r) = r \cup i_r - d_r$. Therefore, without any loss of generality we will represent a transaction applied to a base relation $\mathcal{T}(R)$ by $insert(R, i_r)$ and $delete(R, d_r)$, where R is the name of the base relation with instance r such that r, i_r, d_r are mutually disjoint.

It is assumed that all attributes are defined on discrete and finite domains. Since such a domain can be mapped to a subset of natural numbers, we use integer values in all examples.

4 Relevant and Irrelevant Updates

In certain cases, a set of updates to a base relation has no effect on the state of a view. When this occurs independently of the database state, we call the set of updates *irrelevant*. It is important to provide an efficient mechanism for detecting irrelevant updates so that re-evaluation of the relational expression defining a view can be avoided or the number of tuples considered can be reduced.

Consider a view defined by the expression

$$V = \pi_X(\sigma_{\mathcal{C}(Y)}(R_1 \times R_2 \times \cdots \times R_p))$$

where $\mathcal{C}(Y)$ is a Boolean expression and X and Y are sets of variables denoting the names of (some) attributes for the relations named $R_1, R_2, \ldots, R_p$. The sets X and Y are not necessarily equal (i.e., not all the attributes in the projection participate in the selection condition and *vice versa*), and in fact may be disjoint.

Suppose that a tuple $t = (a_1, a_2, \ldots, a_q)$ is inserted into (or deleted from) relation r_k defined on scheme R_k. Let $Y_1 = R_k \cap Y$, and $Y_2 = Y - Y_1$, so that $Y = Y_1 \cup Y_2$. Let the selection condition $\mathcal{C}(Y)$ be modified by replacing the variables Y_1 by their corresponding values $t(Y_1)$. If the modified condition $\mathcal{C}(Y)$ can be shown to be unsatisfiable regardless of the database state, then inserting or deleting t from r_k has no effect on the view v.

Example 4.1 Consider two relations r and s defined on $R = \{A, B\}$ and $S = \{C, D\}$, respectively, and a view v defined as

$$V = \pi_{A,D}(\sigma_{(A<10)\wedge(C>5)\wedge(B=C)}(R \times S)).$$

That is, $\mathcal{C}(A, B, C) = (A < 10) \wedge (C > 5) \wedge (B = C)$.

$$
\begin{array}{llllll}
r: & \begin{array}{cc} A & B \\ \hline 1 & 2 \\ 5 & 10 \\ 12 & 15 \end{array} &
s: & \begin{array}{cc} C & D \\ \hline 2 & 10 \\ 10 & 20 \end{array} &
v: & \begin{array}{cc} A & D \\ \hline 5 & 20 \end{array}
\end{array}
$$

Suppose that the tuple $(9, 10)$ is inserted into relation r. We can substitute the values $(9, 10)$ for the variables A and B in $\mathcal{C}(A, B, C)$ to obtain the modified condition $\mathcal{C}(9, 10, C) = (9 < 10) \wedge (C > 5) \wedge (10 = C)$. The selection condition $\mathcal{C}(9, 10, C)$ is satisfiable, that is, there exist instances of the relations named R and S containing the tuples $(9, 10)$ and $(10, \delta)$, for some value of δ such that $\mathcal{C}(9, 10, \delta) = True$. Therefore, inserting the tuple $(9, 10)$ into relation r is *relevant* to the view v. Notice that there may be some state of s that contains no matching tuple $(10, \delta)$, in which case the tuple $(9, 10)$ will have no effect on the view. However, the only way of verifying this is by checking the contents of the database.

On the other hand, suppose that the tuple $(11, 10)$ is inserted into relation r. After substituting the values $(11, 10)$ for the variables A and B in $\mathcal{C}(A, B, C)$ we obtain

$$
\mathcal{C}(11, 10, C) = (11 < 10) \wedge (C > 5) \wedge (10 = C).
$$

We can see that $\mathcal{C}$ is now unsatisfiable regardless of the database state. Therefore, inserting the tuple $(11, 10)$ into relation r is (provably) irrelevant to the view v. $\square$

The same argument applies for deletions. That is, if substituting the values of the deleted tuple in the selection condition makes the selection condition unsatisfiable regardless of the database state, then the deleted tuple is irrelevant to the view. In other words, the deleted tuple is not visible in the view. Similarly, if substituting the values of the deleted tuple in the selection condition makes the selection condition satisfiable, then the deleted tuple may need to be removed from the view.

Definition 4.1 Consider a view

$$
v = \pi_X(\sigma_{\mathcal{C}(Y)}(r_1 \times r_2 \times \cdots \times r_p)),
$$

and a tuple $t = (a_1, a_2, \ldots, a_q) \in r_i$ defined on R_i for some $i, 1 \le i \le p$. Let $Y_1 = Y \cap R_i$ and $Y_2 = Y - Y_1$. Denote by $\mathcal{C}(t, Y_2)$ the modified selection condition $\mathcal{C}(Y)$ obtained when substituting the value $t(A)$ for each occurrence of the variable $A \in Y_1$ in $\mathcal{C}(Y)$. $\mathcal{C}(t, Y_2)$ is said to be a *substitution* of t for Y_1 in $\mathcal{C}$.

Theorem 4.1 Consider a view

$$
v = \pi_X(\sigma_{\mathcal{C}(Y)}(r_1 \times r_2 \times \cdots \times r_p)),
$$

and a tuple t inserted into (or deleted from) r_i defined on R_i for some $i, 1 \le i \le p$. Let $Y_1 = Y \cap R_i$ and $Y_2 = Y - Y_1$. The update involving tuple t is *irrelevant* to the view v (for every database instance $\mathcal{D}$) if and only if $\mathcal{C}(t, Y_2)$ is unsatisfiable.

Proof: (if) If the substitution of $\mathcal{C}(t, Y_2)$ is unsatisfiable, then no matter what the current state of the database is, $\mathcal{C}(t, Y_2)$ evaluates to false and therefore does not affect the view. That is, if t were inserted it could not cause any new tuples to become visible in the view, and if t were deleted it could not cause any tuples to be deleted from the view. Hence, the tuple t is irrelevant to the view v.

(only if) Assume that the tuple t is irrelevant to the view and that $\mathcal{C}(t, Y_2)$ is satisfiable. $\mathcal{C}(t, Y_2)$ being satisfiable means that there exists a database instance $\mathcal{D}_0$ for which a substitution of values u for Y_2 in $\mathcal{C}(t, Y_2)$ makes the selection condition true. To construct such a database instance we need to find at least $p - 1$ tuples $t_j \in r_j, 1 \leq j \leq p$ and $j \neq i$ (since $t \in r_i$), in such a way that

$$\pi_X(\sigma_{\mathcal{C}(Y)}(\{t_1\} \times \{t_2\} \times \cdots \times \{t\} \times \cdots \times \{t_p\})) \neq \phi.$$

i) For all attributes A such that $A \in R_i$ and $A \in Y_1$, replace $t_j(A), 1 \leq j \leq p, j \neq i$ by $t(A)$.

ii) For all attributes $B \notin Y$, replace $t_j(B), 1 \leq j \leq p, j \neq i$ by any value, say *one*.

iii) For all attributes $C \in Y_2$, replace $t_j(C), 1 \leq j \leq p, j \neq i$ by any value in the domain of C that makes $\mathcal{C}(t, Y_2)$ true. Such values are guaranteed to exist because $\mathcal{C}(t, Y_2)$ is satisfiable.

The database instance $\mathcal{D}_0$ consists of p relations

$$r_1 = \{t_1\}, r_2 = \{t_2\}, \ldots, r_i = \phi, \ldots, r_p = \{t_p\}.$$

Clearly, the view state that corresponds to $\mathcal{D}_0$ has no tuples. Creating $\mathcal{D}_1$ from $\mathcal{D}_0$ by inserting t into r_i produces a view state with one tuple. Thus the insertion of t is relevant to the view v. Similarly, deleting t from $\mathcal{D}_1$ shows that the deletion of t is also relevant to the view v. This proves that the condition is necessary. $\square$

Deciding the satisfiability of Boolean expressions is in general *NP*-complete. However, there is a large class of Boolean expressions for which satisfiability can be decided efficiently, as shown by Rosenkrantz and Hunt [RH80]. This class corresponds to expressions formed from the conjunction of atomic formulae of the form x *op* y, x *op* c, and x *op* $y + c$, where x and y are variables defined on discrete and infinite domains, c is a positive or negative constant, and $op \in \{=, <, >, \leq, \geq\}$. The improved efficiency arises from not allowing the operator $\neq$ in *op*.

Deciding whether a conjunctive expression in the class described above is satisfiable can be done in time $O(n^3)$ where n is the number of variables contained in the expression. The sketch of the algorithm is as follows: (1) the conjunctive expression is normalized, that is, it is transformed into an equivalent one where only the operators $\leq$ or $\geq$ are used in the atomic formulae; (2) a directed weighted graph is constructed to represent the normalized expression; and (3) if the directed graph contains a cycle for which the sum of its weights is negative then the expression is unsatisfiable, otherwise it is satisfiable. To find whether a directed weighted graph contains a negative cycle one can use Floyd's algorithm [Flo62], which finds all the shortest paths between any two nodes in a directed weighted graph.

We can also decide efficiently the satisfiability of Boolean expressions of the form

$$\mathcal{C} = \mathcal{C}_1 \vee \mathcal{C}_2 \vee \cdots \vee \mathcal{C}_m$$

where, $\mathcal{C}_i$, $i = 1, \ldots, m$, is a conjunctive expression in the class described above. The expression $\mathcal{C}$ is satisfiable if and only if at least one of the conjunctive expressions $\mathcal{C}_i$ is satisfiable. Similarly, $\mathcal{C}$ is unsatisfiable if and only if each of the conjunctive expressions $\mathcal{C}_i$ is unsatisfiable. We can apply Rosenkrantz and Hunt's algorithm to each of the conjunctive expressions $\mathcal{C}_i$; this takes time $O(mn^3)$ in the worst case, where n is the number of different variables mentioned in $\mathcal{C}$.

4.1   Detection of Relevant Updates

This section presents an algorithm to detect those relation updates that are relevant to a view. Before describing the algorithm we need another definition.

Definition 4.2 Consider a conjunctive expression $\mathcal{C}(Y)$, and a tuple $t = (a_1, a_2, \ldots, a_q) \in r$ defined on R. Let $\alpha(\mathcal{C})$ denote the set of variables that participate in $\mathcal{C}$, $Y = \alpha(\mathcal{C})$, $Y_1 = Y \cap R$, $Y_2 = Y - Y_1$, and $\mathcal{C}(t, Y_2)$ be the substitution of t for Y_1 in $\mathcal{C}$. We distinguish between two types of atomic formulae in $\mathcal{C}(t, Y_2)$ called *variant* and *invariant* formulae respectively.

(1) Variant formulae are those directly affected by the substitution of $t(A)$ for $A \in Y_1$ in $\mathcal{C}$. This type of formula may have the form $(x \; op \; c)$, or $(c \; op \; d)$; where x is a variable and c, d are constants. Furthermore, formulae of the form $(x \; op \; c)$ are called *variant non-evaluable* formulae, and formulae of the form $(c \; op \; d)$ are called *variant evaluable* formulae. Variant evaluable formulae are either true or false.

(2) Invariant formulae are those that remain invariant with respect to the substitution of t for Y_1 in $\mathcal{C}$. This type of formula may have the form $(x \; op \; c)$, or $(x \; op \; y + c)$; where x, y are variables, and c is a constant. That is, the attributes X, Y represented by the variables x, y are not in Y_1.

Notice that the classification of atomic formulae in $\mathcal{C}$ depends on the relation scheme of the set of tuples t substituting for attributes Y_1 in $\mathcal{C}$.

Algorithm 4.1

The input to the algorithm consists of:

i) a conjunctive Boolean expression $\mathcal{C} = f_1 \wedge f_2 \wedge \cdots \wedge f_n$, where each f_i, $1 \leq i \leq n$, is an atomic formula of the form $(x \; op \; y)$, $(x \; op \; y + c)$, or $(x \; op \; c)$, where x, y are variables (representing attributes) and c is a constant;

ii) a relation scheme R of the updated relation; and

iii) a set of tuples $T_{in} = \{t_1, t_2, \ldots, t_q\}$ on scheme R. T_{in} contains those tuples inserted to or deleted from the relation r.

The output from the algorithm consists of a set of tuples $T_{out} \subseteq T_{in}$ which are relevant to the view.

1. The conjunctive expression $\mathcal{C}$ is normalized.

2. The normalized conjunctive expression $\mathcal{C}_N$ is expressed as $\mathcal{C}_{INV} \wedge \mathcal{C}_{VEVAL} \wedge \mathcal{C}_{VNEVAL}$. $\mathcal{C}_{INV}$ is a conjunctive subexpression containing only invariant formulae. $\mathcal{C}_{VEVAL}$ is a conjunctive subexpression containing only variant evaluable formulae. $\mathcal{C}_{VNEVAL}$ is a conjunctive subexpression containing only variant non-evaluable formulae.

3. Using $\mathcal{C}_{INV}$, build the invariant portion of the directed weighted graph.

4. For each tuple $t \in T_{in}$, substitute the values of t for the appropriate variables in $\mathcal{C}_{VEVAL}$ and $\mathcal{C}_{VNEVAL}$. Build the variant portion of the graph and check whether the substituted conjunctive expression represented by the graph is satisfiable. If the expression is satisfiable, then add t to T_{out}, otherwise ignore it. $\square$

An important component of the algorithm is the construction of a directed weighted graph $G = (n, e)$, where $n = \alpha(\mathcal{C}) \cup \{0\}$ is the set of nodes, and e is the set of directed weighted edges representing atomic formulae in $\mathcal{C}$. Each member of e is a triple (n_o, n_d, w), where n_o, $n_d \in n$ are the *origin* and *destination* nodes respectively, and w is the *weight* of the edge. The atomic formula $(x \leq y + c)$ translates to the edge (x, y, c). The atomic formula $(x \geq y + c)$ translates to the edge $(y, x, -c)$. The atomic formula $(x \leq c)$ translates to the edge $('0', x, c)$. The atomic formula $(x \geq c)$ translates to the edge $(x, '0', -c)$.

The normalization procedure mentioned in the algorithm takes a conjunctive expression and transforms it into an equivalent one where each atomic formula has as comparison operator either $\leq$ or $\geq$. Atomic formulae $(x < y + c)$ are transformed into $(x \leq y + c - 1)$. Atomic formulae $(x > y + c)$ are transformed into $(x \geq y + c + 1)$. Atomic formulae $(x = y + c)$ are transformed into $(x \leq y + c) \wedge (x \geq y + c)$.

The satisfiability test consists of checking whether the directed weighted graph contains a negative weight cycle or not. The expression is unsatisfiable if the graph contains a negative cycle.

We can generalize Definition 4.1 to allow substitutions of several tuples for variables in an expression $\mathcal{C}$.

Definition 4.3 Consider a view

$$v = \pi_X(\sigma_{\mathcal{C}(Y)}(r_1 \times r_2 \times \cdots \times r_p))$$

and tuples $t_i \in r_i, 1 \leq i \leq k$. Assume that $R_i \cap R_j = \phi$ for all $i \neq j$. Let $Y_1 = Y \cap (R_1 \cup R_2 \cup \cdots \cup R_k)$ and $Y_2 = Y - Y_1$. Denote by $\mathcal{C}(t_1, t_2, \ldots, t_k, Y_2)$ the modified selection condition obtained when substituting the values $t_i(X), 1 \leq i \leq k$, for each occurrence of the variable $A \in Y_1$ in $\mathcal{C}(Y)$. $\mathcal{C}(t_1, t_2, \ldots, t_k, Y_2)$ is said to be the *substitution* of $t_1, t_2, \ldots, t_k$ for Y_1 in $\mathcal{C}$.

Theorem 4.2 Consider a view

$$v = \pi_X(\sigma_{\mathcal{C}(Y)}(r_1 \times r_2 \times \cdots \times r_p)),$$

and tuples $t_1, t_2, \ldots, t_k$ *all* either inserted to or deleted from relations $r_1, r_2, \ldots, r_k$ respectively. Let Y_1 and Y_2 be defined as before. The set of tuples $\{t_1, t_2, \ldots, t_k\}$ is *irrelevant* to the view v (for every database instance $\mathcal{D}$) if and only if $\mathcal{C}(t_1, t_2, \ldots, t_k, Y_2)$ is unsatisfiable.

Proof: Similar to the proof of Theorem 4.1.

While we do not propose the statement of Theorem 4.2 as the basis of an implementation for the detection of irrelevant updates, it shows that the detection of irrelevant updates can be taken further by considering combinations of tuples from different relations.

5 Differential Re-evaluation of Views

The purpose of this section is to present an algorithm to update a view differentially as a result of updates to base relations participating in the view definition. *Differential update* means bringing the materialized view up to date by identifying which tuples must be inserted into or deleted from the current instance of the view.

For simplicity, it is assumed that the base relations are updated by transactions and that the differential update mechanism is invoked as the last operation within the transaction (i.e., as part of the *commit* of the transaction). It is also assumed that the information available when the differential view update mechanism is invoked consists of: (a) the contents of each base relation before the execution of the transaction, (b) the set of tuples actually inserted into or deleted from each base relation, (c) the view definition, and (d) the contents of the view that agrees with the contents of the base relations before the execution of the transaction. Notice in particular that (b) only includes the *net* changes to the relations: for example, if a tuple not in the relation is inserted and then deleted within a transaction, it is not represented at all in this set of changes.

5.1   Select Views

A *select view* is defined by the expression $V = \sigma_{C(Y)}(R)$, where C (the selection condition) is a Boolean expression defined on $Y \subseteq R$. Let i_r and d_r denote the set of tuples inserted into or deleted from relation r, respectively. The new state of the view, called v', is computed by the expression $v' = v \cup \sigma_{C(Y)}(i_r) - \sigma_{C(Y)}(d_r)$. That is, the view can be updated by the sequence of operations $insert(V, \sigma_{C(Y)}(i_r))$, $delete(V, \sigma_{C(Y)}(d_r))$. Assuming $|v| \gg |d_r|$, it is cheaper to update the view by the above sequence of operations than re-computing the expression V from scratch.

5.2   Project Views

A *project view* is defined by the expression $V = \pi_X(R)$, where $X \subseteq R$. The project operation introduces the first difficulty to updating views differentially. The difficulty arises when the base relation r is updated through a delete operation.

Example 5.1 Consider a relation scheme $R = \{A, B\}$, a project view defined as $\pi_B(R)$, and the relation r shown below:

$$r: \quad \begin{array}{cc} A & B \\ \hline 1 & 10 \\ 2 & 10 \\ 3 & 20 \end{array} \qquad v: \quad \begin{array}{c} B \\ \hline 10 \\ 20 \end{array}$$

If the operation $delete(R, \{(3, 20)\})$ is applied to relation r, then the view can be updated by the operation $delete(V, \{20\})$. However, if the operation $delete(R, \{(1, 10)\})$ is applied to relation r, then the view cannot be updated by the operation $delete(V, \{10\})$. The reason for this difficulty is that the distributive property of projection over difference does not hold (i.e., $\pi_X(r_1 - r_2) \neq \pi_X(r_1) - \pi_X(r_2)$).   □

There are two alternatives for solving the problem.

1. Attach an additional attribute to each tuple in the view, a multiplicity *counter*, which records the number of operand tuples that contribute to the tuple in the view. Inserting a tuple already in the view causes the counter for that tuple to be incremented by one. Deleting a tuple from the view causes the counter for that tuple to be decremented by one; if the counter becomes zero, then the tuple in the view can be safely deleted.

2. Include the key of the underlying relation within the set of attributes projected in the view. This alternative allows unique identification of each tuple in the view. Insertions or deletions cause no trouble since the tuples in the view are uniquely identified.

We choose alternative (1) since we do not want to impose restrictions on the views other than the class of relational algebra expressions allowed in their definition. In addition, alternative (2) becomes an special case of alternative (1) in which every tuple in the view has a counter value of one.

We require that base relations and views include an additional attribute, which we will denote $\mathcal{N}$. For base relations, this attribute need not be explicitly stored since its value in every tuple is always one. The select operation is not affected by this assumption. The project operation is redefined as $\pi_X(r) = \{t(X') \mid X' = X \cup \{\mathcal{N}\}$ and $\exists u \in r\big((u(X) = t(X)) \wedge (t(\mathcal{N}) = \sum_{w \in W} w(\mathcal{N})$ where $W = \{w \mid w \in r \wedge w(X) = t(X)\})\big)\}$. Notice that by redefining the project operation, the distributive property of projection over difference now holds (i.e., $\pi_X(r_1 - r_2) = \pi_X(r_1) - \pi_X(r_2)$).

To complete the definition of operators to include the multiplicity counter the join operation is redefined as $r \bowtie s = \{t(Y_1) \mid Y_1 = R \cup S$ and $\exists u, v\big((u \in r) \wedge (v \in s) \wedge (t(R - \{\mathcal{N}\}) = u(R - \{\mathcal{N}\})) \wedge (t(S - \{\mathcal{N}\}) = v(S - \{\mathcal{N}\})) \wedge (t(\mathcal{N}) = u(\mathcal{N}) * v(\mathcal{N}))\big)\}$, where '$*$' denotes scalar multiplication.

5.3 Join Views

A *join view* is defined by the expression

$$V = R_1 \bowtie R_2 \bowtie \cdots \bowtie R_p.$$

We consider first changes to the base relations exclusively through insert operations, next we consider changes to the base relations exclusively through delete operations, and finally we consider changes to the base relations through both insert and delete operations.

Example 5.2 Consider two relation schemes $R = \{A, B\}$ and $S = \{B, C\}$, and a view V defined as $V = R \bowtie S$. Suppose that after the view v is materialized, the relation r is updated by the insertion of the set of tuples i_r. Let $r' = r \cup i_r$. The new state of the view, called v', is computed by the expression

$$
\begin{aligned}
v' &= r' \bowtie s \\
&= (r \cup i_r) \bowtie s \\
&= (r \bowtie s) \cup (i_r \bowtie s).
\end{aligned}
$$

If $i_v = i_r \bowtie s$, then $v' = v \cup i_v$. That is, the view can be updated by inserting only the new set of tuples i_v into relation v. In other words, one only needs to compute the contribution of the new tuples in r to the join. Clearly, it is cheaper to compute the view v' by adding i_v to v than to re-compute the join completely from scratch. □

This idea can be generalized to views defined as the join of an arbitrary number of base relations by exploiting the distributive property of join with respect to union.

Consider a database $\mathcal{D} = \{r_1, r_2, \ldots, r_p\}$ and a view V defined as $V = R_1 \bowtie R_2 \bowtie \cdots \bowtie R_p$. Let v denote the materialized view, and the relations $r_1, r_2, \ldots, r_p$ be updated by inserting the sets of tuples $i_{r_1}, i_{r_2}, \ldots, i_{r_p}$. The new state of the view v' can be computed as

$$v' = (r_1 \cup i_{r_1}) \bowtie (r_2 \cup i_{r_2}) \bowtie \cdots \bowtie (r_p \cup i_{r_p}).$$

Let us associate a binary variable B_i with each of the relation schemes $R_i, 1 \le i \le p$. The value *zero* for B_i refers to the tuples of r_i considered during the current materialization of the view v (i.e., the old tuples), and the value *one* for B_i refers to the set of tuples inserted into r_i since the latest materialization of v (i.e., the new tuples i_r). The expansion of the expression for v', using the distributive property of join over union, can be depicted by the truth table of the variables B_i. For example, if $p = 3$ we have

B_1	B_2	B_3		
0	0	0		$r_1 \bowtie r_2 \bowtie r_3$
0	0	1		$r_1 \bowtie r_2 \bowtie i_{r_3}$
0	1	0	which	$r_1 \bowtie i_{r_2} \bowtie r_3$
0	1	1	repre—	$r_1 \bowtie i_{r_2} \bowtie i_{r_3}$
1	0	0	sents	$i_{r_1} \bowtie r_2 \bowtie r_3$
1	0	1		$i_{r_1} \bowtie r_2 \bowtie i_{r_3}$
1	1	0		$i_{r_1} \bowtie i_{r_2} \bowtie r_3$
1	1	1		$i_{r_1} \bowtie i_{r_2} \bowtie i_{r_3}$

where the union of all expressions in the right hand side of the table is equivalent to v'. The first row of the truth table corresponds to the join of the base relations considering only old tuples (i.e., the current state of the view v). Typically, a transaction would not insert tuples into all the relations involved in a view definition. In that case, some of the combinations of joins represented by the rows of the truth table correspond to null relations. Using the table for $p = 3$, suppose that a transaction contains insertions to relations r_1 and r_2 only. One can then discard all the rows of the truth table for which the variable B_3 has a value of one, namely rows 2, 4, 6, and 8. Row 1 can also be discarded, since it corresponds to the current materialization of the view. Therefore, to bring the view up to date we need to compute only the joins represented by rows 3, 5, and 7. That is,

$$
\begin{aligned}
v' \ = \ & v \ \cup \ (r_1 \bowtie i_{r_2} \bowtie r_3) \\
& \cup \ (i_{r_1} \bowtie r_2 \bowtie r_3) \\
& \cup \ (i_{r_1} \bowtie i_{r_2} \bowtie r_3).
\end{aligned}
$$

The computation of this differential update of the view v is certainly cheaper than re-computing the whole join.

So far we have assumed that the base relations change only through the insertion of new tuples. The same idea can be applied when the base relations change only through the deletion of old tuples.

Example 5.3 Consider again two relation schemes $R = \{A, B\}$ and $S = \{B, C\}$, and the view V defined as $V = R \bowtie S$. Suppose that after the view v is materialized, the relation r is updated by the deletion of the set of tuples d_r. Let $r' = r - d_r$. The new state of the view, called v', is computed as

$$
\begin{aligned}
v' \ = \ & r' \bowtie s \\
= \ & (r - d_r) \bowtie s \\
= \ & (r \bowtie s) - (d_r \bowtie s).
\end{aligned}
$$

If $d_v = d_r \bowtie s$, then $v' = v - d_v$. That is, the view can be updated by deleting the new set of tuples d_v from the relation v. It is not always cheaper to compute the view v' by deleting from v only the tuples d_v; however, this is true when $|v| \gg |d_v|$. □

The differential update computation for deletions can also be expressed by means of binary tables. Thus, the computation of differential updates depends on the ability to identify which tuples have been inserted and which tuples have been deleted. From now on, all tuples are assumed to be tagged in such a way that it is possible to identify inserted, deleted, and old tuples.

Example 5.4 Consider two relation schemes $R = \{A, B\}$ and $S = \{B, C\}$, and a view V defined as $V = R \bowtie S$. Let r and s denote instances of the relations named R and S, respectively, and $v = r \bowtie s$. Assume that a transaction $\mathcal{T}$ updates relations r and s.

Case 1: $t \in i_r \bowtie i_s$ is a tuple that has to be inserted into v.
Case 2: $t \in i_r \bowtie d_s$ is a tuple that has no effect in the view v, and can therefore be ignored.
Case 3: $t \in i_r \bowtie s$ is a tuple that has to be inserted into v.
Case 4: $t \in d_r \bowtie d_s$ is a tuple that has to be deleted from v.
Case 5: $t \in d_r \bowtie s$ is a tuple that has to be deleted from v.
Case 6: $t \in r \bowtie s$ is a tuple that already exists in the view v. $\qquad\square$

In general, we can describe the value of the tag field of the tuple resulting from a join of two tuples according to the following table.

r_1	r_2	$r_1 \bowtie r_2$
insert	insert	insert
insert	delete	ignore
insert	old	insert
delete	insert	ignore
delete	delete	delete
delete	old	delete
old	insert	insert
old	delete	delete
old	old	old

where the last column of the table shows the value of the tag attribute for the tuple resulting from the join of two tuples tagged according to the values under columns r_1 and r_2. Tuples tagged as "ignore" are assumed to be discarded when performing the join. In other words, they do not "emerge" from the join.

The semantics of the join operation has to be re-defined once more to compute the tag value of each tuple resulting from the join based on the tag values of the operand tuples. In the presence of projection this will be in addition to the computation of the count value for each tuple resulting from the join as explained in the section on project views. Similarly, the tag value of the tuples resulting from a select or project operation is described in the following table.

r	$\sigma_{C(Y)}(r)$	$\pi_X(r)$
insert	insert	insert
delete	delete	delete
old	old	old

In practice, it is not necessary to build a table with 2^p rows. Instead, by knowing which relations have been modified, we can build only those rows of the table representing the necessary subexpressions to be evaluated. Assuming that only k such relations were modified, $1 \le k \le p$, building the table can be done in time $O(2^k)$.

Once we know what subexpressions must be computed, we can further reduce the cost of materializing the view by using an algorithm to determine a good order for execution of the joins. Notice that a new feature of our problem is the possibility of saving computation by re-using partial subexpressions appearing in multiple rows within the table. Efficient solutions are being investigated.

5.4   Select-Project-Join Views

A *select-project-join view* (SPJ view) is defined by the expression

$$V = \pi_X(\sigma_{C(Y)}(R_1 \bowtie R_2 \bowtie \cdots \bowtie R_p)),$$

where X is a set of attributes and $C(Y)$ is a Boolean expression. We can again exploit the distributive property of join, select, and project over union to provide a differential update algorithm for SPJ views.

Example 5.5 Consider two relation schemes $R = \{A, B\}$ and $S = \{B, C\}$, and a view defined as $V = \pi_A(\sigma_{(C>10)}(R \bowtie S))$. Suppose that after the view v is materialized, the relation r is updated by the insertion of tuples i_r. Let $r' = r \cup i_r$. The new state of the view, called v', is computed by the expression

$$
\begin{aligned}
v' &= \pi_A(\sigma_{(C>10)}(r' \bowtie s)) \\
   &= \pi_A(\sigma_{(C>10)}((r \cup i_r) \bowtie s)) \\
   &= \pi_A(\sigma_{(C>10)}(r \bowtie s)) \cup \pi_A(\sigma_{(C>10)}(i_r \bowtie s)) \\
   &= v \cup \pi_A(\sigma_{(C>10)}(i_r \bowtie s)).
\end{aligned}
$$

If $i_v = \pi_A(\sigma_{(C>10)}(i_r \bowtie s))$, then $v' = v \cup i_v$. That is, the view can be updated by inserting only the new set of tuples i_v into the relation v.   □

We can again use a binary table to find out what portions of the expression have to be computed to bring the materialized view up to date. To evaluate each SPJ expression associated with a row of the table, we can make use of some known algorithm such as QUEL's decomposition algorithm by Wong and Youssefi [WY76]. Once more, there is a possibility of saving computation by re-using partial computations common to several rows in the table.

We now present the outline of an algorithm to update SPJ views differentially.

Algorithm 5.1

The input consists of:

i) the SPJ view definition $V = \pi_X(\sigma_C(R_1 \bowtie R_2 \bowtie \cdots \bowtie R_p))$,

ii) the contents of the base relations $r_j, 1 \leq j \leq p$, and

iii) the sets of updates to the base relations $u_{r_j}, 1 \leq j \leq p$.

The output of the algorithm consists of a transaction to update the view.
1. Build those rows of the truth table with p columns corresponding to the relations being updated.
2. For each row of the table, compute the associated SPJ expression substituting r_j when the binary variable $B_j = 0$, and u_{r_j} when $B_j = 1$.
3. Perform the union of results obtained for each computation in step 2. The transaction consists of inserting all tuples tagged as insert, and deleting all tuples tagged as delete.   □

Observe that: (I) we can use for V an expression with a minimal number of joins. Such expression can be obtained at view definition time by the tableau method of Aho Sagiv and Ullman [ASU79] extended to handle inequality conditions [Klu80]; and (II) step 2 poses an interesting optimization problem, namely, the efficient execution of a set of SPJ expressions (all the same) whose operands represent different relations and where intermediate results can be re-used among several expressions.

6   Conclusions

A new mechanism for the maintenance of materialized views has been presented. The mechanism consists of two major components. First, necessary and sufficient conditions for the detection of database updates that are irrelevant to the view were given. Using previous results by Rosenkrantz and Hunt we defined a class of Boolean expressions for which this detection can be done efficiently. Our detection of irrelevant updates extends previous results presented by Buneman and Clemons and by Hammer and Sarin. Since their papers were presented in the contexts of trigger support and integrity enforcement, our results can be used in those contexts as well. Second, for relevant updates, a differential view update algorithm was given. This algorithm supports the class of views defined by SPJ expressions.

Our differential view update algorithm does not automatically provide the most efficient way of updating the view. Therefore, a next step in this direction is to determine under what circumstances differential re-evaluation is more efficient than complete re-evaluation of the expression defining the view.

This chapter carries the assumption that the views are materialized every time a transaction updates the database. It is also possible to envision a mechanism in which materialized views are updated periodically or only on demand. Such materialized views are known as *snapshots* [AL80] and their maintenance mechanism as *snapshot refresh*[1]. The approach proposed in this chapter also applies to this environment, and further work in this direction is in progress.

Acknowledgments

This work was supported in part by scholarship No. 35957 from Consejo Nacional de Ciencia y Tecnología (México), and by grants A2460 and A9292 from the Natural Sciences and Engineering Research Council of Canada.

---

[1]System R* provides a differential snapshot refresh mechanism for snapshots defined by a selection and projection on a single base relation [BL85]. However, details of this mechanism have not been published.

MAINTAINING VIEWS INCREMENTALLY

Ashish Gupta, Inderpal Singh Mumick, V.S. Subrahmanian

ABSTRACT

We present incremental evaluation algorithms to compute changes to materialized views in relational and deductive database systems, in response to changes (insertions, deletions, and updates) to the relations. The view definitions can be in SQL or Datalog, and may use UNION, negation, aggregation (*e.g.* SUM, MIN), linear recursion, and general recursion.

We first present a *counting* algorithm that tracks the number of alternative derivations (counts) for each derived tuple in a view. The algorithm works with both set and duplicate semantics. We present the algorithm for *nonrecursive views* (with negation and aggregation), and show that the count for a tuple can be computed at little or no cost above the cost of deriving the tuple. The algorithm is optimal in that it computes exactly those view tuples that are inserted or deleted. Note that we store only the *number* of derivations, not the derivations themselves.

We then present the Delete and Rederive algorithm, DRed, for incremental maintenance of recursive views (negation and aggregation are permitted). The algorithm works by first deleting a superset of the tuples that need to be deleted, and then rederiving some of them. The algorithm can also be used when the view definition is itself altered.

1 Introduction

A view is a derived (idb) relation defined in terms of base (stored, or edb) relations. A view can be materialized by storing its extent in the database. Index structures can be built on the materialized view. Consequently, database accesses to materialized view tuples is much faster than by recomputing the view. Materialized views are especially useful in distributed databases. However, deletion, insertions, and updates to the base relations can change the view. Recomputing the view from scratch is too wasteful in most cases. Using the heuristic of inertia (only a part of the view changes in response to changes in the base relations), it is often cheaper to compute only the changes in the view. We stress that the above is only a heuristic. For example, if an entire base relation is deleted, it may be cheaper to recompute a view that depends on the deleted relation (if the new view will quickly evaluate to an empty relation) than to compute the changes to the view.

Algorithms that compute changes to a view in response to changes to the base relations are called *incremental view maintenance* algorithms. Several such algorithms with different applicability domains have been proposed [BC79, NY83, SI84, BLT86, TB88, BCL89, CW91, Kuc91, QW91, WDSY91, CW92a,

DT92, HD92]. View maintenance has applications in integrity constraint maintenance, index maintenance in object-oriented databases (define the index between attributes of interest as a view), persistent queries, active database [SPAM91, RS93] (to check if a rule has fired, we may need to determine if a particular tuple is inserted into a view).

We present two algorithms, *counting* and DRed, for incremental maintenance of a large class of views. Both algorithms use the view definition to produce rules that compute the changes to the view using the changes made to the base relations and the old materialized views. Both algorithms can handle recursive and nonrecursive views (in SQL or Datalog extensions) that use negation, aggregation, and union, and can respond to insertions, deletions and updates to the base relations. However, we are proposing the *counting* algorithm for nonrecursive views, and the DRed algorithm for recursive views, as we believe each is better than the other on the specified domain.

EXAMPLE 1.1 Consider the following view definition. $link(S, D)$ is a base relation and $link(a, b)$ is true if there is a link from source node a to destination b. $hop(c, d)$ is true if c is connected to d via two links *i.e.* there is a link from node c to some node x and a link from x to d.

```
CREATE VIEW hop(S, D) AS
      (SELECT r1.S, r2.D
       FROM link r1, link r2
       WHERE r1.D = r2.S);
```

Given $link = \{(a, b), (b, c), (b, e), (a, d), (d, c)\}$, the view hop evaluates to $\{(a, c), (a, e)\}$. The tuple $hop(a, e)$ has a unique derivation. $hop(a, c)$ on the other hand has two derivations. If the view had duplicate semantics then $hop(a, e)$ would have a count of 1 and $hop(a, c)$ would have a count of 2.

Suppose the tuple $link(a, b)$ is deleted. Then we can re-evaluate hop to $\{(a, c)\}$.

The counting algorithm infers that one derivation of each of the tuples $hop(a, c)$ and $hop(a, e)$ is deleted. The algorithm uses the stored counts to infer that $hop(a, c)$ has one remaining derivation and therefore only deletes $hop(a, e)$, which has no remaining derivation.

The DRed algorithm first deletes tuples $hop(a, c)$ and $hop(a, e)$ since they both depend upon the deleted tuple. The DRed algorithm then looks for alternative derivations for each of the deleted tuples. $hop(a, c)$ is rederived and reinserted into the materialized view in the second step.   □

Counting The counting algorithm works by storing the number of alternative derivations of each tuple t in the materialized view. We call this number $count(t)$. $count(t)$ is derived from the multiplicity of tuple t under duplicate semantics, as defined in [Mum91] for positive programs and in [MS93b] for programs with stratified negation. Given a program T defining a set of views $V_1, \ldots, V_k$, the counting algorithm derives a program T_Δ at compile time. T_Δ uses the changes made to base relations and the old values of the base and view relations to produce as output the set of changes, $\Delta(V_1), \ldots, \Delta(V_k)$, that need to be made to the view relations. We assume that the count value for each tuple is stored in the materialized view. In the set of changes, inserted tuples are represented with positive counts and deleted tuples are represented with negative counts. The new materialized view is obtained by combining the changes $\Delta(V_1), \ldots, \Delta(V_k)$ with the stored views $V_1, \ldots, V_k$ (combining counts as defined in Section 3). The incremental view maintenance algorithm works for both set and duplicate semantics. On nonrecursive views we show that counts can be computed at little or no cost above the cost of evaluating the view (Section 5) for both set and duplicate semantics; hence it can be used for SQL. For recursively defined views, the counting algorithm can be used effectively only if every tuple is guaranteed to have a finite number of derivations,[1] and even then the computation of counts can significantly increase the cost of computation.

We propose to use the *counting* algorithm only for nonrecursive views, and describe the algorithm for nonrecursive views only.

Deletion and Rederivation The DRed algorithm can incrementally maintain (general) recursive views, with negation and aggregation. Given the changes made to base relations, changes to the view relations are computed in three steps. First, the algorithm computes an overestimate of the deleted derived tuples: a tuple t is in this overestimate if the changes made to the base relations invalidate *any* derivation of t. Second, this overestimate is pruned by removing (from the overestimate) those tuples that have alternative derivations in the new database. Finally, the new tuples that need to be added are computed using the partially updated materialized view and the changes made to the base relations. Only set semantics can be used for this algorithm. The algorithm can also maintain materialized views incrementally when rules defining derived relations are inserted or deleted.

Chapter Outline

Section 2 compares the results in this chapter with related work. Section 3 introduces the notation used in this chapter. Section 4 describes the *counting* algorithm for maintaining nonrecursive views. Section 5 describes how the counting algorithm can be implemented efficiently. We show that a computation of counts imposes almost no overhead in execution time and storage. Section 6 explains how negation and aggregation are handled by the counting algorithm of Section 4. Section 7 discusses the DRed algorithm for maintaining general recursive views. The results are summarized in Section 8.

2 Related Work

Ceri and Widom [CW91] describe a strategy to efficiently update views defined in a subset of SQL without negation, aggregation, and duplicate semantics. Their algorithm depends on keys, and cannot be used if the view does not contain the key attributes of a base relation. Qian and Wiederhold [QW91] use algebraic operations to derive the minimal relational expression that computes the change to select-project-join views. The algorithms by Blakeley *et al.* [BLT86] and Nicolas and Yazdanian (The BDGEN system [NY83]) are perhaps most closely related to our counting algorithm. Blakeley's algorithm is a special case of the counting algorithm applied to select-project-join expressions (no negation, aggregation, or recursion). In BDGEN, the counts reflect only certain types of derivations, are multiplied to guarantee an even count for derived tuples, and all recursive queries are given finite counts. Thus the BDGEN counts, unlike our counts, do not correspond to the number of derivations of a tuple, are more expensive to compute, and the BDGEN algorithm cannot be used with (SQL) duplicate semantics or with aggregation, while our algorithm can be.

Kuchenhoff [Kuc91] and Harrison and Dietrich (the PF algorithm [HD92]) discuss recursive view maintenance algorithms related to our *rederivation* algorithm. Both of these algorithms cannot handle aggregation (we can). Where applicable, the PF (Propagation/Filteration) algorithm computes changes in *one* derived predicate due to changes in *one* base predicate, iterating over all derived and base predicates to complete the view maintenance. An attempt to recompute the deleted tuples is made for each small change in each derived relation. In contrast, our *rederivation* algorithm propagates changes from all base predicates onto all derived predicates stratum by stratum, and recomputes deleted tuples only once. The PF algorithm thus fragments computation, can rederive changed and deleted tuples again and again, and

---

[1]An algorithm to check finiteness appears in [MS93b]

can be worse that our *rederivation* algorithm by an order of magnitude (examples in the final section of this chapter). Kuchenhoff's algorithm needs to store auxiliary relations, and fragments computation in a manner similar to the PF algorithm.

Dong and Topor [DT92] derive nonrecursive programs to update right-linear chain views in response to insertions only. Dong and Su [DS92] give nonrecursive transformations to update the transitive closure of specific kinds of graphs in response to insertions and deletions. The algorithm does not apply to all graphs or to general recursive programs. They also need auxiliary derived relations, and cannot handle negation and aggregation. Urpi and Olive [UO92] need to derive functional dependencies, a problem that is known to be undecidable. Wolfson *et al.* [WDSY91] use a rule language with negation in the head and body of rules, along with auxiliary information about the number of certain derivations of each tuple. They do not discuss how to handle recursively defined relations that are derivable in infinitely many iterations, and do not handle aggregation.

3   Notation

We use Datalog, mostly as discussed in [Ull89], extended with stratified negation [Gel86, ABW88], and stratified aggregation [Mum91]. Datalog extended with stratified negation and aggregation can be mapped to a class of recursive SQL queries, and vice versa [Mum91]. We chose Datalog syntax over SQL syntax for conciseness.

Definition 3.1 (Stratum Numbers (SN) and Rule Stratum Number (RSN)): Stratum numbers are assigned as follows: Construct a *reduced dependency graph (RDG)* of the given program by collapsing every strongly connected component (scc) of the dependency graph (as defined by [ABW88]) to a single node. A RDG is guaranteed to be acyclic. A topological sort of the RDG assigns a stratum number to each node. If a node represents a scc, all predicates in the scc are assigned the stratum number of the node. By convention, base predicates have stratum number $= 0$. The rule stratum number of a rule r, $\mathsf{RSN}(r)$, having predicate p in the head is equal to $\mathsf{SN}(p)$.   ∎

P refers to the relation corresponding to predicate p. $P = \{ab, mn\}$ represents tuples $p(a,b)$ and $p(m,n)$.

Definition 3.2 ($\Delta(P)$): For every relation P, relation $\Delta(P)$ contains the changes made to P.   ∎

For each tuple $t \in P$, count(t) represents the number of distinct derivations of tuple t. Similarly every tuple in $\Delta(P)$ has a count associated with it. Negative and positive counts correspond to deletions and insertions respectively. For instance, $\Delta(P) = \{ab * 4, mn * -2\}$ says that four derivations of tuple $p(a,b)$ are inserted into P and two derivations of tuple $p(m,n)$ are deleted.

The union operator, $\uplus$, is defined over sets of tuples with counts. Given two such sets $S1$ and $S2$, $S1 \uplus S2$ is defined as follows:

1. If tuple t appears in only one of $S1$ or $S2$ with a count c, then tuple t appears in $S1 \uplus S2$ with a count c.

2. If a tuple t appears in $S1$ and $S2$ with counts of c_1 and c_2 respectively, and $c_1 + c_2 \neq 0$, then tuple t appears in $S1 \uplus S2$ with a count $c_1 + c_2$. If $c_1 + c_2 = 0$ then t does not appear in $S1 \uplus S2$.

P^ν refers to the relation P after incorporating the changes in $\Delta(P)$. Thus, $P^\nu = P \uplus \Delta(P)$. The correctness of our algorithm guarantees that a tuple in P^ν will not have a negative count; only tuples in relation $\Delta(P)$ will have negative counts. The join operator is also redefined for relations with counts: when two or more tuples join, the count of the resulting tuple is a product of the counts of the tuples joined.

Algorithm 4.1
  Input: A nonrecursive program $\mathcal{P}$.
            Stored materializations of derived relations in $\mathcal{P}$.
            Changes (deletions/insertions) to the base relations occurring in
                    program $\mathcal{P}$.
  Output: Changes (deletions/insertions) to the derived relations in $\mathcal{P}$.
  Method:
        Mark all rules unprocessed.
        For all derived predicates p in program $\mathcal{P}$, **do**
                initialize P^ν to the materialized relation P.
                initialize $\Delta(P) = \{\}$
        While there is an unprocessed rule
        { $Q = \{r \mid$ rule r has the least RSN among all unprocessed rules$\}$
                For every rule $r \in Q$ **do**
                {   Compute $\Delta(P)$ using the delta rules $\Delta_i(r),\ 1 \le i \le n$ derived

from rule r (Definition 4.1)

$$(\Delta_i(r)): \quad \Delta(p) :\!- s_1^\nu,\ \ldots\ ,\ s_{i-1}^\nu,\ \Delta(s_i),\ s_{i+1},\ \ldots;$$
$$\ldots\ ,\ s_n \quad \ldots\ldots\ldots\ldots (1)$$

$P^\nu = P \uplus \Delta(P).$ *% Update the predicate that is defined by rule r.*

$\boxed{\Delta(P) = \mathsf{set}(P^\nu) - \mathsf{set}(P)}$ $\ldots\ldots\ldots\ldots (2)$

% For optimization only, discussed in Section 5

                Mark rule r as processed.
        }   } $\diamond$

4   Incremental Maintenance of Nonrecursive Views Using Counting

This section gives an algorithm that can be used to maintain nonrecursive views that use negation and aggregation. We first give the intuition using an example.

EXAMPLE 4.1 Intuition. Consider the view `hop` defined in Example 1.1. We rewrite the view definition using Datalog for succinctness and ease of explanation. Recall that `link` $= \{ab, mn\}$ represents tuples `link`(a, b) and `link`(m, n).

$(v1):$ `hop`$(X, Y) :\!-$ `link`(X, Z) , `link`(Z, Y);

If the base relation `link` changes, the derived relation `hop` may also change. Let the change to the relation `link` be represented as $\Delta($`link`$)$. $\Delta($`link`$)$ contains both inserted and deleted tuples, represented by positive and negative **counts** respectively. The new relation `link`$^\nu$ can be written as: `link`$+\Delta($`link`$)$. The following rule computes the new value for the `hop` relation in terms of the relation `link`$^\nu$:

`hop`$^\nu(X, Y) :\!-$ `link`$^\nu(X, Z)$, `link`$^\nu(Z, Y)$;

Using `link`$^\nu =$ `link` $\uplus \Delta($`link`$)$ and distributing joins over unions, the above rule can alternatively be written as the following set of rules:

`hop`$^\nu(X, Y) :\!-$ `link`(X, Z) , `link`(Z, Y);
`hop`$^\nu(X, Y) :\!-$ $\Delta($`link`$)(X, Z)$, `link`(Z, Y);

```
hopᵛ(X, Y) :- link(X, Z) , Δ(link)(Z, Y);
hopᵛ(X, Y) :- Δ(link)(X, Z) , Δ(link)(Z, Y);
```

The first rule recomputes relation hop. The remaining three rules define $\Delta(\text{hop})$, the changes in relation hop. Of these three rules, the last two can be combined, using the fact that $\text{link}^\nu = \text{link} \uplus \Delta(\text{link})$. The set of rules that defines predicate $\Delta(\text{hop})$ is therefore:

$(d1) : \Delta(\text{hop})(X, Y) :- \Delta(\text{link})(X, Z) , \text{link}(Z, Y) \quad (d2) : \Delta(\text{hop})(X, Y) :- \text{link}^\nu(X, Z) , \Delta(\text{link})(Z, Y)$

□

Definition 4.1 (Delta Rules): With every rule r of the form:

$(r): \quad p :- s_1 , \ldots , s_n;$

we associate n delta rules $\Delta_i(r), 1 \le i \le n$, defining predicate $\Delta(p)$ as follows:

$(\Delta_i(r)): \quad \Delta(p) :- s_1^\nu , \ldots , s_{i-1}^\nu , \Delta(s_i) ,$
$\qquad\qquad\qquad s_{i+1} , \ldots , s_n;$

∎

The counting algorithm is listed as Algorithm 4.1. Ignore statement (2) (surrounded by a box) for now; it will be discussed in Section 5.

EXAMPLE 4.2 Consider the view tri_hop defined using the view hop (rule $v1$, Example 4.1).

$(v2) : \text{tri\_hop}(X, Y) :- \text{hop}(X, Z) , \text{link}(Z, Y)$

The stratum numbers of predicates hop and tri_hop are 1 and 2 respectively. Consider the following base relation link and the associated derived relations hop and tri_hop.

link = {ab, ad, dc, bc, ch, fg};
hop = {ac * 2, dh, bh};
tri_hop = {ah * 2};

Let the base relation link be altered as follows:
$\Delta(\text{link}) = \{ab * -1, df, af\}$;
$\text{link}^\nu = \{ad, af, bc, dc, ch, df, fg\}$;

In order to compute the changes, first consider the rule with the least RSN, namely $v1$.

$(\Delta_1(v1)) : \Delta\text{hop}(X, Y) :- \Delta\text{link}(X, Z) , \text{link}(Z, Y) \quad (\Delta_2(v1)) : \Delta\text{hop}(X, Y) :- \text{link}^\nu(X, Z) , \Delta\text{link}(Z, Y)$

Apply rule $\Delta_1(v1)$: $\Delta(\text{hop}) = \{ac * -1, ag, dg\}$
Apply rule $\Delta_2(v1)$: $\Delta(\text{hop}) = \{af\}$

Combining the above changes, we get:
$\text{hop}^\nu = \{ac, af, ag, dg, dh, bh\}$;

Now consider the rules with RSN 2, namely rule $v2$ that defines predicate tri_hop.

$(\Delta_1(v2)): \quad \Delta\text{tri\_hop}(X, Y) :- \Delta\text{hop}(X, Z) ,$
$\qquad\qquad\qquad\qquad \text{link}(Z, Y);$

$(\Delta_2(v2))$: Δ`tri_hop`(X,Y) :- `hop`$^\nu(X,Z)$,
$$\Delta\texttt{link}(Z,Y);$$

Apply rule $\Delta_1(v2)$: $\Delta(\texttt{tri\_hop}) = \{ah * -1, ag\}$
Apply rule $\Delta_2(v2)$: $\Delta(\texttt{tri\_hop}) = \{\}$

Combining the above changes, we get:
`tri_hop`$^\nu = \{ah, ag\}$;

$\square$

Lemma 4.1 *Let Δ^- be the set of base tuples deleted from E, and t be any ground atom that has* count(t) *derivations w.r.t. program $\mathcal{P}$ and database state (edb) E. If $\Delta^- \subseteq E$ then Algorithm 4.1 derives tuple $\Delta(t)$ with a* count *of at least $-1 * $ count(t).* ∎

That is, given that we insist that the deleted base tuples be a subset of the original database, no more than the original number of derived tuples are deleted from any derived relation during evaluation of Algorithm 4.1. Therefore all non-Δ subgoals have positive counts.

Theorem 4.1 *Let t be any ground atom that has* count(t) *derivations w.r.t. program $\mathcal{P}$ and database state (edb) E. Suppose tuple t has* count(t^ν) *derivations when edb E is altered to a new edb E^ν (by insertions/deletions). Then: Algorithm 4.1 derives tuple $\Delta(t)$ with a* count *of* count$(t^\nu) - $ count(t). ∎

If the program needed set semantics, then Algorithm 4.1 is optimized by propagating changes to predicates in higher strata only if the relation P^ν considered as a set changes from relation P considered as a set. This optimization is done by Statement (2) in Algorithm 4.1 and illustrated in Example 5.1.

5   Implementation Issues and Optimizations

Algorithm 4.1 needs a count of the number of derivations for each tuple. Let us see how counts might be computed during bottom-up evaluation in a database system.

We first consider database systems that implement duplicate semantics, such as DB2 and SQL/DS from IBM, and Nonstop SQL from Tandem. The query language SQL in the above systems requires duplicates to be retained for semantic correctness [ISO90]. In an implementation, duplicates may be represented either by keeping multiple copies of a tuple, or by keeping a count with each tuple. In both cases, our algorithm works without incurring any overhead due to duplicate computation. The $\uplus$ operator in our algorithm is mapped to the union operator of the system when the operands have positive counts. When an operand has negative counts, the $\uplus$ operator is equivalent to multiset difference. Though multiset difference is not provided in any of the above example SQL systems, it can be executed in time $O(n)log(n)$ or $O(n)$ (where n is the size of the operands) depending on the representation of duplicates.

Second, consider systems that have set semantics, such as NAIL-GLUE! and LDL. Such systems can treat duplicates in one of two possible ways during query evaluation: (1) Do not eliminate duplicates since duplicate elimination is expensive, and may not have enough payoff, and (2) Eliminate duplicates after each iteration of the semi-naive evaluation. The first implementation is likely to be useful only for nonrecursive queries because recursive queries may have infinite counts associated with them. The first implementation is similar to computing duplicate semantics since all derivation trees will be derived during evaluation. The second implementation removes duplicates, and so it may seem that our incremental view maintenance algorithm must do extra work to derive all the remaining derivation trees. But it is not so for nonrecursive queries.

Note, if a view depends on intermediate views, then all the intermediate views have to be materialized. Alternatively, all the intermediate view definitions can be expanded out in full and the maintenance algorithm applied subsequently to the flattened out definition.

5.1   Optimization

The boxed statement 2 in Algorithm 4.1 optimizes the counting algorithm for views where duplicate semantics is not desired, and for implementations that eliminate duplicates.

First, note that duplicate elimination is an expensive operation, and we can augment the operation to count the number of duplicates eliminated without increasing the cost of the operation. counts can then be associated with each tuple in the relation obtained after duplicate elimination. Let us assume that we do full duplicate computation within a stratum (by extending the evaluation method in some way), and then do duplicate elimination and obtain counts for each tuple computed by the stratum. When computing the next higher stratum $i + 1$, we do not need to make derivations once for each count of a tuple in stratum i or less. We do not even need to carry the counts of tuples in stratum i or lower while evaluating tuples in stratum $i + 1$. We assume that each tuple of stratum i or less has a count of one, and compute the duplicate semantics of stratum $i + 1$. Consequently, the count value for each tuple t corresponds to the number of derivations for tuple t assuming that all tuples of lower strata have count 0 or 1. Maintaining counts as above influences the propagation of changes in a positive manner. For instance, let predicate p in stratum 1 have 20 derivations for a tuple $p(a)$, and let changes to the base tuples delete 10 of them. However the changes need not be cascaded to a predicate q in stratum 2 because as far as derivations of q are concerned, $p(a)$ has a count of one as long as its actual count is positive. The incremental computation therefore stops at stratum 1. The boxed statement 2 in Algorithm 4.1 causes us to maintain counts as above. Consider Example 4.2 if the views had set semantics.

EXAMPLE 5.1 Consider relations $\mathtt{hop}^\nu$ and $\mathtt{hop}$ after the rules $\Delta_1(v1)$ and $\Delta_2(v1)$ have been applied. In order to compute $\Delta(\mathtt{hop})$ we apply the optimization of Statement 2 from Algorithm 4.1.

$$\begin{aligned}
\Delta(\mathtt{hop}) &= set(\mathtt{hop}^\nu) - set(\mathtt{hop}) \\
&= \{ac, af, ag, dg, dh, bh\} - \{ac, dh, bh\} \\
&= \{af, ag, dg\};
\end{aligned}$$

Note that unlike Example 4.2, the tuple $\mathtt{hop}(ac * -1)$ does not appear in $\Delta(\mathtt{hop})$ and is not cascaded to relation $\mathtt{tri\_hop}$. Consequently the tuple $(ah * -1)$ will not be derived for $\Delta(\mathtt{tri\_hop})$.   □

Using the above optimizations, the extra evaluation cost incurred by our incremental view maintenance algorithm is in computing the duplicate semantics of each stratum. For a nonrecursive stratum there is usually no extra cost in computing the duplicate semantics. A nonrecursive stratum consists of a single predicate defined using one or more rules, evaluated by a sequence of select, join, project, and union operators. Each of these operators derives one tuple for each derivation. Thus, tracking counts for a nonrecursive view is almost as efficient as evaluating the nonrecursive view.

Even in SQL systems implementing duplicate semantics, it is possible for a query to require set semantics (by using the DISTINCT operator). The implementation issues for such queries are similar to the case of systems implementing set semantics.

6 Negation and Aggregation

Algorithm 4.1 can be used to incrementally maintain views defined using negation and aggregation. However, we need to describe how statement 1 in Algorithm 4.1 is executed for rules with negated and aggregated subgoals, specifically how $\Delta(S)$ is evaluated for a negated or GROUPBY subgoal s in rule r.

6.1 Negation

We consider safe stratified negation. Negation is safe as long as the variables that occur in a negated subgoal also occur in some positive subgoal of the same rule. Negation is stratified if whenever a derived predicate q depends negatively on predicate p, then $\mathsf{SN}(p) < \mathsf{SN}(q)$ where $\mathsf{SN}(p)$ is the stratum number of predicate p. Nonrecursive programs are always stratified.

The following Example 6.1 gives the intuition for computing counts with negated subgoals. A negated subgoal is computed in the same way for both set and duplicate semantics.[2]

EXAMPLE 6.1 Consider view `only_tri_hop` that uses views `tri_hop` and `hop` as defined in Example 4.2. `only_tri_hop` contains all pairs of nodes that are connected using three links but not using just two.

   $(v3)$:   `only_tri_hop`(X, Y) :- `tri_hop`(X, Y) , $\neg$`hop`(X, Y);

Consider the relation `link` $= \{ab, ae, af, ag, bc,\ cd, ck, ed, fd, gh, hk\}$. The relations `hop` and `tri_hop` are $\{ac, ad * 2, ah, bd, bk, gk\}$ and $\{ad, ak * 2\}$ respectively. The relation `only_tri_hop` $= \{ak * 2\}$. Tuple (a, d) does not appear in `only_tri_hop` because `hop`(a, d) is true. Note that `hop`(a, d) is true as long as `count`$(\text{hop}(a, d)) > 0$. Therefore even if `count`$(\text{hop}(a, d))$ was 1 or 5 (as against the indicated value of 2), relation `only_tri_hop` would not have tuple (a, d). $\square$

Consider a negated subgoal $\neg q(X, Y)$ in rule r defining a view. Because negation is safe, the variables X and Y also occur in positive subgoals in rule r. We represent the relation corresponding to the subgoal $\neg q$ as $\bar{Q}$. The relation $\bar{Q}$ is computed using relation Q and the particular bindings for variables X and Y provided by the positive subgoals in rule r. A tuple (a, b) is in $\bar{Q}$ with a `count` of 1 if, and only if, (i) the positive subgoals in rule r assign the values a and b to the variables X and Y, and (ii) the tuple $q(a, b)$ is false $((a, b) \notin Q)$.

Recall that Algorithm 4.1 creates and evaluates Delta rules of the form $\Delta_i(r)$:

   $(\Delta_i(r))$: $\Delta(p)$:- s_1^{ν} , $\ldots$, s_{i-1}^{ν} , $\Delta(s_i)$, s_{i+1} , $\ldots$, s_n;

In order to define how rule $\Delta_i(r)$ is evaluated, we exhaustively consider all the positions where a negated subgoal can occur in rule $\Delta_i(r)$ and define how the subgoal will be computed:

<u>Case 1: **Subgoal** $s_j = \neg q$, j between $i + 1$ and n</u>: The relation $\bar{Q}$ is computed as described above.

<u>Case 2: **Subgoal** $s_j^{\nu} = (\neg q)^{\nu}$, j between 1 and $i - 1$</u>: The relation $\bar{Q}^{\nu}$ is equal to the relation $\bar{Q}^{\nu}$ by the following Lemma:

Lemma 6.1 *For a negated subgoal, $\neg q$, predicate $(\neg q)^{\nu}$ is equivalent to predicate $\neg(q^{\nu})$.*   ∎

Because negation is stratified, relation Q^{ν} is computed before rule $\Delta_i(r)$ is used. Relation $\bar{Q}^{\nu}$ is computed from Q^{ν} in the same way that $\bar{Q}$ is computed from Q.

---

[2]Formal semantics of Duplicate Datalog with negation is given in [MS93b]

<u>Case 3:</u> **Subgoal** $\Delta(s_i) = \Delta(\neg q)$**:** The relation $\Delta(\bar{Q})$ is computed from relations $\Delta(Q)$ and Q according to Definition 6.1.

Definition 6.1 $(\Delta(\bar{Q}))$**:** Say Q represents the relation for predicate q and $\Delta(Q)$ represents the changes made to Q. A tuple t is in $\Delta(\bar{Q})$ with $\mathsf{count}(t) = 1$ if

$$t \in \Delta(Q) \text{ and } t \notin Q \uplus \Delta(Q),$$

and with $\mathsf{count}(t) = -1$ if

$$t \in \Delta(Q) \text{ and } t \notin Q.$$

Note that $t \in \Delta(\bar{Q})$ only if $t \in \Delta(Q)$.   ■

Note that Definition 6.1 allows $\Delta(Q)$ to be computed without having to evaluate the positive subgoals in rule $\Delta_i(r)$. This is important for efficiency, since the Δ-subgoal is usually the most restrictive subgoal in the rule and would be used first in the join order.

Theorem 6.1 *Algorithm 4.1 works correctly in the presence of negated subgoals.*   ■

6.2 Aggregation

Aggregation is often used to reduce large amounts of data to more usable form. In this section we use the semantics for aggregation as discussed in [Mum91]. The following example illustrates the notation and semantics.

EXAMPLE 6.2 Consider the relation `link` from Example 1.1 and let tuples in `link` also have a cost associated with them, *i.e.* $\mathtt{link}(s, d, c)$ represents a link from source s to destination d of cost c. We now redefine the relation `hop` as follows:

$$\mathtt{hop}(S, D, C_1 + C_2) \ \text{:--} \ \mathtt{link}(S, I, C_1) \ , \mathtt{link}(I, D, C_2)$$

Using `hop` we now define the relation `min_cost_hop` as follows:
  $(v4)$: $\mathtt{min\_cost\_hop}(S, D, M) \ \text{:--} \ \mathtt{GROUPBY}(\mathtt{hop}(S, D, C), [S, D], M = \mathtt{MIN}(C));$

Relation `min_cost_hop` contains pairs of nodes along with the minimum cost of a hop between them.   □

Consider a rule r that contains a `GROUPBY` subgoal defined over relation U. The `GROUPBY` subgoal represents a relation T whose attributes are the variables defined by the aggregation, and the variables $\bar{Y}$ over which the groupby occurs. In Example 6.2, the variable defined by the aggregation is M, and the groupby occurs over the variables $\{S, D\}$. The `GROUPBY` subgoal $\mathtt{GROUPBY}(\mathtt{hop}(S, D, C), [S, D], M = \mathtt{MIN}(C))$ thus defines a relation over variables $\{S, D, M\}$. The relation T contains one tuple for every distinct value of the groupby attributes. All tuples in the grouped relation U that have the same values for the grouping attributes in set $\bar{Y}$, say $\bar{y}$, contribute one tuple to relation T, a tuple we denote by $T_{\bar{y}}$. In Example 6.2, the relation for the `GROUPBY` subgoal has one tuple for every distinct pair of nodes $[S, D]$.

Like negation, aggregation subgoals are non-monotonic. Consider inserting tuple μ into the relation U where the values of the $\bar{Y}$ attributes in tuple μ are $= \bar{c}$. Inserting μ can possibly change the value of the aggregate tuple in relation T that corresponds to $\bar{c}$, *i.e.* tuple $T_{\bar{c}}$. For instance, in Example 6.2, inserting the tuple $\mathtt{hop}(a, b, 10)$ can only change the $\mathtt{min\_cost\_hop}$ tuple from a to b. The change actually occurs if the previous minimum cost from a to b had a cost more than 10. A similar potential change can occur to tuple $T_{\bar{c}}$ if an existing tuple μ is deleted from relation U. Using the old tuple $T_{\bar{c}}$ and the tuples in $\Delta(U)$, the new tuple corresponding to the groupby attribute value $\bar{c}$ can be computed incrementally for each of the aggregate functions $\mathtt{COUNT}$, $\mathtt{SUM}$, and for any other incrementally computable function [DAJ91]. For instance consider the aggregation operation $\mathtt{SUM}$. The sum of the attribute A of the tuples in a group can be computed using the old sum when a new tuple is added to the group by adding $\mu.A$ to the old sum. Functions like $\mathtt{AVERAGE}$ and $\mathtt{VARIANCE}$ that can be decomposed into incrementally computable functions can also be incrementally computed. For aggregations like $\mathtt{MIN}$, $\mathtt{MAX}$ incremental computation is not possible with respect to deletions from the underlying relation. However, the aggregates can be incrementally computed in response to insertions into the underlying relation.

To apply Algorithm 4.1 we need to specify how a $\mathtt{GROUPBY}$ subgoal is evaluated in a Delta rule $\Delta_i(r)$:

$(\Delta_i(r))$: $\Delta(p) :- s_1^\nu , \ldots , s_{i-1}^\nu , \Delta(s_i) , s_{i+1} , \ldots , s_n;$

$\Delta_i(r)$ could have one or more aggregate subgoals. If an aggregate subgoal t occurs between positions $i+1$ and n, then the relation T for the subgoal is computed as in the case of a normal aggregate subgoal. If an aggregate subgoal occurs between positions $1, \ldots, i-1$ then the relation T^ν for the subgoal can be computed as before using relation U^ν. If the aggregate subgoal occurs in position j, then the following algorithm is used to compute the relation $\Delta(T)$:

Algorithm 6.1
Input: An aggregate subgoal:
$\qquad t = \mathtt{GROUPBY}(U, \bar{Y}, \bar{Z} = \ldots).$
$\qquad\quad$ Changes to the relation for the grouped
$\qquad$ predicate u: $\Delta(U)$.
Output: $\Delta(T)$.
Method:
$\qquad$ **For** every grouping value $\bar{y} \in \pi_{\bar{Y}} \Delta(U)$
$\qquad\qquad$ Incrementally compute $T_{\bar{y}}^\nu$ from $T_{\bar{y}}$ (old)
$\qquad\qquad\quad$ and $\Delta(U)$.
$\qquad\qquad$ **If** $T_{\bar{y}}^\nu$ and $T_{\bar{y}}$ are different **then**
$\qquad\qquad\qquad \Delta(T) = \Delta(T) \uplus \{(T_{\bar{y}}, -1)\}$ $\qquad$ *% Insert old tuple $T_{\bar{y}}$ into $\Delta(T)$ with a $\mathsf{count} = -1$.*
$\qquad\qquad\qquad \Delta(T) = \Delta(T) \uplus \{(T_{\bar{y}}^\nu, 1)\}$ $\qquad\qquad$ *% Insert new $T_{\bar{y}}^\nu$ into $\Delta(T)$ with a $\mathsf{count} = 1$.*
$\qquad\qquad\qquad\qquad$ *% **Else** the aggregate tuple is unchanged and nothing needs to be done.*

$\diamond$

If the aggregation function is not incrementally computable [DAJ91], and is not even decomposable into incrementally computable functions, then the computation of $T_{\bar{y}}^\nu$ may be more expensive. Also note that relation U has to be materialized for efficient incremental computation of $T_{\bar{y}}^\nu$. For non incrementally computable aggregate functions, the tuple $T_{\bar{y}}^\nu$ has to be computed using the tuples of relation U^ν that have the value $\bar{y}$ for the variables $\bar{Y}$.

Lemma 6.2 *For an aggregate subgoal t, relation T^ν is equivalent to $T \uplus \Delta(T)$.* ∎

Theorem 6.2 *Algorithm 4.1 works correctly in the presence of aggregate subgoals.* ∎

7   Incremental Maintenance of Recursive Views

We present the DRed algorithm to incrementally maintain recursive views that use negation and aggregation and have set semantics.[3] The DRed algorithm can also be used to maintain nonrecursive views; however the counting algorithm is expected to be more efficient for nonrecursive views. Conversely, we note that the counting algorithm can also be used to incrementally maintain certain recursive views [GKM92].

A semi-naive [Ull89] computation is sufficient to compute new inserted tuples for a recursively defined view when insertions are made to base relations. In the case of deletions however, simple semi-naive computation would delete a derived tuple that depends upon a deleted base tuple *i.e.* if tuple t has even one derivation tree that contains a deleted tuple, then t is deleted. Alternative derivations of t are not considered. Semi-naive therefore computes an overestimate of the tuples that actually need to be deleted. The DRed algorithm refines this overestimate by considering alternative derivations of the deleted tuples (in the overestimate) as follows:

1. Delete a superset of the derived tuples that need to be deleted:

2. Put back those deleted tuples that have alternative derivations:

If base tuples are inserted into the database, then a third step is used to compute new derived tuples. This three step process is formalized as an algorithm, and proved correct, in [GMS92].

A recursive program $\mathcal{P}$ can be fragmented into programs $\mathcal{P}_1, \dots, \mathcal{P}_n$, where $\mathcal{P}_i = \{r | \mathsf{RSN}(r) = i\}$ constitutes stratum i. The DRed algorithm computes change to a view defined by a recursive program $\mathcal{P}$, by applying the above three steps successively to every stratum of $\mathcal{P}$. Every derived predicate in program $\mathcal{P}_i$ depends only on predicates that are defined in $\mathcal{P}_1, \dots, \mathcal{P}_{i-1}$. All base tuples are in stratum 0 *i.e.* in $\mathcal{P}_0$. Changes made to stratum i affect only those strata whose SN is $\geq i$. Propagating the changes stratum by stratum avoids propagating spurious changes across strata. Let Del_{i-1} (Add_{i-1}) be the set of tuples that have been deleted (inserted) from strata $1, \dots, i-1$ respectively. Consider stratum i after strata $1, \dots, i-1$ have been updated. Tuples are deleted from stratum i based on the set of deleted tuples Del_{i-1}. New tuples are inserted into stratum i based on the set of inserted tuples Add_{i-1}.

Theorem 7.1 *Let Δ^- and Δ^+ be the set of base tuples deleted and inserted respectively, from the original set of base tuples E. The new derived view computed by the DRed algorithm contains tuple t if and only if t has a derivation in the database $E^\nu = (E - \Delta^-) \cup \Delta^+$.*   ∎

The DRed algorithm can be applied to recursive views with stratified negation and aggregation also. The details of the algorithm are given in [GMS92].

8   Conclusions and Future Work

We have presented general techniques for maintaining views in relational and deductive databases, including SQL with duplicate semantics, when view definitions include negation, aggregation and general recursion. The algorithms compute changes to a materialized view in response to insertions, deletions and updates to the base relations.

---

[3]The DRed algorithm is similar to an algorithm developed independently, and at the same time as our work, by Ceri and Widom [CW92a], though their algorithm is presented in a production rule framework, and they don't handle aggregation and insertions/deletions of rules.

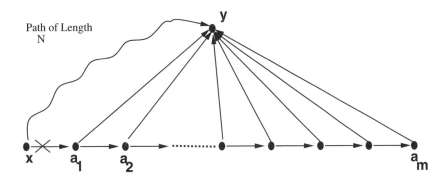

Figure 1 When DRed beats PF

The counting algorithm is presented for nonrecursive views. We show how this incremental view maintenance algorithm fits nicely into existing systems with both set and multiset semantics. The counting algorithm is a general-purpose algorithm that uniformly applies to all nonrecursive views, and is the first to handle aggregation. The DRed algorithm is presented for maintaining recursive views. DRed is the first algorithm to handle aggregation in recursive views. The algorithm first computes an over estimate of tuples that need to be deleted in response to changes to the underlying database. This estimate is refined to obtain an exact answer. New derived tuples are computed subsequently.

Counting can be used to maintain recursive views also. However computing counts for recursive views is expensive and furthermore counting may not terminate on some views. Techniques to detect finiteness [MS93b] and to use partial derivations for counting are being explored. Similarly DRed can be used for nonrecursive views also but it is less efficient than counting.

The techniques to handle negation and aggregation as described in this chapter can be used to extend many other existing view maintenance techniques.

Examples comparing PF with DRed

The view maintenance algorithm described in [HD92] is called the PF algorithm.

EXAMPLE 8.1 This example shows that DRed can beat PF by a factor of n. Consider the derived view tc to be the transitive closure of a given edge predicate e. Consider the graph shown in Figure 1.

Say that tuple $e(x, a_1)$ is deleted (the crossed out edge). The tuples $tc(x, a_i), 1 \leq i \leq m$ should also be deleted. Whenever PF concludes that a tuple $tc(x, a_i)$ is deleted, it also concludes that tuple $tc(x, y)$ is deleted and then derives $tc(x, y)$ using the alternative derivation of $tc(x, y)$ of length N. Therefore PF rederives the tuple m times. DRed on the other hand rederives tuple $tc(x, y)$ once and that too using just one inference that involves the tc tuples for the valid paths of length $N - 1$ on the alternative derivation of $tc(x, y)$. □

EXAMPLE 8.2 This example show that PF can beat DRed by a factor of n. Consider the graph shown in Figure 2.

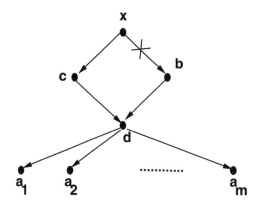

Figure 2   When PF beats DRed

Say that tuple $e(x, b)$ is deleted (the crossed out edge). PF concludes that $tc(x, d)$ is not deleted using the alternative path through c. None of the tuples $tc(x, a_i)$ is therefore considered potentially deleted. However, DRed propagates the deletion of $tc(x, d)$ to each of the a_is and later rederives them.   □

If DRed is applied to a nonrecursive program, then DRed always does as well as PF because both PF and DRed derive the same overestimate of deleted tuples. However, PF can still do worse because it propagates changes predicate by predicate and strata are not completely computed at intermediate stages. Therefore to find alternative derivations for a tuple in the kth stratum PF uses the base predicates and recomputes (some) tuples in strata $1, \ldots, k - 1$. For nonrecursive programs, PF can easily be modified to address this problem. However, PF faces another problem if a tuple t can be deleted because of n base tuples and has an alternative derivation, then the alternative derivation will be computed n times.

INCREMENTAL MAINTENANCE OF VIEWS WITH DUPLICATES

Timothy Griffin, Leonid Libkin

ABSTRACT

We study the problem of efficient maintenance of materialized views that may contain duplicates. This problem is particularly important when queries against such views involve aggregate functions, which need duplicates to produce correct results. Unlike most work on the view maintenance problem that is based on an algorithmic approach, our approach is algebraic and based on equational reasoning. This approach has a number of advantages: it is robust and easily extendible to new language constructs, it produces output that can be used by query optimizers, and it simplifies correctness proofs.

We use a natural extension of the relational algebra operations to bags (multisets) as our basic language. We present an algorithm that propagates changes from base relations to materialized views. This algorithm is based on reasoning about equivalence of bag-valued expressions. We prove that it is correct and preserves a certain notion of minimality that ensures that no unnecessary tuples are computed. Although it is generally only a heuristic that computing changes to the view rather than recomputing the view from scratch is more efficient, we prove results saying that under normal circumstances one should expect the change propagation algorithm to be significantly faster and more space efficient than complete recomputing of the view. We also show that our approach interacts nicely with aggregate functions, allowing their correct evaluation on views that change.

1 Introduction

In database management systems base relations are often used to compute views. Views are derived data that can be materialized (stored in a database) and subsequently queried against. If some of the base relations are changed, materialized views must be recomputed to ensure correctness of answers to queries against them. However, recomputing the whole view from scratch may be very expensive. Instead one often tries to determine the changes that must be made to the view, given the changes to the base relations and the expression that defines the view.

The problem of finding such changes to the views based on changes to the base relations has come to be known as the *view maintenance problem*, and has been studied extensively [BC79, BLT86, Han87, QW91, GMS93, CW91, Kuc91, SI84]. The name is slightly misleading since, as a reading of this literature will indicate, any solution to the problem is applicable in a large number of practical problems, including integrity constraint maintenance, the implementation of active queries, triggers and monitors.

191

Most of the work on view maintenance has assumed that relations are set-valued, that is, duplicates are eliminated. However, most practical database systems use bags (multisets) as the underlying model. They do handle duplicates, which is particularly important for evaluation of aggregate functions. For instance, if the average salary of employees is to be computed, then one applies the aggregate AVG to Π_{Salary}(Employees). Duplicates cannot be removed from the projection since the result would be wrong when at least two employees had the same salary. Not eliminating duplicates also speeds up query evaluation, as duplicate elimination is generally a rather expensive operation.

Many theoretical results obtained for set-theoretic semantics do not carry over to bags. In trying to bridge the gap between theoretical database research and practical languages, one active research topic has been the design of bag languages [Klu82, OOM87, KG85]. Bag primitives [Alb91] formed the basis for the algebras suggested by [GM93, LW93b]. These algebras turned out to be equivalent and accepted as the basic bag algebra. In this chapter we use the basic bag algebra from [GM93, LW93b]. It was also shown that the basic bag algebra essentially adds the correct evaluation of aggregate functions to the relational algebra, and this continues to hold when nested relations are present [LW93a]. There are a number of deep results on the complexity and expressive power of bag languages [GM93, Alb91, LW93b, LW93a, LW94a, LW94b, JVdB91].

The main goal of this chapter is to lay the foundation for incremental maintenance of views defined in the bag algebra. We advocate an approach based on *equational reasoning*. That is, for each primitive in the bag algebra we derive an equation that shows how the result of applying this primitive changes if some changes are made to its arguments. We do it independently for each primitive in the language; then, if an expression is given, the change propagation algorithm calculates changes to the view by recursively applying those rules.

Our approach can be seen as generalizing [BLT86, Han87] to unrestricted queries in the the full bag algebra. A similar equational approach was used in [GLT97] for the relational algebra. That work grew out of an analysis of [QW91], which presented an iterative algorithm for propagating changes. This was improved in [GLT97] with a recursive algorithm that is similar in style to the one we present here for the bag algebra. The recursive form of these algorithms allows correctness to be proved with a simple proof by induction. In addition, our approach has a number of other positive features. In particular:

- As we shall see in section 4, the recursive form of our algorithm allows us to use invariants concerning minimality to further simplify change expressions. Such assumptions would not be available to a later phase of query optimization.

- The approach is robust: if language changes (e.g. new primitives are added), one only has to derive new rules for the added primitives, leaving all other rules intact. As long as the new rules are correct, the correctness of the change propagation algorithm is not affected.

- The resulting changes to the view are obtained in form of expressions in the same language used to define the view. This makes additional optimizations possible. For example, the expressions for changes that are to be made (e.g. for sets/bags of tuples to be deleted/added) can be given as an input to any query optimizer that might find an efficient way of calculating them.

In contrast, these features may be very difficult to obtain in a purely *algorithmic* approach to view maintenance. In section 7 we will outline the difference between our approach and a more algorithmic presented in [GMS93].

Example. Suppose we have a database with the relations S1(Pid, Cost, Date) and S2(Pid, Cost, Date) for recording shipments of parts received from two different suppliers. The attribute Pid is a unique identifier for parts, Cost is the associated cost of a part, and Date is the day the shipment arrived. In addition we

S1		
Pid	Cost	Date
P1	1,200	09/12
P2	2,100	08/27
P3	1,300	09/11
P4	1,400	08/25

S2		
Pid	Cost	Date
P1	1,200	09/05
P4	1,400	08/24
P5	4,000	09/03

Paid		
Pid	Cost	S
P1	1,200	1
P5	4,000	2

Unpaid	
Pid	Cost
P1	1,200
P2	2,100
P3	1,300
P4	1,400
P4	1,400

Figure 1 Relations S1, S2, Paid and view Unpaid

have the relation Paid(Pid, Cost, S), which registers parts that have been paid for. The attribute S must have the value 1 or 2, indicating which supplier was paid (see Figure 1).

We would like to compute the total amount of money we owe — the cost of all parts received by not yet paid for. One way of doing this is to define a view Unpaid as

$$V_1 \overset{\text{def}}{=} (\Pi_{\text{Pid,Cost}}(S1) \uplus \Pi_{\text{Pid,Cost}}(S2))$$

$$V_2 \overset{\text{def}}{=} \Pi_{\text{Pid,Cost}}(\text{Paid})$$

$$\text{Unpaid} \overset{\text{def}}{=} V_1 \dot{-} V_2$$

Here $\uplus$ is the additive union that adds up multiplicities of elements in bags. In particular, it will produce two copies of the record [Pid $\Rightarrow P1$, Cost $\Rightarrow 1,200$] in calculating V_1. The modified subtraction monus $\dot{-}$ subtracts multiplicities. If a record r occurs n times in S and m times in T, then the number of occurrences of r in $S \dot{-} T$ is $n - m$ if $n \geq m$ and 0 if $n < m$.

Assume that the derived data that we are interested in is the amount still owed:

$$\text{Owe} = \text{TOTAL}(\Pi_{\text{Cost}}(\text{Unpaid}))$$

Note that multiset semantics gives the correct answer here, while set-theoretic semantics would not. For example, for relations shown in figure 1, the amount Owe is \$7,400. However, if we switch to set semantics and calculate Unpaid as $(\Pi_{\text{Pid,Cost}}(S1) \cup \Pi_{\text{Pid,Cost}}(S2)) - \Pi_{\text{Pid,Cost}}(\text{Paid})$, then Owe calculated by the same formula equals \$4,800. Thus, we do need multiset semantics for maintaining the view Unpaid in a correct manner.

Suppose that a transaction changes Paid by deleting the bag $\triangledown$Paid and inserting the bag $\triangle$Paid. That is,

$$\text{Paid}^{\text{new}} = (\text{Paid} \dot{-} \triangledown\text{Paid}) \uplus \triangle\text{Paid}.$$

Rather than recomputing the entire view Unpaid from scratch, we would like to find expressions $\triangledown$Unpaid and $\triangle$Unpaid such that

$$\text{Unpaid}^{\text{new}} = (\text{Unpaid} \dot{-} \triangledown\text{Unpaid}) \uplus \triangle\text{Unpaid}.$$

This has the potential of greatly reducing the amount of computational resources needed to recompute this new value.

For example, let $\triangledown$Paid contain the single record [Pid $\Rightarrow$ P5, Cost $\Rightarrow$ 4, 000, S $\Rightarrow$ 2] and $\triangle$Paid contain the single record [Pid $\Rightarrow$ P3, Cost $\Rightarrow$ 1, 300, S $\Rightarrow$ 1]. (That is, we discovered that a payment was made to the first supplier for P3 rather than the second for P5.) Then it is fairly easy to see that $\triangledown$Unpaid should evaluate to [Pid $\Rightarrow$ P3, Cost $\Rightarrow$ 1, 300] and that $\triangle$Unpaid should evaluate to [Pid $\Rightarrow$ P5, Cost $\Rightarrow$ 4, 000].

Our algorithm treats the changes to base relations as black boxes. For this example it produces the delete bag, $\triangledown$Unpaid,

$$[\Pi_{\text{Pid,Cost}}(\triangle\text{Paid}) \dot{-} \Pi_{\text{Pid,Cost}}(\triangledown\text{Paid})] \min \text{Unpaid},$$

and the insert bag, $\triangle$Unpaid,

$$(\Pi_{\text{Pid,Cost}}(\triangledown\text{Paid}) \dot{-} \Pi_{\text{Pid,Cost}}(\triangle\text{Paid})) \dot{-} (V_2 \dot{-} V_1).$$

Here $S \min T$ is a multiset such that the number of occurrences of a record r in it is $\min(n, m)$, where n and m are numbers of occurrences in S and T respectively. Notice that the evaluation of the expressions for $\triangledown$Unpaid and $\triangle$Unpaid can be made very efficient. First we assume that all relations S1, S2 and Unpaid have an index built on the them that uses Pid as a key. Then, in order to evaluate the expressions for $\triangledown$Unpaid and $\triangle$Unpaid we only have to find the numbers of occurrences of elements of $\Pi_{\text{Pid,Cost}}(\triangledown\text{Paid})$ and $\Pi_{\text{Pid,Cost}}(\triangle\text{Paid})$ in V_1, V_2 and $\Pi_{\text{Pid,Cost}}(\text{Paid})$. For example, to find $\triangledown$Unpaid, for each $r \in \triangle$Paid we find x, y, z, v as the numbers of occurrences of r in $\triangle$Paid, $\triangledown$Paid, V_1 and V_2. Then R occurs $\min\{(x \dot{-} y), (z \dot{-} v)\}$ times in $\triangledown$Unpaid. Thus, the complexity of such evaluation depends on how fast we can access elements of the *base* relations. Access to the base relations is typically fast, compared to access to views.

Even if no index exists, the time complexity is still linear in the sizes of the base relations. The big win here is in space usage. Whereas recomputing the whole view Unpaid would require space linear in the size of base relations, the propagation algorithm only requires that we find the number of occurrences of certain records in base relations and then evaluate an arithmetic expression. Therefore, space needed for updating the view Unpaid is linear in the size of *changes* to the base relations. Typically, these changes are relatively small compared to the size of the relations. Thus, calculating changes to the view as opposed to reconstructing the view from scratch leads at least to substantial improvement in space usage.

Once changes to Unpaid are calculated, the new value of Owe is found as

$$\begin{aligned} \text{Owe}^{\text{new}} \quad &= \quad (\text{Owe} - \text{TOTAL}(\Pi_{\text{Cost}}(\triangledown\text{Unpaid}))) \\ &+ \quad \text{TOTAL}(\Pi_{\text{Cost}}(\triangle\text{Unpaid})). \end{aligned}$$

The correctness of this is guaranteed for our solution. Indeed, Owe^{new} calculated above is $10,100, and one can see that it is the correct amount still owed once changes to Paid have been made.

Organization. In Section 2 we introduce our notation, describe our basic bag algebra, and state the problem. We present some basic facts concerning equational reasoning for our bag algebra in Section 3. In Section 4 we present our change propagation algorithm for view maintenance. We then address aggregate functions in Section 5. In Section 6 we analyze the complexity of the results produced by our algorithm. We discuss related work in Section 7. Finally, we conclude in Section 8 with some remarks concerning future work. All proofs can be found in [GL95].

2   Basic Notation

2.1   The Bag Algebra, $\mathcal{BA}$

As we mentioned in the introduction, several equivalent approaches to bag-based database languages have been proposed [GM93, LW93b, LW94b]. As our basic language in which we formulate the change propagation algorithm we take a restriction of those languages to flat bags (that is, bag-valued attributes are not allowed).

In what follows, base relation names are denoted by the symbols R, R_1, R_2, …. Let p range over quantifier-free predicates, and A range over sets of attribute names. $\mathcal{BA}$ expressions are generated by the following grammar.

$$
\begin{array}{lllr}
S & ::= & \phi & \text{empty bag} \\
  & | & R & \text{name of stored bag} \\
  & | & \sigma_p(S) & \text{selection} \\
  & | & \Pi_A(S) & \text{projection} \\
  & | & S \uplus S & \text{additive union} \\
  & | & S \mathbin{\dot{-}} S & \text{monus} \\
  & | & S \min S & \text{minimum intersection} \\
  & | & S \max S & \text{maximum union} \\
  & | & \epsilon(S) & \text{duplicate elimination} \\
  & | & S \times S & \text{cartesian product}
\end{array}
$$

To define the semantics of these operations, let $count(x, S)$ be the number of occurrences of x in a bag S. Then, for any operation e in the language, we define $count(x, e(S, T))$ or $count(x, e(S))$ as a function of $count(x, S)$ and $count(x, T)$ as follows:

$$
count(x, \sigma_p(S)) = \begin{cases} count(x, S) & p(x) \text{ is true} \\ 0 & p(x) \text{ is false} \end{cases}
$$

$$
count(x, \Pi_A(S)) = \sum_{y \in S, \Pi_A(y) = x} count(y, S)
$$

$$
count(x, S \uplus T) = count(x, S) + count(x, T)
$$

$$
count(x, S \mathbin{\dot{-}} T) = \max(count(x, S) - count(x, T), 0)
$$

$$
count(x, S \min T) = \min(count(x, S), count(x, T))
$$

$$
count(x, S \max T) = \max(count(x, S), count(x, T))
$$

$$
count(x, \epsilon(S)) = \begin{cases} 1 & count(x, S) > 0 \\ 0 & count(x, S) = 0 \end{cases}
$$

$$
count((x, y), S \times T) = count(x, S) \times count(y, T)
$$

This language is not intended to be minimal. For example, min can be defined as $S \min T \stackrel{\text{def}}{=} S \mathbin{\dot{-}} (S \mathbin{\dot{-}} T)$. For the full characterization of interdefinability of the operations of $\mathcal{BA}$, consult [LW93b].

We use the symbols S, T, W, and Z to denote arbitrary $\mathcal{BA}$ expressions, and s to denote a database state, that is, a partial map from relation names to multisets. If s is a database state and T is a $\mathcal{BA}$ expression such that s is defined on all relation names mentioned in T, then $s(T)$ denotes the multiset resulting from evaluating T in the state s. (Note that s is a function, so we consider evaluating T in s as the result of applying s to T.) The notation $T =_b S$ means that for all database states s, if s is defined on all relation names mentioned in S and T, then $s(T) = s(S)$.

2.2 Transactions

A transaction is a program that changes the state of a database in one atomic step. There are many approaches to languages for specifying transactions, (see for example [AV88, Qia90, Ull89]). In this chapter we prefer to adopt an abstract view of transactions, in order to make the results independent of a particular language used, but at the same time readily applicable to any such language.

The abstract transactions to be considered are of the form

$$t \quad = \quad \{R_1 \leftarrow (R_1 \mathbin{\dot-} \triangledown R_1) \uplus \triangle R_1,$$
$$\cdots,$$
$$R_n \leftarrow (R_n \mathbin{\dot-} \triangledown R_n) \uplus \triangle R_n\}.$$

The expressions $\triangledown R_i$ and $\triangle R_i$ represent the multisets deleted from and inserted into base relation R_i. More formally, when transaction t is executed in state s, then value of R_i in state $t(s)$ becomes $s((R_i \mathbin{\dot-} \triangledown R_i) \uplus \triangle R_i)$.

The expression T is a *pre-expression* of S w.r.t. t if for every database state s we have $s(T) =_b t(s)(S)$. It is easy to check that

$$\mathrm{pre}(t, S) \quad \stackrel{\mathrm{def}}{=} \quad S((R_1 \mathbin{\dot-} \triangledown R_1) \uplus \triangle R_1,$$
$$\cdots,$$
$$(R_n \mathbin{\dot-} \triangledown R_n) \uplus \triangle R_n))$$

is a pre-expression of S w.r.t. t. In other words, we can evaluate $\mathrm{pre}(t, S)$ *before* we execute t in order to determine the value that S will have *afterwards*.

2.3 Problem Statement

Suppose $S(R_1, \cdots, R_n)$ is a $\mathcal{BA}$ expression and t is a transaction. We would like to determine how t's changes to the base relations propagate to changes in the value of S. In particular, we seek to construct expressions $\triangle S$ and $\triangledown S$, called a *solution* for $\mathrm{pre}(t, S)$, such that

$$\mathrm{pre}(t, S) =_b (S \mathbin{\dot-} \triangledown S) \uplus \triangle S.$$

Note that the expressions $\triangledown S$ and $\triangle S$ are to be evaluated before t is executed (and committed). These solutions can be used in many applications involving the maintenance of derived data. For example, in the case of view maintenance this allows us to recompute the value of S in the new state from its value in the old state and the values of $\triangledown S$ and $\triangle S$. For integrity maintenance it allows us to check data integrity *before* a transaction is committed, thus allowing for the transaction to be aborted without the expense of a roll-back operation.

Clearly, not all solutions are equally acceptable. For example, $\triangledown S = S$ and $\triangle S = \mathrm{pre}(t, S)$ is always a solution. How can we determine which are "good" solutions? First, if S is a materialized view, then it should be generally cheaper to evaluate $(S \mathbin{\dot-} \triangledown S) \uplus \triangle S$ than to evaluate $\mathrm{pre}(t, S)$ in the current state (or to evaluate S after t has been executed). Second, we should impose some "minimality" conditions on $\triangledown S$ and $\triangle S$ to make sure that no unnecessary tuples are produced. In particular,

1. $\triangledown S \mathbin{\dot-} S =_b \phi$: We only delete tuples that are in S.

2. $\triangle S \min \triangledown S =_b \phi$: We do not delete a tuple and then reinsert it.

A solution meeting condition (1) will be called *weakly minimal*, while a solution meeting both conditions (1) and (2) will be called *strongly minimal*. Note that, in contrast to the relational case [QW91], it does not make sense to insist that S be disjoint from $\triangle S$ since a transaction may increase the multipliicities of elements in S.

We will argue that minimality (weak or strong) is especially desirable due to the way in which changes interact with aggregate functions. For example, we have

$$\mathsf{TOTAL}((S \mathbin{\dot-} \triangledown S) \uplus \triangle S) = (\mathsf{TOTAL}(S) - \mathsf{TOTAL}(\triangledown S)) + \mathsf{TOTAL}(\triangle S)$$

assuming a (weakly or strongly) minimal solution.

Again, not all strongly minimal solutions are equally acceptable. For example, the pair

$$\triangledown Q = Q \mathbin{\dot-} \mathrm{pre}(t, Q)$$

and

$$\triangle Q = \mathrm{pre}(t, Q) \mathbin{\dot-} Q$$

is a strongly minimal solution. However, one does not win by using it for maintaining the view given by Q.

The main goal of this chapter is to present an algorithm for generating (at compile time) strongly minimal solutions to the view maintenance problem and demonstrate that they are computationally more efficient than recomputing the view (at run-time).

3   Preliminaries

This section presents the equational theory underlying our change propagation algorithm. A change propagation algorithm for the relational algebra was presented in [QW91], based on a collection of equations that are used to "bubble up" change sets to the top of an expression. For example, [QW91] uses the equation

$$(S \cup \triangle S) - T = (S - T) \cup (\triangle S - T)$$

to take the insertion $\triangle S$ into S and propagate it upward to the insertion $\triangle S - T$ into $S - T$.

Our first step is to define a collection of such propagation rules for bag expressions. The situation is more complicated for *BA* expressions since they do not obey the familiar laws of boolean algebra that we are accustomed to using with set-valued relational expressions. For bag expression, the above example now becomes

$$(S \uplus \triangle S) \mathbin{\dot-} T = (S \mathbin{\dot-} T) \uplus (\triangle S \mathbin{\dot-} (T \mathbin{\dot-} S)),$$

which is not immediately obvious.

Figure 2 contains our equations for change propagation in bag expressions. Some subexpressions are annotated with a $\triangledown$ (for a deletion bag) or a $\triangle$ (for an insertion bag). This annotation simply emphasizes the intended application of these equations: when read as left-to-right rewrite rules, they tell us how to propagate changes upward in an expression. Note that the correctness of these equations involves no assumptions concerning minimality of the change bags.

Theorem 1 *The equations of Figure 2 are correct.*

Example. By repeated applications of the rules in figure 2 we can propagate any number of changes upward. Consider the expression $U = S \uplus T$. Suppose that

$$\mathrm{pre}(t, U) =_b ((S \mathbin{\dot-} \triangledown S) \uplus \triangle S) \uplus ((T \mathbin{\dot-} \triangledown T) \uplus \triangle T).$$

P1. $\sigma_p(S \mathbin{\dot-} \triangledown S) =_b \sigma_p(S) \mathbin{\dot-} \sigma_p(\triangledown S)$

P2. $\sigma_p(S \uplus \triangle S) =_b \sigma_p(S) \uplus \sigma_p(\triangle S)$

P3. $\Pi_A(S \mathbin{\dot-} \triangledown S) =_b \Pi_A(S) \mathbin{\dot-} \Pi_A(\triangledown S \min S)$

P4. $\Pi_A(S \uplus \triangle S) =_b \Pi_A(S) \uplus \Pi_A(\triangle S)$

P5. $(S \mathbin{\dot-} \triangledown S) \uplus T =_b (S \uplus T) \mathbin{\dot-} (\triangledown S \min S)$

P6. $(S \uplus \triangle S) \uplus T =_b (S \uplus T) \uplus \triangle S$

P7. $(S \mathbin{\dot-} \triangledown S) \mathbin{\dot-} T =_b (S \mathbin{\dot-} T) \mathbin{\dot-} \triangledown S$

P8. $S \mathbin{\dot-} (T \mathbin{\dot-} \triangledown T) =_b (S \mathbin{\dot-} T) \uplus ((\triangledown T \min T) \mathbin{\dot-} (T \mathbin{\dot-} S))$

P9. $(S \uplus \triangle S) \mathbin{\dot-} T =_b (S \mathbin{\dot-} T) \uplus (\triangle S \mathbin{\dot-} (T \mathbin{\dot-} S))$

P10. $S \mathbin{\dot-} (T \uplus \triangle T) =_b (S \mathbin{\dot-} T) \mathbin{\dot-} \triangle T$

P11. $(S \mathbin{\dot-} \triangledown S) \min T =_b (S \min T) \mathbin{\dot-} (\triangledown S \mathbin{\dot-} (S \mathbin{\dot-} T))$

P12. $(S \uplus \triangle S) \min T =_b (S \min T) \uplus (\triangle S \min (T \mathbin{\dot-} S))$

P13. $(S \mathbin{\dot-} \triangledown S) \max T =_b (S \max T) \mathbin{\dot-} (\triangledown S \min (S \mathbin{\dot-} T))$

P14. $(S \uplus \triangle S) \max T =_b (S \max T) \uplus (\triangle S \mathbin{\dot-} (T \mathbin{\dot-} S))$

P15. $\epsilon(S \mathbin{\dot-} \triangledown S) =_b \epsilon(S) \mathbin{\dot-} (\epsilon(\triangledown S \min S) \mathbin{\dot-} (S \mathbin{\dot-} \triangledown S))$

P16. $\epsilon(S \uplus \triangle S) =_b \epsilon(S) \uplus (\epsilon(\triangle S) \mathbin{\dot-} S)$

P17. $(S \mathbin{\dot-} \triangledown S) \times T =_b (S \times T) \mathbin{\dot-} (\triangledown S \times T)$

P18. $(S \uplus \triangle S) \times T =_b (S \times T) \uplus (\triangle S \times T)$

Figure 2   Change propagation equations for bag expressions

The changes to S and T can be propagated upward and expressed as changes to U as follows:

$$((S \mathbin{\dot-} \triangledown S) \uplus \triangle S) \uplus ((T \mathbin{\dot-} \triangledown T) \uplus \triangle T)$$

$$\overset{P6}{=_b} (((S \mathbin{\dot-} \triangledown S) \uplus \triangle S) \uplus (T \mathbin{\dot-} \triangledown T)) \uplus \triangle T$$

$$\overset{P6}{=_b} (((S \mathbin{\dot-} \triangledown S) \uplus (T \mathbin{\dot-} \triangledown T)) \uplus \triangle S) \uplus \triangle T$$

$$\overset{P5}{=_b} ((((S \mathbin{\dot-} \triangledown S) \uplus T) \mathbin{\dot-} (\triangledown T \min T)) \uplus \triangle S) \uplus \triangle T$$

$$\overset{P5}{=_b} ((((S \uplus T) \mathbin{\dot-} (\triangledown S \min S)) \mathbin{\dot-} (\triangledown T \min T)) \uplus \triangle S) \uplus \triangle T$$

$$=_b (U \mathbin{\dot-} \triangledown_1 U) \uplus \triangle_1 U$$

where $\triangledown_1 U = (\triangledown S \min S) \uplus (\triangledown T \min T)$ and $\triangle_1 U = \triangle S \uplus \triangle T$. The last step is simply an application of the general rules

G1. $(S \uplus T) \uplus W =_b S \uplus (T \uplus W)$

G2. $(S \mathbin{\dot-} T) \mathbin{\dot-} W =_b S \mathbin{\dot-} (T \uplus W)$

which are applied in order to collect all deletions into one delete bag and all insertions into one insert bag.

Repeated application of the rules of figure 2 guarantees a solution, but not necessarily a strongly minimal one. However, the following theorem tells us that any solution can be transformed into a strongly minimal one.

Theorem 2 *Suppose that* $W =_b (Q \mathbin{\dot-} \triangledown_1 Q) \uplus \triangle_1 Q$. *Let*

$$\triangledown_2 Q = (Q \min \triangledown_1 Q) \mathbin{\dot-} \triangle_1 Q$$

and

$$\triangle_2 Q = \triangle_1 Q \mathbin{\dot{-}} (Q \min \triangledown_1 Q).$$

Then it follows that

    a) $W =_b (Q \mathbin{\dot{-}} \triangledown_2 Q) \uplus \triangle_2 Q$

    b) $\triangledown_2 Q \mathbin{\dot{-}} Q =_b \phi$

    c) $\triangledown_2 Q \min \triangle_2 Q =_b \phi.$

Returning to the example from above, $\triangledown_1 U$ and $\triangle_1 U$ can be transformed to a strongly minimal solution by taking $\triangledown_2 U$ to be

$$(U \min ((\triangledown S \min S) \uplus (\triangledown T \min T))) \mathbin{\dot{-}} (\triangle S \uplus \triangle T)$$

and $\triangle_2 U$ to be

$$(\triangle S \uplus \triangle T) \mathbin{\dot{-}} (U \min ((\triangledown S \min S) \uplus (\triangledown T \min T)))$$

Although these expressions are rather complex, they can be greatly simplified to

$$\triangledown_3 U \stackrel{\text{def}}{=} (\triangledown S \mathbin{\dot{-}} \triangle T) \uplus (\triangledown T \mathbin{\dot{-}} \triangle S)$$

$$\triangle_3 U \stackrel{\text{def}}{=} (\triangle S \mathbin{\dot{-}} \triangledown T) \uplus (\triangle T \mathbin{\dot{-}} \triangledown S)$$

under the assumption that the solutions $(\triangledown S, \triangle S)$ and $(\triangledown T, \triangle T)$ are strongly minimal (details omitted).

This example illustrates the three-step process that was used to derive the recursive algorithm presented in the next section. First, a general solution is derived by repeated application of the propagation rules of figure 2. Second, a strongly minimal solution is obtained by application of theorem 2. Third, the results are simplified under the assumption that all solutions for subexpressions are strongly minimal.

Note that if we are *only* concerned with correctness, then there is considerable freedom in the design of the propagation rules presented figure 2. For example, we could replace rule P8 with

$$S \mathbin{\dot{-}} (T \mathbin{\dot{-}} \triangledown T) =_b (S \mathbin{\dot{-}} T) \uplus ((S \mathbin{\dot{-}} (T \mathbin{\dot{-}} \triangledown T)) \mathbin{\dot{-}} (S \mathbin{\dot{-}} T))$$

However, we have designed our rules from a *computational* point of view. Note that the structure of each equation in figure 2 follows the same pattern. For any operation e and its value $V = e(R_1, \ldots, R_n)$, $n = 1$ or $n = 2$, if one of its arguments changes, then its value V' on changed arguments is obtained as either $V \mathbin{\dot{-}} \triangledown$ or $V \uplus \triangle$. The expressions for $\triangledown$ and $\triangle$ are always of special form. Intuitively, they are "controlled" by $\triangledown R_i$s and $\triangle R_i$s, that is, could be computed by iterating over them and fetching corresponding elements from base relations, rather than by iterating over base relations. Furthermore, this special form is preserved in the transformations defined in theorem 2.

For example, to compute $Z = ((\triangledown T \min T) \mathbin{\dot{-}} (T \mathbin{\dot{-}} S))$ (rule P8 in figure 2), for each element $x \in \triangledown T$, let n, m and k be numbers of occurrences of x in $\triangledown T$, T and S respectively. Then x occurs $\min(n, m) \mathbin{\dot{-}} (m \mathbin{\dot{-}} k)$ times in Z. Thus, to compute Z, we only fetch elements in $\triangledown T$ from T and S. Since $\triangledown R_i$s and $\triangle R_i$s are generally small compared to the size of base relations R_is, this special form of expressions for $\triangledown$ and $\triangle$ will make the change propagation algorithm suitable for maintaining large views. This intuition will be made more precise in the analysis of section 6.

4   Change Propagation Algorithm

This section presents our algorithm for computing a strongly minimal solution to a given view maintenance problem. That is, given a transaction t and a $\mathcal{BA}$ expression Q, we will compute expressions $\triangledown Q$ and $\triangle Q$ such that $\text{pre}(t, Q) =_b (Q \mathbin{\dot{-}} \triangledown Q) \uplus \triangle Q$.

We first define two mutually recursive functions $\triangledown(t, Q)$ and $\triangle(t, Q)$ such that for any transaction t $\text{pre}(t, Q) =_b (Q \mathbin{\dot{-}} \triangledown(t, Q)) \uplus \triangle(t, Q)$. These functions are presented in figure 3. For readability, we use the abbreviations $\text{add}(t, S)$ for $S \uplus \triangle(t, S)$ and $\text{del}(t, S)$ for $S \mathbin{\dot{-}} \triangledown(t, S)$.

We derived the clauses of these recursive functions in three steps: a) a general solution was obtained by repeated applications of the propagation rules of figure 2, b) theorem 2 was applied to obtain a strongly minimal solution, c) the results were further simplified by assuming that all recursively derived solutions are strongly minimal.

This last step is quite important since the assumptions of strong minimality would not be available to a query optimizer at a later stage. It is also why we want to apply theorem 2 at every stage, rather than just once at the end. The three steps were outlined in the previous section for the $S \uplus T$ case.

Algorithm. Our algorithm is simply this: given inputs t and Q, use the functions $\triangledown(t, Q)$ and $\triangle(t, Q)$ to compute a solution for $\text{pre}(t, Q)$. Note that in an actual implementation $\triangledown(t, Q)$ and $\triangle(t, Q)$ could be combined into one recursive function. Thus the algorithm requires only one pass over the expression Q.

The following theorem shows that the functions $\triangledown$ and $\triangle$ correctly compute a solution to the view maintenance problem and that they preserve strong minimality.

Theorem 3 *Let t be a strongly minimal transaction. That is, $\triangledown R \mathbin{\dot{-}} R =_b \phi$ and $\triangledown R \min \triangle R =_b \phi$ for any $R \leftarrow (R \mathbin{\dot{-}} \triangledown R) \uplus \triangle R$ in t. Let Q be a $\mathcal{BA}$ expression. Then*

1. $\text{pre}(t, Q) =_b (Q \mathbin{\dot{-}} \triangledown(t, Q)) \uplus \triangle(t, Q)$

2. $\triangledown(t, Q) \mathbin{\dot{-}} Q =_b \phi$

3. $\triangle(t, Q) \min \triangledown(t, Q) =_b \phi$

Although some of the clauses in the definition of functions $\triangledown$ and $\triangle$ are rather complex, we believe that in practice many of the subexpressions will be ϕ or will easily simplify to ϕ. To illustrate this, recall the example from section 1:

$$V_1 \stackrel{\text{def}}{=} (\Pi_{\text{Pid,Cost}}(\text{S1}) \uplus \Pi_{\text{Pid,Cost}}(\text{S2}))$$

$$V_2 \stackrel{\text{def}}{=} \Pi_{\text{Pid,Cost}}(\text{Paid})$$

$$\text{Unpaid} \stackrel{\text{def}}{=} V_1 \mathbin{\dot{-}} V_2$$

where the t is a transaction that changes Paid to $(\text{Paid} \mathbin{\dot{-}} \triangledown\text{Paid}) \uplus \triangle\text{Paid}$. Using our change propagation functions, the delete bag can be calculated as follows.

Q	$\triangledown(t, Q)$	#
R	$\triangledown R$, if $R \leftarrow (R \doteq \triangledown R) \uplus \triangle R$ is in t, and ϕ otherwise	$\triangledown 1$
$\sigma_p(S)$	$\sigma_p(\triangledown(t, S))$	$\triangledown 2$
$\Pi_A(S)$	$\Pi_A(\triangledown(t, S)) \doteq \Pi_A(\triangle(t, S))$	$\triangledown 3$
$S \uplus T$	$(\triangledown(t, S) \doteq \triangle(t, T)) \uplus (\triangledown(t, T) \doteq \triangle(t, S))$	$\triangledown 4$
$S \doteq T$	$((\triangledown(t, S) \doteq \triangledown(t, T)) \uplus (\triangle(t, T) \doteq \triangle(t, S))) \min Q$	$\triangledown 5$
$S \min T$	$(\triangledown S \doteq (S \doteq T)) \max (\triangledown T \doteq (T \doteq S))$	$\triangledown 6$
$S \max T$	$(\triangledown(t, S) \uplus (\triangledown(t, T) \min (T \doteq \mathrm{add}(t, S)))) \max$ $(\triangledown(t, T) \uplus (\triangledown(t, S) \min (S \doteq \mathrm{add}(t, T))))$	$\triangledown 7$
$\epsilon(S)$	$\epsilon(\triangledown(t, S)) \doteq \mathrm{del}(t, S)$	$\triangledown 8$
$S \times T$	$(\triangledown(t, S) \times \triangledown(t, T)) \uplus$ $((\mathrm{del}(t, S) \times \triangledown(t, T)) \doteq (\triangle(t, S) \times \mathrm{del}(t, T))) \uplus$ $((\triangledown(t, S) \times \mathrm{del}(t, T)) \doteq (\mathrm{del}(t, S) \times \triangle(t, T)))$	$\triangledown 9$

Q	$\triangle(t, Q)$	#
R	$\triangle R$, if $R \leftarrow (R \doteq \triangledown R) \uplus \triangle R$ is in t, and ϕ otherwise	$\triangle 1$
$\sigma_p(S)$	$\sigma_p(\triangle(t, S))$	$\triangle 2$
$\Pi_A(S)$	$\Pi_A(\triangle(t, S)) \doteq \Pi_A(\triangledown(t, S))$	$\triangle 3$
$S \uplus T$	$(\triangle(t, S) \doteq \triangledown(t, T)) \uplus (\triangle(t, T) \doteq \triangledown(t, S))$	$\triangle 4$
$S \doteq T$	$((\triangle(t, S) \doteq \triangle(t, T)) \uplus (\triangledown(t, T) \doteq \triangledown(t, S))) \doteq (T \doteq S)$	$\triangle 5$
$S \min T$	$(\triangle(t, S) \uplus (\triangle(t, T) \min (\mathrm{del}(t, S) \doteq T))) \min$ $(\triangle(t, T) \uplus (\triangle(t, S) \min (\mathrm{del}(t, T) \doteq S)))$	$\triangle 6$
$S \max T$	$(\triangle S \doteq (T \doteq S)) \max (\triangle T \doteq (S \doteq T))$	$\triangle 7$
$\epsilon(S)$	$\epsilon(\triangle(t, S)) \doteq S$	$\triangle 8$
$S \times T$	$(\triangle(t, S) \times \triangle(t, T)) \uplus$ $((\mathrm{del}(t, S) \times \triangle(t, T)) \doteq (\triangledown(t, S) \times T)) \uplus$ $((\triangle(t, S) \times \mathrm{del}(t, T)) \doteq S \times \triangledown(t, T))$	$\triangle 9$

Figure 3 Mutually recursive functions $\triangledown$ and $\triangle$.

$$
\begin{aligned}
& \triangledown(t, \mathrm{Unpaid}) \\
={}& \triangledown(t, V_1 \doteq V_2) \\
\stackrel{\triangledown 5}{=}{}& ((\triangledown(t, V_1) \doteq \triangledown(t, V_2)) \uplus (\triangle(t, V_2) \doteq \triangle(t, V_1))) \\
& \min \mathrm{Unpaid} \\
={}& ((\phi \doteq \triangledown(t, V_2)) \uplus (\triangle(t, V_2) \doteq \phi)) \min \mathrm{Unpaid} \\
={}& \triangle(t, V_2) \min \mathrm{Unpaid} \\
={}& \triangle(t, \Pi_{\mathrm{Pid, Cost}}(\mathrm{Paid})) \min \mathrm{Unpaid} \\
\stackrel{\triangle 3}{=}{}& [\Pi_{\mathrm{Pid, Cost}}(\triangle(t, \mathrm{Paid})) \doteq \Pi_{\mathrm{Pid, Cost}}(\triangledown(t, \mathrm{Paid}))] \\
& \min \mathrm{Unpaid} \\
\stackrel{\triangledown 1, \triangle 10}{=}{}& [\Pi_{\mathrm{Pid, Cost}}(\triangle \mathrm{Paid}) \doteq \Pi_{\mathrm{Pid, Cost}}(\triangledown \mathrm{Paid})] \min \mathrm{Unpaid}
\end{aligned}
$$

In a similar way we can compute the change bag for insertions, $\triangle(t, \text{Unpaid})$, to be

$$[\Pi_{\text{Pid,Cost}}(\triangledown\text{Paid}) \dot- \Pi_{\text{Pid,Cost}}(\triangle\text{Paid})] \dot- (V_2 \dot- V_1).$$

One advantage of our approach is that it produces queries that can be further optimized by a query optimizer. Consider the following example. Suppose that we have a view WellPaid defined as

$$\text{WellPaid} = \Pi_{\text{Name}}(\sigma_{\text{Salary}>50,000}(\text{Employees}))$$

Now if a deletion has been made to Employees, then we compute

$$\triangledown\text{WellPaid} = \Pi_{\text{Name}}(\sigma_{\text{Salary}>50,000}(\triangledown\text{Employees}))$$

We have treated deletions and insertions as black boxes, but often they are specified in some transaction language or as queries. For example, if $\triangledown\text{Employees} = \sigma_{\text{Salary}<5,000}(\text{Employees})$, then we can substitute this value for $\triangledown\text{Employees}$ in the equation for $\triangledown\text{WellPaid}$, obtaining

$$\Pi_{\text{Name}}(\sigma_{\text{Salary}>50,000}(\sigma_{\text{Salary}<5,000}(\text{Employees})))$$

for $\triangledown\text{WellPaid}$. A query optimizer that "knows" that $\sigma_{p_1}(\sigma_{p_2}(S)) = \sigma_{p_1 \& p_2}(S)$ and that $5 < 50$ will figure out that $\triangledown\text{WellPaid} = \phi$ and no computation needs to be done.

5   Top-Level Aggregate Functions

Most database query languages provide a number of aggregate functions such as COUNT, TOTAL, AVG, STDEV, MIN, MAX [MPR90, GMS93, Ull89]. It was noticed in [LW93a, LW94b] that a number of aggregates (in fact, all of the above except MIN and MAX) can be expressed if the query language is endowed with arithmetic operations and the following summation operator:

$$\Sigma_f \; \{|x_1, \ldots, x_n|\} \; = \; f(x_1) + \ldots + f(x_n)$$

For example, COUNT is Σ_1 where the function 1 always returns 1; TOTAL is Σ_{id}, AVG is TOTAL/COUNT. For more complex examples, see [LW93a, LW94a].

Any strongly minimal solution for the view maintenance problem allows us to handle duplicates correctly because the following will hold:

$$\Sigma_f \; ((S \dot- \triangledown S) \uplus \triangle S) \; = \; (\Sigma_f(S) - \Sigma_f(\triangledown S)) + \Sigma_f(\triangle S)$$

Now if an aggregate function is defined as $\text{AGR}(S) = \varphi(\Sigma_{f_1}(S), \ldots, \Sigma_{f_k}(S))$ where φ is an arithmetic expression in k arguments, to be able to maintain the value of AGR when the view S changes, one has to keep k numbers, $\Sigma_{f_i}(S)$, $i = 1, \ldots, k$. Once changes to the view ($\triangledown S$ and $\triangle S$) become known, the values of Σ_{f_i} are recomputed by the formula above and then φ is applied to obtain the value of AGR.

For example, $\text{AVG}(S) = \text{TOTAL}(S)/\text{COUNT}(S) = \Sigma_{id}(S)/\Sigma_1(S)$. Assume that $n = \text{TOTAL}(S)$ and $m = \text{COUNT}(S)$. If S changes and a strongly minimal solution $S^n = (S \dot- \triangledown S) \uplus \triangle S$ is computed, let $n_1 = \Sigma_{id}(\triangledown S)$, $n_2 = \Sigma_{id}(\triangle S)$, $m_1 = \Sigma_1(\triangledown S)$, $m_2 = \Sigma_1(\triangle S)$. Then $\text{AVG}(S^n)$ can be computed as $(n - n_1 + n_2)/(m - m_1 + m_2)$. Notice that all additional computation of aggregates is performed on changes to the views, so one may expect it to be fast.

Two aggregates that require special treatment are MIN and MAX. Assume that $\mathsf{MIN}(S) = n$, and we want to compute $\mathsf{MIN}(S^n)$ where $S^n = (S \mathbin{\dot{-}} \triangledown S) \uplus \triangle S$ is strongly minimal. If we compute $m = \mathsf{MIN}(\triangledown S)$ and $k = \mathsf{MIN}(\triangle S)$, then $k \leq n$ implies $\mathsf{MIN}(S^n) = k$ and $m > n$ implies $\mathsf{MIN}(S^n) = \min(n, k)$. However, if $n = m$ and $k \geq n$, then there is no way to say what the value of $\mathsf{MIN}(S^n)$ is for the minimal value n can be reached at several elements of S and we do not know if *all* of them were deleted in $\triangledown S$. Thus, in only this case one has to recompute S^n in order to evaluate MIN correctly.

6 Complexity Analysis

While it is generally faster to compute changes to the view from changes to base relations rather than recompute the whole view from scratch, this is only a heuristic and need not be true in all cases. Changes to base relations are also typically small, but it is conceivable that in some situations a base relation R can be replaced by another relation R'. In this case $\triangledown R = R$ and $\triangle R = R'$, so changes to R are not small compared to R itself. If these changes "dominate" computing $\triangledown(t, Q)$ and $\triangle(t, Q)$, then one should not expect a significant improvement in time and space efficiency from using the change propagation algorithm.

All this tells us that it is impossible to prove a general statement saying that it is better to use the change propagation algorithm rather than recompute the view. This is also one of the reasons why so little effort has been devoted to the complexity analysis of the view maintenance problem. But intuitively, if changes are small, computing solutions for pre-expressions should be easier than computing pre-expressions themselves. In particular, one may expect that in most cases the sizes of $\triangle S$ and $\triangledown S$ are small compared to the size of S, and these are relatively easy to compute. In this section we present an attempt to formalize this statement.

Our approach is the following. We define two functions on $\mathcal{BA}$ expressions. These functions give a reasonable time (or space) estimate for computing the delta-expressions for the change propagation algorithm (the function $\mathsf{t}_\triangle$) and for recomputing the view from scratch (the function t_{view}). Then we shall prove that if changes to base relations are small, the expected complexity of evaluating $\triangle(t, Q)$ and $\triangledown(t, Q)$ is small compared to the expected complexity of re-evaluating Q on changed arguments. In other words, $\mathsf{t}_\triangle(\triangle(t, Q)) + \mathsf{t}_\triangle(\triangledown(t, Q))$ is small compared to $\mathsf{t}_{view}(\mathrm{pre}(t)Q)$. The special form of $\triangledown(t, Q)$ and $\triangle(t, Q)$ where all expressions that are hard to evaluate occur inside the scope of a simpler $\triangledown$ or $\triangle$ will play the crucial role.

Our first step is to define t_{view}. We give an *optimistic* estimate for t_{view}, because our goal is to prove that generally recomputing the view is more expensive than maintaining it. We first define $\mathsf{t}_{view}(R) = \mathsf{size}(R)$ for any base relation R. For binary operation define

$$\mathsf{t}_{view}(S \min T) = \mathsf{t}_{view}(S \uplus T) = \mathsf{t}_{view}(S \min T)$$
$$= \mathsf{t}_{view}(S \max T) = \mathsf{t}_{view}(S) + \mathsf{t}_{view}(T)$$

The idea is that to compute the new view, we have to compute S and T, and then, being optimistic, we disregard the time needed to compute min, max, $\uplus$ or $\dot{-}$. For cartesian product, define $\mathsf{t}_{view}(S \times T) = \mathsf{t}_{view}(S) \cdot \mathsf{t}_{view}(T)$. Finally, for unary operations we use the optimistic estimate again, and disregard overhead for doing computation on the argument. That is,

$$\mathsf{t}_{view}(\sigma_p(S)) = \mathsf{t}_{view}(\Pi_A(S)) = \mathsf{t}_{view}(\epsilon(S)) = \mathsf{t}_{view}(S)$$

To define the function $\mathsf{t}_\triangle$ that estimates a reasonable evaluation time for expressions used in the change propagation algorithm, we use the special form of the expressions in figure 3 that allow us to iterate over subexpressions in scope of $\bigtriangledown$ or $\triangle$, as was explain before. To do this, as the first step, we define a new function $\mathsf{fetch}(S)$ that estimates the complexity of *retrieving* a given element from the value of $S(R_1, \ldots, R_n)$. We assume that $\mathsf{fetch}(R_i)$s are given and bounded above by some number F. Then for any binary operation $* \in \mathcal{BA}$ we define $\mathsf{fetch}(S * T) = \mathsf{fetch}(S) + \mathsf{fetch}(T)$. For example, to retrieve x from $S \times T$, we first retrieve x's projection onto attributes of S from S, and then x's projection onto T's attributes from T, and use the result to obtain the right number of x's duplicates in $S \times T$. For $\sigma_p(\cdot)$ and $\epsilon(\cdot)$ we assume $\mathsf{fetch}(\sigma_p(S)) = \mathsf{fetch}(\epsilon(S)) = \mathsf{fetch}(S)$ as an upper bound. Finally, we make an assumption that $\mathsf{fetch}(\Pi_A(S)) = \mathsf{fetch}(S)$ which need not be true in general but holds if the index on S is not projected out. As we explained in the introduction, if the index does get projected out, there is no guarantee of winning in terms of time, but we still win in terms of space. Indeed, the space occupied by $\Pi_A(S)$ is bounded by the space needed for S itself, and then the following theorem can be seen as a confirmation of the fact that one should expect to reduce the *space* complexity.

Now we define inductively the estimated time complexity of evaluation of $\triangle S$ and $\bigtriangledown S$. First, we assume that for any base relation R, $\mathsf{t}_\triangle(\triangle R) = \mathsf{size}(\triangle R)$ and $\mathsf{t}_\triangle(\bigtriangledown R) = \mathsf{size}(\bigtriangledown R)$. In the definitions for $\mathcal{BA}$ operations we disregard time needed for projecting out some fields or checking the selection conditions, assuming that it is constant. We also assume that the number of duplicates is known for all elements, and disregard the computational overhead of duplicate elimination. That is,

$$\mathsf{t}_\triangle(\sigma_p(S)) \;=\; \mathsf{t}_\triangle(\Pi_A(S)) \;=\; \mathsf{t}_\triangle(\epsilon(S)) \;=\; \mathsf{t}_\triangle(S).$$

For operations $\uplus, \max$ and $\times$ we define

$$\mathsf{t}_\triangle(S \uplus T) = \mathsf{t}_\triangle(S \max T) = \mathsf{t}_\triangle(S) + \mathsf{t}_\triangle(T)$$

and

$$\mathsf{t}_\triangle(S \times T) = \mathsf{t}_\triangle(S) \cdot \mathsf{t}_\triangle(T).$$

The only thing out of ordinary in the definition of $\mathsf{t}_\triangle$ is the clauses for min and monus:

$$\begin{aligned}
\mathsf{t}_\triangle(S \mathbin{\dot{-}} T) &= \mathsf{t}_\triangle(S) \cdot \mathsf{fetch}(T) \\
\mathsf{t}_\triangle(S \min T) &= \min(\mathsf{t}_\triangle(S) \cdot \mathsf{fetch}(T), \mathsf{t}_\triangle(T) \cdot \mathsf{fetch}(S))
\end{aligned}$$

Unlike in the case of $\uplus, \max$ and $\times$, elements of T need not be stored as they are only used to reduce the size of S. Hence, to compute $S \mathbin{\dot{-}} T$ or $S \min T$, one only has to fetch elements of the computed value S from T, and that requires $\mathsf{fetch}(T)$ rather than $\mathsf{t}_\triangle(T)$ time for each element in S. In the case of min, which is a symmetric operation, we can alternatively iterate over T; the estimated time complexity is obtained by taking the minimum of the two possible iterations.

Let $\mathcal{D} = \{R_1, \ldots, R_n\}$ be a family of base relations stored in a database. We assume that a transaction t is fixed for the remainder of the section, and omit it in all definitions. Define

$$c(\mathcal{D}) \;=\; \max_{i=1,\ldots,n} \frac{\mathsf{size}(\bigtriangledown R_i) + \mathsf{size}(\triangle R_i)}{\mathsf{size}(R_i)}$$

That is, $c(\mathcal{D})$ gives the upper bound on the relative size of the changes to base relations. The following result shows that if $c(\mathcal{D})$ is small, then one should expect to win in terms of time (or space) by using the change propagation algorithm.

Theorem 4 *Let $Q(R_1, \ldots, R_n)$ be a $\mathcal{BA}$ expression. Let $\triangle Q$ and $\bigtriangledown Q$ be calculated according to the change propagation algorithm. Then*

$$\lim_{c(\mathcal{D}) \to 0} \frac{\mathsf{t}_\triangle(\bigtriangledown Q) + \mathsf{t}_\triangle(\triangle Q)}{\mathsf{t}_{view}(\mathrm{pre}(Q))} = 0$$

Let us apply this theorem to our working example. Recall that the positive change to the view Unpaid was calculated as

$$\triangle \text{Unpaid} = (\Pi_{\text{Pid,Cost}}(\triangledown\text{Paid}) \doteq \Pi_{\text{Pid,Cost}}(\triangle\text{Paid})) \doteq (V_2 \doteq V_1)$$

Assuming that for base relations the value of the fetch function equals F, we obtain

$$t_\triangle(\triangle\text{Unpaid}) = \text{size}(\triangledown\text{Paid}) \cdot 2F^2 = O(\text{size}(\triangledown\text{Paid})).$$

Similarly,

$$t_\triangle(\triangledown\text{Unpaid}) = O(\text{size}(\triangle\text{Paid})).$$

Therefore, it is expected that modifications to the table Unpaid can be calculated in $O(\text{size}(\triangledown\text{Paid}) + \text{size}(\triangle\text{Paid}))$ time. One can derive the same result just by looking at the expressions for $\triangledown\text{Unpaid}$ and $\triangle\text{Unpaid}$. Indeed, to calculate $\triangle\text{Unpaid}$, we iterate over $\triangledown\text{Paid}$ and fetch its elements from $\triangle\text{Paid}$, V_1 and V_2 and then compute the value of an arithmetic expression. The time needed for that is linear in the size of $\triangledown\text{Paid}$, assuming F is constant.

On the other hand, to recompute the view Unpaid, one should expect to spend time $O(\text{size}(S_1) + \text{size}(S_2))$, and this is exactly what $t_{view}(\text{pre}(\text{Unpaid}))$ is. If sizes of $\triangledown\text{Paid}$ and $\triangle\text{Paid}$ are small, this tells us that it is better to compute $\triangledown\text{Unpaid}$ and $\triangle\text{Unpaid}$ than to recompute Unpaid.

One may ask what happens if one tries to use the same evaluation strategy for both change propagation and recomputing the view. It should not be surprising that in several cases the complexity of both is the same, as we should not always expect to win by propagating changes. To give an example, let R_1, R_2 and R_3 be base relations, where R_1's attributes are a_1, a_2, R_2's sole attribute is a_1 and R_3's attribute is a_2. Define our view as $V := R_1 \min(R_2 \times R_3)$. Now assume that $\text{size}(R_i) = n$, $i = 1, 2, 3$. Assume that $\text{fetch}(R_i) = F$ is constant. Then it is easy to see that $t_\triangle(\triangledown V) = O(n)$ and $t_\triangle(\triangle V) = O(n)$.

Now assume that changes to base relations R_is are small. Then one can use the evaluation strategy that gave us the function $t_\triangle$ and calculate that $t_\triangle(\text{pre}(V)) = O(n)$, where $\text{pre}(V) = ((R_1 \doteq \triangledown R_1) \uplus \triangle R_1) \min(((R_2 \doteq \triangledown R_2) \uplus \triangle R_2) \times ((R_2 \doteq \triangledown R_2) \uplus \triangle R_2))$. The reason for this is that it is not necessary to calculate the second argument of min as we only have to retrieve certain elements from it.

This example shows that even for a simple view definition it may be the case that using the change propagation algorithm is as complex as recomputing the view from scratch, provided that we do not use a straightforward evaluation strategy (corresponding to t_{view}).

7 Related Work

In [BLT86, Han87], only views of the form

$$V = \pi_Y(\sigma_X(R_i \times R_2 \times \cdots \times R_n))$$

are considered. The tables R_i are defined to be sets, although the resulting view is, in general, a multiset. This can be viewed as a special case of our more general algorithm.

Our approach is closest to that of [GLT97], which treats the standard relational algebra. That work grew out of an analysis of [QW91], which in turn was influenced by the notion of 'finite differencing' of [Pai84]. The algorithm for change propagation in [QW91] is an iterative one that propagates changes, one-by-one, to the top of an expression. It was shown in [GLT97] that this is not enough to guarantee strong minimality.

Instead [GLT97] defines recursive functions to compute change sets, as we have done here, and proves correctness by induction.

Another change propagation algorithm for multisets was presented in [GMS93] in the context of a modified Datalog where programs produce multisets. Informally, a tuple's multiplicity in the multiset resulting from the evaluation of a program P indicates the number of different possible *derivations* showing that it was produced by P using Datalog semantics (see [GMS93]).

Given a program P and a transaction t, the change propagation algorithm of [GMS93] produces a program P^{n} by concatenating the clauses of program P with the clauses of a new program $\triangle^{\pm}P$. Concatenation corresponds to the additive union operation. The program $\triangle^{\pm}P$ is defined so that for any database state s, the evaluation of P^{n} in state s will result in the same multiset as the evaluation of program P in the new state $t(s)$. If P is a materialized query, then in order to evaluate P in the new state we need only evaluate the clauses of $\triangle^{\pm}P$ in the old state and form this union with the old (stored) value of P. In order to make this work with deletions, the semantics of [GMS93] allows for *negative* multiplicities in the change sets $\triangle^{\pm}P(s)$.

For example, consider the program

$$\mathrm{minus}(X) \quad :- \quad S(X) \;\&\; \neg T(X).$$

If we have a database transaction that induces changes to both S and T, then the algorithm of [GMS93] produces the program $\triangle^{\pm}\mathrm{minus}$ with clauses

$$\mathrm{minus}(X) \quad :- \quad \triangle^{\pm}S(X) \;\&\; \neg T(X).$$
$$\mathrm{minus}(X) \quad :- \quad S^{\mathrm{n}}(X) \;\&\; \overline{\triangle^{\pm}T}(X).$$

where $\overline{\triangle^{\pm}T}$ computes a set W such that

$$count(x, W) = \begin{cases} -1 & \text{if } x \in \triangle^{\pm}T \text{ and } x \notin T \uplus \triangle^{\pm}T \\ 1 & \text{if } x \in \triangle^{\pm}T \text{ and } x \notin T \\ 0 & \text{otherwise} \end{cases}$$

There are many differences between our approach and that of [GMS93]. First, we are treating different query languages. The nonrecursive fragment of the language of [GMS93] cannot represent our operations of duplicate elimination, monus, min, and max. This follows from general results on the expressive power of bag languages [LW93b]. On the other hand, our language does not handle GROUPBY or recursive queries, as does [GMS93].

Our approach does not require negative multiplicities. If a program P can be represented as a $\mathcal{BA}$ expression $\hat{P}$, then an incremental change program $\triangle^{\pm}P$ can be represented in $\mathcal{BA}$ as a pair of queries $(\triangledown\hat{P}, \triangle\hat{P})$ where $\triangledown\hat{P}$ $(\triangle\hat{P})$ represents those tuples of $\triangle^{\pm}P$ with a negative (positive) multiplicity. Then program P^{n} corresponds to $(\hat{P} \mathbin{\dot{-}} \triangledown\hat{P}) \uplus \triangle\hat{P}$.

This highlights the fact that our approach is *linguistically closed*. That is, we give explicit algebraic representations to *all* expressions generated in change propagation, and these are represented in the language $\mathcal{BA}$. For example, while [GMS93] must extend their language with a new operation in order to evaluate the program $\overline{\triangle^{\pm}T}$, we would represented this operation explicitly as the pair of queries

$$(\epsilon(\triangle(t, T)) \mathbin{\dot{-}} T, \quad \epsilon(\triangledown T) \mathbin{\dot{-}} (T \mathbin{\dot{-}} \triangledown T)).$$

This makes additional optimizations possible, both in the process of generating change expressions and in any later optimization stages.

Next, our approach gives a declarative semantics to change propagation that is not tightly bound to one computational model. That is, we have an *algebraic* approach rather than an *algorithmic* one. This makes correctness proofs much easier, and also simplifies the process of extending the algorithm to new constructs. It also allows us to apply our results to problems other than view maintenance. For example, suppose that we are given the integrity constraint

$$\sigma \overset{\text{def}}{=} (\forall x \in R_1) \; x.a = \text{count} \underbrace{\{|z \in R_2 : z.b = x.b|\}}_{\text{multiset}}$$

and a strongly minimal transaction $t = \{R_2 \leftarrow (R_2 \doteq \triangledown R_2) \uplus \triangle R_2\}$. Furthermore, suppose that we would like to transform t to a *safe* transaction,

$$t' = \; \text{if } \alpha \text{ then } t \text{ else } abort,$$

that can never leave the database in a state violating σ. If we assume that σ will always hold before t' is executed, then we can use our algorithm, together with some logical manipulations, to produce

$$(\forall x \in R_1) \; \text{count}\{|z \in \triangledown R_2 : z.b = x.b|\} = \text{count}\{|z \in \triangle R_2 : z.b = x.b|\}$$

as the formula α. Indeed, this type of problem provided the original motivation for our work [GT94].

Finally, we are able to use the inductive assumptions of strong minimality to further simplify our solutions. Since this information is not available to a general purpose query optimizer, it may fail to produce an efficient solution that can be found with our approach.

A comparison of performance must wait for implementations of the two approaches.

8 Further Work

Our use of strong minimality in the simplification of queries suggests that this information should be available to a *specialized* query optimizer. We are currently working on the design of such an optimizer based on a collection of inference rules for deriving disjointness (for example, if S is disjoint form T, then $S \doteq W$ is disjoint from $T \doteq Z$) and simplification rules that exploit disjointness (for example, if S is disjoint from T, then $S \doteq T$ simplifies to S). The optimization process is initiated by recognizing that all pairs produced by our algorithm, $(\triangledown S, \triangle S)$, are disjoint.

The work of [GMS93] does handle recursive Datalog programs. One current drawback to our approach is that, as with the relational algebra, bag languages such as $\mathcal{BA}$ cannot express recursive queries [LW94b]. We hope to address this issue in the future by extending $\mathcal{BA}$ with loops or a fixed-point operator, as in [GG92, LW93b].

The other extension of our approach deals with complex objects. Our bag algebra $\mathcal{BA}$ is the flat fragment of what was originally designed as an algebra for nested bags. We are currently working on an approach that allows us to extend the equations of the change propagation algorithm to complex objects.

Acknowledgments. We would like to thank Rick Hull for directing our attention to some of the relevant literature, Inderpal Mumick for his very helpful discussions, and Doug McIlroy and Jon Riecke for their careful reading of our working drafts.

16

ALGORITHMS FOR DEFERRED VIEW MAINTENANCE

Latha Colby, Timothy Griffin, Leonid Libkin, Inderpal Singh Mumick, Howard Trickey

ABSTRACT

Materialized views and view maintenance are important for data warehouses, retailing, banking, and billing applications. We consider two related view maintenance problems: 1) how to maintain views after the base tables have already been modified, and 2) how to minimize the time for which the view is inaccessible during maintenance.

Typically, a view is maintained *immediately*, as a part of the transaction that updates the base tables. Immediate maintenance imposes a significant overhead on update transactions that cannot be tolerated in many applications. In contrast, *deferred* maintenance allows a view to become inconsistent with its definition. A *refresh* operation is used to reestablish consistency. We present new algorithms to incrementally refresh a view during deferred maintenance. Our algorithms avoid a *state bug* that has artificially limited techniques previously used for deferred maintenance.

Incremental deferred view maintenance requires auxiliary tables that contain information recorded since the last view refresh. We present three scenarios for the use of auxiliary tables and show how these impact per-transaction overhead and view refresh time. Each scenario is described by an invariant that is required to hold in all database states. We then show that, with the proper choice of auxiliary tables, it is possible to lower both per-transaction overhead and view refresh time.

1 Introduction

Interest in materialized views has increased in recent years [GM96], primarily due to the expanding range of their applications [GM95]. Most of the research on materialized views has focussed on techniques for incrementally updating materialized views when the base tables used to derive the views are updated [BLT86, CW91, GL95, GMS93, Han87, QW91, RK86b, SI84, SP89b].

Maintenance of a view may involve several steps, one of which brings the view table up-to-date. We call this step *refresh*. There may be other steps involved in the process of maintaining a view. For example, it may be necessary to maintain auxiliary tables that store the history of updates to the base tables. View maintenance techniques depend on *when* the view is refreshed. A view can be refreshed within the transaction that updates the base tables, or the refresh can be delayed. The former case is referred to as *immediate* view maintenance, while the latter is called *deferred* view maintenance. Deferred maintenance may be done periodically or on-demand when certain conditions arise. In the past, the term deferred maintenance has sometimes been used for on-demand maintenance.

Most of the work on view maintenance has involved the immediate case [BLT86, CW91, GL95, QW91]. The immediate maintenance approach has the disadvantage that each update transaction incurs the overhead of updating the view. The overhead increases with the number of views and their complexity.

In some applications, immediate view maintenance is simply not possible. For example, in a data warehousing system, if a component database does not know what views exist at the warehouse, it cannot modify transactions updating base tables so that they also refresh materialized views. Even in a centralized system where all the views are known, it may be necessary to minimize the per-transaction overhead imposed by view maintenance. In such cases, deferred maintenance is most appropriate.

Other applications may have a certain tolerance for out-of-date data, or even require that the view be frozen for analysis and other functions [AL80]. In this case, the view could be refreshed periodically or just before querying. Deferred maintenance also allows several updates to be batched together.

This chapter contributes to the work on deferred view maintenance by presenting solutions to the following problems.

Minimize View Downtime By *downtime* we mean the execution time required by the transaction that refreshes the view table. While the view is being refreshed, an exclusive write lock is typically held over the view, and all queries and scans against the view are disallowed. Therefore, we would like to do maintenance in a manner that minimizes the time for which access to the view is blocked (during refresh), and at the same time minimizes the overhead on update transactions.

Avoid the State Bug Incremental view maintenance is typically based on "incremental queries" that avoid the need to recompute a materialized view from scratch. These queries use the updates made to base tables to compute changes that can be directly applied to a materialized view table to bring it up-to-date. Such queries can be evaluated in one of two states: the pre-update state where the base-table changes have not yet been applied, or the post-update state where the base-table changes have been applied. Most of the algorithms for view maintenance assume that the incremental queries are evaluated in the pre-update state. In the deferred case, since the base tables have already been modified, the pre-update algorithms are not directly applicable. In fact, direct application of pre-update algorithms in the post-update state can result in incorrect answers, a fact we call the *state bug*. The state bug can be avoided by severely restricting the class of updates and views considered. However, such restrictions limit the scope of deferred maintenance techniques. What is required is a general post-update algorithm that avoids the state bug and allows a large class of updates and views.

In the rest of the introduction, we elaborate on the above points and outline the contributions of the chapter.

1.1   Minimizing view downtime

Consider the following example, patterned after a real application at a large retailing company.

Example 1.1 Point-of-sale information is collected in a `sales` table, and a `customer` table is used to keep records pertaining to customers. The `sales` table can be very large and can contain duplicates.

$$\texttt{sales}(\text{custId, itemNo, quantity, salesPrice})$$
$$\texttt{customer}(\text{custId, name, address, score})$$

```
CREATE VIEW V (custId, name, score, itemNo, quantity) AS
      SELECT  c.custId, c.name, c.score, s.itemNo,
             s.quantity
      FROM customer c, sales s
      WHERE c.custId = s.custId AND
            s.quantity ! = 0 AND
            c.score = "High" ;
```

Suppose that insertions into the **sales** table are made continuously. The view V, defined above, uses a join of these tables to compute sales made to highly valued customers. (In practice, views with aggregation are more likely. For simplicity, we omit aggregation since it is orthogonal to the problems that we discuss.) Suppose further that this view is materialized in a table MV, and that it is refreshed once every 24 hours. Between refreshes, the table MV is used by decision support applications for market analysis. If we assume that the entire view is write-locked during refresh, then it is important to minimize this view downtime. □

Contribution 1:   We define consistency for databases that support deferred view maintenance in terms of invariants that describe relationships between base tables, materialized views, and auxiliary tables. Solutions to the deferred view maintenance problem are algorithms for extending user transactions with auxiliary operations needed to maintain the view invariants, and additional operations for refreshing materialized view tables. We present three such invariants together with associated algorithms for deferred view maintenance. Each solution can accommodate various update policies, and we present policies that differ in their impact on refresh times and update transaction overhead. One of these policies provides for minimal view downtime while also minimizing the overhead on update transactions.

1.2   Avoiding the state bug

We illustrate the state bug by applying the algorithm of [BLT86] in both pre- and post-update states.

Example 1.2 Let us suppose that we have a view U defined as follows and materialized in table MU (we assume SQL duplicate semantics).

```
CREATE VIEW U (A) AS
      SELECT R.A
      FROM R, S
      WHERE R.B = S.B ;
```

Suppose that the contents of R, S and MU are as shown below.

R:

A	B
a_1	b_1

S:

B	C
b_1	c_1
b_1	c_2
b_2	c_1

MU:

A
a_1
a_1

Suppose that R and S are to be updated by inserting the tuple $[a_1, b_2]$ in R and the tuple $[b_2, c_2]$ in S. We can use the algorithm of [BLT86, Han87] for calculating the incremental update to MU. The algorithm of [BLT86] is a pre-update algorithm that is based on the availability of the base tables before the update. The changes to the view are computed with the incremental query $\triangle MU$, given below (the symbols $\triangle R$ and $\triangle S$ denote bags of tuples inserted into tables R and S):

$$\pi_{R.A}(R \bowtie (\triangle S)) \cup \pi_{R.A}((\triangle R) \bowtie S) \cup \pi_{R.A}((\triangle R) \bowtie (\triangle S))$$

To be consistent with SQL semantics, we assume that all operators have multiset (bag) semantics. Using this equation, the incremental insert to MU can be calculated correctly as $\{[a_1], [a_1]\}$. Now suppose that the same equation is evaluated in a post-update state, i.e., after the tuples $[a_1, b_2]$ and $[b_2, c_2]$ have been inserted in R and S. Then $\triangle MU$ would incorrectly evaluate to $\{[a_1], [a_1], [a_1], [a_1]\}$. □

Example 1.3 We present another example that shows how the state bug can lead to wrong answers other than incorrect multiplicities. Consider a view U defined as $R - S$. Let $R = \{[a], [b], [c]\}$ and $S = \{[c], [d]\}$. In the current state, U is materialized in a table MU that contains tuples $[a]$ and $[b]$. Let t be a transaction that deletes the tuple $[b]$ from R and inserts it into S. Then the algorithms of [QW91, GL95] that extend [BLT86, Han87] to the full relational and bag algebra calculate the delete bag for the view using the following equation (the symbols ∇R, and ∇MU denote bags of tuples deleted from tables R and MU):

$$\nabla MU \;=\; (\nabla R - S) \cup (\triangle S \cap R) \;=\; (\{[b]\} - S) \cup (\{[b]\} \cap R).$$

Note that it is irrelevant which semantics (set or bag) we use as no duplicates are present in any of the tables before or after the transaction. If ∇MU is evaluated in the pre-update state, the result is $\{[b]\}$ and then MU becomes $\{[a]\}$ (which is correct). However, the same expression for ∇MU evaluated in the post-update state, *after* transaction t is applied, yields $\nabla MU = \{\}$, which means that MU is not updated and keeps the incorrect tuple $[b]$! □

In the past, the same algorithm has been used in both pre-update and post-update states. However, the state bug has been avoided either by assuming availability of pre-update base tables in the post-update state, or by considering only restricted classes of views and updates. The first approach is illustrated in [Han87], where *differential tables* are maintained on base tables that contain the *suspended* updates that have not actually been applied to the database state. One problem with this approach is that it slows down the evaluation of all queries over base tables.

As an example of the second approach, [ZGMHW95] investigates view maintenance in a warehousing environment. Their algorithms comprise a standard view maintenance part and a compensating part. The view maintenance part is based on the pre-update algorithm of [BLT86, Han87], but is applied in the post-update state. The state bug is not encountered since their solution imposes restrictions that require (1) updates to change only *one* table, and (2) view definitions to be SPJ queries without self-joins. Their algorithms would yield incorrect results if these restrictions were relaxed.

Other papers dealing with deferred maintenance [KR87, LHM⁺86, SP89b] have considered even smaller (select-project) classes of views. Select-project views are self-maintainable [GJM96] in the sense that such views can be maintained without looking at base tables. Consequently, the issue of pre-update state vs. post-update state of base tables is irrelevant for maintaining select-project views.

Contribution 2:   Our second contribution is to derive algorithms for view maintenance in the post-update state that avoid the state bug. These algorithms work for the full multiset algebra and permit insertions and deletions to any number of tables.

Chapter Outline: After introducing the notation and basic concepts in Section 2, we present, in Section 3, a framework that casts the problem of view maintenance as that of maintaining database invariants.

Four different scenarios are discussed – one for the immediate update of materialized views and three variations on deferred maintenance. In Section 4, we exploit a duality between pre-and post-update states to arrive at incremental algorithms that avoid the state bug and work for a large class of updates and views. Section 5 presents algorithms for solving the three scenarios of deferred view maintenance described in Section 3. We present refresh policies that use these algorithms and solve the problem of minimizing view downtime. Related work is discussed in Section 6. All proofs can be found in the full paper [CGL+96].

2 Preliminaries

2.1 The bag algebra, $\mathcal{BA}$

A bag (or multiset) X is like a set, except that multiple occurrences of elements are allowed. An element x is said to have multiplicity n in the bag X if X contains exactly n copies of x. The notation $x \in X$ means that x has multiplicity $n > 0$ in X, and $x \notin X$ means that x has multiplicity 0 in X.

A database schema is a collection of base table names $\{R_1, \ldots, R_n\}$. A *database state* is a mapping from table names $\{R_1, \ldots, R_n\}$ to finite bags of tuples. We write $R_i(s)$ to denote the value of table R_i in the state s.

Our query language will be the bag algebra of [GM93, LW94c], restricted to flat bags (bags of tuples, i.e., no bag-valued attributes). Let p range over quantifier-free predicates, and A range over sets of attribute names. $\mathcal{BA}$ expressions are generated by the following grammar.

$$
\begin{array}{llll}
Q & ::= & \phi & \text{empty bag} \\
  & | & \{x\} & \text{singleton bag} \\
  & | & R & \text{table name} \\
  & | & \sigma_p(Q) & \text{selection} \\
  & | & \Pi_A(Q) & \text{projection} \\
  & | & \epsilon(Q) & \text{duplicate elimination} \\
  & | & Q_1 \uplus Q_2 & \text{additive union} \\
  & | & Q_1 \dot{-} Q_2 & \text{monus} \\
  & | & Q_1 \times Q_2 & \text{cartesian product}
\end{array}
$$

We will use the symbols Q, Q_1, Q_2, E, and F to denote $\mathcal{BA}$ expressions, which will usually be called *queries*. If s is a database state and Q is a query, then $Q(s)$ denotes the multiset resulting from evaluating Q in the state s.

The only operation that may require explanation is monus. If x occurs n times in Q_1 and m times in Q_2, then the number of occurrences of x in $Q_1 \dot{-} Q_2$ is the maximum of 0 and $n - m$. Monus corresponds to the `EXCEPT ALL` operation in SQL-92 [MS93a]. The SQL `EXCEPT` operator differs in that Q_1 `EXCEPT` Q_2 eliminates *all* tuples that occur in Q_2, no matter what their multiplicity, and in addition this operation eliminates duplicates in the result. The `EXCEPT` operation can be defined in our bag language as

$$Q_1 \text{ EXCEPT } Q_2 \stackrel{\text{def}}{=} \epsilon(Q_1) \dot{-} Q_2$$

We include monus in our bag algebra because it cannot be defined using `EXCEPT` and the rest of $\mathcal{BA}$. This follows from the characterization of interdefinability of the operations of $\mathcal{BA}$ in [GM93, LW94c].

We will also use the operations $Q_1 \min Q_2$ (minimal intersection) and $Q_1 \max Q_2$ (maximal union) that create bags in which the multiplicity of any tuple is the minimum (maximum) of its multiplicities in Q_1 and Q_2. These can be defined in $\mathcal{BA}$ as $Q_1 \min Q_2 \stackrel{\text{def}}{=} Q_1 \dot{-} (Q_1 \dot{-} Q_2)$ and $Q_1 \max Q_2 \stackrel{\text{def}}{=} Q_1 \uplus (Q_2 \dot{-} Q_1)$.

For arbitrary queries Q_1 and Q_2 we use the notation $Q_1 \equiv Q_2$ to mean that for all database states s, $Q_1(s) = Q_2(s)$. The notation $Q_1 \subseteq Q_2$ means that for all database states s, $Q_1(s)$ is a subbag of $Q_2(s)$.

2.2   Transactions

Transactions $\mathcal{T}$ are functions from states to states. If s is a database state, then $\mathcal{T}(s)$ is the state resulting from the execution of transaction $\mathcal{T}$ in state s. $Q(\mathcal{T}(s))$ represents the value of query Q after $\mathcal{T}$ is executed in state s.

We consider *abstract transactions* defined with the notation

$$\mathcal{T} = \{R_1 := Q_1, \ldots, R_n := Q_n\},$$

abbreviated as $\mathcal{T} = \{R_i := Q_i\}$. When $\mathcal{T}$ is executed in state s, then the value of R_i in state $\mathcal{T}(s)$ becomes $Q_i(s)$. That is, $\mathcal{T}$ executed in state s has the effect of simultaneously replacing the contents of each R_i with the result of evaluating query Q_i in state s.

Since we only consider view maintenance in response to insertions and deletions into base tables caused by a transaction, we will consider only *simple transactions* $\mathcal{T}$ of the form

$$\{R_1 := (R_1 \doteq \nabla R_1) \uplus \triangle R_1, \ldots, R_n := (R_n \doteq \nabla R_n) \uplus \triangle R_n\}.$$

In other words, the value of R_i in state $\mathcal{T}(s)$ is $((R_i \doteq \nabla R_i) \uplus \triangle R_i)(s)$. This is without loss of generality since any abstract transaction can be transformed to an equivalent simple transaction.

2.3   Logs and differential tables

A log $\mathcal{L}$ is a collection of auxiliary base tables $\blacktriangledown R_1, \blacktriangle R_1, \ldots, \blacktriangledown R_n, \blacktriangle R_n$. Suppose that database states are ordered and $s_p \leq s_c$, where s_p represents a state of the database that existed before the database entered state s_c. Informally, think of s_p as a *past* state and s_c as the *current state*. A log $\mathcal{L}$ *records the transition from state s_p to the state s_c*, written $s_p \xrightarrow{\mathcal{L}} s_c$, if, for each table R_i,

$$R_i(s_p) = ((R_i \doteq \blacktriangle R_i) \uplus \blacktriangledown R_i)(s_c).$$

That is, log $\mathcal{L}$ records all deletions ($\blacktriangledown R_i$) from and insertions ($\blacktriangle R_i$) into each table R_i that comprise the transition from state s_p to state s_c. Note that in order to compute the past value of R_i from the value of R_i in the current state, we must *delete* the bag that was inserted and *insert* the bag that was deleted. A similar technique is used in [CW91] with transition tables, which can be thought of as transient logs.

Our notion of logs is not the same as that of differential tables introduced in [SL76]. The tables B, A, and D are differential tables for table R if $R = (B \doteq D) \uplus A$. In this approach, every "base table" R is treated as a virtual table (view). Tables D and A can be thought of as suspended deletions and insertions, while B represents an "old" value of the table R. In contrast, our notion of a log assumes that the changes have been applied to the base tables.

A word about our use of white triangles (∇ and $\triangle$) and black triangles ($\blacktriangledown$ and $\blacktriangle$). The white triangles represent changes specified by the transactions, or changes computed from those specified in the transactions. The black triangles represent changes in the log or changes computed from the log.

2.4 Substitutions

We will denote general substitutions with the notation $\eta = [Q_1/R_1, \cdots, Q_n/R_n]$. The notation $\eta(Q)$ denotes the query that results from simultaneously replacing every occurrence of R_i in Q by Q_i. For example, if η is $[\epsilon(R_2)/R_1, \sigma_q(R_1)/R_2]$ and Q is $\sigma_p(R_1 \times R_2)$, then $\eta(Q)$ is $\sigma_p(\epsilon(R_2) \times \sigma_q(R_1))$.

The next subsection will make use of two substitutions $\widehat{\mathcal{T}}$ and $\widehat{\mathcal{L}}$ that are derived from simple transactions $\mathcal{T}$ and logs $\mathcal{L}$ as:

$$[((R_1 \div \nabla R_1) \uplus \triangle R_1)/R_1, \ldots, ((R_n \div \nabla R_n) \uplus \triangle R_n)/R_n]$$

and

$$[((R_1 \div \blacktriangle R_1) \uplus \blacktriangledown R_1)/R_1, \ldots, ((R_n \div \blacktriangle R_n) \uplus \blacktriangledown R_n)/R_n]$$

2.5 Past and future queries

Past and future queries are the key concepts of view maintenance as they allow us to compute the value of a query in a state that is different from the current one.

Sambadefinition 1 (Past and Future Queries):

1. Suppose s_p is a state that precedes state s_c. A query PQ is a *past-query* at state s_c for a query Q at s_p if $Q(s_p) = PQ(s_c)$. Informally, we can evaluate a past-query PQ in the current state in order to determine the value that Q had in an earlier state.

2. A query FQ is called a *future-query* at state s_p for Q at state s_c if $FQ(s_p) = Q(s_c)$. We call FQ a *future-query* for Q with respect to a transaction $\mathcal{T}$ if for every database state s we have $FQ(s) = Q(\mathcal{T}(s))$. That is, if the database is currently in state s, then we can evaluate FQ in order to determine the "future" value that query Q will have in the state immediately after $\mathcal{T}$ is executed. $\square$

Transactions and logs can be used to compute future- and past-queries. If $\mathcal{T}$ is a simple transaction, then FUTURE$(\mathcal{T}, Q)$ defined as

$$\widehat{\mathcal{T}}(Q) \equiv Q((R_1 \div \nabla R_1) \uplus \triangle R_1, \ldots, (R_n \div \nabla R_n) \uplus \triangle R_n)$$

is a future-query for $Q(R_1, \ldots, R_n)$ with respect to $\mathcal{T}$. Indeed, for any state s, $(\text{FUTURE}(\mathcal{T}, Q))(s) = Q(\mathcal{T}(s))$.

If $\mathcal{L}$ is a log from state s_p to state s_c, then the values of R_i at s_p can be computed from the values of R_i at s_c and the log as $R_i(s_p) = ((R_i \div \blacktriangle R_i) \uplus \blacktriangledown R_i)(s_c)$. Therefore, PAST$(\mathcal{L}, Q)$ defined as

$$\widehat{\mathcal{L}}(Q) \equiv Q((R_1 \div \blacktriangle R_1) \uplus \blacktriangledown R_1, \ldots, (R_n \div \blacktriangle R_n) \uplus \blacktriangledown R_n)$$

is a past-query, at state s_c for Q at state s_p. That is, $Q(s_p) = (\text{PAST}(\mathcal{L}, Q))(s_c)$.

In summary, future-queries allow us to *anticipate* state changes, while past-queries allow us to *compensate* for changes that have already been made.

3   View Maintenance Scenarios

In what follows, the view V is defined by a query Q and materialized in the table MV. A materialized view is said to be consistent with its definition in state s if $Q(s) = MV(s)$.

Any correct solution to the immediate view maintenance problem must guarantee that the contents of the view table MV always be consistent with the definition of the view V. In other words, the formula $Q \equiv MV$ is an *invariant* that should hold in all database states. Any solution to the immediate view maintenance problem must then employ some method of augmenting user transactions with the updates to table MV needed to maintain this invariant.

This section demonstrates that the same approach can be used to characterize deferred view maintenance problems. We use database invariants to specify three deferred view maintenance scenarios. For each invariant, we specify algorithms for transforming user transactions into ones that maintain the invariant. These invariants are more complex than the immediate case since they must relate table MV to query Q as well as auxiliary tables. Unlike the immediate case, the deferred scenarios also require additional algorithms for refreshing view tables as well as for propagating changes to auxiliary tables. For each scenario considered, we explain the main idea behind the associated view maintenance algorithms. The details of the algorithms will be given in Section 5.

3.1   Database invariants

First, we need to introduce some terminology. For formula α and database state s, the notation $s \models \alpha$ means that α holds in state s. Given formulas α, β, and a transaction T, we will use the *Hoare triple* $\{\alpha\}T\{\beta\}$ (see [Gri81]) to assert that for every state s, if $s \models \alpha$, then $T(s) \models \beta$. A transaction T is said to be *safe for* α if $\{\alpha\}T\{\alpha\}$. That is, if α holds in a given state, then it will hold in the state after T is executed.

We assume that the database tables are partitioned into *external* tables that can be changed by user transactions (user-defined base tables) and *internal* tables that are used to store and support materialized views (such as MV, log tables, and view differential files). User transactions are not allowed to directly update internal tables.

A formula is called a *database invariant* if it is guaranteed to hold in every state. We shall denote database invariants by $\mathbb{INV}_*$ where the index $*$ specifies a named scenario for view maintenance. Given an invariant $\mathbb{INV}_*$ and a user transaction T, it cannot be expected that T will be safe for $\mathbb{INV}_*$. Thus, each scenario requires an algorithm for transforming any user transaction T into a transaction $\mathsf{makesafe}_*[T]$ that is safe for $\mathbb{INV}_*$. This transaction should have the same behavior as T on external tables. Hence, $\mathsf{makesafe}_*[T]$ will augment T with changes to internal tables.

The scenarios describing deferred maintenance will also require various auxiliary functions to *refresh* view tables. For each $\mathbb{INV}_*$, we will define a transaction $\mathsf{refresh}_*$ such that $\{\mathbb{INV}_*\}\mathsf{refresh}_*\{Q \equiv MV\}$.

3.2   Immediate maintenance

We review the immediate update scenario in order to facilitate comparison with the deferred scenarios.

Suppose that we require that the table MV always be consistent with its definition. As noted, this amounts to declaring the formula below to be a database invariant.

$\mathbb{INV}_{\mathrm{IM}}$
$$\boxed{Q \equiv MV}$$

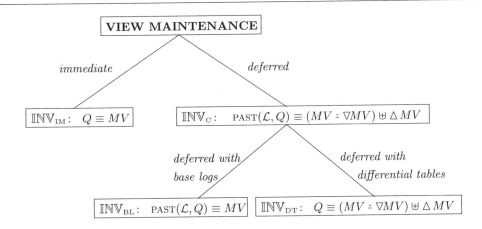

Figure 1 Invariants for view maintenance

The literature on immediate view maintenance [BLT86, CW91, GL95, QW91, SI84] presents various approaches to converting any transaction $\mathcal{T}$ to a transaction $\mathsf{makesafe}_{\mathrm{IM}}[\mathcal{T}]$ that is guaranteed to maintain $\mathbb{INV}_{\mathrm{IM}}$. The method of choice is to produce *incremental queries*, $\nabla(\mathcal{T}, Q)$ and $\triangle(\mathcal{T}, Q)$, such that augmenting $\mathcal{T}$ with

$$MV := (MV \doteq \nabla(\mathcal{T}, Q)) \uplus \triangle(\mathcal{T}, Q)$$

correctly maintains the view. Note that the incremental queries are typically evaluated in the state *before* the updates of $\mathcal{T}$ have been applied.

Although incremental queries can avoid the work of recomputing Q from scratch, their evaluation can still impose a large per-transaction overhead.

3.3   Deferred maintenance with base logs

Suppose that the table MV is allowed to become inconsistent with the definition of view V. This means that the content of table MV is equal to the value of Q in some *past* state when MV was last refreshed or was initialized. Suppose that log $\mathcal{L}$ records the changes made to base tables that make up the transition from this past state to the current state. This scenario can be captured with the invariant

$$\mathbb{INV}_{\mathrm{BL}} \qquad \boxed{\mathrm{PAST}(\mathcal{L}, Q) \;\equiv\; MV}$$

Note that if the log is empty, then the view table is consistent since in this case $Q \equiv \mathrm{PAST}(\mathcal{L}, Q)$. A solution to this scenario involves defining the transformation $\mathsf{makesafe}_{\mathrm{BL}}[.]$ that maintains the invariant and a function $\mathsf{refresh}_{\mathrm{BL}}$ that brings the view up-to-date.

For any user transaction $\mathcal{T}$, $\mathsf{makesafe}_{\mathrm{BL}}[\mathcal{T}]$ must do two things: (1) execute $\mathcal{T}$, and (2) correctly extend the log $\mathcal{L}$ in order to maintain the invariant. This imposes little overhead on each transaction since we only need to record the changes made to base tables.

The refresh function must satisfy the specification $\{\mathbb{INV}_{\text{BL}}\}\text{refresh}_{\text{BL}}\{Q \equiv MV\}$. In a manner similar to the immediate case, we could formulate incremental queries, $\blacktriangledown(\mathcal{L}, Q)$ and $\blacktriangle(\mathcal{L}, Q)$, such that the transaction

$$MV := (MV \doteq \blacktriangledown(\mathcal{L}, Q)) \uplus \blacktriangle(\mathcal{L}, Q)$$

correctly refreshes the table MV. Unlike the immediate case, these incremental queries must be evaluated in a post-update state that reflects the changes recorded in log $\mathcal{L}$. In Section 4, we present a technique for computing incremental queries for post-update states.

We should expect that in most cases this incremental approach will be much less expensive than recomputing Q from scratch. However, the computation of the incremental queries still may be costly, which implies a high refresh time.

3.4 Deferred maintenance with differential tables for views

Many applications require a low refresh time. One way to minimize view downtime is to precompute the changes necessary for refreshing table MV and store them in "differential tables." This scenario can be captured with the invariant

$\mathbb{INV}_{\text{DT}}$
$$\boxed{Q \equiv (MV \doteq \triangledown MV) \uplus \triangle MV}$$

where $\triangledown MV$ and $\triangle MV$ are the differential tables that maintain the changes needed to bring the view table up-to-date. Another way of saying this is that the differential tables record the difference of the past value of Q (stored in MV) and its current value. Note that if the differential tables are empty, then the view table MV is consistent.

The refresh function in this case applies the differential tables to MV,

$$MV := (MV \doteq \triangledown MV) \uplus \triangle MV,$$

and empties them. If the differential tables contain exactly the *net change* needed to refresh MV (that is, $\triangledown MV \subseteq MV$ and $\triangledown MV \min \triangle MV \equiv \phi$), then this represents the *minimal* possible refresh time for MV.

However, as in the immediate update case, the per-transaction overhead for maintaining the invariant may be high since $\text{makesafe}_{\text{DT}}[\mathcal{T}]$ must maintain correct values for $\triangledown MV$ and $\triangle MV$.

3.5 Deferred maintenance with differential tables and base logs

One of our goals is to present a new solution to the deferred view maintenance problem that provides (1) a fast refresh algorithm, and (2) low per-transaction overhead for maintaining auxiliary information.

Our solution combines the last two approaches. We maintain *both* a log $\mathcal{L}$ on base tables *and* a pair of differential tables, $\triangledown MV$ and $\triangle MV$, for the view table MV. The combined invariant is

$\mathbb{INV}_{\text{C}}$
$$\boxed{\text{PAST}(\mathcal{L}, Q) \equiv (MV \doteq \triangledown MV) \uplus \triangle MV}$$

To understand this scenario, it helps to keep in mind three different states: (1) a past state s_p such that the table MV is consistent with Q in state s_p, (2) the current database state s_c, and (3) an intermediate state s_i, with $s_p \leq s_i \leq s_c$. The log $\mathcal{L}$ records the transition from s_i to s_c. That is, in this scenario the log is used to maintain the *view differential tables* (∇MV and $\triangle MV$), and records the changes to the base tables made since the last refresh of the differential tables (in state s_i). If the differential tables are applied to the view table MV to refresh it, then the contents of the table MV will correspond to the value that Q had in state s_i, when the log was initialized. That is, updating MV using the differential tables gives us the value of the past query for Q, $\text{PAST}(\mathcal{L}, Q)$.

The transaction $\mathsf{makesafe}_{\text{C}}[T]$ is essentially the same as $\mathsf{makesafe}_{\text{BL}}[T]$ — it only needs to update the log in order to maintain invariant $\mathbb{INV}_{\text{C}}$. The refresh function for this scenario must satisfy the specification $\{\mathbb{INV}_{\text{C}}\}\mathsf{refresh}_{\text{C}}\{Q \equiv MV\}$. In addition, this scenario suggests two auxiliary transactions: a transaction $\mathsf{propagate}_{\text{C}}$, that propagates to the differential tables the changes recorded in the log $\mathcal{L}$, and a transaction $\mathsf{partial\_refresh}_{\text{C}}$, that partially refreshes the view table by applying the differential tables. These transactions have the specifications:

$$\{\mathbb{INV}_{\text{C}}\} \ \mathsf{propagate}_{\text{C}} \ \{Q \equiv (MV \dot{-} \nabla MV) \uplus \triangle MV\},$$

$$\{\mathbb{INV}_{\text{C}}\} \ \mathsf{partial\_refresh}_{\text{C}} \ \{\text{PAST}(\mathcal{L}, Q) \equiv MV\}.$$

By decoupling incremental computation from *both* $\mathsf{refresh}_{\text{C}}$ and $\mathsf{makesafe}_{\text{C}}[T]$, these auxiliary transactions will allow us to achieve our goal of low refresh time while simultaneously obtaining low per-transaction overhead. A more detailed discussion is presented in Section 5. Here we are only interested in a formal specification of this scenario.

Figure 1 summarizes the four invariants that describe different scenarios for view maintenance. Note that both the $\mathbb{INV}_{\text{BL}}$ and $\mathbb{INV}_{\text{DT}}$ scenarios can be considered as special cases of the $\mathbb{INV}_{\text{C}}$ scenario.

4 Exploiting Duality

As mentioned in the previous section, the method of choice for solving the immediate view maintenance problem involves finding incremental queries $\nabla(T, Q)$ and $\triangle(T, Q)$ such that the operation

$$MV := (MV \dot{-} \nabla(T, Q)) \uplus \triangle(T, Q)$$

will correctly update the materialized view, provided that the queries $\nabla(T, Q)$ and $\triangle(T, Q)$ are evaluated in the *pre-update* database state. This amounts to solving for $\nabla(T, Q)$ and $\triangle(T, Q)$ in the equation

(1) $$\text{FUTURE}(T, Q) \equiv (Q \dot{-} \nabla(T, Q)) \uplus \triangle(T, Q)$$

since table MV is assumed to contain the current value of Q and we wish to update MV to contain the value that Q will have in the future, after T is executed. An example of such an algorithm for the bag algebra can be found in [GL95].

Now let us turn to the simple case of deferred maintenance. Suppose that MV was initialized or last refreshed at state s_p and the database is currently in state s_c. Suppose that $\mathcal{L}$ is a log from s_p to s_c. In order to incrementally refresh MV we want to find two queries $\blacktriangledown(\mathcal{L}, Q)$ and $\blacktriangle(\mathcal{L}, Q)$ such that the operation

$$MV := (MV \dot{-} \blacktriangledown(\mathcal{L}, Q)) \uplus \blacktriangle(\mathcal{L}, Q)$$

will correctly update the materialized view.

Note that these incremental queries must be evaluated in the *post-update* database state that reflects all of the changes recorded in $\mathcal{L}$. Finding such incremental queries amounts to solving for $\blacktriangledown(\mathcal{L}, Q)$ and $\blacktriangle(\mathcal{L}, Q)$ in the equation

$$(2) \qquad\qquad Q \equiv (\text{PAST}(\mathcal{L}, Q) \dot{-} \blacktriangledown(\mathcal{L}, Q)) \uplus \blacktriangle(\mathcal{L}, Q)$$

since table MV is assumed to contain the past value of Q and we wish to update MV to contain the current value of Q.

Can we use the same algorithm for the pre- and post-update states? As we have indicated (see Section 1.2), this cannot be done directly without producing incorrect results. There is, however, a natural *duality* between future- and past-queries that can be exploited to solve this problem. Recall from Section 2.5 that both of these queries are formed as substitution instances,

$$\text{FUTURE}(\mathcal{T}, Q) \stackrel{\text{def}}{=} \widehat{\mathcal{T}}(Q), \quad \text{PAST}(\mathcal{L}, Q) \stackrel{\text{def}}{=} \widehat{\mathcal{L}}(Q)$$

and that each query is formed by replacing every occurrence of a base table name R_i with a query of the form $(R_i \dot{-} D_i) \uplus A_i$. However, the roles of insertions and deletions are reversed since future-queries anticipate the changes that a transaction will make, while past-queries compensate for changes that have already been made.

Suppose that η is a substitution (see Section 2.4), and suppose that we have a method for constructing queries $\text{DEL}(\eta, Q)$ and $\text{ADD}(\eta, Q)$ such that

$$(3) \qquad\qquad \eta(Q) \equiv (Q \dot{-} \text{DEL}(\eta, Q)) \uplus \text{ADD}(\eta, Q).$$

Algorithms that produce the queries $\text{DEL}(\eta, Q)$ and $\text{ADD}(\eta, Q)$ are called *differential algorithms* (terminology is from [Pai84]). Solving Equation (1) is then simply a matter of defining $\triangledown(\mathcal{T}, Q)$ and $\triangle(\mathcal{T}, Q)$ as

$$\triangledown(\mathcal{T}, Q) \stackrel{\text{def}}{=} \text{DEL}(\widehat{\mathcal{T}}, Q), \quad \triangle(\mathcal{T}, Q) \stackrel{\text{def}}{=} \text{ADD}(\widehat{\mathcal{T}}, Q).$$

Solving (2) for $\blacktriangledown(\mathcal{L}, Q)$ and $\blacktriangle(\mathcal{L}, Q)$ is not quite so simple. First, applying Equation (3) with $\eta = \widehat{\mathcal{L}}$ results in

$$\text{PAST}(\mathcal{L}, Q) \equiv \widehat{\mathcal{L}}(Q) \equiv (Q \dot{-} \text{DEL}(\widehat{\mathcal{L}}, Q)) \uplus \text{ADD}(\widehat{\mathcal{L}}, Q).$$

Now in order to solve Equation (2) we must "cancel" the incremental queries. We can do this using the following lemma.

Lemma 1 (cancellation) *Suppose that N, O, I, and D are queries. If $N \equiv (O \dot{-} D) \uplus I$, then $O \equiv (N \dot{-} I) \uplus (O \min D)$.* $\qquad\square$

Applying this lemma to the above equation yields

$$Q \equiv (\text{PAST}(\mathcal{L}, Q) \dot{-} \text{ADD}(\widehat{\mathcal{L}}, Q)) \uplus (Q \min \text{DEL}(\widehat{\mathcal{L}}, Q)).$$

Therefore, (2) can be solved by defining the queries $\blacktriangledown(\mathcal{L}, Q)$ and $\blacktriangle(\mathcal{L}, Q)$ as

$$\blacktriangledown(\mathcal{L}, Q) \stackrel{\text{def}}{=} \text{ADD}(\widehat{\mathcal{L}}, Q)$$

$$\blacktriangle(\mathcal{L}, Q) \stackrel{\text{def}}{=} Q \min \text{DEL}(\widehat{\mathcal{L}}, Q).$$

4.1 Incremental computation

Note that the query $\blacktriangle(\mathcal{L}, Q) \stackrel{\text{def}}{=} Q \min \text{DEL}(\widehat{\mathcal{L}}, Q)$ could be rewritten to the simpler form $\text{DEL}(\widehat{\mathcal{L}}, Q)$, if we knew that $\text{DEL}(\widehat{\mathcal{L}}, Q) \subseteq Q$. This is related to the "minimality" conditions of [GL95, QW91]. These conditions limit the number of unnecessary tuples produced by the incremental change queries.

The minimality constraints typically imposed on $\text{DEL}(\eta, Q)$ and $\text{ADD}(\eta, Q)$ are

(a) $\text{DEL}(\eta, Q) \subseteq Q$: Only tuples actually in Q are in the deleted bag.

(b) $\text{DEL}(\eta, Q) \min \text{ADD}(\eta, Q) \equiv \phi$: No tuple is deleted and then reinserted.

The design of differential algorithms to compute $\text{DEL}(\eta, Q)$ and $\text{ADD}(\eta, Q)$ then involves a choice of imposing none of these constraints, or of imposing one of the three possible combinations of them. A solution meeting condition (a) will be called *weakly minimal*, while a solution meeting both conditions (a) and (b) will be called *strongly minimal*. In this chapter, we present algorithms that produce weakly minimal solutions, for which the following simpler equations hold:

$$\blacktriangledown(\mathcal{L}, Q) \stackrel{\text{def}}{=} \text{ADD}(\widehat{\mathcal{L}}, Q)$$

$$\blacktriangle(\mathcal{L}, Q) \stackrel{\text{def}}{=} \text{DEL}(\widehat{\mathcal{L}}, Q).$$

We will assume that every substitution $\eta = [Q_1/R_1, \cdots, Q_n/R_n]$ has a *factored* form. That is, every query Q_i is of the form $(R_i \dotdiv D_i) \uplus A_i$. Note that (1) if $\eta = \widehat{\mathcal{T}}$, then $D_i = \nabla R_i$ and $A_i = \triangle R_i$, and (2) if $\eta = \widehat{\mathcal{L}}$, then $D_i = \blacktriangle R_i$ and $A_i = \blacktriangledown R_i$.

A factored substitution is called *weakly minimal* if $D_i \subseteq R_i$. Note that any factored substitution η can be transformed into an equivalent weakly or strongly minimal substitution.

A simple transaction is called weakly minimal if $\widehat{\mathcal{T}}$ is a weakly minimal substitution. Similarly, a log $\mathcal{L}$ is called weakly minimal if $\widehat{\mathcal{L}}$ is a weakly minimal substitution. This amounts to declaring that $\blacktriangle R_i \subseteq R_i$ is a database invariant, for each table R_i. As we will see in the next section, care must be taken to guarantee that these invariants are maintained.

Figure 2 presents our algorithm for calculating $\text{DEL}(\eta, Q)$ and $\text{ADD}(\eta, Q)$ for weakly minimal substitutions. When Q is ϕ or $\{x\}$, then $\text{DEL}(\eta, Q) \equiv \text{ADD}(\eta, Q) \equiv \phi$. This algorithm is derived from the same change propagation rules for the bag algebra that were used in [GL95] to derive a strongly minimal algorithm. The functions $\nabla(\mathcal{T}, Q), \triangle(\mathcal{T}, Q), \blacktriangledown(\mathcal{L}, Q), \blacktriangle(\mathcal{L}, Q)$ can be derived straightforwardly from Figure 2. For example, the equation for $\text{DEL}(\eta, E \dotdiv F)$ in Figure 2 gives rise to the equation

$$\nabla(\mathcal{T}, E \dotdiv F) \stackrel{\text{def}}{=} (\nabla(\mathcal{T}, E) \uplus \triangle(\mathcal{T}, F)) \min (E \dotdiv F),$$

as well as its dual equation

$$\blacktriangle(\mathcal{L}, E \dotdiv F) \stackrel{\text{def}}{=} (\blacktriangle(\mathcal{L}, E) \uplus \blacktriangledown(\mathcal{L}, F)) \min (E \dotdiv F).$$

Theorem 2 (Correctness of Differentiation) *For any query Q and any weakly minimal substitution η,*

(a) $\eta(Q) \equiv (Q \dotdiv \text{DEL}(\eta, Q)) \uplus \text{ADD}(\eta, Q),$

Q	$\text{DEL}(\eta, Q)$
R_i	$D_i, \qquad$ where $\eta(R_i) = (R_i \doteq D_i) \uplus A_i$
$\sigma_p(E)$	$\sigma_p(\text{DEL}(\eta, E))$
$\Pi_A(E)$	$\Pi_A(\text{DEL}(\eta, E))$
$\epsilon(E)$	$\epsilon(\text{DEL}(\eta, E)) \doteq (E \doteq \text{DEL}(\eta, E))$
$E \uplus F$	$\text{DEL}(\eta, E) \uplus \text{DEL}(\eta, F)$
$E \doteq F$	$(\text{DEL}(\eta, E) \uplus \text{ADD}(\eta, F)) \min (E \doteq F)$
$E \times F$	$(\text{DEL}(\eta, E) \times \text{DEL}(\eta, F)) \uplus$ $(\text{DEL}(\eta, E) \times (F \doteq \text{DEL}(\eta, F))) \uplus$ $((E \doteq \text{DEL}(\eta, E)) \times \text{DEL}(\eta, F))$

Q	$\text{ADD}(\eta, Q)$
R_i	$A_i, \qquad$ where $\eta(R_i) = (R_i \doteq D_i) \uplus A_i$
$\sigma_p(E)$	$\sigma_p(\text{ADD}(\eta, E))$
$\Pi_A(E)$	$\Pi_A(\text{ADD}(\eta, E))$
$\epsilon(E)$	$\epsilon(\text{ADD}(\eta, E)) \doteq (E \doteq \text{DEL}(\eta, E))$
$E \uplus F$	$\text{ADD}(\eta, E) \uplus \text{ADD}(\eta, F)$
$E \doteq F$	$((\text{ADD}(\eta, E) \uplus \text{DEL}(\eta, F)) \doteq (F \doteq E)) \doteq$ $((\text{DEL}(\eta, E) \uplus \text{ADD}(\eta, F)) \doteq (E \doteq F))$
$E \times F$	$(\text{ADD}(\eta, E) \times \text{ADD}(\eta, F)) \uplus$ $(\text{ADD}(\eta, E) \times (F \doteq \text{DEL}(\eta, F))) \uplus$ $((E \doteq \text{DEL}(\eta, E)) \times \text{ADD}(\eta, F))$

Figure 2   Mutually Recursive functions $\text{DEL}(\eta, Q)$ and $\text{ADD}(\eta, Q)$.

(b) $\text{DEL}(\eta, Q) \subseteq Q$. $\square$

It can be verified that our post-update algorithm gives the correct answers in the examples presented in Section 1.2.

One of the reasons that we chose to use a weakly minimal solution in this chapter is that the expressions are somewhat less complicated than for other solutions, and the algorithm can be seen as a generalization of [BLT86, Han87] to the full bag algebra $\mathcal{BA}$.

It should be emphasized that the issue of minimality of incremental algorithms is completely *orthogonal* to the problem of maintaining views in a deferred manner. Any abstract transaction can be transformed into an equivalent (weakly or strongly) minimal simple transaction, and the same is true for logs. The algorithms in Figure 2, and those of Section 5.1 could be modified to maintain any combination of the minimality conditions (a) and (b), including no minimality constraints at all. For example, in order to produce a strongly minimal solution, one could use the strongly minimal incremental algorithm presented in [GL95], and then modify the algorithms in Figure 3 by enforcing strong minimality.

4.2   How the state bug has been avoided

There are two ways of directly using the pre-update algorithm in the post-update state. The first is exemplified by [Han87], where differential tables are used to suspend the application of changes to database tables. In other words, updates are not actually applied but simply stored in differential tables. Past values of base tables are directly available and do not have to be computed. In this way, the pre-update algorithm will give the correct result. However, this approach is not sufficiently general since it assumes that all database tables are implemented with differential tables. This assumption may be unrealistic in many applications.

The second method can be explained with this observation:

Remark 1 *For certain* restricted *classes of views and updates, the equations derived by the pre-update and post-update algorithms produce the same results upon evaluation in the post-update state.*

For example, it can be shown that if Q is an SPJ query without self-joins, $\mathcal{T}$ is a weakly minimal transaction that inserts into and/or deletes from a single table R, and log $\mathcal{L}$ records only the changes of one such transaction $\mathcal{T}$, then $\triangledown(\mathcal{T}, Q) \equiv \blacktriangledown(\mathcal{L}, Q)$ and $\triangle(\mathcal{T}, Q) \equiv \blacktriangle(\mathcal{L}, Q)$.

If these restrictions are relaxed even slightly (i.e., an SPJ query is allowed to have self-joins, or multiple tables are updated), then it is easy to find examples of views and/or updates for which the pre-update algorithms of [BLT86, GL95, Han87, QW91] will give incorrect results if the incremental queries are evaluated in the post-update state.

5   Algorithms and Policies

This section presents algorithmic solutions for the three scenarios of deferred view maintenance described in Section 3. Each set of algorithms can be used to implement a wide range of view update *policies*. By a *policy* we mean a scheme by which the refresh functions are actually invoked for a given view. For example, in the simple scenario defined by invariant $\mathbb{INV}_{\text{BL}}$, the function $\mathsf{refresh}_{\text{BL}}$ could be invoked (1) only on demand by a user, (2) whenever the table MV is queried, or (3) in a periodic way. The section ends with a presentation of two policies for the $\mathbb{INV}_{\text{C}}$ scenario that can be used to minimize view downtime.

5.1   Algorithms

Figure 3 presents algorithmic solutions for the three scenarios of deferred view maintenance described in Section 3. The notation $\mathcal{L}:=\phi$ is used to abbreviate the operations needed to empty log tables ($\blacktriangledown R_1:=\phi, \dots,$ $\blacktriangle R_n:=\phi$). If $\mathcal{T}_1$ and $\mathcal{T}_2$ are transactions, then $\mathcal{T}_1 + \mathcal{T}_2$ denotes the transaction that has the same behavior as performing the operations of $\mathcal{T}_1$ and $\mathcal{T}_2$ simultaneously. That is, we may view $\mathcal{T}_1 + \mathcal{T}_2$ as performing $\mathcal{T}_1$ and $\mathcal{T}_2$ in a way that operations in $\mathcal{T}_1$ do not see the effect of operations in $\mathcal{T}_2$, and vice versa.

These high-level algorithms are built from two main components: the pre- and post-update differential algorithms presented in Section 4, and a method for composing two sequential updates into a single update. The latter is provided by the following lemma.

Lemma 3 (Weakly Minimal Composition) *Suppose that O, I_1, I_2, D_1 and D_2 are queries such that $D_1 \subseteq O$ and $D_2 \subseteq (O \doteq D_1) \uplus I_1$. Let $D_3 \stackrel{\text{def}}{=} D_1 \uplus (D_2 \doteq I_1)$ and $I_3 \stackrel{\text{def}}{=} (I_1 \doteq D_2) \uplus I_2$. Then*

(a) $(((O \doteq D_1) \uplus I_1) \doteq D_2) \uplus I_2 \equiv (O \doteq D_3) \uplus I_3,$

$$\mathbb{INV}_{\mathrm{BL}}:\ \mathrm{PAST}(\mathcal{L}, Q)\ \equiv\ MV$$

$$\mathsf{makesafe}_{\mathrm{BL}}[\mathcal{T}]\ =\ \left\{\begin{array}{l} \blacktriangledown R_i := \blacktriangledown R_i \uplus (\triangledown R_i \dotdiv \blacktriangle R_i),\\ \blacktriangle R_i := (\blacktriangle R_i \dotdiv \triangledown R_i) \uplus \triangle R_i \end{array}\right\}\ +\ \mathcal{T}$$

$$\mathsf{refresh}_{\mathrm{BL}}\ =\ \{MV := (MV \dotdiv \blacktriangledown(\mathcal{L}, Q)) \uplus \blacktriangle(\mathcal{L}, Q),\quad \mathcal{L} := \phi\}$$

$$\mathbb{INV}_{\mathrm{DT}}:\ Q \equiv (MV \dotdiv \triangledown MV) \uplus \triangle MV$$

$$\mathsf{makesafe}_{\mathrm{DT}}[\mathcal{T}]\ =\ \left\{\begin{array}{l} \triangledown MV := \triangledown MV \uplus (\triangledown(\mathcal{T}, Q) \dotdiv \triangle MV),\\ \triangle MV := (\triangle MV \dotdiv \triangledown(\mathcal{T}, Q)) \uplus \triangle(\mathcal{T}, Q) \end{array}\right\}\ +\ \mathcal{T}$$

$$\mathsf{refresh}_{\mathrm{DT}}\ =\ \{MV := (MV \dotdiv \triangledown MV) \uplus \triangle MV,\quad \triangledown MV := \phi,\quad \triangle MV := \phi\}$$

$$\mathbb{INV}_{\mathrm{C}}:\ \mathrm{PAST}(\mathcal{L}, Q) \equiv (MV \dotdiv \triangledown MV) \uplus \triangle MV$$

$$\mathsf{makesafe}_{\mathrm{C}}[\mathcal{T}]\ =\ \mathsf{makesafe}_{\mathrm{BL}}[\mathcal{T}]$$

$$\mathsf{propagate}_{\mathrm{C}}\ =\ \left\{\begin{array}{l} \triangledown MV := \triangledown MV \uplus (\blacktriangledown(\mathcal{L}, Q) \dotdiv \triangle MV),\\ \triangle MV := (\triangle MV \dotdiv \blacktriangledown(\mathcal{L}, Q)) \uplus \blacktriangle(\mathcal{L}, Q),\\ \mathcal{L} := \phi \end{array}\right\}$$

$$\mathsf{partial\_refresh}_{\mathrm{C}}\ =\ \mathsf{refresh}_{\mathrm{DT}}$$

$$\mathsf{refresh}_{\mathrm{C}}\ =\ \begin{array}{l}(\mathsf{propagate}_{\mathrm{C}}\ \text{followed by}\ \mathsf{partial\_refresh}_{\mathrm{C}})\quad \text{or}\\ (\mathsf{partial\_refresh}_{\mathrm{C}}\ \text{followed by}\ \mathsf{refresh}_{\mathrm{BL}})\end{array}$$

Figure 3   Deferred View Maintenance Algorithms

(b) $D_3 \subseteq O$.

As an example, we show how $\mathsf{propagate}_{\mathrm{C}}$ from Figure 3 is derived. Equation (2) in Section 4 tells us that

$$Q\ \equiv\ (\mathrm{PAST}(\mathcal{L}, Q) \dotdiv \blacktriangledown(\mathcal{L}, Q)) \uplus \blacktriangle(\mathcal{L}, Q),$$

and invariant $\mathbb{INV}_{\mathrm{C}}$ tells us that

$$\mathrm{PAST}(\mathcal{L}, Q)\ \equiv\ (MV \dotdiv \triangledown MV) \uplus \triangle MV.$$

This implies that

$$Q\ \equiv\ (((MV \dotdiv \triangledown MV) \uplus \triangle MV) \dotdiv \blacktriangledown(\mathcal{L}, Q)) \uplus \blacktriangle(\mathcal{L}, Q).$$

By the composition lemma, we then get

$$Q \equiv (MV \dotdiv (\triangledown MV \uplus (\blacktriangledown(\mathcal{L}, Q) \dotdiv \triangle MV))) \uplus\\ ((\triangle MV \dotdiv \blacktriangledown(\mathcal{L}, Q)) \uplus \blacktriangle(\mathcal{L}, Q)).$$

5.2   Correctness

As discussed in Section 4.1 our solutions will impose the following *minimality invariants*, in addition to the invariants described in Figure 1. In the two cases that use a log $\mathcal{L}$, we require that the invariants $\blacktriangle R_i \subseteq R_i$

be maintained. In the two cases that use differential tables we will require that the invariant $\triangledown MV \subseteq MV$ be maintained.

The following lemma tells us that the transactions of Figure 3 correctly extend the log and maintain the minimality invariants.

Lemma 4 *Suppose that $\mathcal{L}$ is a weakly minimal log, $s_p \xrightarrow{\mathcal{L}} s_c$, and $\mathcal{T}$ is a weakly minimal transaction. Then $s_p \xrightarrow{\mathcal{L}} (\mathsf{makesafe}_{\mathrm{BL}}[\mathcal{T}])(s_c)$. Furthermore, the transaction $\mathsf{makesafe}_{\mathrm{BL}}[\mathcal{T}]$ is safe for $\blacktriangle R_i \subseteq R_i$ for each table R_i, and the transactions $\mathsf{makesafe}_{\mathrm{DT}}[\mathcal{T}]$ and $\mathsf{propagate}_{\mathrm{C}}$ are safe for $\triangledown MV \subseteq MV$.* $\square$

The following theorem tells us that our algorithms meet the specifications given in Section 3.

Theorem 5 *The algorithms of Figure 3 are correct. That is, every transaction $\mathsf{makesafe}_*[\mathcal{T}]$ is safe for $\mathbb{INV}_*$ for $*$ being BL, DT and C. The refresh transactions are correct:*

$$\{\mathbb{INV}_*\}\mathsf{refresh}_*\{Q \equiv MV\}$$

In addition, the following holds:

$$\{\mathbb{INV}_{\mathrm{C}}\}\,\mathsf{propagate}_{\mathrm{C}}\,\{Q \equiv (MV \doteq \triangledown MV) \uplus \triangle MV\}$$
$$\{\mathbb{INV}_{\mathrm{C}}\}\,\mathsf{partial\_refresh}_{\mathrm{C}}\,\{\mathrm{PAST}(\mathcal{L}, Q) \equiv MV\} \qquad \square$$

5.3 Minimizing view downtime

The two transactions, $\mathsf{propagate}_{\mathrm{C}}$ and $\mathsf{partial\_refresh}_{\mathrm{C}}$, of the $\mathbb{INV}_{\mathrm{C}}$ scenario allow for a very rich set of maintenance policies. We now present two policies for that scenario and describe how they minimize view downtime.

Policy 1: Every k time units, the transaction $\mathsf{propagate}_{\mathrm{C}}$ is invoked to propagate changes from the log $\mathcal{L}$ to the differential tables, $\triangledown MV$ and $\triangle MV$. Every m time units ($m > k$), the view table MV is brought up-to-date using $\mathsf{refresh}_{\mathrm{C}}$.

Policy 2: The use of $\mathsf{propagate}_{\mathrm{C}}$ is the same as that in Policy 1. Every m time units ($m > k$), the view table MV is *partially refreshed* using $\mathsf{partial\_refresh}_{\mathrm{C}}$.

With both policies, per-transaction overhead is minimized since $\mathsf{makesafe}_{\mathrm{C}}[\mathcal{T}]$ only adds the work required to update the log tables. Policy 1 can be expected to have a refresh time much lower than that of the $\mathbb{INV}_{\mathrm{BL}}$ scenario. This is because much of the work of computing incremental changes has already been done during periodic propagation. Policy 2 has the least downtime since it merely applies the precomputed differential tables to the view table. Policy 2 refreshes the view to a state that is at most k time units out-of-date. This policy is appropriate for applications that can tolerate data that is slightly out-of-date (assuming k is small).

One can minimize view downtime further by removing, from $\triangledown MV$ and $\triangle MV$, tuples that exist in both $\triangledown MV$ and $\triangle MV$. Such a solution would be generated by using strong minimality (Section 3.4), and requires a strongly minimal analog of Lemma 3.

Example 5.1 Again we consider the retail application of Section 1.1. Suppose that we use the $\mathbb{INV}_{\mathrm{C}}$ scenario for the materialized view MV, and maintain logs on the changes to the sales table. In this example, the refresh period is 24 hours ($m = 24$). Suppose that propagation is done every hour ($k = 1$).

Using Policy 1, we can expect the downtime to be much smaller than it would be in the $\mathbb{INV}_{\mathrm{BL}}$ scenario, since the log would contain at most an hour's worth of changes rather than a day's worth. The refresh of Policy 2 results in a view table that is no more than one hour out-of-date, and has the minimal downtime.

□

Of course, there are many possible variations on these two policies. For example, rather than using a fixed interval k, the transaction $\mathsf{propagate}_{\mathrm{C}}$ could be invoked asynchronously whenever any free cycles are available. Similarly, $\mathsf{refresh}_{\mathrm{C}}$ or $\mathsf{partial\_refresh}_{\mathrm{C}}$ could be invoked only when a user queries the view.

6   Related Work

Several incremental view maintenance algorithms for immediate maintenance have been proposed [BLT86, GL95, Han87, QW91]. These algorithms are based on the assumption that access to the pre-update base tables is available. Equations that involve both pre-update and post-update base tables are presented in [CW91, GMS93]. In [CW91], the incremental changes are computed in the post-update state. The pre-update state of a table is computed from its post-update state and from the transition tables that contain update information. Our future queries are similar to the when-clause of [GHJ96].

Research related to deferred view maintenance has focussed on two main issues: (a) computing the changes to the view and (b) applying the changes to the view. The work on computing updates has involved issues such as the types of auxiliary information needed to compute incremental changes, and detecting relevant updates. All of this work, however, has been done in the context of restrictive classes of views. Database snapshots were proposed in [AL80] as a means of providing access to old database states and also as a way of optimizing the performance of large, distributed databases. An algorithm for determining the changes that should be made to snapshots (restricted to select-project views over base tables) is presented in [LHM+86]. Techniques for maintaining update logs to allow efficient detection of relevant updates to select-project views are given in [KR87] and [SP89b]. Deferred maintenance for select-join views is implemented in ADMS [RK86b].

Issues related to the process of applying the computed updates to the view have been studied in [SR88] and [AGMK95]. The problem of determining the optimal refresh frequency, based on queueing models and parameterization of response time and processing cost constraints, has been investigated in [SR88]. View refresh strategies based on different priorities for transactions that apply computed updates to a view and transactions that read a view are presented in [AGMK95]. While this chapter is also concerned with the issue of balancing the costs of refresh with the constraints of other transactions, the focus is on high-level algorithms for incremental maintenance based on the various methods of keeping auxiliary information to achieve this balance. A comparison of view processing techniques based on non-materialization, and immediate and deferred view maintenance is presented in [Han87]. The algorithms for deferred maintenance used in that paper are based on future updates and hypothetical tables.

7   Future Work

There are many directions for future work. For example, are there algorithms to refresh only those parts of a view needed by a given query? How should log information be stored so that the work done by makesafe$_{\text{BL}}[\mathcal{T}]$ is minimal, and independent of the number of views supported? What are the problems related to concurrency control in the presence of materialized views?

Acknowledgments. We would like to thank Teradata/Walmart Support Group and Dave Belanger for the initial discussions that led to this work, and Dan Lieuwen and the referees for helpful comments.

INCREMENTAL EVALUATION
OF DATALOG QUERIES

Guozhu Dong, Rodney Topor

1 Introduction

We consider the problem of repeatedly evaluating the same (computationally expensive) query to a database that is being updated between successive query requests. In this situation, it should be possible to use the difference between successive database states and the answer to the query in one state to reduce the cost of evaluating the query in the next state. We call this process "incremental query evaluation."

We show how and when incremental query evaluation can be performed for Datalog queries to a relational database and updates that are insertions of finite sets of facts.

The problem is analogous to and can be viewed as a generalization of the problem of reducing the cost of checking integrity constraint satisfaction in one state by using (i) database updates and (ii) the fact that the integrity constraint was satisfied in the state prior to the updates [BDM88, LST87, Nic82].

Our task is closely related to the problem of efficiently updating the standard model [ABW88] of a definite or more generally stratified database [AP87, Kuc91]. It is also closely related to the problem of partially evaluating definite logic programs [LS91]. Finally, when restricted to standard transitive closure programs, our task can be viewed as solving the incremental transitive closure computation problem for graphs [BKV90, IK83, Ita86], where the incremental algorithm is a nonrecursive Datalog program and where no recursive algorithm or elaborate data structure is used.

In general, all these optimization approaches store extra information to reduce the time required for subsequent computations. In our case, we store the answer to the query in one database state (and possibly additional derived facts) to reduce the cost of evaluating the query in subsequent database states.

Informally, the idea of incremental query evaluation is as follows. Let Q be a Datalog query, D an initial database state, $Q(D)$ the answer to query Q in database D, A a set of facts to be inserted, and D' the resulting database state. Then our approach is to store $Q(D)$ (and possibly additional derived facts), to use the update A to transform the query Q to a new "incremental query" Q' with the property that $Q(D') = Q'(Q(D) \cup D') \cup Q(D)$.

Using incremental evaluation, the task of evaluating Q is replaced by the task of evaluating Q'. Naturally, our aim is to construct a query Q' that can be evaluated as efficiently as possible, and whose answer contains only new facts (irredundancy): $Q'(Q(D) \cup D') \cap Q(D) = \phi$.

As we shall see, for these goals to be achievable, it is necessary to store facts (not necessarily defined by Q) in addition to the query answer $Q(D)$.

Our main contribution is an algorithm for transforming any regular chain query and update into an incremental query that is correct, irredundant (for a reasonable class of database states), and, most importantly, nonrecursive. Nonrecursive Datalog programs can be evaluated very efficiently. (Much attention has been given in the database field to conditions under which programs are equivalent to nonrecursive programs. See [HKMV91] for recent advances on this issue.)

Thus, our main result implies that regular chain queries can be evaluated incrementally by using nonrecursive programs only. Furthermore, as shall be seen, we can construct a bounded number of (nonrecursive) incremental programs (one for each EDB predicate) as our base of incremental programs; after each update, we need only apply an incremental program from this base.

We also present an algorithm for transforming an arbitrary Datalog query and update into an incremental query that is correct and irredundant (for some database states), but which is not in general nonrecursive.

Section 2 defines the above concepts in more detail; Section 3 presents our incremental query construction algorithm for regular chain queries and the proof of its properties; Section 4 describes our results for arbitrary Datalog queries; and Section 5 discusses the connection between our results and related work, and suggests some directions for future research.

2   Basic Concepts

After briefly reviewing definitions of databases, queries, and answers, we introduce the main concept of the chapter, i.e., an incremental evaluation system.

A *database* is a finite set of ground atomic formulas (facts) in some first-order function-free language. The predicates that occur in a database are called *extensional* or *EDB predicates*. A Datalog program is a finite set of rules of the form $A \leftarrow A_1, \ldots, A_n$, where A and $A_1, \ldots, A_n$ are atomic formulas. (We disallow built-in predicates.) Predicates that occur in the heads of such rules are called *intensional* or *IDB predicates*. A *Datalog query Q* is a pair (Π, p), where Π is a Datalog program and p is a (*query*) predicate symbol.

The result $\Pi(D)$ of applying a Datalog program Π to a database D is the least (Herbrand) model for $\Pi \cup D$ or, equivalently, the set of facts that are logical consequences of $\Pi \cup D$ [vEK76]. The *answer $Q(D)$* to a query $Q = (\Pi, p)$ in a database D is simply the set[1] of facts $\Pi(D)|_p$.

Definition 2.1 (Incremental Evaluation System (IES)): Let $Q = (\Pi, p)$ be a Datalog query and A a finite set of facts. An *incremental evaluation system* (or *IES*) *for Q with respect to A* is a triple $\langle \Pi_p, S, \Pi_A \rangle$, where:

- Π_p is a Datalog program, called the *initial program for Q*, such that $\Pi_p(D)|_p = \Pi(D)|_p$ for each (extensional) database D;

- S is a set of IDB predicate symbols containing p; and

- Π_A is a Datalog program, called the *incremental program for Q and A*, such that $\Pi_p(D \cup A)|_S = \Pi_A(\sigma[\Pi_p(D)|_S \cup D] \cup A)|_S \cup \Pi_p(D)|_S$ for each extensional database D, where σ is a function that systematically maps each predicate symbol q to a new symbol q^o. (Symbol q^o denotes the relation q in the state before inserting the facts in A.)

■

---

[1] For each set S of predicate symbols, the restriction of a set F of facts to those with predicate in S is denoted $F|_S$. We write $F|_p$ for $F|_{\{p\}}$.

As indicated in the introduction, we store $\Pi_p(D)|_S$ to reduce the cost of evaluating $\Pi_p(D{\cup}A)|_S$. This is intended to avoid recomputing the facts in $\Pi_p(D)|_S$ after inserting A. Note that $\Pi_p(D{\cup}A)|_p = (\Pi_p(D{\cup}A)|_S)|_p$.

The benefits that can be achieved by incremental evaluation depend on the choice of Π_p, S and Π_A, and particularly on Π_A, the program used to compute the new facts in the answer to the query in the updated database. We would like this program to be efficient, i.e., to be nonrecursive, and to be irredundant (defined later).

The following example attempts to illustrate the above concepts.

EXAMPLE 2.1 Consider the query $Q = (\Pi, path)$, where Π is the program

$path(x, z) \leftarrow edge(x, z)$
$path(x, z) \leftarrow edge(x, y), path(y, z)$

Let $S = \{path\}$, $\Pi_p = \Pi$, $A = \{edge(a, b)\}$, and Π_A be the program

$path(x, z) \leftarrow edge(x, z)$
$path(x, z) \leftarrow edge(x, y), path^o(y, z)$
$path(x, z) \leftarrow path^o(x, y), edge(y, z)$
$path(x, z) \leftarrow path^o(x, y_1), edge(y_1, y_2), path^o(y_2, z)$

Then $\langle \Pi_p, S, \Pi_A \rangle$ is an incremental evaluation system for A. (The correctness will follow from Theorem 3.2.) Thus we have transformed the computation of a recursive program into the computation of a nonrecursive program (with the help of stored results). [Recall that each predicate of the form p^o in Π_A denotes the subset of facts for predicate p in the model before inserting the facts in A. Each predicate of the form p (without the superscript o) denotes the additional set of facts for predicate p following the insertion of the facts in A.]

To illustrate incremental evaluation, suppose D is the database $\{edge(1, 2), edge(2, 3), edge(4, 5), edge(5, 6)\}$, and A is $\{edge(3, 4)\}$. (That is, $a = 3$ and $b = 4$.) Then $\Pi_p(D) = \{path(1, 2), path(2, 3), path(1, 3), path(4, 5), path(5, 6), path(4, 6)\}$. To compute $\Pi_p(D \cup A)$ from $\Pi_p(D)$ using Π_A, the facts in $\Pi_p(D) \cup D$ are marked with a superscript o to indicate that they were facts in the state before inserting the facts in A; the predicate $edge$ (resp., $path$) in Π_A denotes the additional set of facts that are added (resp., derived) for $edge$ (resp. $path$). Thus, the additional fact for $edge$ is $\{edge(3, 4)\}$, and the additional facts for $path$ are $\{path(i, j) \mid 1 \leq i \leq 3 \text{ and } 4 \leq j \leq 6\}$.

As an aside, we can transform Π_A into a more efficient program by instantiating Π_A with the specific fact in A. The resulting rules are: $path(a, z) \leftarrow path^o(b, z)$; $path(x, b) \leftarrow path^o(x, a)$ and $path(x, z) \leftarrow path^o(x, a), path^o(b, z)$. This technique also applies to other examples described below. □

The next example illustrates why it is sometimes necessary to use an initial program Π_p different from Π, and why it is sometimes necessary to store the set of facts $\Pi_p(D)|_S$ instead of the query answer $\Pi(D)|_p$.

EXAMPLE 2.2 Consider the query $Q = (\Pi, p)$, where Π is the following program that represents the propagation of signals p on wires x, y, z through a network of logical OR gates s with inputs r.

$p(x) \leftarrow s(x, y, z), p(y)$
$p(x) \leftarrow s(x, y, z), p(z)$
$p(x) \leftarrow r(x)$

For no update A is there a nonrecursive incremental program Π_A if we let Π_p be Π. However, by using a different Π_p, and storing derived facts (for a new predicate) in addition to the derived facts for p, we can construct an IES for Q with a nonrecursive incremental program as shown below. Indeed, let Π_p be the program

$$t(x,y) \leftarrow s(x,y,z) \qquad\qquad p(x) \leftarrow r(x)$$
$$t(x,z) \leftarrow s(x,y,z) \qquad\qquad p(x) \leftarrow t(x,y), r(y)$$
$$t(x,z) \leftarrow t(x,y), t(y,z)$$

and let S be the set $\{p, t\}$ (not simply $\{p\}$). Here, $t(x, y)$ is true if x is "on" whenever y is "on". Now, if $A = \{r(a)\}$, we can define Π_A to be the program consisting of the single rule $p(x) \leftarrow t^o(x, a)$. Then $\langle \Pi_p, S, \Pi_A \rangle$ is an IES for Q with respect to A, and Π_A is a nonrecursive incremental program. Furthermore, $\Pi_A(\sigma[\Pi_p(D)|_S \cup D] \cup A)$ can be evaluated using, in effect, a single selection operation!

Alternatively, if $A = \{s(a, b, c)\}$, we can define Π_A to be the program

$$t(a,b) \qquad\qquad\qquad\qquad t(y,c) \leftarrow t^o(y,a)$$
$$t(a,c) \qquad\qquad\qquad\qquad t(x,y) \leftarrow t^o(x,a), t^o(b,y)$$
$$t(a,y) \leftarrow t^o(b,y) \qquad\qquad t(x,y) \leftarrow t^o(x,a), t^o(c,y)$$
$$t(a,y) \leftarrow t^o(c,y)$$
$$t(y,b) \leftarrow t^o(y,a) \qquad\qquad p(x) \leftarrow t(x,y), r^o(y)$$

(Recall that atoms with predicate symbol t denote facts computed by Π_A after inserting A, whereas atoms with predicate symbol t^o denote facts in the state before A is inserted.) Then $\langle \Pi_p, S, \Pi_A \rangle$ is an IES for Q with respect to A, and Π_A is a nonrecursive incremental program. The nonrecursive incremental programs when A is an arbitrary finite set of facts can be constructed using the approach for regular chain queries given in the next section. $\square$

We are especially interested in incremental evaluation systems $\langle \Pi_p, S, \Pi_A \rangle$ that are *irredundant* in the sense that, for each extensional database D and each A disjoint from D, $\Pi_A(\sigma[\Pi_p(D)|_S \cup D] \cup A)|_S$ is disjoint from $\Pi_p(D)|_S$. Note that, in the above example, because there can be several proofs that some $p(b)$ holds, for neither update is the resulting incremental evaluation system irredundant. Thus it is necessary to refine the concept to make irredundancy a realistic goal.

Definition 2.2 (Irredundant IES): An incremental evaluation system $\langle \Pi_p, S, \Pi_A \rangle$ is called *irredundant with respect to* a class $\mathcal{D}$ of extensional databases if $\Pi_A(\sigma[\Pi_p(D)|_S \cup D] \cup A)|_S$ is disjoint form $\Pi_p(D)|_S$ for each $D \in \mathcal{D}$ disjoint from A.   ∎

EXAMPLE 2.3 The incremental evaluation system $\langle \Pi, S, \Pi_A \rangle$ of Example 2.1 is irredundant with respect to extensional databases whose underlying directed graph has the following "forest property": there is at most one path between each pair of nodes in the updated database $D \cup A$. $\square$

3   Regular Chain Programs

In this section we consider the incremental evaluation of Datalog queries associated with "regular chain programs". The main result is an algorithm for constructing for each regular query and each insertion an IES with a nonrecursive incremental program. We assume familiarity with the elements of formal language theory.

A *chain Datalog program* is a finite set of *chain rule*s of the form

$$q(x, z) \leftarrow q_1(x, y_1), q_2(y_1, y_2), \ldots, q_k(y_{k-1}, z) \tag{17.1}$$

where $k \geq 1$ and x, $y_1, \ldots, y_{k-1}$, and z are distinct variables. Note that chain Datalog programs contain only variables and binary predicate symbols.

Chain Datalog programs and generalizations allow special optimization techniques. Indeed, several papers have considered efficiency issues of such programs [AC89, Don91, Don92]. The current chapter also explores such possibilities.

It is well known that, for each chain Datalog program Π, the query (Π, p) is associated with a context-free grammar G which can be constructed as follows. The terminal (resp., nonterminal) symbols are the EDB (resp., IDB) predicates; the start nonterminal is the query predicate p; and for each rule in Π of the form (17.1) there is a production of the form $q \rightarrow q_1 q_2 \cdots q_k$.

Definition 3.1 (Regular Query): A Datalog query (Π, p) is called *regular* if Π is a chain Datalog program and the context-free grammar associated with the query is right-linear[2]. ∎

The standard edge-path query $(\Pi, path)$ given in Example 2.1 is regular, whereas the standard same-generation query (see Section 4) is not.

Our main result of this chapter is as follows:

Theorem 3.1 *(Main) Let Q be a regular chain query and A a finite set of facts. Then there exists an algorithm that constructs an incremental evaluation system for Q wrt A whose incremental program is nonrecursive.* ∎

This theorem will be a direct consequence of Theorem 3.2, as the incremental program constructed by Algorithm 3.1 below is indeed nonrecursive.

We first need an auxiliary notion (given next) and a key lemma (Lemma 3.1). We can regard a database D over a set of binary EDB predicates as a directed graph whose vertices are constant symbols and whose edges are labelled by EDB predicates such that there is an edge labelled p from a to b in the graph if and only if $p(a, b) \in D$. Let L be an ϵ-free regular language over the alphabet of binary EDB predicates. For each directed graph D, an *L-path from c_0 to c_k* is an expression of the form "$q_1(c_0, c_1)q_2(c_1, c_2) \cdots q_k(c_{k-1}, c_k)$" where each $q_i(c_{i-1}, c_i)$ is in D. For example, for $D = \{edge(1, 2), edge(2, 3)\}$, $edge(1, 2)edge(2, 3)$ is an $L(edge^+)$-path from 1 to 3.

Lemma 3.1 *Let D be a labeled directed graph, $q(a_1, a_2)$ be a labeled edge in D, E be a $\{*, \epsilon, \phi\}$-free regular expression, and b_1 and b_2 be nodes. If there is an $L(E)$-path in D from b_1 to b_2, then there is such a path in which $q(a_1, a_2)$ occurs at most $\#_q(E)$ times[3].* ∎

Proof Let Σ be the set of labels appearing in E and $n = \text{Sum}_{x \in \Sigma} \#_x(E)$. Then $n \geq 1$. For each $i \in [1..n]$, we replace the ith occurrence of symbols in E from Σ by i. Let $\hat{E}$ be the resulting regular expression.

---

[2]A grammar is right-linear if the only nonterminal symbol in the right hand side of each production is the rightmost symbol.

[3]$\#_q(E)$ denotes the number of occurrences of symbol q in regular expression E.

Clearly, no terminal symbol occurs in $\hat{E}$ twice. Let f be the homomorphic mapping from $[1..n]$ to Σ such that $f(\hat{E}) = E$. Then $f(L(\hat{E})) = L(E)$.

Suppose there exists an $L(E)$-path $q_1(c_0, c_1) \cdots q_k(c_{k-1}, c_k)$ from b_1 to b_2. Let m be the number of occurrences of $q(a_1, a_2)$ in this path. It suffices to assume $m > \#_q(E)$. Since $q_1 \cdots q_k$ is in $L(E)$ and since $f(L(\hat{E})) = L(E)$, there exists a word $i_1 \cdots i_k$ in $L(\hat{E})$ such that $f(i_1 \cdots i_k) = q_1 \cdots q_k$. Since $m > \#_q(E)$, there exist $1 \leq \rho < \rho' \leq k$ such that $i_\rho = i_{\rho'}$ and $q_\rho(c_{\rho-1}, c_\rho) = q_{\rho'}(c_{\rho'-1}, c_{\rho'}) = q(a_1, a_2)$. Intuitively, the two equations mean that $q(a, b)$ appears at the "position" i_ρ in E twice. It can be verified (using an automata-theoretic argument) that $i_1 \cdots i_\rho i_{\rho'+1} \cdots i_k$ is in $L(\hat{E})$. Since $q_1 \cdots q_\rho q_{\rho'+1} \cdots q_k = f(i_1 \cdots i_\rho i_{\rho'+1} \cdots i_k)$, $q_1 \cdots q_\rho q_{\rho'+1} \cdots q_k$ is in $L(E)$. Since $c_\rho = c_{\rho'} = a_2$, it follows that $q_1(c_0, c_1) \cdots q_\rho(c_{\rho-1}, c_\rho) q_{\rho'+1}(c_{\rho'}, c_{\rho'+1}) \cdots q_k(c_{k-1}, c_k)$ is an $L(E)$-path from b_1 to b_2. Clearly, $q(a_1, a_2)$ occurs in this path at most $m - 1$ times. Repeating the above argument, one ultimately obtains a desired $L(E)$-path.

EXAMPLE 3.1 We now illustrate the construction used in the proof of the lemma. Let $E = (qr \cup q^+ t)^+$. Then $n = 4$, $\hat{\Sigma} = \{1, 2, 3, 4\}$, $\hat{E} = (1\,2 \cup 3^+\,4)^+$, and $f(1) = f(3) = q$, $f(2) = r$, and $f(4) = t$.

Suppose the following $L(E)$-path is in graph D:

$$q(c_0, c_1) q(c_1, c_2) t(c_2, a_1) q(a_1, a_2) r(a_2, a_1) q(a_1, a_2)$$
$$t(a_2, a_1) q(a_1, a_2) r(a_2, a_5) q(a_5, a_6) t(a_6, a_7)$$

Then the word w in $L(\hat{E})$ such that $f(w) = qqtqrqtqrqt$ is $w = 33412341234$. The edge $q(a_1, a_2)$ occurs three times in the path, and $\#_q(E) = 2$. We observe that the first and third usages of $q(a_1, a_2)$ correspond to the same integer 1 in $\hat{E}$. (The second usage corresponds to integer 3 in $\hat{E}$.) By removing 1234, we get the shorter word 3341234 in $L(\hat{E})$. The corresponding $L(E)$-path from c_0 to a_7 is

$$q(c_0, c_1) q(c_1, c_2) t(c_2, a_1) q(a_1, a_2) r(a_2, a_5) q(a_5, a_6) t(a_6, a_7).$$

Note that $q(a_1, a_2)$ now occurs only once in this L(E)-path.   □

We are now ready to present the main algorithm.

Algorithm 3.1 (IES) Let $Q = (\Pi, p)$ be a regular chain query and A a finite set of facts. We construct an IES $\langle \Pi_p, S, \Pi_A \rangle$ for Q with respect to A as follows:

Step 1: Construct a regular expression E' from Q such that the associated grammar of Q generates $L(E')$.

Step 2: Construct a $\{*, \epsilon, \phi\}$-free regular expression E such that $L(E) = L(E')$.

Step 3: For each regular expression e occurring in E, let p_e be a predicate symbol. Assume that $p_E = p$, and $p_r = r$ for each EDB predicate symbol r. Let Π_p consist of the following rules:

- $p_e(x, z) \leftarrow p_{e_1}(x, y_1), p_{e_2}(y_1, y_2), \ldots, p_{e_k}(y_{k-1}, z)$, if $e = e_1 \cdots e_k$ $(k \geq 2)$.

- $p_e(x, z) \leftarrow p_{e_i}(x, z)$ for each $i \in [1..k]$, if $e = e_1 \cup \cdots \cup e_k$ $(k \geq 2)$.

- $p_e(x, z) \leftarrow p_{e_1}(x, z)$ and $p_e(x, z) \leftarrow p_{e_1}(x, y), p_e(y, z)$, if $e = e_1^+$.

- $p_E(x, z) \leftarrow r(x, z)$, if $E = r$ for some EDB predicate r.

Let S be the set of all IDB predicate symbols of Π_p.

Step 4: We use the predicate symbols occurring in Π_p together with their "old" versions of the form p_e^o. Let Π_A consist of the following rules:

- $p_e(x, z) \leftarrow p_1(x, y_1), p_2(y_1, y_2), \ldots, p_k(y_{k-1}, z)$, for each sequence $p_1, \cdots, p_k$ such that each $p_i \in \{p_{e_i}, p_{e_i}^o\}$ and at least one $p_i = p_{e_i}$, if $e = e_1 \cdots e_k$ $(k \geq 2)$.

- $p_e(x, z) \leftarrow p_{e_i}(x, z)$ for each $i \in [1..k]$, if $e = e_1 \cup \cdots \cup e_k$ $(k \geq 2)$.

- $p_e(x, z) \leftarrow p_1(x, y_1) \cdots p_k(y_{k-1}, z)$ for each subsequence[4] $p_1 \cdots p_k$ of $(p_e^o p_{e_1})^m p_e^o$ (where $m = |A| max\{\#_q(e) \mid q$ is a predicate symbol occurring in $A\}$[5]) such that (i) there is at least one j such that $p_j = p_{e_1}$, and (ii) there are no consecutive p_e^o's, if $e = e_1^+$.

- $p_E(x, z) \leftarrow r(x, z)$, if $E = r$ for some EDB predicate r.

□

The program Π_A constructed by this algorithm computes the new facts for predicates of the form p_e, by using the old facts for p_e in the state before the facts in A were inserted.

Note that the incremental program Π_A constructed by the above algorithm is nonrecursive. Furthermore, Π_A only depends on the predicate symbols occurring in A and the size of A; it does not depend on the constants occurring in facts in A. Thus, if we restrict A to singleton sets, the number of incremental programs for Π (which form the incremental program base for Π) is the number of EDB predicates occurring in Π.

Note that Π_p and Π_A do not correspond to right-linear grammars in general.

Example 2.1 illustrated the construction applied to the standard edge-path query. A more involved example follows.

EXAMPLE 3.2 Suppose $Q = (\Pi, p)$ is a regular query and $A = \{q(a, b)\}$. Suppose the first two steps of Algorithm 3.1 yield the regular expression $E = (qr \cup q^+t)^+$. Let $e_1 = qr$, $e_2 = q^+$, $e_3 = e_2 t$, $e_4 = e_1 \cup e_3$, and $e_5 = e_4^+$. Then $S = \{p_{e_i} \mid 1 \leq i \leq 5\}$, Π_p is the program

$$p_{e_1}(x, z) \leftarrow q(x, y), r(y, z) \qquad\qquad p_{e_4}(x, z) \leftarrow p_{e_1}(x, z)$$
$$p_{e_2}(x, z) \leftarrow q(x, z) \qquad\qquad\qquad p_{e_4}(x, z) \leftarrow p_{e_3}(x, z)$$
$$p_{e_2}(x, z) \leftarrow q(x, y), p_{e_2}(y, z) \qquad\quad p_{e_5}(x, z) \leftarrow p_{e_4}(x, z)$$
$$p_{e_3}(x, z) \leftarrow p_{e_2}(x, y), t(y, z) \qquad\quad p_{e_5}(x, z) \leftarrow p_{e_4}(x, y), p_{e_5}(y, z)$$

and Π_A is the program

$$p_{e_1}(x, z) \leftarrow q(x, y), r^o(y, z) \qquad\qquad\qquad p_{e_3}(x, z) \leftarrow p_{e_2}(x, y), t^o(y, z)$$
$$p_{e_2}(x, z) \leftarrow q(x, z) \qquad\qquad\qquad\qquad\quad p_{e_4}(x, z) \leftarrow p_{e_1}(x, z)$$
$$p_{e_2}(x, z) \leftarrow q(x, y), p_{e_2}^o(y, z) \qquad\qquad\quad p_{e_4}(x, z) \leftarrow p_{e_3}(x, z)$$
$$p_{e_2}(x, z) \leftarrow p_{e_2}^o(x, y), q(y, z) \qquad\qquad\quad p_{e_5}(x, z) \leftarrow p_{e_4}(x, z)$$
$$p_{e_2}(x, z) \leftarrow p_{e_2}^o(x, y_1), q(y_1, y_2), p_{e_2}^o(y_2, z) \qquad \text{(10 other rules defining } p_{e_5})$$
$$p_{e_5}(x, z) \leftarrow p_{e_5}^o(x, y_1), p_{e_4}(y_1, y_2), p_{e_5}^o(y_2, y_3), p_{e_4}(y_3, y_4), p_{e_5}^o(y_4, z)$$

---

[4] Given a sequence or word $s = s_1 s_2 \cdots s_k$, a subsequence of s is a sequence $s_{i_1} s_{i_2} \cdots s_{i_j}$, where $j \geq 1$ and $1 \leq i_1 < i_2 < \cdots < i_j \leq k$.

[5] $|A|$ denotes the cardinality of A and $\#_q(e)$ denotes the number of occurrences of q in e.

Recall that p_e in Π_A denotes the newly derived or added atoms for p_e after inserting A, and p_e^o represents the atoms for p_e before inserting A. $\square$

Theorem 3.2 *Let Q be a regular chain query and A a finite set of facts. Then Algorithm 3.1 constructs an IES for Q with respect to A whose incremental program is nonrecursive.* $\blacksquare$

Proof   For simplicity, we only consider the case where A is a singleton set. By an abuse of notation, we use A to denote the fact. We need to verify the two equations in the definition of an IES. To this end, let D be an arbitrary extensional database, E the $\{*, \epsilon, \phi\}$-free regular expression constructed in steps 1 and 2, and Π_p the program constructed in step 3 of Algorithm 3.1. It is then straightforward to verify that $\Pi_p(D)|_p = \Pi(D)|_p$ holds.

We now verify the other equation, namely,

$$\Pi_p(D \cup A)|_S = \Pi_A(\sigma[\Pi_p(D)|_S \cup D] \cup \{A\})|_S \cup \Pi_p(D)|_S.$$

We first prove that the right hand side is contained in the left hand side. Due to monotonicity, $\Pi_p(D)|_S \subseteq \Pi_p(D \cup \{A\})|_S$. Observe that every (bottom-up) derivation of a fact F from the database $\sigma[\Pi_p(D)|_S \cup D] \cup \{A\}$ using the program Π_A can be transformed into a derivation of F from $D \cup \{A\}$ using Π_p by deriving each atom of the form $p_e^o(\ldots)$ from D using Π_p. Hence $\Pi_A(\sigma[\Pi_p(D)|_S \cup D] \cup \{A\})|_S \subseteq \Pi_p(D \cup \{A\})|_S$.

To prove the reverse containment, it suffices to assume $A \notin D$. Let q be the predicate symbol occurring in A. By induction, we show that for each regular subexpression e of E,
($\dagger$) if $p_e(a,b)$ is in $\Pi_p(D \cup \{A\}) - \Pi_p(D)$, then $p_e(a,b)$ is in $\Pi_A(\sigma[\Pi_p(D)|_S \cup D] \cup \{A\})$.

The following is easy to verify.
($\ddagger$) For each regular subexpression e of E using at least one operator, $p_e(a,b)$ is in $\Pi_p(D \cup A)|_S$ if and only if there is an $L(e)$-path in $D \cup \{A\}$.

Basis (Zero operators) e is an EDB predicate symbol. Then ($\dagger$) holds trivially because there is no EDB fact in $\Pi_p(D \cup \{A\})$.

Induction (One or more operators) Assume ($\dagger$) holds for all regular subexpressions of E with fewer than i operators, $i \geq 1$. Let e be a regular subexpression of E with i operators.

Case 1: $e = e_1 \cup \cdots \cup e_k$. Suppose $p_e(a,b) \in \Pi_p(D \cup \{A\}) - \Pi_p(D)$. By the construction of Π_p, there exists $j \in [1..k]$ such that $p_{e_j}(a,b) \in [\Pi_p(D \cup \{A\}) \cup \{A\}] - \Pi_p(D)$. Then either $p_{e_j}(a,b) = A$ or, by the induction hypothesis, $p_{e_j}(a,b) \in \Pi_A(\sigma[\Pi_p(D)|_S \cup D] \cup \{A\})$. Since $p_e(x,z) \leftarrow p_{e_j}(x,z)$ is a rule in Π_A, $p_e(a,b) \in \Pi_A(\sigma[\Pi_p(D)|_S \cup D] \cup \{A\})$ as desired.

Case 2: $e = e_1 \cdots e_k$. Suppose $p_e(a,b)$ is in $\Pi_p(D \cup \{A\}) - \Pi_p(D)$. Then there exist facts $p_{e_1}(a,c_1), \cdots,$ $p_{e_k}(c_{k-1}, b)$ in $D \cup \{A\} \cup \Pi_p(D \cup \{A\})$. Since the rule $p_e(x,z) \leftarrow p_{e_1}(x, y_1), \cdots, p_{e_k}(y_{k-1}, z)$ is in Π_p and $p_e(a,b)$ is not in $\Pi_p(D)$, at least one of these facts is not in $\Pi_p(D) \cup D$. By the induction hypothesis, all these facts are in $\Pi_A(\sigma[\Pi_p(D)|_S \cup D] \cup \{A\}) \cup D \cup \{A\}$. Let $c_0 = a$ and $c_k = b$. Consider the rule $p_e(x,z) \leftarrow p_1(x, y_1), \cdots, p_k(y_{k-1}, z)$ in Π_A, where p_j is p_{e_j} if $p_{e_j}(c_{j-1}, c_j)$ is in $[\{A\} \cup \Pi_p(D \cup \{A\})] - \Pi_p(D)$, and $p_j = p_{e_j}^o$ otherwise. Clearly, an application of the rule yields $p_e(a,b)$. Thus $p_e(a,b)$ is in $\Pi_A(\sigma[\Pi_p(D)|_S \cup D] \cup \{A\})$.

Case 3: $e = e_1^+$. Suppose $p_e(a,b)$ is in $\Pi_p(D \cup \{A\}) - \Pi_p(D)$. By ($\ddagger$), there is an $L(e)$-path from a to b. By Lemma 3.1, there exists an $L(e)$-path P using A at most $\#_q(e)$ times. Let $P_1', \ldots, P_n'$ be $L(e_1)$-paths such that $P = P_1' \cdots P_n'$. We combine the consecutive $L(e_1)$-paths not using A to form $L(e)$-paths. As a result, we obtain $L(e)$-paths not using A and $L(e_1)$-paths that use A. Let $P_1, \ldots, P_k$ be those $L(e)$ or $L(e_1)$ paths such that $P = P_1 \cdots P_k$. Note that, for each $i < k$, if P_i does not use A then P_{i+1} uses A. (But P_{i+1} may use A if P_i uses A.) Let $c_0 = a$, $c_k = b$, and $c_2, \ldots, c_{k-1}$ be the constants such that P_i is from c_{i-1} to c_i. Let i be fixed. If P_i does not use A, then it is an $L(e)$-path in D, and thus $p_e(c_{i-1}, c_i)$ is in $\Pi_p(D)$. Suppose P_i uses A. Then it is an $L(e_1)$-path in $D \cup \{A\}$, and thus $p_{e_1}(c_{i-1}, c_i)$ is in $[\{A\} \cup \Pi_p(D \cup \{A\})] - \Pi_p(D)$ by ($\ddagger$). By the induction hypothesis, $p_{e_1}(c_{i-1}, c_i)$ is in $\{A\} \cup \Pi_A(\sigma[\Pi_p(D)|_S \cup D] \cup \{A\})$. Let $p_e(x, z) \leftarrow p_1(x, y_1), \ldots, p_k(y_{k-1}, z)$ be the rule in Π_A where $p_j = p_{e_1}$ if P_i uses A and $p_j = p_e^o$ otherwise. Clearly an application of this rule yields $p_e(a, b)$. Thus $p_e(a, b)$ is in $\Pi_A(\sigma[\Pi_p(D)|_S \cup D] \cup \{A\})$.

Observe that the program Π_A constructed by Algorithm 3.1 is irredundant with respect to the class of databases that satisfy the forest property. It seems difficult, if not impossible, to improve on this result. For example, an old path may exist between a pair of nodes a and b, and a new edge from c to d may bridge the only gap in a new path from a to b.

4 Arbitrary Datalog Programs

In the previous section we presented an algorithm to construct IES's with nonrecursive incremental programs for regular chain queries. We note that Algorithm 3.1 is only applicable to regular chain queries. However, as illustrated in Example 2.2, other Datalog programs may have IESs.

In this section we present an algorithm to construct an IES for an arbitrary Datalog program. The algorithm is as follows.

Algorithm 4.1 Let $Q = (\Pi, p)$ be a Datalog query and A a finite set of facts. Then $\langle \Pi, S, \Pi_A \rangle$ is an IES for Q wrt A, where S is the set of IDB predicates of Π, and Π_A is constructed as follows.

For each rule of the form $q(\vec{x}) \leftarrow q_1(\vec{x_1}), \ldots, q_k(\vec{x_k})$ in Π, Π_A contains all rules of the form $q(\vec{x}) \leftarrow p_1(\vec{x_1}), \ldots, p_k(\vec{x_k})$, where (i) each p_i is either q_i or q_i^o, (ii) at least one p_i is q_i, and (iii) p_i is q_i^o if q_i is a base predicate that does not occur in A. $\square$

Essentially, for each rule in Π_A, the rule body contains at least one atom that can only be unified with new facts derived from A. Thus Π_A computes the new facts by using at least one new fact at each step (in a bottom-up computation). It is not difficult to see that Π_A computes all facts in $\Pi(D \cup A)$ not in $\Pi(D)$, and that the algorithm is thus correct.

We illustrate the behaviour of this algorithm with the following examples.

EXAMPLE 4.1 Let $Q = (\Pi, path)$ be the query given in Example 2.1 and A an arbitrary finite set of facts. Applying the above algorithm we find S is $\{path\}$ and Π_A is the program

$path(x, z) \leftarrow edge(x, z)$
$path(x, z) \leftarrow edge(x, y), path^o(y, z)$
$path(x, z) \leftarrow edge^o(x, y), path(y, z)$

Then $\langle \Pi, S, \Pi_A \rangle$ is an incremental evaluation system for Q wrt A. Note that the resulting incremental program Π_A is recursive. $\square$

EXAMPLE 4.2 Consider the query $Q = (\Pi, p)$, where Π is the following program that represents the propagation of signals through a network of AND gates, analogously to Example 2.2.

$$p(x) \leftarrow s(x,y,z), p(y), p(z)$$
$$p(x) \leftarrow r(x)$$

Let $A = \{s(a,b,c), r(d)\}$. Applying the above algorithm we find S is $\{p\}$ and Π_A is the program

$$
\begin{array}{ll}
p(x) \leftarrow s(x,y,z), p^o(y), p^o(z) & \qquad p(x) \leftarrow s(x,y,z), p^o(y), p(z) \\
p(x) \leftarrow s^o(x,y,z), p(y), p^o(z) & \qquad p(x) \leftarrow s^o(x,y,z), p(y), p(z) \\
p(x) \leftarrow s^o(x,y,z), p^o(y), p(z) & \qquad p(x) \leftarrow s(x,y,z), p(y), p(z) \\
p(x) \leftarrow s(x,y,z), p(y), p^o(z) & \qquad p(x) \leftarrow r(x)
\end{array}
$$

Then $\langle \Pi, \{p\}, \Pi_A \rangle$ is an IES for Q wrt A. Again, Π_A is recursive. $\square$

EXAMPLE 4.3 Consider the standard same-generation query $Q = (\Pi, sg)$, where Π is the following program.

$$sg(x,y) \leftarrow p(x,z), q(z,y)$$
$$sg(x,y) \leftarrow p(x,z), sg(z,v), q(v,y)$$

If $A = \{p(a,b)\}$, the algorithm yields $S = \{sg\}$ and the following incremental program Π_A.

$$sg(x_1,y) \leftarrow p(x,z), q^o(z,y)$$
$$sg(x,y) \leftarrow p(x,z), sg^o(z,v), q^o(v,y)$$
$$sg(x,y) \leftarrow p^o(x,z), sg(z,v), q^o(v,y)$$
$$sg(x,y) \leftarrow p(x,z), sg(z,v), q^o(v,y)$$

$\square$

Superficially, the incremental programs constructed by Algorithm 4.1 are similar to the (relational algebra) programs used in the semi-naive method for evaluating Datalog queries [Ban85]. However, it should be noted that our method is a program transformation rather than an alternative evaluation procedure, and that our "new" facts are consequences of the inserted facts rather than facts computed in the previous (bottom-up) iteration. In fact, semi-naive evaluation can be applied to speed up the evaluation of our incremental programs.

5   Conclusions and Discussion

We have considered the incremental evaluation problem for Datalog queries. The main idea is to use the tuples computed in one state to reduce the cost of computing the answer to the same query after the insertion of a set of facts. Our main result is an algorithm to construct an IES with a nonrecursive incremental program for each regular chain query and each insertion. For general queries, we proposed an alternative method to construct IESs, though these are not as efficient in general as IESs for regular chain queries.

We now briefly compare our approach with other related work. Our incremental evaluation approach is based on the ideas of (i) transforming the original program into a new program, and (ii) storing derived relations for reuse after updates. Combining program transformation with storage of derived facts, our work is similar to the following in aim and methodology.

Semi-naive evaluation [Ban85]. The basic idea of semi-naive evaluation is in each (bottom-up) iteration to compute only those facts that depend on at least one fact computed in the previous iteration. It is thus similar to our approach in avoiding repeated computation. However, both Algorithms 3.1 and 4.1 are program transformations rather than alternative evaluation procedures, and our "new" facts are consequences of the inserted facts rather than facts computed in the previous iteration.

Integrity constraint simplification [BDM88, LST87, Nic82]. The basic idea of integrity constraint simplification is to use an update to determine a simplified set of constraint instances that need to be checked after the update. It is similar to our approach in using the information that the constraint was satisfied in a previous database state and propagating the effect of an update to transform (and simplify) the constraint to be checked. Our approach differs, however, in storing previous derived relations and in transforming the programs used in query evaluation.

Efficient maintenance of (stratified) databases [AP87, Kuc91]. The goal of this approach is to efficiently compute the standard model of a stratified database after a database update. It is similar to our approach in using the previous standard model (analogous to our stored relations) to simplify the task of computing the standard model (query answer) after the update. Our approach differs by storing intermediate relations rather than reasons (or "supports") for including computed facts [AP87], by not using meta-programs to compute the difference between successive models [Kuc91], and by transforming the programs used in query evaluation. Our approach is, however, more restricted as it does not allow negation in rules and queries.

Partial evaluation in logic programming [LS91]. The idea of partial evaluation is to propagate given facts into programs so that subsequent queries involving those facts can be evaluated more efficiently. In this sense, this approach is also similar to ours, though it does not involve database updates or storage of derived relations. Our results may contribute to research on partial evaluation.

Our incremental approach differs considerably from approaches such as the magic set approach [BMSU86] to query optimization. Indeed, incremental query evaluation is driven by anticipation, whereas magic set evaluation is driven by need. Consequently, it is difficult to combine the two approaches. To see this, consider the path problem in Example 2.1. Suppose that we want to find all nodes reachable from a given node, say 1. Suppose further that our old set of facts contains two connected components such that 1 is in one component, and suppose the inserted fact connects the two components in some way. Since the magic set approach is driven by need, reachable nodes in the component not containing 1 must be computed from the *beginning* in an unbounded number of iterations depending on the original facts. In the incremental approach only one or two joins are necessary since the needed steps have previously been computed in *anticipation*.

Several problems for future research suggest themselves immediately. These include the following.

Incremental evaluation can compute more facts than computation using the original programs. Although such increased computation is amortized or "evenly distributed" over a number of queries, it would be of interest to know when we should use incremental evaluation and when should we avoid using it.

Can IESs with nonrecursive incremental programs be constructed for classes of Datalog programs larger than regular chain programs?

Can more efficient IESs be constructed for arbitrary Datalog programs?

For which classes of programs can irredundancy of incremental evaluation be achieved for all extensional databases?

Can efficient (or any) IESs be constructed for stratified Datalog programs?

What are the exact relationships between incremental evaluation and (i) efficient maintenance of stratified databases and (ii) partial evaluation of logic programs?

We believe that the methods described in this chapter are valuable and deserve further study along these and similar lines.

Acknowledgments

Guozhu Dong gratefully acknowledges the support of the Australian Research Council and of Griffith University (through a travel grant).

VIEW MAINTENANCE ISSUES FOR THE CHRONICLE DATA MODEL

H. V. Jagadish, Inderpal Singh Mumick, Abraham Silberschatz

ABSTRACT

To meet the stringent performance requirements of transaction recording systems, much of the recording and query processing functionality, which should preferably be in the database, is actually implemented in the procedural application code, with the attendant difficulties in development, modularization, maintenance, and evolution. To combat this deficiency, we propose a new data model, the *chronicle* model, which permits the capture, within the data model, of many computations common to transactional data recording systems. A central issue in our model is the incremental maintenance of materialized views in time independent of the size of the recorded stream.

Within the chronicle model we study the type of summary queries that can be answered by using persistent views. We measure the complexity of a chronicle model by the complexity of incrementally maintaining its persistent views, and develop languages that ensure a low maintenance complexity independent of the sequence sizes.

1 Introduction

Motivation: Many database systems are used to record a stream of transactional information, such as credit card transactions, telephone calls, stock trades, flights taken, sensor outputs in a control system, etc. Applications that deal primarily with transactional data have the following common characteristics:

- An incoming sequence of transaction records, each record having several attributes of the transaction to be recorded. The sequence of records can be very large, and grows in an unbounded fashion. The transaction records are stored in a database for some latest time window, as it is beyond the capacity of any database system to store and provide access to this sequence for an indefinite amount of time.

  For example, a major telecommunications company is known to collect 75GB of sequence data every day, or 27TB of sequence data every year. No current database system can even store so much data, far less make it accessible in an interactive manner.

- Queries over the stored sequence of transaction records, with stringent response time requirements. Of particular interest are **summary queries**, that access summarization, or aggregation information of past transactional activity.

  For example, a cellular phone company may want to provide a facility for a summary query that computes the total number of minutes of calls made in the current billing month from a phone number. This query could be executed whenever a cellular phone is turned on, and the result could be displayed on the customer's phone instrument. Another example of a summary query that a customer care agent in the cellular company may want to execute is: What is the total number of minutes of calls made from a given cellular number since the number was assigned to the current customer.

These applications can be (and are) implemented using commercially available relational databases. However, the relational model is not suitable to capture and exploit the peculiar characteristics of a transaction recording system. For example, there is no support for answering a summary query over a sequence that is not stored in the database in its entirety. Even if the sequence is stored, there is no support for answering a summary query over a large sequence, with the speed needed to process a banking transaction, or to display the answer on the customer's phone at power-on time.

These summary queries are therefore supported in today's systems by procedural application code. For example, an application program may define a few summary fields (*e.g.*, *minutes_called*, *dollar_balance*) for each customer, and update these fields whenever a new transaction is processed for this purpose. Summary queries are then answered by looking up the summary fields, rather than going to the sequence of transaction records. This gives the applications a fast response time, as well as independence from the need to lookup past transactional data. Some applications, such as ATM withdrawals, require that a summary field (dollar_balance) be updated as the transaction is executed, since the summary query needs to be made before the next ATM withdrawal. Some applications may choose to use triggers to invoke the updating code; others may update the summary fields as they process transaction in batch. In all cases, the logic to update the summary fields due to a transaction is encoded procedurally, and the burden of writing this code is with the application programmer. This updating code is known to be very tricky, and has been the cause of well-publicized banking disasters (*e.g.*, Chemical bank ATM withdrawals caused incorrect updates on February 18, 1994, leading to several bounced checks and frustrated customers [Tim94]).

The need to define summary fields and to write the update procedures within the application code is one of the reasons for the complexity of banking, billing, and other similar systems. Would it not be much better if these summary fields could be defined declaratively, and then updated automatically by the system as each transaction is processed? The *chronicle data model,* which we are advocating in this chapter, has this goal in mind. In particular, we capture within the chronicle model the above needs of a transactional system, and thereby enable inexpensive, bug-free, and fast development of enhanced transactional systems. As the examples above illustrate, one feature that must be provided the chronicle model is support for summary queries that are specified declaratively (an SQL like language may be used), so that these queries can be answered without requiring the entire transactional history to be stored, and without accessing even the portion of the transactional history that is actually stored. The chronicle data model was inspired by our study of the complexities of a major transactional system within AT&T. However, our model is applicable to numerous other application domains, including credit cards, cellular telephone calls, stock trading, consumer banking, industrial control systems, retailing, frequent flyer programs, etc.

Results: We refer to the growing sequence of transaction records a *chronicle*. Our major contributions are:

■   We present a new data model, called the chronicle data model.

■   The model enables computation of summary queries over the chronicle, without requiring that the entire chronicle be stored in the database, and without requiring the application programmers to write procedural code.

■   The model permits summary queries over arbitrarily large chronicles to be answered in subseconds, without requiring the application programmers to write procedural code.

■   The chronicle model elevates persistent views to first class citizens in a database.

- We derive languages "Summarized Chronicle Algebra" and SCA$_\bowtie$, such that views defined in these language can be maintained incrementally without accessing any of the chronicles. Further, SCA$_\bowtie$ can be maintained incrementally in almost constant time, modulo index look ups. We have found SCA$_\bowtie$ to be very useful in our application of the chronicle model within AT&T.

- We show that the language chronicle algebra, a component of the "Summarized Chronicle Algebra", and the language CA$_\bowtie$, a component of SCA$_\bowtie$, are the largest possible subsets of the relational algebra *operations* that derive chronicles and are in their respective incremental maintenance complexity classes.

- We list several research and systems issues that can add functionality, currently not available in databases, to a chronicle model and make the chronicle model even more appealing to the transactional systems.

The chronicle data model, in effect, is both an enhancement and a restriction of the relational data model, and can be built on top of the relational model. The manner of its realization is, however, orthogonal to the central theme that, in either case, we can reduce the complexity of a large class of applications.

Chapter Outline The remainder of this extended abstract is organized as follows. In Section 2, we define the chronicle model. Section 3 defines complexity of a chronicle model as the complexity of incrementally maintaining its persistent views. We define a summarized chronicle algebra in Section 4, and derive several interesting results about this language, such as a low incremental complexity independent of the chronicle size, and maximal expressiveness while being limited to the relational algebra operations. We discuss some of the other research issues in the chronicle model in Section 5. Discussions concerning related work are offered in Section 6, which lead us to the conclusion in Section 7. Proofs of selected theorems are presented in the Appendix.

Preliminaries

We assume familiarity with relational algebra, and with grouping and aggregation operations of SQL. We use the following syntax [MPR90] to express the grouping operation:

$$\text{GROUPBY}(R, [G_1, \ldots, G_m], [A_1, \ldots, A_n]),$$

where R is the relation being grouped, $[G_1, \ldots, G_m]$ is the list of grouping attributes, and $[A_1, \ldots, A_n]$ is the list of aggregation functions. This expression defines a result relation with attributes in GL and with one attribute for each aggregation function. We will consider only those aggregation functions A_i that are incrementally computable, or are decomposable into incremental computation functions. For our complexity analysis, we will assume that each aggregation function can be computed in time $O(n)$ over a group of size n, and can be computed incrementally in time $O(1)$ over an increment of size 1. MIN, MAX, SUM, and COUNT are examples of such functions.

2   The Chronicle Data Model

We now define the chronicle model, discuss how queries may be posed on a chronicle database, and describe how updates to relations and chronicle must be handled in a chronicle database.

2.1   Model Definition

A chronicle database consists of *relations*, *chronicles*, and *persistent views*. *Relations* are standard, as in any relational database. Each relation may have several temporal versions (at least conceptually).

A *chronicle* is similar to a relation, except that a chronicle is a *sequence*, rather than an unordered set, of tuples. A chronicle can be represented by a relation with an extra *sequencing* attribute, whose values are drawn from an infinite ordered domain. The only update permissible to a chronicle is an insertion of tuples, with the sequence number of the inserted tuples being greater than any existing sequence number in the chronicle. There is no requirement that the sequence numbers be dense. Chronicles can be very large, and the entire chronicle may not be stored in the system.

There is a temporal instant (or chronon) associated with each sequence number. All operations on a tuple of a chronicle are with respect to the database as it was at that point in time. Thus, any join of a chronicle C and a relation R is a union of the corresponding joins of each tuple in C with the version of R that existed at the temporal instant of the tuple in C.

The database maintains a fixed number of *persistent views*, which are views that are materialized into relations, and are always maintained current in response to changes to the underlying database. Each persistent view is materialized when it is initially defined, and it is kept up-to-date, reflecting all the changes that occur in the database, as soon as these changes occur. Of particular concern is the maintenance of a persistent view after every append to a chronicle.

Persistent views are defined in a view definition language $\mathcal{L}$, and correspond to the procedurally computed summary fields in the current transaction systems. Each choice of $\mathcal{L}$ derives a particular instance of the chronicle data model. Formally,

Definition 2.1: (Chronicle database system) A chronicle database system is a quadruple:

$$(\mathcal{C}, \mathcal{R}, \mathcal{L}, \mathcal{V}),$$

where $\mathcal{C} = \{C_0, C_1, \ldots, C_n\}$ is a set of chronicles, $\mathcal{R} = \{R_0, R_1, \ldots, R_m\}$ is a set of relations, and $\mathcal{V} = \{V_0, V_1, \ldots, V_l\}$ is a set of persistent views defined in a language $\mathcal{L}$. $\square$

Example 2.1: Consider an airline database for tracking frequent flyer miles. There is one chronicle – the sequence of mileage transactions posted to the database. There is at least one relation containing information about customers, including their account number, name, and address. There are at least three persistent views to hold the mileage balance, the miles actually flown, and the premier status (bronze, silver, gold) of each customer. In order to define these persistent views, the language must allow for aggregation and joins between the chronicle and the relation. $\square$

2.2   Queries

Queries that access the relations and persistent views can be written in any language — relational algebra, SQL, Datalog, etc. The choice of this language is orthogonal to the chronicle model. The chronicle model enables fast response to queries that access the persistent views; these queries may otherwise have been defined as complex SQL queries over the relations and chronicles and thus would not likely have been answerable with acceptable performance. Further, a system would typically provide detailed queries over some latest window on the chronicle; again the choice of the window and the query language are orthogonal to our discussion.

2.3 Updates

There are two types of updates in our model: those that modify the relations and those that append to chronicles. An update to a relation R can be an insert, delete, or modification of a tuple in R. An update to a chronicle C can only be the insertion of a new tuple (or tuples) to C with a sequence number greater than the sequence number of all existing tuples in C. We consider these updates in turn below.

Each relation conceptually has multiple temporal versions, one after every update. In any persistent view defined in language $\mathcal{L}$, any joins between the relations and chronicles have an implicit temporal join on the sequencing attribute: We can associate a temporal version of the relations with each sequence number in the chronicles. Each tuple of a chronicle is then joined with the version of the relations associated with the same sequence number.

If an update to a relation affects only the versions corresponding to sequence numbers not seen as yet, then it is a *proactive* update; such an update does not affect the persistent views. Only subsequent chronicle updates see the new relation values. Since maintainability of persistent views is critical in the chronicle model, we have chosen to limit the language $\mathcal{L}$ so that only proactive updates to relations are allowed.

In contrast, a *retroactive* update to a relation would require older tuples in the chronicle to be re-processed. Such updates, when necessary, are computationally expensive to maintain, may not be maintainable if the entire past chronicle is unavailable, and are not included as part of the chronicle model.

Example 2.2: Consider again the frequent flyer example. Suppose that each customer living in New Jersey gets a bonus of 500 miles on each flight. The customer relation is updated whenever a customer changes his/her address. A flight tuple in the chronicle qualifies for the bonus only if the flight was made during the period of residence in New Jersey. Thus, the join between the chronicle and the relation is based on the temporal version of the relation associated with the sequence number in the chronicle. An update to the relation is proactive if the address update occurs before the associated tuples are appended to the chronicle. □

An update to a chronicle may cause a change in each persistent view, and we discuss maintenance of persistent views in the next two sections.

3 Complexity of a Chronicle Model

Each time a transaction completes, a record for the transaction is appended to the chronicle, and one or more persistent views may have to be maintained. The transaction rate that can be supported by a chronicle system is determined by the complexity of incremental maintenance of its persistent views. Thus, it is important to choose a language $\mathcal{L}$ that ensures that incremental view maintenance can be done efficiently. Moreover, since chronicles may not be stored in the system, the language $\mathcal{L}$ should allow incremental maintenance without having access to the entire chronicles. Ideally, the complexity of maintaining a view defined in $\mathcal{L}$ should be low – independent of the size of the relations and the view itself, modulo the overhead of index lookups.

We define the complexity of a chronicle system as the complexity of incremental computation of the language $\mathcal{L}$ used to express the persistent views. A class IM-T means that all persistent views defined in the language can be maintained in time $O(T)$ in response to a single append into a chronicle (IM for incremental maintenance). The incremental complexity classes are similar to the dynamic complexity classes of Patnaik and Immerman [PI94].

The following incremental complexity classes may be defined:

IM-Constant: A language is in the class IM-Constant if any persistent view defined in the language can be maintained incrementally in response to a single append into the chronicle in constant time.

IM-log(R): A language is in the class IM-log(R) if any persistent view defined in the language can be maintained incrementally in response to a single append into the chronicle in time logarithmic in the size of the relations.

IM-R^k: A language is in the class IM-R^k if any persistent view defined in the language can be maintained incrementally in response to a single append into the chronicle in time polynomial in the size of the relations.

IM-C^k: A language is in the class IM-C^k if any persistent view defined in the language can be maintained incrementally in response to a single append into the chronicle in time polynomial in the size of the chronicle and the relations.

It is easy to show that the following relationships hold between the sets of views that can be described by languages in each class:

$$\text{IM-Constant} \subset \text{IM-log}(R) \subset \text{IM-}R^k \subset \text{IM-}C^k$$

In a high throughput system, a complexity of IM-Constant is desired, which implies that even index lookups are not permitted, and is thus difficult to achieve. At the other end of the spectrum, a chronicle model with complexity IM-C^k would permit arbitrary access to the chronicle. Such a complexity is totally impractical for an operation to be executed after each append into each chronicle. The size of the relations, $| R |$, is assumed to be much smaller than the size of the chronicle $| C |$, so complexity class IM-R^k is the largest that has the possibility of being manageable.

The choice of language $\mathcal{L}$ for defining persistent views with a low IM complexity is crucial. One obvious candidate is relational algebra with grouping and incrementally computable aggregate operators. However, relational algebra is not an acceptable choice for $\mathcal{L}$, as the following result indicates.

Proposition 3.1: Relational algebra, extended with grouping and aggregation, applied to chronicles and relations, is in the class IM-C^k, and is not in the class IM-R^k. □

4   Summarized Chronicle Algebra

In this section, we derive the largest subsets of a set of relation algebra operators that define languages in the first three IM complexity classes, which are all independent of the size of the chronicle. We present our development in two steps. First, we define an intermediate chronicle algebra that maps chronicles and relations into chronicles. Then, we add a summarization step that maps chronicle algebra expressions into relations by projecting out the sequencing attribute, possibly doing a grouping and aggregation alongside.

All inserted tuples into a chronicle must have a sequence number greater than all existing sequence numbers, but multiple tuples with the same sequence number can be inserted simultaneously. For instance, when a tuple is inserted into a base chronicle, each of the two operands of a union may derive a distinct tuple with the same sequence number. The union expression can then have two distinct tuples with the same sequence number.

We define a *chronicle group* as a collection of chronicles whose sequence numbers are drawn from the same domain, along with the requirement that an insert into any chronicle in a chronicle group must have a sequence number greater than the sequence number of any tuple in the chronicle group. Operations like union, difference, and join are permitted amongst chronicles of the same chronicle group.

Definition 4.1: The chronicle algebra (CA) consists of the following operators (C is a chronicle or a chronicle algebra expression, $A_1, \ldots, A_n$ are attributes of the chronicle, and p is a predicate):

- A selection on a chronicle, $\sigma_p(C)$, where p is a predicate of the form $A_1 \theta A_2$, or $A_1 \theta k$, or a disjunction of such terms, k is a constant, and θ is one of $\{=, \neq, \leq, <, >, \geq\}$. $\sigma_p(C)$ selects chronicle tuples that satisfy the predicate p. The resulting chronicle has the same type as the chronicle C.

- Projection of a chronicle on attributes that include the sequencing attribute, $\Pi_{A_1, \ldots, A_n}(C)$.

- A natural equijoin between two chronicles on the sequencing attribute, $C_1 \bowtie_{C_1.SN = C_2.SN} C_2$, where SN is the sequencing attribute, C_1 and C_2 are chronicles in the same chronicle group, and one of the sequencing attributes is projected out from the result.

- Union of two chronicles, $C_1 \cup C_2$, where C_1 and C_2 are chronicles in the same chronicle group, and have the same type.

- Difference of two chronicles, $C_1 - C_2$, where C_1 and C_2 are chronicles in the same chronicle group, and have the same type.

- A groupby with aggregation, with the sequence number as one of the grouping attributes: GROUPBY(C, GL, AL), where C is a chronicle being grouped, GL is the list of grouping attributes (which must include the sequencing attribute), and AL is the list of aggregation functions.

- A cartesian product between a chronicle C, and any relation R, $C \times R$. Though this operation is written as a cross product, recall (from Sec. 2.3 and Example 2.2) that an implicit temporal join on the sequencing attribute exists between C and R. $\square$

Theorem 4.1: A view defined by the chronicle algebra is monotonic with respect to insertions into the base chronicles. Whenever tuples with sequence numbers greater than all existing sequence numbers are added to the base chronicles, the effect is to add tuples with some of these new sequence numbers to the view. $\square$

Lemma 4.1: Each view defined using a chronicle algebra expression is a chronicle in the same chronicle group as the operand chronicles. $\square$

Definition 4.2:

- CA$_1$ is chronicle algebra, without the cross product operation between chronicles and relations.

- CA$_\bowtie$ is chronicle algebra, where the cross product operation between chronicles and relations is replaced by a join, with a guarantee (based on the schema and integrity constraints on the database) that at most a constant number of relation tuples join with each chronicle tuple. A sufficient condition for the guarantee is that the join be on a key of the relation R. $\square$

Theorem 4.2: The changes, due to insertions into the base chronicles, for a chronicle view defined by:

- CA can be computed in time and space independent of the size of the chronicles and independent of the size of the view. Time $= O((u \mid R \mid)^j \log(\mid R \mid))$, and Space $= O((u \mid R \mid)^j)$, where u is the number of unions in the expression defining the view, $\mid R \mid$ is the size of the relation R, and j is the number of equijoins and cross products in the expression defining the view.

- $\mathsf{CA}_{\bowtie}$ can be computed in Time $= O(u^j \log(\mid R \mid))$, and Space $= O(u^j)$.

- CA_1 can be computed in Time $= O(u^j)$, and Space $= O(u^j)$ $\square$

In all cases, neither the chronicle view nor the chronicles need to be stored or accessed for the view maintenance; and this is the reason for obtaining a complexity which is independent of both the sizes of the chronicle and the sizes of the view.

Theorem 4.3: An extension of the chronicle algebra with either of (1) projection without including the sequencing attribute, or (2) a groupby operation without including the sequencing attribute as a grouping attribute leads to an algebra that can define an expression that is not a chronicle. Further, an extension of the chronicle algebra with either of (1) cross product between chronicles, or (2) a non-equijoin between two chronicles leads to an algebra that can define an expression for which the time for incremental view maintenance is dependent on the size of a chronicle. $\square$

Note that this theorem implies that the chronicle algebra is the largest subset of relational algebra operations that is in $\mathsf{IM}\text{-}R^k$, and that $\mathsf{CA}_{\bowtie}$ is the largest subset of relational algebra operations that is in $\mathsf{IM}\text{-}\log(R)$. It is important to note that we can define expressions using the cross product or non-equijoin between chronicles that are in $\mathsf{IM}\text{-}R^k$. Theorem 4.3 simply states that there also exist expressions one can define using the cross product or non-equijoins that are not in $\mathsf{IM}\text{-}R^k$.

Next, we present a summarization step that maps chronicles produced by chronicle algebra into persistent views, which are relations without the sequencing attributes. The persistent view is then stored, and it is updated whenever an insert occurs into the chronicles on which the persistent view depends.

Definition 4.3: The *summarized chronicle algebra* (SCA), has the two basic operations that can eliminate the sequence attribute and map a chronicle algebra expression χ into a relation.

- Projection, with the sequencing attribute projected out; that is, $\Pi_{A_1,\ldots,A_n}(\chi)$, where the attributes $A_1,\ldots,A_n$ do not include the sequencing attribute.

- Grouping with aggregation, where the sequencing attribute is not included in the grouping list, and where the aggregation functions are incrementally computable (or decomposable into incrementally computable functions); represented as $\mathsf{GROUPBY}(\chi, GL, AL)$ where the grouping list GL does not include the sequencing attribute of χ.

If the expression χ is in CA_1, then the resulting language is called SCA_1; if the expression χ is in $\mathsf{CA}_{\bowtie}$, then the resulting language is called $\mathsf{SCA}_{\bowtie}$. $\square$

From Definition 4.3, it follows that every persistent view expressed in SCA produces a relation (not a chronicle) that does not have the sequence number as an attribute. Once a relation is defined using SCA, it could be further manipulated by using relational algebra and the other relations in the system, to define a persistent view. However, since incremental maintenance is the key, we have to be careful to store a persistent view that can be maintained without accessing the full chronicles over which the summarization step is defined.

Theorem 4.4: Given a set of changes to chronicle algebra expression, incremental maintenance of a persistent view written in SCA in response to insertions to a chronicle can be done in

- Space equal to the size of the view.

- Time $= O(t \log(\mid V \mid))$, where $\mid V \mid$ is the size of the persistent view V, and t is the number of tuples inserted into the chronicle algebra (or CA_1 or $\mathsf{CA}_{\bowtie}$) expression χ. $\square$

Theorem 4.5: SCA is contained in class IM-R^k, SCA$_\bowtie$ is contained in class IM-log(R), and SCA$_1$ is contained in class IM-Constant. □

Thus, though the result of a chronicle algebra expression contains sequence numbers, and therefore may have a size that is polynomial in $\mid C \mid$, incremental maintenance of summarized chronicle algebra expressions can be done in time independent of $\mid C \mid$, since the chronicle view is not accessed during maintenance.

5   Issues in the Chronicle Model

We briefly outline several additional research issues that need to be considered in designing a chronicle system.

5.1   Periodic Persistent Views

The applications targeted by the chronicle model require the definition of a view that is computed over several, potentially overlapping, intervals on a chronicle, one view computation for each interval. To address this need, we introduce a *periodic summarized chronicle algebra* by adding, to the chronicle algebra, features in the spirit of [SS92, CSS94] to construct sets of time intervals over which the persistent views can be computed. A mapping from sequence numbers in a chronicle to time intervals must be made for the periodic summarized chronicle algebra to be defined.

Given a view V in summary algebra, and a calendar D (*i.e.*, a set of time intervals), $V < D >$ specifies a set of views $V_1, \ldots, V_k$, one for each interval in the calendar D. The view V_i for interval i is defined as in V, but with a selection on the chronicle, which requires that all chronicle tuples be within the interval i, under the mapping defined from sequence numbers to time intervals. If the calendar D has an infinite number of intervals, there will be an infinite number of views V_i. The view expression $V < D >$ is called a *periodic view*. When the calendar D has only one interval, the periodic view corresponds to a single view defined using an extra selection on the chronicle.

The periodic summarized chronicle algebra also provides for an expiration time for a view, after which the view is not needed. Expiration dates allow the system to implement an infinite number of periodic views, provided only a finite number of them are current at any one instant.

Many applications require periodic views over non-overlapping intervals. (For instance, a new billing statement is generated each month, by banks, telephone companies, credit card companies, etc.) The evaluation of these can be optimized by starting to maintain a view as soon as its time interval starts, and stopping its maintenance as soon as its interval ends. Periodic views over overlapping intervals can be defined to compute moving averages over the transactions in a chronicle. Optimization of such views is even more challenging. For example, consider a periodic view for every day that computes the total number of shares of a stock sold during the 30 days preceding that day. The computation of these views can be optimized by noticing that the sum of shares is an incrementally computable function. This suggests that we should keep the total number of shares sold for each of the last 30 days separately, and derive the view as the sum of these 30 numbers. Moving from one periodic view to the next one involves shifting a cyclic buffer of these 30 numbers. Further, if an expiration date is given, the space for the periodic view can be reused. How would such a computation be derived automatically by the system for a generic periodic view expressed over any given set of overlapping time intervals?

5.2   Identifying affected persistent views

When multiple views are to be maintained over the same chronicle, each update to the chronicle would require checking all the views to determine if they need to be updated. To do so, we must:

- Identify the persistent views V that will be affected. We need to filter these out early so as not to waste computation resources. This problem is similar to determining when a query is independent of an update [LS93]. The problem is similar to detecting the active rules that must be checked after a database update.

- For each persistent view V, identify the tuples that will be affected. Thus, the persistent views need to have indices. What indices should be constructed?

- When periodic views are used, we must be able to easily identify the persistent views that are *active* – these are the views defined for the *current* time interval, and only these periodic views need to be maintained upon insertions into the chronicle.

Efficient storage structures are needed for fast access to the updated persistent view tuples. We have developed an efficient storage structure in our implementation of the chronicle model at AT&T Bell Labs.

5.3   Batch to Incremental Updates

Applications often define computations applying to a batch of transactions. For example, a bank may charge a fee based upon the total number of transactions within a period, a telephone company may offer a discount based upon the total calls within a period, an airline may give bonus miles based upon total activity within a certain period. For instance, a popular telephone discounting plan in the USA gives a discount of 10% on all calls made if the monthly undiscounted expenses exceed \$10, a discount of 20% if the expenses exceed \$25, and so on. In such applications, a common assumption is that the computations are performed once at the end of the period. This leads to two problems:

- The results of these computations are either out-of-date, or inaccurate before the end of the period over which the discount applies.

- The transactions need to be processed, for computing these attributes, in batch.

Converting computations on a batch of records to an equivalent incremental computation on individual records is an exercise akin to devising algorithms for incremental view maintenance. For example, for the telephone discount plan, there is a nontrivial mapping for incrementally computing a persistent view for total_expenses.

6   Related Work

The notion of incremental differences has been studied extensively, beginning with [SL76], continuing with work on delayed updates, and most recently with work on languages (*e.g.*, [GHJ96]). Incremental differences have been used effectively in the active database context [BW94], and in the constraint maintenance context [Qia88]. Incrementally computable aggregation functions are used in [DAJ91, GMS93, RRSS94]. Our work here deals with incremental view maintenance. However, we differ from the past view maintenance work [BLT86, CW91, GMS93, JMR91, JM93] in that (1) we assume that the modified relation (the chronicle) is not accessible during maintenance, (2) we require that all intermediate views defined in chronicle algebra not be materialized, and (3) we make special use of the sequencing and temporal join properties of a chronicle.

The temporal data model [TCG+93] builds in a model of time into the data, and allows complex queries that relate data across time. Several versions of data are stored to support these queries. However, as in the relational model, queries or persistent views over data that is not completely stored in the database are not modeled. The concept of time in the chronicle model is much simpler – a sequence number for chronicle records, and an implicit temporal join with the relations when defining views. The implicit temporal join is always with the most *current* version of the relations, and versions of relations do not need to be stored. Seshadri *et al.* [SLR94] look at optimizing queries over sequences, assuming the full sequence is stored.

Patnaik and Immerman [PI94] define the dynamic complexity of a query as the complexity of maintaining a materialized view against which the query can be answered with the same complexity. They focused on a class of queries that can be incrementally maintained using a relational algebra expression (the Dyn-FO class), and show that several queries that cannot be expressed in relational algebra can be maintained using a relational algebra expression. The notion of dynamic complexity is similar to the idea of incremental complexity (Section 3) of a persistent view; however, the later does not include the complexity of querying the view, and is a computational measure, while the former is a descriptive measure. We focus on incremental complexity classes that are more efficient than Dyn-FO, and we exploit the special properties of a chronicle to make the incremental complexity independent of the chronicle size.

Incarnations of the chronicle model may be applicable to domains other than transactional systems. For example, in active databases, the recognition of complex events to be fired is done on a chronicle of events. The notion of history-less evaluation [Cho92a, Cho92b, GJS92b, GJS92a] is simply the idea of incremental maintenance of the persistent views defined by the event algebra. The language $\mathcal{L}$ in these cases is either a variant of temporal logic [Cho92a, Cho92b], or a variant of regular expressions [GJS92b, GJS92a].

7 Conclusions

Transaction recording systems are an important class of database applications. To meet the stringent performance requirements of these applications, much of the recording and query processing functionality, which should preferably be in the database, is actually implemented in the procedural application code, with the attendant difficulties in development, modularization, maintenance, and evolution.

To combat this deficiency, we proposed a new data model, the *chronicle* model, which permits the capture, within the data model, of many computations common to transactional recording systems. The database maintains a set of chronicles, each of which is a log of the transactions records of a particular type. A chronicle, in contrast to a regular relation, need not be stored in its entirety in the system. To capture the essential information about the records in the chronicles we allow one to define a materialized (persistent) view over a chronicle. The persistent views must be maintained in response to each new transaction. One major concern is the efficient and automatic maintenance of persistent views in order to meet the performance requirements of transaction recording systems. With this in mind, we defined incremental complexity classes. A language belongs to an incremental class if all views defined using the language can be maintained incrementally in the time specified by the class. The complexity of the chronicle model was itself defined in terms of the incremental complexity of its language for defining persistent views.

We introduced a summarized chronicle algebra (SCA) that can be used to define persistent views. Aggregation is permitted, and is an important operation for the applications. We showed that all SCA views can be maintained incrementally without reference to the chronicle, in time polynomial in the size of the relations. We further derived a condition under which the language SCA$_\bowtie$, by restricting joins to be on a key, can be incrementally maintained in time logarithmic in the size of the relations. We showed that our proposed summarized chronicle algebra and its variants are in fact the largest fragments of relational algebra with these incremental complexities.

The chronicle data model has been implemented for a large transactional system in AT&T. We believe that our model is applicable to numerous other application domains, including credit cards, billing for telephone calls, cellular phones, advanced telephone services, stock trading, consumer banking, industrial control systems, retailing, and frequent flyer programs.

Acknowledgments: We thank Jan Chomicki and Kenneth Ross for valuable suggestions.

19

VIEW MAINTENANCE
IN A
WAREHOUSING ENVIRONMENT

Yue Zhuge, Hector Garcia-Molina
Joachim Hammer, Jennifer Widom

ABSTRACT

A warehouse is a repository of integrated information drawn from remote data sources. Since a warehouse effectively implements materialized views, we must maintain the views as the data sources are updated. This view maintenance problem differs from the traditional one in that the view definition and the base data are now decoupled. We show that this decoupling can result in anomalies if traditional algorithms are applied. We introduce a new algorithm, ECA (for "Eager Compensating Algorithm"), that eliminates the anomalies. ECA is based on previous incremental view maintenance algorithms, but extra "compensating" queries are used to eliminate anomalies. We also introduce two streamlined versions of ECA for special cases of views and updates, and we present an initial performance study that compares ECA to a view recomputation algorithm in terms of messages transmitted, data transferred, and I/O costs.

1 Introduction

Warehousing is an emerging technique for retrieval and integration of data from distributed, autonomous, possibly heterogeneous, information sources. A *data warehouse* is a repository of integrated information, available for queries and analysis (e.g., decision support, or data mining) [IK93]. As relevant information becomes available from a source, or when relevant information is modified, the information is extracted from the source, translated into a common model (e.g., the relational model), and integrated with existing data at the warehouse. Queries can be answered and analysis can be performed quickly and efficiently since the integrated information is directly available at the warehouse, with differences already resolved.

1.1 The Problem

One can think of a data warehouse as defining and storing integrated *materialized views* over the data from multiple, autonomous information sources. An important issue is the prompt and correct propagation of updates at the sources to the views at the warehouse. Numerous methods have been developed for materialized view maintenance in conventional database systems; these methods are discussed in Section 2.

Unfortunately, existing materialized view maintenance algorithms fail in a warehousing environment. Existing approaches assume that each source understands view management and knows the relevant view definitions. Thus, when an update occurs at a source, the source knows exactly what data is needed for updating the view.

253

However, in a warehousing environment, the sources can be legacy or unsophisticated systems that do not understand views. Sources can inform the warehouse when an update occurs, e.g., a new employee has been hired, or a patient has paid her bill. However, they cannot determine what additional data may or may not be necessary for incorporating the update into the warehouse views. When the simple update information arrives at the warehouse, we may discover that some additional source data is necessary to update the views. Thus, the warehouse may have to issue queries to some of the sources, as illustrated in Figure 1. The queries are evaluated at the sources later than the corresponding updates, so the source states may have changed. This decoupling between the base data on the one hand (at the sources), and the view definition and view maintenance machinery on the other (at the warehouse), can lead the warehouse to compute incorrect views.

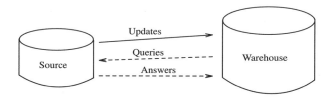

Figure 1 Update processing in a single source model

We illustrate the problems with three examples. For these examples, and for the rest of this chapter, we use the relational model for data and relational algebra select-project-join queries for views. Although we are using relational algebra, we assume that duplicates are retained in the materialized views. Duplicate retention (or at least a replication count) is essential if deletions are to be handled incrementally [BLT86, GMS93]. Note that the type of solution we propose here can be extended to other data models and view specification languages.

Also, in the examples and in this chapter we focus on a single source, and a single view over several base relations. Our methods extend to multiple views directly. Handling a view that spans several sources requires the same type of solution, but introduces additional issues; see Section 7 for a brief discussion.

Example 1:   Correct View Maintenance

Suppose our source contains two base relations r_1 and r_2 as follows:

$r_1:$

W	X
1	2

$r_2:$

X	Y
2	4

The view at the warehouse is defined by the expression: $V = \Pi_W(r_1 \bowtie r_2)$. Initially the materialized view at the warehouse, MV, contains the single tuple [1]. Now suppose tuple [2,3] is inserted into r_2 at the source. For notation, we use $insert(r, t)$ to denote the insertion of tuple t into relation r (similarly for $delete(r, t)$), and we use $([t_1], [t_2], \ldots, [t_n])$ to denote a relation with tuples $t_1, t_2, \ldots, t_n$. The following events occur:

1. Update $U_1 = insert(r_2, [2, 3])$ occurs at the source. Since the source does not know the details or contents of the view managed by the warehouse, it simply sends a notification to the warehouse that update U_1 occurred.

2. The warehouse receives U_1. Applying an incremental view maintenance algorithm, it sends query $Q_1 = \Pi_W(r_1 \bowtie [2,3])$ to the source. (That is, the warehouse asks the source which r_1 tuples match with the new [2,3] tuple in r_2.)

3. The source receives Q_1 and evaluates it using the current base relations. It returns the answer relation $A_1 = ([1])$ to the warehouse.

4. The warehouse receives answer A_1 and adds ([1]) to the materialized view, obtaining ([1],[1]).

The final view at the warehouse is correct, i.e., it is equivalent to what one would obtain using a conventional view maintenance algorithm directly at the source.[1] The next two examples show how the final view can be incorrect.

Example 2:   A View Maintenance Anomaly

Assume we have the same relations as in Example 1, but initially r_2 is empty:

$$r_1: \quad \begin{array}{|c|c|} \hline W & X \\ \hline 1 & 2 \\ \hline \end{array} \qquad\qquad r_2: \quad \begin{array}{|c|c|} \hline X & Y \\ \hline - & - \\ \hline \end{array}$$

Consider the same view definition as in Example 1: $V = \Pi_W(r_1 \bowtie r_2)$, and now suppose there are two consecutive updates: $U_1 = insert(r_2, [2,3])$ and $U_2 = insert(r_1, [4,2])$. The following events occur. Note that initially $MV = \phi$.

1. The source executes $U_1 = insert(r_2, [2,3])$ and sends U_1 to the warehouse.

2. The warehouse receives U_1 and sends $Q_1 = \Pi_W(r_1 \bowtie [2,3])$ to the source.

3. The source executes $U_2 = insert(r_1, [4,2])$ and sends U_2 to the warehouse.

4. The warehouse receives U_2 and sends $Q_2 = \Pi_W([4,2] \bowtie r_2)$ to the source.

5. The source receives Q_1 and evaluates it on the current base relations: $r_1 = ([1,2], [4,2])$ and $r_2 = ([2,3])$. The resulting answer relation is $A_1 = ([1], [4])$, which is sent to the warehouse.

6. The warehouse receives A_1 and updates the view to $MV \cup A_1 = ([1], [4])$.

7. The source receives Q_2 and evaluates it on the current base relations r_1 and r_2. The resulting answer relation is $A_2 = ([4])$, which is sent to the warehouse.

8. The warehouse receives answer A_2 and updates the view to $MV \cup A_2 = ([1], [4], [4])$.

If the view had been maintained using a conventional algorithm directly at the source, then it would be ([1]) after U_1 and ([1],[4]) after U_2. However, the warehouse first changes the view to ([1],[4]) (in step 6) and to ([1],[4],[4]) (in step 8), which is an incorrect final state. The problem is that the query Q_1 issued in step 4 is evaluated using a state of the base relations that differs from the state at the time of the update (U_1) that caused Q_1 to be issued. $\square$

We call the behavior exhibited by this example a *distributed incremental view maintenance anomaly*, or *anomaly* for short. Anomalies occur when the warehouse attempts to update a view while base data at the

---

[1] As stated earlier, for incremental handling of deletions we need to keep both [1] tuples in the view. For instance, if [2,4] is later deleted from r_2, one (but not both) of the [1] tuples should be deleted from the view.

source is changing. Anomalies arise in a warehousing environment because of the decoupling between the information sources, which are updating the base data, and the warehouse, which is performing the view update.

Example 3:   Deletion Anomaly

Our third example shows that deletions can also cause anomalies. Consider source relations:

$$r_1: \quad \frac{\text{W} \quad \text{X}}{1 \quad 2} \qquad\qquad\qquad\qquad r_2: \quad \frac{\text{X} \quad \text{Y}}{2 \quad 3}$$

Suppose that the view definition is $V = \Pi_{W,Y}(r_1 \bowtie r_2)$. The following events occur. Note that initially $MV = ([1,3])$.

1. The source executes $U_1 = delete(r_1, [1,2])$ and notifies the warehouse.

2. The warehouse receives U_1 and emits $Q_1 = \Pi_{W,Y}([1,2] \bowtie r_2)$.

3. The source executes $U_2 = delete(r_2, [2,3])$ and notifies the warehouse.

4. The warehouse receives U_2 and emits $Q_2 = \Pi_{W,Y}(r_1 \bowtie [2,3])$.

5. The source receives Q_1. The answer it returns is $A_1 = \phi$ since both relations are now empty.

6. The warehouse receives A_1 and replaces the view by $MV - A_1 = ([1,3])$. (Difference is used here since the update to the base relation was a deletion [BLT86].)

7. Similarly, the source evaluates Q_2, returns $A_2 = \phi$, and the warehouse replaces the view by $MV - A_2 = ([1,3])$.

This final view is incorrect: since r_1 and r_2 are empty, the view should be empty too. □

1.2   Possible Solutions

There are a number of mechanisms for avoiding anomalies. As argued above, we are interested only in mechanisms where the source, which may be a legacy or unsophisticated system, does not perform any "view management." The source will only notify the warehouse of relevant updates, and answer queries asked by the warehouse. We also are not interested in, for example, solutions where the source must lock data while the warehouse updates its views, or in solutions where the source must maintain timestamps for its data in order to detect "stale" queries from the warehouse. In the following potential solutions, view maintenance is autonomous from source updating:

- *Recompute the view* (RV). The warehouse can either recompute the full view whenever an update occurs at the source, or it can recompute the view periodically. In Example 2, if the warehouse sends a query to the source to recompute the view after it receives U_2, then the source will compute the answer relation $A = ([1],[4])$ (assuming no further updates) and the warehouse will correctly set $MV = ([1],[4])$. Recomputing views is usually time and resource consuming, particularly in a distributed environment where a large amount of data might need to be transferred from the source to the warehouse. In Section 6 we compare the performance of our proposed solution to this one.

- *Store at the warehouse copies of all relations involved in views* (SC). In Example 2, suppose that the warehouse keeps up-to-date copies of r_1 and r_2. When U_1 arrives, Q_1 can be evaluated "locally," and no anomaly arises. The disadvantages of this approach are: (1) the warehouse needs to store copies of all base relations used in its views, and (2) copied relations at the warehouse need to be updated whenever an update occurs at the source.

- *The Eager Compensating Algorithm* (ECA). The solution we advocate avoids the overhead of recomputing the view or of storing copies of base relations. The basic idea is to add to queries sent to the source *compensating queries* to offset the effect of concurrent updates. For instance, in Example 2, consider the receipt of $U_2 = insert(r_1, [4, 2])$ in step 4. If we assume that messages are delivered in order, and that the source handles requests atomically, then when the warehouse receives U_2 it can deduce that its previous query Q_1 will be evaluated in an "incorrect" state—Q_1 will see the [4,2] tuple of the second insert. (Otherwise, the warehouse would have received the answer to Q_1 before it received the notification of U_2.) To compensate, the warehouse sends query:

$$Q_2 = \Pi_W([4, 2] \bowtie r_2) - \Pi_W([4, 2] \bowtie [2, 3])$$

The first part of Q_2 is as before; the second part compensates for the extra tuple that Q_1 will see. We call this an "eager" algorithm because the warehouse is compensating (in step 4) even before the answer for Q_1 has arrived (in step 6). In Section 5.2 we briefly discuss a "lazy" version of this approach. Continuing with the example, we see that indeed the answer received in step 6, $A_1 = ([1], [4])$, contains the extra tuple [4]. But, because of the compensation, the A_2 answer received in step 8 is empty, and the final view is correct. In Section 5.2 we present the Eager Compensating Algorithm in detail, showing how the compensating queries are determined for an arbitrary view, and how query answers are integrated into the view.

We also consider two improvements to the basic ECA algorithm:

- *The ECA-Key Algorithm* (ECA^K). If a view includes a key from every base relation involved in the view, then we can streamline the ECA algorithm in two ways: (1) Deletions can be handled at the warehouse without issuing a query to the source. (2) Insertions require queries to the source, but compensating queries are unnecessary. To illustrate point (1), consider Example 3, and suppose W and Y are keys for r_1 and r_2. When the warehouse receives $U_1 = delete(r_1, [1, 2])$ (step 1), it can immediately determine that all tuples of the form [1,x] are deleted from the view (where x denotes any value)—no query needs to be sent to the source. Similarly, $U_2 = delete(r_2, [2, 3])$ causes all [x,3] tuples to be deleted from the view, without querying the source. The final empty view is correct. Section 5.4 provides an example illustrating point (2), and a description of ECA^K. Note that ECA^K does have the disadvantage that it can only be used for a subset of all possible views—those that contain keys for all base relations.

- *The ECA-Local Algorithm* (ECA^L). In ECA^K, the warehouse processes deletes locally, without sending any queries to the source, but inserts still require queries to be sent to the source. Generalizing this idea, for a given view definition and a given update, it is possible to determine whether or not the update can be handled locally; see, e.g., [GB95, BLT86]. We outline ECA^L, which combines local handling of updates with the compensation approach for maintenance of arbitrary views.

1.3 Outline of Chapter

In the next section we briefly review related research. Then, in Section 3, we provide a formal definition of correctness for view maintenance in a warehousing environment. As we will see, there are a variety of "levels" of correctness that may be of interest to different applications. In Sections 4 and 5 we present our new algorithms, along with a number of examples. In Section 6 we compare the performance of our ECA algorithm to the view recomputation approach. In Section 7 we conclude and discuss future directions of our work. Additional details—additional examples, proofs, analyses, etc.—that are too lengthy and intricate to be included in the body of the chapter are presented in [ZGMHW94] (available via anonymous ftp from host `db.stanford.edu`).

2   Related Research

Many incremental view maintenance algorithms have been developed. Most of them are designed for a traditional, centralized database environment, where it is assumed that view maintenance is performed by a system that has full control and knowledge of the view definition, the base relations, the updated tuples, and the view [HD92, QW91, SI84]. These algorithms differ somewhat in the view definitions they handle. For example, [BLT86] considers select-project-join (SPJ) views only, while algorithms in [GMS93] handle views defined by any SQL or Datalog expression. Some algorithms depend on key information to deal with duplicate tuples [CW91], while others use a counting approach [GMS93].

A series of papers by Segev et al. studies materialized views in distributed systems [SF90, SF91, SP89a, SP89b]. All algorithms in these papers are based on timestamping the updated tuples, and the algorithms assume there is only one base table. Other incremental algorithms, such as the "snapshot" procedure in [LHM+86], also assume timestamping and a single base table. In contrast, our algorithms have no restrictions on the number of base tables, and they require no additional information. Note that although we describe our algorithms for SPJ views, our approach can be applied to adapt any existing centralized view maintenance algorithm to the warehousing environment.

In both centralized and distributed systems, there are three general approaches to the timing of view maintenance: *immediate* update [BLT86], which updates the view after each base relation is updated, *deferred* update [RK86a], which updates the view only when a query is issued against the view, and *periodic* update [LHM+86], which updates the view at periodic intervals. Performance studies on these strategies have determined that the efficiency of an approach depends heavily on the structure of the base relations and on update patterns [Han87]. We assume immediate update in this chapter, but we observe that with little or no modification our algorithms can be applied to deferred and periodic update as well.

The algorithms in this chapter could be viewed as a specialized concurrency control mechanism for a multidatabase system. Our algorithms exploit the semantics of the application (relational views) to provide a certain type of consistency without traditional locking. Paper [BGMS92] provides a survey of related work.

3   Correctness

Our first task is to define what correctness means in an environment where activity at the source is decoupled from the view at the warehouse. We start by defining the notion of *events*. In our context, an event corresponds to a sequence of operations performed at the same site. There are two types of events at the source:

1. S_up: the source executes an update U, then sends an update notification to the warehouse.

2. S_qu: the source evaluates a query Q using its current base relations, then sends the answer relation A back to the warehouse.

There are two types of events at the warehouse:

1. *W_up*: the warehouse receives an update U, generates a query Q, and sends Q to the source for evaluation.

2. *W_ans*: the warehouse receives the answer relation A for a query Q and updates the view based on A.

We will assume that events are atomic. That is, we assume there is a local concurrency control mechanism (or only a single user) at each site to ensure that conflicting operations do not overlap. With some extensions to our algorithms, this assumption could be relaxed. We also assume that, within an event, actions always follow the order described above. For example, within an event *S_up*, the source always executes the update operation first, then sends the update notification to the warehouse.

We use e to denote an arbitrary event, se to denote a source event, and we to denote a warehouse event. Event types are subscripted to indicate a specific event, e.g., S_up_i, or W_up_j. For each event, relevant information about the event is denoted using a functional notation: For an event e, $query(e)$, $update(e)$, and $answer(e)$ denote respectively the query, update, and answer associated with event e (when relevant). If event e is caused ("triggered") by another event, then $trigger(e)$ denotes the event that triggered e. For example, $trigger(W\_up_j)$ is an event of type *S_up*. The state of the data after an event e is denoted by $state(e)$.

It is useful to immediately rule out algorithms that are trivially incorrect; for example, where the source does not propagate updates to the warehouse, or refuses to execute queries. These two examples are captured formally by the following rules:

- $\forall U = update(S\_up_i)$: $\exists W\_up_j$ such that $update(W\_up_j) = U$.

- $\forall Q = query(W\_up_i)$: $\exists S\_qu_j$ such that $query(S\_qu_j) = Q$.

There are a number of other obvious rules such as these that we omit for brevity.

Finally, we define the binary event operator "$<$" to mean "occurs before". We assume that messages are delivered in order and are processed in order. In particular, let e_1, e_2, e_3, e_4 be four events. If $trigger(e_2) = e_1$, $trigger(e_4) = e_3$, and e_1 and e_3 occurred at the same site, then $e_1 < e_3$ iff $e_2 < e_4$. We also use the $<$ relation to order states. That is, we say that $s_i < s_j$ if $state(e_i) = s_i$, $state(e_j) = s_j$, and $e_i < e_j$.

3.1 Levels of Correctness

During the execution of a view maintenance algorithm, the system will process a sequence of updates $U_1, U_2, \ldots, U_n$. In doing so, the source executes events $se_1, se_2, \ldots se_p$ with corresponding resulting states $ss_1, ss_2, \ldots, ss_p$. At the warehouse the triggered events are $we_1, we_2, \ldots we_q$ with corresponding resulting states $ws_1, ws_2, \ldots, ws_q$. When we define the notion of *convergence* (below), we consider executions that are finite, i.e., that have a last update U_n and last events se_p and we_k. However, in general executions may be finite or infinite.

At the warehouse, the state of materialized view V after event we_i is given by $V[ws_i]$, where V is the view definition. Similarly, at the source, $Q[ss_i]$ is the result of evaluating query expression Q on the relations existing after event se_i. If we apply the view definition V to a source state, $V[ss_i]$, we get the state of the view had it been evaluated at the source after event se_i.

An algorithm for warehouse view maintenance may exhibit the following properties:

- *Convergence*: For all finite executions, $V[ws_q] = V[ss_p]$. That is, after the last update and after all activity has ceased, the view is consistent with the relations at the source.

- *Weak Consistency:* For all executions and for all ws_i, there exists an ss_j such that $V[ws_i] = V[ss_j]$. That is, every state of the view corresponds to some valid state of the relations at the source.

- *Consistency:* For all executions and for every pair $ws_i < ws_j$, there exist $ss_k \leq ss_l$ such that $V[ws_i] = V[ss_k]$ and $V[ws_j] = V[ss_l]$. That is, every state of the view corresponds to a valid source state, and in a corresponding order.

- *Strong consistency:* Consistency and convergence.

- *Completeness:* Strong consistency, and for each ss_i there exists a ws_j such that $V[ws_j] = V[ss_i]$. That is, there is a complete order-preserving mapping between the states of the view and the states of the source.

Although completeness is a nice property since it states that the view "tracks" the base data exactly, we believe it is too strong a requirement and unnecessary in most practical warehousing scenarios. In some cases, convergence may be sufficient, i.e., knowing that "eventually" the warehouse will have a valid state, even if it passes through intermediate states that are invalid. In other cases, consistency (weak or not) may be required, i.e., knowing that every warehouse state is valid with respect to some source state. Examples 2 and 3 showed that a straightforward incremental view maintenance algorithm is not even weakly consistent in the environments we consider. We will show that our Eager Compensating Algorithm is strongly consistent, and hence a satisfactory approach for most warehousing scenarios.

4   Views and Queries

Before presenting our algorithms, we must define the warehouse views we handle and the types of queries generated. In this chapter, we consider views defined as:

$$V = \Pi_{proj}(\sigma_{cond}(r_1 \times r_2 \times \ldots \times r_n))$$

where *proj* is a set of attribute names, *cond* is a boolean expression, and $r_1, \ldots, r_n$ are base relations. Note that any relational algebra expression constructed with select, project, and join operations can be transformed into an equivalent expression of this form. For simplicity, we assume that $r_1, \ldots, r_n$ are distinct relations. Our algorithms can be extended to allow multiple occurrences of the same relation (e.g., by handling updates to such relations once for each appearance of the relation).

4.1   Signs

Our warehouse algorithms will handle two types of updates: insertions and deletions. (Modifications must be treated as deletions followed by insertions, although extensions to our approach could permit modifications to be treated directly.) For convenience, we adopt an approach similar to [BLT86] and use *signs* on tuples: + to denote an inserted or an existing tuple, and − to denote a deleted tuple. Tuple signs are propagated through relational operations, as we will illustrate.

Consider an update $U_1 = delete(r_1, [1, 2])$, which causes the warehouse to issue a query $Q_1 = \Pi_W([1, 2] \bowtie r_2)$. Using signs, we instead issue the query $Q_1 = \Pi_W(-[1, 2] \bowtie r_2)$, where "−" attached to tuple [1,2] represents that this is a deleted tuple. Suppose that at the source there is an r_2 tuple [2,3] (which by default has a + sign). The result of Q_1, which we call A_1, will contain the tuple $-[1]$, i.e., the minus sign carries through. Relation A_1 is then returned to the warehouse, where it is combined with the existing view by an operation (explained below): $MV \leftarrow MV + A_1$. Because of the minus sign, the [1] tuple in A_1 is removed from the view. Note that if the original update U_1 had been an insert, the tuple [1,2] would have a plus sign, and tuple [1] would instead have been added to the view. Using tuple signs allows us to handle inserts and deletes uniformly and compactly in our algorithms.

More formally, existing tuples and inserted tuples always have a plus sign, while deleted tuples always have a minus sign. When a relational algebra expression operates on signed tuples, the sign of the result tuples is given by the following tables, where t, t_1 and t_2 are signed tuples:

t	$\sigma_{cond}(t)$	$\Pi_{proj}(t)$
$+$	$+$	$+$
$-$	$-$	$-$

t_1	t_2	$t_1 \times t_2$
$+$	$+$	$+$
$+$	$-$	$-$
$-$	$-$	$+$
$-$	$+$	$-$

In addition, we define two binary operators, also called $+$ and $-$, which operate on relations with signed tuples. For a relation r, let $pos(r)$ denote the tuples in r with a plus sign and let $neg(r)$ denote the tuples with a minus sign. Then:

$$r_1 + r_2 = (pos(r_1) \cup pos(r_2)) - (neg(r_1) \cup neg(r_2))$$
$$r_1 - r_2 = r_1 + (-r_2)$$

Operators $+$ and $-$ are commutative and associative, and they generalize to relational expressions and to single tuples in the obvious way. The cross product $\times$ is distributive over $+$ and $-$.

Note that the use of signed tuples is a notational convenience only—it is not necessary for sources to handle signed tuples in order to participate in our algorithms.

4.2 Query Expressions

In maintaining a view over relations $r_1, \ldots, r_n$, our algorithms will generate queries that contain a collection of terms. Each term is of the form:

$$T = \Pi_{proj}(\sigma_{cond}(\tilde{r}_1 \times \tilde{r}_2 \times \ldots \times \tilde{r}_n)) \tag{4.1}$$

where each $\tilde{r}_i$ is either a relation r_i or an updated tuple t_i of r_i. A query is formed by a sum of terms:

$$Q = \sum_i T_i. \tag{4.2}$$

As an example, the following relational algebra expression is query we might generate:

$$\begin{aligned} Q \quad = \quad & \Pi_{proj}(\sigma_{cond}(r_1 \times [2,3] \times r_3)) \\ & + \Pi_{proj}(\sigma_{cond}(-[1,2] \times [2,3] \times r_3)) \end{aligned}$$

In our algorithms we often derive queries from earlier queries or from view definitions. For example, say we are given a view definition $V = \Pi_{proj}(\sigma_{cond}(r_1 \times r_2))$, and we receive a deletion $U = delete(r_2, [3,4])$. Then the query we want to send to the source is V with r_2 substituted by $-[3, 4]$, i.e., $Q = \Pi_{proj}(\sigma_{cond}(r_1 \times -[3, 4]))$. We use $V\langle U \rangle$ to denote view expression V with the updated tuple of U substituted for U's relation.

More formally, consider any query (or view definition) of the form $Q = \sum_i T_i$ (recall Equation 4.2). Let U be an update involving relation r_k, and let $tuple(U)$ be the updated tuple. Then $Q\langle U \rangle = \sum_i T_i\langle U \rangle$, where for each T_i (recall Equation 4.1):

$$
T_i\langle U \rangle = \begin{cases} \phi & \text{if } \tilde{r}_k \text{ is an updated tuple} \\ \Pi_{proj}(\sigma_{cond}(\tilde{r}_1 \times \ldots \times \tilde{r}_{k-1} \times tuple(U) & \\ \quad \times \tilde{r}_{k+1} \times \ldots \times \tilde{r}_n)) & \text{if } \tilde{r}_k \text{ is relation } r_k \end{cases}
$$

We also recursively define $Q\langle U_1, U_2 \ldots U_k \rangle$ to be $(Q\langle U_1, U_2, \ldots U_{k-1} \rangle)\langle U_k \rangle$. That is, $Q\langle U_1, U_2 \ldots, U_k \rangle$ is the query in which all updated relations have been replaced by the corresponding updated tuples. Note that, by definition, if any two or more of the updates $U_1, U_2, \ldots U_k$ occur on the same relation, then $Q\langle U_1, U_2, \ldots U_k \rangle = \phi$.

5 The ECA Algorithm

In this section we present the details of our *Eager Compensating Algorithm* (ECA), introduced in Section 1 as a solution to the anomaly problem. ECA is an incremental view maintenance algorithm based on the centralized view maintenance algorithm described in [BLT86]. ECA anticipates the anomalies that arise due to the decoupling between base relation updates and view modification, and ECA compensates for the anomalies as needed to ensure correct view maintenance. Before we present ECA and its extensions, we first review the original incremental view maintenance algorithm.

5.1 The Basic Algorithm

The view maintenance algorithm described in [BLT86] applies incremental changes to a view each time changes are made to relevant base relations. We adapt this algorithm to the warehousing environment and use our event-based notation:

algorithm 5.1 (Basic Algorithm)
At the source:

- S_up_i: execute U_i;
  send U_i to the warehouse;
  trigger event W_up_i at the warehouse

- S_qu_i: receive query Q_i;
  let $A_i = Q_i[ss_i]$;   (ss_i is the current source state)
  send A_i to the warehouse;
  trigger event W_ans_i at the warehouse

At the warehouse:

- W_up_i: receive update U_i;
  let $Q_i = V\langle U_i \rangle$;
  send Q_i to the source;
  trigger event S_qu_i at the source

- W_ans_i: receive A_i;
  update view: $MV = MV + A_i$

(end algorithm)

Notice that each update at the source triggers an S_up event, which then triggers a W_up event at the warehouse, triggering an S_qu event back at the source, and finally a W_ans event at the warehouse (recall Figure 1). As shown in Examples 2 and 3, this algorithm may lead to anomalies. Consequently, using our definitions from Section 3, this basic algorithm is neither convergent nor weakly consistent in a warehousing environment.

5.2   The Eager Compensating Algorithm

We start by defining the set of "pending" queries at the warehouse:

Definition: Consider the processing of an event we at the warehouse. Let the *unanswered query set* for we, $UQS(we)$, be the set of queries that were sent by the warehouse before we occurred, but whose answers have not been received before we. We shorten $UQS(we)$ to UQS when we refers to the event being processed.   □

When the warehouse receives an update U_i and UQS is not empty, then U_i may cause queries Q_j in UQS to be evaluated incorrectly. The incorrectness arises because the queries Q_j are assumed to be computed before U_i, but are actually computed after U_i. Thus, all queries in UQS will "see" a source state that already reflects update U_i. (Recall our assumption that messages are processed and delivered in order, so if a query's answer has not yet been received, the query will be evaluated after U_i.) ECA takes this behavior into account: When ECA issues its query in response to update U_i, ECA incorporates one "compensating query" for each query in UQS. The compensating queries offset the effects of U_i on the results of queries in UQS.

algorithm 5.2 (Eager Compensating Algorithm(ECA))
The source events behave exactly as in Algorithm 5.1.
At the warehouse, COLLECT $= \phi$ initially.

- W_up_i: receive U_i;
    let $Q_i = V\langle U_i \rangle - \sum_{Q_j \in UQS} Q_j \langle U_i \rangle$
    send Q_i to the source;
    trigger event S_qu_i at the source

- W_ans_i: receive A_i;
    let COLLECT $=$ COLLECT $+ A_i$;
    if $UQS = \phi$
       then $\{ MV \leftarrow MV + $ COLLECT;
                 COLLECT $\leftarrow \phi \}$
    else do nothing

(end algorithm)

An important and subtle consequence of using compensating queries is that the results of queries should be applied to the view only after the answer to this query and all related compensating queries have been received. If instead we updated the view after the receipt of each answer, then the view might temporarily assume an invalid state. (That is, in the terminology of Section 3.1, the algorithm would be convergent but not consistent.) To avoid invalid view states, ECA collects all intermediate answers in a temporary relation called COLLECT, and only updates the view when all answers to pending queries have been received (i.e. when $UQS = \phi$).

5.3 Example

The following example illustrates ECA handling three insertions to three different base relations. A number of additional ECA examples are given in [ZGMHW94].

Example 4: ECA

Consider source relations:

$$r_1: \quad \frac{\text{W} \quad \text{X}}{1 \quad 2} \qquad\qquad r_2: \quad \frac{\text{X} \quad \text{Y}}{\text{-} \quad \text{-}} \qquad\qquad r_3: \quad \frac{\text{Y} \quad \text{Z}}{\text{-} \quad \text{-}}$$

Let the view definition be $V = \Pi_W(r_1 \bowtie r_2 \bowtie r_3)$, and suppose the following events occur. Initially, the materialized view at the warehouse is empty, and COLLECT is initialized to empty. For brevity, we omit the source events, only listing events occurring at the warehouse. We assume that the three updates occur at the source before any queries are answered.

1. Warehouse receives $U_1 = insert(r_1, [4, 2])$

   Warehouse sends $Q_1 = V\langle U_1 \rangle = \Pi_W([4, 2] \bowtie r_2 \bowtie r_3)$

2. Warehouse receives $U_2 = insert(r_3, [5, 3])$.

   Currently, $UQS = \{Q_1\}$. Warehouse sends

   $Q_2 = V\langle U_2 \rangle - Q_1 \langle U_2 \rangle$

$$= \Pi_W(r_1 \bowtie r_2 \bowtie [5,3]) - \Pi_W([4,2] \bowtie r_2 \bowtie [5,3])$$

3. Warehouse receives $U_3 = insert(r_2, [2,5])$

   $UQS = \{Q_1, Q_2\}$. Warehouse sends

   $$\begin{aligned} Q_3 &= V\langle U_3 \rangle - Q_1\langle U_3 \rangle - Q_2\langle U_3 \rangle \\ &= \Pi_W(r_1 \bowtie [2,5] \bowtie r_3) - \Pi_W([4,2] \bowtie [2,5] \bowtie r_3) \\ &\quad - \Pi_W((r_1 - [4,2]) \bowtie [2,5] \bowtie [5,3]) \end{aligned}$$

4. Warehouse receives $A_1 = [4]$

   COLLECT $= \phi + ([4]) = ([4])$, $UQS = \{Q_2, Q_3\}$

5. Warehouse receives $A_2 = [1]$

   COLLECT $= ([4]) + ([1]) = ([1],[4])$, $UQS = \{Q_3\}$

6. Warehouse receives $A_3 = \phi$

   COLLECT $= ([1],[4]) + \phi = ([1],[4])$, $UQS = \phi$

   Warehouse updates $MV = \phi +$ COLLECT $= ([1],[4])$, which is correct. $\square$

A complete proof showing that the algorithm is strongly consistent is given in [ZGMHW94]. Notice, however, that ECA is not complete. Recalling Section 3.1, completeness requires that every source state be reflected in some view state. Clearly some source states may be "missed" by the ECA algorithm while it collects query answers. We can modify ECA to obtain a complete algorithm that we call the *Lazy Compensating Algorithm* (LCA). For each source update, LCA waits until it has received all query answers (including compensation) for the update, then applies the changes for that update to the view. A detailed description of LCA is beyond the scope of this chapter. LCA is less efficient than ECA, and we believe that strong consistency is sufficient for most environments and completeness is generally not needed. Hence, we expect that ECA will be more useful than LCA in practice.

5.4 The ECA-Key Algorithm

We can "streamline" ECA in the case where the attributes in the projection list of the view definition (recall Section 4) contain key attributes for each of the base tables. (In fact, it could be advisable to design warehouse view definitions with this property in mind, for more efficient maintenance.) The *ECA-Key Algorithm* (ECA^K) proceeds as follows:

1. COLLECT is initialized with the current materialized view (not the empty set). Instead of storing modifications to MV, COLLECT is a "working copy" of MV.

2. When a delete is received at the warehouse, no query is sent to the source. Instead, the delete is applied to COLLECT immediately, using a special *key-delete* operation defined below. Also, if a pending query (in UQS) is triggered by the insertion of the same tuple as the deleted tuple, then mark the answer of this query "ignore".

3. When an insert is received at the warehouse, a query is sent to the source. However, no compensating queries are added. Thus, when an insert U is received, the query sent to the source is simply $V\langle U \rangle$.

4. As answers are received, they are accumulated in the COLLECT set, as in the original ECA. However, those answers that are marked "ignore" are not added to COLLECT. Also, duplicate tuples are not added to the COLLECT set. When the view contains keys for all base relations, there can be no duplicates in the view. Thus, if a duplicate occurs, it is due to an anomaly and can be ignored.

5. When UQS is empty, the materialized view is updated, replacing it with the tuples in COLLECT.

Example 5: $\mathbf{ECA}^K$

Consider the following source relations, where W and Y are key attributes.

$$r_1 : \quad \frac{\text{W} \quad \text{X}}{1 \quad 2} \qquad\qquad\qquad r_2 : \quad \frac{\text{X} \quad \text{Y}}{2 \quad 3}$$

Suppose that the warehouse view definition is $V = \Pi_{W,Y}(r_1 \bowtie r_2)$, and the following events occur. Initially, the materialized view at the warehouse is $MV = ([1,3])$, and COLLECT $= MV$.

1. $U_1 = insert(r_2, [2,4])$

   Warehouse sends $Q_1 = V\langle U_1 \rangle = \Pi_{W,Y}(r_1 \bowtie [2,4])$

2. $U_2 = insert(r_1, [3,2])$

   Warehouse sends $Q_2 = V\langle U_2 \rangle = \Pi_{W,Y}([3,2] \bowtie r_2)$

3. $U_3 = delete(r_1, [1,2])$

   Operation $key\text{-}delete$(V, r_1, [1,2]) (see below) deletes tuples of the form [1,x], obtaining COLLECT $=$ COLLECT $- ([1,3]) = \phi$, $UQS = \{Q_1, Q_2\}$

4. Warehouse receives $A_1 = ([3,4])$

   COLLECT $=$ COLLECT $+ ([3,4]) = ([3,4])$, $UQS = \{Q_2\}$

5. Warehouse receives $A_2 = ([3,3], [3,4])$

   First, A_2 is added to COLLECT: duplicate tuple [3,4] is not added, so COLLECT $= ([3,3],[3,4])$. Next, since $UQS = \phi$, MV is set to COLLECT, so $MV = ([3,3],[3,4])$. Note that COLLECT is not reset to empty.

The special operation $key\text{-}delete(MV, r_1, [1,2])$ deletes from MV all tuples whose attribute corresponding to r_1's key (i.e., attribute W) is equal to the key value in tuple [1,2] (i.e., 1).

Observe that if we had installed COLLECT into MV in steps 3 or 4, without waiting for $UQS = \phi$, then the view would have temporarily assumed an invalid state (resulting in convergence but not consistency).

It is the presence of keys in the view definition that makes it possible to perform deletes at the warehouse without issuing queries to the source, and that eliminates the need for compensating queries in the case of inserts. Consider deletions first. Since each view tuple contains key values for all base relations, when a base relation tuple t is deleted, we can use the key values in t to identify which tuples in the view were derived using t. These are the view tuples that must be deleted.

Now consider insertions. Since insertions cause queries to be sent to the source, anomalies can still arise. However, all such anomalies result in either duplicate view tuples (which we can detect and ignore), or missing tuples that would have been deleted anyway. As illustration, suppose Q_1 of Example 5 had been executed when U_1 occurred; it would have evaluated to $([1,4])$. Instead, because of the delay, we have $A_1 = ([3,4])$. A_1 is incorrect in two ways: (1) It contains an extra tuple $[3,4]$ produced because Q_1 was evaluated after insert U_2. (2) It is missing tuple $[1,4]$ because Q_1 was evaluated after delete U_3. However, both of these problems are resolved at the warehouse: (1) The extra tuple $[3,4]$ is identified as a duplicate when A_2 is received. (2) The missing tuple $[1,4]$ would have been deleted by U_3. Details and a sketch for the ECA^K correctness proof appear in [ZGMHW94].

5.5 The ECA-Local Algorithm

The original ECA uses compensating queries to avoid the anomalies that may occur when queries are sent to the source. ECA^K relies on key properties to avoid compensating queries; furthermore, ECA^K introduces the concept of *local updates* (deletions, in the case of ECA^K), which can be handled at the warehouse without sending queries to the source. The last algorithm we discuss, the *ECA-Local Algorithm* (ECA^L) combines the compensating queries of ECA with the local updates of ECA^K to produce a streamlined algorithm that applies to general views.

In ECA^L, each update is handled either locally or non-locally. A number of papers, e.g., [BLT86, GB95, TB88], describe conditions when, for a particular view definition and a particular base relation update, the view can be updated without further access to base relations (i.e., the view is *autonomously computable*, using the terminology of [BLT86]). These results can be used to identify which updates ECA^L will process locally. For updates that cannot be processed locally, ECA is used (assuming the key condition for ECA^K does not hold), with compensating queries whenever necessary.

Unfortunately, maintaining the correct order of execution among local and non-local processing in ECA^L is not straightforward. Intuitively, we can process a local update as soon as all queries for previous updates have been answered and applied to the view. However, consider three updates, U_1, U_2, and U_3, where U_2 is the only local update. Suppose we process U_2 as soon as the query Q_1 for U_1 is answered. Since ECA^L uses compensating queries, the "true" view update corresponding to U_1 may include not only the answer for Q_1, but also compensations appearing in queries for later updates (such as U_3). To correctly handle this scenario, ECA^L must buffer updates and, in some cases, "split" query results (separating compensation from original), in order to process local updates on a correct version of the view. The details of ECA^L, and determining whether the additional overhead is worthwhile, is left as future work.

5.6 Properties of the ECA family

ECA, and its extensions ECA^K and ECA^L, have the following desirable properties:

1. They are incremental, meaning that they update the warehouse based on updates to the source, rather than recomputing the complete warehouse view from scratch.

2. They do not place any additional burden on the sources (e.g., timestamps, locks, etc.).

3. When the update frequency is low, i.e., when the answer to a warehouse query comes back before the next update occurs at the source, then the ECA algorithms behave exactly like the original incremental view maintenance algorithm. (Compensating queries are used only when the answer to a query has not been received before the next update occurs at the source.)

6   Performance Evaluation

In Section 1.2 we outlined several strategies for view maintenance in a warehousing environment: recomputing the view (RV), storing copies of all base relations (SC), our Eager Compensating Algorithm (ECA), and our extensions ECA-Key (ECA^K) and ECA-Local (ECA^L). All of these approaches provide strong consistency (recall Section 3.1). Thus, a natural issue to explore is the relative performance of these strategies. In this chapter we evaluate only the basic algorithms, RV and ECA. From the performance perspective, ECA^K is simply an enhancement to ECA that eliminates querying the source in certain cases. Since there is very little additional overhead in ECA^K, ECA^K should certainly be used when it is possible to arrange for warehouse views to include all base relation keys. Storing copies of base relations (SC) can be seen as an enhancement to any of our algorithms, requiring an "orthogonal" performance comparison (based on warehouse storage costs, etc.) that is beyond the scope of this chapter. As discussed in Section 5.5, ECA^L requires complex processing at the warehouse, the measurement of which falls outside the scope of our performance evaluation. We plan to address performance issues for SC and ECA^L, along with a more extensive evaluation of ECA, as future work.

When we intuitively compare RV and ECA, it seems that ECA should certainly outperform RV, since ECA is an incremental update algorithm while RV recomputes the view from scratch. However, ECA may need to send many more queries to the source than RV. In addition, ECA's queries grow in complexity as compensations upon compensations are added. Hence, we seek to determine when it is more effective to recompute the entire view, rather than maintaining it incrementally with the associated extra activity.

To answer this question, we provide an initial performance analysis of RV and ECA. We note that this is not a comprehensive analysis, as there are a number of parameters we have not fully studied (ranging from the number of relations, to the exact sequence and timing of the updates, to the way queries are optimized at the source). Rather, we have selected a "representative" scenario that serves to illustrate the performance tradeoffs.

For the analysis, we focus on three separate cost factors: M, the number of messages sent between the source and warehouse, B, the number of bytes transferred from the source to the warehouse, and IO, the number of I/O's performed at the source. In RV and ECA, identical update notification messages are sent to the warehouse, so these costs are not included in our calculations. Throughout this section, we use the variables listed in Table 1, shown with their default values. The RV algorithm is described informally in Section 1.2; a formal specification is provided in [ZGMHW94].

	Variable Description	**Default**
M	Number of messages sent	N/A
B	Total number of bytes transferred	N/A
IO	Number of I/O's	N/A
C	Cardinality of a relation	100
S	Size of projected attributes	4 bytes
σ	Selection factor	1/2
J	Join factor	4
k	# of updates at the source	N/A

Table 1   List of variables.

6.1   Performance Based on Number of Messages

Assume there is a sequence of k updates. For RV, assume the warehouse sends a query message to the source asking it to recompute the view after every s updates, $s \leq k$. Counting both the query and answer messages, the total number of messages is $M_{RV} = \lceil \frac{k}{s} \rceil \times 2$. Thus, RV generates at least 2 messages (if the view is only recomputed once; $s = k$) and at most $2k$ messages (if the view is recomputed after every update; $s = 1$). For ECA, if there are k updates, we always have k queries and k answers, so there are $2k$ messages.[2]

Thus, in the situation least favorable for ECA, ECA sends $2k$ messages while RV sends 2 messages. Of course, the price of the RV approach in this case is that the state of the warehouse view lags well behind the state of the base relations. In the most favorable situation for ECA, ECA and RV both send $2k$ messages.

6.2   Performance Based on Data Transferred

To analyze the number of bytes transferred (and later on the number of I/O's), we introduce a sample scenario consisting of a particular view and a particular sequence of update operations. As mentioned earlier, we have chosen to focus on a sample scenario to illustrate the performance tradeoffs while keeping the number of parameters manageable.

Example 6:   Example warehouse scenario

Base relation schema: $r_1(W, X)$, $r_2(X, Y)$, $r_3(Y, Z)$

View definition: $V = \Pi_{W,Z}(\sigma_{cond}(r_1 \bowtie r_2 \bowtie r_3))$

Updates: $U_1 = \text{insert}[r_1, t_1]$, $U_2 = \text{insert}[r_2, t_2]$, $U_3 = \text{insert}[r_3, t_3]$ □

The condition *cond* involves a comparison between attributes W and Z (e.g., $W > Z$). (This condition has an impact on the derivation of the the number of I/O's performed.) Later we extend this example to a sequence of k updates.

We make the following assumptions in our analysis:

1. The cardinality (number of tuples) of each relation is some constant C.

2. The size of the combined W, Z attributes is S bytes.

3. The join factor $J(r_i, a)$ is the expected number of tuples in r_i that have a particular value for attribute a. We assume that the join factor is a constant J in all cases. For example, if we join a 20-tuple relation with a second relation, we expect to get $20J$ tuples.

4. The selectivity for the condition *cond* is given by σ, $0 \leq \sigma \leq 1$.

5. We assume that C, J and our other parameters do not change as updates occur. This closely approximates their behavior in practice when the updates are single-tuple inserts and deletes (so the size and selectivity do not change significantly), or when C and J are so large that the effect of updates is insignificant.

---

[2]Because ECA uses signed queries (recall Section 4.1), and some sources—such as an SQL server—may need to handle the positive and negative parts of such queries separately, we may need to send a pair of queries for some updates instead of a single query. We assume the pair of queries is "packaged" as one message, and the pair of answers also is returned in a single message.

Not surprisingly, for RV the fewest bytes are transferred (B_{RVBest}) when the view is recomputed only once, after U_3 has occurred. The worst case ($B_{RVWorst}$) is when the view is recomputed after each update. For ECA, the best case ($B_{ECABest}$) is when no compensating queries are needed, i.e., the updates are sufficiently spaced so that each query is processed before the next update occurs at the source. Note that in this case, ECA performs as efficiently as the original incremental algorithm (Algorithm 5.1). The worst case for ECA ($B_{ECAWorst}$) is when all updates occur before the first query arrives at the source. Intuitively, the difference between the best and worst cases of ECA represents the "compensation cost."

The calculations for analyzing our algorithms are rather complex and therefore omitted here; the complete derivations can be found in [ZGMHW94]. In particular, the expressions derived in [ZGMHW94] for the number of bytes transferred are:

$$
\begin{aligned}
B_{RVBest} &= S\sigma C J^2 \\
B_{RVWorst} &= 3S\sigma C J^2 \\
B_{ECABest} &= 3S\sigma J^2 \\
B_{ECAWorst} &= 3S\sigma J(J+1)
\end{aligned}
$$

Figure 2 shows the number B of bytes transferred as a function of the cardinality C. (In all of our graphs, parameters have the default values of Table 1 unless otherwise indicated.) Best and worst cases are shown for both algorithms. Thus, for each algorithm, actual performance will be somewhere in between the best and worst case curves, depending on the timing of update arrivals (for ECA) and the frequency of view recomputation (for RV).

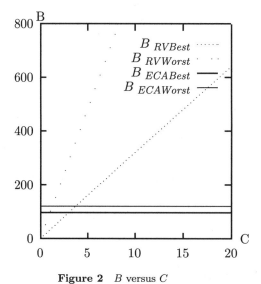

Figure 2 B versus C

From Figure 2 we see that in spite of the compensating queries, ECA is much more efficient than RV (in terms of data transferred), unless the relations involved are extremely small (less than approximately 5 tuples each). This result continues to hold over wide ranges of the join selectivity J, except if J is very small (see equations above).

One of the reasons ECA appears to perform so well is that we are considering only three updates, so the amount of "compensation work" is limited. In [ZGMHW94] we extend our analysis to an arbitrary number k of updates and obtain the following equations:

$$
\begin{array}{rcl}
B_{RVBest} & = & S\sigma CJ^2 \\
B_{RVWorst} & = & kS\sigma CJ^2 \\
B_{ECABest} & = & kS\sigma J^2 \\
B_{ECAWorst} & = & kS\sigma J^2 + k(k-1)S\sigma J/3
\end{array}
$$

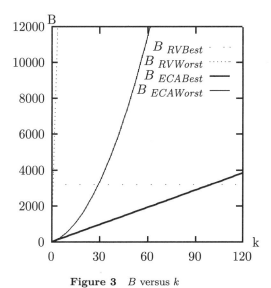

Figure 3 B versus k

Figure 3 shows the number of bytes transferred as a function of k when $C = 100$. As expected, there is a crossover point beyond which recomputing the view once (RV's best case) is superior to even the best case for ECA. For our example, this crossover is at 100 updates. In the ECA worst case, when all updates occur at the source before any of the warehouse queries arrive, each warehouse query must compensate every preceding update. This behavior results in ECA transmitting additional data that is quadratic on the number of updates. Hence, in the situation least favorable for ECA, RV outperforms ECA when 30 or more updates are involved. Bear in mind that this situation occurs only if all updates precede all queries. If updates and queries are interleaved at the source, then performance will be somewhere between the ECA best and worst cases, and the crossover point will be somewhere between 30 and 100 updates.

Also notice that Figure 3 is for relatively small relations ($C = 100$); for larger cardinalities the crossover points will be at larger number of updates. Finally, note that the RV best case we have been comparing against assumes the view is recomputed once, no matter how many updates occur. If RV recomputes the view more frequently (such as once per some number of updates), then its cost will be substantially higher. In particular, $B_{RVWorst}$ is very expensive and always substantially worst than $B_{ECAWorst}$.

6.3 Performance Based on I/O

Estimating the number of I/O's performed at the source is similar to estimating the number of bytes transferred. Details of the estimation are discussed in [ZGMHW94]. We consider two extreme scenarios there: when indexing is used and ample memory is available, and when memory is very limited and there are no indexes. Studying these extremes lets us discover the conditions that are most favorable for the algorithms we consider. Due to the space limitations, we only present one graph to illustrate the type of results obtained. Figure 4 gives the number of I/O's as a function of the number of updates for the second scenario studied (limited memory and no indexes).

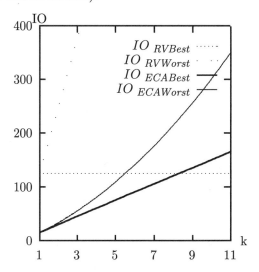

Figure 4 *IO* versus k, Scenario 2

The shape of the curves in Figure 4 is similar to those in Figure 3, and thus our conclusions for I/O costs are similar to those for data transmission. The main difference is that the crossover points occur with smaller update sequences: $5 < k < 8$ in this case, as opposed to a crossover between $k = 30$ and $k = 100$ when data transfer is the metric. Intuitively, this means that ECA is not as effective at reducing I/O costs as it is at reducing data transfer. However, ECA can still reduce I/O costs over RV significantly, especially if relations are larger than the 100 tuples considered for these figures. Also, we expect that the I/O performance of ECA would improve if we incorporated multiple term optimization or caching into the analysis.

As a final note, we remind the reader that our results are for a particular three-relation view. In spite of this, we believe that our results are indicative of the performance issues faced in choosing between RV and ECA. Our results indicate that when the view involves more relations, ECA should still generally outperform RV.

7   Conclusion

Data warehousing is an emerging (and already very popular) technique used in many applications for retrieval and integration of data from autonomous information sources. However, warehousing typically is implemented in an ad-hoc way. We have shown that standard algorithms for maintaining a materialized view at a warehouse can lead to anomalies and inconsistent modifications to the view. The anomalies are due to the fact that view maintenance at the warehouse is decoupled from updates at the data sources, and we cannot expect the data sources to perform sophisticated functions in support of view management. Consequently, previously proposed view maintenance algorithms cannot be used in this environment.

We have presented a new algorithm, and outlined two extensions, for correctly maintaining materialized views in a warehousing environment. Our Eager Compensating Algorithm, ECA, and its streamlined versions, ECA^K and ECA^L, are all strongly consistent, meaning that the warehouse data always corresponds to a meaningful state of the source data. An initial performance study analyzing three different cost factors (messages, data traffic, and I/O) suggests that, except for very small relations, ECA is consistently more efficient than periodically recomputing the warehouse view from scratch.

Although in this chapter we have addressed a restricted warehousing environment with only one source and one view, ECA can readily be adapted to more general scenarios. For example, in a warehouse consisting of multiple views where each view is over data from a single source, ECA is simply applied to each view separately.

In the future we plan to address the following additional issues.

- We will consider how ECA (and its extensions) can be adapted to views over multiple sources. Many aspects of the anomaly problem remain the same. However, additional issues are raised because warehouse queries (both regular queries and compensating queries) must be fragmented for execution at multiple sources. While fragmenting itself does not pose a novel problem (at least in the straightforward relational case), coordinating the query results and the necessary compensations for anomaly-causing updates may require some intricate algorithms.

- We will consider how ECA can be extended to handle a set of updates at once, rather than one update at a time. Since we expect that in practice many source updates will be "batched," this extension should result in a very useful performance enhancement.

- We will modify the algorithms to handle views defined by more complex relational algebra expressions (e.g., using union and/or difference) as well as other relational query languages (e.g., SQL or Datalog).

- We will explore how the algorithms can be adapted to other data models (e.g., an object-based data model).

EFFICIENT MAINTENANCE OF MATERIALIZED MEDIATED VIEWS

James Lu, Guido Moerkotte,
Joachim Schü, V.S. Subrahmanian

ABSTRACT

Integrating data and knowledge from multiple heterogeneous sources -like databases, knowledge bases or specific software packages - is often required for answering certain queries. Recently, a powerful framework for defining mediated views spanning multiple knowledge bases by a set of constrained rules was proposed [Sub94a, AS94, Jam96]. We investigate the materialization of these views by unfolding the view definition and the efficient maintenance of the resulting materialized mediated view in case of updates. Thereby, we consider two kinds of updates: updates to the view and updates to the underlying sources. For each of these two cases several efficient algorithms maintaining materialized mediated views are given. We improve on previous algorithms like the DRed algorithm [GMS93] and introduce a new fixpoint operator W_P which — opposed to the standard fixpoint operator T_P [GL91] — allows us to correctly capture the update's semantics without any recomputation of the materialized view.

1 Introduction

Integrating data and knowledge from multiple heterogeneous sources, each one possibly with a different underlying data model, is not only an important aspect of automated reasoning, but also of retrieval systems — in the widest sense — whose queries can span multiple such sources. These sources can be as different as relational or deductive databases, object bases, (constraint) knowledge bases, or even (structured) files and arbitrary program packages encapsulating specific knowledge, often in a hard-wired form accessible only through function calls. Many queries can only be answered if data and knowledge from these different sources are available. (For a motivating example see Sec. 2.2.) In order to answer these queries, it is necessary to define a mediator [Wie93] integrating the different sources on a semantic level by providing an integrated view spanning these sources.

Traditional research on view or schema integration, and interoperability of databases concentrates on integrating databases, possibly with different underlying schemata or even data models. The basic idea often is to aim for a global integrating schema or view whose definition mediates between different databases. Only lately, investigations started to integrate other sources of data available. The most prominent example of such a source is the file. Recently, it was proposed to integrate (structured) files and object bases by providing an object base view on the file and a file view upon the object base [ACM93, GJR94].

Another powerful technique for integrating multiple knowledge bases is introduced in [Sub94a, AS94, Jam96]. While this work examines a framework for expressing mediated views, the paper [SAB+94] describes a concrete implementation of one such mediating system called HERMES (HEterogeneous Reasoning and MEdiator System). HERMES supports the integration of multiple databases and reasoning paradigms on both the PC/Windows and the SUN/Unix platforms and provides an environment which allows flexibility in adding new databases and software packages. In HERMES, mediators are expressed in a rule-based language containing a special predicate in used to achieve logical integration at the semantic level. It enables access to data contained in external databases, and gives HERMES the ability to execute functions in existing software – the current implementation of HERMES integrates PARADOX, INGRES, DBASE with third-party path planning packages, numerical computation packages, face recognition packages, and multimedia application packages.

As in the case of traditional views, mediated views are materialized for efficiency reasons. A materialized view can be affected by two kinds of Updates, namely updates to the materialized view, and updates to the underlying sources.

If an update of the first kind occurs to a view, whether materialized or not, the problem of reflecting the update correctly by changing the base tables appropriately needs to be addressed. This problem is called the *view update problem* and has been discussed extensively for relational, deductive, and object-oriented databases. However, our objective is slightly different. As motivated by an example in Section 2.2, we do not necessarily assume that an update occurring to a view has to be reflected within some underlying source. Instead, we assume that the view itself — or, to be more precise, its definition — is affected by the update. This kind of update affecting the view's definition is typically not treated within the view update literature. One exception are deductive databases, where the addition or deletion of rules to the definition of an intensional predicate is discussed [Ern95]. However, they neither materialize nor preprocess the view for efficiency reasons.

Within the traditional context, the second case occurs if an update to a base table occurs which possibly affects a materialized view. The resulting problem — preserving the consistency of the view — is called *view maintenance* and has been discussed for, e.g., for (extended) relational [BCL89, Han87, SJGP90] and deductive databases [Kuc91, HD92, GKM92, UO92, SI84]. The same problem occurs also for the materialization of functions within object bases [KKM94]: if the values of some object's attributes change, the materialized function value becomes invalid. However, since we do not necessarily materialize the view upon the underlying sources of our mediated views but instead perform materialization by unfolding the view definition as independent as possible from the underlying sources, the traditional view maintenance problem occurs quite differently to us. Hence, the traditional view maintenance problem and our problem do not intersect but complement each other.

Subsequently, we treat both kinds of updates to materialized mediated views and show how they can be handled efficiently. More specifically, the primary aim is to specify how to efficiently maintain views of mediated systems such as those that may be constructed in HERMES when insertion and deletion requests of both of the above two kinds are made. As in the standard case, a *materialized view* in mediated systems may be thought of as a set of facts that can be concluded from the mediator rules. However, we show that more generally, a materialized mediated view may be regarded as a set of *constraint* atoms that are not necessarily ground. Taking materialized views to be sets of constrained atoms leads to a number of advantages:

1. First of all, it allows us to perform updates to *constrained databases* such as those described by Kanellakis et. al. [KKR90]. To our knowledge, there are currently no methods to incrementally maintain views in constrained databases.

2. We show for updates of the second kind that even in the case of unconstrained databases, such as those considered by Gupta, Mumick and Subrahmanian [GMS93], this approach leads to a simpler and more efficient deletion algorithm than the deletion algorithm, DRed presented in [GMS93].

3. For updates of the first kind, we depart from using the standard fixpoint operation T_P as defined by Gabrielli and Levi [GL91]. Instead, we introduce the fixpoint operator W_P. W_P is able to capture updates of the second kind without any recomputation of the materialized mediated view while maintaining the semantics of T_P and correctly capturing the update.

The rest of the chapter is organized as follows. Section 2.1 gives the preliminaries, including a motivating example. Section 2.2 introduces the running example which also motivates the integration of multiple sources for answering a single query as well as the two kinds of updates. Section 2.3 formally defines the notion of materialized mediated view. Section 3 treats updates of the first kind whereas Section 4 treats updates of the second kind. Section 5 discusses related work and Section 6 concludes the chapter.

2 Preliminaries

2.1 Syntax and Semantics

In this section, we will briefly describe the basic theory behind mediated systems proposed in [Jam96, Sub94a, AS96, AS94, AE95]. Illustration is provided via the HERMES implementation.

A *domain*, $\mathcal{D}$, is an abstraction of databases and software packages and consists of three components: (1) a set, Σ whose elements may be thought of as the data-objects that are being manipulated by the package in question, (2) a set $\mathcal{F}$ of functions on Σ – these functions take objects in Σ as input, and return, as output, objects from their range (which needs to be specified). The functions in $\mathcal{F}$ may be thought of as the predefined functions that have been implemented in the software package being considered, (3) a set of relations on the data-objects in Σ – intuitively, these relations may be thought of as the predefined relations in the domain, $\mathcal{D}$.

A constraint Ξ over D is a first order formula where the symbols are interpreted over D. Ξ is either true or false in D, in which case we say that Ξ is solvable, or respectively unsolvable in D, where the reference to D will be eliminated if it is clear from context. The key idea behind a mediated system is that constraints provide the link to external sources, whether they be databases, object bases, or other knowledge sources.

For example in HERMES, a *domain call* is a syntactic expression of the form

$$\text{domainname} : \langle \text{domainfunction} \rangle (\langle \text{arg1}, \ldots, \text{argn} \rangle)$$

where domainfunction is the name of the function, and $\langle \text{arg1}, \ldots, \text{argn} \rangle$ are the arguments it takes. Intuitively, a domain call may be read as: in the domain called domainname, execute the function domainfunction defined therein on the arguments $(\text{arg1}, \ldots, \text{argn})$. The *result* of executing this domain call is coerced into a set of entities that have the same type as the output type of the function domainfunction on the arguments $(\text{arg1}, \ldots, \text{argn})$

A *domain-call atom* (DCA-atom) is of the form

$$\text{in}(\text{X}, \text{domainname} : \text{domainfunction}(\langle \text{arg1}, \ldots, \text{argn} \rangle)$$

where in is a constraint that is satisfied just in case the entity X is in the set returned by the domain call in the second argument of in(-,-). In other words, in is the polymorphic set membership predicate. More concretely,

in(A,paradox:select_eq('phone book',"name","jo smith"))

is a DCA-atom that is true just in case A is a tuple in the result of executing a selection operation (finding tuples where the name field is jo smith) on a relation called phonebook maintained in a PARADOX database system.

A *mediator/constrained database* is a set of rules of the form

$$A \leftarrow D_1 \wedge \ldots \wedge D_m || A_1, \ldots, A_n.$$

where $A, A_1, \ldots, A_n$ are atoms, and $D_1, \ldots, D_m$ are DCA-atoms. It can be shown (cf. Example 2.2) that all the kinds of constraints considered by Kanellakis et. al. can be captured within this framework (Lu, Nerode, Subrahmanian present further details [Jam96]).

2.2 Motivating Example

We introduce a running example which also motivates our approach. This example has been addressed in the existing HERMES implementation [Sub94b].

EXAMPLE 2.1 (Law-Enforcement Example) Consider the problem of identifying all people P who have been recorded, by surveillance cameras, as having met with an individual X (for instance, X may be a Mafia chief like Don Corleone), who live within a hundred mile radius of Washington DC, and who work for a suspected front company "ABC Corp." Solving this problem may require access to a wide variety of data structures, databases, and furthermore, require recourse to diverse *reasoning paradigms* as well. For instance, it may be necessary to access:

- a background **face database** containing pictures (e.g. passport pictures) of individuals. In this face database, the identity of the photographed individuals is known.

- a database of **surveillance photographs**. These photographs may have been obtained by using surveillance cameras.

- **face-extraction algorithms** that extract the "prominent" faces from the images generated by the surveillance camera.

- methods of **matching** faces extracted from the surveillance data by the face-extraction algorithm, so as to be able to figure out who appears in which images.

- a **relational database** (e.g. a phone and address book database) specifying the names, addresses, and phone numbers of individuals. This database may be stored as a relation in a well known relational DBMS, say PARADOX.

- a **spatial database** in order to determine whether a given address lies within 100 miles of Washington DC.

- a **relational database** about the employees of ABC Corp. Note that this relational database may be completely different from the phone and address book relational database alluded to earlier in this example, and may be stored as a DBASE relation.

In order to answer the above query, we must be able to integrate the above software packages at the software level, as well as at the logical level. In this chapter, we will not go into the software integration scheme – it is described in [SAB+94], but we will go into some details about the mediator syntax itself in order to define what "soundness and completeness" of view maintenance means, and in order to develop algorithms for view maintenance that are sound and complete. For this example, the mediator may be expressed as three clauses:

$$
\begin{aligned}
\texttt{seenwith(X,Y)} &\leftarrow \Xi \\
\texttt{swlndc(X,Y)} &\leftarrow \Xi' \, || \, \texttt{seenwith(X,Y)} \\
\texttt{suspect(X,Y)} &\leftarrow \Xi'' \, || \, \texttt{swlndc(X,Y)}
\end{aligned}
$$

where the constraints have the form

$$
\begin{aligned}
\Xi \quad = \quad &\text{in}(\text{P1}, \text{facextract} : \text{segmentface}(\text{'surveillancedata'})) \wedge \\
&\text{in}(\text{P2}, \text{facextract} : \text{segmentface}(\text{'surveillancedata'})) \wedge \\
&= (\text{P1.origin}, \text{P2.origin}) \wedge \text{P1} \neq \text{P2} \wedge \\
&\text{in}(\text{P3}, \text{facedb} : \text{findface}(\text{X})) \wedge \\
&\text{in}(\text{true}, \text{facextract} : \text{matchface}(\text{P1}, \text{P3})) \wedge \\
&\text{in}(\text{Y}, \text{facedb} : \text{findname}(\text{P2}))
\end{aligned}
\tag{2.1}
$$

$$
\begin{aligned}
\Xi' \quad = \quad &\text{in}(\text{A}, \text{paradox} : \text{select\_eq}(\text{'phonebook'}, "name", \text{Y})) \wedge \\
&\text{in}(\text{Pt1}, \text{spatialdb} : \text{locateaddress}(\text{A.streetnum}, \\
&\text{A.streetname}, \text{A.cityname}) \wedge \\
&\text{in}(\text{true}, \text{spatialdb} : \text{range}(\text{'dcareamap'}, \text{Pt1.X}, \text{Pt1.Y}, 100))
\end{aligned}
\tag{2.2}
$$

$$
\Xi'' \quad = \quad \text{in}(\text{Tuple}, \text{dbase} : \text{select\_eq}(\text{'empl\_abc'}, "name", \text{Y}))
\tag{2.3}
$$

The `seenwith` predicate access a domain called `faceextract` which is a pattern recognition package that uses a function called `segmentface` to locate the faces in a set of photographs, and then extracts these faces (leading to "mugshots") which are then stored in files. The extraction procedure returns a list of pairs of the form ($<$ resultfile, origin $>$) specifying which image in the surveillance data, a given face was extracted from (the origin) and where the mugshot/face is now stored. The `faceextract` domain also contains a function called `matchface` that takes as face (such as those extracted by the `faceextract` domain) and checks if this face is identical to another face in the mugshot library. Likewise, the `seenwith` predicate access a domain called `facedb` containing a function called `findface` which determines, given a person's name, whether his face is in a mugshot library. The `facedb` domain also contains a function called `findname` which, given a mugshot in the mugshot library, returns the name of the person involved.

Given that a person Y has been `seenwith` X, `swlndc` (for "seen with and lives near DC"), accesses a relational database to find the address of Y, and then accesses a spatial data management system to determine what (x, y) coordinates, on a map of the DC area, this address corresponds to (using a function called `locateaddr`). It then determines, using a function called `range`, whether this address lies within the specified distance from DC.

Finally, a person Y is a suspect just in case `swlndc`("Don Corleone", Y) is true and if he is an employee of "ABC Corp." For this, a DBASE relation called `empl_abc` is accessed. The above three clauses express the mediator for this example in its entirety.

EXAMPLE 2.2 (Constrained Databases) Kanellakis et. al. [KKR90] have introduced the concept of constrained databases, which can be modeled within our framework (a formal proof is contained in [Jam96]). For instance, if we wish to write constraints over the `arithmetic` domain, then we may have *functions* called `great(X)` that returns as output, the set of all integers greater than X. Note that this may be implementing lazily. Hence the entire, infinite set need not be computed all at once. Likewise, `plus(X, Y)` returns the *singleton set* $\{X + Y\}$.

In the rest of this chapter, we will use these examples to motivate various kinds of updates that may occur and that bear an important relationship to view maintenance in such mediated systems.

2.3   Non-Ground Materialized Mediated Views

In this section, the concept of a materialized mediated view is given. Typically, a materialized view is a set of ground atoms, corresponding to a set of relations whose fields are filled in with (ground) values. In this case, a materialized view will generalize this notion, allowing non-ground atoms to occur in it, as long as the variables in the atom satisfy certain constraints which are defined as follows:

- Any DCA-atom is a constraint.

- If X is a variable symbol and T is either a variable symbol or a constant, then $X = T$ and $X \neq T$ are constraints.

- Any conjunction of constraints is a constraint.

Thus, for example, $X = 2 \wedge Y \neq X \wedge$ in(Y, arith : greater(X)) is a constraint in the domain arith described earlier. A more common way of writing this constraint is $X = 2 \wedge Y \neq X \wedge Y \geq X$. We shall use this notation when referring to the numeric domain.

A *constrained atom* is an expression of the form $A(\vec{X}) \leftarrow \Xi$ where $\vec{X}$ denotes a tuple of variables and Ξ is a constraint.

Given a constrained atom $A(\vec{X}) \leftarrow \Xi$, $[A(\vec{X}) \leftarrow \Xi]$ denotes the set of instances of X that are solutions of Ξ, viz.

$$\{A(\vec{X})\theta \mid \theta \text{ is a solution of } \Xi\}$$

For example, taking the same constraint $\Xi = (X = 2 \wedge Y \neq X \wedge Y \geq X)$ as above, $[p(X, Y) \leftarrow \Xi]$ is the set $\{p(2, 3), p(2, 4), p(2, 5), \ldots\}$. If $\mathcal{C}$ is a set of constrained atoms, $[\mathcal{C}]$ is defined to be $\bigcup_{A(X) \leftarrow \Xi \in \mathcal{C}} [A(X) \leftarrow \Xi]$.

An interpretation for a mediated system P is any set of constrained atoms. A constrained atom $A(\vec{X}) \leftarrow \Xi$ is said to be *true in an interpretation* I iff $[A(\vec{X}) \leftarrow \Xi] \subseteq [I]$. Given a constrained database P it is possible to define an operator, T_P that maps interpretations to interpretations in the following way:

$$
\begin{aligned}
T_P(I) \quad = \quad & \{A(\vec{X}) \leftarrow \Xi \mid \\
& \text{There is a clause } A(t_0) \leftarrow \Xi_0 \| A_1(t_1), \ldots, A_n(t_n) \text{ in P} \\
& \forall 1 \leq i \leq n \; : \; \exists A_i(X_i) \leftarrow \Xi_i \in I, \\
& \text{which share no variable and the constraint} \\
& \Xi = \Xi_0 \wedge \Xi_1 \wedge \ldots \wedge \Xi_n \wedge \\
& \{\vec{X_1} = \vec{t_1}\} \wedge \ldots \wedge \{\vec{X_n} = \vec{t_n}\} \wedge \{\vec{X} = \vec{t_0}\} \text{ is solvable}\}
\end{aligned}
$$

Note that each $\vec{t_i}$ is assumed to be a tuple of terms of the same length as X_i. This operator was originally defined by Gabbrielli and Levi [GL91] who used it to define a non-ground representation of the ground least Herbrand model of a constrained database/logic program. For the types of updates that are considered in the subsequent sections, this non-ground set of constrained atoms constitutes the materialized view of the constrained database which is of interest for being maintained. The iteration of T_P is defined in the usual way and $T_P \uparrow \omega = lfp(T_P)$ gives us the materialized view. For instance, the materialized view from example 1 has the form:

$$
\begin{aligned}
\texttt{seenwith}(X, Y) \quad &\leftarrow \quad \Xi \\
\texttt{swlndc}(X, Y) \quad &\leftarrow \quad \Xi' \wedge \Xi \\
\texttt{suspect}(X, Y) \quad &\leftarrow \quad \Xi'' \wedge \Xi' \wedge \Xi
\end{aligned}
$$

It must be stressed that due to the representation of a view by means of non-ground constraint facts, the materialization and in particular the update of a materialized view does not spawn queries of the remote knowledge sources. Another important point to note is that T_P may often yield a set containing multiple atoms of the form $A(\vec{X}) \leftarrow \Xi_1, \ldots, A(\vec{X}) \leftarrow \Xi_m$ where the constraints, $\Xi_1, \ldots, \Xi_m$ are not necessarily incompatible. This corresponds to an extension, to the case of constrained databases, of the *duplicate semantics* proposed by Mumick [Mum91] in the context of ordinary deductive databases.

3 Updating Views

In our context, view updating deals with the following problem: given a constrained database P, a materialized view MMV, and an update u, compute a new materialized view that accurately reflects this update. Note that we adapt the view and not modify the underlying sources. Remember that a materialized view is a set of constrained atoms. An *update* may take one of the following three forms:

- **Atom Addition:** A constrained atom (involving predicates defined in the mediator) is added to the materialized view. For instance, in the Law Enforcement example, the atom `seenwith("Don Corleone", "Jane Doe")` may be inserted into the materialized view even though this fact is not be derivable from the mediator. This may be due to the fact that some external reasons (e.g. a policeman saw them together and duly reported it) may justify its truth.

- **Atom Deletion:** Suppose the atom `suspect("Don Corleone", "Jo Smith")` was in the materialized view (e.g. it may been derivable from the original constrained database), but we may wish to delete this fact because there is external evidence that Jo Smith has no connection with Don Corleone (e.g. he may have been derived as a suspect because he was in a large crowd of people one of whom was Don Corleone).

- **External Data Changes and Function Modification:** In a mediated system, the mediator accesses (potentially) many different databases and/or data structures. The data contained in those databases/data structures may be updated, triggering changes to the data in the materialized view. For instance, in the Law Enforcement Example, it may turn out that the surveillance data has been extended (through the addition of new photographs, say) and hence, the domain call
`facextract:segmentface('surveillance-db')`
returns a set of objects that are different from what was returned by this function prior to the update. This change in the domain is modeled as a change in the *function* which, in this example, happens to be `segmentface`. Changes of this kind may trigger new changes to the materialized view (for instance, adding new pictures will, presumably, enlarge the pool of suspects). We will show how this intuition of modeling changes in local databases as function updates leads to simple algorithms for updating a mediated materialized view.

Note that we do not consider the problem of adding or deleting a rule from the mediator.

3.1 Deletion of Constrained Atoms

In this section, we will present two algorithms that will compute a materialized view obtained by deleting an existing atom from the mediated materialized view. Both algorithms apply to non-recursive, as well as recursive views. Details and examples may be found in [Sch95].

Delection Semantics: Let $A(\vec{X}) \leftarrow \Theta$ be a constrained atom whose instances are to be deleted from the materialized view M. Let *Del* be the set $\{A(\vec{Y}) \leftarrow \Theta \wedge (\vec{X} = \vec{Y}) \wedge \Lambda \mid$ where $A(\vec{Y}) \leftarrow \Lambda$ is a constrained atom in the materialized view, MMV and $\Xi = \Theta \wedge (\vec{X} = \vec{Y}) \wedge \Lambda$ is satisfiable$\}$. *Del* is the initial input to our deletion algorithm below. Observe that the construction of *Del* ensures that only those constrained atoms that are actually in the existing materialized view will be deleted. We now show how to construct a new constrained database P' which accomplishes the deletion of these atoms as well as the deletion of their consequences. The least model of this constrained database will be the desired materialized view *after* the deletions are performed. Hence, P' provides the declarative semantics of the deletion operation, and we will later show in Algorithm 1, how this declarative semantics can be computed.

| Rewrite the Constrained Database P |

resulting in a *new* constrained database P', as follows.

1. If $A(\vec{X}) \leftarrow \Xi \parallel Body$ is in P and $A(\vec{Y}) \leftarrow \Xi'$ is in Del, then $A(\vec{X}) \leftarrow \Xi \wedge \mathbf{not}(\Xi') \wedge (\vec{X} = \vec{Y}) \parallel Body$ is in P'.

2. Any clause in P with a head different from $A(\vec{X})$ is in P'.

We present two algorithms for accomplishing the above deletion. The first algorithm extends the DRed algorithm of Gupta, Mumick and Subrahmanian [GMS93] to the mediated case. It is efficient when the mediated view is duplicate-free, i.e. when, for all distinct constrained atoms $A(\vec{X}) \leftarrow \Xi_1$ and $A(\vec{Y}) \leftarrow \Xi_2$ in the materialized view, $[A(\vec{X}) \leftarrow \Xi_1] \cap [A(\vec{Y}) \leftarrow \Xi_2] = \phi$. The second algorithm shows how to completely eliminate the expensive rederivation step in this algorithm, thus improving the DRed algorithm. Furthermore, the second algorithm uses the least fixpoint of the Gabbrielli-Levi operator with no changes (in particular, duplicate checking and elimination, required in Algorithm 1, are not required either).

The First Deletion Algorithm

Algorithm 1 (Extended DRed Algorithm)

1. Unfold the constrained atoms to be deleted with respect to the *original* constrained database P, so as to compute a set of constraint base facts, that are to be "possibly deleted".

$$\mathbf{P\_OUT}_0 \;=\; Del$$

$$
\begin{aligned}
\mathbf{P\_OUT}_{k+1} \;=\; \{ B(\vec{X}) \leftarrow \Xi \mid\ &\text{There is a clause} \\
&B(\vec{X}) \leftarrow \Xi_0 \parallel B_1(\vec{X}_1'),\ldots,B_n(\vec{X}_n') \text{ in } P \\
&\text{and for at least one } j \in \{1,\ldots,n\}: \\
&B_j(\vec{X}_j) \leftarrow \Xi_j \in \mathbf{P\_OUT}_k: \\
&\forall i \neq j \in \{1,\ldots,n\}: B_i(\vec{X}_i) \leftarrow \Xi_i \text{ is a constraint} \\
&\text{atom from the materialized view } M = T_P \uparrow \omega(\phi), \\
&\text{and } \Xi = \Xi_0 \wedge \ldots \wedge \Xi_n \wedge \\
&\quad \{\vec{X}_1 = \vec{X}_1'\} \wedge \ldots \wedge \{\vec{X}_n = \vec{X}_n'\} \\
&\text{is satisfiable}\}
\end{aligned}
$$

$$\mathbf{P\_OUT} \;=\; \bigcup_{k \geq 0} \mathbf{P\_OUT}_k$$

Note that the members of $\mathbf{P\_OUT}$ are candidates for deletion from the materialized view, but not all of them will necessarily be deleted.

2. Compute an overestimate, M', of necessary deletions with $[M'] = [M] \setminus [\mathbf{P\_OUT}]$ as follows:

(a) For every $B(X_1) \leftarrow \Xi$ in M for which there exists a $B(\vec{X_2}) \leftarrow \Gamma$ in **P_OUT**,

$$B(\vec{X_2}) \leftarrow \neg(\Gamma) \wedge \Xi \wedge (\vec{X_1} = \vec{X_2}) \text{ is in } M' \tag{3.4}$$

(b) For each remaining constraint fact $B(\vec{X}) \leftarrow \Xi$ in M, $B(\vec{X}) \leftarrow \Xi$ is in M'.

3. Rederive the new view by computing $T_{P'} \uparrow \omega(M')$.
   Return this as output.

   The fixpoint computation of $T_{P'} \uparrow \omega(M')$ can be speeded up by transforming each clause $C \equiv A(\vec{X}) \leftarrow \Xi \| B_1(\vec{Y_1}) \ldots, B_n(\vec{Y_n})$ of the program P'. It is important to note that we assume only one constrained atom in M' with a possibly *disjunctive* constraint.

   (a) If $[A \leftarrow \Xi] \subseteq [A \leftarrow \Xi_i]$ where $A \leftarrow \Xi_i \in M'$, then delete C from P'. Note that the empty constraint subsumes every other constraint. For instance a clause $A(X) \leftarrow B(X)$ gets only deleted in this step iff $A(X) \leftarrow$ is in M'.

   (b) Otherwise, unfold all constraint atoms $B_i \leftarrow \Theta_i$ which are true in M' into the body of this clause.

   (c) If all rules involving a predicate A have been eliminated by Step 3a, then eliminate all clauses with that predicate in the body. This process should be repeated until no more rules can be eliminated.

The above algorithm is incremental because Step 3 eliminates a large part of the constrained database from consideration by either eliminating rules, or eliminating various preconditions in the bodies of rules. The proof of the following theorem can be found in [Sch95].

Theorem 3.1 *Let $X = T_{P'} \uparrow \omega(M')$ be the output of Algorithm 1. Then: $[X] = [T_{P'} \uparrow \omega(\phi)]$, i.e. the algorithm is correct.*

Note that there are multiple ways of representing equivalent constraint atoms (e.g. $p(X, Y) \leftarrow X = Y + 1$ and $p(X, Y) \leftarrow Y = X - 1$ are syntactically different, but semantically equivalent). The above result says that the set of solutions of the constraint atoms returned by the algorithm coincide with the intended declarative semantics.

EXAMPLE 3.1 Suppose the materialized mediated view associated with the Law Enforcement example contains:
   1. `seenwith("Don Corleone", "Jo")`
   2. `seenwith("Don Corleone", "Ed")`
   3. `swlndc("Don Corleone", "Jo")`
   4. `swlndc("Don Corleone", "Ed")`

Suppose we are interested in deleting `seenwith("Don Corleone", "Jo")`; this may be due to external information (e.g. that the photograph was a forgery intended to frame Jo) then the materialized view will be updated by the deletion of the first and the third atoms. These two atoms constitute the set P_OUT. In this example, all atoms in P_OUT are in fact deleted.

EXAMPLE 3.2 Suppose there is *constrained database* containing:

$$
\begin{aligned}
A(X) &\leftarrow X \le 3 \\
B(X) &\leftarrow X \le 5 \\
A(X) &\leftarrow B(X) \\
C(X) &\leftarrow A(X)
\end{aligned}
$$

the *duplicate-free* materialized view associated with this is:

$$A(X) \ \leftarrow \ X \leq 5$$
$$B(X) \ \leftarrow \ X \leq 5$$
$$C(X) \ \leftarrow \ X \leq 5$$

Suppose now one would like to delete $B(X) \leftarrow X = 3$. Then

$$Del = \{B(X) \leftarrow X = 3\}$$

and

$$\mathbf{P\_OUT} = \{B(X) \ \leftarrow \ X = 3,$$
$$A(X) \ \leftarrow \ X = 3,$$
$$C(X) \ \leftarrow \ X = 3\}$$

(actually in this example, we are showing a simplified version of the constraints). Note that in this case, $A(X) \leftarrow X = 3$ and $C(X) \leftarrow X = 3$ should *not* be eliminated from the view because $A(X) \leftarrow X = 3$ has a proof independently of the proof that depends upon $B(X) \leftarrow X = 3$. M', as presented in the Extended DRed algorithm now becomes

$$A(X) \ \leftarrow \ X \leq 5 \wedge X \neq 3$$
$$B(X) \ \leftarrow \ X \leq 5 \wedge X \neq 3$$
$$C(X) \ \leftarrow \ X \leq 5 \wedge X \neq 3$$

The constrained database P' used in the definition of the view is identical to P except that $B(X) \leftarrow X \leq 5$ is replaced by $B(X) \leftarrow X \leq 5 \wedge X \neq 3$; P' is then the constrained database that contains just the following rules since $B(X) \leftarrow X \leq 5 \wedge X \neq 3$ in P' is subsumed by $B(X) \leftarrow X \leq 5 \wedge X \neq 3$ in M'.

$$A(X) \ \leftarrow \ X \leq 3$$
$$C(X) \ \leftarrow \ A(X)$$
$$A(X) \ \leftarrow \ B(X)$$

$T_{P'} \uparrow \omega(M')$ quickly evaluates to the materialized view,

$$A(X) \ \leftarrow \ X \leq 5$$
$$B(X) \ \leftarrow \ X \leq 5$$
$$C(X) \ \leftarrow \ X \leq 5$$

which is the correct, final materialized view.

The Second Deletion Algorithm

We now present a second algorithm to accomplish the deletion of constrained atoms from materialized mediated views in which duplicates are retained. The important advantage of the new algorithm is the elimination of the rederivation step (Step 3) of the first algorithm. To achieve this, we assume that each constraint atom in the materialized view is "indexed" by a sequence of clauses representing the derivation of the constraint atom in T_P. For simplicity we may assume that clauses are numbered in the constrained database and we use $Cn(C)$ to denote the clause number of the clause C.

For each constraint atom $A(\vec{X}) \leftarrow \Xi$ in the materialized view $T_P \uparrow \omega(\phi)$, we associate an "index" sequence, called the *support* of $A(\vec{X}) \leftarrow \Xi$ and denoted $spt(A(\vec{X}) \leftarrow \Xi)$, as follows:

1. If $A(\vec{X}) \leftarrow \Xi \in T_P \uparrow 0$, then $spt(A(\vec{X}) \leftarrow \Xi) = \langle Cn(C) \rangle$ where C is the clause from which $A(\vec{X}) \leftarrow \Xi$ is derived in T_P.

2. Suppose $A(\vec{X}) \leftarrow \Xi \in T_P \uparrow n$. By definition there is a clause $C \in P$ of the form $A(\vec{Y}) \leftarrow \Xi_0 \| B_1(\vec{X}_1), ..., B_k(\vec{X}_k)$ such that $B_i(\vec{Y}_i) \leftarrow \Xi_i \in T_P \uparrow (n-1)$ and $\Xi = \Xi_0 \wedge_{i=1}^k \Xi_i \wedge (\vec{X} = \vec{Y}) \wedge_{i=1}^k (\vec{X}_i = \vec{Y}_i)$ is solvable. Then $spt(A(\vec{X}) \leftarrow \Xi) = \langle Cn(C), spt(B_1(\vec{Y}_1) \leftarrow \Xi_1), \ldots, spt(B_k(\vec{Y}_k) \leftarrow \Xi_k) \rangle$.

Observe that the support of any constraint atom is always finite. Moreover, each constraint atom in $T_P \uparrow \omega(\phi)$ possesses a unique support.

Lemma 3.1 Suppose $spt(F_1) = spt(F_2)$. Then F_1 and F_2 are the same constraint atom in $T_P \uparrow \omega(\phi)$.

The input to the algorithm is the same set Del given to Algorithm 1. The intuitive idea behind the algorithm is that the support of a constraint atom F is used for determining whether an earlier deletion affects the deletion of F. We present the algorithm first followed by several examples.

Algorithm 2 (The Straight Delete (StDel) Algorithm)

1. Let M be the materialized view given by $T_P \uparrow \omega(\phi)$ and mark each constraint atom in M.

2. For each constraint atom $F = A(\vec{X}) \leftarrow \Xi$ in M where there exists $A(\vec{Y}) \leftarrow \Gamma \in Del$, such that $\Xi \wedge (\vec{X} = \vec{Y}) \wedge \Gamma$ is solvable, replace F with the new constraint atom $A(\vec{X}) \leftarrow \Xi \wedge (\vec{X} = \vec{Y}) \wedge not(\Gamma)$. In addition, put the pair $(A(\vec{Y}) \leftarrow \Xi \wedge (\vec{X} = \vec{Y}) \wedge \Gamma, spt(F))$ into P_OUT.

3. **repeat**

   For each constraint atom $F = A(\vec{X}) \leftarrow \Xi$ in M that is marked. Suppose $spt(F) = \langle Cn(C), s_1, ..., s_n \rangle$ for some constrained clause C having the form
   $A(\vec{Y}) \leftarrow \Xi_0 \| B_1(\vec{t}_1), ..., B_j(\vec{t}_j), ...B(\vec{t})_m$, and
   (a) The constraint atom $(B_j(\vec{Y}_j) \leftarrow \Xi_j, s_j)$, for some $1 \leq j \leq n$, is in P_OUT.
   (b) For each $1 \leq i \leq n$ such that $i \neq j$, the constraint fact $F_i = B_i(\vec{Y}_i) \leftarrow \Xi_i$ with $s_i = spt(F_i)$ is in M.
   (c) The constraint $\Xi_0 \wedge \Xi \wedge (\vec{X} = \vec{Y}) \wedge \wedge_{i=1}^n (\vec{Y}_i = \vec{t}_i \wedge \Xi_i)$ is solvable.

   Then replace F with $A(\vec{X}) \leftarrow \Xi_0 \wedge \Xi \wedge (\vec{X} = \vec{Y}) \wedge \wedge_{i=1}^n (\vec{Y}_i = \vec{t}_i) \wedge \Xi_1 \wedge ... \wedge not(\Xi_j) \wedge ... \wedge \Xi_n$. In addition, put the pair $(A(\vec{X}) \leftarrow \Xi \wedge (\vec{X} = \vec{Y}) \wedge \wedge_{i=1}^n (\vec{Y}_i = \vec{t}_i \wedge \Xi_i), spt(F))$ into P_OUT.

   Until no remaining marked elements can be replaced.

4. Remove any constraint atom from M whose constraint is not solvable.

Note that the constraints that are created in step 3 of the algorithm will often contain redundancy. But as the next example illustrates, in many cases the redundancy can be removed by simplification of the constraints.

EXAMPLE 3.3 Suppose P is the constrained database of example 3.2

The materialized view (containing duplicates) of P is shown below on the left, where the corresponding support for each constraint atom is shown to the right.

$A(X) \leftarrow X \leq 3$	$\langle 1 \rangle$
$A(X) \leftarrow X \leq 5$	$\langle 2, \langle 3 \rangle \rangle$
$B(X) \leftarrow X \leq 5$	$\langle 3 \rangle$
$C(X) \leftarrow X \leq 3$	$\langle 4, \langle 1 \rangle \rangle$
$C(X) \leftarrow X \leq 5$	$\langle 4, \langle 2, \langle 3 \rangle \rangle \rangle$

In the example every instance of $[A(X) \leftarrow X \leq 3]$ occurs twice in the materialized view. For certain constraint domains the elimination of duplicates may become a tedious task, if possible at all. In our case when the underlying constraint domains are external knowledge sources, duplicate elimination in the mediatory knowledge base is not required. In the mediatory knowledge base we explicitly specify in a declarative manner the equality of objects from different knowledge sources. Elimination of duplicates emerging from a *single* knowledge source depends on whether two objects of the same type can be tested for *equality*. This is possible if the underlying constraint domain itself provides an equality test predicate or if an object from an external knowledge source can be converted into a common exchange format.

Suppose the constraint atom $B(X) \leftarrow X = 3$ is specified for deletion. The declarative semantics of this deletion is given by the least fixpoint of the constrained database P':

$$
\begin{aligned}
A(X) &\leftarrow X \leq 3 \\
A(X) &\leftarrow B(X) \\
B(X) &\leftarrow X \leq 5 \wedge X \neq 3 \\
C(X) &\leftarrow A(X)
\end{aligned}
$$

The corresponding materialized view $T_{P'} \uparrow \omega(\phi)$ contains the constraint atoms

$$
\begin{aligned}
A(X) &\leftarrow X \leq 3 \\
A(X) &\leftarrow X \leq 5 \wedge X \neq 3 \\
B(X) &\leftarrow X \leq 5 \wedge X \neq 3 \\
C(X) &\leftarrow X \leq 3 \\
C(X) &\leftarrow X \leq 5 \wedge X \neq 3
\end{aligned}
$$

The StDel algorithm achieves the equivalent view working as follows. Initially, each of the five constraint atoms in M is marked. In the second step, we replace $B(X) \leftarrow X \leq 5$ by the new constraint atom $B(X) \leftarrow X \leq 5, X \neq 3$, and put $(B(X) \leftarrow X \leq 5 \wedge X = 3, \langle 3 \rangle)$ into **P_OUT** where $\langle 3 \rangle$ is the support of the replaced constraint atom.

Next according to step 3 of the algorithm, we search for marked constraint atoms in M whose support contains $\langle 3 \rangle$. The only constraint atom that satisfies this condition is $A(X) \leftarrow X \leq 5$, whose support is $\langle 2, \langle 3 \rangle \rangle$. We construct from constrained clause 2 the new constraint atom $A(X) \leftarrow (X \leq 5) \wedge \neg(X \leq 5 \wedge X = 3)$ that replaces $A(X) \leftarrow X \leq 5$. Simplification of the constraint yields $A(X) \leftarrow X \leq 5 \wedge X \neq 3$. The pair $(A(X) \leftarrow X \leq 5 \wedge X = 3, \langle 2, \langle 3 \rangle \rangle)$ is then placed in **P_OUT**.

The next iteration of the algorithm finds that the support for the marked constraint atom $C(X) \leftarrow X \leq 5$ contains the support $\langle 2, \langle 3 \rangle \rangle$. Hence by a similar analysis as the previous paragraph, a replacement of this constraint atom by $C(X) \leftarrow X \leq 5 \wedge X = 3$ is made. The pair $(C(X) \leftarrow X \leq 5 \wedge X = 3, \langle 4, \langle 2, \langle 3 \rangle \rangle \rangle)$ is put into **P_OUT**.

The final iteration of step 3 does not produce any new replacement since the only remaining marked constraint atoms are $A(X) \leftarrow X \leq 3$ and $C(X) \leftarrow X \leq 3$. Neither of these possesses a support that contains a sub-support in **P_OUT**. Hence the algorithm terminates.

Several observations are in order here. First, the supports that we use are similar to *justifications* used in reason-maintenance systems [Doy79] in that they provide a "history" of the derivation of constraint atoms. Our algorithm can be seen as a variant of justification-based reason maintenance tailored to updates in mediatory knowledge bases. The main difference is that usually the reason maintenance component is separated from the actual problem solver (which in this case is the inference engine of the mediator) and that there is no support due to the *absence* of an atom. Another difference between reason maintenance systems (RMSs) and view maintenance systems (VMSs) is that in RMSs, one attempts to delete an atom A by making it unprovable; in contrast, in view maintenance, one tries to determine what atoms need to be deleted based on deleting A. For instance, let $P = \{a \leftarrow b; a \leftarrow c; b; c; d \leftarrow a\}$ and suppose a is to be deleted from the original materialized view $\{a, b, c, d\}$. Then view maintenance simply says that the new materialized view is $\{b, d\}$; in contrast, RMSs would find three "extensions" for this problem based on different ways of eliminating the derivability of a; these extensions lead to the *multiple* materialized views $\{b, c\}$ obtained by eliminating the first two formulas in P; $\{b\}$ obtained by eliminating the first and fourth formulas in P; and $\{b\}$ again obtained by eliminating the second and fourth formulas in P. Since in a mediated system one would rather have a unique answer to a query (as opposed to agent-oriented systems) we have chosen an appropriate update semantics which keeps the unique-answer property instead of dealing with multiple extensions.

Secondly, the algorithm differs from the counting algorithm of [GKM92] since here, each constraint atom in the materialized view corresponds to a single proof. The counting algorithm maintains a count of the number of proofs of an atom, but does not distinguish between different derivations. In contrast, in this algorithm, given any constrained atom $A(X) \leftarrow \Xi$, we maintain a *list* of supports. This reveals another difference with respect reason maintenance systems where cycles of support are disallowed while in view maintenance those atoms are made explicit (for instance an infinite count may be attached to an atom).

EXAMPLE 3.4 (Recursive Views) Suppose we consider the constrained database:

1. $P(X, Y) \leftarrow \quad X = a \wedge Y = b$
2. $P(X, Y) \leftarrow \quad X = a \wedge Y = c$
3. $P(X, Y) \leftarrow \quad X = c \wedge Y = d$
4. $A(X, Y) \leftarrow \quad P(X, Y)$
5. $A(X, Y) \leftarrow \quad P(X, Z), A(Z, Y)$

The materialized view M is displayed below.

1. $P(X, Y) \leftarrow$	$X = a \wedge Y = b$	$\langle 1 \rangle$
2. $P(X, Y) \leftarrow$	$X = a \wedge Y = c$	$\langle 2 \rangle$
3. $P(X, Y) \leftarrow$	$X = c \wedge Y = d$	$\langle 3 \rangle$
4. $A(X, Y) \leftarrow$	$X = a \wedge Y = b$	$\langle 4, \langle 1 \rangle \rangle$
5. $A(X, Y) \leftarrow$	$X = a \wedge Y = c$	$\langle 4, \langle 2 \rangle \rangle$
6. $A(X, Y) \leftarrow$	$X = c \wedge Y = d$	$\langle 4, \langle 3 \rangle \rangle$
7. $A(X, Y) \leftarrow$	$X = X' \wedge Z = Y' \wedge X' = a \wedge$ $Y' = c \wedge Z = X'' \wedge Y = Y'' \wedge$ $X'' = c \wedge Y'' = d$	$\langle 5, \langle 2 \rangle, \langle 4, \langle 3 \rangle \rangle \rangle$

Suppose $Del = \{P(X, Y) \leftarrow X = c \wedge Y = d\}$. The view of the modified program P', when materialized, yields the set M'

$P(X, Y) \leftarrow$	$X = a \wedge Y = b$	$\langle 1 \rangle$
$P(X, Y) \leftarrow$	$X = a \wedge Y = c$	$\langle 2 \rangle$
$A(X, Y) \leftarrow$	$X = a \wedge Y = b$	$\langle 4, \langle 1 \rangle \rangle$
$A(X, Y) \leftarrow$	$X = c \wedge Y = d$	$\langle 4, \langle 3 \rangle \rangle$

Note that constraint atoms 3, 6, and 7 are no longer derivable since the constraint part of clause 3 in the modified program, $X = c \wedge Y = d \wedge \neg(X = c \wedge Y = d)$ is not solvable.

The computation of Algorithm 2 proceeds as follows. First constraint atom 3 in M is replaced by

$$P(X,Y) \leftarrow X = c \wedge Y = d \wedge \neg(X = c \wedge Y = d)$$

and the pair $(P(X,Y) \leftarrow X = c \wedge Y = d, \langle 3 \rangle)$ is placed in **P_OUT**.

Next constraint atom 6 in M, due to the match within its support with the support $\langle 3 \rangle$ from the above pair, is replaced by

$$A(X,Y) \leftarrow X = c \wedge Y = d \wedge \neg(X = c \wedge Y = d)$$

while simultaneously, the pair $(A(X,Y) \leftarrow X = c \wedge Y = d, \langle 4, \langle 3 \rangle \rangle)$ is added to **P_OUT**.

Finally, standardizing variables apart, constraint atom 7 in M is replaced by

$$\begin{aligned}
A(X,Y) \quad \leftarrow \quad & X = X' \wedge Z = Y' \wedge X' = a \wedge Y' = c \wedge \\
& Z = X'' \wedge Y = Y'' \wedge X'' = c \wedge Y'' = d \wedge \\
& Z = X''' \wedge Y = Y''' \wedge \neg(X''' = c \wedge Y''' = d)
\end{aligned}$$

Though a new pair is added to the set **P_OUT**, no more replacement is made to M and hence the final view is:

1. $P(X,Y) \leftarrow X = a \wedge Y = b$ $\qquad\qquad\qquad\qquad\quad$ $\langle 1 \rangle$
2. $P(X,Y) \leftarrow X = a \wedge Y = c$ $\qquad\qquad\qquad\qquad\quad$ $\langle 2 \rangle$
3. $P(X,Y) \leftarrow X = c \wedge Y = d \wedge \neg(X = c \wedge Y = d)$ $\qquad$ $\langle 3 \rangle$
4. $A(X,Y) \leftarrow X = a \wedge Y = b$ $\qquad\qquad\qquad\qquad\quad$ $\langle 4, \langle 1 \rangle \rangle$
5. $A(X,Y) \leftarrow X = a \wedge Y = c$ $\qquad\qquad\qquad\qquad\quad$ $\langle 4, \langle 2 \rangle \rangle$
6. $A(X,Y) \leftarrow X = c \wedge Y = d \wedge \neg(X = c \wedge Y = d)$ $\qquad$ $\langle 4, \langle 3 \rangle \rangle$
7. $A(X,Y) \leftarrow X = X' \wedge Z = Y' \wedge X' = a \wedge$
   $\qquad Y' = c \wedge Z = X'' \wedge Y = Y'' \wedge$
   $\qquad X'' = c \wedge Y'' = d \wedge Z = X''' \wedge$
   $\qquad Y = Y''' \wedge \neg(X''' = c \wedge Y''' = d)$ $\qquad\qquad$ $\langle 5, \langle 2 \rangle, \langle 4, \langle 3 \rangle \rangle \rangle$

The constraints of each of constraint atoms 3, 6, and 7 are not solvable. Hence these atoms may be removed. This produces the same materialized view as M'.

Suppose in the program above, that instead of the constraint atom 3, there is a constraint atom $P(X,Y) \leftarrow X = c \wedge Y = d$. Consequently atom 7 would be $A(X,Y) \leftarrow X = a \wedge Y = a$ with support $\langle 5, \langle 2 \rangle, \langle 4, \langle 3 \rangle \rangle \rangle$. In the subsequent step an atom $P(X,Y) \leftarrow X = c \wedge Y = a$ with support $\langle 5, \langle 3 \rangle 5, \langle 2 \rangle, \langle 4, \langle 3 \rangle \rangle \rangle$ is derived.

Theorem 3.2 *The Straight Deletion Algorithm is correct, i.e. the output M of the algorithm satisfies* $[M] = [T_{P'} \uparrow \omega(\phi)]$.

The theorem has been proven in [Sch95].

3.2   Insertion of Constrained Atoms

To insert the constrained atom $A(\vec{X}) \leftarrow \Theta$ into the mediated materialized view, we first construct the input *Add*, which is the set $\{A(\vec{X}) \leftarrow \textbf{not}(\Lambda) \wedge \Theta$ such that $A(X) \leftarrow \Lambda$ is in M and $\textbf{not}(\Lambda) \wedge \Theta$ is solvable $\}$. The set *Add* consists of all constrained atoms whose solutions correspond to the instances to be inserted into the materialized view.

Declarative Semantics: We now specify the meaning of an insertion of $A(\vec{X}) \leftarrow \Theta$ into a mediated materialized view, M, w.r.t. constrained database P – this meaning is the meaning of a constrained database $P^\flat$ constructed as follows.

$\boxed{\text{Rewrite the Constrained Database } P}$ into a *new* constrained database $P^\flat$ as follows:

$$\begin{aligned}
P^\flat = P \quad &\cup \quad Add \\
&\cup \quad \{A(\vec{X}) \leftarrow \neg(\Lambda) \wedge \Theta \,||\, B_1(\vec{t_1}), \ldots, B_n(\vec{t_n}) \,| \\
&\quad\quad A(\vec{X}) \leftarrow \Gamma \,||\, B_1(\vec{t_1}), \ldots, B_n(\vec{t_n}) \in P, n > 0, \\
&\quad\quad A(\vec{X}) \leftarrow \Lambda \in M\}
\end{aligned}$$

Note that in the third component of the above union, for every constrained atom $A(X) \leftarrow \Lambda$ in M, and for every clause C in P with A in the head, we are replacing C's constraint part (which may have been, say, Γ) by the constraint $\neg(\Lambda) \wedge \Theta$.

The least model of the above constrained database $P^\flat$ specifies the desired semantics after the insertion is accomplished. The reader may specifically note that even though negation occurs in the body of clauses in $P^\flat$, this negation occurs in the *constraint* part of the clause, and hence, the resulting constrained database still has a least fixpoint [JL87]. We now present an algorithm that incrementally inserts a constrained atom into a materialized view.

Algorithm 3 (Constrained Atom Insertion)

1. Unfold the constraint base fact to be inserted with respect to the *original* constrained database P.

$$\begin{aligned}
\mathbf{P\_ADD}_0 \quad = \quad & Add \\
\mathbf{P\_ADD}_{k+1} \quad = \quad & \mathbf{P\_ADD}_k \cup \{B(\vec{X}) \leftarrow \Xi \,| \\
& \text{There is a clause} \\
& \quad B(\vec{X}) \leftarrow \Xi_0 \,||\, B_1(\vec{t_1}), \ldots, B_n(\vec{t_n}) \text{ in } P \\
& \text{where for at least one } j \in \{1, \ldots, n\}: \\
& \text{There is a } B_j(\vec{X_j}) \leftarrow \Xi_j \in \mathbf{P\_ADD}_k, \\
& \text{and for each } i \in \{1, \ldots, n\} \text{ where} \\
& B_i(\vec{X_i}) \leftarrow \Xi_i \notin \mathbf{P\_ADD}_k \\
& B_i(\vec{X_i}) \leftarrow \Xi_i \text{ is a constraint atom} \\
& \text{in the materialized view } M = T_P \uparrow \omega(\phi), \text{ and} \\
& \Xi = \Xi_0 \wedge \ldots \wedge \Xi_n \wedge (\vec{X_1} = \vec{t_1}) \wedge \ldots \wedge (\vec{X_n} = \vec{t_n}) \\
& \text{is satisfiable}\} \\
\mathbf{P\_ADD} \quad = \quad & \mathbf{P\_ADD}_\omega
\end{aligned}$$

2. Set $M' = M \cup \mathbf{P\_ADD}$, which is then the new view.

Observe that an important difference between the deletion and the insertion algorithms is that in the condition defining P_Add_{k+1}, the number of body literals B_i that are contained in P_ADD_k is one *or more*. Recall that in the construction of P_OUT_{k+1}, we require the number of body literals contained in P_OUT_k to be exactly one.

The next theorem establishes the correctness of this algorithm, i.e. the incrementally computed view, M', is the same as the least fixpoint of $T_{P^\flat}$ where $P^\flat$ is the rewritten constraint database.

Theorem 3.3 The insertion algorithm is correct. i.e. $[T_{P^b} \uparrow \omega(\phi)] = [M']$.

4 Maintaining Views when External Changes Occur

Suppose we consider a mediator that integrates information in domains Σ_i, $i = 1 \ldots n$. For instance, these domains may be relational database systems like PARADOX or DBASE, or non-traditional systems like the facedb and spatialdb domains specified in the law enforcement example. When an update occurs *within* one or more of the domains being integrated (e.g. a PARADOX table gets updated), this could be viewed as a modification of the *behavior* of the functions that access these domains. For instance, the select function in the PARADOX domain may return a new set of tuples (after the update of the PARADOX tables). Another possibility is that the code implementing functions may also have been updated (e.g. to remove bugs in older versions of the software package). In this section, we analyze how updates to the integrated domains may affect the materialized mediated view and how they can be handled efficiently. For this, it is important to always remember that we do not materialize the functions occurring within the in predicate but instead materialize the mediated view by unfolding its defining rules.

As the behavior of functions is changing over time, we will use $d : f_t$ to denote the behavior of the function f of domain d at time t. In order to capture the behavioral difference of f between two successive time points, we define

$$\Delta f^+_{t,t+1}(<\text{args}>) = f_{t+1}(<\text{args}>) - f_t(<\text{args}>)$$

$$\Delta f^-_{t,t+1}(<\text{args}>) = f_t(<\text{args}>) - f_{t+1}(<\text{args}>)$$

Thus, $\Delta f^+_{t,t+1}(<args>)$ is the set of values returned by executing function f at time $t + 1$ that were not returned when f was executed at time t. Likewise, $\Delta f^-_{t,t+1}(<args>)$ is the set of objects returned by executing function f at time t that are not returned when f is executed at time $t + 1$. Note that the efficient computation of the difference between two successive database states has been extensively studied [BCL89, KKM94, Kuc91, Han87, SJGP90]. However, as we will see, we do not need the difference explicitly for our view maintenance mechanism. We only use it to investigate the effects of an update to an external function onto a materialized mediated view if T_P is used.

For a constraint atom to be introduced into the materialized mediated view defined by T_P, we require that the constraint be be satisfiable; hence, we should not be surprised that the materialized mediated view changes if the functions invoked within in change. Let
$REM = \{\text{in}(\text{a}, \text{d} : \text{f(b)}) \mid \text{a} \in \Delta f^-_{t,t+1}\}$ and
$ADD = \{\text{in}(\text{a}, \text{d} : \text{f(b)}) \mid \text{a} \in \Delta f^+_{t,t+1}\}$.
Then, intuitively, we may regard the problem of function updates as being equivalent to the insertion and the deletion of the ground instance that correspond to the DCA-atoms in the sets ADD and REM, respectively. However, as we are working with non-ground constrained atoms, the situation is less straightforward.

The set ADD does not introduce any technical complications. In contrast, the set REM needs to be treated with care. The following example provides an illustration.

EXAMPLE 4.1 Suppose we have a constrained database that contains the single clause $B(X) \leftarrow in(X, d : g(b))$. The function g is a call in the domain d. Assuming the initial set of values returned by g for the argument b is the singleton $\{a\}$, then according to the definition of T_P, we would have the constraint atom $B(X) \leftarrow in(X, d : g(b))$ in the original materialized view. Now suppose at time $t+1$, the result a is removed from the output of g. So $g(b) = \phi$. According to T_P, the materialized view at $t + 1$ would be empty since the constraint $in(X, d : g(b))$ is unsolvable.

This example illustrates that the set *REM* may cause subsequent modifications in the materialized view. However, the requirement that changes in functions of constraint domains be reflected in the materialized view appears to only incur computational overhead with little theoretical benefits. *A better approach is to regard the materialized view as a syntactic construct where each constraint atom $A(X) \leftarrow \Xi$ defines an access into the set of solutions represented by Ξ.* In particular, if f occurs in the constraint Ξ, then at time t, f will be interpreted as if it denotes the function f_t; at time $(t+1)$ it will denote the function f_{t+1}. Then, we may eliminate, from the definition of T_P, the condition that constraints be satisfiable, and instead, may defer the satisfiability test to query-evaluation time. As we demonstrate shortly, the elimination of the requirement that the constraint Ξ is satisfiable will simplify immensely the updating process. *Indeed, maintaining a materialized view requires no action whatsoever when this point of view is adopted, even if external changes occur.* We first adapt the operator T_P to the following simpler version, called W_P.

$W_P(I) = \{A(\vec{X}) \leftarrow \Xi \mid$ There is a clause $A(t_0) \leftarrow \Xi_0 || A_1(t_1), \ldots, A_n(t_n)$ in P and $\forall 1 \leq i \leq n : \exists A_i(X_i) \leftarrow \Xi_i \in I$ which share no variables and the constraint Ξ is $\Xi_0 \wedge \Xi_1 \wedge \ldots \wedge \Xi_n \wedge \{\vec{X}_1 = \vec{t}_1\} \wedge \ldots \wedge \{\vec{X}_n = \vec{t}_n\} \wedge \{\vec{X} = \vec{t}_0\}\}$.

Observe that the only difference between W_P and T_P is that the constraint Ξ is not required to be solvable. The materialized view of a constrained database is defined to be $W_P \uparrow \omega(\phi)$. Given now that the materialized view is only a syntactic construction where constraints that appear in constraint atoms are not necessarily solvable, it is clear to see that no changes to the solution sets of functions in any constraint domain will affect the syntactic form of the materialized view, as proved in the next theorem.

Theorem 4.1 Suppose M_t is the materialized view of the constrained database P at time point t. Then M_{t+1}, the materialized view of the constrained database P at time point $t+1$, is syntactically identical to M_t.

The *reason for this is that when we construct our materialized mediated views, we are storing atoms in the form $A \leftarrow \Xi$ where Ξ may contain some external function calls (let's say f is one such external call). At time t, the syntactic symbol f occurring in Ξ denotes the function f_t, i.e. it denotes the behavior of function f at time t. At time $t+1$, the syntactically identical constraint Ξ is evaluated with the syntactic entity f interpreted as the function f_{t+1}. The reason this approach works with W_P and not with T_P is that T_P determines solvability of constraints at time t, which means that the meaning, f_t of functions at time t may be used to "eliminate" constrained atoms from the materialized view.* In contrast, when no such eliminations are performed, as in the case of W_P, we can use the same syntactic form because evaluation of solvability of constraints is done using the "current meaning" of f, i.e. the meaning of f at time $t+1$.

Hence no action is required in view maintenance as the result of changes to domain functions. More important than the fact that the syntactic form of the materialized view remains static is that semantically, the instances represented by this single view accurately reflects the instances that should be true for the given constrained database at any time point. More specifically, the instances of the view that is constructed using W_P will coincide with the instances of the view constructed using T_P.

Corollary 1 Let $M = W_P \uparrow \omega(\phi)$. Suppose M_t represents the materialized view of the constrained database constructed using T_P and where the function calls to domains are evaluated at time point t, for any t. Then $[M] = [M_t]$.

EXAMPLE 4.2 Let P contain the single rule

$$A(X) \leftarrow in(X, \Sigma_1 : f(X)) \, || \, B(X, Y)$$

and the two facts $\{B(a, b), B(b, b)\}$. Suppose the function f evaluated at time t behaves as $f_t(b) = \{b\}$ and $f_t(X) = \phi$ for $X \neq b$. The materialized view M constructed under W_P is

$$\{\ B(a,b), B(b,b),$$
$$A(X) \leftarrow in(X, \Sigma_1 : f(X)) \wedge X = a \wedge Y = b$$
$$A(X) \leftarrow in(X, \Sigma_1 : f(X)) \wedge X = b \wedge Y = b\}$$

and its instances $[M]$ is the set $\{B(a,b), B(b,b), A(b)\}$. Using T_P, M_t is identical to M with the exception that it does not contain the third constraint atom as listed above for M. Clearly, $[M] = [M_t]$.

Now suppose the behavior of f at time $t + 1$ is $f_{t+1}(a) = a$ and $f_{t+1}(X) = \phi$ for $X \neq a$. M remains unchanged while the new materialized view according to T_P will be $M - \{A(X) \leftarrow in(X, \Sigma_1 : f(X)) \wedge X = b \wedge Y = b\}$. Again, we have $[M] = [M_{t+1}]$ which is now the set $\{B(a,b), B(b,b), A(a)\}$.

5   Discussion

Materialization of mediated views is performed by unfolding the rules defining the view. An update of type one, that is an update to the view, invalidates the materialized mediated view but — in our case — is *not* propagated to the integrated domains as incorporated by the **in** predicate. This makes our approach different from work on view updates on relational, deductive and object-oriented databases as partially cited and discussed in the introduction of this chapter. Note that none of this work is based on a language as powerful as constrained logic. However, considering the orthogonality of the approaches, it might be worthwhile to investigate an integration of this work with our approach. To some extent, this has already been done in this chapter – for instance, the DRed algorithm presented in [GMS93] has been extended to handle deletions in constrained and mediated databases. The relationship between the DRed algorithm and algorithms in [CW91, CW92a, UO92, Kuc91] has been discussed in detail in [GMS93] – however, none of these algorithms deal with constraints, and they all assume that a materialized view contains only *ground, fully instantiated* tuples – assumptions that are removed in this chapter.

As we have seen, an update of the second kind — a change to one of the integrated domains — affects the materialized mediated view if the T_P fixpoint operator is used. By replacing it with W_P, we eliminate the implied recomputation. Again, this differs from the traditional approach to view maintenance, since only the unfolding process of the rules which is *independent* of the actual evaluation of the **in** predicate might be affected. However, the work on view maintenance which was partially cited in the introduction (e.g. [KKM94]) of this chapter becomes relevant as soon as we want to guarantee an efficient evaluation of the **in** predicate by materializing the external function calls.

6   Conclusion and Future Work

The HERMES system at the University of Maryland is based on the intuition that constraints can be used to integrate multiple databases, multiple data structures, and multiple reasoning paradigms. In its current form, HERMES integrates INGRES, PARADOX, path planning packages developed by the US Army, Face Recognition packages, spatial data structures, a text database, and a pictorial database. Descriptions of the theory of HERMES may be found in [Sub94b, AS96, AS94, Sub94a, Sub94b, SAB+94] – in particular, [Jam96] shows that HERMES generalizes constrained databases as proposed by Kanellakis et. al. [KKR90].

In this chapter, we have dealt with the problem of efficiently maintaining materialized mediated views such as those that may occur when any constrained database system is updated. To our knowledge, this is the first work that addresses the view maintenance problem for constrained databases and/or for heterogeneous, mediated systems. The main contributions we have made are the following:

■   We have shown how the DRed deletion algorithm of Gupta et. al. [GMS93] may be extended to handle constraints.

- We have developed a unique *straight delete* algorithm for deletion that uses *supports* to accomplish deletions of constrained atoms; this algorithm is brand new, and, even when constraints are absent, it improves upon the counting method (that can lead to infinite counts) [GKM92] and also improves upon the re-derivation algorithm (as it requires no re-derivations. In addition, as shown in this chapter, it also applies to databases with constraints in it, including mediated systems.

- We have developed algorithms for inserting *constrained* atoms into an existing materialized view.

- We have shown that when we eliminate the constraint-satisfiability check from the Gabbrielli-Levi operator, then the problem of maintaining views in mediated systems (when changes occur in different programs/databases participating in the mediated framework) can be handled very easily indeed – no change to the mediated view, whatsoever, is needed, when the notion of mediated view defined by W_P is adopted ! This makes our approach eminently suitable for mediated systems.

Acknowledgments. This research was supported by ARO grant DAAL-03-92-G-0225, by AFOSR grant F49620-93-1-0065, by ARPA/Rome Labs contract Nr. F30602-93-C-0241 (Order Nr. A716), and by an NSF Young Investigator award IRI-93-57756. James Lu was supported by the NSF under grant number CCR9225037.

UPDATING DERIVED RELATIONS: DETECTING IRRELEVANT AND AUTONOMOUSLY COMPUTABLE UPDATES

José A. Blakeley,

Neil Coburn, Per-Åke Larson

ABSTRACT

Consider a database containing not only base relations but also stored derived relations (also called materialized or concrete views). When a base relation is updated, it may also be necessary to update some of the derived relations. This chapter gives sufficient and necessary conditions for detecting when an update of a base relation cannot affect a derived relation (an irrelevant update), and for detecting when a derived relation can be correctly updated using no data other than the derived relation itself and the given update operation (an autonomously computable update). The class of derived relations considered is restricted to those defined by *PSJ*-expressions, that is, any relational algebra expression constructed from an arbitrary number of project, select and join operations (but containing no self-joins). The class of update operations consists of insertions, deletions, and modifications, where the set of tuples to be deleted or modified is specified by a selection condition on attributes of the relation being updated.

1 Introduction

In a relational database system, the database may contain *derived relations* in addition to base relations. A derived relation is defined by a relational expression (query) over the base relations. A derived relation may be *virtual*, which corresponds to the traditional concept of a view, or *materialized*, meaning that the relation resulting from evaluating the expression over the current database instance is actually stored. In the sequel all derived relations are assumed to be materialized. As base relations are modified by update operations, the derived relations may also have to be changed. A derived relation can always be brought up to date by re-evaluating the relational expression defining it, provided that the necessary base relations are available. However, complete re-evaluation of the expression is often wasteful, and the cost involved may be unacceptable.

Consider a database scheme $\mathbf{D} = (D, S)$ consisting of a set of base relation schemes $D = \{R_1, R_2, \ldots, R_m\}$ and a set of derived relation definitions $S = \{E_1, E_2, \ldots, E_n\}$, where each $E_i \in S$ is a relational algebra expression over some subset of D. Suppose that an update operation $\mathcal{U}$ is posed against the database d on D specifying an update of base relation r_u on $R_u \in D$. To keep the derived relations consistent with the base relations, those derived relations whose definition involve R_u may have to be updated as well. The general *maintenance problem for derived relations* consists of: (1) determining which derived relations may be affected by the update $\mathcal{U}$, and (2) performing the necessary updates to the affected derived relations efficiently.

As a first step towards the solution of this problem, we consider the following two important subproblems: Given an update operation $\mathcal{U}$ and a potentially affected derived relation E_i,

- determine the conditions under which the update $\mathcal{U}$ cannot have any effect on the derived relation E_i, regardless of the database instance. In this case, the update $\mathcal{U}$ is said to be *irrelevant* to E_i.

- if the update $\mathcal{U}$ is not irrelevant to E_i, then determine the conditions under which E_i can be correctly updated using only $\mathcal{U}$ and the current instance of E_i, for every instance of the database. That is, no additional data from the base relations D is required. In this case, the effect of $\mathcal{U}$ on E_i is said to be *autonomously computable*.

In this chapter we give necessary and sufficient conditions for detecting irrelevant and autonomously computable updates.[1] The class of derived relations is restricted to those defined by *PSJ*-expressions, that is, any relational algebra expression constructed from an arbitrary number of project, select, and join operations. However, multiple occurrences of the same relation in the expression are not allowed (self-joins). The class of update operations consists of insertions, deletions, and modifications where the set of tuples to be deleted or modified is specified by a selection condition on the attributes of the relation being updated. We have implemented a simple prototype capable of detecting irrelevant and autonomously computable updates (see [BCL86]). Testing the conditions eventually requires testing the satisfiability of certain Boolean expressions, which, in general, is an *NP*-complete problem. Even though we impose some restrictions on the atomic conditions from which the Boolean expressions are built, we cannot avoid the exponential growth characteristic of *NP*-complete problems. However, the exponential growth depends on the number of attributes and atomic conditions in the selection conditions of the update operation and the derived relation. Experimental results indicate that, normally, this is not a severe problem.

The maintenance problem for derived relations is part of an ongoing project at the University of Waterloo on the use of derived relations. The project is investigating a new approach to structuring the database in a relational system at the internal level. In current systems there is, typically, a one-to-one correspondence, in terms of data contents, between conceptual relations and stored relations. (However, an implementation may map stored relations into physical files in various ways, see [Bat85].) This is a simple and straightforward solution, but its drawback is that the processing of a query often requires data to be collected from several stored relations. Instead of directly storing each conceptual relation, we propose structuring the stored database as a set of derived relations. The choice of stored relations should be guided by the actual or anticipated query load so that frequently occurring queries can be processed rapidly. To speed up query processing, some data may be redundantly stored in several derived relations.

The structure of the stored database should be completely transparent at the user level. This requires a system capable of automatically transforming any user update against a conceptual relation, into equivalent updates against all stored relations affected. The same type of transformation is necessary to process user queries. That is, any query posed against the conceptual relations must be transformed into an equivalent query against the stored relations. The query transformation problem has been addressed in papers by Larson and Yang [LY85, Tra87, YL87].

Although our main motivation for studying the problem stems from the above project, its solution also has applications in other areas of relational databases. Buneman and Clemons [BC79] proposed using views (that is, virtual derived relations) for the support of alerters. An alerter monitors the database and reports when a certain state (defined by the view associated with the alerter) has been reached. Hammer and Sarin [HS77] proposed a method for detecting violations of integrity constraints. Certain types of integrity constraints can be seen as defining a view. If we can show that an update operation has no effect on the view associated with an alerter or integrity constraint, then the update cannot possibly trigger the alerter or

---

[1]Reference [BCL86] is an early and incomplete version of this chapter. Reference [BCL86] contains some implementation details and experimental results not reported here.

result in a database instance violating the integrity constraint. The use of derived relations for the support of real-time queries was suggested by Gardarin et al. [GSV84] and by Dayal et al. [DBB+88]. Stonebraker et al. [SAH85] suggest that the results of database procedures be stored for future use; updating the stored results is similar to updating a derived relation. Our results have direct application in each these areas.

The detection of irrelevant or autonomously computable updates also has applications in distributed databases. Suppose that a derived relation is stored at some site and that an update request, possible affecting the derived relation, is submitted at the same site. If the update is autonomously computable, then the derived relation can be correctly updated locally without requiring data from remote sites. If the request is submitted at a remote site, then we need to send only the update request itself to the site of the derived relation. As well, the results presented here provide a starting point for devising a general mechanism for database snapshot refresh [AL80, BLT86, LHM+86].

In the next section we outline the assumptions and notation used in this chapter. In Section 3 we define when an update is irrelevant to a derived relation; and then give necessary and sufficient conditions for each type of update—insert, delete, modify. In a similar fashion, we deal with autonomously computable updates in Section 4. We conclude the chapter with a discussion in Section 5. The satisfiability algorithm we use is given as an Appendix.

2 Notation and Basic Assumptions

A *database scheme* $\mathbf{D} = (D, S)$ consists of a set of (*base*) *relation schemes* $D = \{R_1, R_2, \ldots, R_m\}$, and a set of derived relation definitions $S = \{E_1, E_2, \ldots, E_n\}$, where each $E_i \in S$ is a relational algebra expression over some subset of D. A *database instance* d, consists of a set of *relation instances* $r_1, r_2, \ldots, r_m$, one for each $R_i \in D$. We impose no constraints (e.g., keys or functional dependencies) on the relation instances allowed. A *derived relation* $v(E_i, d)$ is a relation instance resulting from the evaluation of a relational algebra expression E_i against the database d. We consider a restricted but important class of derived relations, namely those defined by a relational algebra expression constructed from any combination of project, select and join operations, called a *PSJ-expression*. In addition, we impose the restriction that no relation occurs as an operand more than once in the expression. In other words, a relation cannot be joined with itself (a *self-join*). We often identify a derived relation with its defining expression even though, strictly speaking, the derived relation is the result of evaluating that expression.

We state the following without proof: every valid *PSJ*-expression without self-joins can be transformed into an equivalent expression in a standard form consisting of a Cartesian product, followed by a selection, followed by a projection. It is easy to see this by considering the operator tree corresponding to a *PSJ*-expression. The standard form is obtained by first pushing all projections to the root of the tree and thereafter all selection and join conditions. From this it follows that any *PSJ*-expression can be written in the form $E = \pi_{\mathbf{A}} \sigma_{\mathcal{C}}(R_{i_1} \times R_{i_2} \times \cdots \times R_{i_k})$, where $R_{i_1}, R_{i_2}, \ldots, R_{i_k}$ are relation schemes, $\mathcal{C}$ is a selection condition, and $\mathbf{A} = \{A_1, A_2, \ldots, A_l\}$ are the attributes of the projection. We can therefore represent any *PSJ*-expression by a triple $E = (\mathbf{A}, \mathbf{R}, \mathcal{C})$, where $\mathbf{A} = \{A_1, A_2, \ldots, A_l\}$ is called the *attribute set*, $\mathbf{R} = \{R_{i_1}, R_{i_2}, \ldots, R_{i_k}\}$ is the *relation set* or *base*, and $\mathcal{C}$ is a *selection condition* composed from the conditions of all the select and join operations of the relational algebra expression defining E. The attributes in $\mathbf{A}$ will often be referred to as the *visible* attributes of the derived relation. A *selection condition* is a Boolean combination of atomic (selection) conditions. We also use the notation:

$\alpha(\mathcal{C})$ the set of all attributes appearing in condition $\mathcal{C}$

$\alpha(R)$ the set of all attributes of relation R

$\alpha(\mathbf{R})$ the set of all attributes mentioned in the set of relation schemes $\mathbf{R}$ (i.e., $\bigcup_{R_i \in \mathbf{R}} \alpha(R_i)$)

$t[X]$ the projection of the tuple t onto the attributes in set X.

For simplicity, all attribute names are taken to be unique (over the set of base relations). Current systems are capable of handling only discrete and finite domains. Any such domain can be mapped onto an interval of integers, and therefore we will in the sequel treat all attributes as being defined over some interval of integers. It will often be necessary to identify exactly from which set of attributes a tuple may take its value. Let $\mathbf{A} = \{A_1, \dots, A_k\}$ be a set of attributes. We will use the phrase, *tuple t is defined over set $\mathbf{A}$*, to describe a situation where t is a tuple defined over the attributes $A_1, \dots, A_k$; or more simply t *is over* $\mathbf{A}$, if no confusion will arise.

The update operations considered are insertions, deletions, and modifications. Each update operation affects only one (conceptual) relation. The following notation will be used for update operations:

INSERT(R_u, T): Insert into relation r_u the set of tuples T, where each $t \in T$ is defined over $\alpha(R_u)$.

DELETE$(R_u, \mathcal{C}_D)$: Delete from relation r_u all tuples satisfying condition $\mathcal{C}_D$, where $\mathcal{C}_D$ is a selection condition over $\alpha(R_u)$.

MODIFY$(R_u, \mathcal{C}_M, \mathbf{F}_M)$: Modify all tuples in r_u that satisfy the condition $\mathcal{C}_M$, where $\mathcal{C}_M$ is a selection condition over $\alpha(R_u)$. $\mathbf{F}_M$ is a set of expressions, each expression specifying how an attribute of r_u is to be modified.

Note that we make the assumption that all the attributes involved in the update expressions are from relation R_u. That is, both the attributes modified and the attributes from which the new values are computed, are from relation R_u. The set of expressions $\mathbf{F}_M$ of a MODIFY operation is assumed to contain an update expression for each attribute in R_u. An *update expression* is of the form $A_i := g_i(A_{i_1}, A_{i_2}, \dots, A_{i_k})$ where $A_{i_1}, A_{i_2}, \dots, A_{i_k}$ are attributes in R_u and g_i is a function over $A_{i_1}, A_{i_2}, \dots, A_{i_k}$. This function, g_i, is called the *update function* of attribute A_i. Again, the theory developed makes no other assumptions about update functions than that they are (computable) functions on the attributes in R_u. However, in practice, additional restrictions must be placed on them in order to be able to actually test the conditions.

Note that in [BCL86] we considered a more general class of update operations where the selection condition of DELETE and MODIFY operations may involve attributes in relations other than R_u. (Autonomously computable modifications were not considered in detail in [BCL86].) Further work revealed that the results presented in [BCL86] do not always hold for this more general class. However, the results are valid if the selection condition involves only attributes from R_u. This is the class of update operations considered in this chapter.

Conditions are Boolean expressions built from atomic conditions and logical connectives. An atomic condition is a function from the Cartesian product of the domains of a set of attributes (variables) to the set $\{true, false\}$. However, to be able to actually test the conditions stated in the theorems, further restrictions must be imposed on the atomic conditions allowed; this is discussed further below. The logical connectives will be denoted by "$\vee$" for OR, juxtaposition or "$\wedge$" for AND, "$\neg$" for NOT, "$\Rightarrow$" for implication, and "$\Leftrightarrow$" for equivalence. To indicate that all variables of a condition $\mathcal{C}$ are universally quantified we write $\forall \mathcal{C}$, and similarly for existential quantification $\exists \mathcal{C}$. If we need to explicitly identify which variables are quantified, we write $\forall X (\mathcal{C})$ or $\exists X (\mathcal{C})$ where X is a set of variables.

An *evaluation* of a condition is obtained by replacing all the variable names (attribute names) by values from the appropriate domains. The result is either *true* or *false*. A *partial evaluation* (or *substitution*) of a condition is obtained by replacing some of its variables by values from the appropriate domains. Let $\mathcal{C}$ be a condition and t a tuple over some set of attributes. The partial evaluation of $\mathcal{C}$ with respect to t is denoted by $\mathcal{C}[t]$. The result is a new condition with fewer variables.

Detecting whether an update operation is irrelevant or autonomously computable involves testing whether certain Boolean expressions are valid, or equivalently, whether related Boolean expressions are unsatisfiable.

A Boolean expression is valid if it always evaluates to *true*, unsatisfiable if it never evaluates to *true*, and satisfiable if it evaluates to *true* for some values of its variables. Proving the validity of a Boolean expression is equivalent to disproving the satisfiability of its complement.

Proving the satisfiability of Boolean expressions is, in general, *NP*-complete. The theory presented in this chapter requires the ability to test the satisfiability of Boolean expressions. Therefore, we assume that an algorithm for testing satisfiability, for the class of Boolean expressions of interest, is available. We also assume the algorithm returns a set of values and if the given expression is satisfiable then the values satisfy the expression. Since we have imposed the restriction that attributes have finite domains and we assume that any functions used are computable we are guaranteed the existence of a satisfiability testing algorithm—though it may not be efficient.

For a restricted class of Boolean expressions, polynomial algorithms exist. Rosenkrantz and Hunt [RH80] developed such an algorithm for conjunctive Boolean expressions. Each expression B must be of the form: $B = B_1 \wedge B_2 \wedge \cdots \wedge B_m$ where each B_i is an atomic condition. An atomic condition must be of the form $(x \, \theta \, y + c)$ or $(x \, \theta \, c)$, where $\theta \in \{=, <, \leq, >, \geq\}$, x and y are variables representing attributes, and c is a (positive or negative) constant. Variables and constants are assumed to range over the integers. The algorithm runs in $O(n^3)$ time where n is the number of distinct variables in B.

In this chapter, we are interested in the case when each variable ranges over a finite *interval* of integers. We have developed a modified version of the algorithm by Rosenkrantz and Hunt for this case. Details of the modified algorithm are given in the Appendix; however, we wish to stress that this algorithm is applicable only when the atomic conditions are of the form $(x \, \theta \, y + c)$ or $(x \, \theta \, c)$.

An expression not in conjunctive form can be handled by first converting it into disjunctive normal form and then testing each disjunct separately. In the worst case, this may cause the number of atomic conditions to grow exponentially. Several of the theorems in Sections 3 and 4 will require testing the validity of expressions of the form $\mathcal{C}_1 \Rightarrow \mathcal{C}_2$. The implication can be eliminated by converting to the form $(\neg\mathcal{C}_1) \vee \mathcal{C}_2$. Similarly, expressions of the form $\mathcal{C}_1 \Leftrightarrow \mathcal{C}_2$ can be converted to $\mathcal{C}_1\mathcal{C}_2 \vee (\neg\mathcal{C}_1)(\neg\mathcal{C}_2)$. Atomic conditions of the form $(x \neq y + c)$ must be converted to $(x < y + c) \vee (x > y + c)$ to satisfy the input requirements of the Rosenkrantz and Hunt algorithm; similarly, for $(x \neq c)$.

3   Irrelevant Updates

In certain cases, an update operation applied to a relation has no effect on the state of a derived relation. When this occurs independently of the database state, we call the update operation *irrelevant* to the derived relation. This section presents necessary and sufficient conditions for the detection of irrelevant updates. The conditions are given for insert, delete, and modify operations as introduced in the previous section. First we define what it means for an update to be irrelevant.

Definition 3.1 Let d be an instance on the set of relation schemes D, and let d' be the resulting instance after applying the update operation $\mathcal{U}$ to d. Let $E = (\mathbf{A}, \mathbf{R}, \mathcal{C})$ be a derived relation definition. The update operation $\mathcal{U}$ is *irrelevant* to E if $v(E, d') = v(E, d)$ for all instances d. $\qquad\Box$

If the update $\mathcal{U}$ does not modify any relations over which the derived relation is defined then $\mathcal{U}$ cannot have any effect on the derived relation. In this case $\mathcal{U}$ is said to be *trivially irrelevant* to the derived relation.

The fact that an update is not irrelevant does not imply that the update will, in fact, affect the current instance of the derived relation. However, determining whether it does, requires accessing the data in the database.

3.1   Irrelevant insertions

An insert operation into a base relation is irrelevant to a derived relation if it causes no tuple to be inserted into the derived relation.

Theorem 3.1 *The operation* INSERT(R_u, T) *is irrelevant to the derived relation defined by* $E = (\mathbf{A}, \mathbf{R}, \mathcal{C})$, $R_u \in \mathbf{R}$, *if and only if* $\mathcal{C}[t]$ *is unsatisfiable for every tuple* $t \in T$.

Proof: (Sufficiency) Consider an arbitrary tuple $t \in T$. If $\mathcal{C}[t]$ is unsatisfiable, then $\mathcal{C}[t]$ will evaluate to *false* regardless of the assignment of values to the variables remaining in $\mathcal{C}[t]$. Therefore, there cannot exist any tuple defined over the Cartesian product of the relations in $\mathbf{R} - \{R_u\}$ that would combine with t to satisfy $\mathcal{C}$ and hence cause an insertion into $v(E, d)$.

(Necessity) Consider a tuple $t \in T$, and assume that $\mathcal{C}[t]$ is satisfiable. $\mathcal{C}[t]$ being satisfiable means that there exists a tuple s defined over $\alpha(\mathbf{R})$ such that $s[\alpha(R_u)] = t$, $s[A] = \mu_A$ for every attribute $A \notin \alpha(R_u) \cup \alpha(\mathcal{C})$, where μ_A is the lowest value in the domain of A, and the rest of the values $s[A]$, $A \in \alpha(\mathcal{C}) - \alpha(R_u)$ are assigned in such a way that $\mathcal{C}[s] = true$. The fact that $\mathcal{C}[t]$ is satisfiable guarantees the existence of such values for attributes in $\alpha(\mathcal{C}) - \alpha(R_u)$. We can then construct a database instance d using s, such that the insertion of t into r_u will cause a new tuple to be inserted into the derived relation $v(E, d)$.

To construct d, we build a relation instance r_i for each relation scheme $R_i \in \mathbf{R} - \{R_u\}$. Each relation r_i contains a single tuple t_i, where $t_i = s[\alpha(R_i)]$. The database instance d consists of the relation $r_u = \phi$ and relations $r_i = \{t_i\}$ for each $R_i \in \mathbf{R} - \{R_u\}$. Clearly, $v(E, d) = \phi$. However, if we obtain d' from d by inserting tuple t into r_u, then $v(E, d')$ will contain one tuple. Therefore, the INSERT operation is not irrelevant to the derived relation. $\square$

3.2   Irrelevant deletions

A delete operation on a base relation is irrelevant to a derived relation if none of the tuples in the derived relation will be deleted as a result of the operation.

Theorem 3.2 *The operation* DELETE$(R_u, \mathcal{C}_D)$ *is irrelevant to the derived relation defined by* $E = (\mathbf{A}, \mathbf{R}, \mathcal{C})$, $R_u \in \mathbf{R}$, *if and only if the condition* $\mathcal{C}_D \wedge \mathcal{C}$ *is unsatisfiable.*

Proof: (Sufficiency) If $\mathcal{C}_D \wedge \mathcal{C}$ is unsatisfiable, then no tuple t defined over $\alpha(\mathbf{R})$ can have values such that $\mathcal{C}_D[t]$ and $\mathcal{C}[t]$ are simultaneously *true*. Assume that t contains values such that $\mathcal{C}_D[t]$ is *true*, meaning that the delete operation causes the deletion of the tuple $t[\alpha(R_u)]$ from r_u. Since t cannot at the same time satisfy $\mathcal{C}$, then t could not have contributed to a tuple in the derived relation. Thus the deletion of $t[\alpha(R_u)]$ from r_u will not cause any data to be deleted from the derived relation defined by E. Therefore, the delete operation is irrelevant.

(Necessity) Assume that $\mathcal{C}_D \wedge \mathcal{C}$ is satisfiable. Thus, there exists a tuple s over $\alpha(\mathbf{R})$ such that $\mathcal{C}_D[s] \wedge \mathcal{C}[s]$ is *true*. As in the proof of the previous theorem we can construct a database instance, d, for relations in $\mathbf{R}$ such that deleting one tuple from r_u will indeed change the derived relation. Of course, in this case r_u initially contains the single tuple $s[\alpha(R_u)]$. Hence, $v(E, d)$ will contain one tuple. Applying the delete operation to d then gives an instance d' where the tuple in relation r_u has been deleted. Clearly, $v(E, d') = \phi$. This proves that the deletion is not irrelevant. $\qquad\square$

Example 3.1 Consider two relation schemes $R_1(H, I, J)$ and $R_2(K, L)$, and the following derived relation and delete operation:

$$E = (\{H, L\}, \{R_1, R_2\}, (I > J)(J = K)(K > 10))$$

$$\text{DELETE } (R_1, (I < 5)).$$

To show that the deletion is irrelevant to the derived relation we must prove that the following condition holds:

$$\nexists \, H, I, J, K, L \, [(I > J)(J = K)(K > 10) \wedge (I < 5)].$$

Clearly, the condition holds because the condition $(I > J)(J = K)(K > 10)$ implies that $(I > 11)$, which contradicts $(I < 5)$. Hence, the delete operation is irrelevant to the derived relation. $\qquad\square$

3.3   Irrelevant modifications

The detection of irrelevant modifications is somewhat more complicated than insertions or deletions. Consider a tuple that is to be modified. It will not affect the derived relation if one of the following conditions applies:

- it does not qualify for the derived relation, neither before nor after the modification;

- it does qualify for the derived relation both before and after the modification, but all the attributes visible in the derived relation remain unchanged.

Theorem 3.3 introduced in this section covers the two cases mentioned above, but before we state the theorem, we need some additional notation.

Consider a modify operation $\text{MODIFY}(R_u, \mathcal{C}_M, \mathbf{F}_M)$ and a derived relation defined by $E = (\mathbf{A}, \mathbf{R}, \mathcal{C})$. Let $\alpha(R_u) = \{A_1, A_2, \ldots, A_l\}$. As mentioned in Section 2, we will associate an update expression with every attribute in R_u, that is, $\mathbf{F}_M = \{f_{A_1}, f_{A_2}, \ldots, f_{A_l}\}$. Each update expression is of the form $f_{A_i} \equiv (A_i := g_i(A_{i_1}, A_{i_2}, \ldots, A_{i_k}))$. If an attribute A_i is not to be modified, we associate with it a *trivial update expression* of the form $f_{A_i} \equiv (A_i := A_i)$. If the attribute is assigned a fixed value c, then the corresponding update expression is $f_{A_i} \equiv (A_i := c)$. The notation $\rho(f_{A_i})$ will be used to denote the right hand side of the update expression f_{A_i}, that is, the function after the assignment operator. The notation $\alpha(\rho(f_{A_i}))$ denotes the variables mentioned in $\rho(f_{A_i})$. For example, if $f_{A_i} \equiv (A_i := A_j + c)$ then $\rho(f_{A_i}) = A_j + c$ and $\alpha(\rho(f_{A_i})) = \{A_j\}$.

By substituting every occurrence of an attribute A_i in $\mathcal{C}$ by $\rho(f_{A_i})$ a new condition is obtained. We will use the notation $\mathcal{C}(\mathbf{F}_M)$ to denote the condition obtained by performing this substitution for every variable $A_i \in \alpha(R_u) \cap \alpha(\mathcal{C})$.

An update expression $\rho(f_{A_i})$ may produce a value outside the domain of A_i. We make the assumption that such a modification will not be performed, that is, the entire tuple will remain unchanged. Each attribute A_i of R_u must satisfy a condition of the form $(A_i \le U_{A_i})(A_i \ge L_{A_i})$ where L_{A_i} and U_{A_i} are the lower and upper bound, respectively, of its domain. Consequently, the updated value of A_i must satisfy the condition

$(\rho(f_{A_i}) \leq U_{A_i})(\rho(f_{A_i}) \geq L_{A_i})$ and this must hold for every $A_i \in \alpha(R_u)$. The conjunction of all these conditions will be denoted by $\mathcal{C}_B(\mathbf{F}_M)$, that is,

$$\mathcal{C}_B(\mathbf{F}_M) \equiv \bigwedge_{A_i \in \alpha(R_u)} (\rho(f_{A_i}) \leq U_{A_i})(\rho(f_{A_i}) \geq L_{A_i}).$$

Therefore, to be chosen for modification a tuple must satisfy both $\mathcal{C}_M$ and $\mathcal{C}_B(\mathbf{F}_M)$. Thus, the selection condition for a modification is effectively $\mathcal{C}_M \wedge \mathcal{C}_B(\mathbf{F}_M)$.

Example 3.2 Consider a relation schema $R(H, I, J)$ and the following modify operation:

$$\text{MODIFY}(R, (H > 5) \wedge (I \geq J), \{H := H + 20, I := 15, J := J\}).$$

For this modify operation we have:

$$\begin{array}{lll} f_H \equiv (H := H + 20) & \rho(f_H) \equiv H + 20 & \alpha(\rho(f_H)) = \{H\} \\ f_I \equiv (I := 15) & \rho(f_I) \equiv 15 & \alpha(\rho(f_I)) = \phi \\ f_J \equiv (J := J) & \rho(f_J) \equiv J & \alpha(\rho(f_J)) = \{J\} \end{array}$$

$$\mathcal{C}_M \equiv (H > 5) \wedge (I \geq J).$$

If the selection condition $\mathcal{C}$ of a derived relation is $\mathcal{C} \equiv (H > 30) \wedge (I = J)$, then

$$\mathcal{C}(\mathbf{F}_M) \equiv (H + 20 > 30) \wedge (15 = J).$$

Assuming that the domains of the variables H, I, and J are given by the ranges $[0, 50]$, $[10, 100]$, and $[10, 100]$, respectively, we obtain:

$$\begin{aligned} \mathcal{C}_B(\mathbf{F}_M) &\equiv (H + 20 \geq 0) \wedge (H + 20 \leq 50) \wedge (15 \geq 10) \\ &\wedge (15 \leq 100) \wedge (J \geq 10) \wedge (J \leq 100). \end{aligned}$$

$\square$

We make no assumptions about the types of update functions allowed. Hence, the conditions $\mathcal{C}(\mathbf{F}_M)$ and $\mathcal{C}_B(\mathbf{F}_M)$ may not be in the class of Boolean expressions of interest to us. Therefore, the satisfiability algorithm we wish to use may not be able to handle these conditions.

Theorem 3.3 *The operation* $\text{MODIFY}(R_u, \mathcal{C}_M, \mathbf{F}_M)$ *is irrelevant to the derived relation defined by* $E = (\mathbf{A}, \mathbf{R}, \mathcal{C}), R_u \in \mathbf{R}$, *if and only if*

$$\forall [\mathcal{C}_M \wedge \mathcal{C}_B(\mathbf{F}_M) \Rightarrow (\neg \mathcal{C} \wedge \neg \mathcal{C}(\mathbf{F}_M)) \vee (\mathcal{C} \wedge \mathcal{C}(\mathbf{F}_M) \wedge (\bigwedge_{A_i \in \mathbf{A} \cap \alpha(R_u)} (A_i = \rho(f_{A_i}))))]. \quad (3.1)$$

Proof: (Sufficiency) Consider a tuple t over $\alpha(\mathbf{R})$ such that t satisfies $\mathcal{C}_M$ and $\mathcal{C}_B(\mathbf{F}_M)$. Denoted the corresponding modified tuple by t'. Because condition (3.1) holds for every tuple, it must also hold for t. Hence, either the first or the second disjunct of the consequent must evaluate to *true*. (They cannot both be *true* simultaneously.)

If the first disjunct is *true*, both $\mathcal{C}[t]$ and $\mathcal{C}[t']$ must be *false*. (Note that, $\mathcal{C}[t'] \equiv \mathcal{C}(\mathbf{F}_M)[t]$.) This means that neither the original tuple t, nor the modified tuple t', will contribute to the derived relation. Hence changing t to t' will not affect the derived relation.

If the second disjunct is *true*, both $\mathcal{C}[t]$ and $\mathcal{C}[t']$ must be *true*. In other words, the tuple t contributed to the derived relation and after being modified to t', it still remains in the derived relation. The last conjunct must also be satisfied, which ensures that all attributes of R_u visible in the derived relation have the same values in t and t'. Hence the derived relation will not be affected.

(Necessity) Assume that condition (3.1) does not hold. That means that there exists at least one assignment of values to the attributes, i.e., a tuple t, such that the antecedent is *true* but the consequent is *false*. Denote the corresponding modified tuple by t'. Since the consequent of condition (3.1) is *false*, $C[t]$ and $C[t']$ cannot both be *false*; thus there are three cases to consider.

Case 1: $\mathcal{C}[t] = false$ and $\mathcal{C}[t'] = true$. In the same way as in the proof of Theorem 3.1, we can then construct a database instance d from t, where each relation in $\mathbf{R}$ contains a single tuple and such that the resulting derived relation is empty. For this database instance, the modification operation will produce a new instance d' where the only change is to the tuple in relation r_u. The Cartesian product of the relations in $\mathbf{R}$ then contains exactly one tuple, which agrees with t on all attributes except on the attributes changed by the update. Hence, the derived relation $v(E, d')$ will contain one tuple since $\mathcal{C}[t'] = true$. This proves that the modify operation is not irrelevant to the derived relation.

Case 2: $\mathcal{C}[t] = true$ and $\mathcal{C}[t'] = false$. Can be proven in the same way as Case 1, with the difference that the derived relation contains originally one tuple and the modification results in a deletion of that tuple from the derived relation.

Case 3: $\mathcal{C}[t] = true$, $\mathcal{C}[t'] = true$ but $\bigwedge_{A_i \in \mathbf{A} \cap \alpha(R_u)}(A_i = \rho(f_{A_i}))$ is *false*, that is, $t[A_i] \neq t'[A_i]$ for some $A_i \in \mathbf{A} \cap \alpha(R_u)$. We can construct an instance where each relation in $\mathbf{R}$ contains only a single tuple, and where the derived relation also contains a single tuple, both before and after the modification. However, in this case the value of attribute A_i will change as a result of performing the MODIFY operation. Since $A_i \in \mathbf{A}$, this change will be visible in the derived relation. This proves that the update is not irrelevant to the derived relation. $\qquad\square$

Example 3.3 Suppose the database consists of the two relations $R_1(H, I)$ and $R_2(J, K)$ where H, I, J and K all have the domain $[0, 30]$. Let the derived relation and modify operation be defined as:

$$E = (\{I, J\}, \{R_1, R_2\}, (H > 10)(I = K))$$
$$\text{MODIFY } (R_1, (H > 20), \{(H := H + 5), (I := I)\}).$$

Thus the condition given in Theorem 3.3 becomes

$$
\begin{aligned}
\forall \quad & H, I, J, K \; [(H > 20) \wedge (H + 5 \geq 0)(H + 5 \leq 30)(I \geq 0)(I \leq 30) \\
& \Rightarrow \; (\neg((H > 10)(I = K))) \wedge (\neg((H + 5 > 10)(I = K))) \\
& \vee (H > 10)(I = K)(H + 5 > 10)(I = K)(I = I)]
\end{aligned}
$$

which can be simplified to

$$
\begin{aligned}
\forall \quad & H, I, K \; [(H > 20)(H \leq 25)(I \geq 0)(I \leq 30) \\
& \Rightarrow \; (\neg((H > 10)(I = K))) \wedge (\neg((H > 5)(I = K))) \\
& \vee (H > 10)(I = K)].
\end{aligned}
$$

If $I = K$, then the second term of the consequent will be satisfied whenever the antecedent is satisfied. If $I \neq K$, the first term of the consequent is always satisfied. Hence, the implication is valid and we conclude that the update is irrelevant to the derived relation.   □

The idea of detecting irrelevant updates is not new. In the work by Buneman and Clemons [BC79], on the support of triggers and alerters, they are called *readily ignorable updates* and in the work by Bernstein and Blaustein [BB91], on the support of integrity constraints, they are called *trivial tests*.

Maier and Ullman [MU83] study updates to relation fragments. In their work a fragment may be a physical or virtual relation over a single relation scheme, defined by selection and union operators on physical or other virtual relations. A fragment f_1 is related to fragment f_2 through a *transfer predicate* β_{12}; a Boolean expression defining which tuples from f_1 also belong to f_2. When a set of tuples is (say) inserted into f_1 only those tuples which satisfy β_{12} will be transferred to f_2. Tuples not satisfying β_{12} are irrelevant to f_2.

Our work improves upon previous work in several respects: (1) the update operations we support are more general than the ones supported in any of the above related papers, (2) we provide necessary and sufficient conditions for the detection of irrelevant updates, and (3) we provide an algorithm, for actually testing these conditions, which handles a large and commonly occurring class of atomic conditions.

4   Autonomously Computable Updates

Throughout this section we assume that for a given update operation and derived relation the update is not irrelevant to the derived relation. We formalize this with the following statement:

Property 1 Given an update operation $\mathcal{U}$ and the derived relation defined by $E = (\mathbf{A}, \mathbf{R}, \mathcal{C})$ then $\mathcal{U}$ is not irrelevant with respect to E.

If an update operation is not irrelevant to a derived relation, then some data from the base relations may be needed to update the derived relation. An important case to consider is one in which all the data needed is contained in the derived relation itself. In other words, the new state of the derived relation can be computed solely from the derived relation definition, the current state of the derived relation, and the information contained in the update operation. We call updates of this type *autonomously computable updates*. Within this case, two subcases can be further distinguished depending on whether the decision is *unconditional* (scheme-based) or *conditional* (instance-based).

When the decision is unconditional, the new state of the derived relation can be computed using the definition and the current instance of the derived relation, and the information contained in the update operation, *for every database instance*. When the decision is conditional, the new state of the derived relation can be computed using the definition and the current instance of the derived relation, and the information contained in the update operation, *for the current database instance* but not necessarily for other instances. In this chapter we concentrate only on the study of unconditionally autonomously computable updates, hence, we will often omit the word "unconditionally". For results on conditionally autonomously computable updates the reader is referred to [Bla87].

Definition 4.1 Consider a derived relation definition E and an update operation $\mathcal{U}$, both defined over the database scheme D. Let d denote an instance of D before applying $\mathcal{U}$ and d' the corresponding instance after applying $\mathcal{U}$.

The effect of the operation $\mathcal{U}$ on E is said to be *unconditionally autonomously computable* if there exists a function $F_{\mathcal{U},E}$ such that $v(E, d') = F_{\mathcal{U},E}(v(E, d))$ for every database instance d.   □

The important aspect of this definition is the requirement that $F_{\mathcal{U},E}$ be a *function* of the instance $v(E,d)$. In other words, if d_1 and d_2 are database instances where $v(E,d_1) = v(E,d_2)$ then it must follow that $F_{\mathcal{U},E}(v(E,d_1)) = F_{\mathcal{U},E}(v(E,d_2))$. The following simple but important lemma will be used in several proofs in this section.

Lemma 4.1 Consider a derived relation definition E and an update operation $\mathcal{U}$, both defined over the database scheme D. Let d_1 and d_2 be database instances and d_1' and d_2', respectively, be the corresponding instances after applying $\mathcal{U}$. If $v(E,d_1) = v(E,d_2)$ and $v(E,d_1') \neq v(E,d_2')$ then $\mathcal{U}$ is not autonomously computable on E.

Proof: Assume that there exists a function $F_{\mathcal{U},E}$, as in Definition 4.1, such that $v(E,d') = F_{\mathcal{U},E}(v(E,d))$ for every database instance d. Now consider the instances d_1 and d_2. It follows that $F_{\mathcal{U},E}(v(E,d_1)) = v(E,d_1')$ and $F_{\mathcal{U},E}(v(E,d_2)) = v(E,d_2')$. Since $F_{\mathcal{U},E}$ is a function and $v(E,d_1) = v(E,d_2)$, it follows (from the definition of a function) that $F_{\mathcal{U},E}(v(E,d_1)) = F_{\mathcal{U},E}(v(E,d_2))$, that is, $v(E,d_1') = v(E,d_2')$. This contradicts the conditions given and proves the lemma. $\qquad\square$

4.1   Basic concepts

The concepts covered by the following definitions are required in the rest of this section. They were originally introduced by Larson and Yang [LY85].

Definition 4.2 Let $\mathcal{C}_0$ and $\mathcal{C}_1$ be Boolean expressions over the variables $x_1, x_2, \ldots, x_n$. The variables $x_1, x_2, \ldots, x_k$, $k \leq n$, are said to be *computationally nonessential* in $\mathcal{C}_0$ *with respect to* $\mathcal{C}_1$ if

$$\forall x_1, \ldots, x_k, x_{k+1}, \ldots, x_n, x_1', \ldots, x_k'$$
$$[\mathcal{C}_1(x_1, \ldots, x_k, x_{k+1}, \ldots, x_n) \wedge \mathcal{C}_1(x_1', \ldots, x_k', x_{k+1}, \ldots, x_n)$$
$$\Rightarrow (\mathcal{C}_0(x_1, \ldots, x_k, x_{k+1}, \ldots, x_n) \Leftrightarrow \mathcal{C}_0(x_1', \ldots, x_k', x_{k+1}, \ldots, x_n))].$$

Otherwise, $x_1, x_2, \ldots, x_k$ are *computationally essential* in $\mathcal{C}_0$ with respect to $\mathcal{C}_1$. $\qquad\square$

The idea behind this definition is that if a set of variables $x_1, x_2, \ldots, x_k$ are computationally nonessential in $\mathcal{C}_0$ with respect to $\mathcal{C}_1$, then given any tuple defined over the variables $x_1, x_2, \ldots, x_n$ satisfying the condition $\mathcal{C}_1$, where the variables $x_1, x_2, \ldots, x_k$ have been projected out, we can still correctly evaluate whether the tuple satisfies the condition $\mathcal{C}_0$ without knowing the exact values for the missing variables $x_1, x_2, \ldots, x_k$. This is done by assigning surrogate values to the variables $x_1, x_2, \ldots, x_k$ as explained by Larson and Yang [LY85].

Example 4.1 Let $\mathcal{C}_1 \equiv (H > 5)$ and $\mathcal{C}_0 \equiv (H > 0)(I = 5)(J > 10)$. It is easy to see that if we are given a tuple $\langle i, j \rangle$ for which it is known that the full tuple $\langle h, i, j \rangle$ satisfies $\mathcal{C}_1$, then we can correctly evaluate $\mathcal{C}_0$. If $\langle h, i, j \rangle$ satisfies $\mathcal{C}_1$ then the value h must be greater than 5, and consequently it also satisfies $(H > 0)$. Hence, we can correctly evaluate $\mathcal{C}_0$ for the tuple $\langle i, j \rangle$ by assigning to H any (surrogate) value greater than 5. $\qquad\square$

Here is a brief description of the procedure for determining surrogate values. Consider a derived relation defined by $E = (\mathbf{A}, \mathbf{R}, \mathcal{C}_1)$, and suppose that we want to find which tuples in $v(E,d)$ satisfy some condition $\mathcal{C}_0$. For example, $\mathcal{C}_0$ may be the selection condition of a DELETE operation. Since every tuple in the derived relation satisfies $\mathcal{C}_1$ we are interested in the case where all variables in the set $\mathbf{S} = (\alpha(\mathcal{C}_0) \cup \alpha(\mathcal{C}_1)) - \mathbf{A}$ are computationally nonessential in $\mathcal{C}_0$ with respect to $\mathcal{C}_1$. Let $\mathbf{S} = \{x_1, x_2, \ldots, x_k\}$ and $\alpha(\mathcal{C}_0) \cup \alpha(\mathcal{C}_1) = \{x_1, x_2, \ldots, x_n\}, n \geq k$. For each $t \in v(E, d)$ surrogate values for $x_1, x_2, \ldots, x_k$ can be computed by invoking an appropriate satisfiability testing algorithm with input $\mathcal{C}_1[t]$. For each tuple t the algorithm returns a set of values $x_1^0, x_2^0, \ldots, x_n^0$ where $x_i^0 = t[x_i]$, for $k + 1 \leq i \leq n$. The values $x_1^0, x_2^0, \ldots, x_k^0$ are the required surrogate values needed to evaluate $\mathcal{C}_0$ on tuple t. We are guaranteed that surrogate values for the variables $x_1, \ldots, x_k$ exist, since $t \in v(E, d)$ implies that $\mathcal{C}_1[t]$ is satisfiable.

Definition 4.3 Let $\mathcal{C}$ be a Boolean expression over variables $x_1, x_2, \ldots, x_n, y_1, y_2, \ldots, y_m$. The variable $y_i, 1 \leq i \leq m$, is said to be *uniquely determined* by $x_1, x_2, \ldots, x_n$ and $\mathcal{C}$ if

$$\forall x_1, \ldots, x_n, y_1, \ldots, y_m, y_1', \ldots, y_m'$$
$$[\mathcal{C}(x_1, \ldots, x_n, y_1, \ldots, y_m) \wedge \mathcal{C}(x_1, \ldots, x_n, y_1', \ldots, y_m') \Rightarrow (y_i = y_i')].$$

$\square$

If a variable y_i (or a subset of the variables $y_1, y_2, \ldots, y_m$) is uniquely determined by a condition $\mathcal{C}$ and the variables $x_1, \ldots, x_n$, then given any tuple $t = (x_1, \ldots, x_n)$, such that the full tuple $(x_1, \ldots, x_n, y_1, \ldots, y_m)$ is known to satisfy $\mathcal{C}$, the missing value of the variable y_i can be correctly reconstructed. A procedure for computing uniquely determined values can be found in [LY85] and in more detail in [Tra87]. It is similar to the way surrogate values are derived for computationally nonessential variables. If the variable y_i is not uniquely determined, then we cannot guarantee that its value is reconstructible for *every* tuple. However, it may still be reconstructible for *some* tuples.

Example 4.2 Let $\mathcal{C} \equiv (I = H)(H > 7)(K = 5)$. It is easy to prove that I and K are uniquely determined by H and the condition $\mathcal{C}$. Suppose that we are given a tuple that satisfies $\mathcal{C}$ but only the value of H is known. Assume that $H = 10$. Then we can immediately determine that the values of I and K must be 10 and 5, respectively.

$\square$

Definition 4.4 Let $E = (\mathbf{A}, \mathbf{R}, \mathcal{C})$ be a derived relation and let $\mathbf{A}_E$ be the set of all attributes in $\alpha(\mathbf{R})$ that are uniquely determined by the attributes in $\mathbf{A}$ and the condition $\mathcal{C}$. Then $\mathbf{A}^+ = \mathbf{A} \cup \mathbf{A}_E$ is called the *extended attribute set* of E.

$\square$

Larson and Yang [LY85] proved that $\mathbf{A}^+$ is the maximal set of attributes for which values can be reconstructed for *every* tuple of E. $\mathbf{A}^+$ can easily be computed by testing, one by one, which of the attributes in $\alpha(\mathcal{C}) - \mathbf{A}$ are uniquely determined by $\mathcal{C}$ and the attributes in $\mathbf{A}$. An attribute not mentioned in $\mathcal{C}$ cannot be uniquely determined and, thus, cannot be in $\mathbf{A}_E$.

4.2   Insertions

It should be stressed that if the update $\mathcal{U}$ on a derived relation defined by E is autonomously computable, then the update can be performed for every derived relation instance $v(E, d)$. This characterization is important primarily because of the potential cost savings realized by updating the derived relation using only the information in its current instance.

Consider an operation INSERT (R_u, T) where T is a set of tuples to be inserted into r_u. Let a derived relation be defined by $E = (\mathbf{A}, \mathbf{R}, \mathcal{C}), R_u \in \mathbf{R}$. The effect of the INSERT operation[2] on the derived relation is autonomously computable if

---

[2]Recall that if $R_u \notin \mathbf{R}$, then the update cannot have any effect on the derived relation.

A. for each tuple $t \in T$ we can correctly decide whether t will (regardless of the database instance) satisfy the selection condition $\mathcal{C}$ and hence should be inserted into the derived relation, and

B. the values for all attributes visible in the derived relation can be obtained from t only.

Theorem 4.1 *Consider a derived relation defined by* $E = (\mathbf{A}, \mathbf{R}, \mathcal{C})$, $\mathbf{R} = \{R_1, \ldots, R_m\}$, *and the update* INSERT$(R_u, \{t\})$ *where* E *and the update operation satisfy Property 1. The effect of the insert operation on the derived relation* E *is autonomously computable if and only if* $\mathbf{R} = \{R_u\}$.

Proof: (Sufficiency) If $\mathbf{R} = \{R_u\}$, then all attributes required to compute the selection condition $\mathcal{C}$ as well as all the visible attributes $\mathbf{A}$ are contained in the new tuple t. Hence, the function $F_{\mathcal{U},E}$ required by Definition 4.1 trivially exists and we conclude that the effect of the insertion is autonomously computable.

(Necessity) If $\mathbf{R}$ includes other base relation schemes in addition to R_u, then the insertion of tuple t into r_u may affect the derived relation defined by E. Whether it does depends on the existence of tuples in relations whose schemes are in $\mathbf{R} - \{R_u\}$. We can easily construct database instances where it is necessary to access the database to verify the existence of such tuples, even for the case when $\alpha(\mathcal{C}) \subseteq \alpha(R_u)$ and $\mathbf{A} \subseteq \alpha(R_u)$. A database instance $d_1 = \{r_1, r_2, \ldots, r_m\}$ is constructed as follows. Each relation r_i, $1 \leq i \leq m$, $i \notin \{u, j\}$, contains a single tuple t_i, and relations r_u and r_j are empty. Similarly, construct another instance d_2 in the same manner with the one exception that r_j now contains a single tuple t_j. Clearly $v(E, d_1) = v(E, d_2) = \phi$. Now suppose that tuple t is inserted into r_u and furthermore, assume that $\mathcal{C}[t] = true$. The existence of such a tuple is guaranteed by the fact that the INSERT is not irrelevant. Even though t satisfies the selection condition of the derived relation and contains all visible attributes, it will not create an insertion into the derived relation in instance d_1 (because relation r_j is empty) whereas it will create an insertion in d_2. Therefore, by Lemma 4.1, the update is not autonomously computable. $\qquad\square$

4.3 Deletions

To handle deletions autonomously, we must be able to determine, for every tuple in the derived relation, whether it satisfies the delete condition. This is covered by the following theorem.

Theorem 4.2 *The effect of the operation* DELETE$(R_u, \mathcal{C}_D)$ *on the derived relation* $E = (\mathbf{A}, \mathbf{R}, \mathcal{C})$, *where* E *and the update operation satisfy Property 1, is autonomously computable if and only if the attributes in*

$$[\alpha(\mathcal{C}_D) \cup \alpha(\mathcal{C})] - \mathbf{A}^+$$

are computationally nonessential in $\mathcal{C}_D$ *with respect to* $\mathcal{C}$.

Proof: (Sufficiency) If the attributes in $[\alpha(\mathcal{C}_D) \cup \alpha(\mathcal{C})] - \mathbf{A}^+$ are computationally nonessential in $\mathcal{C}_D$ with respect to $\mathcal{C}$, then we can correctly evaluate the condition $\mathcal{C}_D$ on every tuple in the derived relation $v(E, d)$ by assigning surrogate values to the attributes in $\alpha(\mathcal{C}_D) - \mathbf{A}^+$. Hence, the function $F_{\mathcal{U},E}$ required by Definition 4.1 exists.

(Necessity) Assume that $[\alpha(\mathcal{C}_D) \cup \alpha(\mathcal{C})] - \mathbf{A}^+$ contains an attribute x, and assume that x is computationally essential in $\mathcal{C}_D$ with respect to $\mathcal{C}$. We can construct two tuples t_1 and t_2 over $\alpha(\mathbf{R})$ such that they both satisfy $\mathcal{C}$, t_1 satisfies $\mathcal{C}_D$ but t_2 does not, and t_1 and t_2 agree on all attributes except attribute x. The existence of two such tuples follows from the fact that the update is not irrelevant and from the definition of computationally nonessential attributes. By projection, we can create two instances of D, d_1 and d_2, from t_1 and t_2 respectively. In both instances, each relation contains a single tuple. Both instances will give the same instance of the derived relation, consisting of a single tuple $t_1[\mathbf{A}] = t_2[\mathbf{A}]$. In one instance, the tuple should be deleted from the derived relation, in the other one it should not, resulting in two different (updated) instances. Hence, by Lemma 4.1, the DELETE is not autonomously computable. $\square$

Example 4.3 Consider two relation schemes $R_1(H, I)$ and $R_2(J, K)$. Let the derived relation and the delete operation be defined as:

$$E = (\{J, K\}, \{R_1, R_2\}, (I = J)(H < 20))$$
$$\text{DELETE}(R_1, (I = 20)(H < 30))$$

For every tuple t in E we have $\mathbf{A}^+ = \{I, J, K\}$ hence the attributes in $(\alpha(\mathcal{C}_D) \cup \alpha(\mathcal{C})) - \mathbf{A}^+ = \{H, I, J\} - \{I, J, K\} = \{H\}$. In order for the effect of the deletion to be autonomously computable H must be computationally nonessential in $\mathcal{C}_D$ with respect to $\mathcal{C}$. That is, the following condition must hold:

$$\forall \quad H, I, J, K, H' \quad [(I = J)(H < 20) \wedge (I = J)(H' < 20)$$
$$\Rightarrow \quad ((I = 20)(H < 30) \Leftrightarrow (I = 20)(H' < 30))].$$

The conditions $(H < 30)$ and $(H' < 30)$ will both be *true* whenever $(H < 20)$ and $(H' < 20)$ are *true*. For any choice of values that make the antecedent *true*, we must have $J = I$. Any value taken on by the variable I will make the condition $I = 20$ either *true* or *false*, and hence the consequent will always be satisfied. Therefore, the variable H is computationally nonessential in $\mathcal{C}_D$ with respect to $\mathcal{C}$. This guarantees that for any tuple in the derived relation we can always correctly evaluate the delete condition by assigning surrogate values to the variable H. Note that, since $I \in \alpha(\mathcal{C}_D)$ we must reconstruct each tuple's value for I. This is possible because I is uniquely determined by $\mathcal{C}$ and $\mathbf{A}$.

To further clarify these concepts, consider the following instance of the derived relation E.

$$v(E, d): \quad \begin{array}{c|c} J & K \\ \hline 10 & 15 \\ 20 & 25 \end{array}$$

We now have to determine on a tuple by tuple basis which tuples in the derived relation should be deleted. Consider tuple $t_1 = \langle 10, 15 \rangle$ and the condition $\mathcal{C} \equiv (I = J)(H < 20)$. We substitute for the variables J and K in $\mathcal{C}$ the values 10 and 15, respectively, to obtain $\mathcal{C}[t_1] \equiv (I = 10)(H < 20)$. Any values for H and I that make $\mathcal{C}[t_1] = true$, are valid (surrogate) values. For I the only value that can be assigned is 10 and for H we can assign, for example, the value 19. We can then evaluate $\mathcal{C}_D$ using these values, and find that $(10 = 20)(19 < 30) = false$. Therefore, tuple t_1 should not be deleted from $v(E, d)$. Similarly, for $t_2 = \langle 20, 25 \rangle$ we obtain $\mathcal{C}[t_2] \equiv (I = 20)(H < 20)$. Values for H and I that make $\mathcal{C}[t_2] = true$ are $I = 20$ and $H = 19$. We then evaluate $\mathcal{C}_D$ using these values and find that $(20 = 20)(19 < 30) = true$. Therefore, tuple t_2 should be deleted from $v(E, d)$. $\square$

4.4 Modifications

Deciding whether modifications can be performed autonomously is more complicated than deciding whether insertions or deletions can. In general, a modify operation may generate insertions into, deletions from, and modifications of existing tuples in the derived relation. In the next three sections we will state necessary and sufficient conditions for determining when a MODIFY update is autonomously computable. In Section 4.4 we characterize what may happen to tuples which are not in the current instance of a given derived relation; in Section 1 to tuples which are in the current instance. These two sections present conditions which are necessary for a MODIFY to be autonomously computable; in Section 3 we show that those same conditions are, collectively, also sufficient. Intuitively, the procedure required to decide whether a MODIFY is autonomously computable consists of the following steps:

A. Prove that every tuple selected for modification which does not satisfy $\mathcal{C}$ before modification, will not satisfy $\mathcal{C}$ after modification. This means that no new tuples will be inserted into the derived relation.

B. Prove that we can correctly select which tuples in the derived relation are to be modified. Call this the *modify set* (to be formally defined in Definition 4.6).

C. Prove that we can correctly select which tuples in the modify set will not satisfy $\mathcal{C}$ after modification and hence can be deleted from the derived relation.

D. Prove that, for every tuple in the modify set which will not be deleted, we can (autonomously) compute the new values for all attributes in $\mathbf{A}$.

The subsequent discussion is easier to follow if the reader keeps these steps in mind.

Tuples Outside the Derived Relation

In this section we investigate the possible outcomes for a tuple which is not in the current instance of a given derived relation. Let the derived relation of interest be defined by $E = (\mathbf{A}, \mathbf{R}, \mathcal{C})$ and the update by $\mathcal{U} = \text{MODIFY}(R_u, \mathcal{C}_M, \mathbf{F}_M)$. We consider the possible outcomes of evaluating the conditions $\mathcal{C}_M \wedge \mathcal{C}_B(\mathbf{F}_M)$ and $\mathcal{C}(\mathbf{F}_M)$ for a tuple t, defined over set $\alpha(\mathbf{R})$. The outcomes are given in Table 1; for completeness we include $\mathcal{C}[t]$ even though it is never satisfied. Recall the assumption that a tuple must satisfy both $\mathcal{C}_M$ and $\mathcal{C}_B(\mathbf{F}_M)$ in order to be modified. Let us consider each line of the table. If $\mathcal{C}_M[t] \wedge \mathcal{C}_B(\mathbf{F}_M)[t]$ is *false*

$\mathcal{C}[t]$	$\mathcal{C}_M[t] \wedge \mathcal{C}_B(\mathbf{F}_M)[t]$	$\mathcal{C}(\mathbf{F}_M)[t]$	Comments
false	*false*	*false*	No change
false	*false*	*true*	No change
false	*true*	*false*	No change
false	*true*	*true*	Insert t

Table 1 Possible results for tuples not in $v(E, d)$.

then, t is not modified and obviously cannot cause any change in the instance of E. Note that, in this case, the value of $\mathcal{C}(\mathbf{F}_M)$ is immaterial. This explains the first and second lines. If $\mathcal{C}_M[t] \wedge \mathcal{C}_B(\mathbf{F}_M)[t]$ is *true* then, since $\mathcal{C}[t]$ is *false*, whether t requires a change in the instance of E depends on whether $\mathcal{C}(\mathbf{F}_M)[t]$ is satisfied. That is, on whether t satisfies $\mathcal{C}$ after it is modified. Intuitively, if a new tuple should enter $v(E, d)$ we may not be able to determine the appropriate values for that tuple from $v(E, d)$. That is, we may need to obtain values from elsewhere in the database. Hence, to guarantee that $\mathcal{U}$ is autonomously computable we must guarantee that no tuples will be inserted into $v(E, d)$. This is the intention of the following property and subsequent theorem.

Property 2 Given the update operation MODIFY($R_u, \mathcal{C}_M, \mathbf{F}_M$) and the derived relation defined by $E = (\mathbf{A}, \mathbf{R}, \mathcal{C})$, $R_u \in \mathbf{R}$, the following implication is valid,

$$\forall \, (\neg\mathcal{C} \wedge \mathcal{C}_M \wedge \mathcal{C}_B(\mathbf{F}_M) \Rightarrow \neg\mathcal{C}(\mathbf{F}_M)).$$

Example 4.4 Suppose a database consists of the relation scheme $R(H, I)$ where H and I each have the domain $[0, 50]$. Let the derived relation and modify operation be defined as:

$$E = (\{H, I\}, \{R\}, (H = 20)(I < 10))$$
$$\text{MODIFY}(R, (I < 30), \{(H := H), (I := I + 1)\}).$$

The condition stated in Property 2 is then

$$\forall \, H, I$$
$$(\neg((H = 20)(I < 10))) \wedge (I < 30)$$
$$\wedge (H \geq 0)(H \leq 50)(I + 1 \geq 0)(I + 1 \leq 50)$$
$$\Rightarrow \neg((H = 20)(I + 1 < 10))$$

which can be written as
$$\forall \, H, I$$
$$((H \neq 20) \vee (I \geq 10)) \wedge (I < 30) \wedge (H \geq 0)(H \leq 50)(I \geq -1)(I \leq 49)$$
$$\Rightarrow ((H \neq 20) \vee (I \geq 9)).$$

The first two atomic conditions in the antecedent are sufficient to guarantee that the consequent will evaluate to *true*. Hence, the property is satisfied for this update and derived relation and we are guaranteed that a tuple outside E will not enter E due to this update. To see why, consider the condition $(H = 20)(I < 10)$ used to select tuples for the derived relation. A tuple which does not satisfy $H = 20$ before $\mathcal{U}$ is applied will still not satisfy it after, since the value of H is not modified by $\mathcal{U}$. Similarly, since $\mathcal{U}$ *increases* the value of I, a tuple which does not satisfy $I < 10$ originally will not satisfy it after modification. □

Theorem 4.3 *If the operation* MODIFY($R_u, \mathcal{C}_M, \mathbf{F}_M$) *is autonomously computable with respect to the derived relation defined by* $E = (\mathbf{A}, \mathbf{R}, \mathcal{C})$, *where* E *and the update operation satisfy Property 1, then Property 2 must be satisfied.*

Proof: Assume that Property 2 is not valid. Therefore, there exists a tuple s over $\alpha(\mathbf{R})$ such that $\neg\mathcal{C}[s] \wedge \mathcal{C}_M[s] \wedge \mathcal{C}_B(\mathbf{F}_M)[s] \wedge \mathcal{C}(\mathbf{F}_M)[s]$ is *true*. By projection we can create a database instance, d_1, from tuple s. Thus, initially each relation instance contains a single tuple and since $\neg\mathcal{C}[s]$ is *true* we know that $v(E, d_1)$ is empty. Applying the modify operation to d_1 then gives an instance d_1' where the tuple in relation r_u has been modified, since $\mathcal{C}_M[s] \wedge \mathcal{C}_B(\mathbf{F}_M)[s]$ is *true*. However, $v(E, d_1')$ will contain one tuple since $\mathcal{C}(\mathbf{F}_M)[s]$ is *true*. We construct a second database instance d_2 from d_1 where all relation instances are the same, except instance r_u which is empty. Now, $v(E, d_2)$ is empty and $v(E, d_2')$ is empty. Hence, by Lemma 4.1 the MODIFY cannot be autonomously computable. □

Tuples Inside the Derived Relation

In this section we investigate the possible outcomes, under a MODIFY operation, for a tuple which is in the current instance of a given derived relation. We again consider the possible outcomes of evaluating the

$\mathcal{C}[t]$	$\mathcal{C}_M[t] \wedge \mathcal{C}_B(\mathbf{F}_M)[t]$	$\mathcal{C}(\mathbf{F}_M)[t]$	Comments
true	*false*	*false*	No change
true	*false*	*true*	No change
true	*true*	*false*	Delete t
true	*true*	*true*	Modify t

Table 2 Possible results for tuples in $v(E,d)$.

conditions $\mathcal{C}_M \wedge \mathcal{C}_B(\mathbf{F}_M)$ and $\mathcal{C}(\mathbf{F}_M)$ for tuple t, defined over $\alpha(\mathbf{R})$; for completeness we include $\mathcal{C}[t]$ in Table 2. Again we consider each line of the table. If $\mathcal{C}_M[t] \wedge \mathcal{C}_B(\mathbf{F}_M)[t]$ is *false* then t is not modified and obviously cannot cause any change in the instance of E. This situation is depicted by the first two lines of the table. Note that, in this case, the value of $\mathcal{C}(\mathbf{F}_M)$ is immaterial. Since t is already visible in $v(E,d)$ we need to be able to identify it as a tuple which will be unaffected by the update. Hence, it appears that we only need to distinguish, within $v(E,d)$, those tuples which are characterized by line one or two, and those characterized by line three or four. That is, it seems we need to evaluate $\mathcal{C}_M \wedge \mathcal{C}_B(\mathbf{F}_M)$ for each tuple in $v(E,d)$. This requires that all the attributes in $(\alpha(\mathcal{C}) \cup \alpha(\mathcal{C}_M) \cup \alpha(\mathcal{C}_B(\mathbf{F}_M))) - \mathbf{A}^+$ be computationally nonessential in $\mathcal{C}_M \wedge \mathcal{C}_B(\mathbf{F}_M)$ with respect to $\mathcal{C}$. However, as the following example illustrates, this is a slightly stronger condition than is necessary.

Example 4.5 Suppose a database consists of the relation scheme $R(H,I,J)$ where H, I, and J each have the domain $[0,50]$. Let the derived relation and modify operation be defined as:

$$E = (\{H\}, \{R\}, ((H = I)(H < 30)(J < 20)) \vee (H > 40))$$
$$\text{MODIFY}(R, (I < 40), \{(H := H), (I := I), (J := J + 5)\}).$$

Therefore, the set $(\alpha(\mathcal{C}) \cup \alpha(\mathcal{C}_M) \cup \alpha(\mathcal{C}_B(\mathbf{F}_M))) - \mathbf{A}^+$ is $\{I, J\}$. The test to determine if $\{I, J\}$ is computationally nonessential in $\mathcal{C}_M \wedge \mathcal{C}_B(\mathbf{F}_M)$ with respect to $\mathcal{C}$ is:

$$\forall\, H, I, J, I', J'$$
$$[(((H = I)(H < 30)(J < 20)) \vee (H > 40))$$
$$\wedge(((H = I')(H < 30)(J' < 20)) \vee (H > 40))]$$
$$\Rightarrow [((I < 40) \wedge (H \geq 0)(H \leq 50)(I \geq 0)(I \leq 50)(J + 5 \geq 0)(J + 5 \leq 50))$$
$$\Leftrightarrow ((I' < 40) \wedge (H \geq 0)(H \leq 50)(I' \geq 0)(I' \leq 50)$$
$$(J' + 5 \geq 0)(J' + 5 \leq 50))].$$

The assignment $H = 45, I = 39, I' = 41$, and $J = J' = 0$ satisfies the antecedent but not the consequent of this implication. Therefore, the implications in not valid and we conclude that $\{I, J\}$ is computationally essential in $\mathcal{C}_M \wedge \mathcal{C}_B(\mathbf{F}_M)$ with respect to $\mathcal{C}$.

Consider a particular tuple s over $\alpha(R)$ where $s[H] = t$ for some t in E. Since $H \in \mathbf{A}$ then we know the value of $s[H]$. If $s[H] < 30$ then we know that $s[I] = s[H]$ and $s[J] < 20$ and therefore we can evaluate $\mathcal{C}_M \wedge \mathcal{C}_B(\mathbf{F}_M)$ for tuple s and hence for t. The reason I is computationally essential in $\mathcal{C}_M$ is because for $s[H] > 40$ we do not know the value of $s[I]$ and hence cannot evaluate $\mathcal{C}_M$. However, consider what would happen even if s were modified, say to s'. The value of J would change, that is $s[J] \neq s'[J]$, but this value is neither visible in E nor used in the term $(H > 40)$. As this term would still be satisfied then s' would remain in the new instance of E and $s[H] = s'[H] = t$. In other words, for tuples which satisfy $(H > 40)$, it does not matter whether or not they are modified; in either case they will remain in the instance with no visible changes. Hence, the fact that we cannot evaluate $\mathcal{C}_M$ for these tuples does not impair our ability to determine the new instance from the current one. $\square$

In terms of Table 2 the tuples which create this situation are some of those characterized by the fourth line. Simply because t is chosen for modification does not mean it will be *visibly* changed. In other words, if we can prove that even if t is modified it will remain in $v(E, d')$ with all the same attribute values as it had in $v(E, d)$ then it does not matter whether $\mathcal{C}_M[t] \wedge \mathcal{C}_B(\mathbf{F}_M)[t]$ is satisfied. Hence, we only need to evaluate $\mathcal{C}_M \wedge \mathcal{C}_B(\mathbf{F}_M)$ for those tuples which may be visibly modified. Property 3 and the theorem which follows it are intended to provide a procedure which will enable us to do this.

Property 3 Given the update operation MODIFY($R_u, \mathcal{C}_M, \mathbf{F}_M$) and the derived relation defined by $E = (\mathbf{A}, \mathbf{R}, \mathcal{C})$, $R_u \in \mathbf{R}$, the following condition holds

$$\forall\, t_1, t_2$$
$$[((\mathcal{C}[t_1] \wedge \mathcal{C}_M[t_1] \wedge \mathcal{C}_B(\mathbf{F}_M)[t_1])$$
$$\Rightarrow (\mathcal{C}(\mathbf{F}_M)[t_1] \wedge (\bigwedge_{A_i \in (\alpha(R_u) \cap \mathbf{A})} (A_i = \rho(f_{A_i}))[t_1])))$$
$$\vee ((\mathcal{C}[t_1] \wedge \mathcal{C}[t_2]) \Rightarrow ((\mathcal{C}_M[t_1] \wedge \mathcal{C}_B(\mathbf{F}_M)[t_1]) \Leftrightarrow (\mathcal{C}_M[t_2] \wedge \mathcal{C}_B(\mathbf{F}_M)[t_2])))].$$

for t_1, t_2 over $\alpha(\mathbf{R})$ and $t_1[\mathbf{A}^+] = t_2[\mathbf{A}^+]$.

Theorem 4.4 *If the operation* MODIFY($R_u, \mathcal{C}_M, \mathbf{F}_M$) *is autonomously computable with respect to the derived relation defined by $E = (\mathbf{A}, \mathbf{R}, \mathcal{C})$, where E and the update operation satisfy Property 1, then Property 3 must be satisfied.*

Proof: Assume that neither term of the condition in Property 3 is satisfied. This means that for some tuple s_1 we cannot guarantee that if s_1 is in E and is modified then it will have no visible changes nor can we guarantee that $s_1[\mathbf{A}^+]$ will contain all the attribute values required to evaluate $\mathcal{C}_M \wedge \mathcal{C}_B(\mathbf{F}_M)$. Hence, there exist two tuples s_1 and s_2 over the attributes in $\alpha(\mathbf{R})$ such that they both satisfy $\mathcal{C}$, s_1 satisfies $\mathcal{C}_M \wedge \mathcal{C}_B(\mathbf{F}_M)$ but s_2 does not, s_1 satisfies $\neg \mathcal{C}(\mathbf{F}_M)$ or $\neg[\bigwedge_{A_i \in (\alpha(R_u) \cap \mathbf{A})}(A_i = \rho(f_{A_i}))]$, and s_1 and s_2 agree on all attributes in $\mathbf{A}^+$. By projection we can create two database instances d_1 and d_2, from s_1 and s_2 respectively, where each relation contains a single tuple. Both instances will give the same instance of the derived relation, consisting of the single tuple $s_1[\mathbf{A}] = s_2[\mathbf{A}]$. In d_1 the tuple in the derived relation will be modified. Hence, the tuple $s_1[\mathbf{A}]$ will either be deleted or a change will be made to some visible attribute; depending on whether s_1 satisfies $\neg \mathcal{C}(\mathbf{F}_M)$ or $\neg[\bigwedge_{A_i \in (\alpha(R_u) \cap \mathbf{A})}(A_i = \rho(f_{A_i}))]$. In either case $v(E, d_1) \neq v(E, d'_1)$. On the other hand, in the instance obtained from s_2 the tuple in the derived relation will not be modified; so $v(E, d_2) = v(E, d'_2)$. Therefore, by Lemma 4.1, $\mathcal{U}$ is not autonomously computable. $\square$

Returning to Table 2, the previous property and theorem give us a necessary condition for determining which tuples in $v(E, d)$ are placed in the modify set and which are not. That is, for distinguishing tuples which will not be visibly changed, and hence remain in $v(E, d')$, from those that should be placed in the modify set. The next property and theorem give a necessary condition for distinguishing between those tuples in the modify set which satisfy line three and those which satisfy line four. That is, we need to determine which tuples will not still satisfy the selection condition of the derived relation after modification and should be deleted.

Property 4 Given the update operation MODIFY$(R_u, \mathcal{C}_M, \mathbf{F}_M)$ and the derived relation defined by $E = (\mathbf{A}, \mathbf{R}, \mathcal{C})$, $R_u \in \mathbf{R}$, the attributes in the set[3] $[\alpha(\mathcal{C}) \cup \alpha(\mathcal{C}_M) \cup \alpha(\mathcal{C}_B(\mathbf{F}_M))] - \mathbf{A}^+$ are computationally nonessential in $\mathcal{C}(\mathbf{F}_M)$ with respect to the condition $\mathcal{C} \wedge \mathcal{C}_M \wedge \mathcal{C}_B(\mathbf{F}_M) \wedge (\neg(\mathcal{C}(\mathbf{F}_M) \wedge (\bigwedge_{A_i \in (\alpha(R_u) \cap \mathbf{A})}(A_i = \rho(f_{A_i}))))).$

Before we state the corresponding theorem we give a lemma that will simplify the proof of the theorem.

Lemma 4.2 Consider an update operation MODIFY$(R_u, \mathcal{C}_M, \mathbf{F}_M)$ and a derived relation defined by $E = (\mathbf{A}, \mathbf{R}, \mathcal{C})$ where $R_u \in \mathbf{R}$. Given two tuples, t_1 and t_2, over $\alpha(\mathcal{C}) \cup \alpha(\mathcal{C}_M) \cup \alpha(\mathcal{C}_B(\mathbf{F}_M))$ then there are only four assignments of truth values to the expressions in

$$
\begin{aligned}
(\quad \neg \quad & (\mathcal{C}(\mathbf{F}_M)[t_1] \wedge (\bigwedge_{A_i \in (\alpha(R_u) \cap \mathbf{A})} (A_i = \rho(f_{A_i}))[t_1]))) \\
\wedge \quad & (\neg(\mathcal{C}(\mathbf{F}_M)[t_2] \wedge (\bigwedge_{A_i \in (\alpha(R_u) \cap \mathbf{A})} (A_i = \rho(f_{A_i}))[t_2]))) \\
\wedge \quad & (\neg(\mathcal{C}(\mathbf{F}_M)[t_1] \Leftrightarrow \mathcal{C}(\mathbf{F}_M)[t_2]))
\end{aligned}
\tag{4.2}
$$

which will make this statement evaluate to *true*.

Proof: There are four component expressions in Expression 4.2, each representing a column of Table 3. Since each may take a truth value from the set {*true*, *false*} this yields sixteen possible assignments. Since $(\neg(\mathcal{C}(\mathbf{F}_M)[t_1] \Leftrightarrow \mathcal{C}(\mathbf{F}_M)[t_2]))$ must be *true* then the values given to $\mathcal{C}(\mathbf{F}_M)[t_1]$ and $\mathcal{C}(\mathbf{F}_M)[t_2]$ must be different. This eliminates eight of the sixteen assignments. Also, both factors of the conjunction in $(\neg(\mathcal{C}(\mathbf{F}_M)[t_1] \wedge (\bigwedge_{A_i \in (\alpha(R_u) \cap \mathbf{A})}(A_i = \rho(f_{A_i}))[t_1])))$ cannot be *true* if this condition is to be satisfied; this eliminates two more of the remaining eight assignments. Similarly, the condition $(\neg(\mathcal{C}(\mathbf{F}_M)[t_2] \wedge (\bigwedge_{A_i \in (\alpha(R_u) \cap \mathbf{A})}(A_i = \rho(f_{A_i}))[t_2])))$ eliminates a further two assignments. Hence, the only assignments that will satisfy Expression 4.2 are the four given in Table 3. □

$\mathcal{C}(\mathbf{F}_M)[t_1]$	$(\bigwedge_{A_i \in (\alpha(R_u) \cap \mathbf{A})}$ $(A_i = \rho(f_{A_i})))[t_1]$	$\mathcal{C}(\mathbf{F}_M)[t_2]$	$(\bigwedge_{A_i \in (\alpha(R_u) \cap \mathbf{A})}$ $(A_i = \rho(f_{A_i})))[t_2]$
true	*false*	*false*	*false*
true	*false*	*false*	*true*
false	*false*	*true*	*false*
false	*true*	*true*	*false*

Table 3 Assignments which satisfy Expression 4.2

Theorem 4.5 *If the operation* MODIFY$(R_u, \mathcal{C}_M, \mathbf{F}_M)$ *is autonomously computable with respect to the derived relation defined by* $E = (\mathbf{A}, \mathbf{R}, \mathcal{C})$, *where* E *and the update operation satisfy Properties 1 and 3, then Property 4 must be satisfied.*

---

[3]We do not need to include the attributes in $\alpha(\mathcal{C}(\mathbf{F}_M))$ in the set as they are all contained in $\alpha(\mathcal{C}) \cup \alpha(\mathcal{C}_B(\mathbf{F}_M))$.

Proof: Assume that the update is autonomously computable, that Property 3 is satisfied but that Property 4 is not. This means that $[\alpha(\mathcal{C}) \cup \alpha(\mathcal{C}_M) \cup \alpha(\mathcal{C}_B(\mathbf{F}_M))] - \mathbf{A}^+$ contains an attribute x that is computationally essential in $\mathcal{C}(\mathbf{F}_M)$ with respect to the condition $\mathcal{C} \wedge \mathcal{C}_M \wedge \mathcal{C}_B(\mathbf{F}_M) \wedge [\neg(\mathcal{C}(\mathbf{F}_M) \wedge (\bigwedge_{A_i \in (\alpha(R_u) \cap \mathbf{A})}(A_i = \rho(f_{A_i}))))]$. We construct two tuples t_1 and t_2 over the attributes in $\mathbf{A}^+ \cup \alpha(\mathcal{C}) \cup \alpha(\mathcal{C}_M) \cup \alpha(\mathcal{C}_B(\mathbf{F}_M))$. This is done in such a way that $t_1[x] \neq t_2[x]$ but they agree on the values of all other attributes. We require both t_1 and t_2 to satisfy the conditions $\mathcal{C}, \mathcal{C}_M, \mathcal{C}_B(\mathbf{F}_M)$, and $[\neg(\mathcal{C}(\mathbf{F}_M) \wedge (\bigwedge_{A_i \in (\alpha(R_u) \cap \mathbf{A})}(A_i = \rho(f_{A_i}))))]$. Since we wish x to be computationally essential we would also like $(\neg(\mathcal{C}(\mathbf{F}_M)[t_1] \Leftrightarrow \mathcal{C}(\mathbf{F}_M)[t_2]))$ to be satisfied. Therefore, by Lemma 4.2 there are four possible assignments to consider. Due to the symmetry of the truth values in these four assignments (see Table 3) we can, without loss of generality, require that t_1 satisfy $\mathcal{C}(\mathbf{F}_M)$, and t_2 not satisfy $\mathcal{C}(\mathbf{F}_M)$. Thus $(\bigwedge_{A_i \in (\alpha(R_u) \cap \mathbf{A})}(A_i = \rho(f_{A_i})))[t_2]$ may be either *true* or *false*; it will not affect the rest of the proof. The fact that x is computationally essential in $\mathcal{C}(\mathbf{F}_M)$ with respect to the condition $\mathcal{C} \wedge \mathcal{C}_M \wedge \mathcal{C}_B(\mathbf{F}_M) \wedge (\neg(\mathcal{C}(\mathbf{F}_M) \wedge (\bigwedge_{A_i \in (\alpha(R_u) \cap \mathbf{A})}(A_i = \rho(f_{A_i})))))$ guarantees that such values exist. We can now extend t_1 and t_2 to obtain two different database instances where each relation contains only one tuple. In both cases the derived relation contains the same tuple and the tuple is selected for modification. In one case (for the instance obtained from t_2) the single tuple in the derived relation will be deleted after the modification, while in the other case it will not. Hence, by Lemma 4.1, the update $\mathcal{U}$ is not autonomously computable. □

The only tuples still of interest are those that satisfy the conditions characterized by line four of Table 2 and are in the modify set. These tuples are visibly modified and remain in the updated instance so we need to be able to determine the updated values of all visible attributes. The next property and theorem establish the necessary conditions under which the modified values for the attributes in $\mathbf{A}$ can be correctly computed. But, before we state them we need a new definition which extends the concept of uniquely determined to apply to functions.

Definition 4.5 Consider a set of variables $\{x_1, \ldots, x_j, x_{j+1}, \ldots, x_k\}$. Let $\mathcal{C}$ be a Boolean expression over some of the variables in this set, that is, $\alpha(\mathcal{C}) \subseteq \{x_1, \ldots, x_k\}$. As well, let f represent a function over variables in the set $\{x_1, \ldots, x_k\}$. The value of the function f is said to be *uniquely determined* by condition $\mathcal{C}$ and the set of variables $\{x_1, \ldots, x_j\}$ if

$$\forall x_1, \ldots, x_j, x_{j+1}, \ldots, x_k, x'_{j+1}, \ldots, x'_k$$
$$[\mathcal{C}(x_1, \ldots, x_j, x_{j+1}, \ldots, x_k) \wedge \mathcal{C}(x_1, \ldots, x_j, x'_{j+1}, \ldots, x'_k)$$
$$\Rightarrow (f(x_1, \ldots, x_j, x_{j+1}, \ldots, x_k) = f(x_1, \ldots, x_j, x'_{j+1}, \ldots, x'_k))].$$

□

Example 4.6 Let $\mathcal{C} \equiv (H = 5)(I = 10 - J)$ and $f(I, J) = (I + J)$. For any values of I and J that satisfy $\mathcal{C}$ we are guaranteed that the value of $I + J$, and hence f, is 10. In other words the condition of Definition 4.5 becomes

$$\forall \quad H, I, J, I', J'$$
$$[(H = 5)(I = 10 - J) \wedge (H = 5)(I' = 10 - J')$$
$$\Rightarrow ((I + J) = (I' + J'))].$$

As this is a valid implication we conclude that f is uniquely determined by $\mathcal{C}$. Note, that we can state this in spite of the fact that we do not know the value of either I or J. □

Property 5 Given the update operation MODIFY($R_u, \mathcal{C}_M, \mathbf{F}_M$) and the derived relation defined by $E = (\mathbf{A}, \mathbf{R}, \mathcal{C})$, $R_u \in \mathbf{R}$, the value of the function $\rho(f_{A_i})$ is uniquely determined by the condition $\mathcal{C} \wedge \mathcal{C}_M \wedge \mathcal{C}_B(\mathbf{F}_M) \wedge \mathcal{C}(\mathbf{F}_M) \wedge (\neg(\bigwedge_{A_i \in (\alpha(R_u) \cap \mathbf{A})} (A_i = \rho(f_{A_i}))))$ and the attributes in $\mathbf{A}^+$, for each $A_i \in (\alpha(R_u) \cap \mathbf{A})$.

Theorem 4.6 *If the operation* MODIFY($R_u, \mathcal{C}_M, \mathbf{F}_M$) *is autonomously computable with respect to the derived relation defined by $E = (\mathbf{A}, \mathbf{R}, \mathcal{C})$, where E and the update operation satisfy Properties 1, 3, and 4, then Property 5 must be satisfied.*

Proof: Assume that $\mathcal{U}$ is autonomously computable, that $\mathbf{A} \cap \alpha(R_u)$ contains a single attribute A_j with a non-trivial f_{A_j}, and that $\rho(f_{A_j})$ is not uniquely determined by the condition $\mathcal{C} \wedge \mathcal{C}_M \wedge \mathcal{C}_B(\mathbf{F}_M) \wedge \mathcal{C}(\mathbf{F}_M) \wedge (\neg(\bigwedge_{A_i \in (\alpha(R_u) \cap \mathbf{A})} (A_i = \rho(f_{A_i}))))$ and the attributes in $\mathbf{A}^+$. We can then construct two tuples t_1 and t_2 over the attributes in $\alpha(R_u) \cup \alpha(\mathcal{C})$ such that t_1 and t_2 both satisfy $\mathcal{C}, \mathcal{C}_M, \mathcal{C}_B(\mathbf{F}_M), \mathcal{C}(\mathbf{F}_M)$, and $(\neg(\bigwedge_{A_i \in (\alpha(R_u) \cap \mathbf{A})} (A_i = \rho(f_{A_i}))))$. We also require that t_1 and t_2 agree on the values of all attributes in $\mathbf{A}$; but have some values that make $(\rho(f_{A_j}))[t_1] \neq (\rho(f_{A_j}))[t_2]$. That such a set of values exists is guaranteed by the fact that Property 5 is not satisfied. To find such values one can use the set of values returned by an appropriate satisfiability algorithm used to test the validity of the implication in Definition 4.5. Since $\rho(f_{A_j})$ is not uniquely determined then the implication is *false* when tested for this function. Therefore, the set of values returned by the algorithm will satisfy the antecedent but not the consequent. This is exactly what is required of the values in the tuples t_1 and t_2.

Each of t_1 and t_2 can now be extended into an instance of D, where each relation contains a single tuple. Both instances will give the same instance of the derived relation, consisting of a single tuple $t_1[\mathbf{A}] = t_2[\mathbf{A}]$. In both instances the tuple in the derived relation will be modified; as both tuples satisfy $(\neg(\bigwedge_{A_i \in (\alpha(R_u) \cap \mathbf{A})} (A_i = \rho(f_{A_i}))))$ the modifications will be visible in both cases. However, the value of the modified attribute, A_j, will be different depending on whether we use t_1 or t_2. Hence, by Lemma 4.1, $\mathcal{U}$ is not autonomously computable. $\square$

Updating the Instance

In the previous two sections we gave a number of necessary conditions for an update to be autonomously computable. We will now prove that taken together those conditions are sufficient to guarantee that the update is autonomously computable. However, we first present some notation and then a lemma that will aid in the part of the proof of sufficiency which deals with Property 3.

Recall that the first part of the condition in Property 3 is of the form

$$(\mathcal{C} \wedge \mathcal{C}_M \wedge \mathcal{C}_B(\mathbf{F}_M)) \Rightarrow (\mathcal{C}(\mathbf{F}_M) \wedge (\bigwedge_{A_i \in (\alpha(R_u) \cap \mathbf{A})} (A_i = \rho(f_{A_i})))).$$

Let $\mathcal{C}_{ms}$ represent the negation of this expression, that is,

$$\mathcal{C}_{ms} \equiv \mathcal{C} \wedge \mathcal{C}_M \wedge \mathcal{C}_B(\mathbf{F}_M) \wedge (\neg(\mathcal{C}(\mathbf{F}_M) \wedge (\bigwedge_{A_i \in (\alpha(R_u) \cap \mathbf{A})} (A_i = \rho(f_{A_i}))))).$$

We will use the condition $\mathcal{C}_{ms}$ to determine whether a tuple should be placed in the modify set.

First, we give a formal definition of the modify set then we state and prove a lemma which justifies our use of condition $\mathcal{C}_{ms}$.

Definition 4.6 Let d be an instance of the database D, $\mathcal{U} = \text{MODIFY}(R_u, \mathcal{C}_M, \mathbf{F}_M)$ be an update operation, and $E = (\mathbf{A}, \mathbf{R}, \mathcal{C})$ be a derived relation definition. Those tuples, t, in $v(E, d)$ for which $\mathcal{C}_{ms}[t]$ is satisfiable form the *modify set*. □

Lemma 4.3 Consider a modify operation $\mathcal{U} = \text{MODIFY}(R_u, \mathcal{C}_M, \mathbf{F}_M)$, and a derived relation $E = (\mathbf{A}, \mathbf{R}, \mathcal{C})$ where $\mathcal{U}$ and E satisfy Properties 1 and 3. Let t be a tuple in the current instance of E. Tuple t is guaranteed to be unaffected by update $\mathcal{U}$ if and only if $\mathcal{C}_{ms}[t]$ is unsatisfiable.

Proof: Note that, in order for a tuple to be unaffected by a MODIFY operation it must be neither deleted nor *visibly* changed by the operation.

(Sufficiency) Assume that $\mathcal{C}_{ms}[t]$ is unsatisfiable. Hence, for every tuple s over $\alpha(\mathbf{R})$ such that $s[\mathbf{A}] = t$ we have $\mathcal{C}_{ms}[s] = false$. This means that at least one of the conjuncts is *false* when evaluated on s. If $\mathcal{C}[s]$ is *false* then t is not in the current instance of E, a contradiction. If $\mathcal{C}_M[s] \wedge \mathcal{C}_B(\mathbf{F}_M)[s]$ is *false* then t is not chosen for modification. Finally, if $(\neg(\mathcal{C}(\mathbf{F}_M)[s] \wedge (\bigwedge_{A_i \in (\alpha(R_u) \cap \mathbf{A})}(A_i = \rho(f_{A_i}))[s])))$ is *false* then both $\mathcal{C}(\mathbf{F}_M)[s]$ and $(\bigwedge_{A_i \in (\alpha(R_u) \cap \mathbf{A})}(A_i = \rho(f_{A_i}))[s])$ must be *true*. In this case, t is guaranteed to be in the new instance of E and also to not have any visible modifications. Therefore, in each of these three possibilities we conclude that t should be placed in the new instance of E without any modifications.

(Necessity) Assume that t is not deleted or visibly modified but that $\mathcal{C}_{ms}[t]$ is satisfiable. For this to be the case each of the expressions used to form $\mathcal{C}_{ms}$ must be satisfiable. Hence, there exists a tuple s over $\alpha(\mathbf{R})$ such that $s[\mathbf{A}] = t$ and s satisfies each expression in $\mathcal{C}_{ms}$. Since $\mathcal{C}[s] \wedge \mathcal{C}_M[s] \wedge \mathcal{C}_B(\mathbf{F}_M)[s]$ is satisfied then t is in the current instance of E and is chosen for modification. In addition, since $(\neg(\mathcal{C}(\mathbf{F}_M)[s] \wedge (\bigwedge_{A_i \in (\alpha(R_u) \cap \mathbf{A})}(A_i = \rho(f_{A_i}))[s])))$ is satisfied then at least one of $\mathcal{C}(\mathbf{F}_M)[s]$ or $(\bigwedge_{A_i \in (\alpha(R_u) \cap \mathbf{A})}(A_i = \rho(f_{A_i}))[s])$ is false. Hence, either t will be deleted from the instance after it is modified or it will appear in the new instance but with visible modifications. In either case we reach a contradiction. Hence, it is necessary that $\mathcal{C}_{ms}[t]$ be unsatisfiable. □

Theorem 4.7 *Consider a modify operation $\mathcal{U} = \text{MODIFY}(R_u, \mathcal{C}_M, \mathbf{F}_M)$ and a derived relation $E = (\mathbf{A}, \mathbf{R}, \mathcal{C})$ where $\mathcal{U}$ and E satisfy Property 1. If Properties 2, 3, 4, and 5 are satisfied then the effect of $\mathcal{U}$ is autonomously computable on E.*

Proof: We prove the sufficiency of Properties 2, 3, 4, and 5 by demonstrating how $v(E, d')$ can be determined from $\mathcal{U}$ and $v(E, d)$.

Assume that Property 2 is satisfied. Consider a tuple t in the Cartesian product of the relations in the base $\mathbf{R}$, and assume that t is selected for modification. Let t' denote the corresponding tuple after modification. Assume that t does not satisfy $\mathcal{C}$ and hence will not have created any tuple in the derived relation. Because Property 2 is satisfied for every tuple, it must also hold for t and hence t' cannot satisfy $\mathcal{C}$. Consequently, modifying t to t' does not cause any new tuple to appear in the derived relation. Therefore, the only tuples in $v(E, d')$ are those whose unmodified versions are in $v(E, d)$. In other words, we are assured that $v(E, d)$ contains all the tuples needed to compute $v(E, d')$.

Now consider Property 3. If t is a tuple in $v(E, d)$ then, by Lemma 4.3, testing $\mathcal{C}_{ms}[t]$ will determine whether t should be placed in the modify set. Since this is true for each t in $v(E, d)$, we can decide, for each tuple whether it is in the modify set.

For Property 4, if every attribute $x \in [\alpha(\mathcal{C}) \cup \alpha(\mathcal{C}_M) \cup \alpha(\mathcal{C}_B(\mathbf{F}_M))] - \mathbf{A}^+$ is computationally nonessential in $\mathcal{C}(\mathbf{F}_M)$ with respect to $\mathcal{C} \wedge \mathcal{C}_M \wedge \mathcal{C}_B(\mathbf{F}_M) \wedge (\neg(\mathcal{C}(\mathbf{F}_M) \wedge (\bigwedge_{A_i \in (\alpha(R_u) \cap \mathbf{A})}(A_i = \rho(f_{A_i})))))$ we can correctly evaluate the condition $\mathcal{C}(\mathbf{F}_M)$ on every tuple of the modify set by assigning surrogate values to the attributes in $\alpha(\mathcal{C}(\mathbf{F}_M)) - \mathbf{A}^+$. This means that, for those tuples in the modify set we can determine which tuples will remain in the new instance of $v(E, d)$ and which must be deleted.

Finally, assume that Property 5 is satisfied. Hence, for each t, in $v(E, d)$ which is visibly modified and will remain in the new instance, and for each $A_i \in \mathbf{A} \cap \alpha(R_u)$, the value of the expression $\rho(f_{A_i})$ is uniquely determined by the condition $\mathcal{C} \wedge \mathcal{C}_M \wedge \mathcal{C}_B(\mathbf{F}_M) \wedge \mathcal{C}(\mathbf{F}_M) \wedge (\neg(\bigwedge_{A_i \in (\alpha(R_u) \cap \mathbf{A})}(A_i = \rho(f_{A_i}))))$ and the attributes in $\mathbf{A}^+$. As $\rho(f_{A_i})$ gives the new value for attribute A_i, this means that the given condition and the visible attributes contain sufficient information to determine the updated values of A_i. We have assumed this for each $A_i \in \mathbf{A} \cap \alpha(R_u)$, therefore, the value of every modified attribute in $\mathbf{A}$ is autonomously computable. Hence, for every tuple in $v(E, d)$ which is visibly modified and remains in the updated instance we can calculate the new values of all visible attributes.

The entries in Tables 1 and 2 completely characterize all the possible cases for a tuple t. To distinguish between these cases we have defined four properties. We have shown that these four properties are sufficient to allow us to compute the updated instance from $v(E, d)$, the definition E, and $\mathcal{U}$. The procedure described above defines the function $F_{\mathcal{U}, E}$. Hence, the MODIFY is autonomously computable on E. $\qquad \square$

We give an example which proceeds through the four steps associated with Theorems 4.3 through 4.7, at each step testing the appropriate condition.

Example 4.7 Suppose a database consists of the two relation schemes $R_1(H, I)$ and $R_2(J, K, L)$ where H, I, J, K and L each have the domain $[0, 30]$. Let the derived relation and modify operation be defined as:

$$E = (\{I, J\}, \{R_1, R_2\}, (H < 15)(I = K)(L = 20))$$
$$\text{MODIFY}(R_2, (K > 5)(K \le 22), \{(J := L + 3), (K := K), (L := L)\})$$

and note that Property 1 is satisfied since the value of J, which is visible in E, may be modified. ¿From the definition of the derived relation we can see that $\mathbf{A} = \{I, J\}$ and $\mathbf{A}^+ = \{I, J, K, L\}$.

Test of Property 2:

$$\forall \quad H, I, K, L \ [(\neg((H < 15)(I = K)(L = 20))) \wedge (K > 5)(K \le 22)$$
$$\wedge \ (L + 3 \ge 0)(L + 3 \le 30)(K \ge 0)(K \le 30)(L \ge 0)(L \le 30)$$
$$\Rightarrow \ (\neg((H < 15)(I = K)(L = 20)))]$$

Note that, the consequent $\neg((H < 15)(I = K)(L = 20))$ appears as a condition in the antecedent as well. Therefore, the given implication is valid, and we can conclude that the modify operation will not introduce new tuples into $v(E, d)$.

Test of Property 3:

$$\forall \quad \langle H, I, J, K, L \rangle, \langle H', I, J, K, L \rangle$$
$$[[(H < 15)(I = K)(L = 20) \wedge (K > 5)(K \le 22)$$
$$\wedge (L + 3 \ge 0)(L + 3 \le 30)(K \ge 0)(K \le 30)(L \ge 0)(L \le 30)$$
$$\Rightarrow \ (\neg((H < 15)(I = K)(L = 20) \wedge (J = L + 3)))]$$
$$\vee$$
$$[(H < 15)(I = K)(L = 20) \wedge (H' < 15)(I = K)(L = 20)$$
$$\Rightarrow \ ((K > 5)(K \le 22) \wedge (L + 3 \ge 0)(L + 3 \le 30)(K \ge 0)(K \le 30)$$
$$(L \ge 0)(L \le 30)$$
$$\Leftrightarrow \ (K > 5)(K \le 22) \wedge (L + 3 \ge 0)(L + 3 \le 30)(K \ge 0)(K \le 30)$$
$$(L \ge 0)(L \le 30))]]$$

Consider the implication which is after the disjunction; comprising the last three lines. The right-hand-side of this implication contains an equivalence. Since the two conditions in the equivalence are identical, then clearly, the implication is valid. Thus we can correctly select the tuples in the derived relation that satisfy $\mathcal{C}_M \wedge \mathcal{C}_B(\mathbf{F}_M)$ and will be visibly modified.

Test of Property 4:
We are now interested in the set, $[\alpha(\mathcal{C}) \cup \alpha(\mathcal{C}_M) \cup \alpha(\mathcal{C}_B(\mathbf{F}_M))] - \mathbf{A}^+ = \{H, I, K, L\} - \{I, J, K, L\}$
$= \{H\}$.

$$
\begin{aligned}
\forall \quad & H, I, J, K, L, H' \; [(H < 15)(I = K)(L = 20) \wedge (K > 5)(K \le 22) \\
\wedge \; & (L + 3 \ge 0)(L + 3 \le 30)(K \ge 0)(K \le 30)(L \ge 0)(L \le 30) \\
\wedge \; & (\neg(((H < 15)(I = K)(L = 20) \wedge (J = L + 3))) \\
\wedge \; & (H' < 15)(I = K)(L = 20) \wedge (K > 5)(K \le 22) \\
\wedge \; & (L + 3 \ge 0)(L + 3 \le 30)(K \ge 0)(K \le 30)(L \ge 0)(L \le 30) \\
\wedge \; & (\neg(((H' < 15)(I = K)(L = 20) \wedge (J = L + 3))) \\
\Rightarrow \; & ((H < 15)(I = K)(L = 20) \Leftrightarrow (H' < 15)(I = K)(L = 20))]
\end{aligned}
$$

The conditions $(H < 15)$ and $(H' < 15)$ in the antecedent guarantee that the expressions in the consequent will be equivalent. Therefore, H is computationally nonessential in $\mathcal{C}(\mathbf{F}_M)$ with respect to $\mathcal{C} \wedge \mathcal{C}_M \wedge \mathcal{C}_B(\mathbf{F}_M) \wedge (\neg(\mathcal{C}(\mathbf{F}_M) \wedge (\bigwedge_{A_i \in (\alpha(R_u) \cap \mathbf{A})}(A_i = \rho(f_{A_i}))))))$. Thus, determining the tuples, in the modify set of the current instance, which satisfy $\mathcal{C}(\mathbf{F}_M)$ can be computed autonomously.

Test of Property 5:

$$
\begin{aligned}
\forall \quad & H, I, K, L, H' \; [(H < 15)(I = K)(L = 20) \wedge (K > 5)(K \le 22) \\
\wedge \; & (L + 3 \ge 0)(L + 3 \le 30)(K \ge 0)(K \le 30)(L \ge 0)(L \le 30) \\
\wedge \; & (H < 15)(I = K)(L = 20) \wedge (\neg(J = L + 3)) \\
\wedge \; & (H' < 15)(I = K)(L = 20) \wedge (K > 5)(K \le 22) \\
\wedge \; & (L + 3 \ge 0)(L + 3 \le 30)(K \ge 0)(K \le 30)(L \ge 0)(L \le 30) \\
\wedge \; & (H' < 15)(I = K)(L = 20) \wedge (\neg(J = L + 3)) \\
\Rightarrow \; & ((L + 3) = (L + 3))]
\end{aligned}
$$

By considering the right-hand-side of this implication we see that it is obviously valid. Hence, the above condition verifies that the expression f_J is uniquely determined by the condition $\mathcal{C} \wedge \mathcal{C}_M \wedge \mathcal{C}_B(\mathbf{F}_M) \wedge \mathcal{C}(\mathbf{F}_M) \wedge (\neg(\bigwedge_{A_i \in (\alpha(R_u) \cap \mathbf{A})}(A_i = \rho(f_{A_i}))))$ and the variables $\mathbf{A}^+$. Therefore, the new attribute values for the visibly modified tuples that will remain in $v(E, d)$ are autonomously computable.

To summarize, let us consider a numeric example for the given database scheme.

Before

r_1:	H	I	r_2:	J	K	L	$v(E,d)$:	I	J
	1	5		19	5	20		5	19
	2	15		10	15	29		22	16
	3	22		16	22	20			
	4	20		18	20	29			

After

r_1:	H	I	r_2:	J	K	L	$v(E,d')$:	I	J
	1	5		19	5	20		5	19
	2	15		10	15	29		22	23
	3	22		23	22	20			
	4	20		18	20	29			

Note that the second and fourth tuples do *not* get modified as they do not satisfy $\mathcal{C}_B(\mathbf{F}_M)$. Property 2 provides assurance that the tuples in the Cartesian product of r_1 and r_2, which do not satisfy $\mathcal{C}$ before modification, will not satisfy $\mathcal{C}$ after. For example, consider the last tuple in each of r_1 and r_2. In the Cartesian product these will form $\langle 4, 20, 18, 20, 29 \rangle$. Although this does satisfy $(I = K)$ it does not satisfy $(L = 20)$ and hence will not be in the current instance. Moreover, even though this tuple is modified to become $\langle 4, 20, 32, 20, 29 \rangle$ it still does not satisfy $(L = 20)$ and, hence, remains outside the updated derived relation instance.

Property 3 guarantees that we can determine which tuples in $v(E, d)$ belong in the modify set. For each tuple in $v(E, d)$ we need to test the satisfiability of

$$\mathcal{C}_{ms} \equiv \mathcal{C} \wedge \mathcal{C}_M \wedge \mathcal{C}_B(\mathbf{F}_M) \wedge (\neg(\mathcal{C}(\mathbf{F}_M) \wedge (\bigwedge_{A_i \in (\alpha(R_u) \cap \mathbf{A})} (A_i = \rho(f_{A_i}))))).$$

For this example we have

$$\begin{aligned}
\mathcal{C}_{ms} \equiv [&(H < 15)(I = K)(L = 20) \wedge (K > 5)(K \le 22) \\
&\wedge (L + 3 \ge 0)(L + 3 \le 30)(K \ge 0)(K \le 30)(L \ge 0)(L \le 30) \\
&\wedge (\neg((H < 15)(I = K)(L = 20) \wedge (J = L + 3)))].
\end{aligned}$$

The first tuple in $v(E, d)$ gives us $\langle h, 5, 19, k, l \rangle$ to test. Since, $\mathcal{C}_{ms}[\langle h, 5, 19, k, l \rangle]$ is not satisfiable we conclude that $\langle 5, 19 \rangle$ will not be visibly modified and can be placed in the new instance. The second tuple to test from $v(E, d)$ is $\langle h, 22, 16, k, l \rangle$. Since, $\mathcal{C}_{ms}[\langle h, 22, 16, k, l \rangle]$ is satisfiable we conclude that $\langle 22, 16 \rangle$ belongs in the modify set.

Property 4 allows us to determine which tuples in the modify set will be deleted since they will no longer satisfy condition $\mathcal{C}$. The tuple $\langle 22, 16 \rangle$ satisfies $\mathcal{C}(\mathbf{F}_M)$ and will remain in the updated instance[4].

Property 5 ensures that we can compute the new values for the modified tuples. Here we need to compute $(L + 3)$. Since $\mathcal{C}$ contains the condition $(L = 20)$ we know that for any tuple in the modify set $(L + 3) = 23$. Therefore, $\langle 22, 16 \rangle$ should be updated to $\langle 22, 23 \rangle$ in the new instance. $\qquad \square$

5 Discussion

Necessary and sufficient conditions for detecting when an update operation is irrelevant to a derived relation (or view, or integrity constraint) have not previously been available for any nontrivial class of updates and derived relations. The concept of autonomously computable updates is new. Limiting the class of derived relations to those defined by *PSJ*-expressions does not seem to be a severe restriction, at least not as it applies to structuring the stored database in a relational system. The update operations considered are fairly general. In particular, this seems to be one of a few works on update processing where modify operations are considered explicitly and separately from insert and delete operations. Previously, modifications have commonly been treated as a sequence of deletions followed by insertion of the modified tuples.

Testing the conditions given in the theorems above does not require retrieval of any data from the database. According to our definitions, if an update is irrelevant or autonomously computable, then it is so for *every* instance of the base relations. The fact that an update is not irrelevant does not necessarily mean that

---

[4]Since the attributes in $\mathcal{C}$ have trivial update functions $\mathcal{C}(\mathbf{F}_M) \equiv \mathcal{C}$. Hence, no tuple will be deleted from the derived relation.

it affects the derived relation. Determining whether it does, requires checking the current instance. The same applies for autonomously computable updates.

It should be emphasized that the theorems hold for any class of Boolean expressions. However, actual testing of the conditions requires an algorithm for proving the satisfiability of Boolean expressions. Currently, efficient algorithms exist only for a restricted class of expressions, the restriction being on the atomic conditions allowed. As mentioned above, we have built a prototype system, which uses the algorithm given in the Appendix, to test the conditions for irrelevant and autonomously computable updates. The results obtained from experiments using the prototype are encouraging. It appears that, in practice, the tests for irrelevant and autonomously computable updates can be computed very efficiently. Interested readers are referred to [BCL86] for more details on implementation issues and experimental results.

An important open problem is to find efficient algorithms for more general types of atomic conditions. The core of such an algorithm is a procedure for testing whether a set of inequalities/equalities can all be simultaneously satisfied. The complexity of such a procedure depends on the type of expressions (functions) allowed and the domains of the variables. If linear functions with variables ranging over the real numbers (integers) are allowed, the problem is equivalent to finding a feasible solution to a linear programming (integer programming) problem.

We have not imposed any restrictions on valid instances of base relations, for example, functional dependencies or inclusion dependencies. Any combination of attribute values drawn from their respective domains represents a valid tuple. Any set of valid tuples is a valid instance of a base relation. If relation instances are further restricted, then the given conditions are still sufficient, but they may not be necessary. Current work is aimed at extending the theory to incorporate knowledge about keys, functional dependencies, and referential integrity.

Appendix: Satisfiability Algorithm

The theorems presented in this chapter require that statements be proven at *run-time*, that is, when updates are issued. What is required is that certain types of Boolean expressions be tested for unsatisfiability or that implications involving Boolean expressions be proven valid. The latter problem can be translated into one of showing that a Boolean expression is unsatisfiable. Hence, in either case we can proceed by testing satisfiability.

Rosenkrantz and Hunt [RH80] gave an algorithm for testing the satisfiability of conjunctive Boolean expressions where the atomic conditions come from a restricted class. Their algorithm is based on Floyd's all-pairs-shortest-path algorithm [Flo62] and therefore has an $O(n^3)$ worst case complexity, where n is the number of distinct variables in the expression. The algorithm presented here is a modification of that given by Rosenkrantz and Hunt; there are three main differences. First, we assume that each variable has a finite domain whereas Rosenkrantz and Hunt allow infinite domains. Second, if the expression is satisfiable our algorithm not only verifies the satisfiability but also produces an assignment of values to the variables which satisfies the expression. Third, although the worst case complexity of our algorithm remains $O(n^3)$, for a large sub-class of expressions the runtime is reduced to $O(n^2)$.

The algorithm given here tests the satisfiability of a restricted class of Boolean expressions. Each variable is assumed to take its values from a finite, ordered set. Since there is an obvious mapping from such sets to the set of integers, we always assume that the domain consists of a finite interval of the integers. It is assumed that each Boolean expression, B, over the variables $x_1, x_2, \ldots x_n$, is in conjunctive form, i.e. $B = B_1 \wedge B_2 \wedge \ldots \wedge B_m$, and that each atomic condition, B_i, is of the form $(x_i \ \theta \ x_j + c)$ or $(x_i \ \theta \ c)$ where

$\theta \in \{=, <, \leq, >, \geq\}$ and c is an integer constant. We will outline the algorithm and discuss each step in more detail.

Algorithm **Satisfiable**

Input: A conjunctive Boolean expression B over the variables $x_1, \ldots, x_n$. The variables' domain bounds are given by vectors L and U with $L[i] \leq x_i \leq U[i], 1 \leq i \leq n$.

Output: If B is satisfiable then the value *true* is returned and the assignment $x_i := U[i]$ will satisfy B, otherwise *false* is returned.

Begin

1. Normalize B to obtain N. Check the resulting domain bounds; if $U[i] < L[i]$ for some x_i then return *false*.

2. Initialize A (the adjacency matrix of the directed graph representing N).

3. Reduce A, that is, remove (recursively) rows representing nodes of in-degree zero.

4. Test the trial values against the lower bounds. If $U[i] < L[i]$ for some x_i then return *false*.

5. Test the trial values in N. If they satisfy N return *true*.

6. Execute Floyd's Algorithm on A, after each iteration of the outer loop perform the following:

   (a) If A contains a negative cycle then return *false*.
   (b) Calculate the new trial values.
   (c) Test the trial values against the lower bounds. If $U[i] < L[i]$ for some x_i then return *false*.
   (d) Test the trial values in N. If they satisfy N return *true*.

End

(Step 1) We first must *normalize* B so that the resulting expression, $N = N_1 \wedge N_2 \wedge \ldots \wedge N_{m_N}$, only has atomic conditions of the form $(x_i \leq x_j + c)$. Conditions of the form $(x_i \, \theta \, c)$ are handled by modifying the domain bounds for the variable x_i. If any such modification results in $U[i] < L[i]$, for any $1 \leq i \leq n$, then B is unsatisfiable.

(Step 2) We build a weighted, directed graph $G = (V, E)$ representing N. Without loss of generality we assume that N is defined over the variables $x_1, \ldots, x_{n_N}$ where $n_N \leq n$. Each variable in N is represented by a node in G. For the atomic condition $(x_i \leq x_j + c)$ we construct an arc from node "x_j" to node "x_i" having weight c. Hence, $|V| = n_N$ and $|E| = m_N$. The graph is represented by an $n_N \times n_N$ array A where, initially, $A(i, j) = c$ if and only if N contains an expression of the form $(x_i \leq x_j + c)$. If two nodes do not have an arc between them the corresponding array entry is labeled with ∞ (i.e. an arbitrarily large positive value). If there is more than one arc between a pair of nodes, then use the one with lowest weight.

(Step 3) The graph, G, can be *reduced* in size by removing nodes of in-degree zero. The justification for doing this is that if x_j is such a node then N does not have any conditions of the form $(x_j \leq x_i + c)$. Hence, the upper limit value of x_j is not constrained by the value assigned to any other variable. Therefore, we allow x_j to be assigned its (possibly modified) upper bound $U[j]$. Also, for each node x_i in G, such that there is an arc of weight c from x_j to x_i, we replace the upper bound on x_i with $\min\{U[i], U[j] + c\}$. We can then remove node x_j and its incident arcs from G. This process may be repeated until no nodes of in-degree zero remain in G. If G is acyclic (i.e. if B does not contain a cyclic chain of atomic conditions involving mutually dependent variables) then this process will terminate when there are no edges left in G. The resulting trial assignment of values either proves or disproves that B is satisfiable (Steps 4 and 5). As the reduction process requires examining each element of matrix A at most once, the entire Satisfiable algorithm performs $O(n_N^2)$ operations in this case.

(Step 6) If G is not acyclic then A is used as the input to a modified version of Floyd's algorithm [Flo62] to determine either that N is unsatisfiable or to produce an assignment which satisfies N. The idea is that we give each remaining variable, x_i, an initial *trial* value equal to its (possibly modified) upper bound $U[i]$. At each iteration we adjust the values (downward) to reflect the current values in A and the previous set of trial values. The iterations continue until we find an assignment to the variables which satisfies N or until we determine that N is unsatisfiable. This takes at most n_N iterations.

To be more specific, given a graph with nodes $x_1, \ldots, x_{n_N}$, the kth step of Floyd's algorithm produces the least weight path between each pair of nodes, with intermediate nodes from the set $\{x_1, x_2, \ldots, x_k\}$. In terms of the Boolean expression this corresponds to forming, from the conditions in N, the most restrictive condition between each pair of variables. The only conditions of N which may be used at the kth step are those involving the variables $x_1, \ldots, x_k$. The new trial value, $U[i]$, for x_i is found by taking $\min\{U[j] + A[i,j]\}$ for $1 \leq j \leq n_N$. There are three possible situations that indicate that the algorithm should terminate. We test each of these conditions after each iteration:

1. Is there a negative weight cycle? In this case N is unsatisfiable.

2. Does the current trial assignment violate any variable's lower bound? Again, N is unsatisfiable.

3. Does the current trial assignment satisfy the lower bound for each variable and satisfy N? In this case N is satisfiable.

Since the longest cycle can contain at most n_N arcs we conclude that this is the maximum number of iterations required; hence the $O(n_N^3)$ complexity. If after n_N iterations we have not found a negative weight cycle or violated any bound then the current trial assignment must satisfy N.

Acknowledgments

This research was supported by Cognos, Inc., Ottawa under contract WRI 502-12, by the National Council of Science and Technology of México (CONACYT), by a Natural Sciences and Engineering Research Council of Canada (NSERC) Postgraduate Scholarship and under NSERC grant No. A-2460.

We would like to thank the referees for their constructive and detailed comments which led us to improve the clarity and rigour of this chapter.

QUERIES INDEPENDENT OF UPDATES

Alon Y. Levy and Yehoshua Sagiv

1 Introduction

We consider the problem of detecting independence of queries expressed by datalog programs from updates. Detecting independence is important for several reasons. It can be used in view maintenance to identify that some views are independent of certain updates. In transaction scheduling, we can provide greater flexibility by identifying that one transaction is independent of updates made by another. Finally, we can use independence in query optimization by ignoring parts of the database for which updates do not affect a specific query.

In this chapter, we provide new insight into the independence problem by reducing it to the equivalence problem for datalog programs. Equivalence, as well as independence, is undecidable in general. However, algorithms for equivalence provide sufficient (and sometimes also necessary) conditions for independence. We consider two such conditions, *query reachability* [LS92] and *uniform equivalence* [Sag88].

Earlier work by Blakeley et al. [BCL89] and Elkan [Elk90] focussed on cases for which independence is the same as query reachability. Essentially, these are the cases where the updated predicate has a single occurrence in the query. Blakeley et al. [BCL89] considered only conjunctive queries. Elkan [Elk90] considered a more general framework, but gave an algorithm only for nonrecursive rules without negation; that algorithm is complete only for the case of a single occurrence of the updated predicate. Elkan also gave a proof method for recursive rules, but its power is limited.

Query reachability has recently been shown decidable even for recursive datalog programs with dense-order constraints and negated EDB subgoals [LS92, LMSS93]. We show how query-reachability algorithms generalize the previous results on independence.

In order to use uniform equivalence for detecting independence, we extend the algorithm given in [Sag88] to datalog programs with built-in predicates and stratified negation. As a result, we show new decidable cases of independence; for example, if the update is an insertion, and both the query and the update are given by datalog program with no recursion or negation, then independence is decidable (note that the updated predicate may have multiple occurrences). Our algorithms also provide sufficient conditions for independence in the general case. Aside from their usage in detecting independence, the algorithms we present for uniform equivalence are important for optimizing datalog programs.

Finally, we also characterize new cases for which independence of insertions is the same as independence of deletions. Since the former is, in many cases, easier to detect, these characterizations are of practical importance.

2 Preliminaries

2.1 Datalog Programs

Datalog programs are collections of safe horn-rules with no function symbols (i.e., only constants and variables are allowed). We allow the built-in predicates[1] $<, >, =, \neq, \leq$, and $\geq$ that represent a dense order. Programs may also have stratified negation. Both negation and built-in predicates must be used safely (cf. [Ull89]).

We distinguish between two sets of predicates in a given program: the *extensional predicates* (EDB predicates), which are those that appear only in bodies of rules, and the *intensional predicates* (IDB predicates), which are the predicates appearing in heads of rules. The EDB predicates refer to the database relations while the IDB predicates are defined by the program. We usually denote the EDB predicates as $e_1, \ldots, e_m$ and the IDB predicates as $i_1, \ldots, i_n$. The input to a datalog program is an *extensional database* (EDB) consisting of relations $E_1, \ldots, E_m$ for the EDB predicates $e_1, \ldots, e_m$, respectively. Alternatively, the EDB may also be viewed as a set of ground atoms (or facts) for the EDB predicates. Given a datalog program $\mathcal{P}$ and an EDB $E_1, \ldots, E_m$ as input, a bottom-up evaluation is one in which we start with the ground EDB facts and apply the rules to derive facts for the IDB predicates. We continue applying the rules until no new facts are generated. We distinguish one IDB predicate as the *query* (or goal) predicate, and the *output* (or answer) of program $\mathcal{P}$ for the input $E_1, \ldots, E_m$, denoted $\mathcal{P}(E_1, \ldots, E_m)$, is the set of all ground facts generated for the query predicate in the bottom-up evaluation. The query predicate is usually denoted as q. Note that the bottom-up evaluation computes relations for all the IDB predicates, and $I_1, \ldots, I_n$ usually denote the relations for the IDB predicates $i_1, \ldots, i_n$, respectively.

We say that the query predicate is monotonic (anti-monotonic) in the input if whenever $D_1 \supseteq D_2$ then $P(D_1) \supseteq P(D_2)$ ($P(D_1) \subseteq P(D_2)$). Note that a datalog program without negation is monotonic.

2.2 Containment and Equivalence

Independence of queries from updates can be expressed as an equivalence of two programs: one program that computes the answer to the query before the update and a second program that computes the answer after the update.

Definition 2.1: (Containment) *A datalog program $\mathcal{P}_1$ contains a program $\mathcal{P}_2$, written $\mathcal{P}_2 \subseteq \mathcal{P}_1$, if for all EDBs $E_1, \ldots, E_m$, the output of $\mathcal{P}_1$ contains that of $\mathcal{P}_2$, i.e., $\mathcal{P}_2(E_1, \ldots, E_m) \subseteq \mathcal{P}_1(E_1, \ldots, E_m)$.*

Two programs $\mathcal{P}_1$ and $\mathcal{P}_2$ are *equivalent*, written $\mathcal{P}_1 \equiv \mathcal{P}_2$, if $\mathcal{P}_2 \subseteq \mathcal{P}_1$ and $\mathcal{P}_1 \subseteq \mathcal{P}_2$. Containment of datalog programs is undecidable [Shm87], even for programs without built-in predicates or negation.

A sufficient condition for containment is *uniform containment*, which was introduced and shown to be decidable in [Sag88] for programs without built-in predicates or negation. In defining uniform containment, we assume that the input to a program $\mathcal{P}$ consists of EDB relation $E_1, \ldots, E_m$ as well as *initial* IDB relations $I_1^0, \ldots, I_n^0$ for the IDB predicates. The output of program $\mathcal{P}$ for $E_1, \ldots, E_m, I_1^0, \ldots, I_n^0$, written $\mathcal{P}(E_1, \ldots, E_m, I_1^0, \ldots, I_n^0)$, is computed as earlier by applying rules bottom-up until no new facts are generated. When dealing with uniform containment (equivalence), we assume that the output is not just the relation for the query predicate but rather all the IDB relations $I_1, \ldots, I_n$ computed for the IDB predicates $i_1, \ldots, i_n$, respectively. An output $I_1, \ldots, I_n$ *contains* another output $I_1', \ldots, I_n'$ if $I_j' \subseteq I_j$ ($1 \leq j \leq n$). A

---

[1]The phrase "built-in predicates" refers in this chapter just to those listed above.

program $\mathcal{P}_1$ *uniformly contains* $\mathcal{P}_2$, written $\mathcal{P}_2 \subseteq^u \mathcal{P}_1$, if for all EDBs $E_1, \ldots, E_m$ and for all initial IDBs $I_1^0, \ldots, I_n^0$,

$$\mathcal{P}_2(E_1, \ldots, E_m, I_1^0, \ldots, I_n^0) \subseteq \mathcal{P}_1(E_1, \ldots, E_m, I_1^0, \ldots, I_n^0).$$

Uniform containment can also be explained in model-theoretic terms [Sag88]. For programs without negations, the uniform containment $\mathcal{P}_2 \subseteq^u \mathcal{P}_1$ holds if and only if $M(\mathcal{P}_1) \subseteq M(\mathcal{P}_2)$, where $M(\mathcal{P}_i)$ denotes the set of all models of $\mathcal{P}_i$. Furthermore, for programs having only EDB predicates in bodies of rules, uniform containment is the same as containment. Note that a program with no recursion (and no negation) can be transformed into this form by unfolding the rules.

Query reachability is another notion that provides a sufficient condition for equivalence of programs.

Definition 2.2: (Query Reachability) *Let p be a predicate (either EDB or IDB) of a program $\mathcal{P}$. The predicate p is* query reachable *with respect to $\mathcal{P}$ if there is a derivation d of a fact for the query predicate from some EDB D, such that predicate p is used in d.*

Algorithms for deciding query reachability are discussed in [LS92, LMSS93] for cases that include built-in predicates and negation.

2.3 Updates

Given a Datalog program $\mathcal{P}$, which we call the *query program*, we consider updates to the EDB predicates of $\mathcal{P}$, denoted $e_1, \ldots, e_m$. In an update, we either remove or add ground facts to the extensional database. To simplify notation, we assume that updates are always done on the relation E_1 for the predicate e_1. To specify the set of facts that is updated in E_1, we assume we have another datalog program, called the *update program* and denoted as $\mathcal{P}^u$. The query predicate of $\mathcal{P}^u$ is u and its arity is equal to that of e_1. The relation computed for u will be the set of facts updated in e_1.

We assume that the IDB predicates of $\mathcal{P}^u$ are different from those of $\mathcal{P}$. The EDB predicates of $\mathcal{P}^u$, however, could be EDB predicates of $\mathcal{P}$ as well as predicates not appearing in $\mathcal{P}$. To distinguish the two sets of EDB predicates, from now on the phrase "EDB predicates" refers exclusively to the EDB predicates $e_1, \ldots, e_m$ of the query program $\mathcal{P}$; the other extensional relations that may appear in the update program are referred to as *base predicates*, denoted by $b_1, \ldots, b_l$. We denote the output of the update program $\mathcal{P}^u$ as $\mathcal{P}^u(E_1, \ldots, E_m, B_1, \ldots, B_l)$, even if $\mathcal{P}^u$ does not use all (or any) of the EDB predicates. Sometimes we refer to its output as U.

An update is either an *insertion* or a *deletion* and it applies to the relation E_1 for the EDB predicate e_1. The tuples to be inserted into or deleted from E_1 are those in the relation computed for u. A large class of updates consists of those *not* depending on the EDB relations, as captured by the following definition:

Definition 2.3: (Oblivious Update) *An update specified by an update program $\mathcal{P}^u$ is* oblivious *with respect to a query program $\mathcal{P}$ if $\mathcal{P}^u$ has only base predicates (and no EDB predicates). An update is* nonoblivious *if the update program $\mathcal{P}^u$ has some EDB predicates (and possibly some base predicates).*

To define independence, suppose we are given a query program $\mathcal{P}$ and an update program $\mathcal{P}^u$. The program $\mathcal{P}$ is *independent* of the given update if the update does not change the answer to the query predicate.

More precisely, program $\mathcal{P}$ is independent of the given update if for all EDB relations $E_1, \ldots, E_m$ and for all base relations $B_1, \ldots, B_l$,

$$\mathcal{P}(E_1, E_2, \ldots, E_n) = \mathcal{P}(E'_1, E_2, \ldots, E_n)$$

where E'_1 is the result of applying the update to E_1; that is, $E'_1 = E_1 \cup U$ if the update is an insertion and $E'_1 = E_1 - U$ if the update is a deletion, where $U = \mathcal{P}^u(E_1, \ldots, E_m, B_1, \ldots, B_l)$.

We use the following notation. $In^+(\mathcal{P}, \mathcal{P}^u)$ means that program $\mathcal{P}$ is independent of the insertion specified by the update program $\mathcal{P}^u$. Similarly, $In^-(\mathcal{P}, \mathcal{P}^u)$ means that program $\mathcal{P}$ is independent of the deletion specified by the update program $\mathcal{P}^u$.

Several properties of independence are shown by Elkan [Elk90]. In particular, he showed the following.

Lemma 2.4: *Consider a query program $\mathcal{P}$ and an update program $\mathcal{P}^u$. If $\mathcal{P}^u$ is monotonic in the EDB predicates and $\mathcal{P}$ is either monotonic or anti-monotonic in the EDB predicates, then*

$$In^-(\mathcal{P}, \mathcal{P}^u) \Longrightarrow In^+(\mathcal{P}, \mathcal{P}^u).$$

Similarly to the above lemma, we can also prove the following.

Lemma 2.5: *Consider a query program $\mathcal{P}$ and an update program $\mathcal{P}^u$. If $\mathcal{P}^u$ is anti-monotonic in the EDB predicates and $\mathcal{P}$ is either monotonic or anti-monotonic in the EDB predicates, then*

$$In^+(\mathcal{P}, \mathcal{P}^u) \Longrightarrow In^-(\mathcal{P}, \mathcal{P}^u).$$

Proof: Consider an EDB $E_1, \ldots, E_n$, denoted as $\bar{E}$, and relations $B_1, \ldots, B_m$, denoted as $\bar{B}$, for the base predicates. The tuples of the update are given by $U = \mathcal{P}^u(\bar{E}, \bar{B})$. A deletion update transforms the EDB $\bar{E}$ into the EDB $E_1 - U, \ldots, E_n$, denoted as $\bar{E}^-$. We have to show the following.

$$\mathcal{P}(\bar{E}^-) \;=\; \mathcal{P}(\bar{E})$$

So, consider the EDB $\bar{E}^-$ with the relations $\bar{B}$ for the base predicates. Let $U' = \mathcal{P}^u(\bar{E}^-, \bar{B})$. Since $\mathcal{P}^u$ is anti-monotonic in the EDB, $U \subseteq U'$.

We now apply the insertion update specified by $U' = \mathcal{P}^u(\bar{E}^-, \bar{B})$ to $\bar{E}^-$ yielding the following EDB.

$$(E_1 - U) \cup U', E_2, \ldots, E_n$$

Since $In^+(\mathcal{P}, \mathcal{P}^u)$ is assumed, we get the following.

$$\mathcal{P}(\bar{E}^-) \;=\; \mathcal{P}((E_1 - U) \cup U', E_2, \ldots, E_n) \tag{2.1}$$

Moreover, $U \subseteq U'$ implies the following.

$$E_1 - U \;\subseteq\; E_1 \;\subseteq\; (E_1 - U) \cup U' \tag{2.2}$$

If $\mathcal{P}$ is monotonic in the EDB, then (2.2) implies

$$\mathcal{P}(\bar{E}^-) \;\subseteq\; \mathcal{P}(\bar{E}) \;\subseteq\; \mathcal{P}((E_1 - U) \cup U', E_2, \ldots, E_n)$$

and, so, from (2.1) we get the following.

$$\mathcal{P}(\bar{E}^-) \;=\; \mathcal{P}(\bar{E})$$

Similarly, if $\mathcal{P}$ is anti-monotonic in the EDB, then (2.2) implies

$$\mathcal{P}(\bar{E}^-) \;\supseteq\; \mathcal{P}(\bar{E}) \;\supseteq\; \mathcal{P}((E_1 - U) \cup U', E_2, \ldots, E_n)$$

and, so, from (2.1) we get the following.

$$\mathcal{P}(\bar{E}^-) \;=\; \mathcal{P}(\bar{E})$$

□

Note that if an update is oblivious, then it is both monotonic and anti-monotonic. Therefore, the above two lemmas imply the following corollary.

Corollary 2.6: *Consider a query program $\mathcal{P}$ and an update program $\mathcal{P}^u$. If the update is oblivious (i.e., EDB predicates of $\mathcal{P}$ do not appear in $\mathcal{P}^u$), and $\mathcal{P}$ is either monotonic or anti-monotonic in the updated EDB predicates, then the following equivalence holds:*

$$In^-(\mathcal{P}, \mathcal{P}^u) \Longleftrightarrow In^+(\mathcal{P}, \mathcal{P}^u).$$

The importance of Lemma 2.5 and Corollary 2.6, as we will see in the next section, lies in the fact that testing $In^+(\mathcal{P}, \mathcal{P}^u)$ is usually easier than testing $In^-(\mathcal{P}, \mathcal{P}^u)$.

3 Detecting Independence

To develop algorithms for detecting independence, we will show that the problem can be reformulated as a problem of detecting equivalence of datalog programs. Like independence, detecting equivalence of datalog programs is in general undecidable; however, algorithms that provide sufficient conditions for detecting equivalence can also serve as sufficient conditions for independence. In contrast, previous work reduced the independence problem to satisfiability. The following example illustrates the difference between the approaches.

Example 3.1: Consider the following program P_1. An atom $canDrive(X, Y, A)$ is true if person X can drive car Y and A is the age of X. According to the rule for $canDrive$, person X can drive car Y if X is a driver and there is someone of the age 18 or older in the same car. An adult driver, as computed by the IDB predicate $adultDriver$, is anyone who can drive a car and is of the age 18 or older.

$$
\begin{aligned}
canDrive(X, Y, A) \quad &:- \quad inCar(X, Y, A),\ driver(X),\\
&\qquad inCar(Z, Y, B),\ B \geq 18.\\
adultDriver(X) \quad &:- \quad canDrive(X, Y, A),\ A \geq 18.
\end{aligned}
$$

Let the update program consist of the rule

$$
\begin{aligned}
u_1(X, Y, A) \quad &:- \quad inCar(X, Y, A),\ \neg driver(X),\\
&\qquad A < 18.
\end{aligned}
$$

and suppose that the deletion defined by u_1 is applied to $inCar$; that is, non-drivers under the age of 18 are removed from $inCar$.

Let the query predicate be $adultDriver$ and note that $adultDriver(X)$ is equivalent to the following conjunction, denoted as $\mathcal{C}$.

$$inCar(X, Y, A) \wedge driver(X) \wedge inCar(Z, Y, B) \wedge$$
$$A \geq 18 \wedge B \geq 18$$

An algorithm for detecting independence based on satisfiability (e.g., [Elk90, BCL89]) checks whether an updated fact may appear in any derivation of the query. In our example, an updated fact may appear in a derivation of $adultDriver(X)$ if either the conjunction

$$\mathcal{C} \wedge \neg driver(X) \wedge A < 18$$

or the conjunction

$$\mathcal{C} \wedge \neg driver(Z) \wedge B < 18$$

is satisfiable. Since none of the above is satisfiable, the algorithm would conclude that the query is independent of the update.

Now consider the following update program

$$u_2(X, Y, A) \quad :- \quad inCar(X, Y, A), \ \neg driver(X).$$

and suppose that the deletion defined by u_2 is applied to $inCar$. In this case, the conjunction

$$\mathcal{C} \wedge \neg driver(Z)$$

is satisfiable and the algorithm would *not* detect independence. However, to see that the update is independent, observe that *after* the update, P_1 computes for $adultDriver$ the same relation as the one computed by the following program, P_2, *before* the update.

$$
\begin{aligned}
canDrive(X, Y, A) \quad :- \quad & inCar(X, Y, A), \ driver(X), \\
& inCar(Z, Y, B), \ B \geq 18, \\
& driver(Z). \\
adultDriver(X) \quad :- \quad & canDrive(X, Y, A), \ A \geq 18.
\end{aligned}
$$

Since P_1 and P_2 are equivalent (when the query predicate is $adultDriver$), the deletion update defined by u_2 is independent of the query predicate. $\square$

3.1 Independence and Equivalence

As stated above, the independence problem can be formulated as a problem of detecting equivalence of datalog programs. To show that, we construct a new program that computes the new value of the query predicate q from the old value of the EDB (i.e., the value before the update). One program, $\mathcal{P}^+$, is constructed for the case of insertion, and another program, $\mathcal{P}^-$, is constructed for the case of deletion. Each of $\mathcal{P}^+$ and $\mathcal{P}^-$ consists of three parts:

- The rules of $\mathcal{P}$, after all occurrences of the predicate name e_1 have been replaced by a new predicate name s.

- The rules of the update program $\mathcal{P}^u$.
- Rules for the new predicate s.

$\mathcal{P}^+$ and $\mathcal{P}^-$ differ only in the third part. In the case of insertion, the predicate s in $\mathcal{P}^+$ is intended to represent the relation E_1 after the update, and therefore the rules for s are:

$$s(X_1, \ldots, X_k) \quad :- \quad e_1(X_1, \ldots, X_k).$$
$$s(X_1, \ldots, X_k) \quad :- \quad u(X_1, \ldots, X_k).$$

In the case of deletion, the predicate s in $\mathcal{P}^-$ is intended to represent the deletion update to E_1, and the rule for defining it is

$$s(X_1, \ldots, X_k) \quad :- \quad e_1(X_1, \ldots, X_k), \neg u(X_1, \ldots, X_k).$$

The following propositions are immediate corollaries of the definition of independence.

Proposition 3.2: $In^+(\mathcal{P}, \mathcal{P}^u) \Longleftrightarrow \mathcal{P} \equiv \mathcal{P}^+.$

Proposition 3.3: $In^-(\mathcal{P}, \mathcal{P}^u) \Longleftrightarrow \mathcal{P} \equiv \mathcal{P}^-.$

Proof: Both propositions follow from the observation that the relation computed for s is the updated relation for E_1. Therefore, since e_1 is replaced by s in the rules of the program, the new program will compute the relation for q after the update. Clearly, the independence holds if and only if the new program is equivalent to the original program. $\square$

Example 3.4: Consider the following program $\mathcal{P}_0$ with q as the query predicate:

$$
\begin{aligned}
r_1 &: \quad q(X,Y) \quad :- \quad p(X,Y), \neg e_1(X,Y). \\
r_2 &: \quad p(X,Y) \quad :- \quad e_1(X,Y), \neg e(X). \\
r_3 &: \quad p(X,Y) \quad :- \quad e_1(X,Y), X > 1. \\
r_4 &: \quad p(X,Y) \quad :- \quad e(X), e(W), p(W,Y), W > X.
\end{aligned}
$$

Let the update program $\mathcal{P}^u$ consist of the rule:

$$r^u : \quad u(X,Y) \quad :- \quad b(X,Y), X \leq 1.$$

The program for the insertion update $\mathcal{P}^+$ would be:

$$
\begin{aligned}
r_1' &: \quad q(X,Y) \quad :- \quad p(X,Y), \neg s(X,Y). \\
r_2' &: \quad p(X,Y) \quad :- \quad s(X,Y), \neg e(X). \\
r_3' &: \quad p(X,Y) \quad :- \quad s(X,Y), X > 1. \\
r_4' &: \quad p(X,Y) \quad :- \quad e(X), e(W), p(W,Y), W > X. \\
r_5' &: \quad s(X,Y) \quad :- \quad e_1(X,Y). \\
r_6' &: \quad s(X,Y) \quad :- \quad u(X,Y). \\
r_7' &: \quad u(X,Y) \quad :- \quad b(X,Y), X \leq 1.
\end{aligned}
$$

This program is equivalent to the original one, $\mathcal{P}_0$, and indeed $In^+(\mathcal{P}_0, \mathcal{P}^u)$ does hold. $\square$

In Section 4, we describe algorithms for deciding uniform equivalence for datalog programs with built-in predicates and stratified negation. Based on these algorithms, we get the following decidability results for independence. Note that in the following theorem, the updated predicate may have multiple occurrences, and so, this theorem generalizes earlier results on decidability of independence.

Theorem 3.5: *Independence is decidable in the following cases:*

1. *$In^+(\mathcal{P}, \mathcal{P}^u)$ $(In^-(\mathcal{P}, \mathcal{P}^u))$ is decidable if both $\mathcal{P}^+$ $(\mathcal{P}^-)$ and $\mathcal{P}$ have only built-in and EDB predicates (that may appear positively or negatively) in bodies of rules.*[2]

2. *Both $In^+(\mathcal{P}, \mathcal{P}^u)$ and $In^-(\mathcal{P}, \mathcal{P}^u)$ are decidable if $\mathcal{P}$ has only built-in and EDB predicates (that may appear positively or negatively) in bodies of rules, and $\mathcal{P}^u$ has only rules of the form*

$$u(X_1, \ldots, X_k) \quad :- \quad e_1(X_1, \ldots, X_k), \ c.$$

   where c is a conjunction of built-in predicates.

The theorem follows from the observation that for these classes of programs, uniform equivalence is also a necessary condition for equivalence. The algorithms of Section 4 also apply to arbitrary programs $\mathcal{P}$, $\mathcal{P}^+$ and $\mathcal{P}^-$, but only as a sufficient condition for independence.

3.2   Independence and Query Reachability

Detecting independence based on query reachability is based on the observation that if none of the updated facts can be part of a derivation of the query, then clearly, the query is independent of the update. This is made precise by the following lemma, based on query reachability.

Lemma 3.6: *Suppose that neither $\mathcal{P}$ nor $\mathcal{P}^u$ has negation. If predicate u is not query reachable in $\mathcal{P}^+$, then both $In^+(\mathcal{P}, \mathcal{P}^u)$ and $In^-(\mathcal{P}, \mathcal{P}^u)$ are true.*

Query reachability is decidable for all datalog programs with built-in predicates and negation applied to EDB (and base) predicates [LS92, LMSS93]. If negation is also applied to IDB predicates, then a generalization of the algorithm of [LMSS93] is a sufficient test for query reachability. Thus, the above lemma provides a considerable generalization of previous algorithms for detecting independence.

It should be realized that the independence tests of Elkan [Elk90] and of Blakely et al. [BCL89] are just query reachability tests. Both essentially characterized special cases in which independence is equivalent to query reachability. The result of Blakely et al. [BCL89] applies just to conjunctive queries with no repeated predicates. The work of Elkan [Elk90] entails that, in the case of recursive rules, independence is equivalent to query reachability provided that the updated predicate has a single occurrence; he also required that an insertion update be monotonic. For testing independence, Elkan [Elk90] gave a query-reachability algorithm for the case of nonrecursive, negation-free rules, and suggested a proof method for the recursive case; there is no characterization of the power of that proof method, but it should be noted that it cannot capture all cases detected by the algorithms of [LS92, LMSS93].

---

[2]We prefer to describe this case in terms of $\mathcal{P}$ and $\mathcal{P}^+$, rather than $\mathcal{P}$ and $\mathcal{P}^u$, since it is clearer. Note that if $\mathcal{P}$ and $\mathcal{P}^u$ are nonrecursive then in some, but not all cases, $\mathcal{P}^+$ and $\mathcal{P}$ can be converted by unfolding into forms satisfying this condition.

Example 3.7: The following example shows how query reachability can be used for detecting independence in the case of a recursive datalog program. Consider the following rules:

$$r_1: \quad goodPath(X,Y) \quad :- \quad badPoint(X),$$
$$path(X,Y),$$
$$goodPoint(Y).$$
$$r_2: \quad path(X,Y) \quad :- \quad link(X,Y).$$
$$r_3: \quad path(X,Y) \quad :- \quad link(X,Z), \ path(Z,Y).$$
$$r_4: \quad link(X,Y) \quad :- \quad step(X,Y).$$
$$r_5: \quad link(X,Y) \quad :- \quad bigStep(X,Y).$$

The predicates *step* and *bigStep* describe single links between points in a space. The predicate *path* denotes the paths that can be constructed by composing single links. The predicate *goodPath* denotes paths that go from bad points to good ones. Furthermore, the following constraint are given on the EDB relations:

$badPoint(x) \Rightarrow 100 < x < 200.$
$step(x,y) \Rightarrow x < y.$
$goodPoint(x) \Rightarrow 150 < x < 170.$
$bigStep(x,y) \Rightarrow x < 100 \wedge y > 200.$

Figure 1 show the query-tree representing all possible derivation of the query $goodPath(X,Y)$. The query-tree shows that ground facts of the relation *step* which do not satisfy $100 < x$ and $y < 170$ cannot be part of a derivation of the query. Similarly, facts of the relation *bigStep* cannot be part of derivations of the query. Consequently, the query *goodPath* will be independent of removing or adding facts of that form. □

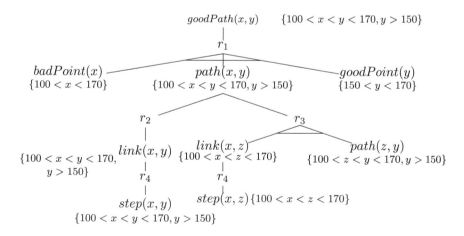

Figure 1 Detecting independence using query reachability

4   Uniform Equivalence

In this section, we describe algorithms for deciding uniform equivalence of programs that have built-in predicates and stratified negation. This extends a previous algorithm [Sag88] that dealt with datalog programs without built-in predicates or negations.

As shown in [Sag88], uniform containment (and equivalence) can be given model-theoretic characterization, namely, the uniform containment $\mathcal{P}_2 \subseteq^u \mathcal{P}_1$ holds if and only if $M(\mathcal{P}_1) \subseteq M(\mathcal{P}_2)$, where $M(\mathcal{P}_i)$ denotes the set of all models of $\mathcal{P}_i$. We note that $M(\mathcal{P}_1) \subseteq M(\mathcal{P}_2)$ holds if and only if $M(\mathcal{P}_1) \subseteq M(r)$ for every rule $r \in \mathcal{P}_2$, since a database D is a model of P_2 if and only if it is a model of every rule $r \in P_2$. Our algorithms will decide whether $M(\mathcal{P}_1) \subseteq M(\mathcal{P}_2)$ by checking whether $M(\mathcal{P}_1) \subseteq M(r)$ for every $r \in \mathcal{P}_2$. We first discuss programs with only built-in predicates.

4.1   Uniform Containment with Built-in Predicates

When the programs have no interpreted predicates, the following algorithm (from [Sag88]) will decide whether a given rule r is uniformly contained in a program $\mathcal{P}$. Given a rule r of the form

$$p \ :- \ q_1, \ \ldots, \ q_n.$$

where p is the head of the rule and $q_1, \ldots, q_n$ are its subgoals, we use a substitution θ that maps every variable in the body of r to a distinct symbol that does not appear in $\mathcal{P}$ or r. We then apply the program $\mathcal{P}$ to the atoms $q_1\theta, \ldots, q_n\theta$. In [Sag88] it is shown that the program $\mathcal{P}$ generates $p\theta$ from $q_1\theta, \ldots, q_n\theta$ if and only if $M(\mathcal{P}) \subseteq M(r)$.

However, there is a problem in applying this algorithm to programs with interpreted predicates. First, the constants used in the input to $\mathcal{P}$, i.e., those that appear in $q_1\theta, \ldots, q_n\theta$, are arbitrary, and therefore, order relations are not defined on them. Consequently, the interpreted subgoals in the rules (that may involve $<, \leq$, etc.) can not be evaluated. Moreover, some of the derivations of $p\theta$ by $\mathcal{P}$ depend on the symbols satisfying the interpreted constraints, and so these cannot be discarded.

We address this problem by associating a constraint with every fact involved in the evaluation of $\mathcal{P}$. The constraints for a given fact f represent the conditions on $q_1\theta, \ldots, q_n\theta$ under which f is derivable. We manipulate these constraints as we evaluate $\mathcal{P}$. Formally, let r be the rule:

$$p \quad :- \quad q_1, \ \ldots, \ q_n, \ c_r. \tag{4.3}$$

We denote the set of variables in r by Y. The subgoal c_r is the conjunction of the subgoals of interpreted predicates in r. We assume that all subgoals in r have distinct variables in every argument position. Note that this requirement can always be fulfilled by introducing appropriate subgoals in rules using the $=$ predicate. As in the original algorithm, we define a mapping θ that maps each variable in r to a distinct symbol not appearing in $\mathcal{P}$ or r. Instead of evaluating $\mathcal{P}$ with the ground atoms $q_1\theta, \ldots, q_n\theta$, we evaluate $\mathcal{P}$ with facts that are pairs of the form (q, c), where q is ground atom and c is a constraint on the symbols in $Y\theta$. The input to $\mathcal{P}$ will be the pairs $(q_i\theta, c_r\theta)$, for $i = 1, 2, \ldots, n$.

An application of a rule $h :- g_1, \ldots, g_l, c$ proceeds as follows. Let $(a_1, c^1), \ldots, (a_l, c^l)$ be pairs generated previously, such that there is a substitution τ for which $g_i\tau = a_i$ $(1 \leq i \leq l)$. Let c_h be the conjunction $c^1 \wedge \ldots \wedge c^l \wedge c\tau$. If c_h is satisfiable, we derive the pair $(h\tau, c_h)$. In words, the constraint of the new fact generated is the conjunction of the constraints on the facts used in the derivation and the constraints of the rule that was applied in that derivation. We apply the rules of $\mathcal{P}$ until no new pairs are generated. Note that there are only a finite number of possible constraints for the generated facts and, therefore, the bottom-up evaluation must terminate.

Finally, let $(p\theta, c_1), \ldots, (p\theta, c_m)$ be all the pairs generated for $p\theta$ in the evaluation of $\mathcal{P}$; recall that p is the head of Rule (4.3) and θ is the substitution used to convert the variables of that rule to new symbols. The containment $M(\mathcal{P}) \subseteq M(r)$ holds if and only if $c_r \models c_1 \vee \ldots \vee c_m$, where c_r is the conjunction of interpreted predicates from the body of Rule (4.3).

Example 4.1: Let $\mathcal{P}_1$ be the program:

$$r_1: \quad p(X,Y) \quad :- \quad e(X,Z), \; p(Z,Y).$$
$$r_2: \quad q(X,Y) \quad :- \quad e(X,Y).$$

Let $\mathcal{P}_2$ be the program:

$$s_1: \quad p(X,Y) \quad :- \quad p(X,Z), \; p(Z,Y).$$
$$s_2: \quad p(X,Y) \quad :- \quad e(X,Y), \; X \leq Y.$$
$$s_3: \quad q(X,Y) \quad :- \quad e(X,Y), \; Y \leq X.$$
$$s_4: \quad q(X,Y) \quad :- \quad p(X,Y).$$

For a variable X of r, we denote the constant $X\theta$ by x_0. *True* denotes the constraint satisfied by all tuples. To check the uniform containment of r_1, the input to $\mathcal{P}_2$ would be $(e(x_0, z_0), \; True)$ and $(p(z_0, y_0), \; True)$. Rule s_2 will derive $(p(x_0, z_0), \; x_0 \leq z_0)$ and rule s_1 will then derive $(p(x_0, y_0), \; x_0 \leq z_0)$. Since $p(x_0, y_0)$ was only generated under the constraint $x_0 \leq z_0$, we say that rule r_1 is not uniformly contained in $\mathcal{P}_2$.

To check the uniform containment of rule r_2, we begin with $(e(x_0, y_0), \; True)$. Rule s_3 will then derive $(q(x_0, y_0), \; y_0 \leq x_0)$. Rule s_2 will derive $(p(x_0, y_0), \; x_0 \leq y_0)$ and rule s_4 will use that to derive $(q(x_0, y_0), \; x_0 \leq y_0)$. Since $q(x_0, y_0)$ was derived for both possible orderings of x_0 and y_0, rule r_2 is uniformly contained in $\mathcal{P}_2$. $\square$

The correctness of the algorithm is established by the following theorem.

Theorem 4.2: $M(\mathcal{P}) \subseteq M(r) \Longleftrightarrow c_r \models c_1 \vee \ldots \vee c_m.$

The theorem is proved by showing the following. Let r be the rule $p :- q_1, \ldots, q_m, c_r$ and Y be the variables appearing in r. If $Y\pi$ is a valid instantiation of the rule r that satisfies c_r, then $p\pi$ is derivable from the database containing the atoms $q_1\pi, \ldots, q_n\pi$ and the program $\mathcal{P}$ if and only if $Y\pi$ satisfies one of $c_1, \ldots, c_m$.

Our bottom-up evaluation of a program with a database containing facts tha are pairs is reminiscent of the procedure used by Kanellakis et al. [KKR90]. In their procedure, an EDB fact may be a generalized tuple specified in the form of a constraint on the arguments of its predicate. However, there is a key difference between the two methods. In [KKR90], every tuple is a constraint *only* on the arguments of the predicate involved. In our procedure, the constraint appearing in a pair is a constraint on all the constants that appear in the database, i.e., all the constants of $Y\theta$, where Y is the set of variables of rule r. Thus, the constraint of a pair may have constants that do not appear in the atom of that pair. The following example illustrates why this difference between the methods is important for detecting uniform containment.

Example 4.3: Consider rules r and s, and let $\mathcal{P}$ consist of rule s.

$$r: \quad p(X,Y) \quad :- \quad q_1(X,Y), \; q_2(U,V).$$
$$s: \quad p(X,Y) \quad :- \quad q_1(X,Y), \; q_2(U,V), \; U \leq V.$$

To show $M(\mathcal{P}) \subseteq M(r)$, we begin with the pairs $(q_1(x_0, y_0),\ True)$ and $(q_2(u_0, v_0),\ True)$, and apply s. If we use the procedure of [KKR90], the result is the pair $(p(x_0, y_0),\ True)$, which has no recording of the fact that its derivation required that $u_0 \leq v_0$. Consequently, we will conclude erroneously that $M(\mathcal{P}) \subseteq M(r)$ holds. In contrast, when our procedure applies rule s to the pairs $(q_1(x_0, y_0),\ True)$ and $(q_2(u_0, v_0),\ True)$, the result is the pair $(p(x_0, y_0),\ u_0 \leq v_0)$, making it clear that s does not contain r, because $True \not\models u_0 \leq v_0$. $\square$

The complexity of the algorithm depends on the number of pairs generated during the evaluation of $\mathcal{P}$. In the worst case, it may be exponential in the number of variables of r. A key component in the efficiency of the algorithm is the complexity of checking whether $c_r \models c_1 \vee \ldots \vee c_m$ holds. In [Lev93] we describe how to reduce this problem to a linear programming problem. The result is an algorithm that decides the entailment in time that is polynomial in the size of the disjunction and exponential in the number of $\neq$'s that appear in $c_r, c_1, \ldots, c_m$.

An interesting special case is containment of conjunctive queries with built-in predicates. Klug [Klu88] showed that if all constraints are left-semiinterval or all constraints are right-semiinterval, then containment of conjunctive queries can be decided by finding a homomorphism from one query to the other. For general conjunctive queries, he pointed out that it could be done by finding a homomorphism for every possible ordering of the variables and constants in the queries (recently, van der Meyden [vdM92] has shown that the containment problem of conjunctive queries with order constraints is Π_2^p-complete). In our algorithm, the complexity depends only on the number of orderings that are actually generated during the evaluation of $\mathcal{P}$. More precisely, our algorithm generates partial rather than complete orderings of the variables and constants in the queries. Essentially, it lumps together complete orderings that need not be distinguished from each other in order to test containment. Therefore, our algorithm is likely to be better in practice, albeit not in the worst case (of course, our algorithm also applies to more than just conjunctive queries).

Beyond Uniform Containment

For testing uniform containment of $\mathcal{P}_1$ in $\mathcal{P}_2$, it is enough to check the containment separately for each rule of $\mathcal{P}_1$. Consequently, uniform containment completely ignores possible interactions between the rules, interactions that may imply containment of $\mathcal{P}_1$ in $\mathcal{P}_2$. Consider the following example.

Example 4.4: Consider the following programs whose query predicate is p. Let $\mathcal{P}_1$ be:

$$r_1: \quad p(X) \quad :- \quad q(X),\ X < 5.$$
$$r_2: \quad q(X) \quad :- \quad e(X),\ X > 0.$$

And let $\mathcal{P}_2$ be the program:

$$r_3: \quad p(X) \quad :- \quad q(X),\ X < 6,\ X > 0.$$
$$r_4: \quad q(X) \quad :- \quad e(X),\ X > 0.$$

The program $\mathcal{P}_1$ is contained in $\mathcal{P}_2$, because whenever $0 < X < 5$, the atom $p(X)$ will be derived from $\mathcal{P}_2$ if $e(X)$ is in the database. However, r_1 is not uniformly contained in $\mathcal{P}_2$ (and, therefore, $\mathcal{P}_1 \not\subseteq^u \mathcal{P}_2$). For example, the model consisting of $\{q(-1), e(-1), \neg p(-1)\}$ is a model of $\mathcal{P}_2$ but not a model of $\mathcal{P}_1$. $\square$

The weakness of uniform containment stems from the fact that it considers all models while for proving (ordinary) containment it is sufficient to consider just minimal models.[3] We may, however, try to transform

---

[3]In our formalism, a set of relations for the EDB and IDB predicates is a minimal model if the IDB part is a minimal model once the EDB facts are added to the program as rules with empty bodies.

$\mathcal{P}_1$ into an equivalent program $\mathcal{P}'$ with a larger set of models (but, of course, the same set of minimal models, since equivalence must be preserved). One way of doing it is by propagating constraints from one rule to another. The query tree of [LS92] is a tool for doing just that; for the type of constraints considered in this chapter the propagation is complete, i.e., each rule ends up having the tightest possible constraint among its variables. In our example, the result of constraint propagation is the following program $\mathcal{P}'$.

$$r'_1: \quad p(X) \quad :- \quad q(X),\ X < 5,\ X > 0.$$
$$r'_2: \quad q(X) \quad :- \quad e(X),\ X > 0.$$

Now we can show that $\mathcal{P}' \subseteq^u \mathcal{P}_2$, and since $\mathcal{P}_1 \equiv \mathcal{P}'$, it follows that $\mathcal{P}_1 \subseteq^u \mathcal{P}_2$.

4.2 Uniform Equivalence with Stratified Negation

In this section, we describe how to test uniform equivalence of datalog programs with safe, stratified negation. We begin with the case of stratified programs with neither constants nor built-in predicates. By definition, two programs P_1 and P_2 are uniformly equivalent, denoted $P_1 \equiv^u P_2$, if for every database D (that may have both EDB and IDB facts), $P_1(D) = P_2(D)$. Note that applying a stratified program to a database that may also have IDB facts is done stratum by stratum, as in the usual case; in other words, $P(D)$ is the perfect model of the program P and the database D (cf. [Ull89]).

Suppose that that P_1 and P_2 are not uniformly equivalent. Hence, there is a database D_0 such that $P_1(D_0) \neq P_2(D_0)$; D_0 is called a *counterexample*. We may assume that $P_1(D_0) \not\subseteq P_2(D_0)$ (the case $P_2(D_0) \not\subseteq P_1(D_0)$ is handled similarly).

We assume that both P_1 and P_2 have the same set of EDB predicates and the same set of IDB predicates, and moreover, there is a partition of the predicates into strata that is a stratification for both P_1 and P_2. In particular, we assume that the lowest stratum consists of just the EDB predicates and we refer to it as the zeroth stratum. We denote by P_1^i the program consisting of those rules of P_1 with head predicates that belong to the first i strata; similarly for P_2^i. Note that P_1^0 is an empty program (i.e., it has no rules). By definition, $P_1^0(D) = D$ for every database D; similarly for P_2^0.

We now assume that for some given i, $P_1^i \equiv^u P_2^i$ and we will show how to test whether $P_1^{i+1} \equiv^u P_2^{i+1}$. The algorithm is based on the following two lemmas.

Lemma 4.5: *Suppose that there is an i, such that $P_1^i \equiv^u P_2^i$. If there is a counterexample database D_0, such that $P_1^{i+1}(D_0) \not\subseteq P_2^{i+1}(D_0)$, then there is some rule r of P_1^{i+1} with a head predicate from stratum $i+1$ and a database D, such that*

1. *D is a model of P_2^{i+1} but not a model of r.*

2. *The number of distinct constants in D is no more than the number of distinct variables in r.*

Proof: Let $D' = P_2^i(D_0)$; note that $D' = P_2^i(D')$. By the assumption in the lemma, $P_1^i(D_0) = P_2^i(D_0)$ and, hence, D' is also a counterexample, i.e., $P_1^{i+1}(D') \not\subseteq P_2^{i+1}(D')$. Now let $\bar{D} = P_2^{i+1}(D')$. Observe that $\bar{D}$ and D' have the same set of facts for predicates of the first i strata, since $D' = P_2^i(D')$. In addition, observe that $D' \subseteq \bar{D}$. These observations imply that $P_1^{i+1}(D') \subseteq P_1^{i+1}(\bar{D})$. Thus, $P_1^{i+1}(\bar{D}) \not\subseteq P_2^{i+1}(\bar{D})$, because $P_1^{i+1}(D') \not\subseteq P_2^{i+1}(D')$ and $P_2^{i+1}(D') = P_2^{i+1}(\bar{D})$.

So, we have shown that $P_1^{i+1}(\bar{D}) \not\subseteq P_2^{i+1}(\bar{D})$ and $\bar{D}$ is a model of P_2^{i+1}. Therefore, there is a rule r in P_1^{i+1} of the form

$$h :- q_1, \ldots, q_m, \neg s_1, \ldots, \neg s_l$$

and a substitution θ, such that

- the predicate of h is from stratum $i + 1$,

- θ is a mapping from the variables of r to constants,

- $q_i\theta \in \bar{D}$ $(1 \leq i \leq m)$,

- $s_j\theta \notin \bar{D}$ $(1 \leq j \leq l)$, and

- $h\theta \notin \bar{D}$.

The above and the fact $\bar{D} = P_2^{i+1}(\bar{D})$ imply that the database $\bar{D}$ is a model of P_2^{i+1} but not of r^{i+1}.

Let D be the database consisting of facts from $\bar{D}$ that have only constants from $r\theta$. Database D is also a model of P_2^{i+1}. In proof, suppose that D is not a model of P_2^{i+1}. Thus, there is a rule $\bar{r}$ of P_2^{i+1} and a substitution τ, such that

1. the head $\bar{h}$ of $\bar{r}$ satisfies $\bar{h}\tau \notin D$,

2. every positive subgoal $\bar{q}$ of $\bar{r}$ satisfies $\bar{q}\tau \in D$, and

3. every negative subgoal $\bar{s}$ of $\bar{r}$ satisfies $\bar{s}\tau \notin D$.

By the definition of D, if g is a ground fact having only constants from D, then $g \in D$ if and only if $g \in \bar{D}$; moreover, for every negative subgoal $\bar{s}$, the constants appearing in $\bar{s}\tau$ are all from D, since rules are safe (cf. [Ull89]). Therefore, items (1)–(3) hold even if we replace D with $\bar{D}$, and so it follows that $\bar{D}$ is not a model of $\bar{r}$—a contradiction, since $\bar{D}$ is a model of P_2^{i+1} and $\bar{r}$ is a rule of P_2^{i+1}. Thus, we have shown that D is a model of P_2^{i+1}. Furthermore, items (1)–(3) above imply that D is not a model of r. So, the lemma is proved. $\square$

Lemma 4.6: *Suppose that $P_1^i \equiv^u P_2^i$. Moreover, suppose that there is a database D that is a model of P_2^{i+1} and is not a model of some rule r of P_1^{i+1} having a head predicate from stratum $i + 1$. Then $P_1(D) \not\subseteq P_2(D)$ and, hence, $P_1 \not\equiv^u P_2$.*

Proof: From the assumptions in the lemma, it follows that rule r can be applied to D to generate a new fact g that is not already in D. Note that $g \notin P_2(D)$, since $P_2^{i+1}(D) = D$ and strata higher than $i + 1$ do not include facts with the same predicate as that of g. If we show that rule r can still generate g even when P_1 is applied to D, it would follow that $g \in P_1(D)$, and hence, $P_1(D) \not\subseteq P_2(D)$. To show that, recall that $P_1^i \equiv^u P_2^i$ and D is a model of P_2^{i+1}; therefore, D is also a model of P_1^i. Thus, rule r can still generate g during the application of P_1 to D, since nothing is generated by rules of lower strata. $\square$

The algorithm of Figure 2 tests whether $P_1 \equiv^u P_2$; its correctness follows from the above two lemmas and the following proposition.

Proposition 4.7: $P_1(D) \not\equiv P_2(D)$ *if and only if there is some i and a database D, such that either $P_1^i(D) \not\subseteq P_2^i(D)$ or $P_2^i(D) \not\subseteq P_1^i(D)$.*

```
procedure check(P₁, P₂);
begin
    for every rule r of P₁ do
    begin
        Let S be a set of v distinct constants,
        where v is the number of variables in r;
        for every database D that includes
            only constants from S do
            if D is a model of P₂ but not of r
            then return false;
    end;
    return true;
end;
begin /* main procedure */
    for i := 1 to max-stratum do
        if not check(P₁ⁱ, P₂ⁱ) or not check(P₂ⁱ, P₁ⁱ)
        then return P₁ ≢ᵘ P₂;
    return P₁ ≡ᵘ P₂;
end.
```

Figure 2   An algorithm for testing $P_1 \equiv^u P_2$.

Note that in the algorithm, it does not matter what are the constants in S as long as their number is equal to the number of distinct variables in the given rule r. Also, if two databases over constants from S are isomorphic, it is sufficient to consider just one of them.

Example 4.8: Let P_1 consist of the rules:

$$
\begin{array}{llll}
r_1: & Iown(X,Y) & :- & own(X,Y). \\
r_2: & Iown(X,Y) & :- & lives(X,Z), \ inHouse(Z,Y). \\
r_3: & Iown(X,U) & :- & own(X,Z), \ lives(Y,Z), \\
 & & & Iown(Y,U). \\
r_4: & buys(X,Y) & :- & likes(X,Y), \ \neg Iown(X,Y).
\end{array}
$$

Let P_2 consist of the rules r_1, r_4 and the rule:

$$
r_5: \quad Iown(X,Y) \quad :- \quad Own(X,Z), \ inHouse(Z,Y).
$$

The EDB relation *own* describes an ownership relationship between persons and objects. The IDB relation *Iown* represents a landlord's perspective of the ownership relation. The programs P_1 and P_2 are not uniformly equivalent. Specifically, consider the database D_0:

$$\{likes(a,o), \ lives(b,h), \ own(b,o), \ own(a,h)\}$$

Rule r_4 (of P_2) and program P_1 satisfy $r_4(D_0) \not\subseteq P_1(D_0)$, since $Iown(a,o) \notin r_4(D_0)$ and therefore $buys(a,o) \in r_4(D_0)$, while the converse is true for $P_1(D_0)$. □

To extend the algorithm to programs with built-in predicates (and constants), we need to check for the possibility that a database may become a counterexample by analyzing the built-in constraints. One conceptually simple (albeit not the most efficient) way of doing it is by using the algorithm of Figure 2, but with the following modifications. Let C be the set of constants appearing in either P_1 or P_2. Instead of considering every database over constants from S, we should consider every database over constants from $S \cup C$. Moreover, for each database we should consider every total order on the constants of the database, such that the order is consistent with any order that may implicitly be defined on C (e.g., if C is a set of integers, then presumably the usual order on integers should apply to C). For each such database and total order defined on its constants, we should apply the given test of the *check* procedure; that is, we should test whether D is a model of P_2 but not of r. The rest of the algorithm is the same as earlier. Thus, we get the following result; for the full details of the proof and for a more efficient algorithm than the one described above see [Lev93].

Theorem 4.9: *Uniform equivalence for datalog programs with safe, stratified negation and built-in predicates is decidable.*

5   Concluding Remarks

We have presented an analysis of the notion of independence and described algorithms for detecting independence of queries from updates. Our formulation of the problem gives us flexibility in the analysis. For example, we can distinguish between the case in which an updates is specified intensionally and the actual tuples to be inserted are computed at update time, and the case in which the set of tuples to be inserted is given a priori. Our framework and algorithms can also be extended to incorporate integrity constraints, as in Elkan [Elk90].

Posing the problem of independence as a problem of equivalence suggests that further algorithms for independence can be found by trying to identify additional sufficient conditions for equivalence. One possibility mentioned in this chapter involves program transformations that increase the set of models but preserve the set of minimal models. Consequently, these transformations increase the possibility of detecting equivalence by an algorithm for uniform equivalence. More powerful transformations can be obtained by considering, for example, only minimal derivations [LS92].

In this chapter, we have considered the problem of detecting independence assuming we have no knowledge of the EDB relations. An important problem, investigated in [BCL89] and [GW93] is detecting independence when some of the EDB relations are known and can be inspected efficiently. Combining our techniques with the ones described in those papers is an intersting area for future research.

6   Acknowledgments

The authors thank Ashish Gupta for many helpful discussions and Jose Blakeley for very useful comments regarding the presentation of the material.

PART IV

MATERIALIZED VIEWS AND OLAP

Views and On Line Analytical Processing

This part of the book contains three chapters on OLAP and views.

OLAP or On Line Analytical Processing has become a hotly researched and developed area to enable decision support applications. OLAP is primarily based on the need for visualizing different aggregations on the same base data. For example, sales information from a store can be aggregated in different ways to give an analyst views like "total sales for a month" and "average sales of each item in each month of 1991." OLAP applications are typically run over warehoused data and require real time response to analysts who ask dynamic queries that. Views play a very important role in such applications because of many reasons: (1) Warehouses are very large and computing results on the fly may be slow - making materialized views attractive. (2) The queries do not require exact answers and tolerate some "out-datedness" - enabling the use of views that can be periodically updated. (3) The queries asked by analysts are frequently interrelated making possible the reuse of intermediate queries that can be materialized - for example partial aggregates are used for further aggregation. (4) The result of a query may need substantial off-line preprocessing for viewing in a non-tabular visualization tool - views enable this preprocessing. (5) Differential computation across time and space is very important to study trends - views provide snapshots at different points that can then be compared. This part includes three chapters that consider three of the steps involved in using views for OLAP. [HRU96] discusses algorithms to identify a set of views to maintain, [AAD+96a] describes how to compute a set of aggregate views, and [MQM97] studies how to incrementally maintain the set. The problem of how to use precomputed views to answer queries is discussed in the previous parts of this book and in [GHQ95, SDJL96].

The first chapter [HRU96] considers the data cube and models it as a lattice of view that captures the dependencies among the views. In this framework, the chapter describes how to identify the views to materialize when the optimization criterion is the response time. The optimization criterion can alternatively be the space available for storing the views, or the number of views that may be materialized. The chapter gives a greedy algorithm with a bounded distance from the optimal solution.

[AAD+96a] discusses how to compute a data cube where all the different nodes in the lattice may not necessarily need be materialized. The chapter considers sort and hash based grouping algorithms along with a variety of optimizationss like combining common operations across multiple group-bys, caching intermediate results, using aggregates "lower" in the lattice to compute further aggregations in the lattice, and pipelining. The different strategies are evaluated on both synthetic and emperical data to determine the factors that determine which strategy does well - for example available size of memory, the sparsity of the data, the reduction obtained by any grouping attribute, the number of scans over the base data.

[MQM97] considers the next step in the problem - that is having materialized a set of views how to efficiently maintain them.

IMPLEMENTING DATA CUBES EFFICIENTLY

Venky Harinarayan, Anand Rajaraman, Jeffrey D. Ullman

ABSTRACT

Decision support applications involve complex queries on very large databases. Since response times should be small, query optimization is critical. Users typically view the data as multidimensional data cubes. Each cell of the data cube is a view consisting of an aggregation of interest, like total sales. The values of many of these cells are dependent on the values of other cells in the data cube. A common and powerful query optimization technique is to materialize some or all of these cells rather than compute them from raw data each time. Commercial systems differ mainly in their approach to materializing the data cube. In this chapter, we investigate the issue of which cells (views) to materialize when it is too expensive to materialize all views. A lattice framework is used to express dependencies among views. We then present greedy algorithms that work off this lattice and determine a good set of views to materialize. The greedy algorithm performs within a small constant factor of optimal under a variety of models. We then consider the most common case of the hypercube lattice and examine the choice of materialized views for hypercubes in detail, giving some good tradeoffs between the space used and the average time to answer a query.

1 Introduction

Decision support systems (DSS) are rapidly becoming a key to gaining competitive advantage for businesses. DSS allow businesses to get at data that is locked away in operational databases and turn that data into useful information. Many corporations have built or are building unified decision-support databases called *data warehouses* on which users can carry out their analysis.

While operational databases maintain state information, data warehouses typically maintain historical information. As a result, data warehouses tend to be very large and to grow over time. Users of DSS are typically interested in identifying trends rather than looking at individual records in isolation. Decision-support queries are thus much more complex than OLTP queries and make heavy use of aggregations.

The size of the data warehouse and the complexity of queries can cause queries to take very long to complete. This delay is unacceptable in most DSS environments, as it severely limits productivity. The usual requirement is query execution times of a few seconds or a few minutes at the most.

There are many ways to achieve such performance goals. Query optimizers and query evaluation techniques can be enhanced to handle aggregations better [CS94], [GHQ95], to use different indexing strategies like bit-mapped indexes and join indexes [OG95], and so on.

A commonly used technique is to materialize (precompute) frequently-asked queries. The data warehouse at the Mervyn's department-store chain, for instance, has a total of 2400 precomputed tables [Rad95] to improve query performance. Picking the right set of queries to materialize is a nontrivial task, since by materializing a query we may be able to answer other queries quickly. For example, we may want to materialize a query that is relatively infrequently asked if it helps us answer many other queries quickly. In this chapter, we present a framework and algorithms that enable us to pick a good set of queries to materialize. Our framework also lets us infer in what order these queries are to be materialized.

1.1   The Data Cube

Users of data warehouses work in a graphical environment and data are usually presented to them as a multidimensional "data cube" whose 2-D, 3-D, or even higher-dimensional sub cubes they explore trying to discover interesting information. The values in each cell of this data cube are some "measures" of interest. As an example consider the TPC-D decision-support benchmark.

EXAMPLE 1.1 The TPC-D benchmark models a business warehouse. Parts are bought from suppliers and then sold to customers at a sale price SP. The database has information about each such transaction over a period of 6 years.

There are three dimensions we are interested in: part, supplier, and customer. The "measure" of interest is the total sales: total sales. So for each cell (p, s, c) in this 3-D data cube, we store the total sales of part p that was bought from supplier s, and sold to customer c. We use the terms dimension and attribute interchangeably in this section. In the general case, a given dimension may have many attributes as we shall see in Section 2.

Users are also interested in consolidated sales: for example, what is the total sales of a given part p to a given customer c? [GBLP96] suggests adding an additional value "ALL" to the domain of each dimension to achieve this. In the question above we want the total sales of a given part p to a given customer c for "ALL" suppliers. The query is answered by looking up the value in cell (p, ALL, c).   ■

We use the TPC-D database of size 1GB as a running example throughout this chapter. For more details on this benchmark refer to [Raa95].

We have only discussed the presentation of the data set as a multi-dimensional data cube to the user. The following implementation alternatives are possible:

1. Physically materialize the whole data cube. This approach gives the best query response time. However, precomputing and storing every cell is not a feasible alternative for large data cubes, as the space consumed becomes excessive. It should be noted that the space consumed by the data cube is also a good indicator of the time it takes to create the data cube, which is important in many applications. The space consumed also impacts indexing and so adds to the overall cost.

2. Materialize nothing. In this case we need to go to the raw data and compute every cell on request. This approach punts the problem of quick query response to the database system where the raw data is stored. No extra space beyond that for the raw data is required.

3. Materialize only part of the data cube. We consider this approach in this chapter. In a data cube, the values of many cells are computable from those of other cells in the data cube. This dependency is similar to a spreadsheet where the value of cells can be expressed as a function of the values of other

cells. We call such cells "dependent" cells. For instance, in Example 1.1, we can compute the value of cell (p, ALL, c) as the sum of the values of cells of $(p, s_1, c), \ldots, (p, s_{N_{\texttt{supplier}}}, c)$, where $N_{\texttt{supplier}}$ is the number of suppliers. The more cells we materialize, the better query performance is. For large data cubes however, we may be able to materialize only a small fraction of the cells of the data cube, due to space and other constraints. It is thus important that we pick the right cells to materialize.

Any cell that has an "ALL" value as one of the components of its address is a dependent cell. The value of this cell is computable from those of other cells in the data cube. If a cell has no "ALL"s in its components, its value cannot be computed from those of other cells, and we must query the raw data to compute its value. The number of cells with "ALL" as one of their components is usually a large fraction of the total number of cells in the data cube. The problem of which dependent cells of to materialize, is a very real one. For example, in the TPC-D database (Example 1.1), seventy percent of all the cells in the data cube are dependent.

There is also the issue of where the materialized data cube is stored: in a relational system or a proprietary MDDB (multi-dimensional database) system. In this chapter, we assume that the data cube is stored in "summary" tables in a relational system. Sets of cells of the data cube are assigned to different tables.

The cells of the data cube are organized into different sets based on the positions of "ALL" in their addresses. Thus, for example, all cells whose addresses match the address (_,ALL,_) are placed in the same set. Here, "_" is a placeholder that matches any value but "ALL". Each of these sets corresponds to a different SQL query. The values in the set of cells (_,ALL,_) is output by the SQL query:

```
SELECT Part,Customer,SUM(SP) AS Sales
FROM R
GROUP BY Part,Customer;
```

Here, R refers to the raw-data relation. The queries corresponding to the different sets of cells, differ only in the GROUP-BY clause. In general, attributes with "ALL" values in the description of the set of cells, do not appear in the GROUP-BY clause of the SQL query above. For example, supplier has an "ALL" value in the set description (_,ALL,_). Hence it does not appear in the GROUP-BY clause of the SQL query. Since the SQL queries of the various sets of cells differ only in the grouping attributes, we use the grouping attributes to identify queries uniquely.

Deciding which sets of cells to materialize is equivalent to deciding which of the corresponding SQL queries (views) to materialize. In the rest of this chapter we thus work with views rather than with sets of cells.

1.2 Motivating Example

The TPC-D database we considered in Example 1.1 has 3 attributes: part, supplier, customer. We thus have 8 possible groupings of the attributes. We list all the queries (views) possible below with the number of rows in their result – "M" denotes million. Note again it suffices to only mention the attributes in the GROUP-BY clause of the view.

1. part, supplier, customer (6M rows)
2. part, customer (6M)
3. part, supplier (0.8M)
4. supplier, customer (6M)
5. part (0.2M)
6. supplier (0.01M)

```
7. customer (0.1M)
8. none (1)
```

none indicates that there are are no attributes in the GROUP-BY clause. Figure 1 shows these eight views organized as a lattice of the type we shall discuss in Section 2. In naming the views in this diagram, we use the abbreviation p for part, s for supplier, and c for customer.

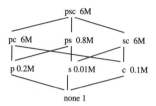

Figure 1   The eight TPC-D views

One possible user query is a request for an entire view. For example, the user may ask for the sales grouped by part. If we have materialized the view that groups only by part (view 5), we only need scan the view and output the answer. We can also answer this query using the view that groups by part and customer (view 2). In this case, since we have the total sales for each customer, for each part we need to sum the sales across all customers to get the result.

In this chapter we assume the cost of answering a query is proportional to the number of rows examined. Thus, the cost of finding the total sales grouped by part, if (view 5) is materialized, is the cost of processing 0.2 million rows (the size of this view). To answer the same query using the part, customer view we would need to process 6 million rows.

Another kind of user query would ask only for the sales for a single part, say "widgets." To answer this query, we still have to scan the entire view (or half on the average). Thus, the same comparison, 0.2M rows for view 5 versus 6M rows for view 2, would apply to this query. Note, in this chapter, we do not consider indexes on the views. We shall discuss the cost model in more detail in Section 3.

There are some interesting questions we can now ask:

1. How many views must we materialize to get reasonable performance?

2. Given that we have space S, what views do we materialize so that we minimize average query cost?

In this chapter, we provide algorithms that help us answer the above questions and provide near optimal results.

In the above example, a fully materialized data cube would have all the views materialized and thus have slightly more than 19 million rows.

Now let us see if we can do better. To avoid going to the raw data, we need to materialize the view grouping by part, supplier, and customer (view 1), since that view cannot be constructed from any of the other views. Now consider the view grouping by part and customer (view 2). Answering any query using this view will require us to process 6 million rows. The same query can always be answered using the view grouping by part, supplier, and customer, which again requires processing of 6 million rows. Thus there is no advantage to materializing the view grouping by part and customer. By similar reasoning, there is no advantage materializing the view grouping by supplier and customer (view 4). Thus we can get almost the same average query cost using only 7 million rows, an improvement of more than 60% in terms of space consumed and thus in the cost of creating the data cube.

Thus by cleverly choosing what parts of the data cube to materialize, we can reap dramatic benefits.

1.3 Related Work

Multi-dimensional data processing (also known as OLAP) has enjoyed spectacular growth of late. There are two basic implementation approaches that facilitate OLAP. The first approach is to eschew SQL and relational databases and to use proprietary multi-dimensional database (MDDB) systems and APIs for OLAP. So while the raw data is in relational data warehouses, the data cube is materialized in an MDDB. Users query the data cube, and the MDDB efficiently retrieves the value of a cell given its address. To allocate only space for those cells present in the raw data and not *every possible cell* of the data cube, a cell-address hashing scheme is used. Arbor's Essbase [Sof] and many other MDDBs are implemented this way. Note, this approach still materializes all the cells of the data cube present in raw data, which can be very large.

The other approach is to use relational database systems and let users directly query the raw data. The issue of query performance is attacked using smart indexes and other conventional relational query optimization strategies. There are many products like BusinessObjects and Microstrategy's DSS Agent that take this tack. However, MDDBs retain a significant performance advantage. Performance in relational database systems though can be improved dramatically by materializing parts of the data cube into summary tables.

The relational approach is very scalable and can handle very large data warehouses. MDDBs on the other hand have much better query performance, but are not very scalable. By materializing only selected parts of the data cube, we can improve performance in the relational database, and improve scalability in MDDBs. There are products in both the relational world [Gro95], and the MDDB world (Sinper's Spreadsheet Connector) that materialize only parts of the data cube. [Gro95] also appears to use a simple greedy algorithm, similar to that given in this chapter. We believe however that this chapter is the first to investigate this fundamental problem in such detail.

[GBLP96] generalizes the SQL GROUP-BY operator to a data cube operator. They introduce the notion of "ALL" that we mention. However, they claim the size of the entire data cube is not much larger than the size of the corresponding GROUP-BY. We believe differently.[1] As we saw in the TPC-D database, the data cube is usually much larger: more than three times larger than the corresponding GROUP-BY *psc*.

1.4 Chapter Organization

The chapter is organized as follows. In Section 2 we introduce the lattice framework to model dependency among views. We also show how the lattice framework models more complex groupings that involve arbitrary hierarchies of attributes. Then in Section 3, we present the query-cost model that we use in this chapter. Section 4 presents a general technique for producing near-optimal selections of materialized views for problems based on arbitrary lattices. In Section 5, we consider the important special case of a "hypercube" lattice, where the views are each associated with a set of attributes on which grouping occurs. The running example of Section 1.2 is such a hypercube.

---

[1] The analysis in [GBLP96], assumes that every possible cell of the data cube exists. However, in many cases, data cubes are sparse: only a small fraction of all possible cells are present. In such cases, the size of the data cube can be much larger than the corresponding GROUP-BY. In fact, the sparser the data cube, the larger is the ratio of the size of the data cube to the size of the corresponding GROUP-BY.

2   The Lattice Framework

In this section we develop the notation for describing when one data-cube query can be answered using the results of another. We denote a view or a query (which is the same thing) by giving its grouping attributes inside parenthesis. For example the query with grouping attributes `part` and `customer` is denoted by (`part`, `customer`). In Section 1.2 we saw that views defined by supersets can be used to answer queries involving subsets.

2.1   The Dependence Relation on Queries

We may generalize the observations of Section 1.2 as follows. Consider two queries Q_1 and Q_2. We say $Q1 \preceq Q2$ if $Q1$ can be answered using only the results of Q_2. We then say that Q_1 is *dependent* on Q_2. For example, in Section 1.2, the query (`part`), can be answered using only the results of the query (`part`, `customer`). Thus (`part`) $\preceq$ (`part`, `customer`). There are certain queries that are not comparable with each other using the $\preceq$ operator. For example: (`part`) $\npreceq$ (`customer`) and (`customer`) $\npreceq$ (`part`).

The $\preceq$ operator imposes a partial ordering on the queries. We shall talk about the views of a data-cube problem as forming a lattice. In order to be a lattice, any two elements (views or queries) must have a least upper bound and a greatest lower bound according to the $\preceq$ ordering. However, in practice, we only need the assumptions that $\preceq$ is a partial order, and that there is a *top* element, a view upon which every view is dependent.

2.2   Lattice Notation

We denote a lattice with set of elements (queries or views in this chapter) L and dependence relation $\preceq$ by $\langle L, \preceq \rangle$. For elements a, b of the lattice, b is an *ancestor* of a, if and only if $a \preceq b$. It is common to represent a lattice by a *lattice diagram*, a graph in which the lattice elements are nodes, and there is a path downward from a to b if and only if $a \preceq b$. The hypercube of Fig. 1 is the lattice diagram of the set of views discussed in Section 1.2.

2.3   Hierarchies

In most real-life applications, dimensions of a data cube consist of more than one attribute, and the dimensions are organized as hierarchies of these attributes. A simple example is organizing the time dimension into the hierarchy: `day`, `month`, and `year`. Hierarchies are very important, as they underlie two very commonly used querying operations: "drill-down" and "roll-up." Drill-down is the process of viewing data at progressively more detailed levels. For example, a user drills down by first looking at the total sales per year and then total sales per month and finally, sales on a given day. Roll-up is just the opposite: it is the process of viewing data in progressively less detail. In roll-up, a user starts with total sales on a given day, then looks at the total sales in that month and finally the total sales in that year.

In the presence of hierarchies, the dependency lattice $\langle L, \preceq \rangle$ is more complex than a hypercube lattice. For example, consider a query that groups on the time dimension and no other. When we use the time hierarchy given earlier, we have the following three queries possible: (`day`), (`month`), (`year`), each of which groups at a different granularity of the time dimension. Further, (`year`) $\preceq$ (`month`) $\preceq$ (`day`). In other words, if we have total sales grouped by `month`, for example, we can use the results to compute the total sales grouped by `year`. Hierarchies introduce query dependencies that we must account for when determining what queries to materialize.

To make things more complex, hierarchies often are not total orders but partial orders on the attributes that make up a dimension. Consider the time dimension with the hierarchy day, week, month, and year. Since months and years cannot be divided evenly into weeks, if we do the grouping by week we cannot determine the grouping by month or year. In other words: $(\text{month}) \npreceq (\text{week})$, $(\text{week}) \npreceq (\text{month})$, and similarly for week and year. When we include the none view corresponding to no time grouping at all, we get the lattice for the time dimension shown in the diagram of Fig. 2.

Figure 2 Hierarchy of time attributes

2.4   Composite Lattices for Multiple, Hierarchical Dimensions

We are faced with query dependencies of two types: query dependencies caused by the interaction of the different dimensions with one another (the example in Section 1.2 and the corresponding lattice in Fig. 1 is an example of this sort of dependency) and query dependencies within a dimension caused by attribute hierarchies.

If we are allowed to create views that independently group by any or no member of the hierarchy for each of n dimensions, then we can represent each view by an n-tuple $(a_1, a_2, \ldots, a_n)$, where each a_i is a point in the hierarchy for the ith dimension. This lattice is called the *direct product* of the dimensional lattices. We directly get a $\preceq$ operator for these views by the rule

$$(a_1, a_2, \ldots, a_n) \preceq (b_1, b_2, \ldots, b_n) \text{ if and only if } a_i \preceq b_i \text{ for all } i$$

We illustrate the building of this direct-product lattice in the presence of hierarchies using an example based on the TPC-D benchmark.

EXAMPLE 2.1 In Example 1.1, we mentioned the TPC-D benchmark database. In this example we focus further on two dimensions: part and customer. Each of these dimensions is organized into hierarchies. The dimensional lattices for the dimension queries are given in Fig. 3. These dimension lattices have already been modified to include the attribute (none) as the lowest element.

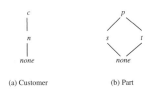

Figure 3 Hierarchies for the customer and part dimensions

The customer dimension is organized into the following hierarchy. We can group by individual customers c. Customers could also be grouped more coarsely based on their nation n. The coarsest level of grouping is none at all — **none**. For the **part** dimension, individual parts p may be grouped based on their size s or based on their type t. Note neither of s and t is $\preceq$ the other. The direct-product lattice is shown in Fig. 4. Note, when a dimension's value is **none** in a query, we do not specify the dimension in the query. Thus for example, $(s,\mathbf{none})$ is written as (s). ∎

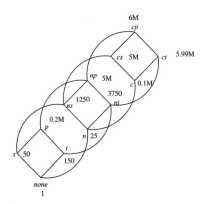

Figure 4 Combining two hierarchical dimensions

The lattice framework, we present and advocate in this chapter, is advantageous for several reasons:

1. It provides a clean framework to reason with dimensional hierarchies, since hierarchies are themselves lattices. As can be seen in Fig. 4, the direct-product lattice is not always a hypercube when hierarchies are not simple.

2. We can model the common queries asked by users better using a lattice framework. Users usually do not jump between unconnected elements in this lattice, they move along the edges of the lattice. In fact, drill-down is going up (going from a lower to higher level) a path in this lattice, while roll-up is going down a path.

3. The lattice approach also tells us in what order to materialize the views. By using views that have already been materialized to materialize other views, we can reduce access to the raw data and so decrease the total materialization time. A simple descending-order topological sort on the $\preceq$ operator gives the required order of materialization. The details are in [HRU95].

3   The Cost Model

In this section, we review and justify our assumptions about the "linear cost model," in which the time to answer a query is taken to be equal to the space occupied by the view from which the query is answered. We then consider some points about estimating sizes of views without materializing them and give some experimental validation of the linear cost model.

3.1   The Linear Cost Model

Let $\langle L, \preceq \rangle$ be a lattice of queries (views). To answer a query Q we choose an ancestor of Q, say Q_A, that has been materialized. We thus need to process the table corresponding to Q_A to answer Q. The cost of answering Q is a function of the size of the table for Q_A. In this chapter, we choose the simplest cost-model:

- The cost of answering Q is the number of rows present in the table for that query Q_A used to construct Q.

As we discussed in Section 1.2, not all queries ask for an entire view, such as a request for the sales of all parts. It is at least as likely that the user would like to see sales for a particular part or for a few parts. If we have the appropriate index structure, and the view (part) is materialized, then we can get our answer in $O(1)$ time. If there is not an appropriate index structure, then we would have to search the entire (part) view, and the query for a single part takes almost as long as producing the entire view.

If, for example, we need to answer a query about a single part from some ancestor view such as (part, supplier) we need to examine the entire view. It can be seen that a single scan of the view is sufficient to get the total sales of a particular part. On the other hand, if we wish to find the total sales for each part from the ancestor view (part, supplier), we need to do an aggregation over this view. We can use either hashing or sorting (with early aggregation) [Gra93] to do this aggregation. The cost of doing the aggregation is a function of the amount of memory available and the ratio of the number of rows in the input to that in the output. In the best case, a single pass of the input is sufficient (for example, when the hash table fits in main memory). In practice, it has been observed that most aggregations take between one and two passes of the input data.

While the actual cost of queries that ask for single cells, or small numbers of cells, rather than a complete view, is thus complex, we feel it is appropriate to make an assumption of uniformity. We provide a rationale for this assumption in [HRU95]. Thus:

- We assume that all queries are identical to some element (view) in the given lattice.

Clearly there are other factors, not considered here, that influence query cost. Among them are the clustering of the materialized views on some attribute, and the indexes that may be present. More complicated cost models are certainly possible, but we believe the cost model we pick, being both simple and realistic, enables us to design and analyze powerful algorithms. Moreover, our analysis of the algorithms we develop in Sections 4 and 5 reflects their performance under other cost models as well as under the model we use here. [GHRU96] investigates a more detailed model incorporating indexes.

3.2 Experimental Examination of the Linear Cost Model

An experimental validation of our cost model is shown in Fig. 5. On the TPC-D data, we asked for the total sales for a single supplier, using views of four different granularities. We find an almost linear relationship between size and running time of the query. This linear relationship can be expressed by the formula: $T = m * S + c$. Here T is the running time of the query on a view of size S, c gives the fixed cost (the overhead of running this query on a view of negligible size), and m is the ratio of the query time to the size of the view, after accounting for the fixed cost. As can be seen in Fig. 5 this ratio is almost the same for the different views.

3.3 Determining View Sizes

Our algorithms require knowledge of the number of rows present in each view. There are many ways of estimating the sizes of the views without materializing all the views. One commonly used approach is to run our algorithms on a statistically representative but small subset of the raw data. In such a case, we can get the sizes of the views by actually materializing the views. We use this subset of raw data to determine which views we want to materialize.

Source	Size	Time	Ratio
From cell itself	1	2.07	-
From view s	10,000	2.38	.000031
From view ps	0.8M	20.77	.000023
From view psc	6M	226.23	.000037

Figure 5   Query response time and view size

We can use sampling and analytical methods to compute the sizes of the different views if we only materialize the largest element v_l in the lattice (the view that groups by the largest attribute in each dimension). For a view, if we know that the grouping attributes are statistically independent, we can estimate the size of the view analytically, given the size of v_l. Otherwise we can sample v_l (or the raw data) to estimate the size of the other views. The size of a given view is the number of distinct values of the attributes it groups by. There are many well-known sampling techniques that we can use to determine the number of distinct values of attributes in a relation [HNSS95].

4   Optimizing Data-Cube Lattices

Our most important objective is to develop techniques for optimizing the space-time tradeoff when implementing a lattice of views. The problem can be approached from many angles, since we may in one situation favor time, in another space, and in a third be willing to trade time for space as long as we get good "value" for what we trade away. In this section, we shall begin with a simple optimization problem, in which

1. We wish to minimize the average time taken to evaluate the set of queries that are identical to the views.

2. We are constrained to materialize a fixed number of views, regardless of the space they use.

Evidently item (2) does not minimize space, but in Section 4.5 we shall show how to adapt our techniques to a model that does optimize space utilization.

Even in this simple setting, the optimization problem is NP-complete; there is a straightforward reduction from Set-Cover. Thus, we are motivated to look at heuristics to produce approximate solutions. The obvious choice of heuristic is a "greedy" algorithm, where we select a sequence of views, each of which is the best choice given what has gone before. We shall see that this approach is always fairly close to optimal and in some cases can be shown to produce the best possible selection of views to materialize.

4.1   The Greedy Algorithm

Suppose we are given a data-cube lattice with space costs associated with each view. In this chapter, the space cost is the number of rows in the view. Let $C(v)$ be the cost of view v. The set of views we materialize should always include the top view, because there is no other view that can be used to answer the query corresponding to that view. Suppose there is a limit k on the number of views, in addition to the top view, that we may select. After selecting some set S of views, the *benefit* of view v relative to S, denoted by $B(v, S)$, is defined as follows.

1. For each $w \preceq v$, define the quantity B_w by:

   (a) Let u be the view of least cost in S such that $w \preceq u$. Note that since the top view is in S, there must be at least one such view in S.

   (b) If $C(v) < C(u)$, then $B_w = C(v) - C(u)$. Otherwise, $B_w = 0$.

2. Define $B(v, S) = \sum_{w \preceq v} B_w$.

That is, we compute the benefit of v by considering how it can improve the cost of evaluating views, including itself. For each view w that v covers, we compare the cost of evaluating w using v and using whatever view from S offered the cheapest way of evaluating w. If v helps, *i.e.*, the cost of v is less than the cost of its competitor, then the difference represents part of the benefit of selecting v as a materialized view. The total benefit $B(v, s)$ is the sum over all views w of the benefit of using v to evaluate w, providing that benefit is positive.

Now, we can define the *Greedy Algorithm* for selecting a set of k views to materialize. The algorithm is shown in Fig. 6.

```
S = {top view};
for i=1 to k do begin
    select that view v not in S such
            that B(v,S) is maximized;
    S = S union {v};
end;
resulting S is the greedy selection;
```

Figure 6   The Greedy Algorithm

EXAMPLE 4.1 Consider the lattice of Fig. 7. Eight views, named a through h have space costs as indicated on the figure. The top view a, with cost 100, must be chosen. Suppose we wish to choose three more views.

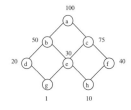

Figure 7   Example lattice with space costs

To execute the greedy algorithm on this lattice, we must make three successive choices of view to materialize. The column headed "First Choice" in Fig. 8 gives us the benefit of each of the views besides a. When calculating the benefit, we begin with the assumption that each view is evaluated using a, and will therefore have a cost of 100.

If we pick view b to materialize first, then we reduce by 50 its cost and that of each of the views d, e, g, and h below it. The benefit is thus 50 times 5, or 250, as indicated in the row b and first column of Fig. 8. As another example, if we pick e first then it and the views below it — g and h — each have their costs reduced by 70, from 100 to 30. Thus, the benefit of e is 210.

	Choice 1	Choice 2	Choice 3
b	$50 \times 5 = 250$		
c	$25 \times 5 = 125$	$25 \times 2 = 50$	$25 \times 1 = 25$
d	$80 \times 2 = 160$	$30 \times 2 = 60$	$30 \times 2 = 60$
e	$70 \times 3 = 210$	$20 \times 3 = 60$	$2 \times 20 + 10 = 50$
f	$60 \times 2 = 120$	$60 + 10 = 70$	
g	$99 \times 1 = 99$	$49 \times 1 = 49$	$49 \times 1 = 49$
h	$90 \times 1 = 90$	$40 \times 1 = 40$	$30 \times 1 = 30$

Figure 8 Benefits of possible choices at each round

Evidently, the winner in the first round is b, so we pick that view as one of the materialized views. Now, we must recalculate the benefit of each view V, given that the view will be created either from b, at a cost of 50, if b is above V, or from a at a cost of 100, if not. The benefits are shown in the second column of Fig. 8.

For example, the benefit of c is now 50, 25 each for itself and f. Choosing c no longer improves the cost of e, g, or h, so we do not count an improvement of 25 for those views. As another example, choosing f yields a benefit of 60 for itself, from 100 to 40. For h, it yields a benefit of 10, from 50 to 40, since the choice of b already improved the cost associated with h to 50. The winner of the second round is thus f, with a benefit of 70. Notice that f wasn't even close to the best choice at the first round.

Our third choice is summarized in the last column of Fig. 8. The winner of the third round is d, with a benefit of 60, gained from the improvement to its own cost and that of g.

The greedy selection is thus b, d, and f. These, together with a, reduces the total cost of evaluating all the views from 800, which would be the case if only a was materialized, to 420. That cost is actually optimal.   ∎

EXAMPLE 4.2 Let us now examine the lattice suggested by Fig. 9. This lattice is, as we shall see, essentially as bad as a lattice can be for the case $k = 2$. The greedy algorithm, starting with only the top view a, first picks c, whose benefit is 4141. That is, c and the 40 views below it are each improved from 200 to 99, when we use c in place of a.

For our second choice, we can pick either b or d. They both have a benefit of 2100. Specifically, consider b. It improves itself and the 20 nodes at the far left by 100 each. Thus, with $k = 2$, the greedy algorithm produces a solution with a benefit of 6241.

However, the optimal choice is to pick b and d. Together, these two views improve, by 100 each, themselves and the 80 views of the four chains. Thus, the optimal solution has a benefit of 8200. the ratio of greedy/optimal is 6241/8200, which is about 3/4. In fact, by making the cost of c closer to 100, and by making the four chains have arbitrarily large numbers of views, we can find examples for $k = 2$ with ratio arbitrarily close to 3/4, but no worse.   ∎

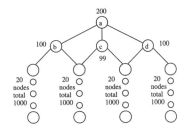

Figure 9   A lattice where the greedy does poorly

4.2   An Experiment With the Greedy Algorithm

We ran the greedy algorithm on the lattice of Fig. 4, using the TPC-D database described earlier. Figure 10 shows the resulting order of views, from the first (top view, which is mandatory) to the twelfth and last view. The units of Benefit, Total Time and Total Space are number of rows. Note, the average query time is the total time divided by the number of views (12 in this case).

	Selection	*Benefit*	*Time*	*Space*
1.	cp	infinite	72M	6M
2.	ns	24M	48M	6M
3.	nt	12M	36M	6M
4.	c	5.9M	30.1M	6.1M
5.	p	5.8M	24.3M	6.3M
6.	cs	1M	23.3M	11.3M
7.	np	1M	22.3M	16.3M
8.	ct	0.01M	22.3M	22.3M
9.	t	small	22.3M	22.3M
10	n	small	22.3M	22.3M
11.	s	small	22.3M	22.3M
12.	none	small	22.3M	22.3M

Figure 10   Greedy order of view selection for TPC-D-based example

This example shows why it is important to materialize some views and also why materializing all views is not a good choice. The graph in Fig. 11 has the total time taken and the space consumed on the Y-axis, and the number of views picked on the X-axis. It is clear that for the first few views we pick, with minimal addition of space, the query time is reduced substantially. After we have picked 5 views however, we cannot improve total query time substantially even by using up large amounts of space. For this example, there is a clear choice of when to stop picking views. If we pick the first five views — cp, ns, nt, c, and p — (*i.e.*, $k = 4$, since the top view is included in the table), then we get almost the minimum possible total time, while the total space used is hardly more than the mandatory space used for just the top view.

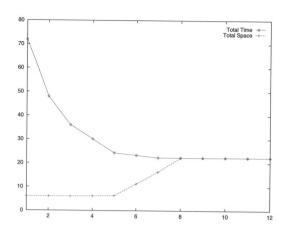

Figure 11   Time and Space versus number of views selected by the greedy algorithm

4.3   A Performance Guarantee for the Greedy Algorithm

We can show that no matter what lattice we are given, the greedy algorithm never performs too badly. Specifically, the *benefit* of the greedy algorithm is at least 63% of the benefit of the optimal algorithm. The precise fraction is $(e-1)/e$, where e is the base of the natural logarithms.

To begin our explanation, we need to develop some notation. Let m be the number of views in the lattice. Suppose we had no views selected except for the top view (which is mandatory). Then the time to answer each query is just the number of rows in the top view. Denote this time by T_ϕ. Suppose that in addition to the top view, we choose a set of views V. Denote the average time to answer a query by T_V. The *benefit* of the set of views V is the reduction in average time to answer a query, that is, $T_\phi - T_V$. Thus minimizing the average time to answer a query is equivalent to maximizing the benefit of a set of views.

Let $v_1, v_2, \ldots, v_k$ be the k views selected in order by the greedy algorithm. Let a_i be the benefit achieved by the selection of v_i, for $i = 1, 2, \ldots, k$. That is, a_i is the benefit of v_i, with respect to the set consisting of the top view and $v_1, v_2, \ldots, v_{i-1}$. Let $V = \{v_1, v_2, \ldots, v_k\}$.

Let $W = \{w_1, w_2, \ldots, w_k\}$ be an optimal set of k views, *i.e.*, those that give the maximum total benefit. The order in which these views appear is arbitrary, but we need to pick an order. Given the w's in order $w_1, w_2, \ldots, w_k$, define b_i to be the benefit of w_i with respect to the set consisting of the top view plus $w_1, w_2, \ldots, w_{i-1}$. Define $A = \sum_{i=1}^{k} a_i$ and $B = \sum_{i=1}^{k} b_i$.

It is easy to show that the benefit of the set V chosen by the greedy algorithm, B_{greedy}, is $T_\phi - T_V = A/m$, and the benefit of the optimal choice W is $B_{opt} = T_\phi - T_W = B/m$. In the full version of this chapter [HRU95], we show that:

$$B_{greedy}/B_{opt} = A/B \geq 1 - (\frac{k-1}{k})^k$$

For example, for $k = 2$ we get $A/B \geq 3/4$; *i.e.*, the greedy algorithm is at least 3/4 of optimal. We saw in Example 4.2 that for $k = 2$ there were specific lattices that approached 3/4 as the ratio of the benefits of the greedy and optimal algorithms. In [HRU95] we show how for any k we can construct a lattice such that the ratio $A/B = 1 - (\frac{k-1}{k})^k$.

As $k \to \infty$, $(\frac{k-1}{k})^k$ approaches $1/e$, so $A/B \geq 1 - \frac{1}{e} = (e-1)/e = 0.63$. That is, for no lattice whatsoever does the greedy algorithm give a benefit less than 63% of the optimal benefit. Conversely, the sequence of bad examples we can construct shows that this ratio cannot be improved upon. We summarize our results in the following theorem:

Theorem 4.1 For any lattice, let B_{greedy} be the benefit of k views chosen by the greedy algorithm and let B_{opt} be the benefit of an optimal set of k views. Then $B_{greedy}/B_{opt} \geq 1 - \frac{1}{e}$. Moreover, this bound is tight: that is, there are lattices such that B_{greedy}/B_{opt} is arbitrarily close to $1 - \frac{1}{e}$. ∎

An interesting point is that the greedy algorithm does as well as we can hope *any* polynomial-time algorithm to do. Chekuri [Che] has shown, using the recently published result of Feige [Fei96], that unless $P = NP$, there is no deterministic polynomial-time algorithm that can guarantee a better bound than the greedy.

4.4 Cases Where Greedy is Optimal

The analysis of Section 4.3 also lets us discover certain cases when the greedy approach is optimal, or very close to optimal. Here are two situations where we never have to look further than the greedy solution.

1. If a_1 is much larger than the other a's, then greedy is close to optimal.

2. If all the a's are equal then greedy is optimal.

The justifications for these claims are based on the proof of Theorem 4.1 and appear in [HRU95].

4.5 Extensions to the Basic Model

There are at least two ways in which our model fails to reflect reality.

1. The views in a lattice are unlikely to have the same probability of being requested in a query. Rather, we might be able to associate some probability with each view, representing the frequency with which it is queried.

2. Instead of asking for some fixed number of views to materialize, we might instead allocate a fixed amount of space to views (other than the top view, which must always be materialized).

Point (1) requires little extra thought. When computing benefits, we weight each view by its probability. The greedy algorithm will then have exactly the same bounds on its performance: at least 63% of optimal.

Point (2) presents an additional problem. If we do not restrict the number of views selected but fix their total space, then we need to consider the benefit of each view *per unit space* used by a materialization of that view. The greedy algorithm again seems appropriate, but there is the additional complication that we might have a very small view with a very high benefit per unit space, and a very large view with almost the same benefit per unit space. Choosing the small view excludes the large view, because there is not enough space available for the large view after we choose the small. However, we can prove the following theorem [HRU95], which says that if we ignore "boundary cases" like the one above, the performance guarantee of the greedy algorithm is the same as in the simple case. The theorem assumes that we use the benefit per unit space in the greedy algorithm as discussed above.

Theorem 4.2 Let B_{greedy} be the benefit and S the space occupied by some set of views chosen using the greedy algorithm, and let B_{opt} be the benefit of an optimal set of views that occupy no more than S units of space. Then $B_{greedy}/B_{opt} \geq 1 - \frac{1}{e}$ and this bound is tight. ∎

5   The Hypercube Lattice

Arguably, the most important class of lattices are the *hypercubes*, in which the views are vertices of an n-dimensional cube for some n. The intuition is that there are n attributes $A_1, A_2, \ldots, A_n$ on which grouping may occur and an $(n+1)$st attribute B whose value is aggregated in each view. Figure 1 was an example of a hypercube lattice with $n = 3$, taken from the TPC-D benchmark database.

The top view groups on all n attributes. We can visualize the views organized by *ranks*, where the ith rank from the bottom is all those views in which we group on i attributes. There are $\binom{n}{i}$ views of rank i.

5.1   The Equal-Domain-Size Case

We can, of course, apply the greedy algorithm to hypercube lattices, either looking for a fixed number of views to materialize, or looking for a fixed amount of space to allocate to views. However, because of the regularity of this lattice, we would like to examine in more detail some of the options for selecting a set of views to materialize.

In our investigations, we shall first make an assumption that is unlikely to be true in practice: all attributes $A_1, A_2, \ldots, A_n$ have the same domain size, which we shall denote r. The consequence of this assumption is that we can easily estimate the size of any view. In Section 5.3, we shall consider what happens when the domain sizes vary. It will be seen that the actual views selected to materialize will vary, but the basic techniques do not change to accommodate this more general situation.

When each domain size is r, and data in the data cube is distributed randomly, then there is a simple way to estimate the sizes of views. The combinatorics involved is complex, but the intuition should be convincing. Suppose only m cells in the top element of our lattice appear in the raw data. If we group on i attributes, then the number of cells in the resulting cube is r^i. To a first approximation, if $r^i \geq m$, then each cell will contain at most one data point, and m of the cells will be nonempty. We can thus use m as the size of any view for which $r^i \geq m$. On the other hand, if $r^i < m$, then almost all r^i cells will have at least one data point. Since we may collapse all the data points in a cell into one aggregate value, the space cost of a view with $r^i < m$ will be approximately r^i. The view size as a function of the number of grouped attributes is shown in Fig. 12.

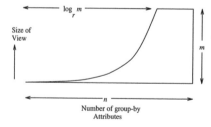

Figure 12   How the size of views grows with number of grouped attributes

The size of views grows exponentially, until it reaches the size of the raw data at rank $\lceil \log_r m \rceil$ (the "cliff" in Fig. 12), and then ceases to grow. Notice that the data in Fig. 1 almost matches this pattern. The top view and the views with two grouping attributes have the same, maximum size, except that the view ps has fewer rows, since the benchmark explicitly sets it to have fewer rows.

k, j, and n	Space	Time
$k > j$	$\left(2r^{r/(r+1)}\right)^n$	$\left(2r^{r/(r+1)}\right)^n$
$k < j$ and $k \leq n/2$	m	$m2^n$
$k < j$ and $k > n/2$	m	$\binom{n}{j}r^j$

Figure 13   Time-optimal strategies for the hypercube

5.2   The Space-Optimal and Time-Optimal Solutions

One natural question to ask when investigating the time/space tradeoff for the hypercube is what is the average time for a query when the space is minimal. Space is minimized when we materialize only the top view. Then every query takes time m, and the total time cost for all 2^n queries is $m2^n$.

At the other extreme, we could minimize time by materializing every query. However, we will not gain much by materializing any view above the cliff in Figure 12, so we might as well avoid materializing those views. The nature of the time-optimal solution depends on the rank $k = \lceil \log_r m \rceil$ at which the cliff occurs, and the rank j such that $r^j \binom{n}{j}$ is maximized. Figure 13 summarizes the time and space used for the three tradeoff points studied. A more detailed discussion of the tradeoff points is in [HRU95].

5.3   Extension to Varying Domain Sizes

Suppose now that the domains of each attribute do not each have r equally-likely values. The next simplest model is to assume that for each dimension, values are equally likely, but the number of values varies, with r_i values in the ith dimension for $i = 1, 2, \ldots, n$.

Now, the "cliff" suggested in Fig. 12 does not occur at a particular rank, but rather the cliff is distributed among ranks. However, the fundamental behavior suggested by Fig. 12 is unchanged. The details are in [HRU95].

6   Conclusions and Future Work

In this chapter we have investigated the problem of deciding which set of cells (views) in the data cube to materialize in order to minimize query response times. Materialization of views is an essential query optimization strategy for decision-support applications. In this chapter, we make the case that the right selection of the views to materialize is critical to the success of this strategy. We use the TPC-D benchmark database as an example database in showing why it is important to materialize some part of the data cube but not all of the cube.

Our second contribution is a lattice framework that models multidimensional analysis very well. Our greedy algorithms work on this lattice and pick the right views to materialize, subject to various constraints. The greedy algorithm we give performs within a small constant factor of the optimal solution for many of the constraints considered. Moreover, [Che] has shown that no polynomial-time algorithm can perform better than the greedy. Finally, we looked at the most common case of the hypercube lattice and investigated the time-space trade-off in detail.

The views, in some sense, form a memory hierarchy with differing access times. In conventional memory hierarchies, data is usually assigned to different memory stores (like cache, or main memory) dynamically based on the run time access patterns. We are currently investigating similar dynamic materialization strategies for the data cube.

Acknowledgments

We thank Bala Iyer and Piyush Goel at IBM for help with the experiments, and Chandra Chekuri and Rajeev Motwani for comments on the chapter.

ON THE COMPUTATION OF MULTIDIMENSIONAL AGGREGATES

Sameet Agarwal, Rakesh Agarwal, Prasad M. Deshpande, Ashish Gupta, Jeffrey F. Naughton, Raghu Ramakrishnan, Sunita Sarawagi

ABSTRACT

At the heart of all OLAP or multidimensional data analysis applications is the ability to simultaneously aggregate across many sets of dimensions. Computing multidimensional aggregates is a performance bottleneck for these applications. This chapter presents fast algorithms for computing a collection of group-bys. We focus on a special case of the aggregation problem — computation of the **CUBE** operator. The **CUBE** operator requires computing group-bys on all possible combinations of a list of attributes, and is equivalent to the union of a number of standard group-by operations. We show how the structure of **CUBE** computation can be viewed in terms of a hierarchy of group-by operations. Our algorithms extend sort-based and hash-based grouping methods with several optimizations, like combining common operations across multiple group-bys, caching, and using pre-computed group-bys for computing other group-bys. Empirical evaluation shows that the resulting algorithms give much better performance compared to straightforward methods.

This chapter combines work done concurrently on computing the data cube by two different teams as reported in [SAG96] and [AAD+96b].

1 Introduction

The group-by operator in SQL is typically used to compute aggregates on a set of attributes. For business data analysis, it is often necessary to aggregate data across many dimensions (attributes) [Fin, Wel95]. For example, in a retail application, one might have a table `Transactions` with attributes `Product(P)`, `Date(D)`, `Customer(C)` and `Sales(S)`. An analyst could then query the data for finding:

- `sum of sales by P, C`:

  For each product, give a breakdown on how much of it was sold to each customer.

- `sum of sales by D, C`:

  For each date, give a breakdown of sales by customer.

- `sum of sales by P`:

  For each product, give total sales.

Speed is a primary goal in these class of applications called On-Line Analytical Processing (OLAP) applications [Cod93]. To make interactive analysis (response time in seconds) possible, OLAP databases often precompute aggregates at various levels of detail and on various combinations of attributes. Speed is critical for this precomputation as well, since the cost and speed of precomputation influences how frequently the aggregates are brought up-to-date.

1.1   What is a CUBE?

Recently, [GBLP96] introduced the **CUBE** operator for conveniently supporting multiple aggregates in OLAP databases. The **CUBE** operator is the n-dimensional generalization of the group-by operator. It computes group-bys corresponding to all possible combinations of a list of attributes. Returning to our retail example, the collection of aggregate queries can be conveniently expressed using the cube-operator as follows:

```
SELECT P, D, C, Sum(S)
FROM Transactions
CUBE-BY P, D, C
```

This query will result in the computation of $2^3 = 8$ group-bys: PDC, PD, PC, DC, D, C, P and all, where all denotes the empty group-by. The straightforward way to support the above query is to rewrite it as a collection of eight group-by queries and execute them separately. There are several ways in which this simple solution can be improved.

In this chapter, we present fast algorithms for computing the data cube. We assume that the aggregating functions are *distributive* [GBLP96], that is, they allow the input set to be partitioned into disjoint sets that can be aggregated separately and later combined. Examples of distributive functions include max, min, count, and sum. The proposed algorithms are also applicable to the *algebraic* aggregate functions [GBLP96], such as average, that can be expressed in terms of other distributive functions (sum and count in the case of average). However, as pointed out in [GBLP96], there are some aggregate functions (*holistic* functions of [GBLP96]) e.g., median, that cannot be computed in parts and combined.

Related Work

Methods of computing *single* group-bys have been well-studied (see [Gra93] for a survey), but little work has been done on optimizing a collection of related aggregates. [GBLP96] gives some rules of thumb to be used in an efficient implementation of the cube operator. These include the smallest parent optimization and partitioning of data by attribute values, which we adopt in our algorithms. However, the primary focus in [GBLP96] is on defining the semantics of the cube operator [GBLP96]. There are reports of ongoing research related to the data cube in directions complementary to ours: [HRU96, GHRU96] presents algorithms for deciding what group-bys to pre-compute and index; [SR96] and [JS96] discuss methods for indexing pre-computed summaries to allow efficient querying.

Aggregate pre-computation is quite common in statistical databases [Sho82]. Research in this area has considered various aspects of the problem starting from developing a model for aggregate computation [CM89], indexing pre-computed aggregates [STL89] and incrementally maintaining them [Mic90]. However, to the best of our knowledge, there is no published work in the statistical database literature on methods for optimizing the computation of related aggregates.

This chapter is in two parts and combines work done concurrently on computing the data cube. Part I[1] presents the methods proposed by [SAG96], whereas the methods proposed by [AAD+96b] are described in Part II[2] . Section 10 presents a summary and brief comparison of the two approaches.

Part I

2 Optimizations Possible

There are two basic methods for computing a group-by: (1) the sort-based method and (2) the hash-based method [Gra93]. We will adapt these methods to compute multiple group-bys by incorporating the following optimizations:

1. **Smallest-parent:** This optimization, first proposed in [GBLP96], aims at computing a group-by from the smallest previously computed group-by. In general, each group-by can be computed from a number of other group-bys. Figure 1 shows a four attribute cube ($ABCD$) and the options for computing a group-by from a group-by having one more attribute called its *parent*. For instance, AB can be computed from ABC, ABD or $ABCD$. ABC or ABD are clearly better choices for computing AB. In addition, even between ABC and ABD, there can often be big difference in size making it critical to consider size in selecting a parent for computing AB.

2. **Cache-results:** This optimization aims at caching (in memory) the results of a group-by from which other group-bys are computed to reduce disk I/O. For instance, for the cube in Figure 1, having computed ABC, we compute AB from it while ABC is still in memory.

3. **Amortize-scans:** This optimization aims at amortizing disk reads by computing as many group-bys as possible, together in memory. For instance, if the group-by $ABCD$ is stored on disk, we could reduce disk read costs if all of ABC, ACD, ABD and BCD were computed in one scan of $ABCD$.

4. **Share-sorts:** This optimization is specific to the sort-based algorithms and aims at sharing sorting cost across multiple group-bys.

5. **Share-partitions:** This optimization is specific to the hash-based algorithms. When the hash-table is too large to fit in memory, data is partitioned and aggregation is done for each partition that fits in memory. We can save on partitioning cost by sharing this cost across multiple group-bys.

For OLAP databases, the size of the data to be aggregated is usually much larger than the available main memory. Under such constraints, the above optimizations are often contradictory. For computing B, for instance, the first optimization will favor BC over AB if BC is smaller but the second optimization will favor AB if AB is in memory and BC is on disk.

Contributions In this part of the chapter, we will present two algorithms for computing the data cube: the sort-based algorithm *PipeSort* (Section 3) and the hash-based algorithm *PipeHash* (Section 4) that includes the optimizations listed above. We have extended these algorithms to two important real-life OLAP cases. The first deals with the useful case of computing a specified subset of the group-bys in a cube. For this case, we identify a reduction of the problem to the *minimum steiner tree* [GJ79] problem.

---

[1]This part presents work done by Sunita Sarawagi, Rakesh Agrawal and Ashish Gupta at IBM Almaden Research Center, San Jose.

[2]This part presents work done by Prasad M. Deshpande, Sameet Agarwal, Jeffrey F. Naughton and Raghu Ramakrishnan; {*pmd, sameet, naughton, raghu*}*@cs.wisc.edu*, University of Wisconsin-Madison. It was supported by a grant from IBM under the University Partnership Programand NSF grant IRI-9157357

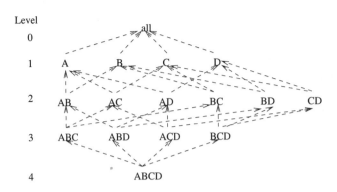

Figure 1 A search lattice for the cube operator

This enables us to find plans that consider computation of intermediate group-bys that are not part of the specified subset but can lead to smaller total cost. The second extension handles the case in which attributes have hierarchies defined on them. Due to space limitation, we have not included these extensions in this chapter, and we refer the reader to [SAG96] for them.

3 Sort-Based Methods

In this section, we present the sort-based algorithm that incorporates the optimizations listed earlier. We include the optimization **share-sort** by using data sorted in a particular order to compute all group-bys that are prefixes of that order. For instance, if we sort the raw data on attribute order $ABCD$, then we can compute group-bys $ABCD$, ABC, AB and A without additional sorts. However, this decision could conflict with the optimization **smallest-parent**. For instance, the smallest parent of AB might be BDA although by generating AB from ABC we are able to share the sorting cost. It is necessary, therefore, to do global planning to decide what group-by is computed from what and the attribute order in which it is computed. We propose an algorithm called *PipeSort* that combines the optimizations share-sorts and smallest-parent to get the minimum total cost.

The PipeSort algorithm also includes the optimizations **cache-results** and **amortize-scans** to reduce disk scan cost by executing multiple group-bys in a *pipelined* fashion. For instance, consider the previous example of using data sorted in the order $ABCD$ to compute prefixes $ABCD$, ABC, AB and A. Instead of computing each of these group-bys separately, we can compute them in a pipelined fashion as follows. Having sorted the raw data in the attribute order $ABCD$, we scan the sorted data to compute group-by $ABCD$. Every time a tuple of $ABCD$ is computed, it is propagated up the pipeline to compute ABC; every time a tuple of ABC is computed, it is propagated up to compute AB, and so on. Thus, each pipeline is a list of group-bys all of which are computed in a single scan of the sort input stream. During the course of execution of a pipeline we need to keep only one tuple per group-by in the pipeline in memory.

Algorithm PipeSort

Assume that for each group-by we have an estimate of the number of distinct values. A number of statistical procedures (e.g., [HNSS95]) can be used for this purpose. The input to the algorithm is the *search lattice* defined as follows.

Search Lattice A search lattice for a data cube is a graph where a vertex represents a group-by of the cube. A directed edge connects group-by i to group-by j whenever j can be generated from i and j has exactly one attribute less than i (i is called the parent of j). Thus, the out-degree of any node with k attributes is k. Figure 1 is an example of a search lattice. Level k of the search lattice denotes all group-bys that contain exactly k attributes. The keyword `all` is used to denote the empty group-by (Level 0). Each edge in the search lattice e_{ij} is labeled with two costs. The first cost $S(e_{ij})$ is the cost of computing j from i when i is not already sorted. The second cost $A(e_{ij})$ is the cost of computing j from i when i is already sorted.

The output, O of the algorithm is a subgraph of the search lattice where each group-by is connected to a single parent group-by from which it will be computed and is associated with an attribute order in which it will be sorted. If the attribute order of a group-by j is a prefix of the order of its parent i, then j can be computed from i without sorting i and in O, edge e_{ij} is marked A and incurs cost $A(e_{ij})$. Otherwise, i has to be sorted to compute j and in O, e_{ij} is marked S and incurs cost S_{ij}. Clearly, for any output O, there can be at most one out-edge marked A from any group-by i, since there can be only one prefix of i in the adjacent level. However, there can be multiple out-edges marked S from i. The objective of the algorithm is to find an output O that has minimum sum of edge costs.

Algorithm The algorithm proceeds level-by-level, starting from level $k = 0$ to level $k = N - 1$, where N is the total number of attributes. For each level k, it finds the best way of computing level k from level $k + 1$ by reducing the problem to a weighted bipartite matching problem[3] [PS82] as follows.

We first transform level $k + 1$ of the original search lattice by making k additional copies of each group-by in that level. Thus each level $k + 1$ group-by has $k + 1$ vertices which is the same as the number of children or out-edges of that group-by. Each replicated vertex is connected to the same set of vertices as the original vertex in the search lattice. The cost on an edge e_{ij} from the original vertex i to a level k vertex j is set to $A(e_{ij})$ whereas all replicated vertices of i have edge cost set to $S(e_{ij})$. We then find the minimum [4] cost matching in the bipartite graph induced by this transformed graph. In the matching so found, each vertex h in level k will be matched to some vertex g in level $k + 1$. If h is connected to g by an $A()$ edge, then h determines the attribute order in which g will be sorted during its computation. On the other hand, if h is connected by an $S()$ edge, g will be re-sorted for computing h.

For illustration, we show how level 1 group-bys are generated from level 2 group-bys for a three attribute search lattice. As shown in Figure 2(a), we first make one additional copy of each level 2 group-by. Solid edges represent the $A()$ edges whereas dashed edges indicate the $S()$ edges. The number underneath each vertex is the cost of all out-edges from this vertex. In the minimum cost matching (Figure 2(b)), A is connected to AB with an $S()$ edge and B by an $A()$ edge. Thus at level 2, group-by AB will be computed in the attribute order BA so that B is generated from it without sorting and A is generated by resorting BA. Similarly, since C is connected to AC by an $A()$ edge, AC will be generated in the attribute order CA. Since, BC is not matched to any level-1 group-by, BC can be computed in any order.

We use the algorithm in [PS82] for finding the minimum cost matching in a bipartite graph[5]. The complexity of this algorithm is $O(((k + 1)M_{k+1})^3)$, where M_{k+1} is the number of group-bys in level $k + 1$.

PipeSort:

Input: search lattice with the A() and S() edges costs

    For level $k = 0$ to $N - 1$

---

[3]The weighted bipartite matching problems is defined as follows: We are given a graph with two disjoint sets of vertices V_1 and V_2 and a set of edges E that connect vertices in set V_1 to vertices in set V_2. Each edge is associated with a fixed weight. The weighted matching problem selects the maximum weight subset of edges from E such that in the selected subgraph each vertex in V_1 is connected to at most one vertex in V_2 and vice-versa.

[4]Note we can covert a minimum weight matching to a maximum weight matching defined earlier by replacing each edge weight w by $max(w) - w$ where $max(w)$ is the maximum edge cost.

[5]The code for the matching algorithm is available from `ftp-request@theory.stanford.edu`

```
/* find how to generate level k from level k + 1 */
Generate-Plan(k + 1 → k);
For each group-by g in level k + 1
        Fix the sort order of g as the order of the
            group-by connected to g by an A() edge;
```

Generate-Plan(k + 1 → k):
    Make k additional copies of each level $k + 1$ vertex;
    Connect each copy vertex to the same set
        of level k vertices as the original vertex;
    Assign cost $A(e_{ij})$ to edge e_{ij} from the original
        vertex and $S(e_{ij})$ to edge from the copy vertex;
    Find the minimum cost matching on the transformed levels.

Example: We illustrate the PipeSort algorithm for the four attribute lattice of Figure 1. For simplicity, assume that for a given group-by g the costs A() and S() are the same for all group-bys computable from g. The pair of numbers underneath each group-by in Figure 3 denote the A() and S() costs. Solid edges denote A() edges and dashed edges denote S() edges. For these costs, the graph in Figure 3(a) shows the final minimum cost plan output by the PipeSort algorithm. Note that the plan in Figure 3(a) is optimal in terms of the *total cost* although the *total number of sorts* is suboptimal. For most real-life datasets there could be a big difference in the sizes of group-bys on a level. Hence, optimizing for the number of sorts alone could lead to poor plans.

In Figure 3(b) we show the pipelines that are executed. Sorts are indicated by ellipses. We would first sort data in the order $CBAD$. In one scan of the sorted data, $CBAD$, CBA, CB, C and all would be computed in a pipelined fashion. Then group-by $ABCD$ would be sorted into the new order $BADC$ and thereafter BAD, BA and B would be computed in a pipelined fashion.

We can make the following claims about algorithm PipeSort.

Claim 3.1 *Generate-plan() finds the best plan to get level k from level $k + 1$.*

PROOF. Follows by construction assuming a cost function where the cost of sorting a group-by does not depend on the order in which the group-by is already sorted. ∎

Claim 3.2 *Generate-plan($k + 1 → k$) does not prevent Generate-plan($k + 2 → k + 1$) from finding the best plan.*

PROOF. After we have fixed the way to generate level k from level $k + 1$ the only constraint we have on level $k + 1$ is the order in which the group-bys should be generated. This ordering does not affect the minimum matching solution for generating level $k + 1$ from $k + 2$. After finding the best solution for generating level $k + 1$ from level $k + 2$, we can always change the order in which each group-by should be generated (as dictated by level k solution) without affecting the minimum cost. ∎

Note that PipeSort computes each group-by from a group-by occurring only in the immediately preceding level. Although the level-by-level approach is not provably optimal, we have not been able to find any case where generating a group-by from a group-by not in the preceding level leads to a better solution. Our experiments reported in Section 5 also show that our solution is very close to empirically estimated lower bounds for several datasets.

Further Enhancements Our implementation of PipeSort includes the usual optimizations of aggregating and removing duplicates while sorting, instead of doing aggregation as a different phase after sorting[Gra93]. Often we can reduce the sorting cost by taking advantage of the partial sorting order. For instance, in Figure 3 for sorting ACD in the attribute order AD, we can get a sorted run of D for each distinct value of AC and for each distinct A we can merge these runs of D. Also, after the PipeSort algorithm has fixed the order in which each group-by is generated we can modify the sort-edges in the output search lattice to take advantage of the partial sorting orders whenever it is advantageous to do so.

4 Hash-Based Methods

We now discuss how we extend the hash-based method for computing a data cube. For hash-based methods, the new challenge is careful memory allocations of multiple hash-tables for incorporating optimizations **cache-results** and **amortize-scans**. For instance, if the hash tables for AB and AC fit in memory then the two group-bys could be computed in one scan of ABC. After AB is computed one could compute A and B while AB is still in memory and thus avoid the disk scan of AB. If memory were not a limitation, we could include all optimizations stated in Section 2 as follows.

> *For* $k = N$ to 0
>> *For* each $k + 1$ attribute group-by, g
>>> Compute in one scan of g all k attribute group-by
>>>> for which g is the smallest parent;
>>>> Save g to disk and destroy hash table of g;

However, the data to be aggregated is usually too large for the hash-tables to fit in memory. The standard way to deal with limited memory when constructing hash tables is to partition the data on one or more attributes. When data is partitioned on some attribute, say A, then all group-bys that contain A can be computed by independently grouping on each partition — the results across multiple partitions need not be combined. We can share the cost of data partitioning across all group-bys that contain the partitioning attribute, leading to the optimization **share-partitions**. We present below the *PipeHash* algorithm that incorporates this optimization and also includes the optimizations **cache-results**, **amortize-scans** and **smallest-parent**.

Algorithm PipeHash

The input to the algorithm is the search lattice described in the previous section. The PipeHash algorithm first chooses for each group-by, the parent group-by with the smallest estimated total size. The outcome is a minimum spanning tree (MST) where each vertex is a group-by and an edge from group-by a to b shows that a is the smallest parent of b. In Figure 4 we show the MST for a four attribute search lattice (the size of each group-by is indicated below the group-by).

In general, the available memory will not be sufficient to compute all the group-bys in the MST together, hence the next step is to decide what group-bys to compute together, when to allocate and deallocate memory for different hash-tables, and what attribute to choose for partitioning data. We conjecture this problem to be NP-complete because solving this problem optimally requires us to solve the following sub-problem optimally: Divide the MST into smaller subtrees each of which can be computed in one scan of the group-by at the root of the MST such that the cost of scanning (from disk) the root group-by is minimized. This problem is similar to well-known NP-complete partitioning problems [GJ79]. Hence, we resort to using a heuristic solution. Later (in Section 5) we show that our solution is very close to empirically estimated lower bounds for several datasets.

Optimizations cache-results and amortize-scans are favored by choosing as large a subtree of the MST as possible so that we can use the method above to compute together the group-bys in the subtree. However, when data needs to be partitioned based on some attribute, the partitioning attribute limits the subtree to only include group-bys containing the partitioning attribute. We therefore, choose a partitioning attribute that allows the choice of the largest subtree as shown in the pseudo-code of the PipeHash algorithm below.

PipeHash:

Input: search lattice with group-by estimated sizes

    Initialize worklist with MST of the search lattice;

    While worklist is not empty

        Pick any tree T from the worklist;

        $T' = $ Select-subtree of T to be executed next;

        Compute-subtree T';

Select-subtree:

    If memory required by T < available, *return T*

    Else let S be the attributes of root(T)

        (We will pick $s \subset S$ for partitioning root(T).

        For any s we get a subtree T_s of T also rooted at

            T including all group-bys that contain s.)

        Let $P_s = $ maximum number of partitions of root(T)

            possible if partitioned on $s \subset S$;

        We choose $s \subset S$ such that

            memory required by T_s/P_s < memory available,

            and T_s is the largest over all subsets of S;

        Remove T_s from T;

        This leaves $T - T_s$, a forest of smaller trees; add

            this to the worklist;

    return T_s;

Compute-subtree:

    $M = $ memory available;

    numParts = memory required by T'*fudge_factor/M;

    Partition root of T' into numParts;

    For each partition of root(T')

        For each node, n in T'

        (scanned in a breadth first manner)

            Compute all children of n in one scan;

            If n is cached, save it to disk and

                release memory occupied by its hash-table;

Example: Figure 4 illustrates the PipeHash algorithm for the four attribute search lattice of Figure 1. The boxed group-bys represent the root of the subtrees. Figure 4(a) shows the minimum spanning tree. Assume there is not enough memory to compute the whole tree in one pass and we need to partition the

Dataset	# grouping attributes	# tuples (in millions)	size (in MB)
Dataset-A	3	5.5	110
Dataset-B	4	7.5	121
Dataset-C	5	9	180
Dataset-D	5	3	121
Dataset-E	6	0.7	18

Table 1   Description of the datasets

data. Figure 4(b) shows the first subtree T_A selected when A is chosen as the partitioning attribute. After removing T_A from the MST, we are left with four subtrees as shown in Figure 4(c). None of the group-bys in these subtrees include A. For computing T_A, we first partition the raw data on A. For each partition we compute first the group-by $ABCD$; then scan $ABCD$ (while it is still in memory) to compute ABC, ABD and ACD together; save $ABCD$ and ABD to disk; compute AD from ACD; save ACD and AD to disk; scan ABC to compute AB and AC; save ABC and AC to disk; scan AB to compute A and save AB and A to disk. After T_A is computed, we compute each of the remaining four subtrees in the worklist.

Note that PipeHash incorporates the optimization share-partitions by computing from the same partition all group-bys that contain the partitioning attribute. Also, when computing a subtree we maintain all hash-tables of group-bys in the subtree (except the root) in memory until all its children are created. Also, for each group-by we compute its children in one scan of the group-by. Thus PipeHash also incorporate the optimizations amortize-scans and cache-results. [6]

PipeHash is biased towards optimizing for the smallest-parent. For each group-by, we first fix the smallest parent and then incorporate the other optimizations. For instance, in Figure 4(c), we could have computed BC from BCD instead of its smallest parent ABC and thus saved the extra scan on ABC. However, in practice, saving on sequential disk scans is less important than reducing the CPU cost of aggregation by choosing the smallest parent.

5   Experimental Evaluation

In this section, we present the performance of our cube algorithms on several real-life datasets and analyze the behavior of these algorithms on tunable synthetic datasets. These experiments were performed on a RS/6000 250 workstation running AIX 3.2.5. The workstation had a total physical memory of 256 MB. We used a buffer of size 32 MB. The datasets were stored as flat files on a local 2GB SCSI 3.5" drive with sequential throughput of about 1.5 MB/second.

Datasets   Table 1 lists the five real-life datasets used in the experiments. These datasets were derived from sales transactions of various department stores and mail order companies. A brief description is given next. The datasets differ in the number of transactions, the number of attributes, and the number of distinct values for each attribute. For each attribute, the number within brackets denotes the number of its distinct values.

---

[6]Refer [SAG96] for a discussion of how we handle the problems of data skew and incorrect size estimates in allocating hash-tables

- **Dataset-A:** This data is about supermarket purchases. Each transaction has three attributes: store id(73), date(16) and item identifier(48510). In addition, two attributes cost and amount are used as aggregation columns.

- **Dataset-B:** This data is from a mail order company. A sales transaction here consists of four attributes: the customer identifier(213972), the order date(2589), the product identifier(15836), and the catalog used for ordering(214).

- **Dataset-C:** This is data about grocery purchases of customers from a supermarket. Each transaction has five attributes: the date of purchase(1092), the shopper type(195), the store code(415), the state in which the store is located(46) and the product group of the item purchased(118).

- **Dataset-D:** This is data from a department store. Each transaction has five attributes: the store identifier(17), the date of purchase(15), the UPC of the product(85161), the department number(44) and the SKU number(63895).

- **Dataset-E:** This data is also from a department store. Each transaction has total of six attributes: the store number(4), the date of purchase(15), the item number(26412), the business center(6), the merchandising group(22496) and a sequence number(255). A seventh attribute: the quantity of purchase was used as the aggregating column.

Algorithms compared For providing a basis of evaluation, we choose the straightforward method of computing each group-by in a cube as a separate group-by resulting in algorithms *NaiveHash* and *NaiveSort* depending on whether group-bys are computed using hash-based or sort-based methods. We further compare our algorithms against easy but possibly unachievable lower-bounds.

For the hash-based method the lower bound is obtained by summing up the following operations: Compute the bottom-most (level-N) group-by by hashing raw-data stored on disk; include the data partitioning cost if any. Compute all other group-bys by hashing the smallest parent assumed to be in memory; ignore data partitioning costs. Save all computed group-bys to disk.

For the sort-based method the lower bound is obtained by summing up the following operations: Compute the bottom-most (level-N) group-by by sorting the raw-data stored on disk. Compute all other group-bys from the smallest parent assumed to be in memory and sorted in the order of the group-by to be computed. Save all computed group-bys.

Performance results Figure 5 shows the performance of the proposed PipeHash and PipeSort relative to the corresponding naive algorithms and estimated lower bounds. The total execution time is normalized by the time taken by the NaiveHash algorithm for each dataset to enable presentation on the same scale. In [SAG96] we discuss the methods we used for estimating the size of each group-by and the hashing function used with NaiveHash and PipeHash. We can make the following observations.

- Our algorithms are two to eight times faster than the naive methods.

- The performance of PipeHash is very close to our calculated lower bound for hash-based algorithms. The maximum difference in performance is 8%.

- PipeSort is also close to the calculated lower bound for sort-based method in most cases. The maximum gap between their performance is 22%.

- For most of the datasets, PipeHash is inferior to the PipeSort algorithms. We suspected this to be an artifact of these datasets. To further investigate the difference between them, therefore, we did a series of experiments on a synthetically generated dataset described next.

5.1 Comparing PipeSort and PipeHash

For the datasets in Table 1, the sort-based method performs better than the hash-based method. For Dataset-D, PipeSort is almost a factor of two better than PipeHash. Based on results in [GLS94], we had expected the hash-based method to be comparable or better than the sort-based method. Careful scrutiny of the performance data revealed that this deviation is because after some parent group-by is sorted we compute more than one group-by from it whereas for the hash-based method we build a different hash table for each group-by. Even though we share the partitioning cost for the hash-based method, the partitioning cost is not a dominant fraction of the total cost unlike sorting.

We conjectured that the hash-based method can perform better than the sort-based method when each group-by results in a considerable reduction in the number of tuples. This is because the cost of hashing at higher levels of aggregations can become a negligible fraction of the total cost when the number of tuples reduces rapidly. To validate our conjecture that the performance difference between the hash-based method and sort-based method is mainly due to the rate of decrease in the number of tuples as we aggregate along more and more attributes, we took a series of measurements on synthetic datasets described below.

Synthetic datasets Each dataset is characterized by four parameters:

1. Number of tuples, T.

2. Number of grouping attributes, N.

3. Ratio amongst the number of distinct values of each attribute $d_1 : d_2 : \ldots : d_N$.

4. A parameter, p, denoting the degree of sparsity of the data. It is defined as the ratio of T to the total number of possible attribute value combinations. Thus, if D_i denotes the number of distinct values of attribute i, then p is defined as $T/(D_1 \times D_2 \ldots D_N)$. Clearly, higher the degree of sparsity (lower value of p), lower the reduction in the number of tuples after aggregation.

Given these four parameters, the dataset is generated as follows. We first determine the total number of values D_i along each dimension i as:

$$D_i = \left(\frac{T}{p}\right)^{\frac{1}{N}} \frac{d_i}{(d_1 \times d_2 \times \ldots \times d_N)^{\frac{1}{N}}}$$

Then, for each of the T tuples, we choose a value for each attribute i randomly between 1 and D_i.

Results We show the results for two sets of synthetic datasets with T is 5 million, N is 5. For dataset in Figure 6(a) the ratio between the number of distinct values of each attribute is 1:2:4:20:300 (large variance in number of distinct values). We vary the sparsity by changing p. The X-axis denotes decreasing levels of sparsity and the Y-axis denotes the ratio between the total running time of algorithms PipeHash and PipeSort. We notice that as the data becomes less and less sparse the hash-based method performs better than the sort-based method. We repeated the same set of measurements for datasets with a different ratio, 1:1:1:1:1 (Figure 6(b)). We notice the same trend for datasets with very different characteristics, empirically confirming that sparsity indeed is a predictor of the relative performance of the PipeHash and PipeSort algorithms.

Part II

6   Contributions of this Part

We present a class of sorting-based methods for computing the CUBE that try to minimize the number of disk accesses by overlapping the computation of the various cuboids. They make use of partially matching sort orders to reduce the number of sorting steps required. Our experiments with an implementation of these methods show that they perform well even with limited amounts of memory. In particular, they always perform substantially better than the *Independent* and *Parent* method of computing the CUBE by a sequence of group-by statements, which is currently the only option in commercial relational database systems.

7   Options for Computing the CUBE

Let R be a relation with $k + 1$ attributes $\{A_1, A_2, \ldots, A_{k+1}\}$. Consider the computation of a CUBE on k attributes $X = \{A_1, A_2, \ldots, A_k\}$ of relation R with aggregate function $F(\cdot)$ applied on A_{k+1}. A *cuboid* on j attributes $S = \{A_{i_1}, A_{i_2}, \ldots, A_{i_j}\}$ is defined as a group-by on the attributes $A_{i_1}, A_{i_2}, \ldots, A_{i_j}$ using the aggregate function F. This cuboid can be represented as a $k + 1$ attribute relation by using the special value ALL for the remaining $k - j$ attributes [GBLP96]. The CUBE on attribute set X is the union of cuboids on all subsets of attributes of X. The cuboid (or group-by) on all attributes in X is called the *base cuboid*.

To compute the CUBE we need to compute all the cuboids that together form the CUBE. The base cuboid has to be computed from the original relation. The other cuboids can be computed from the base cuboid due to the distributive nature of the aggregation. For example, in a retail application relation with attributes *(Product, Year, Customer, Sales)*, *sum of sales by (product, customer)* can be obtained by using *sum of sales by (product, year, customer)*. There are different ways of scheduling the computations of the cuboids:

Multiple Independent Group-By Queries (Independent Method)

A straightforward approach (which we call *Independent*) is to independently compute each cuboid from the base cuboid, using any of the standard group-by techniques. Thus the base cuboid is read and processed for each cuboid to be computed, leading to poor performance.

Hierarchy of Group-By Queries (Parent Method)

Consider the computation of different cuboids for the CUBE on attributes $\{A, B, C, D\}$. The cuboid $\{A, C\}$ can be computed from the cuboid $\{A, B, C\}$ or the cuboid $\{A, C, D\}$, since the aggregation function is distributive. In general, a cuboid on attribute set X (called cuboid X) can be computed from a cuboid on attribute set Y iff $X \subset Y$. One optimization is to choose Y to be as small as possible to reduce cost of computation. We use the heuristic of computing a cuboid with $k - 1$ attributes from a cuboid with k attributes, since cuboid size is likely to increase with additional attributes. For example, it is better to compute *sum of sales by (product)* using *sum of sales by (product, customer)* rather than *sum of sales by (product, year, customer)*.

We can view this hierarchy as a DAG where the nodes are cuboids and there is an edge from a k attribute cuboid to a $k - 1$ attribute cuboid iff the $k - 1$ attribute set is a subset of the k attribute set. The DAG captures the "consider-computing-from" relationship between the cuboids. The DAG for the CUBE on $\{A, B, C, D\}$ is shown in Figure 7.

In the *Parent* method each cuboid is computed from one of its parents in the DAG. This is better than the *Independent* method since the parent is likely to be much smaller than the base cuboid, which is the largest of all the cuboids.

Overlap Method

This is a further extension of the idea behind the *Parent* method. While the *Independent* and *Parent* methods are currently in use by Relational OLAP tools, the *Overlap* method cannot be used directly by a standard SQL database system and to our knowledge it has not appeared in the literature to date. As in the *Parent* method, the *Overlap* method computes each cuboid from one of its parents in the cuboid tree. It tries to do better than *Parent* by overlapping the computation of different cuboids and using partially matching sort orders. This can significantly reduce the number of I/Os required. The details of this scheme are explained in Section 8.

7.1 Computing the Group-bys using Sorting

In relational query processing, there are various methods for computing a group-by, such as sorting or hashing [Eps79, Gra93, SN95]. These methods can be used to compute one cuboid from another. We concentrate on sorting based methods in this chapter, though we believe that hashing could also be used similarly. Computing a CUBE requires computation of a number of cuboids (group-bys). Sorting combined with *Overlap* seems to be a good option due to the following observations which help in reducing the number of sorting steps.

- Cuboids can be computed from a sorted cuboid in sorted order.

- An existing sort order on a cuboid can be used while computing other cuboids from it. For example, consider a cuboid $X = \{A, B, D\}$ to be computed from $Y = \{A, B, C, D\}$. Let Y be sorted in ABCD order which is not the same as ABD order needed to compute X. But Y need not be resorted to compute X. The existing order on Y can be used. The exact details are explained in Section 8.

8 The Overlap Method

The method we propose for CUBE computation is a sort-based overlap method. Computations of different cuboids are overlapped and all cuboids are computed in sorted order. In this chapter we give only a short description of our method. More details can be found in [AAD+96b]. We first define some terms which will be used frequently.

Sorted Runs : Consider a cuboid on j attributes $\{A_1, A_2, \ldots, A_j\}$. We use $(A_1, A_2, \ldots, A_j)$ to denote the cuboid sorted on the attributes A_1, A_2, ..., A_j in that order. Consider the cuboid $S = (A_1, A_2, \ldots, A_{l-1}, A_{l+1}, \ldots, A_j)$ computed using $B = (A_1, A_2, \ldots, A_j)$. A *sorted run* R of S in B is defined as follows: $R = \Pi_{A_1, A_2, \ldots, A_{l-1}, A_{l+1}, \ldots, A_j}(Q)$ where Q is a **maximal** sequence of tuples τ of B such that for each tuple in Q, the first l columns have the same value. Informally a sorted run of S in B is a maximal run of tuples in B whose ordering is consistent with their ordering in the sort order associated with S.

For example, consider $B = [(a, 1, 2), (a, 1, 3), (a, 2, 2), (b, 1, 3), (b, 3, 2), (c, 3, 1)]$. Let S be the cuboid on the first and third attribute. i.e., $S = [(a, 2), (a, 3), (b, 3), (b, 2), (c, 1)]$. The sorted runs for S are $[(a, 2), (a, 3)]$, $[(a, 2)]$, $[(b, 3)]$, $[(b, 2)]$ and $[(c, 1)]$.

Partitions : B and S have a common prefix of $A_1, A_2, \ldots, A_{l-1}$. A *partition* of the cuboid S in B is a union of sorted runs such that the first $l-1$ columns (the common prefix) of all the tuples of the sorted runs have the same value. In the above example, the partitions for S in B will be $[(a,2),(a,3)]$, $[(b,2),(b,3)]$ and $[(c,1)]$.

This definition implies that all tuples of one partition are either less or greater than all tuples of any other partition. Tuples from different partitions will not merge for aggregation. Thus partition becomes a unit of computation and each partition can be computed independently of the others.

8.1   Overview of the Overlap Method

The overlap method is a muti-pass method. In each pass, a set of cuboids is selected for computing under memory constraints. These cuboids are computed in a overlapped manner. The tuples generated for a cuboid are used to compute its descendents in the DAG. This pipelining reduces the number of scans needed. The process is repeated until all cuboids get computed.

The algorithm begins by sorting the base cuboid. All other cuboids can be directly computed in sorted order without any further sorting. Instead of re-sorting for each cuboid, the existing sorted runs are merged to create the cuboid. This reduces the number of comparisons as well. Suppose the base cuboid for the CUBE on $\{A, B, C, D\}$ is sorted in the order (A, B, C, D). This decides the sort order in which the other cuboids get computed. The sort orders for the other cuboids of $\{A, B, C, D\}$ are shown in the Figure 7. A few heuristics for choosing this sort order are mentioned in [AAD+96b].

Computation of each cuboid requires some amount of memory. If there is enough to memory to hold all the cuboids, then the entire CUBE can be computed in one scan of the input relation. But often, this is not the case. The available memory may be insufficient for large CUBEs. Thus, to get the maximum overlap across computations of different cuboids, we could try to reduce the amount of memory needed to compute a particular cuboid. Since partition can be a unit of computation, while computing a cuboid from another sorted cuboid we just need memory sufficient to hold a partition of the cuboid. As soon as a partition is completed, the tuples can be pipelined into the computation of descendant cuboids, or written out to disk; the same memory can then be used to start computation of the next partition. This is a significant reduction since for most cuboids the partition size is much less than the size of the cuboid. For example, while computing (A, B, C) and (A, B, D) from (A, B, C, D) the partition size for (A, B, C) is 1 tuple (since (A, B, C) sort order matches (A, B, C, D) sort order) whereas the partition size for (A, B, D) is bounded by the number of distinct values of D. So for computing these we just need space sufficient to hold a partition. Thus computation of many cuboids can be overlapped in the available memory effectively reducing the number of scans.

8.2   Details

Choosing a Parent to Compute a Cuboid

Each cuboid in the cuboid DAG has more than one parent from which it could be computed. We need to choose one of these parents thus converting the DAG to a rooted tree. The root of the tree is the base cuboid and each cuboid's parent is the cuboid to be used for computing it. For example, one possible tree for computing the DAG in Figure 7 is as shown in Figure 8.

There are many possible trees. The goal in choosing a tree is to minimize the size of the partitions of a cuboid so that minimum memory is needed for its computation. For example, it is better to compute (A, C) from (A, C, D) rather than (A, B, C). This is because (A, C, D) sort order matches the (A, C)

sort order and the partition size is 1. This is generalized to the following heuristic: Consider the cuboid $S = (A_{i_1}, A_{i_2}, \ldots, A_{i_j})$, where the base cuboid is $(A_1, A_2, \ldots, A_k)$. S can be computed from any cuboid with one additional attribute, say A_l. Our heuristic is to choose the cuboid with the largest value of l to compute S. Maximizing the size of the common prefix minimizes the partition size. The tree in Figure 8 is obtained by using this heuristic. Note that among the children of a particular node, the partition sizes increase from left to right. For example, partition size for computing (A, B, C) from (A, B, C, D) is 1 whereas the partition size for (B, C, D) is the maximum (equal to size of the cuboid (B, C, D) itself).

Choosing a Set of Cuboids for Overlapped Computation

The next step is to choose a set of cuboids that can be computed concurrently within the memory constraints. To compute a cuboid in memory, we need memory equal to the size of its partition. We assume that we have estimates of sizes of the cuboids. The partition sizes can be estimated from these using uniform distribution assumption [AAD+96b]. If this much memory can be allocated, the cuboid will be marked to be in *Partition* state. For some other cuboids it may be possible to allocate one page of memory. These cuboids will be *SortRun* state. The allocated page can be used to write out sorted runs for this cuboid on disk. This will save a scan of the parent when the cuboid has to be computed. These sorted runs are merged in further passes to complete the computation.

Given any subtree of a cuboid tree and the size of memory M, we need to mark the cuboids to be computed and allocate memory for their computation. When a cuboid is in *Partition* state, its tuples can be pipelined for computing the descendent cuboids in the same pass. This is not true for *SortRun* state. Thus we have the following constraints:

C1: A cuboid can be considered for computation if either its parent is the root of the subtree (this means either the parent cuboid itself or sorted-runs for the parent cuboid have been materialized on the disk), or the parent has been marked as being in the *Partition* state.

C2: The total memory allocated to all the cuboids should not be more than the available memory M.

There are a large number of options for selecting which cuboids to compute and in what state. The cost of computation depends critically on the choices made. When a cuboid is marked in *SortRun* state there is an additional cost of writing out the sorted runs and reading them to merge and compute the cuboids in the subtree rooted at that node. We have shown that finding an overall optimal allocation scheme for our cuboid tree is NP-hard [AAD+96b] . So, instead of trying to find the optimal allocation we do the allocation by using the heuristic of traversing the tree in a breadth first (BF) search order:

- Cuboids to the left have smaller partition sizes, and require less memory. So consider these before considering cuboids to the right.

- Cuboids at a higher level tend to be bigger. Thus, these should be given higher priority for allocation than cuboids at a lower level in the tree.

Because of the constraints there may be some subtrees that remain uncomputed. These are considered in subsequent passes, using the same algorithm to allocate memory and mark cuboids. Thus, when the algorithm terminates, all cuboids have been computed.

Computing a Cuboid From its Parent

This section describes the actual method of computation for the chosen cuboids. Every cuboid (say S) other than the base cuboid is computed from its parent in the cuboid tree (say B). If a cuboid has been marked in *Partition* state it means that we have sufficient memory to fit the largest partition of S in memory. We can compute the entire cuboid S in one pass over B and also pipeline the tuples generated for further computation if necessary. However, if the cuboid is marked to be in *SortRun* state, we can write out sorted runs of S in this pass. Writing out the sorted runs requires just one page of memory. The algorithm for computing a cuboid is specified below :

ComputeCuboid:

Output: The sorted cuboid S.

    foreach tuple τ of B *do*

        if (state $==$ *Partition*) *then*

            process_partition(τ)

        else

            process_sorted_run(τ)

        endif

        end_of_cuboid()

    endfor

The process_partition() procedure is as follows:

- If the input tuple starts a new partition, output the current partition at the end of the cuboid, start a new one and make it current.

- If the input tuple matches with an existing tuple in the partition then recompute the aggregate of the existing tuple using the old aggregate value and the input tuple.

- If the input tuple is not the same as any existing tuple then insert the input tuple into the current partition at the appropriate location to maintain the sorted order of the partition.

The process_sort_run() procedure is as follows:

- If the input tuple starts a new sorted run, flush all the pages of the current sorted run, start a new sorted run and make it current.

- If the input tuple matches with the last tuple in the sorted run then recompute the aggregate of the last tuple using the old aggregate value and the input tuple.

- If the input tuple does not match with the last tuple of the sorted run, append the tuple to the end of the existing run. If, there is no space in the allocated memory for the sorted run, we flush out the pages in the memory to the end of the current sorted run on disk. Continue the sorted run in memory with the input tuple.

The end_of_cuboid() processing writes the final partition or sorted run currently in memory to disk. For the case of the *Partition* state, the cuboids get computed completely in the first pass. For *SortRun*, we now have a set of sorted runs on disk. We compute such a cuboid by merging these runs, like the merge step of external sort, aggregating duplicates if necessary. This step is combined with the computation of cuboids that are descendants of that cuboid. The runs are merged and the result pipelined for further computation (of descendants). Note that computation of a cuboid in the *SortRun* state involves the additional cost of writing out and merging the runs. Further, the child cuboids cannot be computed during the run-creation phase, and must be computed during the subsequent merging phase, as noted above.

8.3   Example computation of a CUBE

Consider the CUBE to be computed on $\{A, B, C, D\}$. The tree of cuboids and the estimates of the partition sizes of the cuboids are shown in Figure 9. If the memory available is 25 pages, BF allocation will generate three subtrees, each of which is computed in one pass. These subtrees are shown in Figure 10. In the second and third steps the cuboids (B, C, D) and (C, D) are allocated 10 pages as there are 9 sorted runs to merge.

Comparison with Independent and Parent method

The cost of writing out the computed cuboids is common to all the schemes. The only additional cost in this case was of writing the sorted runs of (B, C, D) and (C, D) and merging these sorted runs. The *Independent* scheme would have required 16 scans and sorts of the base cuboid (once for each cuboid to be computed) and the *Parent* scheme would require a number of scans and sorts of each non-leaf cuboid in the tree (one for each of its children). Thus our scheme incurs fewer I/Os and less computation compared to these two.

9   Implementation and Results

To test how well our algorithm performs, we implemented a stand-alone version of the algorithm and tested it for varying memory sizes and data distributions. All the experiments were done on a Sun SPARC 10 machine running SUN-OS or Solaris. The implementation uses the file system provided by the OS. All reads and writes to the files were in terms of blocks corresponding to the page size. Performance was measured in terms of I/Os by counting the number of page read and page write requests generated by the algorithm and is thus independent of the OS. A detailed performance study is described in [AAD+96b]. We mention only a few important experiments here.

Unless otherwise mentioned, the data for the input relation was generated randomly. The values for each attribute is independently chosen uniformly from a domain of values for that attribute. Each tuple has six attributes and the CUBE is computed on five attributes with the aggregation (computing the sum) on the sixth attribute. Each CUBE attribute has 40 distinct values. Each tuple is 24 bytes wide. The page size used was 1K.

9.1   Comparison with Independent and Parent methods

To illustrate the gains of our algorithm over other methods, we compare the performance of our algorithm with the *Independent* and *Parent* methods described before. We varied different parameters like memory size, relation size, data distribution and the number of attributes on which the CUBE is computed.

Different data distributions

In order to run experiments that finished in a reasonable amount of time, for the bulk of our experiments the relation size was kept constant at $100,000$ tuples (2.4 MByte). While this is quite small, the important performance parameter in our algorithm is the ratio of the relation size and the memory size. To compensate for an artificially small input relation size, we used very small memory sizes, varying from a low of 100 pages (100 KByte) to a high of 3000 pages (3 MB). Section 12 shows that the performance characteristics of the algorithms we tested are unchanged if you scale the memory and data size to more realistic levels. For each of the methods, we plotted the sum of the number of reads and writes.

The graph in Figure 11 shows the performance of the three algorithms for uniform data. Figure 12 is for non-uniform data which is generated using zipf distribution for the attribute values. Values for A and B were chosen with a zipf factor of 2, C with a factor of 1, and D and E with a factor of 0 (uniform distribution)

The graphs in Figures 11 and 12 show that our method achieves a significant improvement over the *Independent* and *Parent* methods for both uniform and non-uniform data. There are some spikes in the graph in Figure 12. For example, the I/O performance at memory size 1500K is worse than that at 1250K for our algorithm. This only shows that the breadth-first heuristic that we are using for memory allocation is not always optimal.

The graphs also show that choosing a proper sort order is important. For non-uniform data, sort order 'EDCBA' is better than the order 'ABCDE'. This is due to different degrees of skewness in different attributes.

Scaleup Experiments

We performed some experiments to check how our method scales for larger input sizes with proportionately larger memory sizes. The relation size was varied from 100,000 (2.4M) to 1000,000 tuples (24 M). The memory used for each case was about 10% of the relation size. The graph in Figure 13 shows that the performance characteristics of the algorithms we consider are unchanged when the data sets are scaled to more realistic levels.

9.2   Relation between Memory and Input size for Overlap Method

We performed some experiments to study how our method performs for different ratios of memory to the input size.

Varying Memory

Figure 14 plots the number of Reads and Writes for computing CUBE for a input size of 100,000 tuples (2.4MB). The memory is varied from 100K to 3MB. From the graphs in Figure 14, it is clear that the I/Os decrease with increasing memory since more and more cuboids are computed simultaneously, avoiding excess reading and writing of sorted runs. We observe that even for very low memory sizes, the number of writes is only slightly more than the size of CUBE and the number of reads is within two times the input relation size. This shows that we are getting near optimal performance with respect to number of I/Os.

Varying Relation size

In the other experiment, the memory was kept constant at 500 pages (500K). The input relation size was varied from 10000 to 100,000 tuples. Each attribute has 20 distinct values. The graph is shown in the Figure 15. The X axis represents the size of the relation in bytes. On the Y axis, we plot the following ratios.

1. $\dfrac{Number\ of\ Writes}{Size\ of\ the\ \mathbf{CUBE}\ in\ Pages}$

2. $\dfrac{Number\ of\ Reads}{Size\ of\ the\ Input\ Relation\ in\ Pages}$

Any algorithm to compute the cube has to scan the input and write out the results. Hence these ratios give an idea of how close the algorithm is to ideal. Since the memory size is 500K, for relations of size up to 500K, the performance is ideal. For bigger relations, the performance degrades slowly as the partitions no longer fit in memory and sorted runs have to be written out for many cuboids. The spikes show that the BF allocation may be non-optimal in some cases.

10 Conclusions and Summary

10.1 Summary of Part I

We presented two algorithms for computing the data cube. Our algorithms extend the sort-based and hash-based methods for computing group-bys with five optimizations: *smallest-parent*, *cache-results*, *amortize-scans*, *share-sorts* and *share-partitions*. These optimizations are often conflicting. Our proposed algorithms combine them so as to reduce the total cost. The sort-based algorithm, called *PipeSort*, develops a plan by reducing the problem to a minimum weight matching problem on a bipartite graph. The hash-based algorithm, called *PipeHash*, develops a plan by first creating the minimum spanning tree showing what group-by should be generated from what and then choosing a partitioning that takes into account memory availability.

Measurements on five real-life OLAP datasets yielded a factor of two to eight improvement with our algorithms over straightforward methods of computing each group-by separately. Although the PipeHash and PipeSort algorithms are not provably optimum, comparison with conservatively calculated lower bounds show that the PipeHash algorithm was within 8% and the PipeSort algorithm was within 22% of these lower bounds on several datasets. We further experimented with the PipeHash and PipeSort algorithms using a tunable synthetic dataset and observed that their relative performance depends on the sparsity of data values. PipeHash does better on low sparsity data whereas PipeSort does better on high sparsity data. Thus, we can choose between the PipeHash and PipeSort algorithms for a particular dataset based on estimated sparsity of the dataset.

We extended the cube algorithms to compute a specified subset of the 2^N group-bys instead of all of them. Our proposed extension considers intermediate group-bys that are not in the desired subset for generating the best plan. We also extended our algorithms for computing aggregations in the presence of hierarchies on attributes. These extensions are discussed in [SAG96].

10.2 Summary of Part II

In this part we have examined various schemes to implement the CUBE operator. Sorting-based methods exploit the existing ordering to reduce the number of sorts. Also, pipelining can be used to save on reads.

- We have presented one particular sorting based scheme called *Overlap*. This scheme overlaps the computation of different cuboids and minimizes the number of scans needed. It uses estimates about cuboid sizes to determine a "good" schedule for the computation of the cuboids if the estimates are fairly accurate.

- We implemented the *Overlap* method and compared it with two other schemes.From the performance results, it is clear that our algorithm is a definite improvement over the *Independent* and the *Parent* methods. The idea of partitions allows us to overlap the computation of many cuboids using minimum possible memory for each. By overlapping computations and making use of partially matching sort orders, our algorithms will perform much better than the *Independent* and *Parent* method, irrespective of what heuristic is used for allocation.

- The *Overlap* algorithm gives reasonably good performance even for very limited memory. Though these results are for relatively small relations, the memory used was also relatively small. Scaleup experiments show that similar results should hold for larger relations with more memory available. Very often we may not want to compute all the cuboids. This can be handled in our algorithm by deleting nodes which are not to be computed from the cuboid tree. Results show that the algorithm gives good performance even for this case.

- We have shown that the optimal allocation problem is NP-hard. We have therefore used a heuristic allocation (BF) in our algorithm. The results suggest that the heuristics yield performance close to that of optimal allocation in most cases.

10.3   Comparison of PipeSort and Overlap

The PipeSort method takes into account the size of a group-by while selecting a parent with the aim of reducing both scanning cost and sorting cost. It views this as a matching problem to choose the optimal parent and sort order for each group-by. It may thus use more than one sort order.

The Overlap method on the other hand uses a single sort order. This helps in setting up multiple pipelines (as against the single pipeline of the PipeSort method) to achieve more overlap using Partitions. While choosing a parent, it tries to get maximum match in their sort orders. However, unlike PipeSort, it does not consider the size of the group-bys.

We have not compared the performance of these two methods. As future work, we plan to study their relative merits, and consider how their best features can be combined.

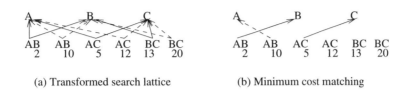

(a) Transformed search lattice   (b) Minimum cost matching

Figure 2   Computing level 1 group-bys from level 2 group-bys in a 3 attribute cube

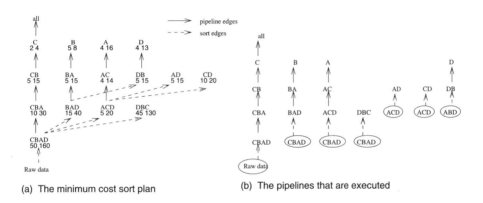

(a) The minimum cost sort plan   (b) The pipelines that are executed

Figure 3   Sort-based method for computing a four attribute cube

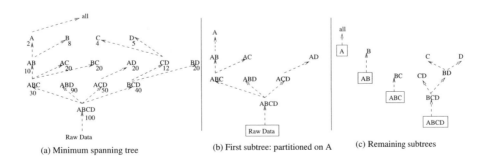

(a) Minimum spanning tree   (b) First subtree: partitioned on A   (c) Remaining subtrees

Figure 4   PipeHash on a four attribute group-by

NH:NaiveHash   PH:PipeHash   NS:NaiveSort   PS:PipeSort

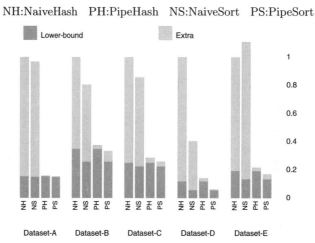

Figure 5   Performance of the cube computation algorithms on the five real life datasets. The y-axis denotes the total time normalized by the time taken by the NaiveHash algorithm for each dataset.

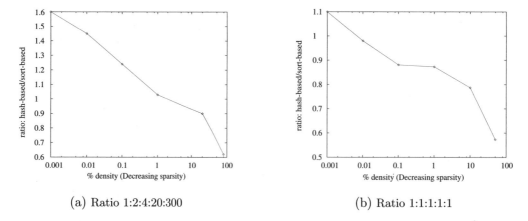

(a) Ratio 1:2:4:20:300   (b) Ratio 1:1:1:1:1

Figure 6   Effect of sparseness on relative performance of PipeSort and PipeHash for a 5 attribute synthetic dataset.

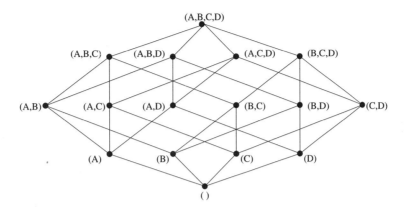

Figure 7 Sort orders enforced on the cuboids

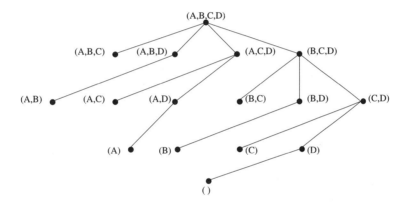

Figure 8 Cuboid Tree obtained from the cuboid DAG

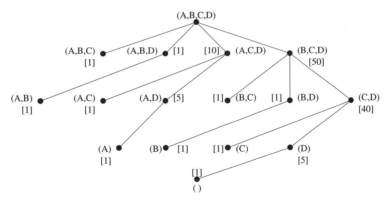

[...] indicates estimated partition size in number of pages

Figure 9 Estimates of Partition Sizes

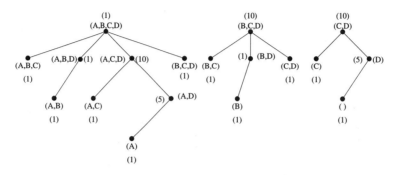

(...) indicates memory allocated in number of pages

Figure 10   Steps of the algorithm

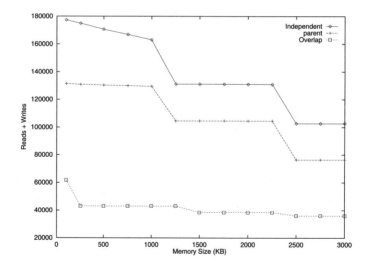

Figure 11   Uniform Data : Varying Memory : Input Size 2.4M, CUBE Size 27.1M

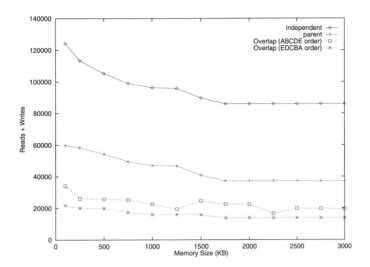

Figure 12   Non-uniform Data : Zipf Distribution : Input Size 2.4M, CUBE Size 10M

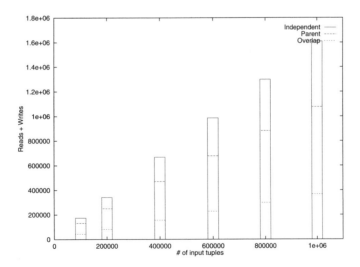

Figure 13   Scale up : I/Os

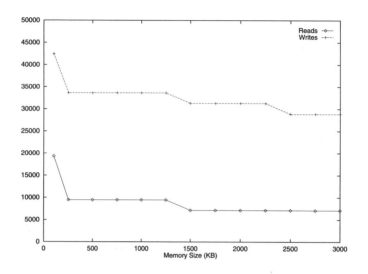

Figure 14   Varying memory : Relation : 2.4M; **CUBE** size : 27.1M

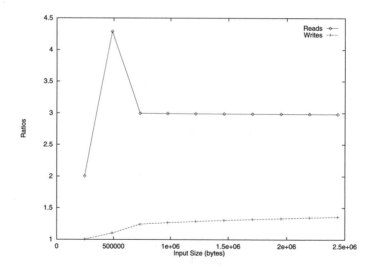

Figure 15   Varying relation sizes: Memory : 500K

25

MAINTENANCE OF DATA CUBES AND SUMMARY TABLES IN A WAREHOUSE

Inderpal Singh Mumick, Dallan Quass,
Barinderpal Singh Mumick

ABSTRACT

Data warehouses contain large amounts of information, often collected from a variety of independent sources. Decision-support functions in a warehouse, such as *on-line analytical processing* (OLAP), involve hundreds of complex aggregate queries over large volumes of data. It is not feasible to compute these queries by scanning the data sets each time. Warehouse applications therefore build a large number of *summary tables*, or materialized aggregate views, to help them increase the system performance.

As changes, most notably new transactional data, are collected at the data sources, all summary tables at the warehouse that depend upon this data need to be updated. Usually, source changes are loaded into the warehouse at regular intervals, usually once a day, in a batch window, and the warehouse is made unavailable for querying while it is updated. Since the number of summary tables that need to be maintained is often large, a critical issue for data warehousing is how to maintain the summary tables efficiently.

In this chapter we propose a method of maintaining aggregate views (the *summary-delta table* method), and use it to solve two problems in maintaining summary tables in a warehouse: (1) how to efficiently maintain a summary table while minimizing the batch window needed for maintenance, and (2) how to maintain a large set of summary tables defined over the same base tables. We show that much of the work required for maintaining one summary table by the summary-delta method can be re-used in maintaining other summary tables, so that a set of summary tables can be maintained efficiently.

While several papers have addressed the issues relating to choosing and materializing a set of summary tables, this is the first chapter to address maintaining summary tables efficiently.

1 Introduction

Data warehouses contain information that is collected from multiple, independent data sources and integrated into a common repository for querying and analysis. Often, data warehouses are designed for *on-line analytical processing* (OLAP), where the queries aggregate large volumes of data in order to detect trends and anomalies. In order to speed up query processing in such environments, warehouses usually contain a large number of *summary tables*, which represent materialized aggregate views of the base data collected from the sources. The summary tables group the base data along various *dimensions*, corresponding to different sets of group-by attributes, and compute various aggregate functions, often called *measures*. As an example, the cube operator [GBLP96] can be used to define several such summary tables with one statement.

As changes are made to the data sources, the warehouse views must be updated to reflect the changed state of the data sources. The views either can be recomputed from scratch, or incremental maintenance techniques [BC79, SI84, RK86b, BLT86, Han87, SP89b, QW91, Qua96, CW91, GMS93, GL95, LMSS95b, ZGMHW95] can be used to calculate the changes to the views due to the source changes. It is common in a data warehousing environment for source changes to be *deferred* and applied to the warehouse views in large batches for efficiency. Source changes received during the day are applied to the views in a nightly batch window, during which time the warehouse is unavailable to readers.

The nightly batch window involves updating the base tables (if any) stored at the warehouse, and maintaining all the materialized summary tables. The problem with this approach is that the warehouse is typically unavailable to readers while the views are being maintained, due to the large number of updates that need to be applied. Since the warehouse must be made available to readers again by the next morning, the time required for maintenance is often a limiting factor in the number of summary tables that can be made available in the warehouse. Because the number of summary tables available has such a significant impact on OLAP query performance, maintaining the summary tables efficiently is crucial.

This chapter addresses the issue of efficiently maintaining a set of summary tables in a data warehouse. Using efficient incremental maintenance techniques, it is possible to increase the number of summary tables available in the warehouse, or alternatively, to decrease the time that the warehouse is unavailable to readers. The chapter includes the following contributions:

- We propose a new method, called the summary-delta tables method, for maintenance of aggregate views. The summary-delta tables method represents a new paradigm for incremental view maintenance.

- A general strategy to minimize the batch time needed for maintenance is to split the maintenance work into *propagate* and *refresh* functions. Propagate can occur outside the batch window, while refresh occurs inside the batch window. The propagate and refresh split for relational algebra was originally presented and formalized in [CGL+96]. We use the propagate and refresh approach of [CGL+96], and extend it to aggregate views by giving algorithms that split the maintenance work required for summary tables into propagate and refresh functions.

- We show how multiple summary tables can be related so that their maintenance can take advantage of the computation done to maintain other summary tables.

Chapter outline: Section 2 presents a motivating example illustrating the importance of efficient incremental maintenance of summary tables. Background and notation is given in Section 3. Section 4 presents propagate and refresh functions for maintaining individual summary tables. Section 5 explains how multiple summary tables can be maintained efficiently together. A performance study of the summary-delta table method, based upon an experimental implementation, is presented in Section 6. Related work and conclusions appear in Section 7.

2 Motivating Example

Consider a warehouse of retail information, with point-of-sale (pos) data from hundreds of stores. The point of sale data is stored in the warehouse in a large pos table, called a *fact table*, that contains a tuple for each item sold in a sales transaction. Each tuple has the format

    pos(storeID, itemID, date, qty, price);

The attributes of the tuple are the id of the store selling the item, the id of the item sold, the date of the sale, the quantity of the item sold, and the selling price of the item. The `pos` table is allowed to contain duplicates, for example, when an item is sold in different transactions in the same store on the same date.

In addition, a warehouse will often store *dimension tables*, which contain information related to the fact table. Let the `stores` and `items` tables contain store information and item information, respectively. The key of `stores` is storeID, and the key of `items` is itemID.

> `stores`(storeID, city, region);
> `items`(itemID, name, category, cost);

Data in dimension tables often represents *dimension hierarchies*. A dimension hierarchy is essentially a set of functional dependencies among the attributes of the dimension table. For our example we will assume that in the stores dimension hierarchy, storeID functionally determines city, and city functionally determines region. In the items dimension hierarchy, itemID functionally determines name, category, and cost.

In order to answer aggregate queries quickly, a warehouse will often store a number of summary tables, which are materialized views that aggregate the data in the fact table, possibly after joining it with one or more dimension tables. Figure 1 shows four summary tables, each defined as a materialized SQL view. We assume that these views have been chosen to be materialized, either by the database administrator, or by using an algorithm such as [HRU96].

Note that the names of the views have been chosen to reflect the group-by attributes. The character S represents storeID, I represents itemID, and D represents date. The notation sC represents the city for a store, sR represents the region for a store, and iC represents the category for an item. For example, the name SiC_sales implies that storeID and category are the group-by attributes in the view definition.

The views of Figure 1 could represent four of the possible points on a "data cube" as described in [GBLP96], except for the use of date as both a dimension and a measure. Another difference between this chapter and previous work on data cubes is that in previous work the data being aggregated comes solely from the fact table, with dimension hierarchy information obtained implicitly. As mentioned earlier, data warehouses typically store dimension hierarchy information explicitly in dimension tables; in this chapter we extend the data-cube concept to include explicit joins with dimension tables (see Section 3.3).

As sales are made, changes representing the new point-of-sale data come into the warehouse. As mentioned in Section 1, most warehouses do not apply the changes immediately. Instead, changes are deferred and applied to the base tables and summary tables in the warehouse at night in a single batch. Deferring the changes allows analysts that query the warehouse to see a consistent snapshot of the data throughout the day, and can make the maintenance more efficient.

Although it is often the case that changes to a warehouse involve only insertions, for the sake of example in this chapter we will assume that the changes involve both insertions and deletions. In order to correctly maintain an aggregate view in the presence of deletions it is necessary to include a COUNT(*) aggregate function in the view. Having COUNT(*) makes it possible to determine when all tuples in a group have been deleted (*i.e.*, when COUNT(*) for the group becomes 0), implying the deletion of the tuple for the group in the view. We have included COUNT(*) explicitly in the example views above, but it also could be added implicitly when the view is materialized in the warehouse.

For simplicity of presentation, we will usually assume in this chapter that maintenance is performed in response to changes only to the fact table, and that the columns being aggregated do not include null values. However, the algorithms we present are easily extended to handle changes also to the dimension tables, as well as nulls in the aggregated columns. The effect of changes to dimension tables is considered in Section 6, and the effect of nulls in the aggregated columns is considered in Section 3.1.

```
CREATE VIEW SID_sales(storeID, itemID, date, TotalCount, TotalQuantity) AS
SELECT storeID, itemID, date, COUNT(*) AS TotalCount, SUM(qty) AS TotalQuantity
FROM pos
GROUPBY storeID, itemID, date


CREATE VIEW sCD_sales(city, date, TotalCount, TotalQuantity) AS
SELECT city, date, COUNT(*) AS TotalCount, SUM(qty) AS TotalQuantity
FROM pos, stores
WHERE pos.storeID = stores.storeID
GROUPBY city, date


CREATE VIEW SiC_sales(storeID, category, TotalCount, EarliestSale, TotalQuantity) AS
SELECT storeID, category, COUNT(*) AS TotalCount, MIN(date) AS EarliestSale, SUM(qty) AS TotalQuantity
FROM pos, items
WHERE pos.itemID = items.itemID
GROUPBY storeID, category


CREATE VIEW sR_sales(region, TotalCount, TotalQuantity) AS
SELECT region, COUNT(*) AS TotalCount, SUM(qty) AS TotalQuantity
FROM pos, stores
WHERE pos.storeID = stores.storeID
GROUPBY region
```

Figure 1   Example summary tables

2.1   Maintaining a single summary table

We will illustrate the summary-delta table method through an example, using it to maintain the SID_sales summary table of Figure 1. Later in Section 2.2, we show that much of the work in maintaining SID_sales can be re-used to maintain the other summary tables in the figure. The complete algorithms for maintaining a single summary table and a set of summary tables appear in Sections 4 and 5 respectively.

An important aspect of our maintenance algorithm is that the maintenance process is divided into two functions: propagate and refresh. The work of computing a summary-delta table happens within the propagate function, which can take place without locking the summary tables so that the warehouse can continue to be made available for querying by analysts. Summary tables are not locked until the refresh function, during which time the summary table is updated from the summary-delta table.

Propagate: The propagate function involves creating a *summary-delta table* from the deferred set of changes. The summary-delta table represents the net changes to the summary table due to the changes to the fact table. Let the deferred set of insertions be stored in table `pos_ins` and the deferred set of deletions be stored in table `pos_del`. Then the summary-delta table is derived using the following SQL statement, without accessing the base `pos` table.

```
CREATE VIEW sd_SID_sales (storeID, itemID, date, sd_Count,
                          sd_Quantity) AS
SELECT storeID, itemID, date, SUM(_count) AS sd_Count,
       SUM(_quantity) AS sd_Quantity
FROM ( (SELECT storeID, itemID, date, 1 as _count,
               qty as _quantity
        FROM pos_ins)
       UNION ALL
       (SELECT storeID, itemID, date, -1 as _count,
               -qty as _quantity
        FROM pos_del) )
GROUPBY storeID, itemID, date
```

To compute the summary-delta table, we first perform a projection on the inserted and deleted tuples so that we have 1 for count and qty for quantity from the inserted tuples, and the negative of those values from the deleted tuples. We then take the union of this result and aggregate it, grouping by the same group-by attributes as in the summary table. The resulting aggregate function values represent the net changes to the corresponding aggregate function values in the summary table. The propagate function is explained fully in Section 4.1.

Refresh: The refresh function applies the net changes represented in the summary-delta table to the summary table. The function to refresh SID_sales appears in Figure 2, and is described below. It takes as input the summary-delta table sd_SID_sales, and the summary table SID_sales, and updates the summary table to reflect the changes in the summary-delta table. For simplicity, we assume here that there are no null values in `pos`. Null values will be considered later when deriving the generic refresh algorithm.

The refresh function has been designed to run quickly. Except for certain cases involving MIN and MAX (see Section 4.2), the refresh function does not require access to the base `pos` table, and all aggregation is performed in the propagate function. Each tuple in the summary-delta table causes a single update to the summary table, and each tuple in the summary table is updated at most once.

Intuitively, the refresh function of Figure 2 can be written as an embedded SQL program using cursors as follows. A cursor c_1 is opened to iterate over each tuple δt in the summary-delta table sd_SID_sales. For each δt, a query is issued and a second cursor c_2 is opened to find a matching tuple t in the summary table SID_sales (there is at most one matching t since the match is on the group-by attributes). If a matching tuple t is not found, then the δt tuple is inserted into the summary table. Otherwise, if t is found it is updated or deleted using cursor c_2, depending upon whether all tuples in t's group have been deleted. The refresh function is explained fully in Section 4.2, including an explanation of how it can be optimized when certain integrity constraints on the changes hold.

2.2 Maintaining multiple summary tables

We now give propagate functions that create summary deltas for the remaining summary tables of Figure 1. Efficiently maintaining multiple summary tables together allows more opportunity for optimization than maintaining each summary table individually, because the summary-delta table computed for the maintenance of one summary table often can be used to compute summary-delta tables for other summary

For each tuple δt in sd_SID_sales:
  Let tuple $t =$
    (SELECT *
    FROM SID_sales d
    WHERE d.storeID $= \delta t$.storeID AND d.date $= \delta t$.date AND d.itemID $= \delta t$.itemID)
  If t is not found,
    Insert tuple δt into SID_sales
  Else /* if t is found */
    If δt.sd_Count $+\ t$.TotalCount $= 0$,
      Delete tuple t from SID_sales
    Else
      Update tuple t.TotalCount $+= \delta t$.sd_Count,
          t.TotalQuantity $+= \delta t$.sd_Quantity

Figure 2 Refresh function for SID_sales.

tables. Since a summary-delta table already involves some aggregation over the changes to the base tables, it is likely to be smaller than the changes themselves, so using a summary-delta table to compute other summary-delta tables will likely require fewer tuple accesses than computing each summary-delta table from the changes directly.

The queries defining summary-delta tables for sCD_sales, SiC_sales, and sR_sales are shown in Figure 3. The summary-delta tables for sCD_sales and SiC_sales both reference the summary-delta table for SID_sales, and the summary-delta table for sR_sales references the summary-delta table for sCD_sales.

Note that the summary-delta table sd_sCD_sales includes the region attribute, which is not necessary to maintain sCD_sales. Region is included so that later in the definition of sd_sR_sales we do not need to join sd_sCD_sales with stores. Including region in sd_sCD_sales does not affect the maintenance of sCD_sales because in the dimension hierarchy for cities we have specified that city functionally determines region, *i.e.*, every city belongs to a single region, so grouping by (city, region, date) results in the same groups as grouping by (city, date).

The refresh functions corresponding to the summary-delta tables of Figure 3 are not given in this section. In general they follow in a straightforward fashion from the example refresh function for SID_sales given in Section 2.1, with the exception of the MIN aggregate function in SiC_sales. In Section 4.2 we show how the refresh function handles MIN and MAX aggregate functions.

3 Background and Notation

In this section we review the concepts of self-maintainable aggregate functions (Section 3.1), data cube (Section 3.2), and the computation lattice corresponding to a data cube (Section 3.3).

3.1 Self-maintainable aggregate functions

In [GBLP96], aggregate functions are divided three classes: *distributive*, *algebraic*, and *holistic*. Distributive aggregate functions can be computed by partitioning their input into disjoint sets, aggregating each set individually, then further aggregating the (partial) results from each set into the final result. Amongst

```
CREATE VIEW sd_sCD_sales(city, region, date, sd_Count, sd_Quantity) AS
SELECT city, region, date, SUM(sd_Count) AS sd_Count, SUM(sd_Quantity) AS sd_Quantity
FROM sd_SID_sales, stores
WHERE sd_SID_sales.storeID = stores.storeID
GROUPBY city, region, date


CREATE VIEW sd_SiC_sales(storeID, category, sd_Count, sd_EarliestSale, sd_Quantity) AS
SELECT storeID, category, SUM(sd_Count) AS sd_Count, MIN(date) AS sd_EarliestSale,
       SUM(sd_Quantity) AS sd_Quantity
FROM sd_SID_sales, items
WHERE sd_SID_sales.itemID = items.itemID
GROUPBY storeID, category


CREATE VIEW sd_sR_sales(region, sd_Count, sd_Quantity) AS
SELECT region, sum(sd_Count) AS sd_Count, SUM(sd_Quantity) AS sd_Quantity
FROM sd_sCD_sales
GROUPBY region
```

Figure 3 Propagate Functions

the aggregate functions found in standard SQL, COUNT, SUM, MIN, and MAX are distributive. For example, COUNT can be computed by summing partial counts. Note however, if the DISTINCT keyword is used, as in COUNT(DISTINCT E) (count the distinct values of E) then these functions are no longer distributive.

Algebraic aggregate functions can be expressed as a scalar function of distributive aggregate functions. Average is algebraic, since it can be expressed as SUM/COUNT. From now on we will assume that if a view is supposed to contain the AVG aggregate function, the materialized view will contain instead the SUM and COUNT functions.

Holistic aggregate functions cannot be computed by dividing into parts. Median is an example of a holistic aggregate function. We will not consider holistic functions in this chapter.

Definition 3.1 (Self-maintainable aggregates): A set of aggregate functions is *self-maintainable* if the new value of the functions can be computed solely from the old values of the aggregation functions and from the changes to the base data. Aggregate functions can be self-maintainable with respect to insertions, with respect to deletions, or both. ∎

In order for an aggregate function to be self-maintainable it must be distributive. In fact, all distributive aggregate functions are self-maintainable with respect to insertions. However, not all distributive aggregate functions are self-maintainable with respect to deletions. The COUNT(*) function can help to make certain aggregate functions self-maintainable with respect to deletions, by helping to determine when all tuples in the group (or in the full table if a group-by is not performed) have been deleted, so that the grouped tuple can be deleted from the view.

The function COUNT(*) is always self-maintainable with respect to deletions. Including COUNT(*) also makes the function COUNT(E), (count the number of non-null values of E), self-maintainable with respect to deletions. If nulls are not allowed in the input, then COUNT(*) also makes SUM(E) self-maintainable with respect to deletions. In the presence of nulls, both COUNT(*) and COUNT(E) are required to make SUM(E) self-maintainable.

MIN and MAX functions: MIN and MAX are not self-maintainable with respect to deletions, and cannot be made self-maintainable. For instance, when a tuple having the minimum (maximum) value is deleted, the new minimum (maximum) value for the group must be recomputed from the changes and the base data. Including COUNT(*) can help a little (if COUNT(*) reaches 0, there is no other tuple in the group, so the group can be deleted), but COUNT(*) cannot make MIN and MAX self-maintainable. (If COUNT(*) > 0 after a tuple having minimum (maximum) value is deleted, we still need to look up the base table.) COUNT(E) can also help in maintaining MIN(E) and MAX(E) (If Count(*) > 0 and COUNT(E) $= 0$, then MIN(E)= null), but COUNT(E) also cannot make MIN and MAX self-maintainable (if Count(*) > 0 and COUNT(E) > 0, and a tuple having minimum (maximum) value is deleted, then we need to look up the base table).

3.2   Data cube

The date cube [GBLP96] is a convenient way of thinking about multiple aggregate views, all derived from a fact table using different sets of group-by attributes. Data cubes are popular in OLAP because they provide an intuitive way for data analysts to navigate various levels of summary information in the database. In a data cube, attributes are categorized into *dimension attributes*, on which grouping may be performed, and *measures*, which are the results of aggregate functions.

Cube Views: A data cube with k dimension attributes is a shorthand for 2^k cube views, each one defined by a single SELECT-FROM-WHERE-GROUPBY block, having identical aggregation functions, identical FROM and WHERE clauses, no HAVING clause, and one of the 2^k subsets of the dimension attributes as the groupby columns.

EXAMPLE 3.1 An example data cube for the pos table of Section 2 is shown in Figure 4 as a lattice structure. Construction of the lattice corresponding to a data cube was first introduced in [HRU96].

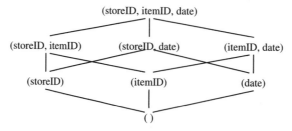

Figure 4   Data Cube Lattice.

The dimension attributes of the data cube are storeID, itemID, and date, and the measures are COUNT(*) and SUM(qty). Since the measures computed are assumed to be the same, each point in the figure is annotated simply by the group-by attributes. Thus, the point (storeID, itemID) represents the cube view corresponding to the query

(SI):   SELECT storeID, itemID, COUNT(*), SUM(qty)
        FROM pos
        GROUPBY storeID, itemID ;

■

Edges in a lattice run from the node above to the node below. Each edge $v1 \rightarrow v2$ implies that $v2$ can be answered using $v1$, instead of accessing the base data. The edge defines a query that derives view $v2$ below from the view $v1$ above by simply replacing the table in the FROM clause with the name of the view above, and by replacing any COUNT aggregate function with the SUM aggregate function. For example, the edge from $v1 = $ (storeID, itemID, date) to $v2 = $ (storeID, itemID) defines the following query equivalent to query SI above (assuming that the aggregate columns in the views are named count and qty).

(SI'):   SELECT storeID, itemID, SUM(count), SUM(qty)
         FROM v1
         GROUPBY storeID, itemID ;

Generalized Cube Views: However, in most warehouses and decision support systems, the set of summary tables do not fit into the structure of cube views—they differ in their aggregation functions and the joins they perform with the fact tables[1]. Further, some views may do aggregation on columns used as dimension attributes in other views. We will call these views *generalized cube views*, and define them as traditional cube-style views that are extended in the following ways:

- different views may compute different aggregate functions,

- some views may compute aggregate functions over attributes that are used as group-by attributes in other views,

- views may join with different combinations of dimension tables (note that dimension-table joins are always along foreign keys).

3.3   Dimension hierarchies and lattices

As mentioned in Section 2, the various dimensions represented by the group-by attributes of a fact table often are organized into dimension hierarchies. For example, in the stores dimension, stores can be grouped into cities, and cities can be grouped into regions. In the items dimension, items can be grouped into categories.

The dimension hierarchy information can be stored in separate dimension tables, as we did in the **stores** and **items** tables. In order to group by attributes further along the dimension hierarchy, the fact table must be joined with the dimension tables before doing the aggregation. The joins between the fact table and dimension tables are always along foreign keys, so each tuple in the fact table is guaranteed to join with one and only one tuple from each dimension table.

A dimension hierarchy can also be represented by a lattice, similar to a data-cube lattice. We can construct a lattice representing the set of views that can be obtained by grouping on each combination of elements from the set of dimension hierarchies. It turns out that a *direct product* of the lattice for the fact table along with the lattices for the dimension hierarchies yields the desired result [HRU96]. For example, given that stores are grouped into cities and then regions, and items are grouped into categories, Figure 5 shows the lattice combining the fact table lattice of Figure 4 with the dimension hierarchy lattices of store and item.

3.4   Partially-materialized lattices

A partially-materialized lattice is obtained by removing some nodes of the lattice, to represent the fact that the corresponding views are not being materialized. When a node n is removed, all incoming and outgoing

---

[1]They may also differ in the WHERE clause, but we do not consider differing WHERE clauses in this chapter.

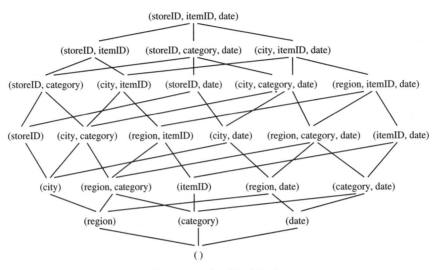

Figure 5 Combined lattice.

edges from node n are also removed, and new edges are added between nodes above and below node n. For every incoming edge $(n1, n)$, and every outgoing edge $(n, n2)$, we add an edge $(n1, n2)$. The query defining view $n2$ along the edge $(n1, n2)$ is obtained from the query along the edge $(n, n2)$ by replacing view n in the FROM clause with view $n1$. Note that if the top and/or bottom elements of the lattice are removed, the resulting partially-materialized lattice may not be a lattice - it represents a partial order between nodes without a top and/or a bottom element.

4   Basic Summary-Delta Maintenance Algorithm

In this section we show how to efficiently maintain a summary table given changes to the base data. Specifically, we give propagate and refresh functions for maintaining a generalized cube view of the type described in Section 3.2, including joins with dimension tables. We require that the aggregate functions calculated in the summary table either be self-maintainable, be made self-maintainable by adding the appropriate COUNT functions as described in Section 3.1, or be MIN or MAX aggregate functions (in which case the circumstances under which they are not self-maintainable are detected and handled in the refresh function). For simplicity, we start out by considering changes (insertions and deletions) only to the base fact table. We consider changes to the dimension tables in Section 6.

4.1   Propagate function

As described briefly in Section 2, the general intuition for the propagate function is to create a *summary-delta table* that contains the net effect of the changes on the summary table. Since the propagate function does not affect the summary table, the summary table can continue to be available to readers while the propagate function is computed. Therefore, the goal of the propagate function is to do as much work as possible so that the time required by the refresh function is minimized.

Preparing changes

In order to make the computation of the summary-delta table easier to understand, we split up some of the work by first defining three *virtual* views: *prepare-changes*, *prepare-insertions* and *prepare-deletions*. The prepare-changes virtual view is defined simply as the union of prepare-insertions and prepare-deletions, which are described below. In Section 6 we will see that the summary-delta table is computed from the prepare-changes virtual view.

The prepare-insertions and prepare-deletions views derive the changes to the aggregate functions caused by individual insertions and deletions, respectively, to the base data. They take a projection of the insertions/deletions to the base data, after applying any selections conditions and joins that appear in the definition of the summary table. The projected attributes include

- each of the group-by attributes of the summary table, and

- *aggregate-source* attributes corresponding to each of the aggregate functions computed in the summary table.

An aggregate-source attribute computes the result of the expression on which the aggregate function is applied. For example, if the summary table included the aggregate function sum(A*B), the prepare-insertions and prepare-deletions virtual views would each include in their select clause an aggregate-source attribute computing either $A * B$ (for prepare-insertions), or $-(A * B)$ (for prepare-deletions). We will see later that the aggregate-source attributes are aggregated when defining the summary-delta table.

The aggregate-source attributes are derived according to Table 1. The column labeled prepare-insertions describes how they are derived for the prepare-insertions view; the column labeled prepare-deletions describes how they are derived for the prepare-deletions view. The COUNT(*expr*) row uses the SQL-92 case statement [MS93a].

	prepare-insertions	prepare-deletions
COUNT(*)	1	-1
COUNT(*expr*)	case when *expr* is null then 0 else 1	case when *expr* is null then 0 else -1
SUM(*expr*)	*expr*	$-expr$
MIN(*expr*)	*expr*	*expr*
MAX(*expr*)	*expr*	*expr*

Table 1   Deriving aggregate-source attributes

EXAMPLE 4.1 Consider the SiC_sales view of Figure 1. The prepare-insertions, prepare-deletions, and the prepare-changes virtual views for SiC_sales are shown in Figure 6. The prepare-insertions view name is prefixed by "pi_," the prepare-deletions view name is prefixed by "pd_," and the prepare-changes view name is prefixed by "pc_." The aggregate sources are named _count, _date, and _quantity, respectively. ∎

Computing the summary-delta table

The summary-delta table is computed by aggregating the prepare-changes virtual view. The summary-delta table has the same schema as the summary table, except that the attributes resulting from aggregate functions in the summary delta represent changes to the corresponding aggregate functions in the summary

```
CREATE VIEW pi_SiC_sales(storeID, category, _count, _date, _quantity) AS
SELECT storeID, category, 1 AS _count, date AS _date, qty AS _quantity
FROM pos_ins, items
WHERE pos_ins.itemID = items.itemID


CREATE VIEW pd_SiC_sales(storeID, category, _count, _date, _quantity) AS
SELECT storeID, category, -1 AS _count, date AS _date, -qty AS _quantity
FROM pos_del, items
WHERE pos_del.itemID = items.itemID


CREATE VIEW pc_SiC_sales(storeID, category, _count, _date, _quantity) AS
SELECT *
FROM (pi_SiC_sales UNION ALL pd_SiC_sales)
```

Figure 6 Prepare changes example

table. For this reason we name attributes resulting from aggregate functions in the summary-delta table after the name of the corresponding attribute in the summary table, prefixed by "sd_."

Each tuple in the summary-delta table describes the effect of the base-data changes on the aggregate functions of a corresponding tuple in the summary table (*i.e.*, a tuple in the summary table having the same values for all group-by attributes as the tuple in the summary-delta table). Note that a corresponding tuple in the summary table may not exist, and in fact it is sometimes necessary in the refresh function to insert a tuple into (or delete a tuple from) the summary table due to the changes represented in the summary-delta table.

The query to compute the summary-delta table follows from the query computing the summary table, with the following differences:

- The **FROM** clause is replaced by prepare-changes.

- The **WHERE** clause is removed. (It is already applied when defining prepare-insertions and prepare-deletions.)

- The expressions on which the aggregate functions are applied are replaced by references to the aggregate-source attributes of prepare-changes.

- **COUNT** aggregate functions are replaced by **SUM**.

Note that computing the summary-delta table involves essentially aggregating the tuples in the changes. Thus, techniques for parallelizing aggregation can be used to speed up computation of the summary-delta table.

EXAMPLE 4.2 Consider again the SiC_sales view of Figure 1. The query computing the summary-delta table for SiC_sales is shown below. It aggregates the changes represented in the prepare-changes virtual view, grouping by the same group-by attributes as the summary table.

```
CREATE VIEW sd_SiC_sales(storeID, category, sd_Count,
                    sd_EarliestSale, sd_Quantity) AS
```

```
SELECT  storeID, category, sum(_count) AS  sd_Count,
        min(_date) AS  sd_EarliestSale,
        sum(_quantity) AS  sd_Quantity
FROM pc_SiC_sales
GROUPBY  storeID, category
```

The astute reader will recall that in Section 2.2 the summary-delta table for SiC_sales was defined using the summary-delta table for SID_sales. In this example we defined the summary-delta table using instead the changes to the base data. ∎

Pre-aggregation

As a potential optimization, it is possible to pre-aggregate the insertions and deletions before joining with some of the dimension tables. In particular, joins with dimension tables whose attributes are not referenced in the aggregate functions, can be delayed until after pre-aggregation. Delaying joins until after pre-aggregation reduces the number of tuples involved in the join, potentially speeding up the computation of the summary-delta table. The decision of whether or not to pre-aggregate could be made in a cost-based manner by a query optimizer. The notion of pre-aggregation follows essentially from the idea of pushing down aggregation presented in [CS94, GHQ95, YL95].

Changes to dimension tables

Up to now we have considered changes only to the fact table. Changes to the dimension tables can also be incorporated into our method. Due to space constraints we will only give the intuition underlying the technique.

Applying the incremental view-maintenance techniques of [GMS93, GL95], we can start with the changes to a dimension table, and derive dimension-table-specific prepare-insertions and prepare-deletions views that represent the changes to the aggregate functions due to changes to the dimension table. For example, the following view definition calculates prepare-insertions for SiC_sales due to insertions to `items` (made available in `items_ins`).

```
CREATE VIEW pi_items_SiC_sales(storeID, category, _count,
                                 _date, _quantity) AS
SELECT  storeID, category, 1 AS  _count, date AS  _date,
        qty AS  _quantity
FROM pos, items_ins
WHERE  pos.itemID = items_ins.itemID
```

Prepare-changes then takes the union of all such prepare-insertions and prepare-deletions views, representing changes to the fact table and all dimension tables, and the summary-delta computation proceeds as before.

4.2   Refresh function

The refresh function applies the changes represented in the summary-delta table to the summary table. Each tuple in the summary-delta table causes a change to a single corresponding tuple in the summary

For each tuple δt in the summary-delta table,
    % get the corresponding tuple in the summary table
    Let tuple t = tuple in the summary table having the same values for its group-by attributes as δt
    If t is not found,
        % insert tuple
        Insert tuple δt into the summary table
    Else
        % check if the tuple needs to be deleted
        If $\delta t.\texttt{COUNT}(*) + t.\texttt{COUNT}(*) = 0$,
          Delete tuple t
        Else
          % check if min/max values must be recomputed
          recompute = false
          For each $\texttt{MIN}$ and $\texttt{MAX}$ aggregate function $m(e)$ in the summary table,
            If ((m is a $\texttt{MIN}$ function AND $\delta t.\texttt{MIN}(e) \leq t.\texttt{MIN}(e)$ AND $t.\texttt{COUNT}(e) + \delta t.\texttt{COUNT}(e) > 0$) OR
              (m is a $\texttt{MAX}$ function AND $\delta t.\texttt{MAX}(e) \geq t.\texttt{MAX}(e)$ AND $t.\texttt{COUNT}(e) + \delta t.\texttt{COUNT}(e) > 0$))
              recompute = true
          If (recompute)
            Update tuple t by recomputing its aggregate functions from the base data for t's group.
          Else
            % update the tuple
            For each aggregate function $a(e)$ in the summary table,
              If $t.\texttt{COUNT}(e) + \delta t.\texttt{COUNT}(e) = 0$,
                $t.a$ = null
              Else If a is $\texttt{COUNT}$ or $\texttt{SUM}$,
                $t.a = t.a + \delta t.a$
              Else If a is $\texttt{MIN}$,
                $t.a = \texttt{MIN}(t.a, \delta t.a)$
              Else If a is $\texttt{MAX}$,
                $t.a = \texttt{MAX}(t.a, \delta t.a)$

Figure 7   The Refresh function

table (by corresponding we mean a tuple in the summary table having the same values for all group-by attributes as the tuple in the summary delta). The corresponding tuple in the summary table is either updated, deleted, or if the corresponding tuple is not found, the summary-delta tuple is inserted into the summary table.

The refresh algorithm is shown in Figure 7. It generalizes and extends the example refresh function given in Section 2.1, by handling the case of nulls in the input and $\texttt{MIN}$ and $\texttt{MAX}$ aggregate functions. In the algorithm, for each tuple δt in the summary-delta table the corresponding tuple t in the summary table is looked up. If t is not found, the summary-delta tuple is inserted into the summary table. If t is found, then if $\texttt{COUNT}(*)$ from t plus $\texttt{COUNT}(*)$ from δt is zero, then t is deleted.[2] Otherwise, a check is performed for each of the $\texttt{MIN}$ and $\texttt{MAX}$ aggregate functions, to see if a value less than or equal to the minimum (greater

---

[2]Note that $\texttt{COUNT}(*)$ from t plus $\texttt{COUNT}(*)$ from δt can never be less than zero, and that if $\texttt{COUNT}(*)$ from δt is less than zero, then the corresponding tuples t must be found in the summary table.

than or equal to the maximum) value was deleted, in which case the new MIN or MAX value of t will probably need to be recomputed. The only exception is if COUNT(e) from t plus COUNT(e) from δt is zero, in which case the new min/max/sum/count(e) values are null.

As the last step in the algorithm, the aggregation functions of tuple t are updated from the values in δt, or (if needed) by recomputing a min/max value from the base data for t's group. For simplicity in the recomputation, we assume that when a summary table is being refreshed, the changes have already been applied to the base data. However, an alternative would be to do the recomputation before the changes have been applied to the base table by issuing a query that subtracts the deletions from the base data and unions the insertions. As written, the refresh function only considers the COUNT, SUM, MIN, and MAX aggregate functions, but it should be easy to see how any self-maintainable aggregation function would be incorporated.

The above refresh function may appear complex, but conceptually it is very simple. One can think of it as a left outer-join between the summary-delta table and the summary table. Each summary table tuple that joins with a summary-delta tuple is updated or deleted as it joins, while a summary-delta tuple that does not join is inserted into the summary table. The only complication in the process is an occasional recomputation of a min/max value. The refresh function could be parallelized by partitioning the summary-delta table and summary table on the group-by attributes. Such a *"summary-delta join"* needs to be implemented in the database server, and should be implemented by database vendors that are targeting the warehouse market.

5 Efficiently Maintaining Multiple Summary Tables

In the previous section we have shown how to compute the summary-delta table for a generalized cube view, directly from the insertions and deletions into the base fact table.

We have also seen that multiple cube views can be arranged into a (partially-materialized) lattice (Section 3.3). We will now show that multiple summary tables, which are generalized cube views, can also be placed in a (partially-materialized) lattice, which we call a $\mathcal{V}$-lattice. Further, all the summary-delta tables can also be written as generalized cube views, and can be placed in a (partially-materialized) lattice, which we call a $\mathcal{D}$-lattice. It turns out that the $\mathcal{D}$-lattice is identical to the $\mathcal{V}$-lattice, modulo renaming of tables.

5.1 Placing generalized cube views into a lattice

The principle behind the placement of cube views in a lattice is that a cube view $v2$ should be derivable from the cube view $v1$ placed above $v2$ in the cube lattice. The same principle can be adapted to place a given set of generalized cube views into a (partially-materialized) lattice. We will show how to define a *derives relation* $v2 \prec v1$ between the given set of generalized cube views. The derives relation, $\prec$, can be used to impose a partial ordering on the set of generalized views, and to place the views into a (partially-materialized) lattice, with v_1 being an ancestor of v_2 in the lattice if and only if $v_2 \prec v_1$.

For two generalized cube views v_1 and v_2, let $v_2 \prec v_1$ if and only if view v_2 can be defined using a single block SELECT–FROM–GROUPBY query over view v_1 possibly joined with one or more dimension tables on the foreign key. The $v_2 \prec v_1$ condition holds if

1. each group-by attribute of v_2 is either a groupby attribute of v_1, or is an attribute of a dimension table whose foreign key is a groupby attribute of v_1, and

2. each aggregate function $a(E)$ of v_2 either appears in v_1, or E is an expression over the groupby attributes of v_1, or E is an expression over attributes of dimension tables whose foreign keys are groupby attributes of v_1.

If the above conditions are satisfied using dimension tables $d_1, \ldots, d_m$, we will superscript the $\prec$ relation as $\prec^{d_1, \ldots, d_m}$.

EXAMPLE 5.1 For our running retailing warehouse example, the following *derives* relationships exist: sCD_sales $\prec^{\texttt{stores}}$ SID_sales,   SiC_sales $\prec^{\texttt{items}}$ SID_sales,   sR_sales $\prec^{\texttt{stores}}$ SID_sales,   sR_sales $\prec^{\texttt{stores}}$ sCD_sales, and sR_sales $\prec^{\texttt{stores}}$ SiC_sales. SID_sales is the top and sR_sales is the bottom of the lattice.   ∎

The query associated with an edge from v_1 to v_2 is obtained from the original query for v_2 by making the following changes:

- The original WHERE clause is removed (it is not needed since the conditions already appear in v_1).

- The FROM clause is replaced by a reference to v_1. Further, if the $\prec$ relation between $v2$ and $v1$ is superscripted with dimension tables, these are joined into $v1$. (The dimension tables will go into the FROM clause, and the join conditions will go into the WHERE clause.)

- The aggregate functions of v_2 need to be rewritten to reference the aggregate function results computed in v_1. In particular,

  - A COUNT aggregate function needs to be changed to a SUM of the counts computed in v_1.
  - If v_1 groups by an attribute A and v_2 computes SUM(A), then SUM(A) will be replaced by SUM($A *$ Y), where Y is the result of COUNT(*) in v_1. Similarly COUNT(A) will be replaced by SUM(Y).

5.2   Making summary tables lattice-friendly

It is also possible to change the definitions of summary tables slightly so that the *derives* relation between them grows larger, and we do not repeat joins along the lattice paths. The summary tables are changed by adding joins with dimension tables, adding dimension attributes, and adding aggregation functions used by other summary tables.

Let us consider the case of dimension tables and dimension attributes. Are joins with dimension tables all performed implicitly at the top-most view, or could they be performed lower down just before grouping by dimension attributes? Because the joins between the fact table and the dimension tables are along foreign keys—so that each tuple in the fact table joins with one and only one tuple from each dimension table—either approach, joining implicitly at the top-most view or just before grouping on dimension attributes, is possible.

Now, consider a dimension hierarchy. An attribute in the hierarchy functionally determines all of its descendents in the hierarchy. Therefore, grouping by an attribute in the hierarchy yields the same groups as grouping by that attribute plus all of its descendent attributes. For example, grouping by (storeID) is the same as grouping by (storeID, city, region).

The above two properties provide the rationale for the following approach to fitting summary tables into a lattice: join the fact table with all dimension tables at the top-most point in the lattice. At each point in the lattice, instead of grouping only by the group-by attributes mentioned at that point, we include as well each dimension attribute functionally determined by the group-by attributes. For example, the top-most point in the lattice of Figure 5 groups by (storeID, city, region, itemID, category, date).

The end result of the process can be to fit the generalized views into a regular cube (partially-materialized) lattice where all the joins are taken once at the top-most point, and all the views have the same aggregation functions.

EXAMPLE 5.2 For our running warehousing example, we can define all four summary tables as a groupby over the join of pos, items, and stores, computing COUNT(*), SUM(qty), and MIN(date) in each view, and retaining some or all of the dimension attributes City, Region, and Category. The resulting lattice represents a portion of the complete lattice shown in Figure 5. ∎

5.3 Optimizing the lattice

Although the approach of Section 5.2 is always correct, it does not yield the most efficient result. An important question is where best to do the joins with the dimension tables. Further, assuming that some of the dimension columns and aggregation functions have been added to the views just so that the view fits into the lattice, where should the aggregation functions and the extra columns be computed? Optimizing a lattice means pushing joins, aggregation functions, and dimension columns as low down into the lattice as possible.

There are two reasons for pushing down joins: First, as one travels down the data cube, the number of tuples at each point is likely to decrease, so fewer tuples need to be involved in the join. Second, joining with all dimension tables at the top-most view results in very wide tuples, which require more room in memory and on disk. For example, when computing the data cube in Figure 5, instead of joining the pos table with stores and items to compute the (storeID, itemID, date) view, it may be better to push down the join with stores until the (city, itemID, date) view is computed from the (storeID, itemID, date) view, and to push down the join with items until the (storeID, category, date) view is computed from the (storeID, itemID, date) view.

EXAMPLE 5.3 For the running retail warehousing example, optimization derives the lattice shown in Figure 8. The lattice edges are labeled with the dimension join required when deriving the lower view. For example, the edge from SID_sales to SiC_sales is labeled items to indicate that SID_sales needs to be joined with items to derive the SiC_sales view. The view sCD_sales is extended by adding the region attribute so

Figure 8 The $\mathcal{V}$-lattice for the retail warehousing example

that the view sR_sales may be derived from it without (re-)joining with the stores table. ∎

5.4 Summary-delta lattice

Following the self-maintenance conditions discussed in Section 3.1, we assume that any view computing an aggregation function is augmented with COUNT(⋆). A view computing SUM(E), MIN(E), and/or MAX(E) is further augmented with COUNT(E).

Given the set of generalized cube views in the partially-materialized $\mathcal{V}$ lattice, we would like to arrange the summary-delta tables for these views into a partially-materialized lattice (the $\mathcal{D}$, or delta, lattice). The hope is that we can then compute the summary-delta tables more efficiently by exploiting the $\mathcal{D}$ lattice structure, just as the views can be computed more efficiently by exploiting the $\mathcal{V}$ lattice structure.

The following theorem follows from the observation that the queries defining the summary-delta tables sd_v (Section 4.1) are similar to the queries defining the views v, except that some of the tables in the FROM clause are uniformly replaced by the *prepare-changes* table. The theorem gives us the desired $\mathcal{D}$-lattice. (A proof of the theorem appears in [Qua97].)

Theorem 5.1 *The $\mathcal{D}$-lattice is identical to the $\mathcal{V}$-lattice, including the queries along each edge, modulo a change in the names of tables at each node.*   ∎

Thus, each summary delta table can be derived from the summary-delta table above it in the partially-materialized lattice, possibly by a join with dimension tables, followed by a simple groupby operation. The queries defining the topmost summary-delta tables in the $\mathcal{D}$-lattice are obtained by defining a *prepare-changes* virtual view (Section 4.1). For example, the summary-delta $\mathcal{D}$-lattice for our warehouse example is the same as the partially-materialized $\mathcal{V}$-lattice of Figure 8.

5.5   Computing the summary-delta lattice

The beauty of our approach is that the summary table maintenance problem has been partitioned into two subproblems — computation of summary-delta tables (propagation), and the application of refresh functions — in such a way that the subproblem of propagation for multiple summary tables can be mapped to the problem of efficiently computing multiple aggregate views in a lattice.

Propagation of changes to multiple summary tables involves computing all the summary-delta tables in the $\mathcal{D}$-lattice derived in Section 5.4. The problem now is how to compute the summary-delta lattice efficiently, since there are possibly several choices for ancestor summary-delta tables from which to compute a summary-delta. It turns out that that this problem maps directly to the problem of computing multiple summary tables from scratch, as addressed in [AAD$^+$96a, SAG96]. We can use their solutions to derive an efficient propagate strategy on how to sort/hash inputs, what order to evaluate summary-delta tables, and which of the incoming lattice edges (if there is more than one) to use to evaluate a summary-delta table. The algorithms of [AAD$^+$96a, SAG96] would be directly applicable but for the fact that they do not consider join annotations in the lattice. However, it is a simple matter to extend their algorithms by including the join cost estimate in the cost of the derivation of the aggregate view along the edge annotated with the join. We omit the details here as the algorithms for materializing a lattice are not the focus of this chapter.

6   Performance

We have implemented the summary-delta algorithm on top of a common PC-based relational database system. We have used the implementation to test the performance improvements obtained by the summary-delta table method over recomputation, and to determine the benefits of using the lattice structure when maintaining multiple summary tables.

The implementation was done in Centura SQL Application Language (SAL) on a Pentium PC. The test database schema is the same as the one used in our running example described in Section 2. We varied the size of the pos table from 100,000 tuples to 500,000 tuples, and the size of the changes from 1,000 tuples to 10,000 tuples. The pos table had a composite index on (storeID, itemID, date), and each of the summary tables had composite indices on their groupby columns. We found that the performance of the refresh operation depended heavily on the number of updates/deletes vs. inserts to the summary tables. Consequently, we considered two types of changes to the pos table:

- **Update-Generating Changes:** Insertions and deletions of an equal number of tuples over existing date, store, and item values. These changes mostly cause updates amongst the existing tuples in summary tables.

- **Insertion-Generating Changes:** Insertions over new dates, but existing store and item values. These changes cause only inserts into two of the four summary tables (for whom date is a groupby column), and mostly cause updates into the other two summary-delta tables.

The insertion-generating changes are very meaningful since in many data warehousing applications the only changes to the fact tables are insertions of tuples for new dates, which leads to insertions, but no updates, into summary tables with date as a groupby column.

Figure 9 shows four graphs illustrating the performance advantage of using the summary-delta table method. The graphs show the time to rematerialize (using the lattice structure), and maintain all four summary tables using the summary-delta table method (using the lattice structure). The maintenance time is split into propagate and refresh, with the lower solid line representing the portion of the maintenance time taken by propagate when using the lattice structure. The upper solid line represents the total maintenance time (propagate + refresh). The time taken by propagate without using the lattice structure is shown with a dotted line for comparison.

Graphs 9(a) and 9(c) plot the variation in elapsed time as the size of the change set changes, for a fixed size (500,000) of the pos table. While 9(a) considers update-generating changes, graph 9(c) considers insertion-generating changes. We note that the incremental maintenance wins for both types of changes, but it wins with a greater margin for the insertion-generating changes. The difference between the two scenarios is mainly in the refresh times for the views SID_sales and sCD_sales; The refresh time going down by 50% in 9(c). The graphs also show that the summary-delta maintenance beats rematerialization, and that propagate benefits by exploiting the lattice structure. Further, the benefit to propagate increases as the size of the change set increases.

Graphs 9(b) and 9(d) plot the variation in elapsed time as the size of the pos table changes, for a fixed size (10,000) of the change set. Graph 9(b) considers update generating changes, and graph 9(d) considers insertion generating changes. We see that the propagate time stays virtually constant with increase in the size of pos table (as one would expect, since propagate does not depend on the pos table); However interestingly the refresh time goes down for the update generating changes. A close look reveals that when the pos table is small, refresh causes a significant number of deletions in addition to updates to the materialized views. When the pos table is large, refresh causes only updates to the materialized views, and this leads to a 20% savings in refresh time.

7 Related Work and Conclusions

Both view maintenance and data warehousing are active areas of research, and this chapter is in the intersection of the two areas, proposing new view maintenance techniques for maintaining multiple summary tables (aggregate views) over a star schema using a new *summary-delta* paradigm.

Earlier view maintenance papers [BLT86, CW91, QW91, GMS93, GL95, JMS95, ZGMHW95, CGL+96, HZ96, Qua96] have all used the *delta* paradigm - compute a set of inserted and deleted tuples that are then used to refresh the materialized view using simple union and difference operations. The new summary-delta paradigm is to compute a summary-delta table that represents a summary of the changes to be applied to the materialized view. The actual refresh of the materialized view is more complex than a

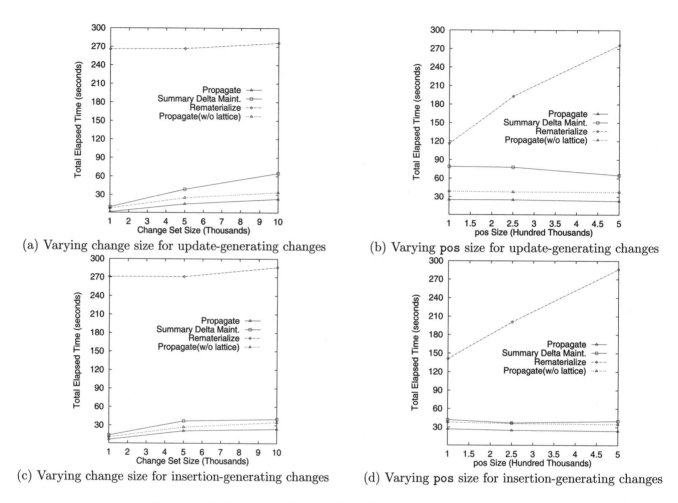

Figure 9 Performance of Summary-Delta Maintenance algorithm

union/difference in the delta paradigm, and can cause updates, insertions, and/or deletions to the materialized view. Amongst the above work on view maintenance algorithms, [GMS93, GL95, JMS95, Qua96] are the only papers that discuss maintenance algorithms for aggregate views. [GMS93, GL95, Qua96] develop algorithms to compute sets of inserted and deleted tuples into an aggregate view, while [JMS95] discusses the computational complexity of immediately maintaining a single aggregate view in response to a single insertion into a *chronicle* (sequence of tuples). It is worth noting that the previous papers do not consider the problem of maintaining multiple aggregate views, and are not as efficient as the summary-delta table method.

A formal split of the maintenance process into propagate and refresh functions was proposed in [CGL⁺96]. We build on the propagate/refresh idea here, extending it to aggregate views and to more complex refresh functions. Our notion of self-maintainable aggregation functions is an extension of self-maintainability for select-project-join views defined in [GJM96, QGMW96].

[GBLP96] proposed the cube operator linking together related aggregate tables into one SQL query, and started a mini-industry in warehousing research. The notion of cube lattices and dimension lattices was proposed in [HRU96], along with an algorithm to determine a subset of cube views to be materialized so as to maximize the querying benefit under a given space constraint. Algorithms to efficiently materialize all or a subset of the cube lattice have been proposed by [AAD$^+$96a, SAG96]. Next, we need a technique to maintain these cube views efficiently, and this chapter provides the summary-delta table method to do so. In fact, we even map a part of the maintenance problem into the problem addressed by [AAD$^+$96a, SAG96].

Our algorithms are geared towards cube views, as well as towards generalizations of cube views that are likely to occur in typical decision-support systems. We have developed techniques to place aggregate views into a lattice, even suggesting small modifications to the views that can help generate a fuller lattice.

Finally, we have tested the feasibility and the performance gains of the summary-delta table method by implementing it on top of a relational database, and doing a performance study comparing the propagate and refresh times of our algorithm to the alternatives of doing rematerializations or using an alternative maintenance algorithm. We found that our algorithm provides an order of magnitude improvement over the alternatives. Another observation we made from the performance study is that our refresh function, when implemented outside the database system, runs much slower than what we had expected (while still being fast). The right way to implement the refresh function is by doing something similar to a *left outer-join* of the summary-delta table with the materialized view, identifying the view tuples to be updated, and updating them as a part of the outer-join. Such a *"summary-delta join"* operation should be built into the database servers that are targeting the warehousing market.

PART V

IMPLEMENTATION AND PERFORMANCE
ANALYSIS OF MATERIALIZED VIEWS

Implementation and Performance

This section of the book contains seven chapters that discuss implementation and performance issues related to materialized views.

The first four chapters discuss systems that have implemented materialized views in a variety of contexts. The implementations span supporting materialized views inside a RDBMS, as a layer on top of the system, and by enhancing a programming language to easily maintain views in an application context. The last chapter contains a performance study of how maintenance of materialized views performs relative to recomputation.

Chapter 26 discusses materialized views in Oracle, *snapshots*, that in 1992 first introduced support for incremental maintenance of materialized views. Snapshots are implemented to support distributed applications over replicated subsets of data. Snapshots support a wide range of functionality - simultaneous updates from multiple users and conflict resolution, constraints on snapshots, automatic periodic refresh and more. In general they can be arbitrary queries but incremental maintenance, or "fast refresh," is supported for SP views. The feature is widely used in the industry and has been enhanced to support more functionality that is not described in this chapter due to confidentiality constraints.

Chapter 27 discusses EKS, a prototype deductive database system that was developed at ECRC. The system is one of the earliest implementations of materialized views, particularly in a deductive framework. It includes an update propagation facility that is used to implement view maintenance and integrity constraint checking. The update propagation facility can deal with recursion, (recursive) aggregates, negation, and quantifiers. The chapter discusses the various issues encountered in implementing update propagation and the design decisions made in EKS—to name a few: how to identify "relevant" updates for interconnected views, how to manipulate only "changes" to views for efficiency purposes, and how to compute the changes in a large system.

Chapter 28 describes how to implement incremental view maintenance using a production rule language. The change-computing queries are expressed as rules and are generated automatically for views expressed in a large subset of SQL that includes *union, intersection*, and *difference* queries. The production rule system is implemented in the Starburst system at IBM. The rules make maintenance efficient by exploiting information about the keys of relations.

Chapter 29 describes the Heraclitus Database programming language that offers another approach for doing view maintenance different from relational, deductive, and production rule systems. Heraclitus extends the C programming language with relational algebra, support for *deltas* as "first-class citizens", and operators to manipulate relations and deltas. Deltas correspond to database updates. The system can be used to provide efficient support for materialized integrated views using deltas to determine when different maintenence rules fire. The system supports multiple other Database constructs like version control, specification of concurrency protocols, resolution of update conflicts, and multiple access methods to the deltas.

Chapter 30 discusses ViewCache and IAM (incremental access method). A ViewCache is a materialized view that does not contain the data in the materialized view; instead it contains the rowids (pointers) for the rows of the base relations that contribute towards the row in the view. The IAM is a deferred maintenance strategy that can be used to maintain a ViewCache as needed by queries. The IAM strategy enables the maintenance costs to be amortized over multiple updates because IAM does not necessarily update the entire ViewCache at maintenance points but only the part needed by the query. The paper also discusses the cost parameters and conditions under which the IAM performs well and the circumstances under which IAM outperforms query modification as the maintenance technique for ViewCaches.

Chapter 31 analyzes performance of different view materialization and maintenance techniques—for example, incremental view maintenance, deferred view maintenance, and query modification (i.e., using the base relations directly to answer queries). The authors evaluate the cost of these different approaches for three kinds of views: SP over one relation, join of two relations, and aggregation over an SPJ view. They show that the choice of the view materialization strategy depends on the percentage of updates, selectivity factor, size of the result set of queries, number of tuples written by each update, and the cost of maintaining the sets of insertions and deletions in storage. The chapter gives detailed models of cost and explains how different combinations of the factors mentioned above determine which materialization strategy is best.

Chapter 32 studies performance of incremental view maintenance by applying them to efficiently compute and maintain a join between two base relations in the presence of queries and updates to the base relation. Of the different ways discussed in the chapter, two correspond to maintaining the join as a materialized view. The paper studies the performance of materialized views relative to hash joins algorithms for computing equi-joins in light of a variety of factors that influence the performance of incremental view maintenance - the frequency of update of the underlying relations, the size of the view (selectivity of the join) and the amount of available memory. The chapter uses equi-join views to yield good insight into how general materialized views will perform compared to rematerialization on demand.

ORACLE7 SNAPSHOTS

Alan Downing, Ashish Gupta,
Robert Jenkins, Harry Sun

1   Introduction

Most research on incremental maintenance of materialized views has focused on how complex views may be efficiently maintained when the base tables are updated [BBC80, BLT86, CW91, DT92, GL95, GM93, HD92, KSS87, LHM$^+$86, NY83, QW91, Rou91, SI84, ZGMHW95]. More recently, warehousing applications are being emphasized wherein maintaining aggregates is especially important. The resulting algorithms often are applicable to an environment where only a few views are incrementally maintained in a local or a very reliable distributed environment. The Oracle RDBMS first introduced support for incremental maintenance of materialized views in late 1992. This feature, called Snapshots, was designed to address a different application domain.

Oracle believes that one of the most important uses for incremental view maintenance is to allow distributed applications to work on a replicated subset of data. Let us illustrate the requirements using a simple sales automation example. In our example, a mobile workforce of salesmen run sales automation software on laptop computers. In general, communication between the laptops and the corporate repository at headquarters is low-bandwidth and unreliable, making client-server software difficult to use. Instead, each laptop locally runs the sales automation software on top of a local copy of a small subset of the data stored at the corporate repository. This approach is also appealing because the easiest way to distribute an existing single-site application is to transparently replicate the data that the application uses. A laptop only stores data of interest to its salesman, such as customers and warehouses in the sales region. If the salesman makes a sale or a new customer contact, the salesman updates his copy of the database. The salesmen connects to the main database server once or twice a day (*e.g.*, once at lunch and once at night) over a modem to exchange updates for all snapshots in a way that maintains transactional consistency.

This example points out several characteristics that are different from most research assumptions:

- There may be several incrementally maintained views (snapshots) per table.

- The snapshots can be updated.

- The update exchange, which Oracle calls a refresh, is driven from the snapshot side.

- Multiple snapshots will need to be refreshed simultaneously in a manner that maintains transactional consistency.

- Horizontal partitioning is used to keep the amount of data exchanged reasonable, but vertical partitioning, set operations, and group functions are not really used.

In the following sections of this chapter, we discuss the design of Oracle7 snapshots and how it satisfies all these intended application domain characteristics. The intent of this chapter is to outline the architecture of the actual implementation of materialized views in Oracle7 and not to compare our maintenance algorithms with those in existing research.

2   Overview of Snapshots in Oracle7

A snapshot is a local materialization of a view on data stored at a master site. The snapshot can reside in the same or different database as the master. A snapshot can be periodically refreshed, after which the snapshot will be a consistent-read instantiation of the view. A snapshot can be completely refreshed by reinstantiating the view from scratch, or fast-refreshed by considering only the changes to the query's base table since the last refresh.

Oracle7 snapshots allow fast refresh of only simple snapshots. Informally, each row in a simple snapshot is based on a single row in a single table. A simple snapshot has a defining query with no distinct or aggregate functions, GROUP BY or CONNECT BY clauses, subqueries, joins, or set operations. If a snapshot's defining query contains any of these clauses or operations, it is referred to as a complex snapshot.

Oracle7 snapshots can be read-only or updatable. Read-only snapshots allow both horizontal and vertical partitioning of master tables. Updatable snapshots only allow horizontal partitioning and must be simple snapshots. Changes to updatable snapshots can be either synchronously or asynchronously propagated to the master by using the same update-propagation method as used for Oracle's peer-to-peer replication facility [DBB+88, Smi95]. Because multiple snapshots can simultaneously update the same replicated data and because the updates can be asynchronously propagated to the master, write-write conflicts are possible at the master. Oracle allows masters to automatically resolve these conflicts using the same conflict resolution mechanism that is used in Oracle's peer-to-peer replication facility [Dow95]. No conflict resolution is required at the snapshot sites because the refresh will pull down the resolved rows from the master so that the snapshot will once again be a consistent-read instantiation of the view after the refresh.

Oracle7 has the concept of refresh groups in which multiple snapshots can have a consistent-read instantiation of their views. Basically, the snapshots in the refresh group will share the same refresh transaction. Refresh groups allow the referential integrity constraints between master tables to be applicable at the snapshot site after a refresh has been completed (although Oracle7's statement-level referential integrity constraints cannot be used on snapshots). A refresh group can contain both simple and complex snapshots based on tables from multiple master databases. Refresh groups can be scheduled to automatically refreshed at user-defined intervals or they can be manually refreshed.

3   System Architecture

Many database objects are created to enable the use of the features described above. Some of these objects are created automatically while others have to be created by the user. In this section we describe the architecture of the system using an example updatable snapshot that is defined on the "customer" table stored on the remote site "master". The snapshot contains all rows of the customer table that correspond to customers in "NY" state. Section 3.2 gives the exact SQL DDL for creating the example snapshot.

3.1   Master-side Objects

Site "master" is the master-side in the above example because it contains the "customer" base table. Figure 1 shows the user-level master-side objects that are used to perform fast refreshes for the example snapshot on table "customer".

A single log table is maintained for every master table that supports one or more simple snapshots. Changes to the master table are recorded in the log by a trigger on the master table. The trigger on the master table is built automatically when the log is created. The following DDL creates the log and trigger for the example "customer" table:

                            create snapshot log on customer;

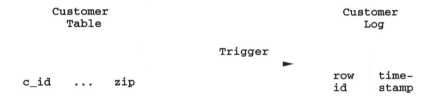

Figure 1 Master Side Objects

The log table contains the rowids of the changed rows of the master and is shared by all fast-refresh snapshots defined on that master table. The timestamp column is used to record the first time each log entry was used in a fast refresh. Normally the master base tables (e.g., customer) will be very large while the logs will be fairly small. The log is not automatically created whenever someone creates a fast-refresh snapshot because the master sites schema should not be automatically altered by snapshot sites. If a log is not explicitly created on a master table then snapshots on that table cannot fast refresh because "incremental" information is not available.

Oracle's approach of using triggers to build the log of changes is different from the "log sniffing" approach where the redo logs of the database are scanned to detect the changes made to a table. Oracle chose this approach because of its potential for better performance and also to avoid interfering with the existing logging mechanisms of the database system that have been built and tuned for other uses.

The master also stores information about the refresh times of different snapshots so that the log can be cleaned up periodically. This information is stored in a data dictionary table and is maintained transparently by the Oracle kernel. If a row has already been used in fast-refreshes by all the snapshots, the row will be deleted from the log. Thus, snapshot logs contain only those entries that are of use to at least one snapshot.

3.2   Snapshot-side Objects

Snapshots are created using SQL DDL as illustrated below for our example snapshot:

create snapshot customer for update as select * from customer@master
where state = "NY";

The above snapshot contains a horizontal partition of the customer table at site "master." Figure 2 shows the user-level snapshot-side objects that are used to perform fast refreshes for the above updatable snapshot.

The above DDL results in the creation of a snapshot table that contains all the columns supposed to be in the snapshot plus an additional column, namely the rowid of the master. Thus, each row in the snapshot table is identified by the rowid of the master row from which it was derived. The snapshot-table is created when the snapshot creation DDL is issued (transparent to the user). The snapshot defined by the user is created as a view on this table where the view projects out the rowid column.

For updatable snapshots, a log table also is created on the snapshot table. Rowids of deleted and modified rows are inserted into the log table. Insertions into the snapshot table are assigned fake rowids and are not logged. Insertions, deletions and updates are also sent to the update propagation mechanism that propagates the changes to the master site. To handle these two separate actions, two triggers also are created – one to insert deleted and updated rowids into the log table and the other to input insertions,

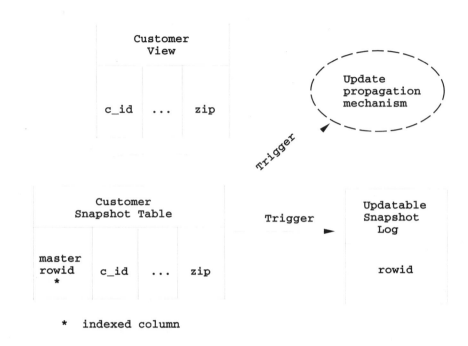

Figure 2 Snapshot-side Objects

deletions and updates into the update propagation mechanism. Fake rowids for inserted rows are resolved when the snapshot is refreshed.

4   Refresh Algorithm

After the logs and the snapshots are created, the snapshots are ready to be refreshed. A simple snapshot is allowed to use a fast refresh as long as the log information predates the snapshot's creation or last refresh. Refreshes can be executed automatically or manually by using a simple command. The implementation of the snapshot refresh algorithm uses a combination of Oracle's distributed query capabilities and the remote procedure call (RPC) capabilities provided by Oracle's programmatic SQL language, PL/SQL. A refresh has multiple distinct phases: update propagation, log set-up, the main transaction to update the snapshots, and log purging. The following is an outline of the fast refresh algorithm:

        For each updatable snapshot in the refresh group:
            If the replication method is asynchronous then
                Propagate local modifications to the master
            Acquire an exclusive lock on the snapshot table
        For each snapshot in the refresh group:
            If the snapshot is fast-refreshable then
                Issue the set_up RPC
        Begin the main refresh transaction
        For each snapshot in the refresh group:
            Validate the timestamp of the snapshot log at the master
            If the snapshot is not fast-refreshable or log validation failed then
                If the complete refresh option is specified then

```
            Delete all rows from the snapshot table
            Reinstantiate the snapshot using "INSERT AS SELECT"
        Else
            Raise error "cannot fast refresh"
    Else
        Select the rowid of rows from master table to delete
        For each row selected:
            Delete the row from the snapshot table
        If the snapshot is updatable then
            Delete locally inserted rows from the snapshot table
        Select the rows from the master to insert or modify
        For each row selected:
            snapshot table as appropriate
Commit main refresh transaction
For each snapshot in the refresh group
    the snapshot if fast-refreshable then
        Issue the wrap_up RPC
```

Since Oracle's read-consistent concurrency model does not require remote locks, Oracle's transparent two-phase commit (2PC) is not used during the refresh. The set_up and wrap_up RPCs actually perform master-site modifications to manage snapshot logs. These modifications are performed in separate single-site transactions. Master-side transactions are serialized by locking the log's row in the data dictionary at the master site. Snapshot-side transactions are serialized by locking a snapshot's row in the data dictionary at the snapshot site. The master tables are not locked during fast refreshes.

The algorithm can tolerate untimely crashes. Crashes that occur before the set_up RPC or between the set_up RPC and the commit of the main refresh transaction just mean that the next fast refresh will have to start over. The set_up RPC is idempotent. Crashes that occur after the refresh but before the wrap_up RPC just means that the snapshot logs cannot be purged at this time and will be purged in a later refresh.

In the following subsections, we discuss details of each of the phases of the fast refresh algorithm.

4.1 Updatable Snapshot Propagation

Each updatable snapshot in a refresh group must have its snapshot table exclusively locked for the length of the refresh. If the snapshot uses asynchronous replication to propagate to the master, the following steps are taken before the main refresh transaction begins:

1. The local updates are propagated to the master site.

2. The snapshot table is locked in exclusive mode.

3. If the more local updates need to be propagated (i.e., a snapshot is updated before the exclusive lock is acquired), repeat steps 1 and 2.

The updates are propagated before the lock is obtained to minimize the time that the snapshot table is locked.

4.2 Set_up RPC

Each snapshot uses a low-watermark timestamp to determine which rows in the snapshot logs should be considered during the fast refresh. To ensure that rows inserted into a snapshot log are not assigned a timestamp until after the rows are committed, the log triggers initially assign a null value to each row.

When the set_up RPC is executed at the master, all null timestamps are reset to the master's current time and the new timestamp is returned to the snapshot site. The set_up RPC performs all updates in a separate transaction that does not involve 2PC. If the refresh is successful, the new timestamp (plus the smallest time increment) will become the snapshot's new low-watermark. All timestamps used during fast refresh are generated at the master site.

Although the low-watermark ensures forward progress for snapshot refreshes, it does not guarantee that a row in the log is not considered twice. Rows inserted into the log between the set_up RPC and the start of the main refresh transaction will not have their null timestamp updated, but they will still be considered during refresh. Considering a row more than once does not result in invalid snapshots.

4.3   Main Refresh Transaction

The main refresh transactions can be further broken down into four phases:

1. Validate the timestamp of the snapshot log at the master site and ensure that the log can be used for a fast refresh.

2. Delete the rows that should no longer be in the snapshot.

3. For updatable snapshots, delete the rows that were inserted at the snapshot site.

4. Update or insert the rows from the master table that have been modified since the last refresh of the snapshot.

Phase one is performed by issuing an RPC to the master site which returns a timestamp indicating the age of the log. This timestamp is then compared to the last refresh date of the snapshot. If the last refresh date of the snapshot is older than the log timestamp, the snapshot may not use the log for a fast refresh. Snapshots that fail log validation must perform a complete refresh before they are able to fast refresh again.

In phase two, the tuples that should no longer be in the snapshot are deleted. The tuples to be deleted are determined by entries in the log at the master site for which the snapshot definition query selects no corresponding row from the master table. The fast refresh algorithm only considers entries in the log that have timestamps later than that of the last refresh time of the snapshot or that have a null timestamp (see section 4.2). The snapshot site deletes tuples based on the rowids retrieved from the master site by a distributed query. The following is an example of the distributed query that returns the rowids:

```
select distinct log.rowid from customer_log@master log
    where log.rowid not in
              (select a.rowid
               from (select customer_columns
                     from customer@master where state = 'NY') cust
               where cust.rowid = log.rowid)
       and  ((log.entry_timestamp > last_refresh_time)
             or (log.entry_timstamp is null))
```

Updatable snapshots need to delete the rows that were inserted at the snapshot site. This is due to the fact that rows inserted at the snapshot site do not map to existing rows in the master table. If the snapshot-site modifications are propagated to the master, the insertions will be reapplied to the snapshot in the last phase of the main refresh transaction. If the inserted rows resulted in errors during propagation or if they were ignored by the master during conflict resolution, then the rows should not remain in the snapshot.

In the last phase of the main transaction, the row that were modified at the master since the last refresh are applied to the snapshot. This application is performed in two steps. First the snapshot site attempts to update a modified row. If the update results in no rows being processed, the modified row is inserted into the snapshot table. The following is an example of the distributed query that returns the modified rows:

```
select customer_columns, log.rowid
    from customer_log@master log,
          (select customer_columns
            from customer@master where state = 'NY') cust
    where(cust.rowid = log.rowid)
    and   ((log.entry_timestamp > last_refresh_time)
            or (log.entry_timestamp is null))
```

The fast refresh queries are optimized so that the following is true:

■ The above example queries are actually processed at the master site, minimizing the amount of data pulled over the network.

■ The remote query is driven by the snapshot log thus requiring only a scan of the log table, which is usually small. Master tables are accessed by the rowids recorded in the snapshot log.

■ Data pulled over the network is batched to reduce network round trips.

4.4   Wrap_up RPC

The main task of the wrap_up RPC is to purge the entries in the snapshot log that are no longer needed. Each successfully refreshed snapshot passes its refresh timestamp to the master. The master site keeps track of the refresh timestamps associated with all snapshots using each log. If the calling snapshot is the least-recently-refreshed snapshot, wrap_up purges all log entries with timestamps older than the timestamp associated with the next-most-recently-refreshed snapshot.

For example, a master table, M1, has two snapshots, S1 and S2, that were last refreshed at time T1 and T2, respectively. When snapshot S1 is refreshed at time T3, the master site's log entries with timestamps younger than T2 are no longer needed. These entries are deleted by the wrap_up RPC during the refresh of snapshot S1 in a separate transaction that does not involve 2PC.

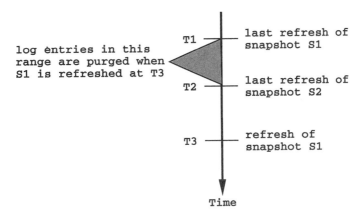

Figure 3 Purging Unused rows in the Snapshot Log

5   Conclusions

Oracle snapshots satisfy all the requirements of the application domain discussed in the introduction:

- Multiple snapshots can efficiently share the same table and log at the master site. Each log at the master site is maintained at a minimal fixed-cost for each row updated at the master so that OLTP transactions do not suffer severe response time delays. Fast refreshes do not require full-table scans of the master tables and pull only changed rows over the network.

- Updates to snapshots can be propagated either synchronously or asynchronously to the master. Conflicting updates are resolved by the master.

- Snapshot sites initiate refreshes. Refreshes can be scheduled to occur automatically by user-defined functions or manually.

- Refresh groups allow multiple snapshots to be consistently refreshed in a manner that can be used to maintains a master's referential integrity relationships at the snapshot site.

- Both read-only and updatable snapshots support fast refreshes of horizontally partitioned data. Read-only snapshots also support fast refreshes of vertically partitioned data.

The combination of Oracle's peer-to-peer replication technology and Oracle Snapshots provides the most complete distributed and replication solutions in the commercial database market. Oracle snapshots continue to be enhanced to address the needs of new applications.

Acknowledgments

The authors would like to acknowledge the entire replication team including Sukanya Balaraman, Dean Daniels, Alan Demers, Lip Doo, Curtis Elsbernd, Gary Hallmark, Sandeep Jain, Huyen Nguyen, Brian Oki, Maria Pratt, Gordon Smith, Benny Souder, and James Stamos.

CHECKING INTEGRITY AND MATERIALIZING VIEWS BY UPDATE PROPAGATION IN THE EKS SYSTEM

Laurent Vieille, Petra Bayer, Volker Küchenhoff, Alexandre Lefebvre

ABSTRACT

EKS is a prototype deductive database system which was developed at ECRC in 1989 and 1990. Its architecture includes in particular an *update propagation* facility. In EKS, this generic and unique facility is used to implement the verification of generalized integrity constraints or the maintenance of materialized predicates; it could also be used for the monitoring of conditions associated with alerters.

Given a transaction adding and/or deleting (base) facts, the task of this facility is to determine the effect of the transaction over the set of derived facts derivable from the database. This update propagation facility is able to deal with recursion, (recursive) aggregates, negation and quantifiers. This chapter discusses the various issues we have encountered and the solutions and/or design decisions we have adopted.

1 Introduction

EKS is a prototype deductive database system [GMN84] developed at ECRC in 1989 and 1990 (EKS stands for ECRC Knowledge Base Management System, see also [BLV93, VBKL90]). The primary objective of the project was to convey the maturity and the practical interest of deductive database systems: EKS has been demonstrated in a number of technical conferences and commercial shows, in Europe and in the United States; it has been used as a support for teaching in several universities; it is a a key technology source for the VALIDITY Deductive and Object-Oriented Database system under development [FGVL+95, FLV96].

EKS presents a number of features, many of which will not be covered in this chapter. Amongst the features relevant to the present chapter, one can note:

1. Integrity constraints are very general: the logical formula expressing a constraint may refer to recursively defined predicates, or to predicates defined by means of aggregate operations. This allows the expression of cardinality constraints and of acyclicity constraints.

2. Rules may include aggregate operations, in particular intertwined with recursion. Such recursive aggregates allow *bill of materials* queries to be expressed [Lef92].

3. Derived predicates can be specified as materialized. In this case, an explicit copy of the derived facts is automatically maintained by the system. We illustrate the interest of this functionality to efficiently handle inclusion queries in geometrical applications.

This chapter focuses on one particular aspect of EKS, its *update propagation* facility. Update propagation is complementary to *fact derivation*: fact derivation is used to derive the set of answers to a query; methods for fact derivation [BR87, CGT90, LV89, Lau89] work in a goal-oriented fashion in order to focus on the data relevant to the query. The aim of update propagation is different. Its task is to determine the changes induced by a set of (explicit) updates over the set of facts derivable from the database.

Update Propagation is a generic facility, used in EKS for both checking general integrity constraints and maintaining the extensions of materialized predicates. It can also be used for the efficient monitoring of the conditions associated with alerters.

At the time EKS was developed, the genericity of update propagation had rarely been noted (except, e.g., in [BC79, BCL89, BM90b]), although it is usable for *integrity checking* [BB82, BDM88, DW89, Dec86, Kuc91, LST87, MB88, Nic82, SK88], *materialized predicates handling* [BCL89, Kuc91, NY83], and *alerter monitoring* [BC79, DBB+88, HD92]. Update propagation had been studied mainly in the context of integrity checking in deductive databases (see [BDM88, BM90b, DW89, Dec86, LST87, MB88, SK88], following earlier contributions [BB82, Nic82]). And, indeed, these works had laid down the basic principles of update propagation. A first step towards a uniform presentation of these basic principles is made in [BM90b, BMM91]. See also [Kuc91, Oli91] ([Kuc91] reports on an alternative study for EKS).

Since the initial version of this chapter was written [VBK91], this topic has become a much more actively researched area. In section 7, we will shortly compare our work with those more recent works.

To be effective, an update propagation method must incorporate solutions to the following issues.

First, it must focus on the changes actually induced by the updates. It is expected that, in most current cases, the set of induced changes will remain (very) small in comparison with the set of all derivable facts. As the volume of the data manipulated is a key factor for efficiency, an update propagation procedure should try to manipulate only data directly or indirectly related to the updates. A natural way to address this issue (as adopted in the early works [Dec86, SK88]) is to design an update-driven, bottom-up method to propagate both additions and deletions through rules. Although such a method bears similarity with a semi-naive execution of a fixed-point procedure [BR86], it has to address a more general setting, as it has to propagate not only fact additions but also fact deletions.

As a second issue, it must avoid doing irrelevant propagation, i.e., propagation through rules on which no constraint and no materialized predicate depends. A blind bottom-up propagation of updates is likely to perform irrelevant propagation (as noted in [BDM88, GL90]). Some kind of top-down reasoning from the constraints and the materialized predicates must identify the relevant propagations.

In EKS, we have developed an original and effective solution to fulfill these two requirements. A top-down analysis is carried out, at compile-time, when the set of constraints, rules and materialized predicates is defined or updated; this analysis generates a so-called *set of relevant propagation rules* which contains all the (and only those) propagation rules modeling relevant propagations. The activation of these propagation rules at transaction commit time performs exactly the relevant propagations. This is done by taking full advantage of the EKS query evaluator kernel, deriving from DedGin* [LV89]. This evaluator is a top-down set-oriented evaluator and permits an elegant task-driven implementation of update propagation.

Third, the *testing policy* of an update propagation method must be designed with care to achieve both correctness and efficiency. A testing policy determines when and what derivability tests must be performed. To understand the role of derivability tests, consider the following examples. Let `head <- b1` and `head <- b2` be two rules. Suppose that `b1` belongs to the database before a transaction adds `b2`; then, an update propagation method will detect that, via the second rule, a new proof for `head` has been added; `head` is not really new, as it was already derivable using the first rule. Similarly, supppose that both `b1` and `b2` belong to the database before a transaction deletes `b1`; then an update propagation will detect that, via the first rule, a proof of `head` has been deleted; however, `head` is not really deleted as it is derivable using the second rule. In the first case, a derivability test checks whether `head` was derivable from the old database. In the first case, it checks whether `head` is still derivable from the new database.

In general, derivability tests are expensive to perform, and the testing policy (what tests should be performed, and when?) may have important impacts on performance. We argue that a minimal requirement for an update propagation method is to return a complete set of *safe updates*; the manipulation of safe updates requires particularly few derivability tests. We have developed (and implemented) a testing policy fitting with this minimal requirement.

Counting-based methods [NY83, GMS93] address this third issue in a different way. The idea is to keep a count of the proofs for each derived fact. The role of the update propagation method is to generate an increment or a decrement to this count, corresponding to the number of proofs added or deleted by a transaction. On the down side, a systematic use of counting in the presence of negation forces the materialization of predicates appearing negatively in the body of rules.

Section 2 presents background on EKS, definitions and examples. In section 3, a synthetic model of update propagation is developed. The concept of safe updates and the adapted testing policy are discussed in section 4. Section 5 defines relevant propagation rules, while section 6 is devoted to their management. In section 7, earlier work is discussed. Section 8 is the conclusion.

2 Background

2.1 EKS

EKS uses a basic *deductive data model*, with no function symbols and no type constructors (set, list, bag): arguments of facts are atomic values (strings or numbers). The predicate symbols of the EKS language are partitioned into *base*, *derived* and *external predicates*. Facts for base predicates are explicitly stored in the database; facts for derived predicates are derived by means of *derivation rules*; facts for external predicates are computed by means of procedures associated to the predicate.

The user language of EKS is based on Datalog and is used to write deduction rules and constraints. It is purely declarative (assertional) in the sense that the user does not need to know how rules and constraints are evaluated. Updates and transactions are required to leave the database consistent with respect to the integrity constraints. This language includes the logical connectives `and`, `or`, `=>` and quantifiers `forall`, `exists`. Constraints are closed first-order formulae, while general formulae can appear in the body of rules. Full Datalog recursion and stratified negation are supported. Aggregate semantics is provided in [Lef92].

Functionally, EKS is a fully persistent deductive database system. Its compile-time components are written in the MegaLog system [Boc91], which is a Prolog system integrating access to the BANG file system [Fre89]. The initial system was single-user (1990). The query evaluator of EKS implements a version of Query/SubQuery [Lau89] and derives from DedGin* [LV89]. The VALIDITY industrial effort mentioned in the introduction is a multi-user system.

2.2 Definitions

The general expressions of the user language are rewritten into an internal extended Datalog form where quantifiers and disjunctions are removed. Both fact derivation and update propagation work on this internal form, and this chapter will focus on this version of the language.

A term is either a variable or a constant. We follow Prolog for the syntax of variables and constants. A positive literal has the form `pred(t`$_1$`, ..., t`$_n$`)` where `t`$_i$ is a term. A negated literal has the form `not lit`, where `lit` is a positive literal. A rule has the form:

    lit₀ <- lit₁, ..., litₙ

where `lit`$_0$ (the head of the rule) is a positive literal and `lit`$_1$, ..., `lit`$_n$ (the body of the rule) are positive or negative literals.

EKS supports a query-dependent version of range-restriction. The rule:

    p(X) <- not q(X)

is accepted in EKS, with the provision that the only queries which can be run on `p` are those with its argument instantiated. This feature of EKS is not marginal as it allows a smooth integration of negation, quantifiers and of those external predicates which require some arguments to be bound. For the purpose of this chapter, however, we will focus on the classical version of range-restriction: any variable appearing in the head of a rule or in a negated literal of its body must occur in a positive literal of its body.

Constraints are expressed as *denials* [SK88]:

    inc-constraint-id <- lit₁, ..., litₙ

where `constraint-id` is an identifier of the constraint (`inc` stands for **inconsistent**). Formally, the distinction of several versions of **inconsistent** does not make sense; this is done here for simplicity. The database is *consistent* if `inc-constraint-id` is not derivable for any constraint.

Updates are either *additions* or *deletions* on base predicates. A *transaction* is abstracted as a set of additions and a set of deletions. We consider the net effect of transactions and suppose that the same fact is not both an addition and a deletion. We do not consider rule updates. We denote by OLD-DB (respectively, NEW-DB) the database before (respectively after) a transaction.

Any derived predicate may be declared as *materialized*. In this case, the set of facts derivable for this predicate (its *extension*) is automatically maintained by the system. We always assume that, in OLD-DB, this extension contains all (and only those) facts actually derivable. We do not consider duplicate facts.

A proof of a fact `F` over a database DB is a tree whose root is labeled by `F` and built as follows:

- Let `F` be a base positive fact contained in DB; then there is a proof (of `F`) reduced to a single node labeled by `F`.

- Let `F` be a (base or derived) fact for which no proof over DB can be constructed; then there is a proof (of `not F`) reduced to a single node labeled by `not F`.

- Let `T`$_i$ be a proof of `F`$_i$ over DB (`F`$_i$ may be negative, i.e., be `not F'` for some `F'`, or positive); let `F <- F`$_1$`, .., F`$_n$ be a ground instance of a rule in DB; then there is a proof (of `F`) over DB the direct subtrees of which are exactly the `T`$_i$'s.

A derived fact is *actually added* by a transaction if it is derivable from NEW-DB but not from OLD-DB. A derived fact is *actually deleted* by a transaction if it is derivable from OLD-DB but not from NEW-DB.

We suppose known the notion of *substitution* and of *most general unifier (mgu)* (see, e.g., [CGT90]).

2.3   Motivating examples

EXAMPLE 2.1 *Consider the constraint:* The owner of a car must hold a driving license. *This can be written in denial form as:*

    inc-1 <- owns_car(Driver, Car), not licensed(Driver)

To check whether the insertion of `owns_car("John", "Lincoln")` *violates the constraint, it is sufficient to check whether* `"John"` *has a driving license. No full scan of the* `licensed` *facts is needed. Also, note that* `licenced` *insertions and* `owns_car` *deletions can not affect the constraint.* □

EXAMPLE 2.2 *As a second constraint, assume that there may not be cycles in a part/subpart hierarchy. This constraint may appear in bill-of-material databases and its verification requires ad-hoc development in current systems. It is expressed with the help of the transitive closure* `part_subpart` *of the base relation* `assembly`:

```
RULES: part_subpart(Part, SubPart) <- assembly(Part, SubPart)
       part_subpart(Part, SubPart) <- assembly(Part, InterPart)
                    and   part_subpart(InterPart, SubPart)

CONSTRAINT:      inc-2   <-  part_subpart(Part, Part)
```
□

EXAMPLE 2.3 *As an example of a materialized predicate, we define a predicate modeling the minimal enclosing box of a polygon. After a transaction, the system recomputes only the minimal enclosing boxes of the polygons modified or defined during the transaction.*

```
min_max_box(Polygon_Id, Xmin, Xmax, Ymin, Ymax) <-
     agg(           polygon_points(Polygon_Id, X, Y)
          group_by [Polygon_Id]
          where    [Xmin is min(X), Xmax is max(X),
                    Ymin is min(Y), Ymax is max(Y)]
         )
```

The materialization of the minimal enclosing boxes is a potentially essential factor for the efficient support of, e.g., inclusion queries: Which are the polygons containing a given point? *Such a query can be modeled as, first, a range query to find the enclosing boxes containing the point and, then, as an exact inclusion test on the polygons returned by the first phase. This query is modeled by the following rule, where the predicate* `check_polygone` *implements the inclusion test and is omitted here.*

```
encl_polygone(Polygone, X0, Y0) <-
        min_max_box(Polygone, Xmin, Xmax, Ymin, Ymax) and
        X0 >= Xmin and X0 =< Xmax and
        Y0 >= Ymin and Y0 =< Ymax and
        check_polygone(Polygone, X0, Y0).
```

If the minimal enclosing boxes were not materialized, then the exact test would have to be performed on every polygon in the database, as it is very difficult to transform a selection criteria on X0 and Y0 on a selection criteria on polygons. Performance tests indicate a factor 10 improvement when materialization is performed.

In this example, materialization and range queries can be seen as modeling specialized structures and algorithms (see [Ore90]). □

3   Basic Notions of Update Propagation

3.1   Transactions Add or Delete Proofs

A transaction can be seen as adding and deleting proofs of derived facts: a proof over NEW-DB is said to be *added by a transaction* if it could not be constructed over OLD-DB; a proof over OLD-DB is said to be *deleted by a transaction* if it can not be constructed over NEW-DB.

As a more precise characterization, a proof over NEW-DB is added by the transaction if one of its leaves is labeled either by a positive *base* fact added by the transaction or by a negated (*base or derived*) fact not F and F is actually deleted by the transaction. Similarly, a proof over OLD-DB is deleted by the transaction if one of its leaves is labeled by a positive *base* fact deleted by the transaction or by a negative (*base or derived*) fact not F and F is actually added by the transaction.

The addition (resp. deletion) of a proof of a derived fact does not imply that this fact is actually added (resp. actually deleted) by the transaction: other proofs may have existed before (resp. may exist after). A fact for which a proof is added, is actually added if and only if it was not derivable from OLD-DB; a fact for which a proof is deleted, is actually deleted if and only if it is not derivable from NEW-DB.

3.2   Propagating Updates

The explicit manipulation of proofs in a database system is complex as it requires the implementation of tree structures, while data managers are usually designed to manipulate flat records. In order to avoid manipulating proofs, one focuses instead on the derived *facts* for which proofs are added or deleted. This is achieved without materializing their proofs, by propagating the updates through the rules.

We first consider propagation through *positive body literals*.

Let R be a rule and L be a positive literal in the body of R. Let Side be the body literals other than L in R (the *side literals*):
```
R:        H <- L, Side.
```

Consider a fact F unifiable with L (mgu σ) and suppose that the transaction adds or deletes a proof for F.

The propagation of this update through the rule R via the body literal L, consists in evaluating Sideσ and in producing instances of H for which proofs are added or deleted. Let θ be the overall substitution resulting from the unification of F and L and from the evaluation of Sideσ. The following properties can easily be checked by the reader:

- If the transaction adds a proof for F and if Sideθ is derivable from NEW-DB, then the transaction adds a proof for Hθ.

- If a transaction deletes a proof for F and if Sideθ was derivable from OLD-DB, then the transaction deletes a proof for Hθ.

We now consider propagation through *negative body literals*.

Let R be a rule of the form:
```
R:        H <- not L, Side.
```
The update considered now is an *actual update*, i.e., the actual addition or actual deletion of a fact F unifiable with L (mgu σ). Actual updates are required here instead of mere additions or deletions of proofs because the definition of added/deleted proofs require negated leaves to be labeled by actual updates. Hence, we have:

- If F is actually deleted by a transaction, and if Sideθ is derivable from NEW-DB, then the transaction adds a proof for Hθ.

- If F is actually added by a transaction, and if Sideθ was derivable from OLD-DB, then the transaction deletes a proof for Hθ.

As a final remark, the above properties have indicated an important asymmetry: when deriving facts for which proofs are added, side literals are evaluated over NEW-DB; when deriving facts for which proofs are deleted, the side literals are evaluated over OLD-DB.

3.3 Summary and Propagation Rules

It is convenient to model update propagation by means of meta-rules [BDM88, SK88], called here *propagation rules*. Let the unary meta-predicates:

    added_proof_for, deleted_proof_for,
    actual_add, actual_del,
    new, old

respectively hold of a fact F if F has an added proof, has a deleted proof, is actually added, is actually deleted, is derivable from NEW-DB or is derivable from OLD-DB. In addition, the meta-predicates **new** and **old** will also apply to conjunctions. The various results of this section can be written as follows.

- Given the rule:
    R: H <- L, Side.
  Propagation through the positive literal L:

  > **if** *added_proof_for(L)* **and** *new(Side)* **then** *added_proof_for(H)*
  > **if** *deleted_proof_for(L)* **and** *old(Side)* **then** *deleted_proof_for(H)*

- Given the rule:
    R: H <- not L, Side.
  Propagation through the negative literal **not** L:

  > **if** *actual_add(L)* **and** *old(Side)* **then** *deleted_proof_for(H)*
  > **if** *actual_del(L)* **and** *new(Side)* **then** *added_proof_for(H)*

- Derivation of actual updates from added and deleted proofs:

  > **if** *added_proof_for(L)* **and** *not old(L)* **then** *actual_add(L)*
  > **if** *deleted_proof_for(L)* **and** *not new(L)* **then** *actual_del(L)*

A construct of the form *type(L)* where *type* is a unary meta-predicate and L is a literal is called a *propagation literal*. The propagation literal after **if** (resp. **then**) is called the *body update* (resp. *head update*) of the propagation rule. Hence, in general, a propagation rule has the form (*state* is either **old** or **new**, and *C* is a conjunction - potentially empty - of literals):

> **if** *body-update* **and** *[not] state(C)* **then** *head-update*

4   Testing Policy

From the previous section, it is clear that it is sometimes necessary to perform *derivability tests*, i.e., to test whether a fact for which a proof is deleted (respectively added) is derivable from NEW-DB (respectively from OLD-DB). However, these tests may be expensive as they may invoke several (if not many) derivation rules. In this section, we discuss a testing policy which minimizes the number of these tests without endangering the correctness of update propagation.

This testing policy has two main characteristics. First, a method applying this policy may produce so-called *safe updates* besides actual updates; the definition of safe updates guarantees the correctness of the procedure. Second, this policy leads to fewer tests than it would be implied by the previous section; for instance, when applying this policy, no test is performed when propagating actual additions through negative body literals.

4.1   Safe Updates

We say that an update propagation method is *correct* if and only if it returns a set of updates on derived predicates such that:

- the returned set of updates contains all actual updates;

- all returned additions are *safe*, i.e., they all correspond to facts which are derivable from NEW-DB;

- all returned deletions are *safe*, i.e., they all correspond to facts which are not derivable from NEW-DB.

Note that the notion of a safe update is rather permissive: a fact may "safely" be deleted, although it has never been derivable from the database; a fact may "safely" be added, although no new proof has been added for it. This permissivity may be confusing at first, but its interest is to allow a reduction of the number of derivability tests.

This notion of correctness is a practical notion: for integrity checking, if *inconsistent* is returned as a safe addition, then it derives from NEW-DB and the database is inconsistent; for materialized predicates, redundant insertions (as it may happen when performing safe additions) or uneffective deletions (as it may happen when performing safe deletions) do not harm.

4.2   Derivability Tests for Safe Updates

Safety of updates is an asymmetrical notion in the sense that OLD-DB and NEW-DB do not play the same role in the definition. This is unlike the notions defined in section 3 which were all symmetrical in OLD-DB and NEW-DB. The reason for this asymmetry is practical: it is the result of the transaction, i.e., NEW-DB, which is of interest, not the state before. This asymmetry is reflected in the testing policy which we describe now.

Additions returned by the procedure are required to be derivable from NEW-DB but not necessarily to be actual additions. This indicates a first decision for the testing policy:

> *Do not check that added derived facts were derivable from OLD-DB.*

As a next step, the testing policy for deletions must guarantee that returned deletions are safe and must be coherent with the first decision above. As we show below, the following design decision will do:

Check whether a potentially deleted fact is not derivable from NEW-DB in two cases: before propagating this fact through a negative literal and when it is to be returned as output of the procedure.

The first case is needed to guarantee that only safe additions be manipulated; the second case is needed to guarantee the correctness of the update propagation method.

This strategy is formalized by the following rules, where **safe-add, safe-del, any-del** are unary predicates holding of a fact if this fact can "safely" be added, deleted or is regarded as a potential deletion ("potential" is not given any formal meaning here).

- Propagation through a positive literal:

if *safe-add(L)*	**and**	*new(Side)*	**then**	*safe-add(H)*
if *any-del(L)*	**and**	*old(Side)*	**then**	*any-del(H)*

- Propagation through a negative literal:

if *safe-add(L)*	**and**	*old(Side)*	**then**	*any-del(H)*
if *safe-del(L)*	**and**	*new(Side)*	**then**	*safe-add(H)*

- Testing the safety of actual deletions:

if *any-del(L)*	**and**	*not new(L)* **then**	*safe-del(L)*

- Finally, check whether deletions are safe before returning a deletion as output of the procedure, i.e., when the deletion is of the form "remove inconsistent"[1] or "delete a fact from the extension of a materialized predicate".

An easy proof by induction on the number of rules applied to generate an addition, shows that all additions are safe. The last point of the strategy guarantees that the deletions returned by the procedure are safe. Note that an update propagation method working along this strategy may internally manipulate unsafe deletions.

We leave the reader convince himself that all actual upates are returned by a procedure implementing this strategy.

EXAMPLE 4.1 *This example illustrates the permissivity of the notion of safe updates. Consider the following set of rules.*

```
p <- q
p <- r
s <- not p
t <- not s
r
```

---

[1] This case will never occur if only relevant propagation is performed - see section 5.

Assume that a transaction adds q. *The propagation of this addition through the first rule produces the actual (thus safe) addition of* p. *By propagating this addition through the literal* not p *of the third rule, one obtains the actual deletion of* s. *Before propagating this deletion through the body literal* not s *in the fourth rule, the derivability of* s *from NEW-DB is tested. As this test fails, the deletion of* s *is considered to be safe and is propagated through the fourth rule. This results in the actual (safe) addition of* t.

Two points are worth noting: s *is regarded as being "safely" deleted, though it was not derivable; similarly,* t *is regarded as being "safely" added, whereas no proof has been added.*   □

5 Relevant Propagation Rules

In this section, we define the set of propagation rules associated with a set of user rules, constraints and materialized predicates. This definition guarantees that only *relevant* propagations are performed, and that update propagation is *complete*. This is achieved by making sure that this set contains all the propagation rules modeling relevant propagations, and only them.

Which derived updates are relevant can be decided on the following basis.

1. The addition (but not the deletion) of *inconsistent* is relevant.

2. Both additions and deletions on materialized predicates are relevant.

3. Recursively, the relevance of an update on a literal H implies the relevance of a corresponding update on the literals in the body of the rules defining H:

   ■   if additions on H are relevant, then additions (resp. deletions) on positive (resp. negative) body literals are relevant;

   ■   if deletions on H are relevant, then deletions (resp. additions) on positive (resp. negative) body literals are relevant.

Further, the above criteria can be refined to take into account constants, or multiple occurrences of a variable in a literal. As an example, consider the denial:

        inc-ic <- p(a,X,X), not q(X)

then only additions of facts matching p(a,X,X) are relevant. The corresponding bindings can be used to generate more restricted propagation rules. ¿From the rule:

        p(X,Y,X) <- r(X,Y,X)

one may generate the propagation rule:

   if *safe-add(r(a,X,X))*   **then**   *safe-add(p(a,X,X))*

However, some care must be taken when generating these more restricted propagation rules: more general updates may be needed elsewhere. For instance, another denial may be:

        inc-ic' <- p(X,Y,Z), not s(X,Y,Z)

In this case, only the more general propagation rule below should be included in the set:

   if *safe-add(r(X,Y,Z))*   **then**   *safe-add(p(X,Y,Z))*

5.1 The Set of Propagation Rules

We say that a set S1 of propagation rules is less general than a set S2 of propagation rules if for each rule R1 in S1, there is a rule R2 in S2 and a substitution σ such that R1 is identical to R2σ, up to body literal reordering. The *set of propagation rules* associated with a set of derivation rules, of integrity constraints and of materialized predicates is the smallest and less general set such that:

1. It contains the following *initial propagation rules* :

    (a) for each constraint of identifier id[2]:

    > **if** *safe-add(inc-id)*   **then**   *set-flag-inc(id)*

    (b) for each materialized predicate `pred` of arity n:

    > **if** *safe-add(pred(X_1,..,X_n))*   **then**   *insert(pred(X_1,..,X_n))*
    > **if** *safe-del(pred(X_1,..,X_n))*   **then**   *delete(pred(X_1,..,X_n))*

2. If *type(Lit)* (*type* may be `safe-add` or `any-del`) appears as body update of a propagation rule, if *Lit* is unifiable (mgu σ) with the head H of a rule R: `H <- Body`, then there must be a propagation rule of head update *type(Hγ)* such that Hγ subsumes Hσ for each literal L in `Body`. There are four cases:

    (a) *type* is `safe-add` and L appears positively in the body of R:

    > **if**   *safe-add(Lγ)*   **and**   *new(Sideγ)*   **then**   *safe-add(Hγ)*

    (b) *type* is `safe-add` and L appears negatively in the body of R:

    > **if**   *safe-del(Lγ)*   **and**   *new(Sideγ)*   **then**   *safe-add(Hγ)*

    (c) *type* is `any-del` and L appears positively in the body of R:

    > **if**   *any-del(Lγ)*   **and**   *old(Sideγ)*   **then**   *any-del(Hγ)*

    (d) *type* is `any-del` and L appears negatively in the body of R:

    > **if**   *safe-add(Lγ)*   **and**   *old(Sideγ)*   **then**   *any-del(Hγ)*

3. Whenever *safe-del(Lit)* appears as body update, there must be a propagation rule of the form given below, such that *L* subsumes *Lit*:

    > **if**   *any-del(L)*   **and**   *not new(L)*   **then**   *safe-del(L)*

---

[2] *set-flag-inc(id)* sets a flag indicating that the constraint of identifier *id* has been violated.

5.2   Examples

EXAMPLE 5.1 IC3:   inc-3 <- p(a)
                p(X) <- q(X,Y), not r(Y,X)   □

In this example, additions on q or deletions on r not unifiable with q(a,Y) and r(Y,a) do *not* need to be propagated, and the propagation rules generated are:

(3-C) **if**   *safe-add(inc-3)*   **then**   *set-flag-inc(3)*
(3-0) **if**   *safe-add(p(a))*   **then**   *safe-add(inc-3)*
(3-1) **if**   *safe-add(q(a,Y))* **and**   *not r(Y,a)*   **then**   *safe-add(p(a))*
(3-2) **if**   *safe-del(r(Y,a))* **and**   *q(a,Y)*   **then**   *safe-add(p(a))*

The system ensures that only the (relatively) most general propagation rules exist in the database. For instance, if the following second constraint is added to the database:

IC4:   inc-4 <- p(X)

then the rules (3-1) and (3-2) will be removed, and the following rules will be added:

(4-C) **if**   *safe-add(inc-4)*   **then**   *set-flag-inc(4)*
(4-0) **if**   *safe-add(p(X))*   **then**   *safe-add(inc-4)*
(4-1) **if**   *safe-add(q(X,Y))* **and**   *not r(Y,X)*   **then**   *safe-add(p(X))*
(4-2) **if**   *safe-del(r(Y,X))* **and**   *q(X,Y)*   **then**   *safe-add(p(X))*

EXAMPLE 5.1   (Continued) The propagation rules generated for the *acyclicity constraint* are:

    if   *safe-add(inc-2)*   **then**   *set-flag-inc(2)*
    if   *safe-add(part-subpart(P,P))*   **then**   *safe-add(inc-2)*
    if   *safe-add(assembly(P, IP))*   **and**   *part-subpart(IP, SP)*
                                    then   *safe-add(part-subpart(P, SP))*
    if   *safe-add(assembly(P, SP))*   **then**   *safe-add(part-subpart(P, SP))*
    if   *safe-add(part-subpart(IP,SP))* **and**   *assembly(P,IP)*
                                    then   *safe-add(part-subpart(P,SP))*

Note first that the propagation rules are recursive, like the initial Datalog rules. Second, the mutual bindings between the two variables of *part-subpart* in the second propagation rule have disappeared in the propagation rules associated with the rules defining *part-subpart*. Indeed, even if, eventually, only facts of the form *part-subpart(Y,Y)* can violate the constraints, *intermediate* facts of the more general form *part-subpart(X,Y)* can also lead (in several steps) to a violation. Hence, most general additions for *part-subpart* need to be propagated.

5.3   Propagation Rules for Aggregate Operations

EKS provides both non-recursive and recursive aggregate facilities (see [Lef92]). We discuss here only non-recursive aggregate rules, and extend the propagation rules framework to deal with them. Their general form, together with an example, is as follows:

```
H <-    agg( Subgoal, Group-variables, List-of-agg-operations)

avg_sal(Dep, AvgSal) <-
        agg( employee(Dept, Name, Salary),
          [Dept],
          [Avgsal is avg(Salary)]
        )
```

The example (*find the average salary by department*) should suffice to explain the meaning of the aggregate construct: *Subgoal (employee)* indicates the input of the aggregate operation, *Group-variables ([Dept])* is the list of grouping attributes, and *List-of-agg-operations* is the list of aggregate operations to perform (of the form *"Var is op(In_Var)"*). We refer to [Lef92] for more details.

In general, *both additions and deletions* over `Subgoal` can imply *both additions and deletions* over `H`. For instance, the addition of an employee to the "toy" department with a given *Salary*, will change the average salary of the "toy" department, i.e., will remove the old value and add the new value. In the case of a deletion, the situation is symmetrical.

Whenever *type(L)* appears as *Body-update* in a propagation rule (L and H being unifiable, mgu σ), there must exist propagation rules of head *type(Hγ)* (Hγ subsumes Hσ). There are two cases:

1. *Type* is `safe-add`:

   > **if** *safe-add(Subgoalγ)* **and** *Hγ*   **then**   *safe-add(Hγ)*
   > **if** *any-del(Subgoalγ)*   **and** *Hγ*   **then**   *safe-add(Hγ)*

2. *Type* is `any-del`:

   > **if** *safe-add(Subgoalγ)* **and** *old(Hγ)*   **then**   *any-del(Hγ)*
   > **if** *any-del(Subgoalγ)*   **and** *old(Hγ)*   **then**   *any-del(Hγ)*

The nature of the side literals (here the head of the initial rule) is different from the case of a normal Datalog rule. Here, the addition and deletion of a fact over `Subgoal` only serves as a *trigger* for the *re-evaluation* of the aggregate function, however restricted to the corresponding grouping values.

6   Managing Propagation Rules

6.1   Maintenance

The set of propagation rules has to be updated when a constraint or a materialized predicate is added or removed. The algorithms to maintain this set reflect the definitions given in the previous section: if an initial propagation rule is added or removed, then other propagation rules are added or deleted in a top-down fashion.

The main difficulty is to take care of the propagation rules subsumed by other propagation rules. Upon additions, propagation rules previously in the set of propagation rules may have to be removed because they are subsumed by the new ones; this will maintain the minimality of the set of propagation rules. Upon deletions, it is necessary to add to the set of propagation rules those propagation rules which were previously subsumed by the propagation rules being deleted; this will maintain the completeness of the set of propagation rules.

Example 5.1 provides an illustration of this issue. When adding (4-1) and (4-2), (3-1) and (3-2) had to be removed. Similarly, if the constraint IC-2 is removed later, then (4-1) and (4-2) are deleted, but (3-1) and (3-2) need to be added.

Adding Propagation Rules

The addition process is triggered by the insertion of one initial propagation rule (point 1 of the definition in section 5.1). Its body update is passed as the argument to the *addition procedure* given below.

This addition procedure takes as input a propagation literal of the form **safe-del(L), safe-add(L)** or **any-del(L)**. Its main purpose is to make sure that the set of propagation rules contains all the rules necessary to generate updates instance of the propagation literal passed as input.

Addition Procedure

1. The argument is of the form `safe-del`(L).
    If there is a propagation rule whose head update subsumes `safe-del`(L), do nothing; otherwise:

    (a) remove the propagation rules whose head updates are subsumed by `safe-del`(L);

    (b) insert the propagation rule:

    > **if** *any-del(L)* **and** *not new(L)* **then** *safe-del(L)*

    (c) call recursively the *addition procedure* with `any-del`(L) as argument.

2. The argument is of the form *type(L)*, where *type* is either `safe-add` or `any-del`.
    For each Datalog rule `R:  H <- Body` such that H and L are unifiable (mgu σ), and for each literal L' in `Body`, do:

    If there is a propagation rule for the same Datalog rule `R` and the same body literal L' whose head update subsumes *type(Hσ)*, do nothing; otherwise:

    (a) remove the propagation rules whose head update are subsumed by *type(Hσ)*;

    (b) generate a propagation rule according to the definition in 5.1;

    (c) insert this propagation rule;

    (d) call recursively the *addition procedure* with the body update of this propagation rule as argument.

The following remark applies both to the addition process and to the deletion process. The subsumption test is not performed on whole propagation rules, but on their head updates; this is sufficient, as propagation rules are compared only if they correspond to the same Datalog rule and to the same body literal, and as only variables appearing in their head may be bound. The cost of this subsumption test is thus limited (subsumption is NP-complete in general).

Deleting Propagation Rules

The deletion process is triggered by the removal of one initial propagation rule (point 1 of the definition in section 5.1). Its body update is passed as the argument of the *deletion procedure* defined below.

This addition procedure takes as input a propagation literal of the form **safe-add, safe-del(L)** or **any-del(L)**. It proceeds in two phases: first, delete all propagation rules which are connected to the initial propagation rule being removed; second, add all the propagation rules which were previously subsumed and thus not present in the database. The second phase starts from the propagation literals affected by the first phase (they are collected in a list -initially empty-, called *remember-list* here).

Deletion Procedure

1. Let the argument of the procedure be *type(L)*.
   For each existing propagation rule whose head update subsumes *type(L)* do:

   (a) remove this propagation rule;

   (b) add its body update to *remember-list*;

   (c) call recursively the *deletion procedure* with its body update as argument;

2. For each update literal *type'(L')* in *remember-list*, if it unifies (mgu σ) with the body update of a propagation rule still present, call the *addition procedure* with *type'(L'σ)* as argument.

6.2   Activation

The activation of propagation rules in a database context involves both optimization and compilation aspects and run-time execution. In order to avoid duplication, the optimization, compilation and execution of propagation rules must use the system's components for basic query optimization, compilation and execution. In this section, we shortly indicate how the EKS core rule evaluator (designed for fact derivation) is used for propagation rules.

Mapping Propagation Rules onto Datalog Rules

The query evaluation kernel of EKS derives from the DedGin* prototype [LV89]. This kernel is made up of a rule optimizing compiler and of a query evaluator. It implements the QSQ execution model [Lau89], which extends top-down by sharing the evaluation of subqueries, thus guaranteeing completeness and termination. All manipulations of data are performed in a set-oriented way.

The propagation rules are rewritten in such a way that the top-down activation of the rewritten rules simulates the bottom-up activation of the initial propagation rules. Our generic propagation rule:

> **if** *Body-update*   **and** *state(Side)*   **then**   *Head-update*

is rewritten as:
> *Body-update $<-$ state(Side) and Head-update*

Implementation wise, new internal predicates are introduced to code propagation literals. For instance, `safe-add(pred(X,Y))` may become `sa-pred(X,Y)`, and the propagation of explicit additions on `pred` is triggered by issuing a query on `sa-pred`.

Only minor changes had to be done to the rule optimizing compiler and to the query evaluator for supporting propagation rules. They concerned (1) the evaluation of (sub)queries over the old state, (2) the systematic selection of *Head-update* as the last literal from rewritten propagation rules, (3) the unfolding of some rewritten propagation rules, to handle non-locally range-restricted rules (this is beyond the scope of this chapter) and (4) allowing some side-effects (strictly controlled by the system), e.g., for updating materialized predicates.

Finally, note that *recursion* and *aggregates* are handled normally by the query evaluation kernel. The control of recursion avoids several propagations of the same update through the same propagation rule.

Run-Time Coordination

Propagation rules represent a uniform framework for integrity checking and for materialized predicates handling. But the coordination of their execution must comply with different requirements: (1) the violation of only one integrity constraint is sufficient for a transaction to be invalid; as soon as such a violation is detected, the remaining propagation rules do not need to be activated; (2) to be complete, the maintenance of materialized predicates must activate all possible propagation rules.

As a consequence, the strategy used to coordinate the activation of propagation rules must be chosen with care. For integrity checking, a "depth-first" coordination strategy is recommended, as it allows early detection of inconsistency while avoiding redundant work. For materialized predicates, where saturation is always needed, there is no such clear winner.

The query evaluator of EKS (see [LV89]) was designed to support both a depth-first and a breadth-first strategy. While DedGin* systematically applied depth-first, EKS systematically applies breadth-first. This choice was made for simplicity; however, this induces redundant work for yes/no queries and integrity violation detections. Dynamic switching between depth-first and breadth-first, although initially planned, has not been implemented.

7   Discussion and Previous Work

7.1   Pattern Propagation

The Role of Side Literal Evaluation

Let us return for a short moment to the context of section 3 and consider the propagation of an update on L through one of the following rules: Consider the following rule:

```
R:        H <- L, Side.
R':       H <- not L, Side.
```

In this context, the goal of propagation is to find out the derived facts for which proofs have been added or deleted by a transaction. In this case, the evaluation of the side literals Side serves two purposes: (1) it permits deriving the instances of H for which proofs are added and deleted, but (2) it also ensures that these instances are *actually* derivable either from NEW-DB or from OLD-DB.

When the focus changes from added and deleted proofs to safe updates, as in sections 4 and following, the role of side literal evaluation is changed accordingly. On one hand, it remains important to guarantee that facts regarded as added are actually derivable from NEW-DB (safe additions). On the other hand, it becomes unnecessary to guarantee that facts regarded as deleted were actually derivable from OLD-DB (we require only that they are not derivable from NEW-DB).

As a consequence, not all side literals need to be evaluated when generating deletions: one needs only to evaluate sufficiently many side literals to produce ground instances of H. The remaining side literals can be regarded as additional tests on the deletion being induced: if their evaluation fails, the potential deletion does not need to be propagated. These tests are thus of the same nature as derivability tests, and a consistent strategy would be to leave them out[3].

As an example, consider the rule:

```
        s(X,Y) <- p(X,Z), q(Z,Y), r(X,Z)
```

---

[3]We could have done so in EKS, but the current implementation evaluates all of them.

Suppose that `q(a,b)` is deleted. In order to provide bindings for `s`, only one of the two side literals (`p(X,Z)` or `r(X,Z)`) needs to be evaluated. The evaluation of the remaining literal is optional.

More radically, one can envisage evaluating even fewer side literals, and generate non-ground instances of `H`. These non-ground instances represent *update patterns*, as they indicate that some of their instances may be added or deleted. These patterns can be propagated in a similar way as ground updates. Consider the rule:

```
R:       H <- L, Side,
```

and an update pattern `P` unifiable with `L` (mgu σ), then the propagation of `P` through `R` generates the update pattern `H`σ on `H` (if no side literal at all is evaluated). `H`σ may be more restricted than `H` or be as general as `H`; `H`σ can be further propagated through rules.

Patterns carry less information than (ground) updates: some bindings are missing and no specific derivability (from NEW-DB, OLD-DB) information is available. Bindings can be regenerated by evaluating the patterns either as stand-alone queries or integrated within larger queries.

It is even possible to mix the propagation of update patterns and ground updates. Suppose that, in the above example, one propagates the pattern `P` through the rule `R` by evaluating the whole expression "`L`σ, `Side`σ" (over OLD-DB or NEW-DB, depending on the type of `P`). As a result, from an update pattern on `L`, one generates ground updates on `H`. Further, if these updates are additions, then they are guaranteed to be derivable from NEW-DB, for the whole body of the rule has been evaluated. Note that the evaluation of "`L`σ, `Side`σ" differs from the evaluation of side literals considered so far because of the presence of `L`σ.

As a result, a wide range of possibilities exists. We discuss below two methods which can be interpreted as combining pattern and (ground) update propagation.

We did not retain such an approach in EKS for the following reason. The propagation of patterns does not focus on induced updates: a pattern is a very loose piece of information and regenerating bindings by re-evaluation will in general regenerate more data than when directly generating ground updates (a similar point is made in [BDM88]).

On Constraint Simplification

The simplification method [Nic82], initially developed for relational databases, has been rather influential and several authors have extended it for deductive databases [BDM88, Dec86, LST87]. Both the initial method and the extension presented in [LST87] can be understood as the following combination of pattern and ground update propagation:

1. Propagate patterns until the body of a denial is reached;

2. Unify the pattern with the corresponding literal of the denial;

3. Evaluate the resulting instance of the denial.

As an example, consider the following constraint (the simplification method works with first-order formulas):

```
        forall X: [p(X) -> exists Y: ( q(X,Y) and r(Y) )]
```

In EKS, as in [LT84], this constraint is rewritten as:

```
        inconsistent <- p(X), not tmp(X)
        tmp(X) <- q(X,Y) , r(Y)
```

As a result of this update/pattern propagation strategy, the body of the following instances of the denial needs to be evaluated upon the updates: addition of `p(a)`; deletion of `q(a,b)`; deletion of `r(b)`:

```
inconsistent <- not tmp(a)
inconsistent <- p(a), not tmp(a)
inconsistent <- p(X), not tmp(X)
```

In the first case, constraint simplification is equivalent to the method presented here. In the second and third cases, our propagation procedure evaluates the side literals in the rule defining `tmp` (resp. `r` and `q`) to produce updates over `tmp`. More propagation work is done, but the method focuses better on induced changes.

Another Combination

As an example of another design, in the method presented in [DW89], side literals are evaluated when generating additions and are not evaluated when generating deletions. In other words, patterns are generated for deletions, while updates are generated for additions. The rationale for this design might be presented as follows: (1) the evaluation of side literals on the old state may be expensive; (2) derivability tests are needed in any case when generating deletions: hence, why not simply re-derive the facts matching the patterns?

We took the view that (1) evaluation on the old state can be efficiently implemented, and (2) the "focus on induced changes" is a practical requirement.

7.2   Combination of Top-down and Bottom-up Requirements

Some authors [BDM88, Kuc91, Oli91] have assumed a top-down activation of (the equivalent of our) propagation rules, rather than the bottom-up activation advocated here. The main rationale for this approach [BDM88] was to avoid the irrelevant propagations performed by a blind bottom-up propagation of updates (recall that this is avoided here by the definition of the set of relevant propagation rules).

In this top-down approach (mainly studied in the context of integrity checking), the activation of propagation rules is triggered by asking the query **?- safe-add(inc-id)** for every constraint. This query is then to be answered by the standard query evaluator.

A first issue in this approach is to ask these queries only for the constraints which may be affected by the update. This is addressed in [BDM88] by using a dependency graph linking base updates to constraints. A second issue is to avoid the activation of irrelevant propagation rules, i.e., of propagation rules not connected to the updates: this issue thus generalizes the first one. A third issue is to use the bindings provided by the updates to actually focus on the induced changes. [Kuc91] addresses these issues by adding a "dependency" literal in the body of the propagation rules. A full comparison between the approach reported here and the one presented in [Kuc91] remains to be done.

7.3   Basic Work on Update Propagation

A couple of basic contributions [BDM88, Dec86, SK88] have isolated the main aspects of update propagation, as we presented in section 3: evaluation over old and new states and derivability tests. Let us recall the tentative uniform view presented in [BMM91, BM90b]. The influence of these basic works on the design of EKS should be clear.

[SK88], followed by [MB88], deal with a uniform representation of expressions as rules and denials. [SK88] and [Dec86] propagate updates in bottom-up manner - our scheme is close to their; however, none of them tackle the issue of avoiding irrelevant propagations, as noted in [BDM88]. [BDM88, Dec86] combine update propagation and constraint simplification; it is now recognized that a uniform view should be adopted [SK88, BM90b, BMM91], as we have done here. [BDM88] provides a first approach to avoiding irrelevant propagation (see above).

More recent presentations of these basic principles include [Kuc91, Oli91]. [Kuc91] presents in an overview various classes of changes for derived predicates that can be obtained using various update propagation schemes.

[LST87] combines pattern propagation and constraint simplification. Works including only detection of irrelevant checks have been proposed in [BCL89]; these proposals fully evaluate a constraint once it has been detected as relevant.

7.4 Counting-like Methods

Counting methods implement an interesting alternative, as they permit avoiding derivability tests. These methods basically work as follows: the number of proofs for each materialized derived fact is stored together with the derived fact. After each transaction, the number of proofs added or removed by the transaction is computed along a mechanism similar to the one described in section 3. The number of proofs added to removed by the transaction thus permits maintaining the extensions of materialized predicates.

As a shortcoming, counting methods need special tricks to handle negation.

The first attempt for a counting method was in the BDGEN prototype [NY83] (without negation). Counting has been considerably improved in [GMS93]. The work presented in [GL95] is related to counting, and addresses the issue not from a deductive setting but from a bag algebra setting.

7.5 Miscellaneous

Ceri and Widom (see [CW94] and papers pointed there), concentrate on the generation of production rules to handle update propagation and on the adequacy of these production rules to extended relational systems.

Harrison and Dietrich [HD92] develop an update propagation approach that they, in particular, apply to condition monitoring in active database systems.

When checking general integrity constraints, update propagation has to be performed at the end of the transaction (so-called *deferred mode*). In some simpler cases, it is possible to do otherwise (check before or after the update, so-called *immediate* mode in SQL databases). In particular, generating pre-conditions has been addressed several works (see [Sto75, BB82]). While the interest of the immediate mode is obvious, in EKS, only the most general case is considered and update propagation is performed at the end of a transaction.

8 Conclusion

In this chapter, we have stressed the genericity of update propagation, as a way to support both integrity checking and materialized predicates; we believe that it can also be used to monitor the conditions associated with alerters. We have developed an original and an effective solution to combine the two main requirements of update propagation: focus on induced changes and avoid irrelevant propagations. We have justified and developed a testing policy which aims at minimizing the number of derivability tests. These techniques have been implemented in the EKS system which supports generalized integrity checking and materialized predicates handling.

As an obvious limitation, EKS does not offer an `update` primitive to modify tuples (to modify a fact, one must perform a deletion and then an insertion). An explicit update facility sometimes allows gains for update propagation. Consider the rule:

        p(X,Y) <- q(X,Y,Z)

Modifications of the third attribute of `q`-facts do not induce changes on `p`. If tuple modifications are performed by one deletion followed by an insertion, the absence of induced changes is difficult to detect. Techniques for update propagation can easily be generalized to support such an `update` primitive.

Acknowledgments

The design and the development of the update propagation component of EKS have largely benefited from the high level of expertise previously acquired within the KB group at ECRC by our fellow researchers Francois Bry, Hendrik Decker, Rainer Manthey and Mark Wallace. We acknowledge the advice of Rainer Manthey. This chapter is a revised version of [VBK91], written while the first author was an employee of Ecole Nationale des Ponts et Chaussées, Paris, France.

28

DERIVING PRODUCTION RULES FOR INCREMENTAL VIEW MAINTENANCE

Stefano Ceri, Jennifer Widom

ABSTRACT

It is widely recognized that production rules in database systems can be used to automatically maintain derived data such as views. However, writing a correct set of rules for efficiently maintaining a given view can be a difficult and ad-hoc process. We provide a facility whereby a user defines a view as an SQL **select** expression, from which the system automatically derives set-oriented production rules that maintain a materialization of that view.

The maintenance rules are triggered by operations on the view's base tables. Generally, the rules perform Incremental view maintenance: the materialized view is modified according to the sets of changes made to the base tables, which are accessible through logical tables provided by the rule language. However, for some operations substantial recomputation may be required. We give algorithms that, based on key information, perform syntactic analysis on a view definition to determine when efficient maintenance is possible.

1 Introduction

In relational database systems, a *view* is a logical table derived from one or more physical (*base*) tables. Views are useful for presenting different levels of abstraction or different portions of a database to different users. Typically, a view is specified as an SQL **select** expression. A retrieval query over a view is written as if the view were a physical table; the query's answer is logically equivalent to evaluating the view's **select** expression, then performing the query using the result. There are two well-known approaches to implementing views. In the first approach, views are *virtual*: queries over views are modified into queries over base tables [Sto75]. In the second approach, views are *materialized*: they are computed from the base tables and stored in the database [BLT86,KP81,SI84]. Different applications favor one or the other approach. In this chapter we consider the problem of view materialization.

Production rules in database systems allow specification of data manipulation operations that are executed automatically when certain events occur or conditions are met, e.g. [DE88,MD89,SJGP90,WF90]. Clearly, production rules can be used to maintain materialized views: when base tables change, rules are triggered that modify the view.[1] Writing a correct set of rules for efficiently maintaining a given view can be a difficult process, however. The rules could simply rematerialize the view from the base tables, but this can be very inefficient. Efficiency is achieved by *incremental* maintenance, in which the changed portions of the base tables are propagated to the view, without full recomputation. We have developed a method that automatically derives incremental maintenance rules for a wide class of views. The rules produced are

---

[1] Production rules also can be used to implement Virtual views, as shown in [SJGP90].

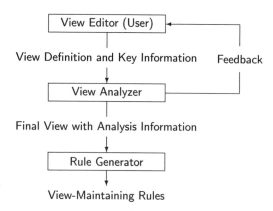

Figure 1 *Rule derivation system*

executable using the rule language of the Starburst database system at the IBM Almaden Research Center [WCL91].

Figure 1 shows the structure of our system, which is invoked at compile-time when a view is created. Initially, the user enters the view as an SQL **select** expression, along with information about keys for the view's base tables.[2] Our system then performs syntactic analysis on the view definition; this analysis determines two things: (1) whether the view may contain duplicates (2) for each base table referenced in the view, whether efficient view maintenance rules are possible for operations on that table. The user is provided with the results of this analysis. The results may indicate that, in order to improve the efficiency of view maintenance, further interaction with the system is necessary prior to rule generation. In particular:

- Views with duplicates cannot be maintained efficiently, as explained in Section 4.3. Hence, if the system detects that the view may contain duplicates, then the user should add **distinct** to the view definition. (In SQL, **distinct** eliminates duplicates.)

- If the system detects that efficient maintenance rules are not possible for some base table operations, this may indicate to the user that not all key information has been included, or the user may choose to modify the view definition.

If changes are made, view analysis is repeated. In practice, we have discovered that efficient rules are possible for most views and operations once all key information is provided. However, there are cases when certain base table operations cannot be supported efficiently. If these operations are expected to occur frequently, view materialization may be inappropriate. The responsibility for considering these trade-offs lies with the user; our system provides all necessary information.

Once the user is satisfied with the view definition and its properties, the system generates the set of view-maintaining rules. Rules are produced for **insert**, **delete**, and **update** operations on each base table referenced in the view. The rule language we use is *set-oriented*, meaning that rules are triggered after arbitrary sets of changes to the database (Section 3). For those operations for which the system

---

[2]Key information is essential for view analysis, as we will show. Functional dependencies could be specified as well, but we assume that keys are more easily understood and specified by the user; in normalized tables, functional dependencies are captured by keys anyway.

has determined that efficiency is possible, the maintenance rules modify the view incrementally according to the changes made to the base tables. These changes are accessible using the rule system's *transition table* mechanism (Section 3). For those operations for which efficiency is not possible, rematerialization is performed.

Note that the view must be computed in its entirety once, after which it is maintained automatically. The frequency of view maintenance depends on the frequency of rule invocation, which is flexible; see Section 3. Our method is directly applicable for simultaneous maintenance of multiple views; see Section 9.

1.1 Related Work

Most other work in incremental view maintenance differs from ours in two ways: (1) It takes an algebraic approach, considering a restricted class of views and operations. In contrast, we consider a practical class of views specified using a standard query language, and we consider arbitrary database operations. (2) It suggests view maintenance mechanisms that must be built into the database system. In contrast, we propose view maintenance as an application of an existing mechanism. In addition, our system provides interaction whereby the user can modify a view so the system will guarantee efficient maintenance.

In [BLT86], views are specified as relational algebra expressions. Algorithms are given for determining when base table changes are irrelevant to the view and for differentially reevaluating a view after a set of insert and delete operations. [Han87] extends this work to exploit common subexpressions and proposes an alternative approach using RETE networks; [Han87] also includes algorithms for incremental aggregate maintenance. In [RCBB89], an algebra of "delta relations" is described, including a "changes" operator that can be applied to views. There is a suggested connection to the production rules of HiPAC [MD89], but rule derivation is not included. In [SP89b], incremental maintenance of single-table views is considered, with emphasis on issues of distribution.

Our work here is loosely related to that reported in [CW90], where we gave a method for deriving production rules that maintain integrity constraints. Our solutions to the two problems differ considerably, but the approaches are similar: In both cases we describe a general compile-time facility in which the user provides a high-level declarative specification, then the system uses syntactic analysis to produce a set of lower-level production rules with certain properties relative to the user's specification.

1.2 Outline

Section 2 defines our SQL-based syntax for view definition and Section 3 provides an overview of our production rule language. Section 4 motivates our approach: it gives an informal overview of view analysis, explains incremental maintenance, and describes certain difficulties encountered with duplicates and updates.[3] Subsequent sections contain the core technical material, formally describing our methods for view analysis and rule generation. We consider *top-level* table references in Section 5, *positively nested* subqueries in Section 6, *negatively nested* subqueries in Section 7, and *set operators* in Section 8. In each of these sections we describe how view analysis can guarantee certain properties, and we show how these properties are used to determine if efficient maintenance is possible. Section 9 addresses system execution, showing that the generated rules behave correctly at run-time. Finally, in Section 10 we conclude and discuss future work.

Due to space constraints, some details have been omitted. For further details and additional examples see [CW91].

---

[3]Note that we are not dealing with the *view update problem*, which addresses how updates on views are propagated to updates on base tables. We are considering how updates on base tables are propagated to updates on views.

1.	*View-Def*	::=	**define view** $V(Col\text{-}List)$:
			View-Exp
2.	*View-Exp*	::=	*Select-Exp* | *Set-Exp*
3.	*Select-Exp*	::=	**select** [**distinct**] *Col-List*
			from *Table-List*
			[**where** *Predicate*]
4.	*Set-Exp*	::=	$Select\text{-}Exp_1$ **union distinct**
			$Select\text{-}Exp_2$ **union distinct**
			... $Select\text{-}Exp_n$
5.		|	$Select\text{-}Exp_1$ **intersect**
			$Select\text{-}Exp_2$ **intersect**
			... $Select\text{-}Exp_n$
6.	*Col-List*	::=	$Col_1, \ldots, Col_n$ | *
7.	*Col*	::=	$[T.]C$ | $[Var.]C$
8.	*Table-List*	::=	$T_1\,[Var_1], \ldots, T_n\,[Var_n]$
9.	*Predicate*	::=	*Item Comp Item*
10.		|	**exists** (*Simple-Select*)
11.		|	**not exists** (*Simple-Select*)
12.		|	*Item* **in** (*Simple-Select*)
13.		|	*Item* **not in** (*Simple-Select*)
14.		|	*Item Comp* **any** (*Simple-Select*)
15.		|	*Predicate* **and** *Predicate*
16.	*Item*	::=	*Col* | ⟨*Col-List*⟩ | constant
17.	*Comp*	::=	= | < | <= | > | >= | !=
18.	*Simple-Select*	::=	**select** *Col-List* **from** *Table-List*
			[**where** *Simple-Pred*]
19.	*Simple-Pred*	::=	*Item Comp Item*
20.		|	*Simple-Pred* **and** *Simple-Pred*

Figure 2 *Grammar for View Definitions*

2   View Definition Language

Views are defined using a subset of the SQL syntax for **select** expressions. The grammar is given in Figure 2 and should be self-explanatory to readers familiar with SQL [SC288].[4] Several examples are given in subsequent sections. Our view definition language is quite powerful, but, for brevity and to make our approach more presentable, the language does include certain restrictions:

- Disjunction in predicates is omitted. (There is little loss of expressive power since **or** usually can be simulated using **union**.)

---

[4]We include multi-column **in** (grammar productions 12 and 16), which is not standard in all SQL implementations.

- Subqueries are limited to one level of nesting.

- Set operators **union** and **intersect** may not be mixed; set operator **minus** is omitted.

- Comparison operators using **all** are omitted.

The reader will see that our method could certainly be extended to eliminate these restrictions, but the details are lengthy. Note also that we have omitted aggregates. Incremental methods for maintaining aggregates have been presented elsewhere [Han87]; these techniques can be adapted for our framework.

3   Production Rule Language

We provide a brief but self-contained overview of the set-oriented, SQL-based production rule language used in the remainder of the chapter. Further details and numerous examples appear in [WF90,WCL91]. Here we describe only the subset of the rule language used by the view maintenance rules.

Our rule facility is fully integrated into the Starburst database system. Hence, all the usual database functionality is available; in addition, a set of rules may be defined. Rules are based on the notion of *transitions*, which are database state changes resulting from execution of a sequence of data manipulation operations. We consider only the net effect of transitions, as in [BLT86,WF90]. The syntax for defining production rules is:[5]

> **create rule** *name*
> **when** *transition predicate*
> **then** *action*
> [**precedes** *rule-list*]

Transition predicates specify one or more operations on tables: **inserted into T**, **deleted from T**, or **updated T**. A rule is *triggered* by a given transition if at least one of the specified operations occurred in the net effect of the transition. The action part of a rule specifies an arbitrary sequence of SQL data manipulation operations to be executed when the rule is triggered. The optional **precedes** clause is used to induce a partial ordering on the set of defined rules. If a rule R_1 specifies R_2 in its **precedes** list, then R_1 is higher than R_2 in the ordering. When no ordering is specified between two rules, their order is arbitrary but deterministic [RAL91].

A rule's action may refer to the current state of the database through top-level or nested SQL **select** operations. In addition, rule actions may refer to *transition tables*. A transition table is a logical table reflecting changes that have occurred during a transition. At the end of a given transition, transition table "**inserted T**" refers to those tuples of table **T** in the current state that were inserted by the transition, transition table "**deleted T**" refers to those tuples of table **T** in the pre-transition state that were deleted by the transition, transition table "**old updated T**" refers to those tuples of table **T** in the pre-transition state that were updated by the transition, and transition table "**new updated T**" refers to the current values of the same tuples. Transition tables may be referenced in place of tables in the **from** clauses of **select** operations.

Rules are activated at *rule assertion points*. There is an assertion point at the end of each transaction, and there may be additional user-specified assertion points within a transaction.[6] We describe the semantics of rule execution at an arbitrary assertion point. The state change resulting from the user-generated

---

[5]Rules also may contain *conditions* in **if** clauses, but these are not needed for view maintenance.

[6]Currently, assertion points are at transaction commit only. We will soon extend the system with a flexible mechanism that supports additional points [WCL91].

database operations executed since the last assertion point (or start of the transaction) create the first relevant transition, and some set of rules are triggered by this transition. A triggered rule R is chosen from this set such that no other triggered rule is higher in the ordering. R's action is executed. After execution of R's action, all other rules are triggered only if their transition predicate holds with respect to the composite transition created by the initial transaction and subsequent execution of R's action. That is, these rules consider R's action as if it were executed as part of the initial transition. Rule R, however, has already "processed" the initial transition; thus, R is triggered again only if its transition predicate holds with respect to the transition created by its action. From the new set of triggered rules, a rule is chosen such that no other triggered rule is higher in the ordering, and its action is executed. At an arbitrary time in rule processing, a given rule is triggered if its transition predicate holds with respect to the (composite) transition since the last time at which its action was executed; if its action has not yet been executed, it is considered with respect to the transition since the last rule assertion point or start of the transaction. When the set of triggered rules is empty, rule processing terminates.

For view maintenance, it sometimes is necessary for a rule to consider the entire pre-transition value of a table (see, e.g., Section 5.4). Currently there is no direct mechanism in the rule language for obtaining this value, but it can be derived from transition tables. In the action part of view maintenance rules, we use "**old T**" to refer to the value of table **T** at the start of the transition triggering the rule. **old T** is translated to:

```
(T minus inserted T minus new updated T)
union deleted T union old updated T
```

This expression may seem rather complex, but one should observe that in most cases the transition tables are small or empty.

4   Motivation

4.1   View Analysis

Initially, the user defines a view using the language of Section 2, and the user specifies a set of (single- or multi-column) keys for the view's base tables. All known keys for each table should be specified, since this provides important information for view analysis. Using the key information, during view analysis the system considers each list of table references in the view definition. For each list, it first computes the "bound columns" of the table references. Based on the bound columns, it then determines for each table reference whether the reference is "safe". When a table reference is safe, Incremental view maintenance rules can be generated for operations on that table, as described in Section 4.2. The system also uses the bound columns for the top-level tables to determine if the view may contain duplicates. Formal definitions for bound columns and safety are based on the context of table references and are given in Sections 5–7.

4.2   Incremental Maintenance

The definition of a view V can be interpreted as an expression mapping base tables to table V. That is, $V = V_{exp}(T_1, .., T_n)$, where $T_1, .., T_n$ are the base tables appearing in V's definition. Efficient maintenance of V is achieved when changes to $T_1, .., T_n$ can be propagated incrementally to V, without substantial recomputation. Consider any table reference T_i in V, and assume for the moment that T_i appears only once in V's definition. If view analysis determines that T_i is safe, then changes to T_i can be propagated incrementally to V. More formally, changes to T_i (sets of insertions, deletions, or updates), denoted ΔT_i, produce changes to V, denoted ΔV, that can be computed using only ΔT_i and the other base tables:

$\Delta V = V'_{exp}(T_1, .., \Delta T_i, .., T_n)$, where V'_{exp} is an expression derived from V_{exp}. Table V is then modified by inserting or deleting tuples from ΔV as appropriate. We assume that ΔT_i is small with respect to T_i and ΔV is small with respect to V; hence, safe table references result in efficient maintenance rules. If T_i appears more than once in V's definition, we separately analyze each reference. If all references are safe, then changes to T_i can be propagated incrementally to V. If any reference is unsafe, changes to T_i may cause rematerialization.

4.3 Duplicates

Our method does not support efficient maintenance of views with duplicates. The main difficulty lies in generating rule actions in SQL that can manipulate exact numbers of duplicates. As an example, the SQL **delete** operation is based on truth of a predicate; hence, if a table contains four copies of a tuple (say), there is no SQL operation that can delete exactly two copies. To correctly maintain views with duplicates, such partial deletions can be necessary. [BLT86] also considers the problem of duplicates in views, proposing two solutions. In the first solution, an extra column is added in the view table to count the number of occurrences of each tuple. We choose not to use this approach because rule generation can become quite complex and the result is not transparent to the user. (The user must reference duplicates in the view through the extra column.) The second solution proposed in [BLT86] ensures that a view will not contain duplicates by requiring it to include key columns for each of the base tables. We have essentially taken this approach, however we have devised algorithms that allow us to loosen the key requirement considerably, yet still guarantee that a view will not contain duplicates.

4.4 Update Operations

When update operations are performed on a view's base tables, we would like to consequently perform an update operation on the view. In many cases, however, this is not the semantic effect. As a simple example, consider two tables T1(A,B) and T2(C,D) where T1 contains tuples (x,y), (z,y), and (u,v), and T2 contains tuples (x,z) and (v,x). Consider the following view:

```
define view V(A): select T1.A from T1, T2
                  where T1.B = T2.C
```

Initially, V contains only one tuple, (u). Now suppose the following two update operations are performed on table T2:

```
update T2 set C = u where D = x ;
update T2 set C = y where D = z
```

The effect of the first update is to remove tuple (u) from view V, while the effect of the second update is to add tuples (x) and (z) to V. There is no way to reflect the update operations on base table T2 as an update operation on view V; rather, the updates must be reflected as delete and insert operations on V. There do exist some cases in which update operations on base tables can be reflected as updates on views. However, for general and automatic rule derivation, in our approach update operations on base tables always result in delete and/or insert operations on the view.

5 Top-Level Table References

Assume now that the user has defined a view and has specified key information for the view's base tables. Assume that the view does not include set operators **union** or **intersect**; views with set operators are covered in Section 8. The system first analyzes the top-level table references, i.e., those references generated from the *Table-List* in grammar production 3 of Figure 2. This analysis reveals both whether the view may contain duplicates and whether efficient maintenance rules are possible for operations on the top-level tables. Consider a view V with the general form:[7]

> **define view** $V(Col\text{-}List)$:
>   **select** $C_1, .., C_n$ **from** $T_1, .., T_m$ **where** P

where $T_1, .., T_m$ are the top-level table references, $C_1, .., C_n$ are columns of $T_1, .., T_m$, and P is a predicate.

5.1   Bound Columns

View analysis relies on the concept of *bound columns*. The bound columns of the top-level table references in view V are denoted $B(V)$ and are computed as follows:

**Definition 5.1 (Bound Columns for Top-Level
Table References)**

1. Initialize $B(V)$ to contain the columns $C_1, .., C_n$ projected in the view definition.

2. Add to $B(V)$ all columns of $T_1, .., T_m$ such that predicate P includes an equality comparison between the column and a constant.

3. Repeat until $B(V)$ is unchanged:

    (a) Add to $B(V)$ all columns of $T_1, .., T_m$ such that predicate P includes an equality comparison between the column and a column in $B(V)$.

    (b) Add to $B(V)$ all columns of any table T_i, $1 \leq i \leq m$, if $B(V)$ includes a key for T_i. □

Bound columns can be computed using syntactic analysis and guarantee the following useful property (Lemma 5.2 below): If two tuples in the cross-product of top-level tables $T_1, .., T_m$ satisfy predicate P and differ in their bound columns, then the tuples also must differ in view columns $C_1, .., C_m$. Let $Proj(t, C_1, .., C_j)$ denote the projection of a tuple t onto a set of columns $C_1, .., C_j$.

Lemma 5.2 (Bound Columns Lemma for Top-Level Tables) Let t_1 and t_2 be tuples in the cross-product of $T_1, .., T_m$ such that t_1 and t_2 both satisfy P. By definition, columns $C_1, .., C_n$ are in $B(V)$. If $D_1, .., D_k$ are additional columns in $B(V)$ such that t_1 and t_2 are guaranteed to differ in $C_1, .., C_n, D_1, .., D_k$, i.e. $Proj(t_1, C_1, .., C_n, D_1, .., D_k) \neq Proj(t_2, C_1, .., C_n, D_1, .., D_k)$, then t_1 and t_2 also are guaranteed to differ in $C_1, .., C_n$, i.e. $Proj(t_1, C_1, .., C_n) \neq Proj(t_2, C_1, .., C_n)$.

Proof: Suppose, for the sake of a contradiction, that $Proj(t_1, C_1, .., C_n) = Proj(t_2, C_1, .., C_n)$. Then there must be some D_i in $D_1, .., D_k$ such that $Proj(t_1, D_i) \neq Proj(t_2, D_i)$. We show that this is impossible. Consider any column D_i in $D_1, .., D_k$. Since D_i is in $B(V)$, by the recursive definition of $B(V)$ and since t_1 and t_2 both satisfy predicate P, the value of column D_i in both t_1 and t_2 must either

1. satisfy an equality with a constant k, or

2. satisfy an equality with a column C_j in $C_1, .., C_n$, or

---

[7]For clarity and without loss of generality, we omit the use of table variables here.

3. be functionally dependent on a constant k or column C_j. (This is the case where D_i was added to $B(V)$ because a key for D_i's table was present; recall that all columns of a table are functionally dependent on any key for that table.)

In the case of a constant, $Proj(t_1, D_i)$ and $Proj(t_2, D_i)$ are both equal to or functionally dependent on the same constant, so $Proj(t_1, D_i) = Proj(t_2, D_i)$. In the case of a column C_j, $Proj(t_1, C_j) = Proj(t_2, C_j)$ by our supposition, so $Proj(t_1, D_i) = Proj(t_2, D_i)$. $\square$

5.2 Duplicate Analysis

If V's definition does not include **distinct**, then our system performs duplicate analysis. If this analysis reveals that V may contain duplicates, then the user is notified that maintenance rules cannot be generated for V unless V's definition is modified to include **distinct**. (The system does not add **distinct** automatically since it may change the view's semantics.) Once the bound columns for top-level table references have been computed, duplicate analysis is straightforward:

Theorem 5.3 (Duplicates) If $B(V)$ includes a key for every top-level table, then V will not contain duplicates.

Proof: Let t_1 and t_2 be two different tuples in the cross-product of the top-level tables in V such that t_1 and t_2 both satisfy predicate P. We must show that t_1 and t_2 cannot produce duplicate tuples in V, i.e. $Proj(t_1, C_1, .., C_n) \neq Proj(t_2, C_1, .., C_n)$. By the theorem's assumption, there must be additional columns $D_1, .., D_k$ in $B(V)$ such that $C_1, .., C_n, D_1, .., D_k$ include a key for every top-level table. Then t_1 and t_2 must differ in $C_1, .., C_n, D_1, .., D_k$. Consequently, by Lemma 5.2, $Proj(t_1, C_1, .., C_n) \neq Proj(t_2, C_1, .., C_n)$. $\square$

5.3 Safety Analysis

Safety of top-level table references is similar to duplicate analysis:

Definition 5.4 (Safety of Top-Level Table References) Top-level table reference T_i is *safe* in V if $B(V)$ includes a key for T_i. $\square$

The following three theorems show that if table reference T_i is safe, then **insert**, **delete**, and **update** operations on T_i can be reflected by incremental changes to V.

Theorem 5.5 (Insertion Theorem for Top-Level Tables) Let T_i be a safe top-level table reference in V and suppose a tuple t is inserted into T_i. If v is a tuple in the cross-product of the top-level tables using tuple t from T_i, and v satisfies predicate P so that $Proj(v, C_1, .., C_n)$ is in view V after the insertion, then $Proj(v, C_1, .., C_n)$ was not in V before the insertion.

Proof: Suppose, for the sake of a contradiction, that there was a tuple v' in V before the insertion such that $Proj(v', C_1, .., C_n) = Proj(v, C_1, .., C_n)$. Let $D_1, .., D_k$ be additional bound columns so that $C_1, .., C_n, D_1, .., D_k$ includes a key for T_i. (We know such columns exist since T_i is safe.) Since v and v' include different tuples from T_i, then $Proj(v, C_1, .., C_n, D_1, .., D_k) \neq Proj(v', C_1, .., C_n, D_1, .., D_k)$. Hence, by Lemma 5.2, $Proj(v, C_1, .., C_n) \neq Proj(v', C_1, .., C_n)$. $\square$

The practical consequence of this theorem is that if a set of tuples ΔT_i are inserted into T_i, then the tuples

ΔV that should be inserted into V can be derived from the cross-product of the top-level tables using ΔT_i instead of T_i. This exactly corresponds to the definition of incremental maintenance in Section 4.2, and is implemented in the rules given below.

Similar theorems with similar consequences apply for delete and update operations. The proofs are omitted since they also are similar [CW91].

Theorem 5.6 (Deletion Theorem for Top-Level Tables) Let T_i be a safe top-level table reference in V and suppose a tuple t is deleted from T_i. If v is a tuple in the cross-product of the top-level tables using tuple t from T_i, and v satisfies predicate P so that $Proj(v, C_1, .., C_n)$ was in view V before the deletion, then $Proj(v, C_1, .., C_n)$ is not in V after the deletion. $\square$

Theorem 5.7 (Update Theorem for Top-Level Tables) Let T_i be a safe top-level table reference in V and suppose a tuple t is updated in T_i. Let v_O be a tuple in the cross-product of the top-level tables using the old value of tuple t from T_i, where v_O satisfies P so that $Proj(v_O, C_1, .., C_n)$ was in view V before the update. Let v_N be a tuple in the cross-product of the top-level tables using the new value of tuple t from T_i, where v_N satisfies P so that $Proj(v_N, C_1, .., C_n)$ is in V after the update. Finally, let v be a tuple in the cross-product of the top-level tables not using t, where v satisfies P so v is in V both before and after the update. Then $Proj(v_O, C_1, .., C_n) \neq Proj(v, C_1, .., C_n)$ and $Proj(v_N, C_1, .., C_n) \neq Proj(v, C_1, .., C_n)$. $\square$

5.4 Rule Generation

We describe how maintenance rules are generated for the top-level tables. We first consider safe table references, then unsafe references. Initially, for each table reference we generate four rules—one triggered by **inserted**, one by **deleted**, and two by **updated**. Subsequently we explain how some rules can be combined and how the entire rule set is ordered.

Let T_i be a safe top-level table reference in view V defined as above. If tuples are inserted into T_i, then we want to insert into V those tuples produced by the view definition using **inserted Ti** instead of **Ti** in the top-level table list. By Theorem 5.5, these insertions cannot create duplicates in the view. However, if a similar rule is applied because tuples also were inserted into a different top-level table, then duplicates could appear. Hence, before inserting a new tuple, the rule must ensure that the tuple has not already been inserted by a different rule. This is checked efficiently using transition table **inserted V**. The rule for **inserted** is:

```
create rule ins-Ti-V
when inserted into Ti
then insert into V
      (select C1,..,Cn
       from T1,..,inserted Ti,..,Tm
       where P and <C1,..,Cn> not in inserted V)
```

If tuples are deleted from T_i, then we want to delete from V those tuples produced by the view definition using **deleted Ti** instead of **Ti** in the top-level table list. By Theorem 5.6, we know that these tuples should no longer be in the view. Again, however, we must remember that other tables in the top-level table list may have been modified. Hence, to identify the correct tuples to delete from V, we must consider the pre-transition value of all other tables, obtained using the **old** feature described in Section 3. For predicate P, let P-*old* denote P with all table references **T** replaced by **old T**. The rule for **deleted** is:

```
create rule del-Ti-V
when deleted from Ti
then delete from V
      where <C1,..,Cn> in
        (select C1,..,Cn
         from old T1,..,deleted Ti,..,old Tm
         where P-old)
```

As explained in Section 4.4, update operations on base tables always cause delete and/or insert operations on views. In fact, we generate two separate rules triggered by **updated**—one to perform deletions and the other to perform insertions. They are similar to the rules for **deleted** and **inserted**, and their correctness follows from Theorem 5.7:

```
create rule old-upd-Ti-V
when updated Ti
then delete from V
      where <C1,..,Cn> in
        (select C1,..,Cn
         from old T1,..,old updated Ti,..,old Tm
         where P-old)

create rule new-upd-Ti-V
when updated Ti
then insert into V
        (select C1,..,Cn
         from T1,..,new updated Ti,..,Tm
         where P and <C1,..,Cn> not in inserted V)
```

If a table appears more than once in the top-level table list, then rules are generated for each reference. Rules with identical triggering operations whose actions perform the same operation (either insert or delete) are merged into one rule by sequencing or combining their actions. Once the entire set of rules is generated (including those for nested table references, described below), they are ordered by adding **precedes** clauses so that all rules performing deletions precede all rules performing insertions.[8]

Now consider the case when a top-level table reference T_i is unsafe, so the properties guaranteed by the theorems may not hold. For insertions, incremental maintenance is still possible; the only difference from the safe case is that all new tuples must be checked against V itself to guarantee that duplicates are not produced. If V is indexed, this can be performed efficiently.

```
create rule ins-Ti-V
when inserted into Ti
then insert into V
        (select C1,..,Cn
         from T1,..,inserted Ti,..,Tm
         where P and <C1,..,Cn> not in V)
```

Delete and update operations are more difficult, and this is where recomputation must occur. If a tuple is deleted from T_i, without Theorem 5.6 we cannot determine whether corresponding tuples should be deleted from V—those tuples still may be produced by other base table tuples that have not been deleted; a similar problem occurs with update. The only solution is to reevaluate the view expression itself. Since

---

[8]This is why we merge only rules with the same action operation and why we create two separate rules for **updated**—for ordering, we cannot generate rule actions that perform both deletions and insertions.

this is equivalent to rematerializing the view, we choose to create a single distinguished rule that performs rematerialization. This rule will be triggered by all operations for which efficient maintenance is impossible. (As mentioned above, if these operations are expected to occur frequently, then materialization may be inappropriate for this view.) The rematerialization rule with triggering operations for T_i is:

```
create rule rematerialize-V
when deleted from Ti,
     updated Ti
then delete from V;
     insert into V
       (select C1,..,Cn from T1,..,Tm where P);
     deactivate-rules(V)
```

This rule will have precedence over all other rules for V. Since execution of the first two rule actions entirely rematerializes V, the rule's final action, `deactivate-rules(V)`, deactivates all other rules for V until the next rule assertion point.[9] Note that when a triggering operation appears in the rematerialization rule, any other rules triggered by that operation can be eliminated.

5.5   Examples

We draw examples from a simple airline reservations database with the following schema:

```
flight (FLIGHT-ID, flight-no, date)
res (RES-ID, psgr-id, flight-id, seat)
psgr (PSGR-ID, name, phone, meal, ffn)
ff (FFN, miles)
```

Most of the schema is self-explanatory, with `res` denoting reservation, `ff` denoting frequent flier, and `ffn` denoting frequent flier number. Primary keys for each table are capitalized; other keys are `<flight-no,date>` for table `flight`, `<psgr-id,flight-id>` or `<flight-id, seat>` for table `res`, and `ffn` for table `psgr`.

Consider the following view, which provides the seat numbers and meal preferences of all passengers on a given flight (FID) who have ordered special meals:

```
define view special-meals(seat, meal):
  select res.seat, psgr.meal
  from res, psgr
  where res.flight-id = FID
  and res.psgr-id = psgr.psgr-id
  and psgr.meal != null
```

Using Definition 5.1, we determine that the bound columns of top-level table references `res` and `psgr` are: projected columns `res.seat` and `psgr.meal`, column `res.flight-id` since it is equated to a constant in the predicate, all remaining columns of `res` since `<flight-id,seat>` is a key, and `psgr.psgr-id` since it is equated to bound column `res.psgr-id`. Since the bound columns include keys for both top-level tables, the view will not contain duplicates, and incremental maintenance rules can be generated for both tables.

---

[9]This feature is not included in the current rule system but can easily be simulated using rule conditions; see [Wid91]. We intend to add this feature in the near future.

The rules triggered by operations on table **res** are given here; the rules for table **psgr** are similar:

```
create rule ins-res-special-meals
when inserted into res
then insert into special-meals
        (select res.seat, psgr.meal
          from inserted res, psgr
          where res.flight-id = FID
          and res.psgr-id = psgr.psgr-id
          and psgr.meal != null
          and <seat,meal> not in
                inserted special-meals)

create rule del-res-special-meals
when deleted from res
then delete from special-meals
      where <seat,meal> in
        (select res.seat, psgr.meal
          from deleted res, old psgr
          where res.flight-id = FID
          and res.psgr-id = psgr.psgr-id
          and psgr.meal != null)

create rule old-upd-res-special-meals
when updated res
then delete from special-meals
where <seat,meal> in
        (select res.seat, psgr.meal
          from old updated res, old psgr
          where res.flight-id = FID
          and res.psgr-id = psgr.psgr-id
          and psgr.meal != null)

create rule new-upd-res-special-meals
when updated res
then insert into special-meals
        (select res.seat, psgr.meal
          from new updated res, psgr
          where res.flight-id = FID
          and res.psgr-id = psgr.psgr-id
          and psgr.meal != null
          and <seat,meal> not in
                inserted special-meals)
```

As a second example, consider the following view, which provides the frequent flier numbers of all passengers currently holding reservations:

```
define view ff-res(ffn):
  select psgr.ffn
  from psgr, res
  where psgr.psgr-id = res.psgr-id
```

The bound columns are all columns of table `psgr` (since `ffn` is a key) and column `res.psgr-id`. Since the bound columns do not include a key for table `res`, the view may contain duplicates, and **distinct** must be added. Table reference `psgr` is safe, so the rules for operations on `psgr` are similar to those in the previous example. Table reference `res` is unsafe, however, so the following rules are generated:

```
create rule ins-res-ff-res
when inserted into res
then insert into ff-res
        (select distinct psgr.ffn
          from psgr, inserted res
          where psgr.psgr-id = res.psgr-id
          and ffn not in ff-res)

create rule rematerialize-ff-res
when deleted from res,
     updated res
then delete from ff-res;
     insert into ff-res
        (select distinct psgr.ffn from psgr, res
          where psgr.psgr-id = res.psgr-id);
     deactivate-rules(ff-res)
```

6 Positively Nested Subqueries

A *positively nested* subquery is a nested **select** expression preceded by **exists**, **in**, or *Comp* **any**, where *Comp* is any comparison operator except `!=`. We first describe safety analysis and rule generation for table references in **exists** subqueries. Similar methods apply for the other positively nested subqueries and are explained in Section 6.3. Consider a view V as follows, where $N_1, .., N_l$ are the table references under consideration:

> **define view** $V(Col\text{-}List)$:
>   **select** $C_1, .., C_n$ **from** $T_1, .., T_m$
>   **where** P' **and exists**
>   (**select** $Cols$ **from** $N_1, .., N_l$ **where** P)

6.1 Bound Columns and Safety Analysis

To analyze nested table references we introduce the concept of columns that are *bound by correlation* to the bound columns of the top-level tables. We assume that set $B(V)$ of top-level bound columns already has been computed. Correlated bound columns are denoted $C(V)$, and for **exists** they are computed as follows:

Definition 6.1 (Correlated Bound Columns for Exists)

1. Initialize $C(V)$ to contain all columns of $N_1, .., N_l$ such that predicate P includes an equality comparison between the column and a column in $B(V)$.

2. Add to $C(V)$ all columns of $N_1, .., N_l$ such that predicate P includes an equality comparison between the column and a constant.

3. Repeat until $C(V)$ is unchanged:

    (a) Add to $C(V)$ all columns of $N_1, .., N_l$ such that predicate P includes an equality comparison between the column and a column in $C(V)$.

    (b) Add to $C(V)$ all columns of any table N_i, $1 \leq i \leq l$, if $C(V)$ includes a key for N_i. $\square$

Correlated bound columns for **exists** guarantee the following property:

Lemma 6.2 (Bound Columns Lemma for Exists) Consider four tuples, t_1 and t_2 in the cross-product of $T_1, .., T_m$ and n_1 and n_2 in the cross-product of $N_1, .., N_l$, such that t_1 and t_2 satisfy predicate P', n_1 satisfies nested predicate P using t_1 for the top-level cross-product, and n_2 satisfies P using t_2 for the top-level cross-product. Let $D_1, .., D_k$ be columns of $N_1, .., N_l$ in $C(V)$ such that n_1 and n_2 are guaranteed to differ in $D_1, .., D_k$, i.e. $Proj(n_1, D_1, .., D_k) \neq Proj(n_2, D_1, .., D_k)$. Then t_1 and t_2 are guaranteed to differ in $C_1, .., C_n$, i.e. $Proj(t_1, C_1, .., C_n) \neq Proj(t_2, C_1, .., C_n)$.

Proof: Suppose, for the sake of a contradiction, that $Proj(t_1, C_1, .., C_n) = Proj(t_2, C_1, .., C_n)$. By supposition there is some D_i in $D_1, .., D_k$ such that $Proj(n_1, D_i) \neq Proj(n_2, D_i)$. D_i is in $C(V)$, so by the recursive definitions of $C(V)$ and $B(V)$, since t_1 and t_2 satisfy P', and since n_1 with t_1 and n_2 with t_2 both satisfy predicate P, the value of column D_i in both n_1 and n_2 must either

1. satisfy an equality with a constant k, or

2. satisfy an equality with a column C_j in $C_1, .., C_n$, or

3. be functionally dependent on a constant k or column C_j.

As in Bound Columns Lemma 5.2, in all cases $Proj(n_1, D_i) = Proj(n_2, D_i)$. $\square$

Safety analysis and rule generation for positively nested subqueries is similar to top-level tables:

Definition 6.3 (Safety of Table References for Exists) Table reference N_i in an **exists** subquery is *safe* in V if $C(V)$ includes a key for N_i. $\square$

The following three theorems show that if N_i is safe, then insert, delete, and update operations on N_i can be reflected by incremental changes to V. We include a proof for the insertion theorem only; the other proofs follow by analogy.

Theorem 6.4 (Insertion Theorem for Exists) Let N_i be a safe table reference in an **exists** subquery in V and suppose a tuple n_i is inserted into N_i. Let v be a tuple in the cross-product of the top-level tables such that v satisfies P' and there is a tuple n in the cross-product of the nested tables using n_i such that n satisfies P using v, so $Proj(v, C_1, .., C_n)$ is in view V after the insertion. Then $Proj(v, C_1, .., C_n)$ was not in V before the insertion.

Proof: Suppose, for the sake of a contradiction, that $Proj(v, C_1, .., C_n)$ was in V before the insertion. Then there must have been a tuple n' in the cross-product of the nested tables before the insertion and a tuple v' in the top-level cross-product such that $Proj(v', C_1, .., C_n) = Proj(v, C_1, .., C_n)$, v' satisfies P', and n' satisfies P using v'. Let $D_1, .., D_k$ be correlated bound columns of $N_1, .., N_l$ such that $D_1, .., D_k$ includes a key for N_i. Since n and n' use different tuples from N_i, $Proj(n, D_1, .., D_k) \neq Proj(n', D_1, .., C_k)$. Then, by Lemma 6.2, $Proj(v', C_1, .., C_n) \neq Proj(v, C_1, .., C_n)$. $\square$

Theorem 6.5 (Deletion Theorem for Exists) Let N_i be a safe table reference in an **exists** subquery in V and suppose a tuple n_i is deleted from N_i. Let v be a tuple in the cross-product of the top-level tables such that v satisfies P' and there is a tuple n in the cross-product of the nested tables using n_i such that n satisfies P using v, so $Proj(v, C_1, .., C_n)$ was in view V before the deletion. Then $Proj(v, C_1, .., C_n)$ is not in V after the deletion. $\square$

Theorem 6.6 (Update Theorem for Exists) Let N_i be a safe table reference in an **exists** subquery in V and suppose a tuple n_i is updated in N_i. Let v_O be a tuple in the cross-product of the top-level tables such that v_O satisfies P' and there is a tuple n_O in the cross-product of the nested tables using the old value of n_i such that n_O satisfies P using v_O, so $Proj(v_O, C_1, .., C_n)$ was in view V before the update. Let v_N be a tuple in the cross-product of the top-level tables such that v_N satisfies P' and there is a tuple n_N in the cross-product of the nested tables using the new value of n_i such that n_N satisfies P using v_N, so $Proj(v_N, C_1, .., C_n)$ is in V after the update. If $Proj(v_O, C_1, .., C_n) \neq Proj(v_N, C_1, .., C_n)$, then $Proj(v_O, C_1, .., C_n)$ is not in V after the update and $Proj(v_N, C_1, .., C_n)$ was not in V before the update. $\square$

6.2   Rule Generation

Consider safe table references. The properties guaranteed by Theorems 6.4–6.6 allow incremental maintenance to be performed just as for safe top-level table references: N_i is replaced by **inserted Ni** in the **inserted** rule, by **deleted Ni** in the **deleted** rule, and by **old updated Ni** and **new updated Ni** in the two **updated** rules. In the rules that perform insertions, we must check that tuples have not already been inserted by another rule; in the rules that perform deletions we must use the **old** value of other tables. If a table appears more than once in $N_1, .., N_l$, or if a table in $N_1, .., N_l$ also appears elsewhere in the view definition, then rules are merged as previously described. Unsafe table references also are handled similarly to top-level tables: If nested table reference N_i is unsafe, triggering operations **deleted from Ni** and **updated Ni** are included in the distinguished rematerialization rule for V. The **inserted** rule is similar to the safe rule, except "`not in V`" is added to the predicate rather than "`not in inserted V`".

6.3   Other Positively Nested Subqueries

Safety analysis and rule generation for subqueries preceded by **<any**, **<=any**, **>any**, and **>=any** is identical to **exists**. The method for **=any** and **in** (which are equivalent) also is identical to **exists**, except the set of correlated bound columns may be larger. Consider a view V of the form:

> **define view** $V(Col\text{-}List)$:
>   **select** $C_1, .., C_n$ **from** $T_1, .., T_m$
>   **where** P' **and** $\langle D_1, .., D_j \rangle$ **in**
>   (**select** $E_1, .., E_j$ **from** $N_1, .., N_l$ **where** P)

Definition 6.1 of correlated bound columns is modified to include the case:

- Add to $C(V)$ every column E_i such that corresponding column D_i is in $B(V)$, $1 \leq i \leq j$.

The reader may note that view V above is equivalent to view V':

> **define view** $V'(Col\text{-}List)$:
>   **select** $C_1, .., C_n$ **from** $T_1, .., T_m$
>   **where** P' **and exists**
>   (**select** $*$ **from** $N_1, .., N_l$ **where** P
>   **and** $D_1 = E_1$ **and** ... **and** $D_j = E_j$)

As expected, the correlated bound columns of view V' using Definition 6.1 for **exists** are equivalent to the correlated bound columns of V using the extended definition for **in**.[10]

6.4 Example

Using the airline reservations database introduced in Section 5.5, the following view provides the ID's of all passengers with more than 50,000 frequent flier miles:

```
define view many-miles(id):
  select psgr-id from psgr
  where psgr.ffn in
    (select ffn from ff where miles > 50,000)
```

All columns of top-level table `psgr` are bound since `psgr-id` is a key. Using our extended definition for **in**, `ff.ffn` is a correlated bound column. Since `ffn` is a key, nested table reference `ff` is safe. The **inserted** and **deleted** rules for table `ff` follow; the **updated** rules are similar.

```
create rule ins-ff-many-miles
when inserted into ff
then insert into many-miles
        (select psgr-id from psgr
          where psgr.ffn in
            (select ffn from inserted ff
              where miles > 50,000)
          and psgr-id not in inserted many-miles)

create rule del-ff-many-miles
when deleted from ff
then delete from many-miles
      where psgr-id in
              (select psgr-id from old psgr
                where psgr.ffn in
                  (select ffn from deleted ff
                    where miles > 50,000))
```

7 Negatively Nested Subqueries

A *negatively nested* subquery is a nested **select** expression preceded by **not exists**, **not in**, or **!=any**. We describe safety analysis and rule generation for table references in **not exists** subqueries. Similar methods apply for the other negatively nested subqueries; see [CW91]. Consider a view V of the form:

> **define view** $V(Col\text{-}List)$:
>   **select** $C_1, .., C_n$ **from** $T_1, .., T_m$
>   **where** P' **and not exists**
>   (**select** $Cols$ **from** $N_1, .., N_l$ **where** P)

With negatively nested subqueries, insert operations on nested tables result in delete operations on the view, while delete operations on nested tables result in insert operations on the view.

---

[10]The reader may also note that **select** expressions with positive subqueries often can be transformed into equivalent **select** expressions without subqueries, as in [CG85,Kim82]. By considering the actual transformations, we see that the maintenance rules produced for any transformed view are equivalent to the maintenance rules produced for the original view.

7.1 Safety Analysis

For a negatively nested table reference N_i, we define two notions of safety: *I-safety* indicates that insert operations on N_i can be reflected by incremental changes to V, and *DU-safety* indicates that delete and update operations on N_i can be reflected by incremental changes to V. The definition of I-safety is somewhat different from previous safety definitions—correlated bound columns are not used, and all nested table references are considered together. Assume that set $B(V)$ of top-level bound columns already has been computed.

Definition 7.1 (I-Safety of Table References for Not Exists) Table references $N_1, .., N_l$ in a **not exists** subquery are *I-safe* in V if predicate P refers only to columns of N_i, $1 \leq i \leq l$, columns in $B(V)$, and constants. □

Using this notion of safety, we prove the following theorem for insertions:

Theorem 7.2 (Insertion Theorem for Not Exists) Let N_i be an I-safe table reference in a **not exists** subquery in V and suppose a tuple n_i is inserted into N_i. Let v be a tuple in the cross-product of the top-level tables such that v satisfies top-level predicate P' and there is a tuple n in the cross-product of the nested tables using n_i such that n satisfies nested predicate P using v. Then $Proj(v, C_1, .., C_n)$ is not in V after the insertion.

Proof: Suppose, for the sake of a contradiction, that $Proj(v, C_1, .., C_n)$ is in V after the insertion. Then there must be a tuple v' other than v in the cross-product of the top-level tables such that $Proj(v', C_1, .., C_n) = Proj(v, C_1, .., C_n)$, v' satisfies P', and there is no tuple n' in the cross-product of the nested tables such that n' satisfies P using v'. We show that there is such an n', namely n. By Definition 5.1 of $B(V)$, since v and v' both satisfy P' and $Proj(v', C_1, .., C_n) = Proj(v, C_1, .., C_n)$, v and v' are equivalent in all columns of $B(V)$. Since N_i is I-safe and since n satisfies P using v, by Definition 7.1 of safety, n also satisfies P using v'. □

For deletes and updates, we combine our new notion of I-safety with the previous notion of safety using keys. Correlated bound columns for negatively nested table references are defined as for positive references (Definition 6.1), and Bound Columns Lemma 6.2 still holds.

Definition 7.3 (DU-Safety of Table References for Not Exists) Table reference N_i in a **not exists** subquery is *DU-safe* in V if it is I-safe and $C(V)$ includes a key for N_i. □

Theorem 7.4 (Deletion Theorem for Not Exists) Let N_i be a DU-safe table reference in a **not exists** subquery in V and suppose a tuple n_i is deleted from N_i. Let v be a tuple in the cross-product of the top-level tables such that v satisfies P' and there is a tuple n in the cross-product of the nested tables using n_i such that n satisfies P using v. Then: (1) $Proj(v, C_1, .., C_n)$ was not in V before the deletion. (2) $Proj(v, C_1, .., C_n)$ is in V after the deletion.

Proof: The proof of (1) is analogous to the proof of Insertion Theorem 7.2. For (2), suppose, for the sake of a contradiction, that $Proj(v, C_1, .., C_n)$ is not in V after the deletion. Then there must be a tuple n' in the cross-product of the nested tables such that n' satisfies P using v. Let $D_1, .., D_k$ be correlated bound columns of $N_1, .., N_l$ such that $D_1, .., D_k$ includes a key for N_i. Since n and n' use different tuples from N_i, $Proj(n, D_1, .., D_k) \neq Proj(n', D_1, .., C_k)$. Then, by Lemma 6.2, $Proj(v, C_1, .., C_n) \neq Proj(v, C_1, .., C_n)$, which is impossible. □

Theorem 7.5 (Update Theorem for Not Exists) Let N_i be a DU-safe table reference in a **not exists** subquery in V and suppose a tuple n_i is updated in N_i. Let v_O be a tuple in the cross-product of the top-level tables such that v_O satisfies P' and there is a tuple n_O in the cross-product of the nested tables using the old value of n_i such that n_O satisfies P using v. Let v_N be a tuple in the cross-product of the top-level tables such that v_N satisfies P' and there is a tuple n_N in the cross-product of the nested tables using the new value of n_i such that n_N satisfies P using v. If $Proj(v_O, C_1, .., C_n) \neq Proj(v_N, C_1, .., C_n)$ then: (1) $Proj(v_N, C_1, .., C_n)$ is not in V after the update. (2) $Proj(v_O, C_1, .., C_n)$ was not in V before the update. (3) $Proj(v_O, C_1, .., C_n)$ is in V after the update.

Proof: Analogous to Theorems 7.2 and 7.4. □

7.2   Rule Generation

If nested table reference N_i is I-safe, then, using Theorem 7.2, the following incremental rule is generated:

```
create rule ins-Ni-V
when inserted into Ni
then delete from V
      where <C1,..,Cn> in
        (select C1,..,Cn from T1,..,Tm
        where P' and exists
          (select Cols
           from N1,..,inserted Ni,..,Nl
           where P))
```

Notice that the subquery's "**not exists**" is converted to "**exists**"; this conversion occurs in the **deleted** and **updated** rules as well. If N_i is not I-safe, then the view expression would need to be reevaluated to determine which tuples should be deleted. Hence in the unsafe case, **inserted into Ni** is included in the rematerialization rule for V.

If N_i is DU-safe, then, using Theorems 7.4 and 7.5, the following incremental rule for **deleted** is generated. The rules for **updated** correspond to the **inserted** and **deleted** rules as previously.

```
create rule del-Ni-V
when deleted from Ni
then insert into V
        (select C1,..,Cn from T1,..,Tm
        where P' and exists
          (select Cols
           from old N1,..,deleted Ni,..,old Nl
           where P)
        and <C1,..Cn> not in inserted V)
```

If table reference N_i is not DU-safe, **updated Ti** is included in the rematerialization rule for V. For **deleted**, however, incremental maintenance still can be performed—as previously, for the unsafe case the rule above is modified to use "**not in V**" rather than "**not in inserted V**".

7.3   Example

Using the airline reservations database introduced in Section 5.5, the following view provides the ID's of all reservations whose `flight-id` is not in table `flight`:

```
define view bad-flight(res-id):
  select res-id from res
  where not exists
    (select * from flight
     where flight.flight-id = res.flight-id)
```

By Definitions 7.1 and 7.3, nested table reference `flight` is both I-safe and DU-safe. The **inserted** and **deleted** rules for table `flight` follow; the **updated** rules are similar.

```
create rule ins-flight-bad-flight
when inserted into flight
then delete from bad-flight
      where res-id in
        (select res-id from res
         where exists
           (select * from inserted flight
            where flight.flight-id =
                  res.flight-id))

create rule del-flight-bad-flight
when deleted from flight
then insert into bad-flight
        (select res-id from res
         where exists
           (select * from deleted flight
            where flight.flight-id =
                  res.flight-id)
         and res-id not in inserted bad-flight)
```

8   Set Operators

Finally, consider views with *set operators*. A view definition may include either **union distinct** or **intersect**. For these views, view analysis and rule generation initially is performed independently on each component **select** expression. The rules are then modified to incorporate the set operators.

8.1   Union Views

Consider a view V of the form:

> **define view** $V(Col\text{-}List)$:
>   **select** $Cols_1$ **from** $Tables_1$ **where** P_1
>   **union distinct** ...
>   **union distinct** **select** $Cols_k$ **from** $Tables_k$ **where** P_k

First, duplicate analysis is performed on each **select** expression as in Section 5.2; if any **select** expression may contain duplicates, the user is required to add **distinct** to that **select** expression. For each **select** expression, an initial set of view-maintaining rules is generated using the methods of the preceding sections. The rules' actions are then modified to incorporate **union**. In actions that perform **insert** operations, if "**not in inserted V**" has been added to predicate P_i due to a safe table reference, it is changed to "**not in V**"; this ensures that duplicates are not added by different **select** expressions. If the rule already includes "not in V" due to an unsafe table reference, it remains unchanged. Modifications for **delete** operations are more complicated. If a tuple no longer is produced by one of the **select** expressions, it should be deleted from V only if it is not produced by any of the other **select** expressions. Without loss of generality, consider a **delete** operation in the action of a rule generated from the first **select** expression in V. The following conjunct must be added to the **delete** operation's **where** clause:

```
and <Cols> not in
      (select Cols2 from Tables2 where P2)
and ...
and <Cols> not in
      (select Colsk from Tablesk where Pk)
```

Clearly, such conjuncts may cause considerable recomputation, depending on the complexity of the **select** expressions. For rules in which the recomputation cost appears large, the user may choose to move the triggering operation to the rematerialization rule for V.

As usual, rules with common triggering and action operations are merged, and rules whose triggering operations also appear in the rematerialization rule are eliminated.

8.2   Intersect Views

A view V with **intersect** operators is handled similarly to views with **union** operators. In rule modification, however, all rules performing **delete** operations remain unchanged. (If a tuple is deleted from any **select** expression, then it always should be deleted from V.) Modifications for **insert** operations are similar to the modifications for **delete** operations in **union** views: If a tuple is newly produced by one of the **select** expressions, it should be inserted into V only if it also is produced by all the other **select** expressions. Consider an **insert** operation in the action of a rule generated from the first **select** expression in V. The following conjunct must be added to the **where** clause of the **insert** operation's **select** expression:

```
and <Cols> in
      (select Cols2 from Tables2 where P2)
and ...
and <Cols> in
      (select Colsk from Tablesk where Pk)
```

Again, if the **select** expressions are sufficiently complex, the user may decide that rematerialization is more appropriate.

9   System Execution

So far, we have described only the compile-time aspects of our facility. View definition, view analysis, and rule generation all occur prior to database system execution. We still must ensure that, at run-time, derived rules will behave as desired, i.e., views will be maintained correctly. Suppose our facility has been used to derive sets of maintenance rules for several views. The system orders the set of rules for each view so that all **delete** operations in rule actions precede all **insert** operations. No ordering is necessary between rules for different views—the action part of each rule modifies only the view itself, so rules for different views have no effect on each other.

Consider the set of rules for a given view V, and suppose an arbitrary set of changes has been made to V's base tables. If the rematerialization rule for V is triggered, the view certainly is maintained correctly: V is recomputed from its base tables; all other rules for V are deactivated, so V cannot be modified until the base tables change again. Suppose the rematerialization rule is not triggered. During rule processing, first some rules delete tuples from V, then other rules insert tuples into V. Consider the deletions. For each type of table reference, our theorems guarantee that the generated **delete** operations never delete tuples that should remain in V. Furthermore, these operations always delete all tuples that should no longer be in V. Consider the insertions. First, notice that all generated **insert** operations use nested **select** expressions based on the view definition itself. Since we know the view definition cannot produce duplicates, the set of tuples in **insert** operations never includes duplicates. Furthermore, our theorems (along with the "not in inserted V" clauses) guarantee that tuples already in V are never inserted. Finally, in each case the **insert** operations produce all tuples that should be added to V.

We must consider that other production rules in addition to view-maintaining rules may be defined in the system. Although these rules cannot modify views, they can modify base tables. Our view-maintaining rules behave correctly even in the presence of other rules, and no additional rule ordering is necessary. Recall the semantics of rule execution (Section 3): a rule is considered with respect to the transition since the last time its action was executed; if its action has not yet been executed, it is considered with respect to the transition since the last rule assertion point (or start of the transaction). Hence, the first time a view-maintaining rule R is triggered during rule processing, it processes all base table changes since the last assertion point. Suppose that, subsequently during rule processing, the base tables are changed by a non-view-maintaining rule. Then R will be triggered again and will modify the view according to the new set of changes. When rule processing terminates, no rules are triggered, so all view-maintaining rules will have processed all relevant changes to base tables.

10   Conclusions and Future Work

We have described a facility that automatically derives a set of production rules to maintain a materialization of a user-defined view. This approach both frees the view definer from handling view maintenance and guarantees that the view remains correct. Through analysis techniques based on key information, incremental maintenance rules are generated whenever possible. Our facility allows the user to interact with the system: view definitions and key information can be modified to guarantee that the system produces efficient maintenance rules for frequent base table operations. In practice, efficient rules are possible for a wide class of views—efficiency relies on safe table references, and it can be seen from our criteria for safety that table references routinely fall into this class. In those cases where efficiency is not possible for the user's desired view, our system provides recognition of this fact; the user either may use the rules produced for automatic rematerialization or may decide that query modification is more appropriate.

We plan to implement our facility using the Starburst Rule System, then conduct experiments to evaluate the run-time efficiency of our approach on a variety of views. Meanwhile, we want to extend view analysis and rule generation so that the full power of SQL **select** statements can be used in view definitions. (We have started this and expect it to be tedious but not difficult.) Currently, the biggest drawback of our approach is that views with duplicates are not handled; we will consider ways to remove this restriction. We would like to add automatic rule optimization as a post-rule-generation component in our system. The rules produced by our method have a standard form, and in some cases can be optimized as in [CW90].

In addition, rules for different views could be merged and common subexpressions could be exploited as in [Han87]. Finally, the properties guaranteed by our algorithms are useful in other areas (such as query optimization), and we intend to explore this connection.

Acknowledgments

Thanks to Guy Lohman and Laura Haas for helpful comments on an initial draft.

THE HERACLITUS DBPL WITH APPLICATION TO ACTIVE DATABASES AND DATA INTEGRATION[1]

Gang Zhou, Richard Hull,
Shahram Ghandeharizadeh

ABSTRACT

The database programming language Heraclitus[Alg,C] is an extension of the C programming language that supports the relational algebra and novel constructs related to the specification of these semantics. In particular, the language supports *deltas* as "first-class citizens" – these are values corresponding to database updates, which may or may not be applied. Unlike previous work on differential files and hypothetical relations, Heraclitus supports operators for combining deltas, and also alternative implementations that incorporate the impact of deltas into conventional database operators (e.g., join).

This chapter describes the design and preliminary implementation of Heraclitus[Alg,C]. Two strategies for providing access to deltas have been implemented, one hash-based and the other sort-based. Initial evaluation of system performance demonstrates the feasibility of the language.

A key issue in active database systems, i.e., database systems that incorporate automatic firing of rules, concerns understanding alternative semantics of rule application. This chapter shows how deltas can be used in representing the effect of rule firings, and for representing virtual database states, as they arise in the specification of these semantics. The chapter also describes how Heraclitus can be used to provide efficient support of materialized integrated views. More generally, the Heraclitus framework appears useful in connection with hypothetical database access, version control, specifying concurrency protocols, and the resolution of update conflicts.

1 Introduction

"Active" databases generally support the automatic triggering of updates as a response to user-requested or system-generated updates. Many active database systems, e.g., [CCCR[+]90,Coh86,MD89,Han89,dMS88, SJGP90,WF90,ZH90], use a paradigm of *rules* to generate these automatic updates, in a manner reminiscent of expert systems. Active databases have been shown useful for constraint maintenance [Mor83,CW90, HJ90], incremental update of materialized views [CW91], query rewriting [SJGP90], database security [SJGP90]; and hold the promise of providing a new family of solutions to the view and derived data update problem [CHM92] and issues in heterogeneous databases [CW92b]. Active database technology will also play an important role in the development of "mediators" [Wie92] for supporting database interoperation.

---

[1]This work was supported in part by the NSF under grants IRI-9318326, IRI-9222926 and NYI award IRI-9258362, and by ARPA under grants NAG2-862 (adminstered through NASA) and 33825-RT-AAS (administered by the Army Research Office).

As discussed in Section 2 (see also [HJ90,HW92,Sto92]), each of the active database systems described in the literature uses a different semantics or "execution model" for rule application. The variety of alternatives found in active database systems highlights the fact that the "knowledge" represented in them stems from two distinct components: the rule base and the execution model [Abi88]. It appears that different execution models will sometimes be appropriate even within a single database, and that a fixed collection of choices is unlikely to suffice. There is a need for high-level constructs that permit database designers and programmers to specify and implement system modules using customized execution models.

The Heraclitus project [HJ91,JH91,GHJ92] is focused on the development of database programming language constructs and techniques that can be used to specify and implement alternative, interchangeable execution models for active database systems. Our current focus is to provide language constructs that support (a) the use of multiple virtual states in rule conditions and (b) a wide variety of semantics for applying rules and combining their effects. This chapter focuses on developing the Heraclitus paradigm in connection with the pure relational model (no duplicates or tuple-ids). Research has also been performed on extending the Heraclitus paradigm to object-oriented databases [BDD+95,DHDD95,DHR96].

The basic novelty in the Heraclitus framework is to elevate *deltas*, i.e., values corresponding to database updates, which may or may not be applied, to be "first-class citizens" in database programming languages. Operators are provided for explicitly constructing, accessing and combining deltas. Of particular importance is the when operator that permits hypothetical expression evaluation: expression E when δ evaluates to the value that E *would* have if the value of δ *were* applied to the current state. This allows deltas to be used to represent virtual states, and also supports hypothetical database access.

We have implemented Heraclitus[Alg,C], a database programming language (DBPL) that extends C to incorporate the relational algebra and deltas and their operators. The implementation has two primary components, a pre-processor and HERALD (HEraclitus Relational ALgebra with Deltas), a library of functions supporting relational and delta operators. Of particular interest is the support of "hypothetical" relational operators, which correspond to the traditional relational operators (e.g., select, join) evaluated under a when. HERALD was initially implemented [GHJ92] on the Wisconsin Storage System (WiSS) [CDKK85], and has now been ported to the Exodus system [CDRS86]. HERALD currently supports two strategies for incorporating the effect of deltas on the relational operators, one hash-based and the other sort-based.

This chapter describes the design and preliminary implementation of Heraclitus[Alg,C], and some applications in connection with active databases and data integration. Section 2 discusses the conceptual underpinnings of deltas and their use in specifying active database execution models and other database applications. Section 3 introduces Heraclitus[Alg,C], presenting both algebraic operators and language constructs. Section 4 describes the current implementation of the language, along with analysis of the expected running times for the various algebraic operators. Section 5 shows that Heraclitus[Alg,C] can be used to conveniently implement rules and their execution model for the maintenance of materialized derived data. Brief conclusions are offered in Section 6.

2   Deltas, Virtual States, and Active Database Execution Models

This section lays a conceptual framework for understanding much of the current research in active databases. In particular, we show how access to both deltas and virtual states are useful in the context of active databases, and illustrate how the Heraclitus paradigm can be used to provide this access. Some of this material also appears in [HJ91], and is included here to make the current chapter more self-contained.

Supplier	Part
Trek	frame
Campy	brakes
Campy	pedals

Suppliers

Part	Quantity	Supplier	Expected
frame	400	Trek	8/31/93
brakes	150	Campy	9/1/93

Orders

Figure 1 Relations for Inventory Control Example

At the end of the section we briefly sketch other database applications where this paradigm may be useful, and compare our deltas with related work on hypothetical relations and differential files.

2.1 Active databases

A wide range of active database systems have been proposed in the literature. The most crucial differences between their execution models stem from choices concerning (a) how and when rules should be fired, (b) the expressive capabilities of the rules, and (c) how the effects of rule firings should be combined. With regards to (a), three approaches have been proposed: (i) *transaction boundary* rule firing, which occurs only at the end of the user transaction (e.g., Starburst, RDL1, LOGRES, AP5); (ii) *interleaved* rule firing, where rule application is interleaved with the atomic commands of a user transaction (e.g., POSTGRES [SJGP90], among others [Han89,KDM88,MP90,MD89]); and (iii) *concurrent* rule firing (e.g., [MD89,BM91]), in which rules may spawn concurrent processes in a recursive fashion. The Heraclitus paradigm can be used to specify many of these design choices; in this subsection we focus on transaction boundary rule firing, and briefly discuss interleaved rule firing.

Under transaction boundary rule firing, rule application constructs a sequence of "virtual states"

$$S_{orig}, \quad S_{prop}, \quad S_2, \quad S_3, \quad \ldots, \quad S_{curr}$$

of the database, where S_{orig} is the "original" state and S_{prop} is the result of applying to S_{orig} the set of user-proposed updates collected during the transaction. The subsequent virtual states result from a sequence of rule firings according to the execution model. S_{curr} denotes the "current" virtual state that is being considered by the execution model. Execution terminates either when the execution model reaches a fixpoint, in which case the final virtual state replaces S_{orig}, or aborts the transaction. Prominent systems following this paradigm include the Starburst Rule System [WF90, CW90], RDL1 [dMS88], LOGRES [CCCR+90] and AP5 [Coh86,ZH90], and also expert systems such as OPS5 [BFKM85]. (Other paradigms shall be considered below.)

As a simple example, consider a relational database for inventory control in manufacturing. Figure 1 shows two relations used by a hypothetical bicycle manufacturer. The Suppliers relation holds suppliers and the parts they supply, and the Orders relation shows currently unfilled orders for parts. Other relations, not shown here, might hold information about the parts usage of different bicycle models, and the expected demand for these parts based on the production schedule of the company.

Consider now the referential integrity constraint stating that if there is an order for part p from supplier s, then the pair (s, p) should be in relation Suppliers. A possible rule for enforcing this might be written as

R1 : if Orders(*part, qty, supp, exp*) and not Suppliers(*supp, part*)
       then −Orders(*part, qty, supp, exp*)

In the pidgen syntax used for this rule we follow the style of many active database systems. In particular, (a) the "if" part, or *condition*, is a boolean expression – the rule can "fire" only if this expression evaluates to true; (b) the "then" part, or *action* is an imperative command that executes when the rule fires; and (c) it is implicit which virtual state(s) are being considered by the conditions and actions. In typical active database systems, if at some point in the application of rules the state S_{curr} satisfies the condition of R1 for some assignment of variables, then the action may be fired, depending on the presence of other rules whose condition is true. We say that rule R1 uses a "one-state" logic, because the rule condition examines a single state, namely the "current" one. RDL1, LOGRES, and most expert systems (e.g., OPS5 [BFKM85]) support only a one-state logic.

In the context of databases, a problem with rule R1 is that the appropriate response to a constraint violation may depend on how the violation arose. Rule R2 below deletes all violating orders if a pair is deleted from the **Suppliers** relation, but if the violation is the result of an update to **Orders**, then R3 undoes that individual update and transmits a warning.

R2 : if $-$**Suppliers**($supp, part$)
      then $-$**Orders**($part, *, supp, *$)

R3 : if $+$**Orders**($part, qty, supp, exp$) and not **Suppliers**($supp, part$)
      then $-$**Orders**($part, qty, supp, exp$) and **send_warning**

The signed atoms in the conditions of these rules refer to proposed updates, rather than any database state. The action of R2 uses "wildcards" (denoted '*'); these match any value.

In essence, the conditions of rules R2 and R3 make explicit reference to the delta between two virtual states. Of course, some design choice needs to be made about which pair of virtual states should be considered. The AP5 system focuses on the delta between S_{orig} and S_{curr}:

$$S_{orig}, \quad S_{prop}, \quad S_2, \quad S_3, \quad \ldots, \quad S_{curr}$$
$$\underbrace{\phantom{S_{orig}, \quad S_{prop}, \quad S_2, \quad S_3, \quad \ldots, \quad S_{curr}}}_{\Delta}$$

Assuming this semantics for a moment, note that a one-state execution model cannot simulate the effect of rules R2 and R3 without using "scratch paper relations" that essentially duplicate the contents of S_{orig}. Another natural semantics for rule conditions supporting explicit access to a delta would be to use the delta between S_{prop} and S_{curr}. The Starburst Rule System is even more intricate: it uses the delta between virtual states S_i and S_{curr}, where i is determined by the rule under consideration and the history of previous firings of that rule.

Consider finally the rule

R4 : if the firing of rules results in a 20% drop in orders
      then **inventory_warning**()

Here we need to consider the change in orders between S_{prop} and S_{curr}:

$$S_{orig}, \quad \boxed{S_{prop}}, \quad S_2, \quad S_3, \quad \ldots, \quad \boxed{S_{curr}}$$

While this could be expressed using explicit access to a delta, it is much easier to express it in terms of the virtual states, i.e., to write:

$$R4' : \quad \text{if} \quad \frac{\text{count(Orders)} \;\; \text{``in } S_{curr}\text{''}}{\text{count(Orders)} \;\; \text{``in } S_{prop}\text{''}} < .8$$

then `inventory_warning()`

In current DBPL's there is no mechanism to write expressions such as the condition of R4′, because they do not provide explicit access to virtual states. The Heraclitus paradigm provides this by using deltas and the special **when** operator. As mentioned in the introduction, the expression E **when** δ evaluates an arbitrary side-effect free expression E in the state that *would* arise if the value of δ *were* applied to the existing database state. Evaluation of such an expression does not change the existing database state. One way to express rule R4′ in the Heraclitus paradigm is to construct deltas corresponding to the virtual states S_{prop} and S_{curr} as follows:

$$S_{orig}, \;\; \boxed{S_{prop}}, \;\; S_2, \;\; S_3, \;\; \dots, \;\; \boxed{S_{curr}}$$

Rule R4′ can be expressed within the Heraclitus paradigm as:

$$R4'' : \quad \text{if} \quad \frac{\text{count(Orders)} \;\; \textbf{when} \;\; \Delta_{curr}}{\text{count(Orders)} \;\; \textbf{when} \;\; \Delta_{prop}} < .8$$

then `inventory_warning()`

We now describe how the Heraclitus paradigm can specify a large family of execution models that use transaction boundary rule firing. During execution, the database state will remain untouched, and deltas will be constructed to represent the virtual states needed for evaluating rule conditions. (An alternative would be to update the database state with each rule firing, and maintain "negative" deltas that simulate previous virtual states in the sequence.) Rules are represented as functions that have as input zero or more deltas (corresponding either to virtual states or deltas between them), and produce as output a delta corresponding to the effect of the rule firing. The rules might also invoke additional procedures such as `inventory_warning()`. Although not done here, triggers (which are logically a part of the condition, but whose value can typically be determined in a very efficient manner) can also be incorporated into the framework. Rules can be arranged to provide either "tuple-at-a-time" or "set-at-a-time" operation [WF90]. Algebraic operators are provided in Heraclitus for manipulating deltas, so that deltas corresponding to new virtual states can be constructed from previous deltas and rule outputs. Using this approach, the execution models of AP5, RDL1, LOGRES and the Starburst Rule System can be specified within Heraclitus[Alg,C] (see also [HJ91]). Variations on this theme can be developed. As a simple example, a rule-base can be "stratified", and the execution model can fire each layer to a fixpoint before moving to the next layer. More complex firing patterns subsuming the rule algebra of [IN88] are easily expressed.

Returning now to the full range of design choices for active database execution models, the Heraclitus paradigm can also specify interleaved rule firing. In this case, the user transaction and the rule actions are broken into a sequence of atomic updates, and rules are invoked immediately upon a condition becoming true. There is the possibility of intricate recursive rule firing, and it is hard to associate an intuitive meaning to the sequence of virtual states constructed. As a result, the rule conditions in these systems typically give explicit access to the "old" and "new" values of certain tuples, but not to multiple virtual states. Heraclitus also permits "hybrid" execution models, which combine aspects of both interleaved and transaction boundary rule firing. At present, the primary focus of the Heraclitus project is on sequential processing; incorporation of concurrent rule firing is a subject of future research.

Heraclitus gives broad latitude with regards to dimensions (b) and (c) mentioned above. For this reason, the Heraclitus paradigm, and Heraclitus[Alg,C] in particular, can serve as a flexible platform for specifying a wide variety of execution models for active databases. We expect this to be useful both in developing customized execution models, and in comparing them, both experimentally and analytically.

2.2   Other applications

We now briefly outline a few other applications of the Heraclitus paradigm. We feel that the Heraclitus paradigm will be useful in implementing and understanding a variety of database issues, including (1) hypothetical database access, (2) version control, (3) concurrency protocols, and (4) update conflict resolution. With regards to (1), it is possible within Heraclitus to specify deltas that have meanings such as "Add 2 weeks to the Expected value for all orders with quantity > 500" or "Cancel all orders with Expected in the month of October". Queries are now easily specified against hypothetical states using arbitrary combinations of these deltas and the when operator (see Subsection 3.3). With regards to (2), alternative versions might be represented using deltas. Because Heraclitus provides explicit access to deltas, it can provide both a flexible platform for developing customized version control frameworks, and for experimentally comparing them. Turning to (3), deltas appear especially useful in connection with long transactions. For example, protocols could be developed in which certain short transactions can be executed during the running of a long transaction, and a delta recording the impact of the short transaction could be stored and applied after the long transaction finishes. This kind of "soft commit" could increase concurrent access to databases. Finally, (4) addresses situations in which multiple conflicting updates are presented to a database system. This could arise, for example, in managing a forest fire, where different observers give conflicting information about current status of the fire. One approach to finding a coherent update is to extend active database techniques, so that rule conditions can explicitly access multiple deltas corresponding to the different proposed updates.

2.3   Related techniques

This section concludes with a brief comparison of the Heraclitus paradigm with related techniques.

Differential files [SL76] are a low-level implementation technique that support efficient representation of multiple versions of a database. Unlike differential files, deltas in the Heraclitus framework are manipulated directly by constructs in the user-level programming language. Furthermore, we support a family of operators for explicitly constructing and combining deltas, in addition to those for explicitly and hypothetically accessing them.

A version of hypothetical relations is introduced in [WS83]. While the work there describes carefully crafted implementation strategies for such relations, it cannot easily be extended to provide the full generality of delta usage supported in the Heraclitus framework.

It has been suggested that a reasonable approach to support the basic functionality of the when operator would be to augment existing concurrency control mechanisms, using the following steps: (a) evaluate E when δ by applying δ it to the database (but don't commit), (b) evaluate E in the context of the new database, and (c) rollback the transaction in order to undo δ. While this rollback technique will be useful in some contexts, it is just one of several feasible implementation strategies that warrant investigation. In the case of complex algebraic expressions involving several not necessarily nested deltas, it may be more efficient to incorporate optimization of when into the conventional optimization of the other algebraic operators, rather than relegating it to the orthogonal rollback mechanism. Also, the use of rollbacks to support hypothetical database access may cause unacceptable delays in the concurrency system, complicate the transaction protocols, and degrade the performance of the system.

3   Heraclitus[Alg,C]

This section describes the language Heraclitus[Alg,C] from a user's perspective. The discussion begins with an abstract perspective on deltas, then presents a specific realization for the relational model of deltas and their algebraic operators, and finally describes how this is embedded into the C language.

3.1   The abstract perspective

The foundation of the Heraclitus paradigm is the notion of *delta values*, sometimes called simply *deltas*; these are functions that map database states to database states. Intuitively, a delta can be thought of as a "delayed update", i.e., a command that can be used to update a given database state, but is not necessarily applied. Three operations are fundamental to deltas: applying them to the current database state to obtain a new one; *composition*, and `when`. The `when` operator provides hypothetical expression evaluation: the value of E `when` δ in state DB is the value of expression E evaluated in the state resulting from the application of the value of delta expression δ on DB.

The notion of delta and these basic operators provide a powerful paradigm for supporting a wide variety of database applications, across a wide spectrum of database models. In the first phase of the Heraclitus project we are focusing on the development of a comprehensive realization of this paradigm and its application for the pure relational model; we plan to extend the paradigm to an object-oriented database model in the near future.

Several factors affect the specific realization of the Heraclitus paradigm. Obviously, we expect that all deltas considered are computable. Furthermore, the family of deltas that can created should be closed under composition. Even in this case, there is a trade-off between the expressive power of the family of deltas incorporated, and the efficiency with which they can be stored, manipulated, and accessed. In Heraclitus[Alg,C] we provide a natural tabular representation for a restricted family of deltas that permits efficient manipulation. Importantly, the family of deltas supported is sufficient to specify a wide variety of active database execution models.

3.2   The algebraic perspective

To understand the family of deltas supported in Heraclitus[Alg,C], we first describe the tabular representation used for them, and the function that each represents.

A *signed atom* is an expression of the form $+<reln\text{-}name><tuple>$ or $-<reln\text{-}name><tuple>$; intuitively these correspond to "insertions" and "deletions", respectively. In the context of Heraclitus[Alg,C], a *delta*, is represented as a finite set of signed atoms (referring to relations in the current database schema) which does not include both positive and negative versions of the same atom. An example is:

$$\Delta_1 = \left\{ \begin{array}{l} +Suppliers(Shimano,\ brakes), \\ +Suppliers(Trek,\ frame), \\ -Orders(brakes,\ 150,\ Campy,\ 9/1/93), \\ +Orders(brakes,\ 150,\ Shimano,\ 9/6/93) \end{array} \right\}$$

We also include a special delta value *fail*, that corresponds to inconsistency.

Supplier	Part
Trek	frame
Campy	brakes
Campy	pedals
Shimano	brakes

Suppliers

Part	Quantity	Supplier	Expected
frame	400	Trek	8/31/93
brakes	150	Shimano	9/6/93

Orders

Figure 2 Result of applying Δ_1

For non-*fail* delta Δ, we set

$$\Delta^+ = \{A \mid +A \in \Delta\}$$
$$\Delta^- = \{A \mid -A \in \Delta\}$$

The consistency requirement on deltas states that $\Delta^+ \cap \Delta^- = \phi$. Δ represents the function which maps a database state [2] DB to $(DB \cup \Delta^+) - \Delta^-$, which, due to the consistency requirement, is equal to $(DB - \Delta^-+) \cup \Delta^+$. Speaking informally, applying Δ has the affect of adding tuples of Δ preceded by a '+', and deletes tuples preceded by a '−'.

The result of applying Δ_1 to the instance of Figure 1 is shown in Figure 2. Because we are working with the pure relational model, the signed tuple $+Suppliers(Trek, frame)$ can be viewed as a "no-op" in this context; it has no impact when `apply` is used on the instance of Figure 1. Deletes are "no-ops" if the associated tuple is not present in the underlying instance. A mechanism to express "modifies" is also incorporated; see Subsection 3.3

We call the composition operator for these deltas *smash*, denoted '!'. The smash of two delta values is basically their union, with conflicts resolved in favor of the second argument. For example, given

$$\Delta_2 = \left\{ \begin{array}{l} +Suppliers(Cat\ Paw,\ light), \\ -Suppliers(Campy,\ pedals), \\ -Orders(brakes,\ 150,\ Shimano,\ 9/6/93), \\ +Orders(brakes,\ 500,\ Shimano,\ 9/20/93) \end{array} \right\}$$

then $\Delta_1!\Delta_2$ equals

$$\left\{ \begin{array}{l} +Suppliers(Shimano,\ brakes), \\ +Suppliers(Trek,\ frame), \\ +Suppliers(Cat\ Paw,\ light), \\ -Suppliers(Campy,\ pedals), \\ -Orders(brakes,\ 150,\ Campy,\ 9/1/93), \\ -Orders(brakes,\ 150,\ Shimano,\ 9/6/93), \\ +Orders(brakes,\ 500,\ Shimano,\ 9/20/93) \end{array} \right\}$$

Formally, for non-*fail* Δ_1 and Δ_2 their smash is defined by

$$(\Delta_1\ !\ \Delta_2)^+ = \Delta_2^+ \cup (\Delta_1^+ - \Delta_2^-)$$
$$(\Delta_1\ !\ \Delta_2)^- = \Delta_2^- \cup (\Delta_1^- - \Delta_2^+)$$

---

[2]In this context, we view the database state to be a set of atoms, e.g., { *Suppliers(Trek, frame)*, *Suppliers(Campy, brakes)*,..., *Orders(frame, 400, Trek, 8/31/93)*, ...}.

It is easily verified that smash realizes function composition for the family of deltas.

Most active database systems use smash when combining the impact of different rule firings. In contrast, AP5 uses a special "merge" operator. The *merge*, denoted '&', of two non-*fail* deltas Δ_1 and Δ_2 is given by:

$$(\Delta_1 \,\&\, \Delta_2) = \begin{cases} \Delta_1 \cup \Delta_2 & \text{if this is consistent} \\ fail & \text{otherwise} \end{cases}$$

Thus, the merge of the two deltas of the previous example is *fail*. The use of merge yields a more declarative flavor than smash; this has been exploited in [ZH90] to obtain sufficient conditions on rule-bases to ensure consistent termination of rule firing sequences.

Several other binary operators for combining deltas can be defined, for example, *weak-merge*, i.e., union but deleting all conflicting pairs of signed atoms (cf. [SdM88, CCCR+90]), or union giving priority to inserts in the case of conflict. At present Heraclitus[Alg,C] provides explicit constructs for smash, merge and weak-merge; other binary operators can be built up from more primitive Heraclitus[Alg,C] constructs.

3.3   Embedding into C

We now describe how relational deltas and the algebraic operators described above are embedded into C. The primary focus is on Heraclitus[Alg,C] expressions for (a) creating deltas, (b) combining deltas, and (c) accessing deltas.

Heraclitus[Alg,C] supports the manipulation of both persistent and transient relations and deltas. Suppose that `Suppliers` and `Orders` are persistent relations as defined in the previous section. The following declares two variables for these, and a variable for transient relation `Big`:

```
relation Supp, Ord, Big;
Supp = access_relation("Suppliers");
Ord = access_relation("Orders");
Big = empty_relation(Part:char[30], Qty:int,
                     Sup:char[30], Exp:int);
```

Signatures for variables `Supp` and `Ord` are taken from the corresponding persistent relations. The signature for transient relation variable `Big` must be specified explicitly upon initialization. While coordinate names may be associated with relation types as indicated here at present the algebra is based on coordinate positions. However, most of our examples will use coordinate names to simplify the exposition. (We assume that `Ord` has the same field names as `Big`, and that `Supp` has field names `Sup` and `Part`.) In Subsection 3.4 we use pure Heraclitus[Alg,C] syntax.

The algebra used is essentially the standard relational algebra, except that system- and user-defined scalar functions can be used in projection target lists, and in selection and join conditions (e.g., `project([Part, Qty*2], select( {foo(Sup)>Qty}, Orders))` for user-defined function `foo`).

Deltas are supported in Heraclitus[Alg,C] by the type `delta`. Deltas can be created using *atomic* commands, such as

```
delta D1, D2;
D1 = [del Supp("Campy","pedals")];
D2 = [ins Big("brakes",500,"Shimano", "9/20/93")];
```

After execution D1 has $\{-Suppliers(Campy, pedals)\}$ and D2 has $\{+temp14(brakes, 500, Shimano, 9/20/93)\}$, where *temp*14 is the relation identifier chosen during program execution for the transient relation `Big`. The *bulk* operator can be used to construct a "large" delta from data currently in the database. For example,

```
bulk(ins Big(Part, Qty, Sup, Exp), select({Qty > 300}, Ord))
```
evaluates in the context of Figure 1 to

$$\{ \ +temp14(frame, 400, Trek, 8/31/93) \ \}$$

More generally, the first argument to bulk must be, what amounts to, an atomic delta expression containing scalar expressions built up from column names and scalar values. These names are assigned possible values by the second argument to bulk, which must be a relation expression. Thus, a `bulk` operator can be viewed as a composition of relational projection followed by parallel creation of atomic delta expressions.

Heraclitus[Alg,C] also supports atomic *modify* expressions, such as `[mod Ord("brakes",150, "Campy", "9/1/93; "brakes", 150, "Shimano", "9/6/93")]`. Evaluation of this expression depends on the current state: if $(brakes, 150, Campy, 9/1/93)$ is present in Orders (as it is in Figure 1) this expression evaluates to

$$\left\{ \begin{array}{l} -Orders(brakes, 150, Campy, 9/1/93), \\ +Orders(brakes, 150, Shimano, 9/6/93) \end{array} \right\}$$

On the other hand, if $(brakes, 150, Campy, 9/1/93)$ is not present in Orders (as in Figure 2) then the expression evaluates to the empty delta. We have experimented with permitting explicit modifies inside of delta values, on an equal footing with deletes and inserts. However, as reported in [GHJ92], the semantics for consistency and for smash become quite cumbersome in that framework. This has lead us to the compromise that they can be written explicitly, but their value depends on the state. Regardless of this decision, the presence of modify expressions in a program may give the compiler opportunities for optimization (e.g., by avoiding two traversals of an index).

Heraclitus[Alg,C] also permits "wildcards" in delete and modify commands. Wildcards, denoted by '*', match any value. Evaluation of expressions with wildcards again depends on the current database state.

Deltas may be combined using smash (!), merge (&), and weak-merge explicitly. A fourth operator, *compose*, is also supported; this is described shortly.

We now turn to the four operators for accessing deltas. The first is *apply*: the command apply δ; first evaluates δ and applies the resulting delta value to the current state. Hypothetical expression evaluation is supported by the when operator. As a simple example,

```
Big = select({Qty > 300}, Ord) when
([mod Ord("brakes",150,"Shimano","9/6/93";
          "brakes",500,"Shimano","9/20/93")] &
 [ins Ord("light",300,"Cat Paw","9/3/93")]);
```
when evaluated in Figure 2 yields $\{(frame, 400, Trek, 8/31/93), (brakes, 500, Shimano, 9/20/93)\}$. Importantly, side-effect free functions can be called within the context of a when. Nesting of when's is also permitted – it is easily verified that

$$(E \text{ when } \delta_1) \text{ when } \delta_2 \ \equiv \ E \text{ when } (\delta_2 \ ! \ (\delta_1 \text{ when } \delta_2))$$

This plays a key role in the implementation of delta expressions consisting of nested when's.

The final operators for accessing deltas are *peeking* expressions; these permit the programmer to directly inspect a delta. The expression $\text{peekins}(R, \delta)$ evaluates to the relation containing all tuples that are to be inserted into R according to the value of δ, and the expression $\text{peekdel}(R, \delta)$ evaluates analogously. For example, peekdel(Supp,[del ("Campy",*)]) evaluates in Figure 2 to $\{(Campy, brakes), (Campy, pedals)\}$.

The *compose* operator, denoted '#', has the property that the command `apply` (δ_1 # δ_2) is equivalent to (`apply` δ_1; `apply` δ_2;). Compose is defined in terms of smash and `when`, by δ_1 # δ_2 = δ_1 ! (δ_2 `when` δ_1). This definition indicates the difference between smash and compose. In δ_1 ! δ_2, both δ_1 and δ_2 are evaluated with respect to the current state, then smashed, and then applied to the current state. In δ_1 # δ_2, δ_2 is evaluated in the state resulting from the application of δ_1 to the current state. This is reminiscent of the "phantom" problem in database transaction processing. It is straightforward to verify that compose is associative.

Compose is especially useful in the context of hypothetical database access. We present an example involving two functions. The first function builds a delta that has the effect of canceling all October orders:

```
delta cancel_Oct_orders()
{return bulk(del Ord(Part,Qty,Sup,Exp),
           select({in_Oct(Exp)},Ord));}
```

The second one builds a delta that delays the expected date by two weeks of all orders with `Qty` > 500:

```
delta delay_big_orders()
{return bulk(mod Ord(Part,Qty,Sup,Exp,
                     Part,Qty,Sup, add_two_weeks(Exp)),
           select({Qty > 500}, Ord));}
```

Suppose that the function `total_brakes_on_order` computes the total number of brakes on order. Then the expression

```
total_brakes_on_order() when
  cancel_Oct_orders() # delay_big_orders()
```

performs a hypothetical evaluation of `total_brakes_on_` order, assuming that first the October orders where canceled, and then the big orders were delayed. Note the value resulting from the call to `delay_big_orders` takes into account the updates proposed by the value of `cancel_Oct_orders`. The following performs the hypothetical evaluation, but with the application of the two delta functions reversed.

```
total_brakes_on_order() when
  delay_big_orders() # cancel_Oct_orders()
```

In general these two expressions will evaluate to different values.

3.4   Active database examples

This subsection provides a brief indication of how Heraclitus[Alg,C] can be used to specify, and thereby implement, a variety of active database execution models. To simplify, we omit consideration of "triggers", and assume rules to have the form:

$$\text{if } <condition> \text{ then } <action>$$

Because Heraclitus[Alg,C] provides explicit peeking, triggers can easily be incorporated into the syntax.

Recall the discussion of Subsection 2.1. We adopt here the convention for this discussion that the original database state remains unchanged during rule firing, and that appropriate virtual states are represented and manipulated using deltas. We now specify in Heraclitus[Alg,C] the rules R2 and R4 of Subsection 2.1. It is assumed that deltas corresponding to S_{prop} and S_{curr} are maintained by the execution model. Both rules will be functions with two arguments, although R2 uses only the delta corresponding to S_{curr}.

In Heraclitus[Alg,C], coordinate positions are indicated using the '@' symbol. Typing information is also included here to simplify the task of pre-processing into C, given the fact that relation signatures can change over the lifetime of a program. Thus, in the rule rule_R2, @c1 refers to the first coordinate of the output of the peekdel, which has type character string.

```
delta rule_R2(prop,curr)
  delta prop,curr;
  { return bulk(del Ord(@c2,*,@c1,*), peekdel(Supp,curr)); }

delta rule_R4(prop,curr)
  delta prop,curr;
  { if ( (count(Ord) when curr) / (count(Ord) when prop) < .8 )
      inventory_warning();
    return empty_delta; }
```

Suppose now that a total of 25 rules are written to capture the purchasing policy for this application, all using input variables corresponding to S_{prop} and S_{curr}. They can be combined into an array of delta functions as follows:

```
delta (*policy[24])();
policy[0] = rule_R1;
policy[1] = rule_R2;
    .
    .
    .
policy[24] = rule_R25;
```

The following function specifies an execution model that takes in a delta corresponding to a user-requested update and applies the rules according to a specific algorithm. Here we use the *copy* ('<<') operator; 'curr << prop;' copies the signed atoms associated with delta variable prop into the delta variable curr. The assignment temp = empty_delta initializes temp as a transient delta holding the empty delta. The expression curr !<< temp; is equivalent to curr << curr ! temp;, and analogously for &<<. The boolean dequiv checks equality of deltas.

```
boolean apply_policy(prop)
delta prop
{
  delta curr, prev, temp;
  if (prop == fail) return (false);
  curr << prop;
  do { prev << curr;
       temp = empty_delta;
       for (i=0; i<25; i++)
         { temp &<< (*policy[i])(prop,curr) };
       curr !<< temp; }
  while ( curr != fail && !dequiv(prev,curr));
  if (curr == fail)
    { return (false); }
  else
    { apply curr;
      return (true); };
}
```

Here, the inner loop corresponds to a single, independent (set-oriented) application of each rule in policy, and combines the results using merge. Note that in the inner loop, each rule is evaluated on prop and `curr`, and the resulting deltas are accumulated in variable `temp`. The outer loop repeatedly performs the inner loop, using smash to fold the results of each iteration into the value of `curr` already obtained. The outer loop is performed until either a fixpoint is reached, or the inner loop produces the delta *fail* (either because one of the rules explicitly called for an abort by producing *fail*, or because in some execution of the inner loop, two rules produced conflicting deltas).

Suppose now that there is a second array `keys` of rule functions capturing key constraints, and that the above execution model is to be modified so that after each execution of the inner loop the rules in `keys` are to be fired until a fixpoint is reached. Suppose further that these rules use only a single input delta, corresponding to S_{curr}. Now let function `apply_rules` have the following signature

```
delta apply_rules(curr, rule_base, size)
  delta curr;
  delta (*rule_base[])();
  int size;
```

and suppose that it applies the rules in `rule_base` until a fixpoint is reached. Then the desired modification to `apply_policy` can be accomplished by adding

```
    curr !<< apply_rules(curr,keys,15);
```

as the last line of the inner loop. This very briefly indicates the kind of flexibility that Heraclitus[Alg,C] provides in specifying active database execution models.

We are currently implementing in Heraclitus[Alg,C] the (kernel of the) execution models of the Starburst Rule System, AP5, and POSTGRES systems. Specifications for Starburst and AP5 in Heraclitus pseudo-code were presented in [HJ91].

4 The Implementation of Heraclitus[Alg,C]

The implementation of Heraclitus[Alg,C] has two components: HERALD, a library of relational and delta operators built on top of Exodus, and a pre-processor that maps Heraclitus[Alg,C] programs into C programs with calls to HERALD. We discuss the pre-processor first.

4.1 The Pre-Processor

We mention here only of several significant aspects of the Heraclitus[Alg,C] pre-processor, namely, the implementation of `when`'s.

Consider the expression `join( <cond> , R, S) when D`. This cannot be evaluated in the traditional bottom-up manner, because the relationships of `D` with `R` and `S` are lost if the join is performed. Instead, the `when` must be "pushed" inwards, through the join operator, to directly modify the relations. A naive approach to this problem is to have the compiler "replace" the above expression by `join( <cond>, R when D, S when D)`. before passing it to HERALD. A complication arises, however, because Heraclitus[Alg,C] permits functions that reference the database state to be called in the context of a `when`, e.g., `goo(u,v) when D`. This means that essentially any expression may have to be evaluated hypothetically, but the relevant delta is known only at runtime. In the current implementation we maintain a "runtime when stack." During the execution of a program the top of the stack holds a delta that reflects the full effect of all deltas relevant to the evaluation of the expression currently under consideration. This has the same impact as pushing `when`'s to the leaves of the syntax tree.

As an aside, we note that in the context of database programming languages such as Heraclitus[Alg,C], queries are generally accessible only at runtime due to the presence of function calls. This highlights one of the key differences between query processing in conventional databases, where the full query tree is available at compile time, and query processing in database programming languages.

4.2   HERALD

A central aspect of the HERALD system is to combine the evaluation of when's with evaluation of the algebraic operators, in a manner reminiscent of the traditional relational optimization of combining selects and projects with joins. For example, HERALD provides a *hypothetical join* function `join_when`, that evaluates the expression `join( <cond>, R when D, S when D).` without materializing `R when D` or `S when D`. HERALD currently supports two strategies for obtaining access to deltas in connection with the hypothetical algebraic operators and other delta operators, one based on hashing and the other on a sort-merge paradigm.

Conceptually, HERALD represents a delta as a collection of pairs (R_Δ^+, R_Δ^-), specifying the proposed inserts and deletes for each relation variable R in the program. Here, R_Δ^+ and R_Δ^- are called *sub-deltas*, and are stored as relations (actually, files) in Exodus. Hash-based access is best suited for the situation where a subdelta pair (R_Δ^+, R_Δ^-) fits into main memory, and sort-based access is better when a subdelta pair is bigger than main memory.

In the remainder of the section we discuss hash-based and sort-based access to deltas.

Hash-based access to deltas

When sub-deltas are small enough to fit in main memory, HERALD maintains a hash index on each sub-delta. The hash index key value to address this hash table is composite and computed based on the values of all fields (or attributes) of a record. This implementation technique is effective as long as a delta fits in main memory. We now describe the low-level algorithms for two representative delta operators, namely `select_when` and `join_when`.

Select_when.   The input arguments of this operator are: a relation R, a selection condition, a delta Δ, and an output relation. Logically, this operator selects tuples of R that satisfy the selection condition in the hypothetical state proposed by Δ and stores the resulting tuples in the output relation. Its implementation is as follows:

1. open a scan on R
2. get the first tuple of R (say t)
3. while not EOF(R) do
   - a. evaluate the selection condition for t. If the tuple does not qualify go to step e.
   - b. probe the hash index of R_Δ^+ with t for a matching tuple, if found go to step e.
   - c. probe the hash index of R_Δ^- with t for a matching tuple, if found go to step e.
   - d. insert t into the output relation.
   - e. get the next tuple t in R.
4. for each tuple t of R_Δ^+ do
   - a. evaluate the selection condition for t. If t satisfies this condition, then insert t into the output relation.

Note that we probe the hash index only if the tuple satisfies the selection condition. This minimizes the number of disk accesses because probing the hash index may result in a disk read operation.

We briefly analyze the expected I/O costs of the implementation of `select_when`. Suppose that R_Δ^+, R_Δ^- are small enough to fit into main memory, and that $s\%$ of the tuples in R satisfy the selection condition. Assuming that $s > 0$, the algorithm will call for the following I/Os:

(a) scan R
(b) scan hash tables for R_Δ^+, R_Δ^+.
(c) probe R_Δ^- for $s\%$ of R
(d) probe R_Δ^+ for $s\%$ of R
(e) scan R_Δ^+
(f) write output relation

Thus, the expected overhead in I/O is roughly equal to the number of pages of the hash tables for R_Δ^+ and R_Δ^+, and the number of pages of R_Δ^+ and R_Δ^- that are read during parts (b) and (c). (An additional scan of all of R_Δ^+ and R_Δ^- is needed if hash tables are not maintained.) This was confirmed in our benchmarking experiments.

Join_when.   In the current implementation, the binary relational operators use sort-based implementations. In the case of hash-based delta access, a key subroutine for all of them is `sort_when`. Suppose that R is unsorted. The conventional approach to sorting R is to use heap-sort on short (e.g., 100 page) segments of R, and then to perform n-way merges of these segments. In `sort_when`, the impact of a delta is incorporated into the heap-sort. For example, on relation R, as portions of R are read in for heap-sorting, a hash-table for R_Δ^- is probed, and the matching tuples are not placed into the heap. Also redundant tuples in R_Δ^+ are marked, to prevent later duplication. After R is completely read, the remainder of R_Δ^+ is also processed by the heap sort to provide additional sorted segments. Then one or more merges is invoked to create a sorted file. In the current implementation for join with hash-based delta access, `sort_when` is used to sort R (as impacted by R_Δ^+, R_Δ^-) and S (as impacted by S_Δ^+, S_Δ^-), and then a binary merge is used to create the join. Although not currently implemented, this could be optimized by combining the final merge with the separate merges inside the two calls to `sort_when`.

When using hash-based delta access for these operators, there is an important interaction between the amount of buffer space used by the heap vs. the hash tables. To illustrate, suppose in the abstract that the total available buffer pool consists of 100 frames (and so the heap-sort can perform 100-way merges). Moreover, assume that R consists of 1000 pages, R^- has about 90 pages that will be probed during a pass of R (termed "hitting" pages), and R^+ is empty. In this case a 10-page heap could be established, and $R - R^-$ would be broken into roughly 100 (or fewer) sorted segments. Now a single 100-way merge will yield a sorted version of $apply(R, R^-)$; total cost is $2|R| + |R^-|$. Suppose now that R has 2000 pages, R^- has about 80 "hitting" pages, and R^+ is empty. It is now optimal to devote 20 pages to the heap-sort and the other 80 to hash probing. (Fewer pages for the heap-sort results in more merge passes; and fewer pages for the hash probing may result in thrashing.) Thus, providing optimal support for hash-based delta access requires the ability to dynamically partition the buffer pool between these two tasks. This capability is supported by Exodus, and we plan to investigate these trade-offs in our future research.

Sort-based access to deltas

A delta may be so large that it does not fit in main memory, in which case the hash-based implementation will thrash. To remedy this, we have designed and implemented algorithms that access deltas using a sort and merge technique. We now present the low level algorithm for the `select_when` operator; the implementation of other operators is analogous. Heraclitus[Alg,C] maintains information on whether relations and subdeltas are sorted, so that one or more of the sorting steps of these sort-based algorithms can be eliminated.

select_when.   The input arguments of this operator are: a relation R, a selection condition, a delta Δ, and an output relation. We assume that no order is maintained for any of the inputs. A key function used here is `select_sort` which takes as input a relation and a selection condition. As with `sort_when`, this implements a two-phase sort, but in the heap-sort phase it deletes all tuples violating the selection condition.

In the following algorithm, if no tuples satisfy the selection condition (i.e., $Temp$ is empty), then R_Δ^+ is scanned for the qualifying tuples and returns. Otherwise, it sorts the qualifying tuples found in each of R_Δ^- and R_Δ^+ into two different temporary relations. Next, it performs a three way merge on these relations, inserting one occurrence of entries of R that match with R_Δ^+ (prevent duplicates) and eliminating those that match with R_Δ^- (tuples proposed to be deleted).

1. `select_sort` (R, selection condition) into a temporary relation $Temp$.
2. if $Temp$ is empty, then
   a. for each tuple t of R_Δ^+, evaluate the selection condition for t. If t satisfies this condition, then insert t into the output relation.
   b. return as the output relation and exit.
3. `select_sort` (R_Δ^-, selection condition) into a temporary relation $Temp^-$.
4. `select_sort` (R_Δ^+, selection condition) into a temporary relation $Temp^+$.
5. retrieve the first tuple in $Temp$ (say r), $Temp^-$ (say $d-$), and $Temp^+$ (say $d+$).
6. while not EOF($Temp$) OR not EOF($Temp^-$) OR not EOF($Temp^+$) do
   a. assign t to be the tuple with minimum value among r, $d+$, and $d-$.
   b. If t is not equivalent to $d-$, then insert t into the output relation.
   c. If t is equivalent to r, then get the next tuple r from $Temp$.
   d. If t is equivalent to $d-$, then get the next tuple $d-$ from $Temp_\Delta^-$.
   e. If t is equivalent to $d+$, then get the next tuple $d+$ from $Temp_\Delta^+$.

We now analyze the expected I/O cost of this implementation of `select_when`, under the assumption that the inputs are not maintained in sorted order. Let $P(R)$ represent the number of disk pages for relation R, $SP(R)$ represents the number of disk pages that satisfy the selection condition, and analogously for R_Δ^+ and R_Δ^-. We assume that $SP(R) \leq$ the square of the number of available pages in the buffer pool (i.e., that only one n-way merge is need to sort R), and similarly for R_Δ^+ and R_Δ^-. The total number of I/Os incurred by the above algorithm can be estimated as the sum of:

$$
\begin{aligned}
select\_sort(R) &: \quad P(R) + 2 * SP(R) \\
select\_sort(R_\Delta^+) &: \quad P(R_\Delta^+) + 2 * SP(R_\Delta^+) \\
select\_sort(R_\Delta^-) &: \quad P(R_\Delta^-) + 2 * SP(R_\Delta^-) \\
merge &: \quad 2 * SP(R) + 2 * SP(R_\Delta^+) + SP(R_\Delta^-)
\end{aligned}
$$

This cost function is a worst case estimate because it assumes: (1) SP(R) is not empty, (2) the tuples of SP(R) are not redundant with those in SP(R_Δ^+), causing all their entries to be written to the output relation, and (3) the tuples of SP(R) do not match with the tuples found in R_Δ^-.

The implementation also handles the case where the input relation and delta are sorted. In this case, only steps (5) and (6) of the algorithm are executed, and the selection condition is incorporated into step (6).

```
interface Student {                        interface Employee {
    extent      students;                      extent      employees;
    string      studName;                      string      empName;
    integer[7]  studID;                        integer[9]  SSN;
    string      major;                         Division    division;
    string      local_address;                 string      address;
    string      permanent_address;         };
    Set<Course> courses_taken;
};                                         interface Division {
                                               extent      divisions;
interface Course {                             string      divName;
    extent      courses;                       ... ...
    string      courseName;                };
    ... ...
};
```

              Subschema of *StudentDB*   Subschema of *EmployeeDB*

Figure 3   Subschemas of `StudentDB` and `EmployeeDB` in ODL syntax

5   Heraclitus and Maintenance of Materialized Data

In this section, we show how the Heraclitus DBPL can be used to conveniently implement rules and their execution model for the maintenance of integrated, materialized derived data. More specifically, we apply these rules and the execution model to supporting data integration involving object matching, that is, determining when object representations in different databases correspond to the same object-in-the-world. Chapter 6 in this book introduces "integration mediators" that support this and more conventional kinds of data integration. One important aspect of integration mediators is that they can materialize, among other things, the correspondence information about object matching. A mediator uses a set of rules to maintain the materialized data. In this section, we focus on using constructs of the Heraclitus DBPL to implement the rules and an execution model for them. For the sake of clarity, we base our discussion here on object matching between pairs of classes from different databases. The execution model can be easily extended to support *n*-ary matching [ZHK96].

Before we present the rules and the execution model, we briefly summarize the Student/Employee example in Section 3 of Chapter 6. In the example, there are two databases, `StudentDB` and `EmployeeDB`, that hold information about students at a university and employees in a corporation, respectively. The relevant subschemas of the two databases are shown in Figure 3. Our example integration mediator maintains correspondence information about persons who are both students and employees.

The example further assumes that a student object *s* *matches* an employee object *e* (i.e., they refer to the same person in the real world) if (1) either $s.\texttt{local\_address} = e.\texttt{address}$ or $s.\texttt{permanent\_address} = e.\texttt{address}$, and (2) their names are "close" to each other according to some metric. The "closeness" of names is determined by a function, called here `close_names()`, that takes two names as arguments and returns a boolean value.

To support the kind of object matching criteria such as those between students and employees, we propose the following general solution. Suppose now that classes A_1, A_2 from two source databases represent the same or overlapping sets of objects-in-the-world. An integration mediator can support matching of objects from these classes by maintaining a match class $match\_A_1\_A_2$. As suggested in Chapter 6 each of the source classes will contribute three kinds of attributes to the match class (these sets may overlap), namely

```
interface match_Stud_Emp {
     string      studName;              string     empName;
     integer[7]  studID;                integer[9] SSN;
     string      local_address;         string     address;
     string      perm_address;                                };
```

Figure 4 The class interface of `match_Stud_Emp`, stored in the integration mediator

identification attributes, match attributes, and export attributes. Speaking loosely, the class $match\_A_1\_A_2$ will hold an "outer join" of the underlying source classes, where each object in $match\_A_1\_A_2$ represents a single object-in-the-world. Each element of $match\_A_1\_A_2$ is called a *surrogate* object. A given surrogate object might represent objects from essentially any subset of the associated source database classes.

The interface of the match class `match_Stud_Emp` for the Student/Employee example in Chapter 6 is shown in Figure 4. The left column of four attributes of this class come from the `Student` class; the other 3 attributes in the right column come from the `Employee` class. The identification attributes are `studID` and `SSN`, which are printable keys; the match attributes are `studName`, `local_address`, `perm_address`, `empName`, and `address`; and the only export attribute is `studName`.

5.1   Rule templates

As detailed in Chapter 6, an integration mediator can be generated from high-level specifications of the view that is to be supported. A key component here is the generation of rules for supporting incremental update propagation within the mediator. This subsection describes the rule "templates" that are used to generate these rules, and the next subsection briefly describes the execution model that is used when applying the rules.

Reference [ZHK96] describes rule templates for a full range of view-defining operations, including relational algebra and object-matching operations. We focus here on the rule templates for supporting the incremental maintenance of the match class in response of the creation of objects for a source class A_i. Analogous rule templates for deletions of source objects are omitted. The two rule templates presented here would be used to generate the rules dealing with the creation of new objects in the classes A_1 and A_2. The modification updates indicated in the second rule action is shorthand for a deletion followed by an insertion. Although the rules generated from the templates described here refer to individual objects, the execution model apply the rules in a set-at-a-time fashion.

rule template for an insertion in A_i:
ON   new ΔA_i
IF   (insert $A_i(x : a_1, \ldots, a_n)$) in ΔA_i
THEN   [insert $match\_A_1\_A_2(new : \ldots, nil, x.m_1, \ldots, x.m_j, nil, \ldots)$];
where $m_1, \ldots, m_j$ are attributes contributed to $match\_A_1\_A_2$ by A_i.

Description: if a new object x of class A_i is inserted, insert a corresponding new object into class $match\_A_1\_A_2$, with nil for non-A_i attributes.

rule template for an insertion in $match\_A_1\_A_2$:
ON   insert $match\_A_1\_A_2(x : \ldots, nil, x.m_1, \ldots, x.m_j, nil, \ldots)$
IF   exists a unique y in $match\_A_1\_A_2$ such that $match(x, y)$
THEN   [delete $match\_A_1\_A_2(x)$;
               modify $match\_A_1\_A_2(y : existing\ attr.\ of\ y, x.m_1, \ldots, x.m_j, \ldots)$];

Description: when a new $match\_A_1\_A_2$ object x is inserted, if an object y of class $match\_A_1\_A_2$ matches x, delete x and modify y by setting the values of attributes $m_1, \ldots, m_j$ to $x.m_1, \ldots, x.m_j$.

Specific rule instances can be created from these templates in a straightforward manner.

5.2 The execution model

A key issue about the execution model is how to maximize the concurrency between the incremental maintenance of the match class and answering queries against it. The incremental maintenance process typically involves firing of multiple rules, and the action part of each rule performs updates to the match class. Traditional approaches would lock the match class during the entire period of an invocation of the incremental maintenance. We propose that the actions do not apply those updates to the matching class, rather the updates are held in a delta $\Delta match\_A_1\_A_2$. Only when all the applicable rules are fired, the match class is then locked and the delta is applied to the match class. Whenever the rules refer to the match class, it refers to ($match\_A_1\_A_2$ **when** $\Delta match\_A_1\_A_2$) rather then simply $match\_A_1\_A_2$.

The execution model has the following steps:

(1) Initialization: Let Δ correspond to the smash of all incremental updates held in the queue that receives relevant net changes reported from the source database. Δ will hold two subdeltas, ΔA_1 and ΔA_2.

(2) Firing the applicable rules. And the proposed updates to $match\_A_1\_A_2$ are held in $\Delta Temp$. Set $\Delta match\_A_1\_A_2 = \Delta match\_A_1\_A_2$ *smash* $\Delta Temp$. Repeat the above steps until $\Delta Temp$ is empty, i.e., a fixpoint is reached.

(3) Apply $\Delta match\_A_1\_A_2$, and delete all entries in the queue that contributed to Δ.

In the general setting [ZHK96], rules for supporting incremental update propagation in an integration mediator are organized by a directed acyclic graph (DAG), called a *View Decomposition Plan*. The execution model fires the rules in a bottom-up fashion according to this DAG. To provide maximum concurrency, the effect of all rules can be recorded in deltas until all rules have been fired. Then the actual data can be locked while the deltas are applied.

6 Conclusions

This chapter describes the current status of the Heraclitus project. A long-range goal is to develop and implement language constructs and techniques for the flexible specification and implementation of a wide variety of execution models for active databases. The current focus has been on the development of the language Heraclitus[Alg,C], that extends C with the relational algebra, deltas, and delta operators, and uses Exodus to provide bulk data access. The main research contributions of the implementation have been (a) understanding feasible physical implementations of the algebraic operators, and (b) understanding the implications of embedding the Heraclitus paradigm for database access into an imperative programming language. As shown here, the delta paradigm and Heraclitus[Alg,C] are especially well-suited for working with virtual states, as arise in several active databases in the literature, and for specifying how the results of fired rules should be combined. The chapter also describes how Heraclitus can be used to provide effective support for materialized data integration.

Current work on the Heraclitus paradigm has involved the development of a prototype object-oriented version of Heraclitus called the Heraclitus[OO] (or H2O) DBPL [DHDD95]; and the study of different "forms" of deltas for the object-oriented context [DHR96]. In connection with data integration, a recent result has been the development of a framework for integration mediators that support a flexible hybrid of the virtual and materialized approaches [HZ96].

Acknowledgments

This chapter is based on parts of [GHJ^{+}93,GHJ96] on Heraclitus[Alg,C] and [ZHKF95,ZHK96] on data integration. In connection with the research and implementation effort on Heraclitus[Alg,C], we would like to thank Jaime Castillo, Hsun-Ko Chan, Elton Chen, Vera Choi, Yuji Enzaki, Martha Escobar-Molano, Sanjay Joshi, Yoram Landau, Michel Liu, Shih-Hui Lu, Junhui Luo, Aris Prassinos, Babar Saeed, Chiu (Simon) Tsang, Howard Ungar and Jackie Yu. More generally We would also like to thank Serge Abiteboul, Omar Boucelma, Jean-Claude Franchitti, Roger King, and Eric Simon for useful discussions a variety of topics in connection with both the Heraclitus project and the work on data integration.

30

AN INCREMENTAL ACCESS METHOD OF VIEW CACHE: CONCEPT, ALGORITHMS, AND COST ANALYSIS[1]

Nicholas Roussopoulos

1 Introduction

The concept of a view that stems from the "closure" of the relational algebra is probably the most important asset of the relational model. Views have been used for providing conceptual subsets of the database to different users and as an implementation tool for efficiency, security, etc. References to work based on relational views abound [AL80,BS81,CP84,DB82,FC85,Kel86,Rou82,Rou82b,Sto75]. Recently Wiederhold, [Wie86], related the commonality of the concept of the view to the concept of collections of objects in programming languages and proposed the concept of views for building complex data objects. Similarly, objects consisting of collections of views and/or other objects have been implemented in [RK89].

There are three principal methods for implementing views. The first and most popular method for supporting views is the query modification approach [Sto75]. The definition of each view is kept in the directory of the system, and queries referring to a view are appropriately modified using the view's definition because only the intention is maintained, any reference to a view implies reexecution of the definition. The second method is storing the result (target relation) of a relational expression involving base relations and other views as shapshots. A previously constructed snapshot can be retrieved directly like a base relation. Finally, the third method is storing, for each view, a collection of indices which point to the records of base relations required to materialize the view [Rou82,Rou82b]. Since indexes are very compact and, in many cases, they can be loaded and kept in main memory, they can be thought of as a form of an I/O cache. For this reason, we will refer to them as *ViewCache* indexes.

The advantage of the query modification technique is that it requires practically no disk storage and no maintenance. Its major disadvantage is its poor performance. The cost of an exhaustive access to a view, or a selective access to a subset of it in answering a follow-up query against that view, includes all of the initial construction cost of the view. And this cost is repeated every time an access to the view is required. Therefore, in the query modification method, views are only naming tools (macros) that cannot be used to enhance the efficiency of frequently accessed database subsets.

The snapshot method achieves high performance at the expense of storage. It redundantly stores query and intermediate results, thus requiring much storage and is very cumbersome for incremental updating. Unless the views have not been affected by updates to the base relations and unless they match the target query exactly, they offer no advantage. Incremental maintenance of outdated materialized views and incorporation of them in higher level views is very expensive in terms of I/O because of their size.

---

[1]This research was supported partially by the National Science Foundation and the Air Force Office of Scientific Research under Grants IRI-8719458 and AFOSR 89-0303.

Additional indexes on the snapshots may have to be generated on the fly during the execution for speeding up the query process. This reduces or diminishes the benefits of the snapshot approach.

The ViewCache method provides a middle-of-the-road approach. It caches access paths of views and intermediate results in terms of pointers to actual data records. The pointers are materialized as needed. The ViewCache's redundancy is comparable to that of indexing and negligible when compared to snapshot redundancy. We will show that it achieves both high performance and efficient incremental updates.

The ViewCache, like any other indexing method, has to *amortize* its maintenance cost over the period that the views remain valid. For relatively static databases such as catalogs, libraries, archived data sets, etc., the cost that has to be amortized is minor because views remain valid for very long periods. For non-static databases, invalidation of a ViewCache (and the same is true for the snapshot approach) occurs as soon as an update to any of the view's underlying relations is made. In an update intensive database, the amortization period of views is very short; therefore, all the benefits from redundancy may be lost. This is also true when irrelevant updates [BLT86] are screened out, a technique that prolongs the amortization period.

This paper presents an *Incremental Access Method (IAM)* for views that allows incremental update and use of derived ViewCaches. The IAM prolongs the amortization period of ViewCaches; in many cases, ViewCaches are cost-effectively maintained indefinitely. The IAM consists of a set of update algorithms for ViewCaches derived via relational operators. We present the incremental update algorithms for the most fundamental operators of the relational model, namely, *selection, projection,* and *join.* Incremental algorithms for intersection, union, and difference are similar to the join algorithm and not included in this paper.

Incremental computations have been successfully applied elsewhere. Paige used *finite differencing* for efficient validation of database constraints [Pai84]. *Differential fixpoint iteration* has been used for efficient processing of deductive queries that have many repetitive computations [GKB87]. In both applications, performance is dramatically improved. In this paper, we apply incremental computation to an access method for dynamically derived views obtained during interactions with the users. Combined with *lazy* update strategies that bear no maintenance overhead for ViewCaches, they offer significant performance improvement over the traditional reexecution approach of query modification.

Section 2 describes the IAM and the ViewCache concept. Section 3 describes the IAM algorithms. Section 4 includes the cost analysis of the IAM and the criteria for deciding when the IAM is cost-effective. Section 5 presents a few experiments on the current implementation of a relational prototype system called *Advanced Database Management System, (ADMS)* [Rou87]. Section 6 has the conclusions.

2   Incremental Access Methods for Views

In the query modification method, the cost of answering a query against the same view V is uniform, approximately the same in each request (assuming that, between requests, the database does not drastically change in size, value distribution and other characteristics affecting V). This is true whether the query scans the entire V or selectively accesses subsets of it. On the contrary, in the ViewCache method, the cost of answering a similar query against the view V for the second time (or other subsequent requests), under prevailing conditions, can be significantly lower than the cost of answering it the first time around. For example, if no updates have occurred between the first and a subsequent request, the cost of the latter is reduced to retrieving only the absolutely needed data for the result. No search cost is incurred. Therefore, in the sequel, we will distinguish between a first time request (FTR) and subsequent ones. We assume that the FTR cost for the ViewCache is approximately the same with that of the query modification technique.[2]

Updates to the underlying base relations, i.e., insertions, deletions, and modifications, may outdate a ViewCache. Therefore, in processing a subsequent request against it, the IAM will be invoked in order to correct its affected pointers before materializing from them. We will refer to this update cost as VCU, the *ViewCache Update* cost, and the cost of materializing the view from the pointers as VCM, the *ViewCache Materialize* cost. In addition, we have to account for the *ViewCache Read* cost, VCR, for reading the ViewCache in before materialization, and the *ViewCache Write* cost, VCW, for writing the modified portion of it back to disk for later requests.

A ViewCache is *cost-effective* if VCR + VCU + VCM + VCW < FTR. In other words, the cost of reading, updating, materializing from, and writing back the modified portion of the ViewCache is less than the cost of reexecuting the view. We will show that ViewCaches are cost-effective provided that the size of the *differential files* [SL76] of the update logs of the underlying base relations, hereafter called *incremental update logs,* are not terribly big. This situation is certainly true in static databases and can be true in dynamic databases depending on the access behavior. We will develop some dynamic, accurate conditions for deciding when an incremental update and use of the ViewCaches is cost-effective. The conditions depend on some readily available parameters and the size of the incremental update logs. Therefore, no overhead is incurred in deciding whether or not a ViewCache is cost-effective. For ViewCaches that are not cost-effective, reexecution of their view definition is assumed.

The comparison between IAM and query reexecution is based on worst case analysis for the IAM. The analysis provided in section 4 assumes that the update of the ViewCache is done first followed by materialization. In our ADMS prototype [Rou87], updating the ViewCache and materialization from it are *interleaved,* and much of the materialization cost is subsumed by the update cost. This is achieved by one-pass implementation of the incremental algorithms of ADMS. The additional savings obtained by this interleaving are not easily quantifiable but are apparent from the experimental runs. The interleaving also permits quick response time, that is, the elapsed time between the submission of the query and the display of the first tuple. Unaffected ViewCache entries are quickly materialized and displayed while the ViewCache update is in progress. This achieves rapid response time even for very complex views.

Note that a pure I/O based cost model makes ineffective those ViewCaches that require a walk through all pages of the underlying relations. For example, the Cartesian product operator requires a total retrieval of both operand relations in order to make up the result; therefore, no I/O can be saved by caching precomputed access paths. A projection operator that does not eliminate duplicate records from the ViewCache pointers is also not cost-effective with respect to an I/O cost model. However, for a different cost model that accounts for CPU and I/O costs, the IAM can be cost-effective for the projection even when a complete walk of the underlying pages is necessary.

The IAM allows for a number of updtae strategies to be implemented:

(a) **Immediate update broadcast.** All affected ViewCaches are immediately updated. This strategy maintains minimal response time at the expense of system overhead. For some applications and some views, this may be desirable for instant response time on view retrieval.

(b) **Periodic update broadcast.** All affected ViewCaches are periodically updated. This strategy can also be used to do updates during periods of low system load or at prespecified times.

---

[2]Assuming the same query optimizer for both the query modification and the incremental approach, the FTR cost for generating the records of a view and writing them on a file/terminal is exactly the same. A 10–12% overhead is associated with the ViewCache for storing it on disk to be used in subsequent queries.

(c) **Event triggered update.** A ViewCache is updated when an event occurs. For example, a particular event can be triggered when the thresholds for the IAM cost-effectiveness on the incremental update logs have been reached (selective update propagation).

(d) **Deferred update.** All ViewCaches stay outdated until a direct or indirect reference to them is made; at that time, the IAM for a ViewCache is invoked if it is cost-effective. This avoids any system overhead associated with immediate propagation of updates.

Strategies (b)–(d) implement the *deferred (lazy)* approach, [RK86b,RK86a], that postpones the incremental update propagation either for a while (strategies (b) and (c)) or indefinitely (strategy (d)) unless a direct or indirect reference to a ViewCache is made.

The algorithms and the results obtained for the IAM are applicable to all strategies (a)–(d). Therefore, the strategies can be combined, allowing the user to specify different strategies for views depending on their importance, frequency of access, and other application dependent criteria. The main difference among these strategies is how they control the size of the incremental update logs. The trade-off is between system overhead and query processing time. The deferred strategies incur less or no overhead on the system at the cost of having to process bigger incremental update logs during the query processing.

2.1   The ViewCache Model

Let $DB = \{R_i\}$ be a set of base relations. A unique tuple identifier (TID) is assigned to each tuple of a relation R_i. The access path for a view consists of a collection of TIDs of records of the underlying base relations or other access paths needed for materializing the view [Rou82,Rou82b]. This section defines an efficient storage organization for such view access paths. This storage structure is called a *ViewCache index* because it inherits properties from both caches and indexes. Like a cache, the system can use it without having to search for the records that correspond to the view. It can follow the TIDs to materialize the view records. Like an index, it stores pointers to the records and is buffered in main memory or read in its entirety.

A ViewCache entry is either a single TID or a pair of TIDs, depending on whether the view corresponds to a unary or binary relational operator, respectively. Each entry in a ViewCache has also its own TID. This allows the definition of multiple level hierarchies of ViewCaches. An example ViewCache hierarchy is shown in figure 1. Materialization of an entry from a ViewCache is done by recursive retrieval of lower ViewCache tuples until base relation tuples are obtained. Views stored as ViewCaches can be referenced by any (SQL) query for selectively retrieving from it or for creating other higher level views.

The hierarchical organization not only permits better sharing of access paths [Rou82b], but also confines the update propagation. If the access paths of views were combined into a monolithic one-level cache, then a single update on any of the underlying base relations affects the entire cache. In a hierarchical organization, if an update to a base relation does not affect ViewCache V, then any ViewCache derived from V remains valid with respect to the same update and no further propagation is necessary.

	V3
	PTR
e1025	d1025
e1026	c1027
e1027	d1029
e1028	d1030

	V2	
	LPTR	RPTR
d1025	c1025	b1026
d1026	c1025	b1031
d1027	c1027	b1025
d1028	c1027	b1027
d1029	c1027	b1030
d1030	c1028	b1029

	V1
	PTR
c1025	a1026
c1026	a1028
c1027	a1029
c1028	a1031

	Suppliers		
	S-NO	S-NAME	RATING
a1025	s01	IBM	fair
a1026	s02	DEC	good
a1027	s03	UNIVAC	poor
a1028	s04	ZENITH	good
a1029	s05	ATARI	good
a1020	s06	APPLE	fair
a1031	s07	MAC	good

	Stock		
	S-NO	P-NO	QTY
b1025	s05	p92	47
b1026	s02	p12	500
b1027	s05	p08	1000
b1028	s03	p02	84
b1029	s07	p06	43
b1030	s05	p12	16
b1031	s02	p64	800

V1 = select from suppliers where RATING = 'good'
V2 = join V1 stock where S-NO = S-NO
V3 = select from V2 where QTY < '800'

Figure 1 Example of a multilevel ViewCache.

2.2   An Incremental Access Method for ViewCache

Let R_i and R_j be two base relations maintained in the database. Let V_σ, V_π, and V be the ViewCaches that are derived by applying a *selection* σ, *projection* π, and a *join*, respectively:

$$V_\sigma = \sigma(R_i)$$
$$V_\pi = \pi(R_i)$$
$$V = (R_i, R_j)$$

Suppose now that after several insertions and deletions, R_i becomes R_i'. We assume that all updates to base relations are applied immediately. Let dlR_i be the *incremental update log* obtained from the log of R_i. dlR_i is a form of *differential file* [SL76]. Respectively, let D_i and I_i be all the deletions and insertions found in dlR_i. D_i stores only a list of TIDs where I_i is a relation compatible with R_i, storing the insertions of dlR_i.[3] We refer to D_i and I_i as *incremental deletion* and *insertion logs*, respectively. Let R_i^- be the relation obtained from R_i after applying all the deletions, D_i; then, $R_i' = R_i^- \cup I_i$. The following rules permit incremental updates of ViewCaches (similar rules have been reported in [BLT86] for materialized views):

Incremental Update Rule for Selection and Projection   Given D_i, I_i, and the ViewCache $V_\sigma(V_\pi)$, we can compute $V_\sigma'(V_\pi')$ by

$$V_\sigma' = \sigma(R_i') = \sigma(R_i^- \cup I_i) = \sigma(R_i^-) \cup \sigma(I_i) = (V_\sigma - D_i) \cup \sigma(I_i)$$
$$V_\pi' = \pi(R_i') = \pi(R_i^- \cup I_i) = \pi(R_i^-) \cup \pi(I_i) = (V_\pi - D_i) \cup \pi(I_i)$$

This holds because the unary relational operators of selection and projection can be distributed over the union operator [Ull82].

The above rule permits the computation of the new result by applying the select operator on the insertions I_i only. We call this `small-select` because it is done on a subset of the operand, namely on the insertions of the incremental update log I_i, instead of the whole relation. Its result is then merged with the ViewCache obtained after deleting the D_i TIDs. Deletions are processed by removing the TIDs of D_i found in V_σ without having to retrieve the deleted tuples.

Projection requires more work for processing both I_i and D_i. For the insertions, the incremental merge has to make sure it does not generate any duplicates. For the deletions, it must either redirect the TID entry of V_π to another tuple of the underlying relation that has the same projected values or eliminate it if no such a tuple exists. In our ADMS implementation, we chose to treat projection like selection, and eliminate duplicates during the output of the result. This simplified both the structure and the incremental maintenance of the ViewCache. For this reason, only selection will be discussed in the rest of the paper.

Incremental Update Rule for Join   Given D_i, I_i, D_j, I_i, and V, we can compute V' by

$$
\begin{aligned}
V' &= (R_i', R_j') \\
&= (R_i', \{R_j^- \cup I_j\}) \\
&= (R_i', R_j^-) \cup R_i', I_j) \\
&= (\{R_i^- \cup I_i\}, R_j^-) \cup (R_i', I_j) \\
&= (R_i^-, R_j^-) \cup (I_i, R_j^-) \cup (R_i', I_j) \\
&= (R_i^-, R_j^-) \cup (I_i, \{R_j' - I_j\}) \cup (R_i', I_j) \\
&= [V - \{D_i, -\} - \{-, D_j\}] \cup (I_i, R_j') - (I_i, I_j) \cup (R_i', I_j) \\
&= [V - \{D_i, -\} - \{-, D_j\}] \cup (I_i, R_j') \cup (R_i' - I_i, I_j) \\
&= [V - \{D_i, -\} - \{-, D_j\}] \cup (I_i, R_j') \cup (R_{i-}', I_j)
\end{aligned}
$$

---

[3]Modification of a tuple is treated as a pair of a deletion and an insertion.

where $\{D_i, -\}$ $(\{-, D_j\})$ are the pairs $< \text{tid}_i, \text{tid}_j >$ of V for which $\text{tid}_i \in D_i(\text{tid}_j \in D_j)$. The above shows that deletions can be removed without accessing R_i or R_j, and that need only be applied to the insertions I_i and I_j against R'_j and R'_{i-}, respectively. We call these `small-joins` simply because they perform a small fraction of the join operation. The rule allows us to avoid the reexecution of (R_i^-, R_j^-), which, in typical cases, is the biggest portion of the total cost.

Note that the last two lines of the join rule suggests an efficient algorithm, namely performing the computation of $(R'_i, I_j) - (I_i, I_j)$ in one step. Some bookkeeping is required to ensure that no tuple of I_j gets joined with a tuple of I_i because this is already done in (I_i, R'_j). If this is not done, the joining tuples of I_i and I_j would be generated twice.

The selection, projection, and join update rules are applicable to all levels of ViewCaches. Thus, ViewCaches on ViewCaches are updated in exactly the same way.

2.3 The Physical Organization of ViewCache

The benefit of the ViewCache depends on the storage organization of TIDs. If a ViewCache is randomly organized, TID materialization can cause thrashing which could reduce or diminish the IAM's benefits. For this reason, we need some criterion for measuring the performance of the ViewCache. On a given system's buffer capacity, a ViewCache is *optimal* if, during its materialization, the same page of the underlying operand relation(s) is never read more than the minimum number of times required. Access is measured in terms of pages read from the files storing base relations and other views. Therefore, an optimal ViewCache implies minimum total I/O.

In this subsection, we discuss the problem of obtaining and maintaining optimal ViewCaches. We will also provide a physical organization that, under a random mix of insertions, deletions, and retrievals, dynamically maintains the ViewCache's performance.

Unary ViewCache Structure

Let V be a unary ViewCache derived from a base relation R_i occupying n_i pages. Further, let pageid be a function that maps a TID of a tuple of relation R_i to the page identifier PID of R_i storing that tuple, that is,

$$\text{PID} = \text{pageid}(R_i, \text{TID}).$$

The TIDs of V are partitioned into equivalence classes in which all TIDs have the same PID, i.e., each partition corresponds to a disk page of R_i. Figure 2 shows an example of the partitions of a unary ViewCache. Across the x-axis are the pages of $R_i, 1, 2, \ldots, n_i$. A * mark on the axis represents a partition that corresponds to a page of the deriving base relation R_i containing one or more tuples satisfying the definition of V. If a page of R_i does not have a *, then none of the tuples stored in this page are in the materialization of V. Thus, materialization of V skips all unmarked pages.

The partitions are grouped and stored into ViewCache disk pages in such a way that for any pair of ViewCache pages u and v for which u *precedes* v, $\text{pageid}(R_i, \text{TID}_i) \leq \text{pageid}(R_i, \text{TID}_j)$ for any $\text{TID}_i \in u$

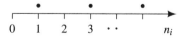

Figure 2

and $\text{TID}_j \in v$. Within the same ViewCache page, the partitions can be stored in any order. This *page-oriented* organization of the partitions of the ViewCache does not require that TIDs be totally ordered within the ViewCache page; they can be inserted in any vacant position of a ViewCache page as long as their partition is greater than or equal to the largest partition of the previous disk page and less than or equal to the smallest partition of the next disk page.

The above storage organization permits optimal materialization of all partitions using a single page buffer. If materialization exhausts all the partitions of each ViewCache page before it starts the next ViewCache page, it is guaranteed that no page from the underlying relation will ever be read more than once. Therefore, the unary ViewCache is optimal.

Binary ViewCache Structure

Optimal ViewCaches for binary views are more complex. Careful storage organization and appropriate sequencing for the materialization of binary ViewCaches is needed.

Let V be a binary ViewCache derived from two base relations R_i and R_j occupying n_i and n_j pages, respectively. The entries of V are now pairs of TIDs, $< \text{TID}_i, \text{TID}_j >$ which point to R_i and R_j, respectively [Rou82]. Let PID_i and PID_j be defined as

$$\text{PID}_i = \text{pageid}(R_i, \text{TID}_i)$$
$$\text{PID}_j = \text{pageid}(R_j, \text{TID}_j)$$

We partition the entries of V into groups of pairs having the same ordered pair, $< \text{PID}_i, \text{PID}_j >$. Figure 3 shows an example of the partitions of a binary ViewCache placed on a grid. The x- and y-axes correspond to the pages of relations R_i and R_j, respectively. A point on the grid with integer coordinates x, y represents a partition and is marked with a * if there is at least one tuple in page x of R_i that is joinable with a tuple in page y of R_i.

Materializing V is equivalent to *traversing* all marked points on the grid, fetching the disk pages of the operand relations that correspond to each partition and joining the tuples in them. Clearly, the smaller the number of partitions, the fewer the I/O accesses needed to materialize a join ViewCache. The materialization cost depends on the traversal sequence because intelligent utilization of the buffers may cause significant reduction in the number of disk page accesses.

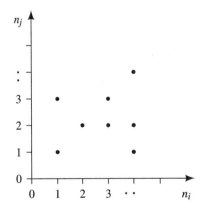

Figure 3

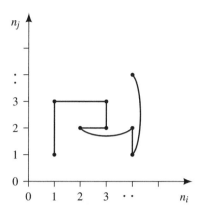

Figure 4

We define a cost function that measures the pages read for materializing a binary ViewCache. Assume a buffer capacity of b pages. The cache cost function for moving from a partition point P_1 to a different point P_2 on the grid (i.e., for materializing partition P_2 after P_1) is

$$C_b(P_1, P_2) = \begin{cases} 0 \text{ if both } \text{PID}_i \text{ and } \text{PID}_j \text{ of } P_2 \text{ are in the buffers} \\ 1 \text{ if one is in the buffers} \\ 2 \text{ otherwise} \end{cases}$$

The simplest cache cost model is obtained when b is two, one buffer for each relation. Then the cache cost function becomes

$$C_2(P_1, P_2) = \begin{cases} 1 \text{ if move is parallel to either axis} \\ 2 \text{ otherwise} \end{cases}$$

If a page corresponding to an axis is already buffered, moving parallel to the opposite axis causes the reading of a single page. This assumes that it costs the same to read the next or any other page along the same axis.

The optimal traversal problem is to find a path that visits all marked points at a minimal total cost C_2. The path can start from any point on the grid. There is a fixed overhead cost of two page accesses for every traversal to get to any starting point. Alternatively, we can think of the starting point being always the origin $(0, 0)$ because moving to any point would cost two units. Figure 4 shows an optimal traversal of all marked points of figure 3 with a cost of 9 reads. Clearly, this is optimal because there are no diagonal moves in this traversal—all moves incur the minimum cost of 1 page read.

It is shown in [AR88] that traversing the above graph in an optimal way is an *NP-complete* problem. Although only exponential algorithms are available for problems in the above class, for relatively static databases, one may be willing to pay the one time cost of finding an optimal traversal and using it every time the ViewCache is materialized. Further improvement for the static case can be obtained by clustering the tuples of both relations on the join attribute values. This will minimize the number of partitions and therefore the cost of the optimal (or suboptimal) traversal.

The number of partitions in a join is what determines the performance in any join algorithm that does not reorganize the underlying relations. The smaller the number the easier it is to compute the join using

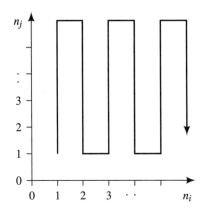

Figure 5

either the reexecution or the incremental method. This number gives a much better estimate on the cost than *join selectivities* [Yao79]. The importance of reducing the number of partitions can be seen from the high performance obtained by the *hash join* algorithm, which by reorganizing the underlying relations, minimizes the number of partitions. It also makes the *'s on the grid concentrate on and around the diagonal $x = y$, thus allowing a linear traversal of all the pages having joined tuples.

In this paper, since the Incremental Access Method is used for dynamic databases, the optimal traversal cost changes with updates. Therefore, recomputing and maintaining the optimal traversal would not be cost-effective. Instead, we group and store the partitions following the *Reverse Inner Nested Loop (RINL)* or the *Nested Loop (NL)* traversals illustrated in figures 5 and 7, respectively (similar nested loops are discussed in [Kim82]). The total ViewCache cost for the RINL and NL traversals on the grid of figure 3 are shown in figures 6 and 8, respectively. Coincidentally, the cost of both RINL and NL traversals is 11 page accesses. The ViewCache RINL or NL traversal reads pages along the x-axis once (and only those that have joining tuples). Therefore, a single buffer for the R_i relation suffices. Along the y-axis, the same page may be read more than once; therefore, we use the remaining buffer capacity $b - 1$ for R_j.[4]

We can now use the above model to bound the deviation of the RINL or NL traversal cost $C_{2\text{RINL/NL}}$ from the optimal one. Let $p_{y=0}$ be the number of distinct projected partition points on the x-axis. Also let C_2, be an optimal traversal cost and p_v be the total number of partitions in the ViewCache (total number of *s on the grid). Then, the following lemma holds.

Lemma: If $n_i \leq n_j$, then

$$C_{2\text{RINL/NL}} \leq C_{2_o} + p_{y=0} - 1.$$

Proof: The worst case for RINL or NL is when there is a diagonal cross for each of the points on $p_{y=0}$. This cost is

$$C_{2_w} = p_{y=0} + p_v.$$

Therefore,

$$C_{2\text{RINL/NL}} \leq C_{2_w} = p_{y=0} + p_v.$$

---

[4]Note that the NL traversal takes advantage of the caching done by the operating system due to reading of larger block sizes along the axes. For this reason, in the implementation of ADMS the NL traversal was used.

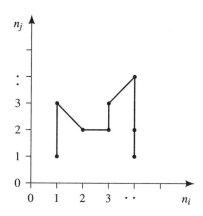

Figure 6

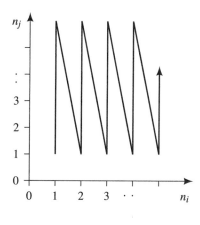

Figure 7

However, the optimal C_2, is no better than a traversal that makes no diagonal moves, i.e.,

$$1 + p_v \leq C_{2_o}.$$

Adding the above inequalities, we obtain the conclusion of the lemma. □

The above lemma gives an upper bound on the additional cost of $C_{2_{\mathrm{RINL/NL}}}$ compared to the optimal caching. Let l_j be the actual total number of distinct times the RINL/NL traversal reads a page of R_j. Then, the following is a corollary of Lemma 1.

Corollary:

$$C_{2_{\mathrm{RINL/NL}}} = p_{y=0} + l_j \leq C_{2_w} = p_{y=0} + p_v$$

or $l_j \leq p_v$ □

The corollary is the basis of the analysis and the comparisons of section 4.

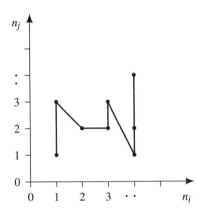

Figure 8

2.4 The Update Logs

As said earlier, updates to each base relation are made immediately, and they are recorded in the relation's update log. Updates propagated to a ViewCache are also recorded in that ViewCache's own update log. From these logs, the incremental update logs are extracted before processing a query.

The update log of a base relation R_i is itself a relation,

$$LR_i(\text{Update-type, PTR-}R_i),$$

where Update-type is set to one of $\{\text{insertion, deletion}\}$, and PTR-$R_i$ is the TID of the inserted/deleted tuple of the base relation R_i.

The update log of a ViewCache V is a relation

$$BV(\text{Update-type, PTR-}V,\ \text{PTR-}V'),$$

where Update-type is set to one of $\{\text{insertion, deletion, move}\}$, and PTR-$V$ is the TID of the inserted/ deleted/moved tuple of V. The move type is used for maintaining the physical structure of high level views, see section 2.5. PTR-V' is a pointer to an address that the PTR-V moved to as a result of a reorganization needed to maintain the ViewCache's organization as discussed in the previous subsections. Moving a tuple in the View Cache means simply that the tuple is still a qualified entry, but it is moved to avoid extra page faults during the materialization of a multilevel ViewCache.

The incremental update logs are processed before the incremental algorithms start. This preprocessing is required to discard any tuples that were first inserted and then deleted. Thus, deleted TIDs of unprocessed insertions are neutralized. In order to speed up the incremental update log preprocessing, the ADMS prototype uses a main memory hash table on the TIDs of the incremental logs.

The size of the update logs does not affect the IAM algorithms because only the increments of the logs are preprocessed. Each ViewCache keeps a pointer to the last log entry which was used to bring the ViewCache up-to-date on its previous update. The update logs are cleaned up when all ViewCaches dependent on them are brought up-to-date. At that time, the entire update log can be archived. Similarly, complete or partial update log cleanups can be carried out off-line by first updating all dependent ViewCaches.

The update cost of the ViewCaches is amortized among views that have common subexpressions, thus, distributing the cost of the incremental log preprocessing. This adds up to a significant performance factor for queries that are based on heavily used views.

2.5   Multi-Level ViewCache Structures

The results of the previous subsections and the improvements obtained by IAM are directly applicable to higher level (two and above) ViewCaches if one assumes that insertions and deletions in level one ViewCaches are random, as assumed to be the case for base relations. Multilevel ViewCaches are built by submitting queries against other views. Multilevel ViewCaches offer even higher performance gains than single level ones because, unlike query reexecution techniques, they do not have to generate and store intermediate results that correspond to subordinate views. This savings is cumulative, and scales up the performance improvement of multilevel ViewCaches compared to the reexecution strategy of query modification. The latter will have to pay a stiff penalty for writing, very often indexing, and reaccessing the intermediate results to process follow up steps.[5] On the contrary, ViewCache entries are very compact and materialization of only a few records are needed for the incremental update (see the second experiment of section 5).

In order to avoid thrashing between levels of multilevel ViewCaches and to achieve locality of pointer referencing, ViewCache pages, when necessary, are split and logically linked to accommodate the new entries caused by insertions to underlying relations or ViewCaches. The split algorithms may vary in sophistication depending on the desired load factor, the performance required, etc. In the ADMS prototype, the split algorithms used for the join ViewCaches are similar to those used in R+-trees [SRF87] and are not included in this paper. During a split, if any ViewCache entries have to be moved to another ViewCache page that logically follows the storage structure, the moves are recorded in the update log in order to propagate them down the ViewCache hierarchy. Note that such moves are inexpensive to handle during the preprocessing of the update log because a move at level k is not treated as an insertion at level $k + 1$; therefore, it does not need to be materialized and joined with the tuples of the other relation.

3   The IAM Algorithms

In this section, we describe the incremental selection and join algorithms. For completeness, we also include the reexecution algorithms.

We assume that secondary indexes are organized as B-trees, although hashing and other indexing methods can be used. The B-tree has an occurrence file that stores all the TIDs that have the same key value. If the indexed attribute is a key, all key values are unique and, therefore, no occurrence file is necessary. To simplify the description of the algorithms, we chose a minimal buffer capacity, one page per base relation or view. Extending the algorithms for higher buffering is straightforward.

The following two queries are assumed in the description of the algorithms:

---

[5]We obtained similar savings by eliminating intermediate results in a Pipelined Distributed N-way Join algorithm.

A: Range Selection
    select   *
    from R_j
    where $val_1 \leq attr_j \leq val_2$

B: Simple Join
    select   *
    from R_i, R_j
    where $attr_i = attr_j$

We assume that there is a B-tree B_j on non-key attribute $attr_j$ of R_j.

Reexecution Loop (RL) Selection

1. For each page r_j of R_j, do `small-select` (r_j).

Reexecution Indexed (RI) Selection

1. Traverse down B_j to reach the smallest value val_1 or the smallest value that covers it.

2. Follow the b_j leaf pages until val_2 is reached and for each leaf entry pointing to a page p in the occurrence file read(p); for each PID = pageid(R_j, TID), read(PID) and display the tuples pointed to by the TIDs in p.

2′ (Alternatively, when most of the occurrence TIDs fit in main memory 2 is replaced by 2′.)
   Separate the occurrence page reads from those of the base relation in step 2. First, traverse all the leaf pages, collect all the TIDs of R_j over the whole range, sort them, and then access the base relation pages. This would require additional I/O if the TIDs do not all fit in main memory, but it would avoid reading the same page more than once.

Incremental Unindexed (IU) Selection

The incremental unary rule needs no indexing to update the view.

1. DO a small-select on the I_j-log and display the qualifying tuples. Save the TIDs of those qualifying tuples.

2. Read each page r_v of the ViewCache.

3. Apply all deletions relevant to R_v.

4. For each partition P in r_v, fetch the corresponding R_j page and display the tuples having their TIDs in P.

5. Insert those TIDs saved from step 1 that belong to any partition that is smaller than the last partition of r_v and greater than the last partition of the previous ViewCache page. If there is no room, then split r_v into two logically connected pages. Read the next ViewCache page r_v and go to step 3.

Reexecution Sort-Merge (RSM) Join

1. Sort R_i and R_j.

2. Merge the sorted relations to generate the join.

Reexecution Nested Loop (RNL) Join

1. For each page r_i of R_i, do `small-join`(r_i, R_j).

Reexecution Indexed Loop (RIL) Join

1. For each page r_i of R_i and for each *val* of the joining attribute found in r_i, find all pages P_j of R_j pointed by an occurrence of the *val* in B_j; do `small-join`(r_i, P_j).

Note that the `small-joins` can minimize page accesses to R_j by collecting all the TIDs from the occurrence file of the B-tree first, and sorting them before accessing R_j. This avoids accessing any R_j page more than once.

Incremental Nested Loop (INL) Join

Let I_i and I_j be the incremental insertion logs of R_i and R_j, respectively.

1. Do `small-join`(R_i, I_j) and save the TID pairs of the joining tuples to be inserted in the ViewCache. Do `small-join`(R_j, I_i) and save the TID pairs of the joining tuples to be inserted in the ViewCache.

2. Read the first ViewCache page, say r_v:

3. Apply all deletions relevant to all partitions stored in r_v;

4. Materialize one by one the partitions following the RINL or NL order;

5. Insert those TID pairs saved from step 1 in r_v if they belong to any partition that is smaller than the last partition of r_v and greater than the last partition of the previous view page. If there is no room, then split r_v into two logically connected pages.

6. Read the next ViewCache page r_v and go to step 2.1.

The above algorithm is two-pass. We can make it one-pass by combining steps 1 and 2, and moving the `small-joins` inside the materialization loop. This is illustrated in the following incremental algorithm in which the first `small-join` is moved inside the loop that starts at step 3.2, while the second is moved outside and uses the B-tree to avoid the loop.

Incremental Indexed Loop (IIL) Join

1. For each page r_i of I_i and for each *val* of the joining attribute found in r_i, find all pages P_j of R_j pointed by an occurrence of the *val* in B_j; do `small-join`(r_i, P_j).

2. /* This step takes care of deletions */

3. Read the first ViewCache page r_v. Let $R_{i_{min}}$ and $R_{i_{max}}$, respectively, be the smallest and largest pages of R_i appearing in a partition of r_v.

4. Apply all deletions relevant to all partitions stored in r_v.

5. /* This step does the incremental joins with the insertions */

6. Read the page $R_{i_{min}}$. Let r_i be $R_{i_{min}}$.

7. small-join(r_i, I_j) and save the TID pairs of the joining tuples.

8. For each r_j of R_j that appears in a partition of r_v, materialize all tuples of partition $< r_i, r_j >$

9. If the last partition in r_v is reached, insert those RID pairs saved from step 1 and 3.2 in r_v if they belong to any partition that is smaller than the last partition of r_v and greater than the last partition of the previous view page. If there is no room, then split r_v into two logically connected pages.

10. Read the next page r_i of R_i that is less than or equal to $R_{i_{max}}$; go to step 3.2.

11. Read the next ViewCache page, r_v; go to step 2.

Incremental Doubly Indexed (IDI) Join

The incremental algorithm can further benefit from a second secondary index B_i on $attr_i$ of R_i. The second index allows us to move the small-join of the previous algorithm outside the loop that starts at 3.2. What remains inside the loop is the processing of deletions and the materialization of the TIDs. Because the changes are straightforward, we have omitted the detailed algorithm description.

We are not aware of any reexecution nested loop join algorithm that effectively uses both secondary indexes on the joining attribute.

4   The IAM Cost Model

The cost model used in this paper is a standard I/O based model. The only important difference with previous ones, such as [Yao79], is that the IAM has accurate information on the number of partitions in the ViewCache. This is not easily attainable in the classical reexecution methods in which analysis and optimization depends on rough estimates, statistics, and the uniformity assumption.

4.1   Model Assumptions

Selecting the best join method is not the subject of this paper. We only compare the incremental approach with established reexecution methods for joins. In the analysis of this section, we assume that the tuples of base relations are randomly placed in the pages, and that the relation cardinalities are large enough to warrant savings by optimization. We also assume that the number of updates does not affect the order of magnitude of the relations and/or views. In other words, the relation sizes do not significantly increase or decrease after updates. This size invariant assumption implies that the cost of reexecuting a query is roughly the same every time. Finally, we assume that the cost of reading the incremental update log, consisting of TIDs of inserted and deleted tuples, is not significant.[6]

---

[6]For a base relation, each entry of its update log is one word for the TID and two bits for the type. Therefore, even for a large number of entries in the incremental update log, the I/O cost is negligible.

4.2 Cost Parameters

The following parameters are used in the cost analysis of the algorithms of the previous subsections.

Parameter	Explanation
N_i	cardinality of base relation R_i
n_i	number of disk pages occupied by R_i
n_v	number of disk pages occupied by ViewCache V
p_v	number of partitions in V
l_j	actual number of distinct times RINL/NL traversal reads pages of R_j
s_j	the selectivity of an attribute, defined as one over the number of distinct values of the attribute
h_j	height of the B-tree B_j defined as a secondary index on an attribute of R_j
t_j	number of leaf-page accesses in a B-tree to satisfy the condition $val_1 \leq attr_j \leq val_2$
b_j	average number of accesses to the occurrence file of a B-tree leaf entry containing a value val to retrieve the TIDs of all qualifying tuples
j_i	average number of distinct values of the join attribute of R_i per page
$K_i = n_i j_i$	total number of times the secondary index has to be accessed to generate the TIDs of all joinable tuples of R_i
I_i	number of insertions stored in the I_i-log of R_i

4.3 Comparison of the Reexecution and Incremental Algorithms

This section compares the reexecution and incremental algorithms and derives the conditions under which incremental execution is cost-effective, that is, $C_{R*} - C_{I*} \geq 0$. The cost-effectiveness conditions are based on the following cost parameters: n_i, n_v, p_v, I_i, and h_j. All of these are dynamically maintained and provide accurate information. In spite of their dynamic nature, they require inexpensive bookkeeping because the number of pages occupied by the relations and the ViewCaches, as well as the height of the B-tree, are all readily available in any implementation. The number of partitions p_v of a ViewCache is computed during the creation of the ViewCache and stored in the directory along with other information. On updates that insert new partitions or delete old ones, the number is updated accordingly. For the decision criteria, the value of p_v prior to the update is needed. At the end of each incremental update p_v is updated for a later query, and this cost is part of the incremental update of the ViewCache. The cost of the reading of the incremental update log to obtain I_i is also insignificant due to the small size of the log entries.

The cost of each of the algorithms is given in terms of I/O, that is, the total number of page reads and writes. In all the incremental algorithms, we assume the worst case of reading and writing the entire ViewCache, that is $2n_v$ pages. As a consequence, the cost of deletions, which require no access to the data values of any tuple, is subsumed by the writing of the modified pages. Furthermore, our analysis is a worst case analysis for the IAM, and thus the obtained conditions are very conservative. In the experiments, we were able to stretch the incremental algorithm thresholds much farther than those suggested by the analysis.

First, we compare the incremental with the reexecution selection algorithms. Then, we compare the most comparable join algorithms. The join algorithms that are compared are illustrated in table 1. An X in the table indicates that the join algorithms of the corresponding row and column are compared.

Reexecution → Incremental ↓	Sort-Merge RSM	Nested-Loop RNL	Indexed-Loop RIL
Nested-Loop INL	X	X	
Indexed-Loop IIL			X
Doubly-Indexed IDI			X

Table 1 Compared Reexecution and Incremental Join Algorithms

Unindexed Selection

$$C_{RL} = n_j$$
$$C_{IU} = 2n_v + p_v$$

where p_v is the number of partitions in the view.

Comparison:

$$C_{RL} - C_{IU} = n_j - 2n_v - p_v \geq 0$$

if $n_v \leq \frac{n_j - p_v}{2}$

Note that in most typical situations, p_v is much smaller than n_j, i.e. tuples satisfying the view do not span all base relation pages. If, on the other hand, the above inequality does not hold during the creation of the view, then no ViewCache is saved.

Indexed Selection

$$C_{RI} = h_j + t_j + b_j(val_2 - val_1 + 1) + L_j$$

where L_j is the cost to access all the pages of R_j containing the qualifying tuples.

Comparison: As shown in the following analysis, incremental selection is unconditionally better than reexecution and cannot further benefit from an index. For this reason we compare the RI with the IU algorithm.

$$C_{RI} - C_{IU} = h_j + t_j + b_j(val_2 - val_1 + 1) + L_j - 2n_v - p_v$$

The following are true:

$$t_j \geq 0$$

and

$$b_j(val_2 - val_1 + 1) \geq n_v$$

because the ViewCache contains only qualifying TIDs which makes it more compact than the occurrence file of the secondary index of R_j that holds pointers for all the values of the attribute. Equality is attained in the above when the occurrence file of the index is clustered. Typically, L_j is much larger than p_v unless the relation is kept sorted (a very expensive assumption). Though we assume that L_j is equal to p_v, $C_{RI} - C_{IU}$ is non-negative if

$$h_j \geq n_v.$$

The above is true for relatively small views.[7] For larger views where $n_v > h_j$, L_j, which has exactly the same pointers as the ViewCache, would have to be sorted first before being materialized to achieve the minimum p_v reads of the IAM. Thus, the cost of materializing from L_j becomes

$$L_j = n_v \log n_v + p_v$$

and therefore

$$C_{RI} - C_{IU} \geq h_j + n_v \log n_v - n_v \geq 0$$

The above implies that, for either small or large views, the incremental cost is unconditionally better than the best case of reexecution.

Unindexed Joins

$$C_{RSM} = 2n_i \log n_i + 2n_j \log n_j + n_i + n_j$$

The 2's are for writing the intermediate results.

$$C_{RNL} = n_i n_j$$
$$C_{INL} = n_i + n_j + l_j + 2n_v$$

where n_i and n_j page reads are required for the `small-joins`. The n_j pages can be saved if no insertions on R_i have been made. But even when this is not the case, a portion of the n_j is subsumed by the l_j in the one-pass algorithm.

Comparison:

$$C_{RSM} - C_{INL} = 2n_i \log n_i + 2n_j \log n_j + n_i + n_j - n_i - n_j - l_j - 2n_v \geq 0$$

Because $l_j \leq p_v$, the above is true if

$$n_v + \frac{p_v}{2} \leq n_i \log n_i + n_j \log n_j$$

Comparison:

$$C_{RNL} - C_{INL} = n_i n_j - n_i - n_j - l_j - 2n_v \geq 0$$

Because $l_j \leq p_v$, the above is true if

$$n_i n_j - n_i - n_j - p_v - 2n_v \geq 0$$

or if

$$n_v + \frac{p_v}{2} \leq \frac{n_i n_j - n_i - n_j}{2}$$

This clearly indicates that the number of partitions is very important for the incremental case. In the extreme case of $p_v = n_i n_j$, i.e., when all possible partitions are present in the ViewCache, then the incremental nested loop will not be cost effective.[8]

---

[7] In our ADMS prototype, a unary ViewCache page can hold up to 1,000 TIDs and a binary one up to 500 pairs of TIDs. Therefore a unary ViewCache derived from a relation whose B-tree height is either 3 or 4 can hold somewhere between 3,000 and 4,000 entries and still satisfy $n_v \leq h_j$.

[8] This may still be cost-effective for a different cost model that takes into account CPU cost because the IAM requires less computation.

Indexed Joins

$$C_{RIL} = n_i + K_i(h_j + s_j b_j) + L_j = n_i + n_i j_i(h_j + s_j b_j) + L_j$$

where L_j is the total number of R_j page accesses needed to generate the join tuples from the occurrence file of the secondary index. L_j could be as bad as the number of tuples in the join.

$$C_{IIL} = n_i + I_i(h_j + s_j b_j) + l_j + 2n_v$$

where l_j is the total number of R_j page accesses needed to generate the unaffected and new join tuples of the view V.

$$C_{IDI} = I_i(h_j + s_j b_j) + I_j(h_i + s_i b_i) + l_i + l_j + 2n_v$$

Comparison:

$$C_{RIL} - C_{IIL} = n_i + K_i(h_j + s_n b_j) + L_j - n_i - I_i(h_j + s_j b_j) - l_j - 2n_v \geq 0.$$

The above is true if

$$I_i \leq K_i + \frac{L_j - l_j - 2n_v}{h_j + s_j b_j}$$

If we assume that $L_j = l_j$ (this is achieved if we sort the occurrence file entries before reading R_j pages), then the above is true if

$$I_i \leq K_i - \frac{2n_v}{h_j + s_j b_j} = n_i j_i - \frac{2n_v}{h_j + s_j b_j}$$

Although j_i is an estimate, $j_i \geq l$, (typical values are a lot higher[9]), even with its lowest possible value, it provides a good upper bound on I_i:

$$I_i \leq n_i - \frac{2n_v}{h_j}$$

In this case, the criterion for deciding whether or not the incremental algorithm is cost-effective is based on the number of insertions in the incremental update log.

Comparison:

$$C_{RIL} - C_{IDI} = n_i + K_i(h_j + s_j b_j) + L_j - I_i(h_j + s_j b_j) - I_j(h_i + s_i b_i) - l_i - l_j - 2n_v \geq 0$$

The best case for the reexecution algorithm is when it scans the smaller relation and uses the secondary index to access the larger. If we assume that R_j is the larger, then $h_j \geq h_i$ is true. It is also true that $l_i \leq n_i$ because the RINL traversal visits R_i pages at most once. Then, the above inequality is true if

$$I_i(h_j + s_j b_j) + I_j(h_i + s_i b_i) \leq n_i + K_i(h_j + s_j b_j) + L_j - n_i - l_j - 2n_v \geq 0$$

or if

$$I_i + f I_j \leq K_i + \frac{L_j - l_j - 2n_v}{h_j + s_j b_j}$$

where $0 < f < 1$. Or if

$$I_i + f I_j \leq K_i - \frac{2n_v}{h_j + 1} = n_i j_j - \frac{2n_v}{h_j}$$

Once again, the cost-effectiveness criterion is based on the number of insertions in the incremental update log.

---

[9]In the Wisconsin Benchmark database with 4KB pages the value is about 16, while in the experiments discussed in the next section the value is about 32.

5 ADMS Implementation and Experiments

The current implementation of ADMS, [Rou87], runs a version of ViewCache and some of the incremental algorithms. ADMS runs on VAXes, SUNs, and other machines under Unix. The experiments described in this section were performed on a Sun 3/280. They compare the reexecution indexed loop join algorithm with the corresponding incremental one. Both alorithms use a single B-tree as a secondary index. The experiments consisted of mixed complexity queries run several times against the database, shown in figure 9. Figure 10 shows the modifications used in this experiment. Each modification to the "usage" relation is equivalent to one deletion and one insertion. The modified attribute values were distributed and applied to attributes that do not affect the cardinalities of the relations and the selectivities of the selection and

$$\begin{array}{ll} \text{user(uname,accno,rank)} & N_{user} = 310 \\ \text{usage(uname,pname,time,date)} & N_{usage} = 6,002 \\ \text{program(pname,directory,size,rate)} & N_{program} = 650 \end{array}$$

q1: **create ViewCache** med,med1 **as**
    select   uname,pname
    from   usage
    and   '200' $\leq$ usage.time $\leq$ '300'

q2: **create ViewCache** usage.program **as**
    select   uname,pname,directory
    from   usage,program
    and   usage.pname = program.pname

q3: **create ViewCache** user.med **as**
    select   uname,rank,time
    from   user,med1
    and   user.uname = med1.uname

q4: **create ViewCache** very_long_users **as**
    select   user.uname,program.pname
    from   usage,user,program
    where   user.uname = usage.uname
    and   usage.pname = program.pname
    and   usage.time $\geq$ '450'

q5: **create ViewCache** long_high_rank_users **as**
    select   uname
    from   usage,user,program
    where   user.uname = usage.uname
    and   usage.pname = program.pname
    and   usage.time $\geq$ '400'
    and   user.rank $\geq$ '7'

Figure 9 Database and queries of the experiment.

/* 4% Increment: (119 modifications) */

modify date **to** '119' **in** usage **where** time ≥ '10' **and** time ≤ time '12'
modify date **to** '119' **in** usage **where** time ≥ '210' **and** time ≤ time '211'
modify date **to** '119' **in** usage **where** time ≥ '310' **and** time ≤ time '312'
modify date **to** '119' **in** usage **where** time ≥ '410' **and** time ≤ time '411'

/* 10% Increment: (305 modifications) */

modify date **to** '305' **in** usage **where** time ≥ '60' **and** time ≤ time '65'
modify date **to** '305' **in** usage **where** time ≥ '260' **and** time ≤ time '265'
modify date **to** '305' **in** usage **where** time ≥ '360' **and** time ≤ time '365'
modify date **to** '305' **in** usage **where** time ≥ '460' **and** time ≤ time '465'

/* 25% Increment: (736 modifications) */

modify date **to** '736' **in** usage **where** time ≥ '30' **and** time ≤ time '44'
modify date **to** '736' **in** usage **where** time ≥ '230' **and** time ≤ time '244'
modify date **to** '736' **in** usage **where** time ≥ '330' **and** time ≤ time '344'
modify date **to** '736' **in** usage **where** time ≥ '430' **and** time ≤ time '443'

Figure 10   Modifications used in the experiment.

join attributes. Queries and modifications were run individually to avoid uneven penalization due to any start up overhead cost.

Note that the values of the selection predicates and the join atttributes were purposely chosen such that the paths were independent of each other. This took away from the IAM the amortization benefits of the subsumed shared subpaths. By replacing "med1" by "med" in q3 and by using the ViewCache "usage.program" of q2 in queries q4 and q5, the update cost of these intermediate ViewCaches is amortized. However, we felt that this would make it an unfair comparison for a reexecution method that cannot benefit from subsumption. Subsumption of the IAM and the benefits obtained by the ViewCache will be fully documented in a forthcoming paper.

Table 2 compares the I/O and CPU cost required for the incremental materialization of the ViewCaches with the reexecution method. In both cases, the results are written into a file. I/O cost is measured in terms of total system "reads" and "writes" obtained by the Unix "profile" utility. The CPU is obtained by the "time" utility of Unix. The column Selects/Joins stores the number of selection and join operators in each of the five queries. The Size of the operands column shows the cardinality of the underlying base relations and intermediate ViewCaches. The "Approximate Size of Increment" column stores the percent value of the incremental update log over the total number of tuples in the base relations. Zero percent increment means that the incremental update log is empty (nothing has been changed); therefore, the ViewCaches used in the queries are up-to-date. 4% corresponds to 119 deletions and 118 insertions. Finally, 25% corresponds to 736 deletions and 736 insertions.

The ratio column for the I/O shows that IAM saves at least 69% of the I/O required by the reexecution method. The CPU time is always better for the incremental except for the last case of q1. The CPU

ADMS TODS Experiment 10/7/89

Print the records of the result into a file   SUN 3/280

Query	Selects/ Joins	Aprx Size of Oprnds	Size of Result	Aprx size of incrment	READS & WRITES			CPU TIME		
					Incr	Re-ex	Ratio	Incr	Re-ex	Ratio
q1	1-0	6002	1233	0%	263	1317	20%	0.86	1.48	58%
				4%	259	1276	20%	1.10	1.36	81%
				10%	265	1226	22%	1.22	1.24	98%
				25%	276	1090	25%	1.46	1.24	118%
q2	0-1	6002, 650	6421	0%	399	5040	8%	4.80	6.74	71%
				4%	433	5109	8%	5.54	6.84	81%
				9%	418	5230	8%	6.06	7.02	86%
				22%	455	5703	8%	7.06	7.34	96%
q3	1-1	6002, 12d33 ,310	1258	0%	291	1812	16%	1.32	48.14	3%
				3%	331	1795	18%	1.86	47.94	4%
				9%	339	1745	19%	2.22	48.12	5%
				21%	359	1590	23%	2.84	47.90	6%
q4	1-2	6002, 650, 665, 711, 310	723	0%	374	1855	20%	1.18	88.96	1%
				3%	386	1754	22%	1.44	88.84	2%
				9%	514	1653	31%	2.56	67.36	4%
				21%	407	1854	22%	1.86	89.00	2%
q5	2-2	6002, 1299 310, 96, 260, 650	281	0%	130	2237	6%	0.34	45.42	1%
				3%	203	2213	9%	1.52	45.56	3%
				9%	214	2165	10%	1.64	45.46	4%
				21%	251	2098	12%	2.22	45.66	5%

Table 2   Comparing Incremental and Reexecution Methods—print

time for higher level ViewCaches is significantly better than reexecution because the time for processing intermediate results is spared by the ViewCache.

Table 3 shows a similar experiment for counting the results of the above queries.[10] In this experiment, the tuples of the ViewCaches do not have to be materialized, but counting invokes the IAM algorithms to update these and all underlying ViewCaches. For the reexecution method, we measured the time to construct and count, but not save the result. Clearly, the effectiveness of the IAM becomes more apparent in this case, because it updates the ViewCache with only a bare minimum of I/O. The main reason for including this experiment is because it illustrates the cumulative gains of the IAM on high level ViewCaches. Selective or exhaustive materialization from such a ViewCache requires an update on all underlying ViewCaches in a fashion that is identical to the count command, namely without manipulating much of the actual data records. Only those tuples required to do the small-selects and small-joins are materialized.

In the second experiment the incremental algorithms save more than 85% of the I/O cost. The CPU time savings for queries that involve at least one join is higher than 50%. And for high level ViewCaches, the CPU savings is higher than 90%.

---

[10]The "Wisconsin Benchmark" [BDT83] measured a similar construction cost.

ADMS TODS Experiment 10/7/89

Count the records of the result   SUN 3/280

Query	Selects/ Joins	Aprx Size of Oprnds	Size of Result	Aprx size of incrment	READS & WRITES			CPU TIME		
					Incr	Re-ex	Ratio	Incr	Re-ex	Ratio
q1	1-0	6002	1233	0%	86	1281	7%	0.14	1.48	9%
				4%	83	1250	7%	0.62	1.36	46%
				10%	129	1200	11%	0.78	1.24	63%
				25%	105	1058	10%	1.04	1.24	84%
q2	0-1	6002, 650	6421	0%	71	4486	2%	0.18	6.68	3%
				4%	138	5057	3%	2.40	6.76	36%
				9%	145	5178	3%	2.70	6.88	39%
				22%	163	5652	3%	3.52	7.20	49%
q3	1-1	6002, 12d33 ,310	1258	0%	87	1768	5%	0.16	48.14	0%
				3%	132	1751	8%	1.20	47.94	3%
				9%	150	1701	9%	1.40	48.12	3%
				21%	163	1547	11%	2.06	47.90	4%
q4	1-2	6002, 650, 665, 711, 310	723	0%	91	1785	5%	0.26	88.96	0%
				3%	128	1734	7%	0.64	88.84	1%
				9%	247	1634	15%	1.82	67.36	3%
				21%	149	1784	8%	1.10	89.00	1%
q5	2-2	6002, 1299 310, 96, 260, 650	281	0%	322	2317	14%	0.86	45.42	2%
				3%	376	2293	16%	1.72	45.56	4%
				9%	383	2245	17%	2.04	45.46	4%
				21%	415	2178	19%	2.56	45.66	6%

Table 3   Comparing Incremental and Reexecution Methods—count

6   Conclusions

We presented an Incremental Access Method for efficient access to views. This method capitalizes on the ViewCache, an efficient pointer structure for storing precomputed access paths that can be incrementally updated and materialized in a cost-effective way. This paper concentrated on defining criteria for deciding whether or not incremental access from ViewCaches is cost-effective. We showed that under some prevailing conditions the IAM performance is significantly better than query reexecution. Exceptionally good performance is obtained for complex queries because the IAM avoids the explicit generation and manipulation of intermediate results. The experiments verified the incremental approach.

The IAM is accompanied by several update propagation strategies. These can be used to tune the performance of the IAM for different classes of ViewCaches dependent on application needs.

The ViewCache structure efficiently simulates database *navigation* by allowing application programs to walk through it a-record-at-a-time. The locality of the interlevel pointers and the buffer management that keeps one or more page buffers per underlying base relation and ViewCache makes the per view tuple cost equal whether one navigates through a ViewCache a-record-at-a-time or extracts all the tuples in one step. It remains to be seen whether the ViewCache with its IAM can achieve the high performance of network and hierarchical systems while offering the simplicity of interface and the dynamic features of relational ones.

Incremental access methods for databases demonstrate that there is a class of problems that can benefit from incremental computation by capitalizing on the unaffected portion of repetitive computations. It is our strong belief that classic optimization techniques based on reexecution models have reached a saturation point, and that a fresh approach is needed for obtaining substantial performance improvement. Incremental computation models provide a novel paradigm that promises high performance and should be further explored.

7   Acknowledgments

I would like to thank a number of students whio contributed to the ideas of this paper and helped in making these ideas a reality in the ADMS project. Among those are Huyanchul Kang, Jim O'Connor, Anthony Stamenas, Young Choi, Christian Bader, Maria Salazar, Hyun Soon Kim, Young Kang, and Nickos Economou. I would also like to thank my colleague Timos Sellis for his valuable comments.

A PERFORMANCE ANALYSIS OF VIEW MATERIALIZATION STRATEGIES[1]

Eric N. Hanson

1 Introduction

A materialized view is a stored copy of the result of retrieving the view from the database. In this paper, the types of materialized views considered are those that could be defined using SELECT, PROJECT, and JOIN, and also simple aggregates such as sum or count over the result of such expressions.

Conventional systems do not materialize views in advance, but rather use query modification to turn a query referring to a view into one on the base relations [Sto75]. An alternate method for materializing views which updates the copy of the view after each transaction [BLT86] will be called immediate view maintenance or simply immediate in this paper. A related differential view update algorithm is described in [HT86]. Another more restricted view maintenance algorithm generates and periodically refreshes database snapshots, which are copies of views consisting of selections and projections of a single base table [AL80, LHM+86]. In the context of evaluating complex trigger and alerter conditions, Buneman and Clemons presented a method for analyzing each update command prior to execution to see whether it could cause a view to change [BC79]. If the system could not rule out the possibility that the command might alter the state of the view, the view would be completely recomputed. Hence, this represents another view refresh algorithm. Lastly, this paper presents a final alternative, called deferred view maintenance, or deferred, that incrementally updates a materialized view just before data is retrieved from it. This algorithm was also proposed by Roussopoulos as a method for materializing copies of views on workstations attached to a mainframe [RK86a]. In that scheme, the mainframe maintains a shared global database, and workstations update local copies of views when they process queries.

An important way to improve the performance of view materialization algorithms is to use a screening algorithm to test each tuple inserted into or deleted from the base relations. If a tuple passes the screening test, then its insertion or deletion may cause the state of the view to change, so the tuple must be used to try to update the view. If the tuple fails the screening test then it cannot cause the view to change, so it does not need to be used to refresh the view. In the scheme described in [BLT86] screening is done by substituting a tuple into a view predicate, which is then tested to see if it is still satisfiable. If so, the tuple passes the screening test, otherwise it fails. This test is performed for every tuple inserted into a relation, incurring a significant CPU cost.

The screening test proposed in [BC79] has a compile-time phase and a run-time phase. In the first phase, when the command for a transaction is compiled, the system checks to see whether any fields the command proposes to update are read by the view definition. If no such fields are updated then the command is

---

[1]This search was sponsored by the National Science Foundation under Grant DMC-6504633 and by the Navy Electronics Systems Command under contract N00039-54-C-0039.

called a readily ignorable update (RIU) with respect to view. If a command is an RIU, it cannot cause the view to change. In the second phase, if the command is not an RIU, the individual tuples updated are screened further at run time. If a command is an RIU, there is only a per-transaction cost associated with this screening test. If it is not an RIU, then there is a per-tuple cost, similar the screening test of [BLT86].

An alternative test that will usually be more efficient than the two just described is to apply the rule wake-up scheme in [SSH86] to the screening problem. Using this mechanism, called rule indexing the index intervals covered by one or more clauses of the view predicate are locked using special markers called trigger-locks or t-locks. When a tuple is inserted into the relation, if an index record containing a t-lock is disturbed, then the tuple passes the screening test. Otherwise, the tuple fails the test implicitly. Since this screening test can produce "false drops" (i.e. tuples which pass the screening test but do not satisfy the view predicate), a second stage screening test, substituting the tuple into the view predicate, is required. This strategy is assumed for both immediate and deferred view maintenance in the performance analysis of this paper.

To provide the background necessary for the performance analysis, Section 2 reviews the immediate view maintenance algorithm and describes the proposed deferred view maintenance scheme in detail. In Section 3, cost formulas for each of the algorithms are derived for three different view models:

1. selection-projection views

2. two-way natural join views

3. aggregates over selection-projection views

The performance of the algorithms is compared for each model. Finally, Section 4 presents conclusions, and suggests directions for future research.

2   View Materialization Strategies

In this section, the algorithm for incrementally updating materialized views after each update transaction is described briefly (see [BLT86] for a complete discussion). The proposed variant of this algorithm to allow deferred view maintenance is then presented. Also, a brief discussion of query modification is given.

The differential view update algorithm (i.e. immediate view maintenance) operates on the following sets of tuples:

$R_1, R_2, \ldots R_N$ the N base relations
$A_1, A_2, \ldots A_N$ the N sets of tuples inserted into the base relations by the current transaction
$D_1, D_2, \ldots D_N$ the N sets of tuples deleted from the base relations by the current transaction

The sets $A_1 \ldots A_N$ and $D_1 \ldots D_N$ must contain the net changes to the database made by one transaction. Hence:

$$A_i \cap D_i = \phi$$
$$A_i \cap R_i = \phi \qquad \text{for } 1 \leq i \leq N$$
$$D_i \subseteq R_i$$

The definition of a view V can be represented by a select-project-cross-product expression as follows, where $sigma_X$ represents selection based on a predicate X, π_g represents projection of the set of attributes Y, and $\times$ represents cross-product.

$$V = \pi_\gamma(\sigma_X(R_1 \times R_2 \times \cdots \times R_N))$$

Consider an example with two relations, $R_1(a, b)$ and $R_2(b, c)$, and a view V defined as follows, where $Y = \{a, c\}$ and $X = (R_1.a = 5$ and $R_1.b = R_2.b)$:

$$V = \pi_\gamma(\sigma_X(R_1 \times R_2))$$

The following expression shows the subsequent value of V, V_1, after an append only transaction updating both R_1 and R_2.

$$V_1 = \pi_\gamma(\sigma_X((R_1 \cup A_1) \times (R_2 \cup A_2)))$$

Selection and projection both distribute over union, so the above expression simplifies as follows:

$$\begin{aligned}
V_1 &= \pi_\gamma(\sigma_X(R_1 \times R_2 \cup A_1 \times R_2 \cup R_1 \times A_2 \cup A_1 \times A_2)) \\
&= \pi_\gamma(\sigma_X(R_1 \times R_2)) \cup \pi_\gamma(\sigma_X(A_1 \times R_2)) \\
&\quad \cup \pi_\gamma(\sigma_X(R_1 \times A_2)) \cup \pi_\gamma(\sigma_X(A_1 \times A_2)) \\
&= V_0 \cup \pi_\gamma(\sigma_X(A_1 \times R_2)) \cup \pi_\gamma(\sigma_X(R_1 \times A_2)) \\
&\quad \cup \pi_\gamma(\sigma_X(A_1 \times A_2))
\end{aligned}$$

This algebraic simplification shows that V can be refreshed by computing the value of the last three expressions shown above, and then unioning the results to the stored copy of V (V_0). In practice, the query optimizer can be used to find the most efficient method available for computing these subexpressions [SALP79]. Since all the subexpressions are computed at the same time, performance advantages can be gained by optimizing them together. The techniques described in [Sel86] can be applied to this problem.

If deletions as well as insert recognitions occur in transactions, the differential update algorithm becomes slightly more complicated. One problem is that tuples in V may have been contributed by more than one source, since the projection operation can map multiple input tuples to the same value. If it appears that a tuple should be deleted from V, but V is stored with duplicates removed, it is impossible to decide what action to take without totally recomputing V from the base relations. To overcome this difficulty without wasting disk space by physically storing duplicates, each tuple in V must contain a *duplicate count* indicating how many potential sources could have contributed the tuple. With the duplicate count, when a tuple is inserted into V, if an identical value is already stored, then its duplicate count is incremented. Otherwise, the tuple is inserted with a duplicate count of 1. Similarly, the duplicate count of the stored value is decremented on tuple deletion. If the count becomes 0, the tuple is physically removed from V.

Extending the previous example, consider a transaction that inserts *and* deletes tuples from both R_1 and R_2. The new version of the view V_1, is thus represented as follows:

$$V_1 = \pi_\gamma(\sigma_X(((R_1 - D_1) \cup A_1) \times ((R_2 - D_2) \cup A_2)))$$

Using

$$\begin{aligned}
R_1' &= (R_1 - D_1) \\
R_2' &= (R_2 - D_2)
\end{aligned}$$

the above can be rewritten as simply

$$V_1 = \pi_\gamma(\sigma_X((R_1 i' \cup A_1) \times (R_2' \cup A_2)))$$

Multiplying out this expression yields

$$V_1 = \pi_\gamma(\sigma_X(R_1' \times R_2' \cup R_1' \times A_2 \cup A_1 \times R_2' \cup A_1 \times A_2))$$

Expanding the $R_1' \times R_2'$ term of the above gives the following (the remaining terms are indicated by ellipses):

$$\begin{aligned}
V_1 &= \pi_\gamma(\sigma_X((R_1 - D_1) \times (R_2 - D_2) \cup \cdots)) \\
&= \pi_\gamma(\sigma_X(R_1 \times (R_2 - D_2) - D_1 \times (R_2 - D_2) \cup \cdots)) \\
&= \pi_\gamma(\sigma_X(R_1 \times R_2 - R_1 \times D_2 - D_1 \times (R_2 - D_2) \cup \cdots))
\end{aligned}$$

Re-writing the second occurrence of R_1 as $(R_1' \cup D_1)$ gives

$$V_1 \quad = \pi_\gamma(\sigma_X(R_1 \times R_2 - (R_1' \cup D_1) \times D_2 \\ - D_1 \times (R_2 - D_2) \cup \cdots))$$

Multiplying the second term through, and substituting R_2' for $(R_2 - D_2)$ leaves

$$V_1 \quad = \pi_\gamma(\sigma_X(R_1 \times R_2 - R_1' \times D_2 \\ - D_1 \times D_2 - D_1 \times R_2' \cup \cdots))$$

If the operator $-$ is implemented as deletion and $\cup$ as insertion using duplicate counts as described previously, then the projection operation π will have the distributive property for *both* $-$ and $\cup$ [BLT86]. Applying these distributive properties to the expression above yields

$$V_1 \quad = \pi_\gamma(\sigma_X(R_1 \times R_2)) - \pi_\gamma(\sigma_X(R_1' \times D_2)) \cdots \\ = V_0 - \pi_\gamma(\sigma_X(R_1' \times D_2)) - \pi_\gamma(\sigma_X(D_1 \times R_2')) \\ - \pi_\gamma(\sigma_X(D_1 \times D_2)) \cup \pi_\gamma(\sigma_X(R_1' \times A_2)) \\ \cup \pi_\gamma(\sigma_X(A_1 \times R_2')) \cup \pi_\gamma(\sigma_X(A_1 \times A_2))$$

As expected, the first term of this expression is V_0, the previous stored value V. To update the stored copy of V so that its value becomes V_1 the remaining expressions must be evaluated, and either inserted into or deleted from V as required maintaining the currect duplicate counts. (The differential view update algorithm presented here is slightly different than that given in [BLT86]. A discussion of the differences appears in Appendix A.)

2.1   Deferred View Maintenance

The immediate view maintenance algorithm is performed after every database update. However, in certain situations, it will be advantageous to save the sets of tuples inserted and deleted for a period of time, and *then* apply the differential update algorithm to the whole group. Given a method to compute the net changes (A_1-net and D_1-net) for each relation, R_1, for $1 \leq i \leq N$, over a period encompassing more than one transaction, incremental view maintenance can be done whenever desired (hence the name *deferred* view maintenance). To refresh the materialized view on a deferred basis, A_1-net and D_1-net must be calculated and then input to the standard differential view update algorithm.

A previously developed technique called *hypothetical relations* [WS83] can be adapted to the purpose of computing A_1-net and D_1-net. The basic algorithm for implementing hypothetical relations is briefly described below. Efficient implementation of hypothetical relations to support deferred view maintenance will be discussed after the basic algorithm is presented.

Hypothetical Relations

Fortunately, the net changes to R_1 to use in deferred refresh can be found using a modified hypothetical relation (HR) algorithm proposed in [AD83]. The HR scheme uses three tables for each relation rather than one. Each relation has associated with it tables R, D and A, for base tuples, deletions and insertions, respectively. The data value of a tuple will simply be called "value." Each tuple will also have a unique identifier field "id." This yields the following schema for each relation:

$$R(\text{id, value})$$
$$D(\text{id, value})$$
$$A(\text{id, value})$$

The true value of the relation (R_T) is $(R \cup A) - D$. The set difference operation "$-$" above has the normal meaning, based on all fields of the tuple, including id.

To append a tuple to R_T, a transaction inserts that tuple in A, placing the value of the system clock or other monotonicly increasing source in the id field. If duplicate-free semantics are desired, the system must ensure that the tuple is not already in $(R \cup A) - D$ before appending it to A. To delete the tuple from the relation, a copy of its value, including the id it had in R or A, is placed in D. To modify an existing tuple, its old value will be put in D, and its new value in A. When retrieving data from R_T, queries are processed against both R and A, and any tuples found are checked to make sure they are not already in D_i (if they are, they are ignored).

Given this structure of the HR, the expressions for computing A-net and D-net from R, A and D as described above are the following:

$$A\text{-net} := A - D$$
$$D\text{-net} := D - A$$

After a view refresh that uses A-net and D-net, the files used to store the hypothetical relation will be reset as follows:

$$R := (R \cup A) - D$$
$$A := \phi$$
$$D := \phi$$

Efficient Implementation of Hypothetical Relations

The problem with the most straightforward implementation of hypothetical relations is that retrieving a tuple from R requires three disk accesses rather than just one, as in a standard relational database. To retrieve a tuple t from R using the HR scheme this way, an attempt must be made to read $t4$ from both R and A, and then D must be read to make sure that t has not been deleted.

Fortunately, a method developed in [SL76] can be used to screen out most accesses to the differential file(s). In this method, a *Bloom filter* [Blo70] is used for each differential file, consisting of an array of bits $B[l..m]$, with each entry initially zero. It is assumed that some subset of the fields of each record called the *key* uniquely identifies the record. For each record in the differential file, a hash function h mapping the key of a record to an integer in the range 1 to m is computed, and the corresponding entry in B is set to 1. Then, to test whether a record t is in the differential file, if $B[(t.key)] = 0$, t is not present; otherwise, if $B[(t.key)] = 01$, it might be present, so the differential file must be searched to see if it is there. Using the method proposed in [SL76] one can design a Bloom filter with any desired ability to screen out accesses to records not present in the differential file by increasing the value of m.

As another measure to help speed up accesses the differential file, A and D for each relation R will be combined into a single file, AD. An extra attribute "role" will be added to tuples in AD to indicate whether they are appended or deleted tuples. This storage structure will speed up the majority of updates, which modify existing records without changing the key. For example, if AD is maintained using a clustered hashing access method on the key, then when a tuple t is updated to T' without having its key changed, t' will hash to the same page as t. Thus, a maximum of only three disk I/Os will be required to update a single tuple t in R given the key for t. This update procedure is as follows:

I/O   Read the tuple. (Check the Bloom filter to see if t could be in AD. If not, read t from R. Otherwise, read AD to see if it is there. If t is not in AD, read R. This might require 2 I/Os, but the probability can be made arbitrarily small by increasing m. Hence, only one I/O is counted here for simplicity.)

I/O   Read the page where the new value of t (t') will lie in AD. (Place both t and t prime on the page. The role values of t and t' are "deleted" and "appended" respectively.)

I/O   Write this page back to disk.

This is only one more I/O than necessary to perform this type of update using a standard relational data structure. If separate files for A and D were used, at least *five* I/Os would be required rather than three since R must be read, and A and D must both be read and written.

In the remainder of the paper, the sets of inserted and deleted tuples will still be referred to as A and D, even though they are stored in the AD table. It is assumed that AD will be partitioned to form A and D when necessary.

2.2   Query Modification

The standard method for processing view queries is query modification, whereby view queries are translated into base relation queries. This can result in efficient view access, since a good query execution plan for the resulting base relation query will be found by the query optimizer [SALP79]. For example, consider the following view ED on the standard EMP and DEPT schema:

EMP(name, age, salary, dept)
DEPT(dname, floor)

define view ED (EMP.all, DEPT.all)
where EMP.dept = DEPT.dname

Suppose that EMP has a hash index on dept and DEPT has hash indexes on dname and floor. Query modification would translate the view query

retrieve (ED.name) **where** ED.floor = 1

into the following base relation query:

retrieve (EMP.name)
where EMP.dept = DEPT.dname
and DEPT.floor = 1

The optimizer might then select the following access plan for the query:

Find all DEPT tuples with floor = 1 using the hash index on DEPT.floor.

Do a nested loop join, with the tuples found above as the OUTER relation, and EMP as INNER, making use of the EMP.dept index.

3   Performance Comparison

Each of the view materialization methods presented will have different performance characteristics. This section discusses the factors affecting performance and derives cost functions for each method for three different view models.

3.1   Models to be Analyzed

Views can be materialized using query modification, or immediate or deferred view maintenance. Here, the situations in which each method performs best are determined. Three different models of the structure

model	view structure
Model 1	selection and projection of a single relation R
Model 2	natural join of two relations, R_1 and R_2, on a key field
Model 3	aggregates (e.g. sum, average) over a Model 1-type view

of views are considered: Only two types of operations will be considered in the models: updates to the base relations, and queries to the view. It is assumed that exactly k update operations, and q queries to the view will be run. For each model, a formula for the *average* cost per query, over all k updates and q queries, will be derived.

The relations involved have the following access methods: Generous assumptions will be made for all view

relation(s)	access method
R, R_1	clustered B^+-tree on field used in view predicate
R_2	clustered hashing on join field
materialized view (V)	clustered B^+-tree on field used in view predicate
differential file (AD)	clustered hashing on a key field

materialization schemes regarding how queries and other operations are performed using these clustered indexes. Since these performance benefits will be given to all algorithms, the results should not be biased toward any one scheme.

The parameters important to the analysis are shown in Figure 1. The default values of these parameters, which will be used unless stated otherwise, are as follows:

N	100,000	f	.1
S	100	f_v	.1
B	4,000	f_{R_2}	.1
k	100	C_1	1
l	25	C_2	30
q	100	C_3	1
n	20		

3.2 Model 1 Cost Analysis

In Model 1, the view is formed by projecting exactly one half of the attributes of tuples from R, and applying a predicate with selectivity f. Thus, the result will contain f times N tuples. The value that will be measured for each view maintenance scheme is the average cost of a query that retrieves a fraction f_v of the tuples in view.

Cost of Deferred View Maintenance Assuming Model 1

In deferred view maintenance, it is assumed that the view is refreshed every time it is queried. After the refresh is finished, the result of the query is computed. The average cost of a query to the view, which will be called TOTAL$_{deferred1}$, has several components. The first is the cost to read the result of the query

parameter	definition
N	number of tuples in relation
S	bytes per tuple
B	bytes per block
b	total blocks ($b = NS/B$)
T	number of tuples per page ($T = B/S$)
n	number of bytes in a B^+-tree index record
k	number of update transactions on base relation
l	number of tuples modified by each update transaction
q	number of times view queried
u	number of tuples updated between view queries ($u = kl/q$)
P	probability that a given operation is an update ($P = k/(k+q)$)
f	view predicate selectivity for Model 1
f_v	fraction of view retrieved per query
f_{R_2}	size of R_2 as a fraction of R_1
C_1	CPU cost to screen a record against a predicate in milliseconds (ms)
C_2	Cost in ms of a disk read or write
C_3	Cost in ms per tuple per transaction to manipulate A and D data structures in immediate view maintenance

Figure 1

from the copy of the view stored on disk. The second is the cost to refresh the view. The third is the cost to screen incoming and deleted tuples to see if they might affect the state of the view. Finally, the fourth is the cost to maintain the hypothetical relation(s). The average value of each of these costs are added together to get the average cost per query, $\text{TOTAL}_{\text{deferred1}}$. In summary,

$\text{TOTAL}_{\text{deferred1}} =$
   (cost to retrieve result of query from stored copy of view)
   +(cost to refresh the view)
   +(average cost per query to screen tuples to see if they affect view)
   +(average cost per query to maintain hypothetical relation(s))

It is assumed that no duplicates are formed by projecting half the attributes, so the view has fN tuples and $fb/2$ pages. A fraction f_v of the view is read during each access, requiring $f_v b/2$ page reads, at a cost of C_2 each. One search of the B^+-tree will also be necessary to locate the position in the view to begin scanning. Since there are n bytes per index record, the height of the B^+-tree, not including the data pages, is determined as follows. The number of index records per page, and thus the index fanout, is B/n. There is one index record for each of the fN tuples in the view. Assuming as a simplification that all pages are packed full, the height of the view index (H_{vi}) is thus

$$H_{vi} = \lceil \log_{\lceil B/n \rceil} fN \rceil$$

Additionally, each tuple read from the view must be screened against the query predicate, at a cost of C_1, for a total cost per view access of $C_1 f_v fN$. Thus, the total cost C_{query1} to query a materialized view is

$$C_{\text{query1}} = C_2 \frac{f f_v b}{2} + C_2 H_{vi} + C_1 f f_v N$$

The next cost to consider is that for the hypothetical relation overhead. It is only necessary to measure the cost in excess of that required to perform normal base relation updates. As a simplification, the assumption is made that only tuples in R are updated, and never tuples in AD. The cost to maintain the HR for a single insertion into R in this situation is the following:

1. read the original tuple from R

2. read the page in AD where the modified tuple will be placed

3. write this page in AD

Step (2) is the only extra I/O required over using just a single table (R). The normal cost to update R would be one read and one write, or $2C_2$, per tuple updated. If the cost of step (2) is averaged over all queries and updates, the cost per query to maintain the HR is at most the cost of one I/O (C_2) times the number of tuples update per view query (u). The total cost is likely to be somewhat less than this, however, since AD often has a small number of pages, and there are l tuples modified per transaction. The cost can be modeled more accurately using a function for estimating the number of pages touched when accessing k out of n records in a file occupying m disk pages. This function, which will be called $y(n, m, k)$, has been previously derived [Yao77] (See Appendix I3 for a description of y). The number of tuples in AD will thus be $2u$ divided by the number of tuples per page (T). The number of pages in AD touched per transaction is thus $y(2u, 2u/T, l)$. Averaged over q queries and k updates, the total case of the extra accesses to AD is thus the following:

$$C_{AD} = C_2 \frac{k}{q} y(2u, \frac{2u}{T}, l)$$

Consider now the cost to refresh the view V once. This first involves the cost to read all of AD. Since s tuples are updated per view query, AD has approximately $2u$ elements. There are T records per page, so AD has $2u/T$ pages. Thus, the cost C_{ADread} of reading AD is

$$C_{ADread} = C_2 \frac{2u}{T}$$

Another cost is incurred to screen updates to see whether they have a chance of affecting the view. Recall that to screen incoming tuples to see whether they can affect a view, rule indexing is used in combination with a more stringent satisfiability test. For the view maintenance methods analyzed, it is assumed that the screening is performed as follows:

if
    (1) a tuple breaks a t-lock for the predicate of view V, and
    (2) the predicate for V with t substituted into it is still satisfiable
then
    a marker indicating this is placed on t.

In both the deferred and immediate view update algorithms, a tuple will be used to update a stored view V only if the tuple has a marker for V. A fraction f of the u tuples inserted into R per query will conflict with a t-lock set for V in step (1) above, and thus must be passed on to step (2). Step (1) has essentially no overhead, and step (2) costs C_1. Thus, the average overhead per query to screen tuples to see if they affect V is:

$$C_{screen} = C_1 f u$$

Also, approximately f_u tuples per query will be inserted into and deleted from the view, respectively, for a total of 2_u tuple updates. Each insertion or deletion from the view requires reading the B^+-tree view index, and reading and writing a data block. However, somewhat less than $2fu$ *pages* of the view may actually have to be updated during a refresh, since there may be more than one record per block in the view. Using the Yao function, since there are fN tuples and $fb/2$ blocks in the view, the number of view blocks accessed (X_1) is approximately

$$X_1 = y(fN, \frac{fb}{2}, 2fu)$$

Each access requires reading the index, reading and writing a data block, and writing a leaf-level index block (splits of internal index pages are infrequent, so their cost will be ignored as a simplification). This requires 3 I/Os, plus a number of I/Os equal to the height of the index on V (H_{vi}). Thus, the cost to refresh the view, $C_{defresh1}$, is as follows

$$C_{def-refresh1} = C_2 \, (3 + H_{vi}) X_1$$

The following is the final expression for the cost per query to the view V using deferred refresh:

$$TOTAL_{deferred1} = C_{AD} + C_{ADread} + C_{query1} + C_{def-refresh1} + C_{screen}$$

Cost of Immediate Assuming Model

The cost per view access of performing immediate view maintenance, $TOTAL_{immediate1}$, is as follows:

$TOTAL_{immediate1} =$
    (cost to query view)
    +(total cost to modify stored view)/(# of view accesses)
    +(total cost to screen tuples inserted into to see if they should enter view)/(# of view accesses)
    +(overhead per query to maintain A and D sets in a data structure during transaction processing)

The cost C_{query} to query the view is the same as for deferred view maintenance. The cost to update the stored view when a transaction modifies R, which will be called $C_{imm-refresh1}$, is computed much like $C_{def-refresh1}$. The difference is that approximately $2fl$ tuples in the view must be modified *once per transaction*, rather than modifying $2fl$ view tuples once per query. Since some of these $2fl$ tuples may lie on the same page, the number of view pages touched (X_2) can be estimated using the Yao function as follows:

$$X_2 = y(fN, \frac{fb}{2}, 2fl)$$

Similar to the case for deferred view maintenance, updating a tuple in V requires a B^+-tree search, the read and write of a data block, and the write of an index block. This requires $(3 + H_{vi})$ I/Os for each view page touched, as before. Since there are k updates for every q queries, the average cost per query to update the view is:

$$C_{imm-refresh1} = \frac{k}{q} C_2 (3 + H_{vi}) \, X_2$$

The cost C_{screen} to screen the kl tuples inserted into R is unchanged.

Finally, since immediate view maintenance must update the view after every transaction, the data structures used to maintain the A and D sets must be reset once per transaction. The overhead per query to do this, which will be called $C_{overhead}$, will be estimated as C_3 for each of the fl tuples in A and D, multiplied by the number of updates per query (k/q), i.e.

$$C_{overhead} = (C_3 2fl) \frac{k}{q}$$

This gives the following expression for the total cost of immediate view maintenance:

$$\text{TOTAL}_{\text{immediate1}} = \text{C}_{\text{query1}} + \text{C}_{\text{imm-refresh1}} + \text{C}_{\text{screen}} + \text{C}_{\text{overhead}}$$

Cost Using Query Modification Assuming Model 1

The cost of using query modification rather than materializing the view in advance is considered here (this option will perform best in some circumstances, e.g. if the ratio of updates to queries is high). Three different methods for retrieving the view from R will be considered:

1. a clustered (primary) index scan for which no extra tuples must be read (**clustered**)

2. an unclustered (secondary) index scan (**unclustered**)

3. a sequential scan of the entire relation (**sequential**)

Using a clustered index scan, the number of pages that must be read from R is equal to the size of the view, which is fb, times the fraction of the view retrieved, f_v. The number of tuples retrieved is ff_vN, and each of these tuples must be tested against the view predicate at a cost of C_1. Thus, for the clustered scan (1), the total cost to retrieve the view per access is

$$\text{TOTAL}_{\text{clustered}} = \text{C}_2 bff_v + \text{C}_1 Nff_v$$

Using an unclustered scan (2), a larger number of pages must be read from R. Searching for ff_vN, tuples out of a total of b pages will require approximately $y(N, b, Nff_v)$ reads. The system must still test Nff_v) tuples against the view predicate. Thus, the total cost for case (2) is

$$\text{TOTAL}_{\text{unclustered}} = \text{C}_2 \cdot y(N, b, Nff_v) + \text{C}_1 Nff_v$$

Using a sequential scan of the entire relation (3), all b pages must be read, and all N tuples must be screened against the view predicate, resulting in the following total cost:

$$\text{TOTAL}_{\text{sequential}} = \text{C}_2 b + \text{C}_1 N$$

3.3   Performance Results for Model 1

To indicate the differences in cost with respect to the probability P that an operation is an update, figure 2 plots the total cost of deferred, immediate, clustered and unclustered vs. P for the standard parameter settings (sequential is not shown since it is off the scale). This setting of the parameters models a situation where the view contains 10,000 tuples, and each query retrieves 1,000 tuples. In this situation, query modification using a clustered access path has performance equal or superior to deferred and immediate. One would expect that clustered would perform well here since the number of pages that must be read is small when using a clustered index. The only advantage that deferred and immediate have over clustered is that there are twice as many tuples per page in the view compared with the base relation. However, the extra overhead paid by deferred and immediate to maintain the materialized copies of the view offsets this.

It is surprising that deferred and immediate view maintenance have almost identical cost under these circumstances. One reason for this is that for low values of P, materialization methods have nearly equal cost for virtually any parameter setting. This occurs since for low update probability, a large fraction of the cost of both algorithms is for processing queries against the materialized view, and both algorithms do this the same way. Another cause of the close match is that the hypothetical relation overhead in deferred view maintenance counteracts the other advantages it holds over immediate view maintenance. If more than one disk is available, and I/O operations can be issued concurrently by a program, then it would be possible to significantly decrease the cost of maintaining hypothetical relations (e.g. by putting R, A and D on separate disks and reading from them simultaneously). This would give deferred maintenance an advantage over the immediate scheme for a wider range of parameter settings. However, these assumptions are not made in this paper since they would require extra hardware, and operating system functionality not readily available in all computer systems.

Assuming the view is maintained with a clustered index on a commonly used access path, the view materialization methods are significantly superior to query modification when only an unclustered access path is available on the base relation. This has implications for database design, since a materialized view could be clustered on one attribute, and the base relation on another. In this situation, a query optimizer could choose to process a view query in one of two ways, depending on the query predicate. If the predicate could be processed most efficiently using the clustered index on the base relation, query modification would be chosen to execute the query. Otherwise, the query could be processed against the materialized view, using the clustered view index as an alternate access path.

An interesting tradeoff among the algorithms centers around the parameters f, P, and f_v. To illustrate the relationship between these parameters, figure 3 plots the region where each algorithm has lowest cost for different values of P and f, with f_v fixed at .1. Although deferred is never the most efficient algorithm under these parameter settings, larger values for f improve the performance of deferred relative to immediate view maintenance. This occurs due to the nature of the Yao function, combined with the fact that increasing f increases the size of A and D proportionately. Larger values of P tend to favor the algorithm with the least overhead per update transaction (i.e. query modification). Reducing the total fraction f_v of the view retrieved also tends to favor using query modification, since the overhead of the view maintenance schemes is independent of f_v, but the cost per query decreases with f_v. When the value of f_v is lowered to .01,

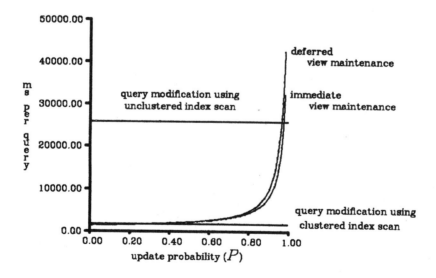

Figure 2

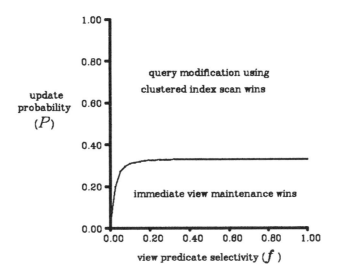

Figure 3

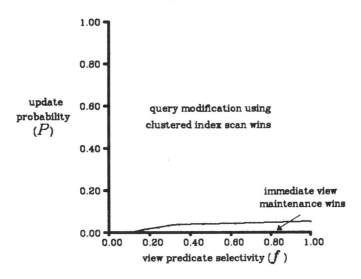

Figure 4

as shown in figure 4, clustered performs best over an even larger area. In figure 5, C_3, the overhead per tuple for maintaining the A and D sets was increased from 1 to 2 ms, while setting $f_v = 1$. The affect of this change can be seen by comparing figure 5 and figure 3. The fact that deferred view maintenance now performs best in part of figure 3 shows that the cost of the view materialization methods is very sensitive to the overhead for maintaining the A and D sets.

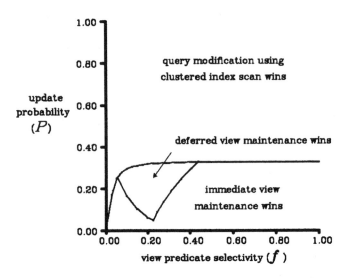

Figure 5

3.4 Model 2: 2-Way Join View

In this section, the performance of the different view maintenance algorithms is compared, assuming a more complex view model. The view V in Model 2 is a join of two relations, R_1 and R_2 where R_1 contains N tuples, and R_2 has $f_{R2}N$ tuples.

The definition of V is:

define view V (R_1.fields, R_2.fields)

where $R_1 x = R_2 y$

and C_f (R_1)

The clause C_f (R_1) in the view predicate restricts relation R_1 with selectivity f. It is assumed that every tuple of R_1 that matches condition C_f joins to exactly one tuple in R_2, so V has $f.N$ tuples total. Also, both R_1 and R_2 contain tuples of size S bytes, and only half the attributes of each relation are projected in the target list of the view definition. Thus, the tuples in V also contain S bytes each. The query and update activity assumed is the same as for Model 1, except that all updates are to R_1 rather than R (R_2 is never updated).

Cost of Deferred Assuming Model 2

For Model 2, the cost per query of doing deferred view maintenance is determined as follows:

$$\text{TOTAL}_{\text{deferred2}} =$$
$$(\text{cost to read } AD)$$
$$+(\text{cost to refresh view})$$
$$+(\text{cost to query view})$$
$$+(\text{cost per query to screen new tuples against view predicate})$$

The costs (C_{AD}) and (C_{ADread}) of updating and reading the HR, respectively, from Model 1 are unchanged for Model 2. The cost to refresh the view before it is queried (using deferred view maintenance), which will be called $C_{def-refresh2}$, will be determined as follows. To refresh V, the value of the following expression must be computed (the notation $V(X, Y)$ means the expression for V evaluated with X and Y in place of R_1 and R_2 respectively:

$$V(R_1, R_2) \cup V(A_1, R_2) - V(D_1, R_2)$$

The $V(R_1, R_2)$ term is already computed and stored as the previous version of the view (V_0). No terms containing A_2 and D_2 are shown since R_2 is never updated. Thus, only $V(A_1, R_@)$ and $V(D_1, R_2)$ must be computed. Recall that there is a clustered hashing index on R_2 that can be used as an access path to join tuples in A_1 and D_1, to R_2. The cost to join the A_1 and D_1, sets to R_2 is determined as follows: R_2 has $f_{R_2}N$ tuples and $f_{R_2}b$ pages, and there are u tuples in each of A_1 and D_1 at refresh time. Thus, the total number of pages that must be read from R_2 to perform these two joins is

$$X_3 = y(f_{R_2}N, f_{R_2}b, 2fu)$$

It is assumed that pages read for the first join stay in the buffer pool for the second.

There is also a CPU cost of C_1 for matching each of the $2u$ tuples in A_1 and D_1 with the joining tuple in R_2. Furthermore, for each joining tuple, a page must be read and written from the stored view. Using the Yao function, since the view has fN tuples of size S bytes, and a fraction f of the tuples in A_1 and D_1 join to exactly one tuple in R_1[2] the actual number of view pages that will be updated is approximately

$$X_4 = y(fN, fb, 2fu)$$

Each page update requires reading the B^+-tree index on the view, as well as reading and writing the data page, and writing the index leaf page (i.e. $3 + H_{vi}$ I/Os). Thus, the total cost $C_{def-refresh2}$ to update the view every time it is queried is:

$$C_{def-refresh2} = C_2X_3 + C_12u + C_2(3 + H_{vi}).X_4$$

When the view is queried, both deferred and immediate view maintenance pay the same cost C_{query2}. This consists of searching the view index to find the starting point, and then performing a clustered index scan to retrieve a fraction f_v of the view. This costs C_2 per page, and C_1 per tuple scanned. Summing the cost of the index search and scan yields the following expression for C_{query2}:

$$C_{query2} = C_2H_{vi} + C_2f_vfb + C_1f_vfN$$

Both deferred and immediate view maintenance pay an average screening cost of C_{screen} per query to the view. Given $C_{def-refresh2}$, and C_{query2}, and C_{screen}, the expression for the total cost using deferred view maintenance assuming Model 2 is

$$TOTAL_{deferred2} = C_{ADread} + C_{def-refresh2} + C_{query2} + C_{screen}$$

Cost of Immediate View Maintenance Assuming Model 2

The cost $TOTAL_{immediate2}$ of doing immediate view maintenance combined with rule indexing in Model 2 is

$$TOTAL_{immediate2} =$$
(cost per query to update view)
+(cost to query view once)
+(total overhead per query to maintain A and D sets)
+(cost to screen new tuples against view predicate)

To find the cost per query $C_{\text{imm-refresh2}}$ of maintaining the materialized view, the cost to refresh the view after each transaction must first be found. The components of this refresh cost are the I/O cost of reading the pages of R_2 to which tuples in A_1 and D_1 join and reading and writing modified pages of V, plus the CPU cost of handling each tuple in A_1 and D_1. Since A_1 and D_1 both contain l tuples at the end of each transaction, and a fraction f of these match the view predicate and must be joined to R_2, the number of pages that must be read from R_2 is

$$X_5 = y(f_{R_2}N, f_{R_2}b, 2fl)$$

Each tuple in A_1 and D_1 joins to some tuple in R_2, so each causes one tuple to enter or leave V. The number of modified pages of V is

$$X_6 = y(fN, fb, 2fl)$$

Again, for each of these pages, the index on V must be read, the page must be read and written, and an index leaf page is written, requiring $3 + H_{vi}$ page I/Os. There is also a CPU cost of C_1 for handling each of the $2l$ tuples in A_1 and D_1. Averaging the per-transaction cost of updating V over k transactions and q queries, the estimated copy per query is as follows:

$$C_{\text{imm-refresh2}} = \frac{k}{q}(C_2 X_5 + C_2(3 + H_{vi})X_6)$$

Given $C_{\text{imm-refresh2}}$ and C_{query2}, the following equation shows the total cost of immediate view maintenance using rule indexing, assuming Model 2

$$\text{TOTAL}_{\text{immediate2}} = C_{\text{imm-refresh2}} + C_{\text{query2}} + C_{\text{overhead}} + C_{\text{screen}}$$

Cost Using Query Modification Assuming Model 2

Another important cost to measure is that to materialize a view directly from the base relations. A frequently used join strategy called *nested-loops* (or *loopjoin*) involves scanning one (outer) relation, and for each of its elements searching the other (inner) relation to find all joining tuples. If an index is present on the join field of the inner relation, it can be used for the search.

It is assumed that the nested-loops join algorithm is used to join R_1 and R_2 in Model 2. R_1 will be the outer relation, and R_2 will be the inner one. Since there is a hash index on the join field of R_2, it will be used for the inner search. The assumption is made that pages of R_2 stay in the buffer pool throughout the computation of the join after they are read the first time. With the advent of very large main memories, this is reasonable since R_2 contains only $f_{R_2}NS$ bytes, which is approximately 1 Mbyte using the standard parameter settings. Under these assumptions, nested loop join has the following cost components, with the actual costs shown below: Summing the above cost components gives the following formula $\text{TOT}_{\text{loopjoin}}$

cost component	actual cost
read B^+-tree on R_1	$C_2\lceil\log_{\lceil B/n\rceil}N\rceil$
read part of R_1 using clustered scan	$C_2 f f_v b$
CPU cost to screen R_1 tuples scanned	$C_1 f f_v N$
read pages from R_2 using has index	$C_2 y(f_{R_2}N, f_{R_2}b, f f_v N)$
CPU cost to match R_1 tuples to R_2 tuples	$C_1 N f f_v$

for the total cost to compute the join using nested loops:

$$\begin{aligned}\text{TOT}_{\text{loopjoin}} &= C_2\lceil\log_{\lceil B/n\rceil}N\rceil + C_2 f f_v b \\ &\quad + C_2 y(f_{R_2}N, f_{R_2}b, f f_v N) + 2C_1 N f f_v\end{aligned}$$

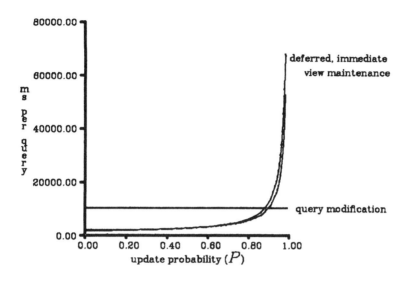

Figure 6

3.5   Performance Results for Model 2

The actual cost per query for deferred view maintenance, immediate view maintenance, and query modification using a nested loop join with an index on the inner relation are plotted in figure 6 using the standard parameter settings. This figure indicates that the results for Model 2 are significantly different than to those for Model 1. When the view joins data from more than one relation, incremental view maintenance algorithms (deferred and immediate) perform better relative to query modification. By maintaining a materialized copy of the view, the query cost is greatly reduced, since each result tuple is stored on exactly one page. In effect, maintaining the view serves as an effective way of *clustering* related data on the same page. However, as the update probability P increases, the overhead for maintaining the materialized view overwhelms the advantage gained by clustering, so query modification becomes more attractive. Also, similar to Model 1, as the fraction of the view retrieved (f_v) is decreased, the advantage of query modification grows. This follows since making f_v smaller reduces the query cost, while the amount of overhead paid by deferred and immediate algorithms for updating the view stays the same. An important special case to consider is when the view is large, and the queries read a small amount of data. This occurs, for example, using the standard EMP and DEPT relations, and view ED joining the two. The majority of queries in this situation might retrieve only a single tuple from ED. Also, updates usually change only one EMP tuple. This example was modeled by setting $f = 1$, $f_v = 1/N$ and $l = 1$, and the results showed that query modification is superior to deferred and immediate under these circumstances for all values of $P \geq .08$. Thus, query modification is almost always the preferred method for answering small queries against large views. Other effects of varying f_v are shown using two figures. Figure 7 plots the area where deferred view maintenance, immediate view maintenance and query modification using nested loops each have best performance for different values of P and f, with f_v set to .1 (recall that the nested loop join uses an index on the inner relation). Figure 8 shows the same information with f_v set to .01.

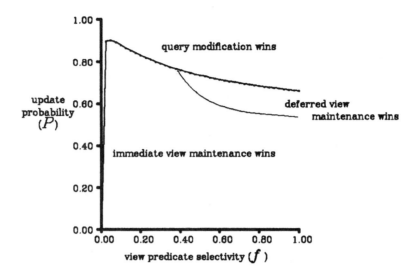

Figure 7

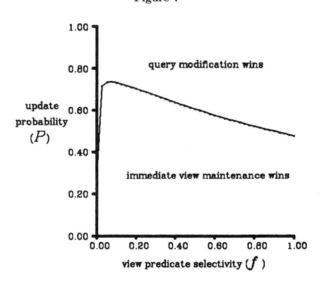

Figure 8

3.6   Model 3: Aggregates Over Model 1 Views

Aggregates such as sum, count and average are an often-used feature of database systems. Many aggregates (including all the ones listed above) can be incrementally updated as changes occur to the data from which they are computed. This is done by defining a *state* for the aggregate, functions for updating it in case of deletion or insertion of values in the set being aggregated, and a function for computing the current value of the aggregate from the state. The notion of incrementally maintaining aggregates is extremely attractive since the aggregate state can be read quickly because it normally requires less than one disk block of storage, while it often takes a large amount of I/O to recompute the aggregate from scratch. Thus, it would appear that an aggregate need not be used often to justify the expense of maintaining a materialized version of it.

To compare the value of maintaining aggregates vs. computing them from scratch, a modified view model (Model 3) is used, in which the views are simply aggregates over views of the same type as Model 1. In Model 3, the tuples for which the aggregate is computed do not need to be kept in a separate materialized view. Only the aggregate state must be stored.

For this model, a query to the view consists of simply reading the state of the aggregate. Using the deferred view maintenance scheme in Model 3, the cost $\text{TOTAL}_{\text{deferred3}}$ per query to the view is

$$\begin{aligned}
\text{TOTAL}_{\text{deferred3}} = \\
\text{(cost to read the hypothetical database)} \\
+\text{(cost to read the aggregate state)} \\
+\text{(cost per query to update the aggregate state if necessary)} \\
+\text{(cost per query of screening tuples to see if aggregate is affected)}
\end{aligned}$$

The cost to read the hypothetical database is C_{ADread}, unchanged from Model 1. The cost to query the aggregate is the cost to read a single page, i.e.

$$\text{C}_{\text{query3}} = \text{C}_2$$

The cost to update the aggregate is the cost of one write times the probability that at least one tuple modified since the last query to the view lies in the set being aggregated (no read is necessary since the aggregate must be read to answer the query). There are $2u$ modified tuples in the hypothetical database per query to the view, and each has probability f of lying in the aggregated set. The probability that at least one of these tuples will lie in the aggregated set is equal to 1 minus the probability that none of the tuples lie in the set. Thus, the probability that at least one of the tuples lies in the set is $(1 - (1 - f)^{2u})$. This yields the following expression for the cost per query to update the view:

$$\text{C}_{\text{def}-\text{refresh3}} = \text{C}_2(1 - (1 - f)^{2u})$$

The final value of $\text{TOTAL}_{\text{deferred3}}$ is the following:

$$\text{TOTAL}_{\text{deferred3}} = \text{CA}_{\text{Dread}} + \text{C}_{\text{query3}} + \text{C}_{\text{def}-\text{refresh3}} + \text{C}_{\text{screen}}$$

Using the intermediate view update algorithm, the cost per query to maintain the aggregate is

$$\begin{aligned}
\text{TOTAL}_{immediate3} = \\
\text{(cost to read the aggregate state)} \\
+\text{(cost per query to update the aggregate state if necessary)} \\
+\text{(cost per query of screening tuples to see if aggregate is affected)}
\end{aligned}$$

The cost to read the aggregate state is C_{query3}. The cost *per transaction* to update the aggregate state is C_2 times the probability that at least one tuple modified by the transaction lies in the aggregate, which is $(1 - (1 - f)^{2u})$. The cost per query to update the aggregate state is thus as follows:

$$\text{C}_{\text{imm}-\text{refresh3}} = \frac{\text{C}_2 k}{q}(1 - (1 - f)^{2l})$$

The cost of screening tuples is again C_{screen}, yielding the following expession for $\text{TOTAL}_{immediate3}$:

$$\text{TOTAL}_{immediate3} = \text{C}_{\text{query3}} + \text{C}_{\text{immrefresh4}} + \text{C}_{\text{screen}}$$

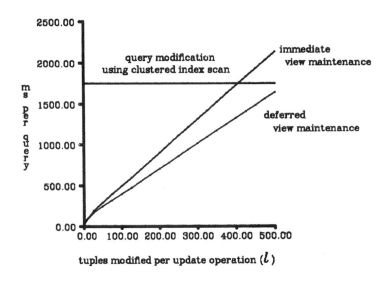

Figure 9

The actual cost of recomputing the aggregate for each query using a clustered index scan is the same as the cost of query modification in Model 1, which is $\text{TOTAL}_{\text{clustered}}$. This cost will be compared to $\text{TOTAL}_{\text{immedate3}}$ and $\text{TOTAL}_{\text{deferred3}}$.

3.7   Performance Results for Model 3

To compare the total cost of using deferred view maintenance, immediate view maintenance and a clustered index scan to compute an aggregate, the total cost of all three is plotted vs. l in figure 9. Note that the most significant part of the curve is for small values of l, e.g. $l < 100$. In this region, maintaining the aggregate costs only a small percentage as much as computing it from scratch.

To show the trade-off between a materialization algorithm and standard aggregate processing, figure 10 plots curves for P vs. L showing where a clustered scan and immediate view maintenance have equal cost for different values of f (the fraction of the relation that is being aggregated). Query modification using the clustered scan performs best above each curve, and immediate maintenance performs best below. It is interesting to note that maintaining materialized aggregates is most attractive when the fraction of the relation being aggregate (f) is largest. Also, since realistically l will probably be small, it is likely to be worthwhile to maintain materialized aggregates even for small values of f. Cost savings can be obtained by materializing aggregates in significantly more cases than for other views.

4   Conclusion

The performance analysis presented has shown that the choice of the most efficient view materialization algorithm is highly application dependent. The results are most sensitive to the following parameters:

1. the total fraction of operations that are updates (P).

2. the selectivity factor of the view predicate (f).

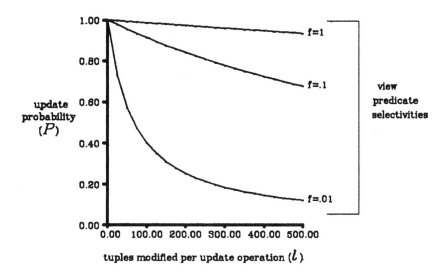

Figure 10

3. the fraction of the view retrieved by each query (f_v).

4. the number of tuples written by each update (l).

5. the cost of maintaining the sets of inserted and deleted tuples (either in main memory, or in disk-based hypothetical relations).

Situations where P is high, f is high, or f_v is small, tend to favor not materializing the view at all. Rather, it is best to perform query modification, and retrieve the result from the base relations using a good access plan selected by the query optimizer. An important example of this is for large views (e.g. the ED view on EMP and DEPT) and queries that always retrieve a single record. When this example was modeled using $f = 1$, $l = 1$, and $f_v = 1/$(number of tuples in the view), it was found that query modification nearly always outperforms materializing the view in advance.

If ff_v is large, and P is not extremely high, then it becomes desirable to maintain views in materialized form. Higher values of P, f_v and l favor defined view maintenance over the immediate scheme. Conversely, if P is low, immediate view maintenance has a slight advantage over deferred maintenance.

An interesting phenomenon observed was that immediate and deferred view maintenance have very nearly equal cost for Models 1 and 2, especially for low values of P. The reason for this is that the advantages and disadvantages of deferred and immediate view maintenance nearly canceled each other. The main advantage of deferred view maintenance is that fewer disk writes to the stored copy of a view must be performed than in immediate view maintenance. The reason for this is that *triangle inequality* holds for the Yao function, which is a main determinant of the number of writes to the view. More precisely,

$$y(n, m, a + b) \leq (a, m, a) + y(n, m, b)$$

for all $a, b > 0$. On the other hand, the advantage of immediate view maintenance is that less overhead is usually required to maintain the A and D sets, since they usually will not have to be written to disk (they should fit in the buffer pool except for transactions that update a large fraction of the database). In deferred view maintenance, the A and D sets must be written to disk, since they may live for more than one transaction. Reducing or increasing the overhead of maintaining A and D in either algorithm could give that algorithm an overall performance advantage.

Also, a valuable strategy is available to deferred view maintenance that cannot be used in the immediate scheme. If there is idle CPU and disk time available, it is likely to be useful to put it to work refreshing views asynchronously. This would improve the response time of view queries in some situations since the views would not have to be refreshed first. It would also allow update transactions to be completed more quickly than using immediate view maintenance, since the view would not have to be updated within the transaction. The evaluation of the usefulness of optimization is an interesting topic for future study.

This paper has shown that the performance benefits of differential view update algorithms relative to query modification are greater for two-way join views (Model 2) than for simple restrictions (Model 1). This is due to the natural clustering of view tuples on a single disk page that occurs when the view is materialized in advance. The performance benefits of view maintenance algorithms are likely to be even greater for views joining three or more relations.

Also, one could speculate that the most significant applications of incremental view update may not be related to processing queries against views, since this study has shown that query modification is still quite effective. Rather, view materialization might have a greater impact in applications where a complete copy of the answer to a query is always needed. For example, materialization could support conditions for complex triggers and alerters, as described in [BC79]. As another example, it could be used as a basis for a "window on a database" facility, where the result of a query would be displayed and updated in real time.

Finally, the performance of different view materialization schemes depends significantly on the database and view structure, and the distribution of queries and updates. Thus, an interesting topic for future research would be to devise an adaptive method to choose the appropriate view materialization algorithm. Future implementation and empirical testing of immediate and deferred view maintenance are also needed to help gain a fuller understanding of the tradeoffs involved.

Appendix A

The method presented in [BLT86] for determining how to refresh the view when both deletions and insertions occur is slightly different than the one shown here, and is in fact not always correct. Using the scheme [BLT86], the expression below would be used to refresh the view:

$$V_1 = \pi_\gamma(\sigma_X(R_1 \times R_2 \cup A_1 \times A_2 \cup A_1 \times R_2 \cup R_1 \times A_2 - D_1 \times D_2 - D_1 \times R_2 - R_1 \times D_2))$$

Using this expression can cause improper update of the duplicate counts. For example, suppose tuples t_1 and R_1 and t_2 and R_2 joined together to produce a result tuple in V_0. If a transaction deleted both T_1 and t_2, then the result of joining t_1 to t_2 would be deleted from V_0 three times, not just one as it should. This happens since t_1 is in both R_1 and D_1 and t_2 is in both R_2 and D_2. The formulation given in this paper (using $R'_1 = R_1 - D_1$ and $R'_2 = R_2 - D_2$) does not have this problem.

Appendix B

Given that there are n total records on m blocks, a formula giving the expected number of blocks that will be accessed to modify k records is as follows [Yao77]. Let C^b_a be the number of ways that b items can be selected from a items ($a \geq b$). If the number of records per block is $p = n/m$, then the formula giving the expected number of block accesses is C_k^{n-p}/C_K^n. An approximation to the above that is very close if the blocking factor is large (e.g. $n/m > 10$) is $m(1 - (1 - 1/m)^k)$ [Car75]. The notation $y(n, m, k)$ is used to represent the Yao function.

32

JOIN INDEX, MATERIALIZED VIEW, AND HYBRID-HASH JOIN: A PERFORMANCE ANALYSIS

José A. Blakeley, Nancy L. Martin

ABSTRACT

This chapter deals with the problem of efficiently computing a join between two base relations in the presence of queries and updates to the base relations. We present a performance analysis of three methods: *join index*, *materialized view*, and *hybrid-hash join*. The first two methods are examples of a strategy based on data caching; they represent two ends of a spectrum of possibilities depending on the attributes projected in the materialization. The third method is an example of a conventional strategy for computing a join from base relations. The results of this study show that the method of choice depends on the environment, in particular, the update activity on base relations, the join selectivity, and the amount of main memory available. A byproduct of this study is a strategy for incrementally maintaining a join index in the presence of updates to the underlying base relations.

1 Introduction

Improving query-processing performance in relational database management systems continues to be a challenging area of research. New application areas of relational systems such as engineering design require the storage of more complex objects than the ones required by conventional business applications [HFLP89, LKM+85]. In addition, designers of object-oriented database systems are choosing to build their systems on top of relational ones [FBC+87, KH87]. Efficient query processing in such systems becomes a more difficult problem because queries involve complex objects which may themselves be composed of complex objects and so on.

Active database systems [MD89] which allow users to specify actions to be taken automatically when certain conditions arise are systems that require very efficient query processing. The completion of many of the actions specified in these systems may be time-constrained in the order of a few milliseconds. In such situations, the system cannot afford to spend a lot of time performing secondary storage accesses, hence caching precomputed queries may be a good strategy.

Several caching mechanisms have recently been suggested to support efficient query processing in extensible relational database systems. Materialized views [AL80, BLT86, LHM+86, SI84] have been suggested by Stonebraker *et al.* [SAH85] and by Hanson [Han88] as an efficient alternative for the support of procedures in Postgres [SR86]. They have also been suggested by several researchers as an alternative approach to structuring the database at the internal level in a relational system [BCL89, LY85, Mar81, TB88, YL87]. Other forms of caching include *links* [Hae78, SB75], *view indices* [Rou82], and *join indices* [Val87]. Valduriez [Val87] has suggested a join index as a data structure to support efficient retrieval of complex objects in object-oriented systems built on top of relational systems.

As a result of these developments, customizers of relational database management systems must decide among several performance improving mechanisms. For example, if the customizer chooses to use auxiliary relations to improve query efficiency, should full tuples be stored (*i.e.*, materialized views) or only the tuple identifiers from the joining relations (*i.e.*, join indices)? On the other hand, the customizer may decide to incorporate more efficient algorithms to compute joins [BE77,Bra84,DKO+84] and rely exclusively on complete re-evaluation of queries.

This chapter represents a step in establishing criteria for selecting among the various approaches mentioned above. Specifically, we concentrate on the performance analysis of two caching strategies: a materialized view defined as an equi-join operation between two relations and the corresponding join index. An alternative to caching is the complete computation of a join from the base relations. We have chosen the hybrid-hash join algorithm as a representative of this approach because it outperforms other methods of its type and allows us to compare our results with those of Valduriez [Val87]. The remainder of this chapter analyzes these three approaches and compares their costs. Section 2 contains a brief description of the methods while Section 3 describes the performance analysis. Section 4 presents results and Section 5 contains our conclusions.

2   Methods

In this section we illustrate how each method works via an example. Consider the two relations shown below. The `Student` relation contains tuples describing student volunteers. Each tuple contains a student's name, major and native country; each tuple also has a unique identifier known as a surrogate. The `Project` relation is used to store data pertaining to the on-going summer projects of a university's archeology department. It has attributes for the project title, the project leader and the project location as well as a surrogate.

Table 1   `Student` relation

Ssur	Name	Major	NativeCountry
010	S. Bando	Music	USA
011	G. Jetson	Art	Great Britain
012	C. Faleri	Math	Italy
013	L. LaPaz	Art	Mexico
014	J. Jones	English	USA
015	P. Valens	CSci	Mexico

Table 2   `Project` relation

Psur	Title	Leader	City	Country
030	Ruins	N. Smith	Coba	Mexico
031	Facade	E. Ruggeri	Venice	Italy
033	Mural	A. Montez	Tulum	Mexico
034	Excavate	M. Cox	Lima	Peru

If the archeology department wished to place student volunteers on projects located in their native country, the following query would be necessary:

```
SELECT Title, Leader, City, Country, Name, Major
FROM Project, Student
WHERE Country = NativeCountry
```

We can now examine the auxiliary relations produced by applying the proposed speed-up methods to the above query.

2.1 Materialized View

The approach used by the materialized view method is to fully evaluate the join once and store the result for future use. Applying this method would create the relation shown in Table 3 as a result of the initial join.

Table 3 Materialized view for query

Title	Leader	City	Country	Name	Major
Ruins	N. Smith	Coba	Mexico	L. LaPaz	Art
Ruins	N. Smith	Coba	Mexico	P. Valens	CSci
Facade	E. Ruggeri	Venice	Italy	C. Faleri	Math
Mural	A. Montez	Tulum	Mexico	L. LaPaz	Art
Mural	A. Montez	Tulum	Mexico	P. Valens	CSci

Subsequent evaluations of the example query would be very quick as they would merely consist of reading the materialized view from the disk. However, updating any attribute of any tuple of `Student` or `Project` would necessitate examining the materialized view to determine if it should also be updated and, when necessary, performing the update.

2.2 Join Index

The join index method tries to store enough information to aid efficient join formation while minimizing the size of the auxiliary relation and the effects of subsequent updates. For each tuple in the join, only the surrogates of its component tuples are stored. Thus, when the join is needed, the appropriate component tuples can be efficiently fetched via a clustered or inverted index. Furthermore, only updates that change the join attributes (in the example, `NativeCountry` and `Country`) need to be checked against and possibly posted to the join index relation. The sample query join index is shown in Table 4.

Table 4 Join index relation for the sample query

Psur	Ssur
030	013
030	015
031	012
033	013
033	015

2.3   Hybrid Hash-Join

The hybrid-hash join algorithm fully utilizes the available main memory to do an efficient yet complete re-evaluation of the join each time the corresponding query occurs. The efficiency is gained by applying the divide-and-conquer principle to the problem of computing a join. The potentially large component relations are hashed on the join attribute into several smaller subfiles (also called buckets) each of which will fit into memory; after this stage, each subfile contains tuples from the base relations that may potentially join. The set of tuples within each subfile are then joined in the appropriate order to produce the final join. This method further takes advantage of the available main memory space by performing the first sub-join while building the subfiles for subsequent manipulation. This algorithm has the advantages of not requiring any permanent auxiliary relations and being uneffected by base-relation updates.

3   Performance Analysis

In this section we analyze the performance of three approaches for computing the join of two relations. The following scenarios will be analyzed: (a) materialized view with deferred updates to the view, (b) join index with deferred updates to the join index, and (c) complete re-evaluation using the hybrid-hash join algorithm. By "deferred updates" we mean that in case the joining base relations are updated many times between subsequent queries, updating a materialized view or a join index will be deferred until the time they are queried. Table 5 summarizes the assumptions made with respect to the storage organization of base relations, join index, and materialized view. These organizations follow Valduriez's assumptions [Val87].

Table 5   Assumptions on the organization of base relations.

Base relations R, S	clustered B^+-tree on surrogate
Base relation S	nonclustered index on join attribute
Join index JI	clustered B^+-tree on surrogate r
	nonclustered B^+-tree on surrogate s
Materialized view V	Linear hash file on join attribute

3.1   Analysis parameters

Table 6 lists the parameters we use to analyze the different scenarios. Similar notation has been used by DeWitt *et al.* [DKO$^+$84], Hanson [Han87], and Valduriez [Val87].

3.2   Analysis formulas

Although the formulas used throughout the analysis are similar to or compatible extensions of those used by Valduriez [Val87], we give a very brief explanation of them. Initial experiments showed that both quicksort and heap merge possess favorable time-space characteristics for sorting and merging, respectively. Costs for these algorithms are based on average case analyses by Knuth [Knu73]. The CPU time to quicksort n tuples is defined by

$$CPU_{st}(n) = 2 * (n+1) * \ln((n+1)/11) * comp \\ + 2/3 * (n+1) * \ln((n+1)/11) * move$$

Table 6 List of parameters.

Database dependent parameters

$\|R\|, \|S\|, \|JI\|, \|V\|$	Number of pages in relations R, S, join index, and materialized view, respectively
$\|\|R\|\|, \|\|S\|\|, \|\|JI\|\|, \|\|V\|\|$	Number of tuples in relations R, S, join index, and materialized view, respectively
JS	Join selectivity, $(\|\|R \bowtie S\|\|)/(\|\|R\|\| * \|\|S\|\|)$
SR	Semijoin selectivity, $(\|\|R \ltimes S\|\|)/\|\|R\|\|$
SS	Semijoin selectivity, $(\|\|S \ltimes R\|\|)/\|\|S\|\|$
T_R, T_S, T_{JI}, T_V	Size (in bytes) of a tuple of R, S, JI, and V, respectively
$n_R, n_S, n_{JI}, n_V, n_{i_R}$	Number of tuples per page in relations R, S, JI, V, and in the insertion (deletion) file, respectively
$N1_M, N1_J$	Number of passes in phase 1 of materialized view and join index algorithms, respectively
$N2_M, N2_J$	Number of passes in phase 2 of materialized view and join index algorithms, respectively
Pr_A	Probability that an update operation modifies the join attribute

System dependent parameters

$\|M\|$	Number of usable pages of main memory
F	Space-overhead factor for hashing
P	Page size in bytes
PO	Average page occupancy factor B^+-tree
FO	Average fan out of an index node in a B^+-tree
ssur	Surrogate size in bytes
sptr	Pointer size in bytes

System performance dependent parameters

IO	Time to perform a random IO operation
comp	Time to compare two keys in memory
hash	Time to hash a key
move	Time to move a tuple (of any size) in memory

if the sort is on a key that is not hashed, or

$$CPU_{st}(n) = 2 * (n+1) * \ln((n+1)/11) * (comp + 2 * hash) \\ + 2/3 * (n+1) * \ln((n+1)/11) * move$$

if the sort is on a key that must be hashed. The number of overhead pages needed to quicksort n memory-resident items is

$$SPACE_{st}(n) = 2 * sptr * \lg(n)/P.$$

Merging n items of size s in a heap of size z requires time and space as shown below. (The n items are assumed to be in a main memory buffer before they are moved to the heap which contains entire items as well as pointers into corresponding buffers.)

$$CPU_{mrg}(n, z) = ((2*n-1)*\lg(z) - 3.042*n)*comp \\ + (n*\lg(z) + 1.13*n + \lfloor n/2 \rfloor - 4)*move$$

if the keys are not hashed, or

$$CPU_{mrg}(n, z) = ((2*n-1)*\lg(z) - 3.042*n) \\ *(comp + 2*hash) \\ + (n*\lg(z) + 1.13*n + \lfloor n/2 \rfloor - 4)*move$$

if the merge keys are hashed. The space required is given by

$$SPACE_{mrg}(z, s) = z*(s + sptr)/P.$$

The number of page accesses needed to get k records randomly distributed in a file of n records stored in m pages given that a page is accessed at most once is given by Yao's formula [Yao77]

$$Yao(k, m, n) = m - m * \prod_{i=1}^{k} \frac{n - (n/m) - i + 1}{n - i + 1}.$$

Based on this formula, we can calculate the IO time for accessing k tuples in a relation having m pages and n tuples via a clustered (IO_{ci}) or inverted index (IO_{ii}) using the following equations.

$$IO_{ci} = [Yao(k, m, n) + Yao(Yao(k, m, n), m/FO, m)] * IO$$

$$IO_{ii} = [Yao(k, m, n) + Yao(k, n/FO, n) \\ + Yao(Yao(k, n/FO, n), n/(FO*FO), n/FO)] * IO$$

These formulas assume B^+-tree indices with two and three levels of index pages when used as clustered and inverted indices, respectively. The root node is assumed to reside in main memory.

3.3   Cost of materialized view with deferred updates

In this subsection we describe the cost of computing a join operation using a materialized view defined as $V = R \bowtie S$. We assume relations R and S are joined on their common attribute A. Let i_R, d_R, i_S, and d_S denote the sets of tuples inserted into or deleted from relations R and S, respectively. Let $R' = R - d_R$ and $S' = S - d_S$. If a transaction updates the base relations R and S, the updated state of the view V' can be computed by

$$V' = V \cup (i_R \bowtie S') \cup (R' \bowtie i_S) \cup (i_r \bowtie i_S) \\ - ((d_R \bowtie S') \cup (R' \bowtie d_S) \cup (d_R \bowtie d_S)).$$

Our analysis assumes that only relation R is updated, thus

$$V' = (V \cup (i_R \bowtie S)) - (d_R \bowtie S).$$

Furthermore, relation R is changed by update operations only, which get translated into a delete followed by an insert, thus $||i_R|| = ||d_R||$. We defer updating the materialized view until the time the join computation is required. Computing the join using the materialized view involves: (1) maintaining the changes to R, (2) computing the changes to V from i_R and d_R, (3) updating V, and (4) reading the new view V'. Because steps (3) and (4) require reading the view, we perform step (3) on the fly at the time the view is read in step (4), thus saving the cost of reading V once. The sets i_R and d_R are stored on disk. Since V is stored as a linear hash file on the join attribute A (see Table 5) and since we want to perform the updates on the fly, we need to have the changes to the view ordered on $hash(A)$. The next subsections describe the cost of computing each of these steps.

(1) Maintaining the sets i_R and d_R. In order to compute changes to the view we need to charge the overhead of moving the sets i_R and d_R to an output buffer and writing them to disk when relation R is updated:

$$C_{1.1} = (||i_R|| + ||d_R||) * move + (|i_R| + |d_R|) * IO.$$

Reading the sets i_R and d_R from disk to update the view costs

$$C_{1.2} = (|i_R| + |d_R|) * IO.$$

All algorithms discussed in this chapter try to make efficient use of the main memory available. We assume that updates to R are logged in main memory as long as possible. Roughly half of the available memory is devoted to deletions while the other half is used to store insertions. The space used is not exactly half because we must also provide overhead space to sort the deletions or insertions by $hash(A)$ before writing them out to disk. The layout of memory for this part of the algorithm is shown in Figure 1. We will say

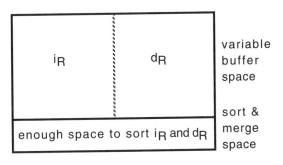

Figure 1   Memory configuration for sorting insertions and deletions.

that Z pages are available for insertions and Z pages are available for deletions where

$$Z = \max_{z \in \{Integer\}} (2 * z + SPACE_{st}(z * n_{i_R})) \leq |M| \tag{3.1}$$

Thus, there will be $f = \lfloor |i_R|/Z \rfloor$ full internal sorts and $p = \lceil (|i_R| - f * Z)/Z \rceil$ partial internal sorts of each of the i_R and d_R sets. The total number of runs of this part of the algorithm is $N1_M = f + p$ and the total internal sorting cost is

$$
\begin{aligned}
C_{1.3} &= 2 * f * CPU_{st}(Z * n_{i_R}) \\
&\quad + 2 * p * CPU_{st}(||i_r|| - f * Z * n_{i_R}).
\end{aligned}
$$

To read the sets i_R and d_R sorted by $hash(A)$ we simply need to merge $N1_M$ subfiles for each of the sets i_R and d_R. Merging is done using a heap data structure of size $N1_M$. The cost is

$$C_{1.4} = CPU_{mrg}(||i_R||, N1_M) + CPU_{mrg}(||d_R||, N1_M).$$

At this point we have a cost of $C_1 = C_{1.1} + C_{1.2} + C_{1.3} + C_{1.4}$.

(2) Compute the changes to V. We only need to compute $i_R \bowtie S$ as the set $d_R \bowtie V$ is deleted from V in step (3); this is accomplished by merely not outputting tuples in V whose R component matches a d_R tuple. As S has an inverted index on the join attribute A, we use main memory to schedule the accesses to S by ordering the inverted index pointers. We collect $|W|$ pages of i_R as they come out of the merge in the previous step. Call these pages relation W_R. Hence, computing $i_R \bowtie S$ requires $N2_M = |i_R|/|W_R|$ passes of the following steps:

2.1 sort W_R by attribute A,

2.2 compute $W_R \bowtie S$ assuming S has an inverted index on A,

2.3 sort $W_R \bowtie S$ by $hash(A)$. Relation $i_R \bowtie S$ is produced in sorted order by $hash(A)$ as the union of $W_R \bowtie S$ of each pass. So, as step (2) produces tuples of $i_R \bowtie S$, step (3) consumes them, avoiding an intermediate read/write of $i_R \bowtie S$.

Since $2 * N1_M$ pages are used to read the different batches of i_R and d_R and we need input buffers for S and V and an output buffer for the updated V, we have $|M| - 2 * N1_M - 3$ pages of available memory left for this step. W_R occupies $|W_R|$ pages. $W_R \bowtie S$ occupies $|W_R| * n_R * ||S|| * JS * (T_R + T_S)/P$ pages. In addition, the necessary merging and sorting will occupy some space. The memory configuration for step (2) is illustrated in Figure 2 and yields the following computation for $|W_R|$:

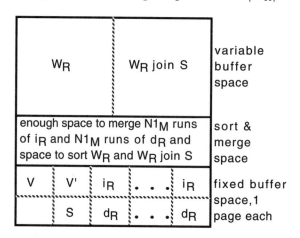

Figure 2 Memory layout for phase 2 of materialized view method.

$$
\begin{aligned}
|W_R| &= \max_{w \in \{Integer\}, w \le |i_R|} (w + \frac{w * n_{i_R} * ||S|| * JS * (T_R + T_S)}{P} \\
&\quad + 2 * SPACE_{mrg}(N1_M, T_R) \\
&\quad + max[SPACE_{st}(w * n_{i_R}), \\
&\quad \quad SPACE_{st}(w * n_{i_R} * ||S|| * JS)]) \\
&\le (|M| - 2 * N1_M - 3).
\end{aligned}
$$

Thus the costs of the steps described above are:

$$
\begin{aligned}
C_{2.1} &= CPU_{st}(||W_R||), \\
C_{2.2} &= IO_{ii}(k, |S|, ||S||) + Yao(k, |S|, ||S||) * n_S * comp \\
&\quad + ||W_R|| * ||S|| * JS * move, \\
C_{2.3} &= CPU_{st}(||W_R|| * ||S|| * JS)
\end{aligned}
$$

where $k = SR * ||W_R||$; $C_2 = (C_{2.1} + C_{2.2} + C_{2.3}) * N2_M$.

(3) Update the view on the fly. This is done while reading V. Reading the whole view costs

$$C_{3.1} = F * |V| * IO.$$

When the updated pages of V are written, some of the $(||i_R|| + ||d_R||) * SR$ groups of adjacent tuples to be inserted or deleted may extend over a page boundary and cause two writes rather than one. While this is a possibility, we assume that it does not occur. Under this assumption, writing the changed pages including inserts and deletes costs

$$C_{3.2} = F * Yao((||i_R|| + ||d_R||) * SR, F * |V|, ||V||) * IO.$$

The cost of merging the tuples is

$$\begin{aligned} C_{3.3} = \ & ((||i_R|| + ||d_R||) * ||S|| * JS + ||V||) * comp \\ & + F * Yao((||i_R|| + ||d_R||) * SR, F * |V|, ||V||) \\ & * n_V * move. \end{aligned}$$

Thus, the total cost of this step is $C_3 = C_{3.1} + C_{3.2} + C_{3.3}$. Finally, the total cost of this scenario is $C = C_1 + C_2 + C_3$.

3.4   Cost of join index with deferred updates

This subsection analyzes the cost of displaying a join where that join is partially materialized via a join index and where updates have occurred since the join index was formed. The algorithm used is based on that of Valduriez [Val87] but has been extended to include incremental, on-the-fly updates of both the join and the join indices. Valduriez's algorithm exploits the available main memory to process as much as possible of JI and the corresponding $R \ltimes JI$ at a single time; if all of JI and $R \ltimes JI$ do not fit into the available memory, the processing is accomplished in several passes. Essentially, we extend the algorithm so that the available memory holds as much as possible of JI and the corresponding $R \ltimes JI$, i_R and $i_R \bowtie S$.

Specifically, on-the-fly update of join indices involves two phases. The first phase is comprised of one or more passes where the insertions and deletions are saved in the available memory until space is exhausted; then each set is sorted on r, its surrogate for R, and written out to disk. The second phase also involves one or more passes. In each pass, "as much as possible" of JI is read into memory. A heap organization is used to merge the possibly several files of deleted tuples to produce just the deletions which correspond to the portion of JI in memory. Any join index entries in JI that match deleted tuples are "marked" so that they will not be processed further. Next a heap is used to merge the possibly several files of insertions to store in memory the pages of i_R which correspond to the memory-resident portion of the JI. These pages of i_R are subsequently sorted on the join attribute A and pages of S are accessed one page at a time to form $i_R \bowtie S$ which is in turn sorted on s, the surrogate for S. Then the necessary pages of R are read one page at a time to form $R \ltimes JI$ for the pages of JI which are memory resident. Also at this time, a pointer is stored with the JI so that the corresponding tuple of R may be accessed quickly. Finally, JI is sorted on s and S is accessed one page at a time. As tuples of S are retrieved, they can be joined with R and merged with $i_R \bowtie S$ to give the join. Also, to keep the join index current, changed pages need to be moved to an output area and rewritten.

The assumptions made in the following analysis are the same as those of the previous section. On-the-fly-update of join indices can be partitioned into four categories: (1) maintaining the changes to R, (2) reading and updating the JI and (3) forming the join using JI, d_R and i_R as well as R and S.

(1) Maintaining the sets i_R and d_R. The method which maintains these sets is similar to the one used for materialized views. However, there are two important differences. As a join index is a "partially materialized view," it is only effected by updates to the join attribute. Thus, if $||i_R||$ tuples are inserted by updates, only $Pr_A * ||i_R||$ need to be saved for future update of the JI. Secondly, since i_R and d_R are ordered by r, no hashing is necessary. Based on these observations and the fact that the memory layout is the same as that in Figure 1, we need only reformulate the cost equations of the corresponding part of the materialized view analysis. The cost of storing the pertinent insertions and deletions and then writing them to disk is

$$
\begin{aligned}
C_{1.1} \ = \ & Pr_A * (||i_R|| + ||d_R||) * move \\
& + Pr_A * (|i_R| + |d_R|) * IO.
\end{aligned}
$$

Reading the pertinent insertions and deletions from disk to update the join and the JI costs

$$
C_{1.2} = Pr_A * (|i_R| + |d_R|) * IO.
$$

There will be $f = \lfloor Pr_A * |i_R|/Z \rfloor$ full runs and $p = \lceil (Pr_A * |i_R| - f * Z)/Z \rceil$ partial runs of sorting for insertions and also for the deletions. This gives a total number of runs of $N1_J = f + p$ and a total internal sort cost of

$$
\begin{aligned}
C_{1.3} \ = \ & 2 * f * CPU_{st}(Z * n_{i_R}) \\
& + 2 * p * CPU_{st}(Pr_A * ||i_R|| - f * Z * ni_R).
\end{aligned}
$$

As the $N1_J$ subfiles for deletions and the $N1_J$ subfiles for insertions are read into memory, we provide two heaps of size $N1_J$ for the merging of these subfile sets. The cost of merging is

$$
\begin{aligned}
C_{1.4} \ = \ & CPU_{mrg}(Pr_A * ||i_R||, N1_J) \\
& + CPU_{mrg}(Pr_A * ||d_R||, N1_J)
\end{aligned}
$$

Thus, the total cost of maintaining the pertinent insertions and deletions is $C_1 = C_{1.1} + C_{1.2} + C_{1.3} + C_{1.4}$.

(2) Reading and updating the JI. Just like merging the sorted deletions and insertions, reading and updating the join index file is actually carried out during a series of one or more passes. However, as the cost of these operations is independent of the number of passes, we show them here in a separate section.

Reading the join index file costs

$$
C_{2.1} = |JI| * IO.
$$

Using the pertinent deletions to "mark" the entries in JI which correspond to deleted items costs

$$
C_{2.2} = (Pr_A * ||d_R|| + ||JI||) * comp.
$$

The step where the join indices for the inserted tuples are merged with the already "marked" join index is actually done as part of forming the join itself. The cost of merging and moving the newly inserted tuples to the joined result output area is

$$
\begin{aligned}
C_{2.3} \ = \ & (||i_R|| * Pr_A * ||S|| * JS + ||J|| - ||d_R|| * Pr_A * ||S|| \\
& * JS) * comp + ||i_R|| * Pr_A * ||S|| * JS * move.
\end{aligned}
$$

The process of forming the join will also identify pages of JI which need to be updated by being moved to the join index output buffer and written. Again, we make the assumption that no i_R or d_R group will overlap page boundaries. The cost is

$$
\begin{aligned}
C_{2.4} \ = \ & Yao((||i_R|| + ||d_R||) * Pr_A, |JI|, ||JI||) \\
& * (IO + n_{JI} * move).
\end{aligned}
$$

Thus the cost apportioned to reading and updating the JI may be summarized as $C_2 = C_{2.1} + C_{2.2} + C_{2.3} + C_{2.4}$.

(3) Forming the join. The join is actually formed in one or more passes. Hence, many of the costs involved are determined by the number of passes required which is in turn determined by how many pages of JI can be read into memory during a given pass. Let $|JI_k|$ denote this quantity. The available memory pages, M, must contain one page to input S, one page to input R, one page to store a portion of $S \bowtie JI_k$, one page to store the join result, one page to form the updated JI, $2 * N1_J$ pages to read in the insertions and deletions, space to merge both the insertions and deletions, as many pages as possible to accommodate the JI and its pointers to the corresponding R tuple, enough pages to store $R \bowtie JI_k$, enough pages to store the insertions pertaining to JI_k, enough pages to store memory-resident $i_R \bowtie S$, and enough space to sort the largest of JI_k, memory-resident i_R and memory-resident $i_R \bowtie S$. This memory requirement is illustrated in Figure 3 and yields the following computation:

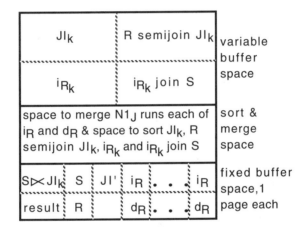

Figure 3   Memory configuration for phase 2 of join index algorithm.

$$
\begin{aligned}
|JI_k| \;=\; & \max_{k \in \{Integer\}, k \le |JI|} (1.5 * k + \frac{k * ||R|| * SR * T_R}{|JI| * P} \\
& + \frac{k * |i_R| * Pr_A}{|JI|} + \frac{k * |i_R| * Pr_A * n_{i_R} * ||S|| * JS * (T_S + T_R)}{|JI| * P} \\
& + 2 * SPACE_{mrg}(N1_J, T_R) \\
& + max[SPACE_{st}(k * n_{JI}), \\
& \quad\quad SPACE_{st}(k * |IR| * n_{i_R}/|JI|), \\
& \quad\quad SPACE_{st}(k * |i_R| * n_{i_R} * ||S|| * JS/|JI|)]) \\
& \le M - 2 * (N1_J) - 5.
\end{aligned}
$$

The number of passes is determined by taking $N2_J = |JI|/|JI_k|$. Likewise, the number of pages of R which are memory-resident during any pass is $|R_k| = |R| * SR/N2_J$ and the number of pages of memory-resident i_R is $|i_{R_k}| = |i_R| * Pr_A/N2_J$.

Once the $|JI_k|$ is read into memory and "marked" by the accumulated deletions and the corresponding pages of i_R are read into memory, the latter pages are sorted on the join attribute A, the corresponding tuples of S are accessed via an indirect index on A to form the join, and this portion of $i_R \bowtie S$ is sorted on s. The cost of this step is

$$
\begin{aligned}
C_{3.1} \;=\; & (CPU_{st}(|i_{R_k}| * n_{i_R}) \\
& + IO_{ii}(SR * |i_{R_k}| * n_{i_R}, |S|, ||S||) \\
& + Yao(SR * |i_{R_K}| * n_{i_R}, |S|, ||S||) * n_S * comp \\
& + |i_{R_k}| * n_{i_R} * ||S|| * JS * move \\
& + CPU_{st}(|i_{R_K}| * n_{i_R} * JS * ||S||)) * N2_J
\end{aligned}
$$

Forming R_k requires reading R using a clustered index, finding which tuples match and moving these to the area reserved for R_k. These operations have an attendant cost of

$$
\begin{aligned}
C_{3.2} \;=\; & (IO_{ci}(||R|| * SR/N2_J, |R|/N2_J, ||R||/N2_J) \\
& + Yao(||R|| * SR/N2_J, |R|/N2_J, ||R||/N2_J) \\
& * n_R * comp) * N2_J + ||R|| * SR * move.
\end{aligned}
$$

Sorting the JI_k on s incurs the following cost:

$$
C_{3.3} = CPU_{st}(|JI_k| * n_{JI}) * N2_J.
$$

Accessing S and moving join tuples to the output area requires

$$
\begin{aligned}
C_{3.4} \;=\; & (IO_{ci}(||S|| * SS/N2_J, |S|, ||S||) \\
& + Yao(||S|| * SS/N2_J, |S|, ||S||)) * N2_J \\
& + ||S|| * SS * move.
\end{aligned}
$$

The cost for forming the join is thus $C_3 = C_{3.1} + C_{3.2} + C_{3.3} + C_{3.4}$ and the full cost for the join index scenario is $C = C_1 + C_2 + C_3$.

3.5   Cost of hash join

As the hybrid-hash join algorithm has been analyzed extensively elsewhere [DKO+84] and adding the complicating factor of updates does not invalidate that analysis, we give only a brief presentation here. The algorithm consists of $B + 1$ steps where

$$
B = \max(0, \frac{|R| * F - |M|}{|M| - 1}).
$$

On the first step R and S are read into memory and hashed into $B + 1$ compatible sets; also, the first sets, $R0$ and $S0$, are joined at this time while the remainder are written out to disk. The remaining B steps consist of processing the sets $R_1, \ldots, R_B$ and $S_1, \ldots, S_B$ by reading them into memory and joining them. q of the tuples will be processed as part of the first pass and $1 - q$ will be processed during the subsequent passes. q is calculated as $|R0|/|R|$ where $|R0| = (|M| - B)/F$. The entire cost is

$$
\begin{aligned}
C \;=\; & (|R| + |S|) * IO + (||R|| + ||S||) * hash \\
& + (||R|| + ||S||) * (1 - q) * move \\
& + (|R| + |S|) * (1 - q) * IO \\
& + (||R|| + ||S||) * (1 - q) * hash + ||S|| * F * comp \\
& + ||R|| * move + (|R| + |S|) * (1 - q) * IO.
\end{aligned}
$$

Table 7 Parameter settings.

$\|R\|, \|S\|$	200,000 tuples	ssur, sptr	4 bytes
$\|M\|$	1000 pages	IO	25 msec
T_R, T_S	200 bytes	comp	3 μsec
PO	0.7	hash	9 μsec
FO	400 entries	move	20 μsec
P	4000 bytes	F	1.2

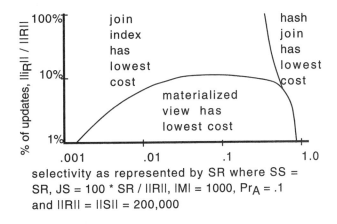

Figure 4 Cheapest method as selectivity and update activity vary.

4 Results

This section presents the performance comparisons of the three methods just analyzed. The default values used for some of the parameters are shown in Table 7 and are the same as those used in previous related studies [DKO+84,Val87].

Figure 4 illustrates the regions where each method performs best for different update activity and join selectivities. The update activity in the system is described by the ratio $\|i_R\|/\|R\|$ which represents the percentage of the tuples from the base relation R modified between two consecutive queries that involve the join. The join selectivity factor JS is proportional to the semijoin selectivities SS and SR ($SS = SR$) as $JS = 100 * SS/\|R\|$. This value has been chosen to produce a resulting join relation of realistic size. For example, when $SR = 0.01$, the resulting join relation has the same cardinality as an operand relation. We have chosen a join selectivity whose proportion to the semijoin is 10 times larger than the proportion used by Valduriez [Val87] to best highlight differences among the three methods. Figure 4 shows that materialized views offer the fastest performance when the selectivity is neither extremely high nor extremely low and the update activity is at most moderate. When the selectivity is extremely high, *e.g.*, the join relation is much larger than the relations used to form the join, the hash join method has the lowest cost. If the selectivity is extremely low or the selectivity is moderate but the update activity is large, then the join index algorithm has the fastest execution time.

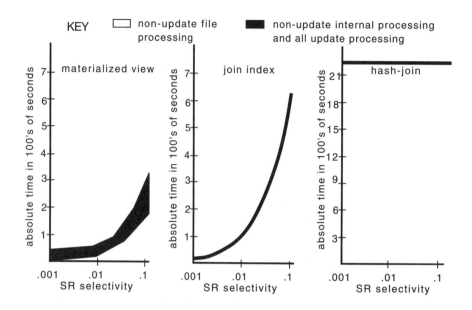

Figure 5 Cost of each method broken down into non-update-related file processing and other costs.

The effect produced in Figure 4 can be best understood by looking at a slightly more detailed cost analysis contained in Figure 5. This diagram breaks down the cost at each selectivity into the file costs that are associated with the basic algorithm and the costs for supporting updates and any non-update-related internal operations. All parameter settings are the same as those used in Figure 4 with the exception that the update activity has been fixed at 6 percent and the values for SR do not range beyond 0.1. For each method, the time associated with the non-updated-related file costs of the basic algorithm is represented by the white area under the total cost curve; the dark area under the curve represents the time associated with update operations and/or non-update-related internal processing. For the materialized view algorithm the dark area under the curve represents only update costs as this method has no internal processing associated with the basic algorithm. In the case of the join index method, the dark area under the curve represents both update costs and internal costs associated with the basic algorithm; however, the internal costs are small and never exceed 3 percent of the total time. The cost curve for the hash join method is constant with the darkened area representing only internal processing costs associated with the basic algorithm; the internal costs are approximately 1 percent of the total cost. Comparison among the three detailed analyses shows that the materialized view method has a competitive advantage because the file time required by its basic algorithm is less – sometimes much less – than the other two approaches. In particular, for low selectivities, reading the relation V takes a fraction of the time to read R and S, rewrite them and then read them again as required by the hash join method. And reading V takes much less time than reading JI, randomly accessing portions of R and several runs of randomly accessing portions of S as required by the join index method. The implication of this observation is that optimizing the internal processing of the hash join or join index algorithms or the update processing of the join index algorithm is unlikely to effect the comparative advantage of the materialized view method. The only way that the hash join method can favorably compete with the materialized view approach is by drastically increasing the size of V, which is exactly what occurs for extremely high selectivities. The only way that the join index algorithm can beat the time performance of the materialized view method is when the latter method spends sufficiently more time in processing updates, which is exactly what occurs when the selectivity is extremely low or the update activity is high.

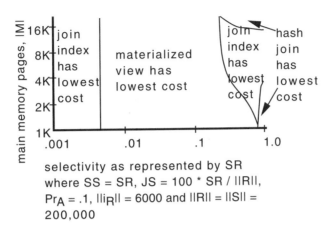

Figure 6 Cheapest method as selectivity and memory size vary.

We conclude this section with some experimental observations about the effects of various parameters which are held constant in Figure 4. As an example of what happens when these constants take on different values, consider the implications of varying the size of main memory. Figure 6 illustrates the regions where each method is better for different join selectivities and amounts of main memory available. Clearly, the join index algorithm is able to use additional main memory more efficiently than the other two algorithms in the sense that the join index algorithm reaches the point where all processing can be accomplished in one iteration, sooner than the other two methods. Thus, moderately increasing the size of main memory in Figure 4 would enlarge the area where the join index algorithm performs best. If the memory size were increased by approximately 20K pages, the area where the hash join method is superior would be increased. Similar effects can be observed for changes in other parameters. These changes do not change the general implications of the results shown in Figure 4 but they may considerably alter the boundaries of various regions of superiority. For instance, the size of V is largely dependent on the value used for JS so varying it within the bounds established by SS and SR have a considerable effect on the cost of the materialized view algorithm. In particular, the size of the area where the materialized view algorithm performs best varies inversely with the value of JS. The join index method gains a competitive advantage from only having to process a percentage of the updates. Therefore, it is not surprising that its area of superiority varies inversely with the probability of an update altering the join attribute. Lastly, we consider the effects upon Figure 4 results when the relation size varies. This can be accomplished either by changing the tuple sizes, T_S or T_R, or the number of tuples, $||R||$ or $||S||$. Varying the relation size has an inverse effect on whatever method is doing the most file process at a given selectivity. The materialized view cost is most effected at low selectivities, the join index method is effected at moderate selectivities, and the hash join method is effected at high selectivities.

5   Conclusion

This study has raised several points regarding the effectiveness of the join index, the materialized view, and the hash join algorithms for computing an equi-join. The method of choice depends upon the values of several parameters. Our results have shown that among these parameters are the selectivity, the update activity, the probability that the joining attribute is updated, and the relation and memory sizes. The observed effects of these parameters can be summarized as follows:

- The hash join algorithm performs well when the selectivity is extremely high. Its performance is adversely effected by an increase in relation size. Increasing the size of available main memory does not help the algorithm's performance until the memory is made extremely large. Although its performance is invariant to the update activity and the join attribute update probability, the hash join gains indirectly because increasing these parameters adversely effects the cost of the other two methods.

- The materialized view approach performs well for what might be described as "typical values." Primarily, these values include selectivities that are neither extremely high nor extremely low and a low to moderate update activity. This method is only slightly slower than the join index algorithm for very low selectivities. Increasing the relation size adversely effects this algorithm at low selectivities but increases its relative goodness at moderate selectivities. The algorithm does not appear to utilize additional main memory as well as the other two approaches. The materialized view approach is unaffected by increasing the join attribute update probability, but it gains relatively when this occurs because the join index method becomes more costly.

- The join index algorithm performs best when the selectivity is low to moderate, the update activity is high and the join attribute update probability is low. This method is favorably effected by an increase in memory and adversely effected by an increase in the attribute update probability. Increasing the relation size favors this method at high and low selectivities but decreases its relative cost effectiveness at moderate selectivities. A byproduct of this analysis is a strategy for incrementally maintaining a join index in the presence of updates to underlying base relations.

These results are important because complete or partial caching of joins is a relevant strategy for efficiently supporting (1) procedures as data types in extensible database systems, (2) situation monitoring in active databases, and (3) querying through methods in object-oriented database systems. Unfortunately, database customizers working in these environments often have only incomplete or imperfect knowledge of critical parameters. We propose the following heuristics based on our results: (a) If the join relation is much larger than the two relations which form it, use the hash join algorithm; (b) If the join relation is smaller or not much larger than its base relations and the update activity is less than or equal to 10 percent, cache the join via the materialized view algorithm; and (c) If the join relation is smaller or not much larger than its base relations but the update activity is more than 10 percent, use the join index algorithm to partially cache the join relation. While these heuristics do not guarantee the quickest join, the actual times obtained will generally not be too far from the optimal time.

Although this work has generated some interesting results, there is much to be done. There are several places where the internal processing could be optimized or further compaction could be applied. Also, the analysis should be generalized to investigate other operators like select and project, joins of more than two relations and arbitrary and possibly unequal sets of insertions and deletions. Eventually, the information gleaned from such an investigation could be incorporated in a system which used the designer's estimates to initially select among algorithms for efficiently supporting queries but also maintained usage statistics so that the system could automatically adapt to the appropriate structures and algorithms after a suitable period.

Acknowledgments

This work has benefited from ideas provided by Pedro Celis in early stages of this project.

References

[Abi88] Serge Abiteboul. Updates, A New Frontier. In Marc Gyssens, Jan Paredaens, and Dirk Van Gucht, editors, *Proceedings of the Second International Conference on Database Theory (ICDT '88)*, pages 1–18, Bruges, Belgium, August 31 - September 2 1988.

[AAD+96a] Sameet Agarwal, Rakesh Agrawal, Prasad Deshpande, Ashish Gupta, Jeffrey F. Naughton, Raghu Ramakrishnan, and Sunita Sarawagi. On the computation of multidimensional aggregates. In T. M. Vijayaraman, C. Mohan, and Alexander Buchman, editors, *Proceedings of the 22nd International Conference on Very Large Databases*, pages 506–521, Mumbai, India, September 3-6 1996.

[AAD+96b] Sameet Agarwal, Rakesh Agrawal, Prasad Deshpande, Ashish Gupta, Jeffrey F. Naughton, Raghu Ramakrishnan, and Sunita Sarawagi. On the Computation of Multidimensional Aggregates. Technical report-1314, University of Wisconsin-Madison, September 3-6 1996.

[AD83] Rakesh Agrawal and David J. DeWitt, "Updating Hypothetical Data Bases," *Information Processing Letters 16* (April 1983), 145146, North Holland.

[ABW88] Krzysztof Apt, Howard Blair, and Adrian Walker. Towards a theory of declarative knowledge. In J. Minker, editor, *Foundations of Deductive Databases and Logic Programming*, pages 89–148, Washington D.C., 1988. Morgan Kaufmann.

[AC89] Foto Afrati and Stavros S. Cosmadakis. Expressiveness of restricted recursive queries. In *Proceedings of the Twenty-First Annual ACM Symposium on Theory of Computing*, pages 113–126, Seattle, WA, May 15–17 1989.

[ACHK93] Yigal Arens, Chin Y. Chee, Chun-Nan Hsu, and Craig A. Knoblock. Retrieving and Integrating Data from Multiple Information Sources. *IJCIS*, 2(2):127–158, June 1993.

[ACM93] Serge Abiteboul, Sophie Cluet, and Tova Milo. Querying and updating the file. In Rakesh Agrawal, Sean Baker, and David Bell, editors, *Proceedings of the Conference on Very Large Databases, Morgan Kaufman pubs. (Los Altos CA) 19, Dublin.*, pages 73–84, Dublin, Ireland, August 1993.

[ADD+91] Rafi Ahmed, Philippe DeSmedt, Weimin Du, William Kent, Mohammad Ketabchi, Witold Litwin, Abbas Rafii, and Ming-Chien Shan. Pegasus heterogeneous multidatabase system. *IEEE Computer*, 24(12):19–27, December 1991.

[AE95] Sibel Adali and Ross Emery. A Uniform Framework for Integrating Knowledge in Heterogeneous Knowledge Systems. In *Proceedings of the Eleventh IEEE International Conference on Data Engineering (ICDE)*, pages 513–520, Taipei, Taiwan, March 6-10 1995.

[AGMK95] Brad Adelberg, Hector Garcia-Molina, and Ben Kao. Applying update streams in a soft real-time database system. In Michael Carey and Donovan Schneider, editors, *Proceedings of ACM SIG-MOD 1995 International Conference on Management of Data*, pages 245–256, San Jose, CA, May 23-25 1995.

[AL80] Michel E. Adiba and Bruce Lindsay. Database snapshots. In *Proceedings of the sixth International Conference on Very Large Databases*, pages 86–91, Montreal, Canada, October 1-3 1980.

[Alb91] Joseph Albert. Algebraic properites of bag data types. In Guy M. Lohman, Amilcar Sernadas, and Rafael Camps, editors, *Proceedings of the Conference on Very Large Databases, Morgan Kaufman pubs. (Los Altos CA) 17, Barcelona.*, pages 211–219, Barcelona, Spain, September 1991.

[AP87] Krzysztof R. Apt and Jean-Marc Pugin. Maintenance of Stratified Databases Viewed as a Belief Revision System. In *Proceedings of the Sixth Symposium on Principles of Database Systems (PODS)*, pages 136–145, San Diego, CA, March 23-25 1987.

[AR88] A. Amir and Nick Roussopoulos, Optimal View Cache, *Submitted to Information Processing Letters*, (January 1988).

[AS94] Sibel Adali and Venkatramanan Siva Subrahmanian. Amalgamating Knowledge Bases, II: Distributed Mediators. *International Journal of Intelligent Cooperative Information Systems*, 3(4):349–383, 1994.

[AS96] Sibel Adali and Venkatramanan Siva Subrahmanian. Amalgamating Knowledge Bases, III: Algorithms, Data Structures, and Query Processing. *Journal of Logic Programming (JLP)*, 28(1):45–88, July 1996.

[ASU79] Alfred.V. Aho, Yehoshua Sagiv, and Jeffrey D. Ullman. Efficient optimization of a class of relational expressions. *ACM Transactions on Database Systems (TODS)*, 4(4):435–454, December 1979.

[AV88] Serge Abiteboul and Victor Vianu. Equivalence and optimization of relational transactions. *Journal of the ACM.*, 35(1):70–120, January 1988.

[AWS92] Christopher Ahlberg, Christopher Williamson, and Ben Shneiderman (1992). Dynamic Queries for Information Exploration: An Implementation and Evaluation. Proc. CHI'92: Human Factors in Comp. Systems, ACM Press.

[AWS93] Christopher Ahlberg, Christopher Williamson, and Ben Shneiderman. Dynamic Queries for information exploration: an implementation and evaluation. In Ben Shneiderman, editor, *Sparks of Innovation in Human-Computer Interaction.* Ablex Publishing Corp, 1993.

[Ban85] F. Bancilhon. Naive evaluation of recursively defined relations. In M. Brodie and J. Mysopoulos, editors, *On Knowledge Base Management Systems \(Em Integrating Database and AI Systems.* Springer-Verlag, 1985.

[Bat85] Don S. Batory. Modeling the storage architectures of commercial database systems. *ACM Transactions on Database Systems (TODS)*, 10(4):463–528, December 1985.

[BB82] Philip A. Bernstein and Barbara T. Blaustein. Fast Methods for Testing Quantified Relational Calculus Assertions. In Mario Schkolnick, editor, *Proceedings of ACM SIGMOD 1982 International Conference on Management of Data*, pages 39–50, Orlando, FL, June 2-4 1982.

[BB91] Philip A. Bernstein and Barbara T. Blaustein. A Simplification Algorithm for Integrity Assertions and Concrete Views. In *In Proceedings of COMPSAC*, pages 90–99, Chicago, 1991.

[BBC80] Philip.A. Bernstein, Barbara T. Blaustein, and Edmund M. Clarke. Fast maintenance of semantic integrity assertions using redundant aggregate data. In *Proceedings of the Conference on Very Large Databases, Morgan Kaufman pubs. (Los Altos CA) 6, Lochovsky and Taylor(eds).*, pages 126–136, Montreal, Canada, October 1980.

[BDT83] Dina Bitton, David DeWitt, and C. Turbyfill, Benchmarking Database Systems: A Systematic Approach, Department of Computer Science, University of Wisconsin at Madison, TR 526 (December 1983).

[Blo70] Bloom, B. H., "Space/Time Trade-offs in Hash Coding with Allowable Errors" Comm. *of the ACM 13, 7* (July 1970).

[BBMR89] Alex Borgida, Ronald J. Brachman, Deborah L. McGuinness, and Lori Alperin Resnick. Classic: A structural data model for objects. In *Proceedings of the 1989 ACM SIGMOD International Conference on Mangement of Data*, pages 58–67. Association for Computing Machinery, June 1989.

[BC79] Peter O. Buneman and Eric K. Clemons. Efficiently monitoring relational databases. *ACM Transactions on Database Systems (TODS)*, 4(3):368–382, September 1979.

[BCL86] Jose A. Blakeley, Neil Coburn, and Per-Ake Larson. Updating derived relations: Detecting irrelevant and autonomously computable updates. *Proceedings of the Conference on Very Large Databases, Morgan Kaufman pubs. (Los Altos CA) 12.*, pages 457–466, August 1986.

[BCL89] Jose A Blakeley, Neil Coburn, and Per-Ake Larson. Updating derived relations: Detecting irrelevant and autonomously computable updates. *ACM Transactions on Database Systems (TODS)*, 14(3):369–400, September 1989.

[BDD+95] Omar Boucelma, J. Dalrymple, M. Doherty, Jean Claude Franchitti, Richard Hull, Roger King, and Gang Zhou. Incorporating Active and Multi-database-state Services into an OSA-Compliant Interoperability Framework. In *The Collected Arcadia Papers, Second Edition*. University of California, Irvine, May 1995.

[BDM88] Francois Bry, Hendrik Decker, and Rainer Manthey. A Uniform Approach to Constraint Satisfaction and Constraint Satisfiability in Deductive Databases. In *Proceedings of the First International Conference on Extending Database Technology (EDBT)*, pages 488–505, Venice, Italy, March 14-18 1988.

[BE77] Mike W. Blasgen and Kapali P. Eswaran. Storage and Access in Relational Data Bases. *IBM Systems Journal*, 16(4):362–377, 1977.

[Bee89] Catriel Beeri. Formal models for object-oriented databases. In Won Kim, Jean-Marie Nicolas, and Shojiro Nishio, editors, *Proceedings of the First International Conference on Deductive and Object-Oriented Databases (DOOD '89)*, pages 405–430, Kyoto, Japan, December 4-6 1989.

[BFKM85] L. Brownston, R. Farrell, E. Kant, and N. Martin. *Programming Expert Systems in OPS5: An Introduction to Rule-Based Programming*. Addison-Wesley, Reading Massachusetts, 1985.

[BGMS92] Yuri Breitbart, Hector Garcia-Molina, and Abraham Silberschatz. Overview of Multidatabase Transaction Management. *VLDB Journal*, 1(2):181–293, 1992.

[BKV90] Adam L. Buchsbaum, Paris C. Kanellakis, and J.S. Vitter. A data structure for arc insertion and regular path finding. In *In* Proc. ACM-SIAM Symp. on Discrete Algorithms, 1990.

[BL85] Jose Blakeley and Bruce G. Lindsay. Personal communications on snapshot refresh in system r*, 1985.

[Bla87] Jose A. Blakeley. Updating materialized database views. Technical report, Un.Waterloo, CSD, Res.R. CS-87-32., May 1987.

[BLN86] Carlo Batini, Maurizio Lenzerini, and Shamkant Navathe. A Comparative Analysis of Methodologies for Database Schema Integration. *Computing Surveys*, 18(4):323–364, 1986.

[BLT86] Jose A. Blakeley, Per-Ake Larson, and Frank W. Tompa. Efficiently Updating Materialized Views. In Carlo Zaniolo, editor, *Proceedings of ACM SIGMOD 1986 International Conference on Management of Data*, pages 61–71, Washington, D.C., May 28-30 1986.

[BLV93] Petra Bayer, Alexandre Lefebvre, , and Laurent Vieille. Architecture and Design of the EKS Deductive Database System. Unpublished Report Bull - ECRC, December 1993.

[BM90a] Jose A. Blakeley and Nancy L. Martin. Join index, materialized view, and hybrid hash join: A performance analysis. In *Proceedings of the Sixth IEEE International Conference on Data Engineering (ICDE)*, pages 256–263, Los Angeles, CA, February 5-9 1990.

[BM90b] Francois Bry and Rainer Manthey. Deductive Databases. In Logic Programming Summer School: tutorial notes, University of Zurich, Switzerland, August 1990.

[BM91] Catriel Beeri and Tova Milo. A model for active object oriented database. In Guy M. Lohman, Amilcar Sernadas, and Rafael Camps, editors, *Proceedings of the Seventeenth International Conference on Very Large Databases*, pages 337–349, Barcelona, Spain, September 3-6 1991.

[BMM91] Francois Bry, Rainer Manthey, and Bern Martens. Integrity Verification in Knowledge Bases. In *Proceedings of the Second Russian Conference on Logic Programming*, pages 114–139, St. Petersburg, Russia, September 1991. Published by Springer-Verlag LNCS.

[BMSU86] Francois Bancilhon, David Maier, Yehoshua Sagiv, and Jeffrey D. Ullman. Magic sets and other strange ways to implement logic programs. In *Proceedings of the Fifth Symposium on Principles of Database Systems (PODS)*, pages 1–16, Cambridge, MA, March 24-26 1986.

[Boc91] Jorge B. Bocca. MegaLog - A platform for developing Knowledge Base Management Systems. In *Proceedings of the Second International Symposium on Database Systems for Advanced Applications (DASFAA)*, pages 374–380, Tokyo, Japan, April 1991.

[BR86] Francois Bancilhon and Raghu Ramakrishnan. An amateur's introduction to recursive query processing strategies. In Carlo Zaniolo, editor, *Proceedings of ACM SIGMOD 1986 International Conference on Management of Data*, pages 16–52, Washington, D.C., May 28-30 1986.

[BR87] Catriel Beeri and Raghu Ramakrishnan. On the power of magic. In *Proceedings of the Sixth Symposium on Principles of Database Systems (PODS)*, pages 269–283, San Diego, CA, March 23-25 1987.

[Bra84] Kjell Bratbergsengen. Hashing Methods and Relational Algebra Operations. In Lim Huat Seng Umeshwar Dayal, Gunter Schlageter, editor, *Proceedings of the Tenth International Conference on Very Large Databases (VLDB)*, pages 323–333, Singapore, August 27-31 1984.

[BS81] Francois Bancihon and Nicolas Spyratos. *Update Semantics of Relational Views*. Transactions on Database Systems 6(4) December 1981, 557–575.

[BST+92] Ronald J. Brachman, Peter G. Selfridge, Loren G. Terveen, Boris Altman, Alex Borgida, Fern Halper, Thomas Kirk, Alan Lazar, Deborah L. McGuinness, and Lori Alperin Resnick. Knowledge representation support for data archeology. In *First International Conference on Information and Knowledge Management*, pages 457–464, November 1992.

[BST+93] Ronald J. Brachman, Peter G. Selfridge, Loren G. Terveen, Boris Altman, Alex Borgida, Fern Halper, Thomas Kirk, Alan Lazar, Deborah L. McGuinness, and Lori Alperin Resnick. Integrated support for data archeology. *International Journal of Intelligent and Cooperative Information Systems*, 2:159–185, 1993.

[BW94] Elena Baralis and Jennifer Widom. An algebraic approach to rule analysis in expert database systems. In Jorge Bocca, Matthias Jarke, and Carlo Zaniolo, editors, *Proceedings of the 20th International Conference on Very Large Databases*, pages 475–486, Santiago, Chile, September 12-15 1994.

[Car75] Alfonso F. Cardenas, "Analysis and Performance of Inverted Data Base Structures," *Comm. of the ACM 18, 5* (May 1975), 253–263.

[Cat93] R.G.G. Cattell. *The Object Database Standard: ODMG-93*. Morgan Kaufmann Publishers, San Mateo, California, 1993.

[CCCR+90] Filippo Cacace, Stefano Ceri, Stefano Crespi-Reghizi, Letizia Tanca, and Roberto Zicari. Integrating object-oriented data modeling with a rule-based programming paradigm. In Hector Garcia-Molina and Hosagrahar V. Jagadish, editors, *Proceedings of ACM SIGMOD 1990 International Conference on Management of Data*, pages 225–236, Atlantic City, NJ, May 23-25 1990.

[CDKK85] Hong-Tai Chou, David DeWitt, Randy Katz, and Anthony Klug. Design and implementation of the wisconsin storage system. *Software Practices and Experience*, 15(10):943–962, October 1985.

[CDRS86] Michael J. Carey, David J. DeWitt, Joel E. Richardson, and Eugene J. Shekita. Object and File Management in the EXODUS Extensible Database System. In Wesley W. Chu, Georges Gardarin, Setsuo Ohsuga, and Yahiko Kambayashi, editors, *Proceedings of the Twelfth International Conference on Very Large Databases (VLDB)*, pages 91–100, Kyoto, Japan, August 25-28 1986.

[CG85] Stefano Ceri and Georg Gottlob. Translating sql into relational algebra: Optimization, semantics, and equivalence of sql queries. *Polit.Milano, Lab.di Calcolatori, TR-84-16.*, pages 324–345, 1985.

[CDN88] J. Chin, V. Diehl, K. Norman. (1988). Development of an instrument measuring user satisfaction of the human-computer interface. in Proc. CHI'88: Human Factors in Comp. Systems Conf., ACM Press, 213–218.

[CGL+96] Latha Colby, Timothy Griffin, Leonid Libkin, Inderpal Singh Mumick, and Howard Trickey. Algorithms for deferred view maintenance. In Hosagrahar V. Jagadish and Inderpal Singh Mumick, editors, *Proceedings of ACM SIGMOD 1996 International Conference on Management of Data*, pages 469–480, Montreal, Canada, June 1996.

[CGM90] Upen S. Chakravarthy, John Grant, and Jack Minker. Logic-Based Approach to Semantic Query Optimization. *ACM Transactions on Database Systems (TODS)*, 15(2):162–207, 1990.

[CGT90] Stefano Ceri, Georg Gottlob, and Letizia Tanca. *Logic Programming and Databases*. Springer-Verlag, Berlin Heidelberg, 1990.

[CH95] Ti-Pin Chang and Richard Hull. Using Witness Generators to Support Bi-directional Update Between Object-Based Databases. In *Proceedings of the Fourteenth Symposium on Principles of Database Systems (PODS)*, pages 196–207, San Jose, CA, May 22-24 1995.

[Cha94] Ti-Pin Chang. *On Incremental Update Propagation Between Object-Based Databases*. PhD thesis, University of Southern California, Los Angeles, CA, 1994.

[Che] Chandra Chekuri. Personal communcation on greedy algorithms for selecting views in a data cube.

[CHM92] I-Min A. Chen, Richard Hull, and Dennis McLeod. Derived data update via limited ambiguity, December 7 1992. Technical Report, University of Southern California, December 7 1992.

[Cho92a] Jan Chomicki. History-less checking of dynamic integrity constraints. In *Proceedings of the Seventh IEEE International Conference on Data Engineering (ICDE)*, pages 557–564, Tempe, AZ, February 3-7 1992.

[Cho92b] Jan Chomicki. Real-time integrity constraints. In *Proceedings of the Eleventh Symposium on Principles of Database Systems (PODS)*, pages 274–282, San Diego, CA, June 2-4 1992.

[CKL+97] Latha Colby, Akira Kawaguchi, Daniel Lieuwen, Inderpal Singh Mumick, and Kenneth A. Ross. Supporting multiple view maintenance policies:concepts, algorithms,and performance analysis. In Patrick Valduriez and Joan Peckham, editors, *Proceedings of ACM SIGMOD 1997 International Conference on Management of Data*, pages 0–, Tucson, AZ, May 1997.

[CKPS95] Surajit Chaudhuri, Ravi Krishnamurthy, Spyros Potamianos, and Kyuseok Shim. Optimizing queries with materialized views. In *Proceedings of the Eleventh IEEE International Conference on Data Engineering (ICDE)*, pages 190–200, Taipei, Taiwan, March 6-10 1995.

[CLR90] Thomas H. Cormen, Charles E. Leiserson, and Ronald L. Rivest. Introduction to Algorithms. MIT Press, Cambridge, MA, 1990.

[CM77] Ashok K. Chandra and Philip M. Merlin. Optimal implementation of conjunctive queries in relational data bases. In *Conference Record of the Ninth Annual ACM Symposium on Theory of Computing*, pages 77–90, Boulder, Colorado, May 1977.

[CM89] Meng Chang Chen and Lawrence McNamee. On the Data Model and Access Method of Summary Data Management. *IEEE Transactions on Knowledge and Data Engineering (TKDE)*, 1(4):519–529, 1989.

[Cod93] E. F. Codd. Providing OLAP: An IT Mandate. Unpublished Manuscript, E.F. Codd and Associates, 1993.

[Coh86] D. Cohen. Programming by specification and annotation. In *Proceedings of AAAI*, 1986.

[CP84] S. Stavros Cosmadakis and Christos H. Papadimitriou, Updates of Relational Views, *Journal of the Assoc. Comput. Mach.*, 31:4(October 1984).

[CR94] Chungmin Melvin Chen and Nick Roussopoulos. The Implementation and Performance Evaluation of the ADMS Query Optimizer: Integrating Query Result Caching and Matching. In *Proceedings of the Fourth International Conference on Extending Database Technology*, pages 323–336, Cambridge, UK, March 28-31 1994.

[CS93] Surajit Chaudhuri and Kyuseok Shim. Query optimization in the presence of foreign functions. In Rakesh Agrawal, Sean Baker, and David Bell, editors, *Proceedings of the Nineteenth International Conference on Very Large Databases*, pages 529–542, Dublin, Ireland, August 24-27 1993.

[CS94] Surajit Chaudhuri and Kyuseok Shim. Including group-by in query optimization. In Jorge Bocca, Matthias Jarke, and Carlo Zaniolo, editors, *Proceedings of the 20th International Conference on Very Large Databases*, pages 354–366, Santiago, Chile, September 12-15 1994.

[CSS94] Rakesh Chandra, Arie Segev, and Michael Stonebraker. Implementing calendars and temporal rules in next-generation databases. In *Proceedings of the Tenth IEEE International Conference on Data Engineering (ICDE)*, pages 264–273, Houston, TX, February 14-18 1994.

[CV93] Surajit Chaudhuri and Moshe Y. Vardi. Optimization of Real Conjunctive Queries. In *Proceedings of the Twelfth Symposium on Principles of Database Systems (PODS)*, pages 59–70, Washington, DC, May 25-27 1993.

[CW90] Stefano Ceri and Jennifer Widom. Deriving Production Rules for Constraint Maintainance. In Dennis McLeod, Ron Sacks-Davis, and Hans Schek, editors, *Proceedings of the Sixteenth International Conference on Very Large Databases*, pages 566–577, Brisbane, Australia, August 13-16 1990.

[CW91] Stefano Ceri and Jennifer Widom. Deriving production rules for incremental view maintenance. In Guy M. Lohman, Amilcar Sernadas, and Rafael Camps, editors, *Proceedings of the Seventeenth International Conference on Very Large Databases*, pages 577–589, Barcelona, Spain, September 3-6 1991.

[CW92a] Stefano Ceri and Jennifer Widom. Deriving Incremental Production Rules for Deductive Data. Technical Report RJ 9071, IBM Research Division, Almaden Research Center, 1992.

[CW92b] Stefano Ceri and Jennifer Widom. Managing semantic heterogeneity with production rules and persistent queues. Technical Report RJ 9064 (80754), IBM Research Division, Almaden Research Center, October 30 1992.

[CW94] Stefano Ceri and Jennifer Widom. Deriving Incremental Production Rules for Deductive Data. *Information Systems*, 19(6):467–490, 1994.

[DAJ91] Shaul Dar, Rakesh Agrawal, and Hosagrahar V. Jagadish. Optimization of generalized transitive closure. In *Proceedings of the Seventh IEEE International Conference on Data Engineering (ICDE)*, pages 345–354, Kobe, Japan, April 8-12 1991.

[Dal95] J. Dalrymple. *Extending Rule Mechanisms for the Construction of Interoperable Systems*. PhD thesis, University of Colorado, Boulder, 1995.

[DB82] Umeshwar Dayal and Philip A. Bernstein, On the Correct Translation of Update Operations on Relational Views, *ACM Trans. on Database Systems*, 7:3(September 1982).

[DB94] Tomasz Imielinski and Daniel Barbara. Sleepers and Workaholics: Caching Strategies in Mobile Environments. In Richard Snodgrass and Marianne Winslett, editors, *Proceedings of ACM SIGMOD 1994 International Conference on Management of Data*, pages 1–12, Minneapolis, MN, May 25-27 1994.

[DBB+88] Umeshwar Dayal, Barbara T. Blaustein, Alejandro P. Buchmann, Upen S. Chakravarthy, M. Hsu, R. Ledin, Dennis R. McCarthy, Arnon Rosenthal, Sunil K. Sarin, Michael J. Carey, Miron Livny, and Rajiv Jauhari. The HiPAC Project: Combining Active Databases and Timing Constraints. *SIGMOD Record*, 17(1):51–70, 1988.

[DE88] Lois M. L. Delcambre and James N. Etheredge. The Relational Production Language: A Production Language for Relational Databases. In *Proceedings from the Second International Conference on Expert Database Systems*, pages 333–351, Virginia, USA, April 1988.

[Dec86] Hendrik Decker. Integrity Enforcement on Deductive Databases. In *Proceedings of the First International Conference on Expert Database Systems*, pages 381–395, Charleston, SC, April 1986.

[DH84] Umeshwar Dayal and Hai-Yann Hwang. View Definition and Generalization for Database Integration in a Multidatabase System. *ACM Transactions on Software Engineering (TSE)*, 10(6):628–645, 1984.

[DHDD95] Michael Doherty, Richard Hull, Marcia A. Derr, and Jacques Durand. On Detecting Conflict Between Proposed Updates. In Paolo Atzeni and Val Tannen, editors, *Proceedings of the Fifth International Workshop on Database Programming Languages*, page 7, Gubbio, Umbria, Italy, September 6-8 1995.

[DHR96] Michael Doherty, Richard Hull, and Mohammed Rupawalla. Structures for Manipulating Proposed Updates in Object-Oriented Databases. In Hosagrahar V. Jagadish and Inderpal Singh Mumick, editors, *Proceedings of ACM SIGMOD 1996 International Conference on Management of Data*, pages 306–317, Montreal, Canada, June 1996.

[DK94] Guozhu Dong and Ramamohanrao Kotagiri. Incrementally evaluating constrained transitive closure by conjunctive queries. Technical report 94/11, Univ of Melbourne, 1994.

[DKO+84] David J. DeWitt, Randy H. Katz, Frank Olken, Leonard D. Shapiro, Michael Stonebraker, and David A. Wood. Implementation Techniques for Main Memory Database Systems. In *Proceedings of ACM SIGMOD 1984 International Conference on Management of Data*, pages 1–8, 1984.

[DLW95] Guozhu Dong, Leonid Libkin, and Limsoon Wong. On Impossibility of Decremental Recomputation of Recursive Queries in Relational Calculus and SQL. In *Proceedings of the International Workshop on Database Programming Languages*, page 7, 1995.

[dMS88] Christophe de Maindreville and Eric Simon. Modelling Non Deterministic Queries and Updates in Deductive Databases. In David J. DeWitt Francois Bancilhon, editor, *Proceedings of the Fourteenth International Conference on Very Large Databases*, pages 395–406, Los Angeles, CA, August 22-25 1988.

[Don91] Guozhu Dong. On datalog linearization of chain queries. In Jeffrey D. Ullman, editor, *Theoretical Studies in Computer Science*, pages 181–206, Academic Press, 1991.

[Don92] Guozhu Dong. Datalog Expressiveness of Chain Queries: Grammar Tools and Characterizations. In *Proceedings of the Eleventh Symposium on Principles of Database Systems (PODS)*, pages 81–90, San Diego, CA, June 2-4 1992.

[Dow95] Alan Downing. Conflict Resolution in Symmetric Replication. In *European Oracle User Group (EOUG)*, Florence, Italy, April 1995.

[Doy79] Jon Doyle. A Truth Maintenance System. *Artificial Intelligence*, 12, 1979.

[DP95] Guozhu Dong and C. Pang. Maintaining transitive closure in first-order after node-set and edge-set deletions. Technical report, Univ of Melbourne, May 1995.

[DS92] Guozhu Dong and Jianwen Su. Incremental and Decremental Evaluation of Transitive Closure by First-Order Queries. Technical Report TRCS 92-18, University of California, Santa Barbara, 1992.

[DS93] Guozhu Dong and Jianwen Su. First-Order Incremental Evaluation of Datalog Queries. In Catriel Beeri, A. Ohori, and Dennis Shasha, editors, *Proceedings of the Fourth International Workshop on Database Programming Languages*, pages 295–308, New York, NY, August 30-September 1 1993.

[DS95a] Guozhu Dong and Jianwen Su. Incremental and Decremental Evaluation of Transitive Closure by First-Order Queries. *Information and Computation*, 120(1):101–106, 1995.

[DS95b] Guozhu Dong and Jianwen Su. Space-Bounded FOIES. In *Proceedings of the Fourteenth Symposium on Principles of Database Systems (PODS)*, pages 139–150, San Jose, CA, May 22-24 1995.

[DS96] Guozhu Dong and Jianwen Su. Deterministic FOIES are strictly weaker. Technical report, Uni of Melbourne, 1996.

[DSR95] Guozhu Dong, Jianwen Su, and Rodney Topor. Nonrecursive incremental evaluation of Datalog queries. *Annals of Mathematics and Artificial Intelligence*, 14(2-4):187–223, 1995.

[DT92] Guozhu Dong and Rodney Topor. Incremental Evaluation of Datalog Queries. In Joachim Biskup and Richard Hull, editors, *Proceedings of the Fourth International Conference on Database Theory (ICDT '92)*, pages 282–296, Berlin, Germany, October 14-16 1992.

[DW89] Subrata K. Das and M. Howard Williams. A Path Finding Method for Constraint Checking in Deductive Databases. *Data & Knowledge Engineering*, 4(3):223–244, 1989.

[EK91] Frank Eliassen and Randi Karlsen. Interoperability and Object Identity. *SIGMOD Record*, 20(4):25–29, 1991.

[Elk90] Charles Elkan. Independence of Logic Database Queries and Updates. In *Proceedings of the Ninth Symposium on Principles of Database Systems (PODS)*, pages 154–160, Nashville, TN, April 2-4 1990.

[Eps79] Robert S. Epstein. Techniques for processing of aggregates in relational database systems. Technical report, UCB, Elec. Res. Lab, M798., February 1979.

[Ern95] Ernest Teniente and Antoni Olive. Updating Knowledge Bases While Maintaining Their Consistency. *VLDB Journal*, 4(2):193–241, 1995.

[FBC+87] Daniel H. Fishman, David Beech, H. P. Cate, E. C. Chow, Tim Connors, J. W. Davis, Nigel Derrett, C. G. Hoch, William Kent, Peter Lyngb k, Brom Mahbod, Marie-Anne Neimat, T. A. Ryan, and Ming-Chien Shan. Iris: An Object-Oriented Database Management System. *ACM Transactions on Office Information Systems (TOIS)*, 5(1):48–69, 1987.

[FC85] Antonio L. Furtado and Marco A. Casanova, *Updating Relational Views in Query Processing in Database Systems*. 1985.

[Fei96] Uriel Feige. A threshold of ln n for approximating set cover. In *Proceedings of the 28th ACM Symposium on the Theory of Computing (STOC)*, 1996.

[FGVL+95] Oris Friesen, Gilles Gauthier-Villars, Alexander Lefebvre, , and Laurent Vieille. Applications of Deductive Object-Oriented Databases using DEL. In Raghu Ramakrishnan, editor, *Applications of Logic Databases*. Kluwer Academic Publishers, 1995.

[FHMS91] Dong Fang, Joachim Hammer, Dennis McLeod, and Antonio Si. Remote-Exchange: An approach to controlled sharing among autonomous, heterogenous database systems. In *Proceedings of IEEE COMPCON 1991*, San Francisco, CA, February 1991.

[Fin] Richard Finkelstein. Understanding the Need for On-Line Analytical Servers. Unpublished Manuscript.

[Fin82] Sheldon Finkelstein. Common Subexpression Analysis in Database Applications. In Mario Schkolnick, editor, *Proceedings of ACM SIGMOD 1982 International Conference on Management of Data*, pages 235–245, Orlando, FL, June 2-4 1982.

[FK93a] Jean-Claude Franchitti and Roger King. A Language for Composing Heterogeneous, Persistent Applications. In *Proceedings of the Workshop on Interoperability of Database Systems and Database Applications*, Fribourg, Switzerland, October 13-14 1993. Springer-Verlag, LNCS. .

[FK93b] Jean-Claude Franchitti and Roger King. Amalgame: A Tool for Creating Interoperating, Persistent, Heterogeneous Components. In Nabil R. Adam and Bharat K. Bhargava, editors, *Advanced Database Systems*, pages 313–336. Springer-Verlag, LNCS #759, 1993. Nabil R. Adam and Bharat K. Bhargava (Eds.).

[FLM97] Tim Finin, Yannis Labrou, and James Mayfield. KQML as an agent communication language. In Jeff Bradshaw, editor, *Software Agents*. MIT Press, 1997.

[Flo62] Robert W. Floyd. Algorithm 97: Shortest path. *Commun. ACM*, 5(6):345, 1962.

[FFW91] Richard Fowler, Wendy A. L. Fowler, Bradley A. Wilson. Integrating Query, Thesaurus, and Documents through a Common Visual Representation. in Proc. SIGIR '91. ACM Press, 142–151.

[FLV96] Oris Friesen, Alexandre Lefebvre, and Laurent Vieille. VALIDITY: Applications of a DOOD System. In *Proceedings of the Fifth International Conference on Extending Database Technology (EDBT)*, pages 131–134, Avignon, France, March 25-29 1996.

[Fre89] Michael Freeston. Advances in the Design of the BANG File. In *Proceedings of the Third International Conference on Foundations of Data Organization and Algorithms*, pages 322–338, Paris, France, June 1989.

[GB95] Ashish Gupta and Jose A. Blakeley. Using partial information to update materialized views. *Information Systems*, 20(8):641–662, 1995.

[GBLP96] Jim Gray, Adam Bosworth, Andrew Layman, and Hamid Pirahesh. Data cube: A relational aggregation operator generalizing group-by, cross-tab, and sub-total. In *Proceedings of the Twelfth IEEE International Conference on Data Engineering (ICDE)*, pages 152–159, New Orleans, LA, February 26 - March 1 1996.

[Gel86] Allen Van Gelder. Negation as Failure Using Tight Derivations for General Logic Programs. In *Proceedings of the 1986 Symposium on Logic Programming*, pages 127–138, Salt Lake City, UT, September 22-25 1986.

[GG92] Marc Gyssens and Dirk Van Gucht. The Powerset Algebra as a Natural Tool to Handle Nested Database Relations. *Journal of Computer and System Sciences (JCSS)*, 45(1):76–103, 1992.

[GHJ92] Shahram Ghandeharizadeh, Richard Hull, and Dean Jacobs. Implementation of Delayed Updates in Heraclitus. In *Proceedings of the Third International Conference on Extending Database Technology*, pages 261–276, Vienna, Austria, March 23-27 1992.

[GHJ+93] Shahram Ghandeharizadeh, Richard Hull, Dean Jacobs, Jaime Castillo, Martha Escobar-Molano, Shih-Hui Lu, Junhui Luo, Chiu Tsang, and Gang Zhou. On Implementing a Language for Specifying Active Database Execution Models. In Rakesh Agrawal, Sean Baker, and David Bell, editors, *Proceedings of the Nineteenth International Conference on Very Large Databases*, pages 441–454, Dublin, Ireland, August 24-27 1993.

[GHJ96] Shahram Ghandeharizadeh, Richard Hull, and Dean Jacobs. Heraclitus: Elevating deltas to be first class citizens in a database programming language. *ACM Transactions on Database Systems*, 21(3):370–426, 1996.

[GHK92] Sumit Ganguly, Waqar Hasan, and Ravi Krishnamurthy. Query Optimization for Parallel Execution. In Michael Stonebraker, editor, *Proceedings of ACM SIGMOD 1992 International Conference on Management of Data*, pages 9–18, San Diego, CA, June 2-5 1992.

[GHQ95] Ashish Gupta, Venky Harinarayan, and Dallan Quass. Aggregate-query processing in data warehousing environments. In Umeshwar Dayal, Peter M.D. Gray, and Shojiro Nishio, editors, *Proceedings of the 21st International Conference on Very Large Databases*, pages 358–369, Zurich, Switzerland, September 11-15 1995.

[GHRU96] Himanshu Gupta, Venky Harinarayan, Anand Rajaraman, and Jeffrey D. Ullman. Index selection for OLAP. Submitted for publication, April 7-11 1996.

[GJ79] Michael R. Garey and David S. Johnson. *Computers and Intractability*. W. H. Freeman and Company, 1979.

[GJM94] Ashish Gupta, Hosagrahar V. Jagadish, and Inderpal Singh Mumick. Data integration using self-maintainable views. Technical Memorandum 113880-941101-32, AT&T Bell Laboratories, November 1994.

[GJM96] Ashish Gupta, Hosagrahar V. Jagadish, and Inderpal Singh Mumick. Data integration using self-maintainable views. In *Proceedings of the Fifth International Conference on Extending Database Technology (EDBT)*, pages 140–144, Avignon, France, March 25-29 1996.

[GJM97] Ashish Gupta, Hosagrahar V. Jagadish, and Inderpal Singh Mumick. Maintenance and self-maintenance of outer-join views. In *Proceedings of the Third International Workshop on Next Generation Information Technologies and Systems (NGITS 97)*. Neve Ilan, Israel, June 1997.

[GJR94] Narain H. Gehani, Hosagrahar V. Jagadish, and William D. Roome. OdeFS: A File System Interface to an Object-Oriented Database. In Jorge Bocca, Matthias Jarke, and Carlo Zaniolo, editors, *Proceedings of the 20th International Conference on Very Large Databases*, pages 249–260, Santiago, Chile, September 12-15 1994.

[GJS92a] Narain Gehani, Hosagrahar V. Jagadish, and Oded Shmueli. Composite event specification in active databases: Model and implementation. In Li-Yan Yuan, editor, *Proceedings of the Eighteenth International Conference on Very Large Databases*, pages 327–338, Vancouver, Canada, August 23-27 1992.

[GJS92b] Narain Gehani, Hosagrahar V. Jagadish, and Oded Shmueli. Event specification in an active object-oriented database. In Michael Stonebraker, editor, *Proceedings of ACM SIGMOD 1992 International Conference on Management of Data*, pages 81–90, San Diego, CA, June 2-5 1992.

[GKB87] Ulrich Guntzer, Werner Kiessling, and Rudolf Bayer, On the Evaluation of Recursion in (Deductive) Database Systems by Efficient Differential Fixpoint Iteration, *Proceedings of the 3-rd Int. Conference on Data Engineering*, (February 3–5, 1987). pp. 120–129

[GKM92] Ashish Gupta, Dinesh Katiyar, and Inderpal Singh Mumick. Counting solutions to the view maintenance problem. In *Proceedings of the Workshop on Deductive Databases, Joint International Conference and Symposium on Logic Programming*, pages 185–194, Washington D. C., USA, November 14 1992.

[GL90] Ulrike Griefahn and Stefan Liittringhaus. Top-down integrity constraint checking for deductive databases. In *Proceedings of the Seventh International Conference on Logic Programming (ICLP)*, pages 130–144, Jerusalem, Israel, June 18-20 1990. MIT Press.

[GL91] Maurizio Gabbrielli and Giorgio Levi. Modeling Answer Constraints in Constraint Logic Programs. In *Proceedings of the Eigth International Conference on Logic Programming (ICLP)*, pages 238–252, Paris, France, June 24-28 1991. MIT Press.

[GL95] Timothy Griffin and Leonid Libkin. Incremental maintenance of views with duplicates. In Michael Carey and Donovan Schneider, editors, *Proceedings of ACM SIGMOD 1995 International Conference on Management of Data*, pages 328–339, San Jose, CA, May 23-25 1995.

[GLS94] Goetz Graefe, Ann Linville, and Leonard D. Shapiro. Sort versus Hash Revisited. *IEEE Transactions on Knowledge and Data Engineering (TKDE)*, 6(6):934–944, 1994.

[GLT97] Timothy Griffin, Leonid Libkin, and Howard Trickey. An improved algorithm for incremental recomputation of active relational expressions. *IEEE Transactions on Knowledge and Data Engineering (TKDE)*, 1997. To Appear.

[GM93] Stephane Grumbach and Tova Milo. Towards tractable algebras for bags. In *Proceedings of the Twelfth Symposium on Principles of Database Systems (PODS)*, pages 49–58, Washington, DC, May 25-27 1993.

[GM95] Ashish Gupta and Inderpal Singh Mumick. Maintenance of Materialized Views: Problems, Techniques, and Applications. *IEEE Data Engineering Bulletin, Special Issue on Materialized Views and Data Warehousing*, 18(2):3–18, June 1995.

[GM96] Ashish Gupta and Inderpal Singh Mumick. What is the Data Warehousing Problem? Are Materialized Views the Answer? In T. M. Vijayaraman, C. Mohan, and Alexander Buchman, editors, *Proceedings of the 22nd International Conference on Very Large Databases*, pages 602–602, Mumbai, India, September 3-6 1996.

[GMN84] Herve Gallaire, Jack Minker, and Jean M. Nicolas. Logic and databases: A deductive approach. *Computing Surveys*, 16:153–185, 1984.

[GMR95a] Ashish Gupta, Inderpal Singh Mumick, and Kenneth A. Ross. Adapting materialized views after redefinitions. In Michael Carey and Donovan Schneider, editors, *Proceedings of ACM SIGMOD 1995 International Conference on Management of Data*, San Jose, CA, May 23-25 1995.

[GMR95b] Ashish Gupta, Inderpal Singh Mumick, and Kenneth A. Ross. Adapting materialized views after redefinitions. In Michael Carey and Donovan Schneider, editors, *Columbia University Technical Report number CUCS-010-95*, pages 211–222, San Jose, CA, March 1995.

[GMS92] Ashish Gupta, Inderpal Singh Mumick, and Venkatramanan Siva Subrahmanian. Maintaining views incrementally. Technical Report 921214-19-TM, AT&T Bell Laboratories, December 1992.

[GMS93] Ashish Gupta, Inderpal Singh Mumick, and Venkatramanan Siva Subrahmanian. Maintaining views incrementally. In Peter Buneman and Sushil Jajodia, editors, *Proceedings of ACM SIGMOD 1993 International Conference on Management of Data*, pages 157–166, Washington, DC, May 26-28 1993.

[Gra93] Goetz Graefe. Query Evaluation Techniques for Large Databases. *Computing Surveys*, 25(2):73–170, 1993.

[Gri81] David Gries. *The Science of Programming*. Springer-Verlag, 1981.

[Gro95] Stanford Technology Group. Designing the data warehouse on relational databases. Unpublished white paper, 1995.

[GSUW94] Ashish Gupta, Shuky Sagiv, Jeffrey D. Ullman, and Jennifer Widom. Checking integrity constraints using partial data. In Inderpal Singh Mumick, editor, *Proceedings of the Thirteenth Symposium on Principles of Database Systems (PODS)*, pages 45–55, Minneapolis, MN, May 24-26 1994.

[GSV84] George Gardarin, Eric Simon, and Lionel Verlaine. Querying real time relational data bases. *IEEE-ICC Int'l Conf.*, pages 757–761, May 1984.

[GT94] Timothy Griffin and Howard Trickey. Integrity maintenance in a telecommunications switch. *IEEE Data Engineering Bulletin, Special Issue on Database Constraint Management*, 17(2):43–46, 1994.

[Gup94] Ashish Gupta. *Partial Information Based Integrity Constraint Checking*. PhD thesis, Stanford University, Department of Computer Science, STAN-CS-TR-95-1534, 1994.

[Gup97] Himanshu Gupta. Selection of Views to Materialize in a Data Warehouse. In Foto N. Afrati and Phokion Kolaitis, editors, *Proceedings of the Sixth International Conference on Database Theory (ICDT '97)*, pages 98–112, Delphi, Greece, January 8-10 1997.

[GW93] Ashish Gupta and Jennifer Widom. Local verification of global integrity constraints in distributed databases. In *ACM SIGMOD Conf. on the Management of Data 93, Washington,DC.*, pages 49–58, May 1993.

[Hae78] Theo Haerder. Implementing a generalized access path structure for a relational database system. *ACM Transactions on Database Systems (TODS)*, 3(3):285–298, 1978.

[Han87] Eric N. Hanson. A performance analysis of view materialization strategies. In Umeshwar Dayal and Irv Traiger, editors, *Proceedings of ACM SIGMOD 1987 International Conference on Management of Data*, pages 440–453, San Francisco, CA, May 27-29 1987.

[Han88] Eric N. Hanson. Processing Queries Against Database Procedures: A Performance Analysis. In Haran Boral and Per ke Larson, editors, *Proceedings of ACM SIGMOD 1988 International Conference on Management of Data*, pages 295–302, Chicago, IL, June 1-3 1988.

[Han89] Eric N. Hanson. An initial report on the design of ariel: A dbms with an integrated production rule system. *SIGMOD Record*, 18(3):12–19, September 1989.

[Hel88] Helander, M. (1988). Handbook of Human-Computer Interaction. Chapter 13. North-Holland, New York.

[HC90] Donna Harman and G. Candela. Bringing natural language information retrieval out of the closet. SIGCHI Bulletin 22, 42–48, 1990.

[HD92] John V. Harrison and Suzanne Dietrich. Maintenance of Materialized Views in a Deductive Database: An Update Propagation Approach. In *Workshop on Deductive Databases, JICSLP 1992*, pages 56–65, 1992.

[HFLP89] Laura M. Haas, Johann C. Freytag, Guy M. Lohman, and Hamid Pirahesh. Extensible query processing in starburst. In *Proceedings of the 1989 ACM SIGMOD International Conference on Mangement of Data*, pages 377–388. Association for Computing Machinery, June 1989.

[HJ90] Richard Hull and Dean Jacobs. On the Semantics of Rules in Database Programming Languages. In J. Schmidt and A. Stogny, editors, *Next Generation Information System Technology: Proc. of the First International East/West Database Workshop*, pages 59–85, Kiev, USSR, October 1990. Springer-Verlag LNCS, Volume 504.

[HJ91] Richard Hull and Dean Jacobs. Language Constructs for Programming Active Databases. In Guy M. Lohman, Amilcar Sernadas, and Rafael Camps, editors, *Proceedings of the Seventeenth International Conference on Very Large Databases*, pages 455–467, Barcelona, Spain, September 3-6 1991.

[HKMV91] Gerd G. Hillebrand, Paris C. Kanellakis, Harry G . Mairson, and Moshe Y. Vardi. Tools for datalog boundedness. In *ACM-PODS 91, Denver CO.*, pages 1–12, Denver, CO, CA, May 1991.

[HM93] Joachim Hammer and Dennis McLeod. An Approach to Resolving Semantic Heterogenity in a Federation of Autonomous, Heterogeneous Database Systems. *International Journal of Cooperative Information Systems (IJCIS)*, 2(1):51–83, 1993.

[HNSS95] Peter J. Haas, Jeffrey F. Naughton, S. Seshadri, and Lynne Stokes. Sampling-Based Estimation of the Number of Distinct Values of an Attribute. In Umeshwar Dayal, Peter M.D. Gray, and Shojiro Nishio, editors, *Proceedings of the 21st International Conference on Very Large Databases*, pages 311–322, Zurich, Switzerland, September 11-15 1995.

[HRU95] Venky Harinarayan, Anand Rajaraman, and Jeffrey D. Ullman. Implementing Data Cubes Efficiently. Technical Report, Stanford University, 1995.

[HRU96] Venkatesh Harinarayan, Anand Rajaraman, and Jeffrey D. Ullman. Implementing data cubes efficiently. In Hosagrahar V. Jagadish and Inderpal Singh Mumick, editors, *Proceedings of ACM SIGMOD 1996 International Conference on Management of Data*, pages 205–216, Montreal, Canada, June 1996.

[HS77] Michael Hammer and Sunil K. Sarin. Efficient monitoring of database assertions. In *Machine Intelligence,* eds: Meltzer o.o., and Michie, vars., pages 159–, December 1977.

[HSW94] Yixiu Huang, A. Prasad Sistla, and Ouri Wolfson. Data Replication for Mobile Computers. In Richard Snodgrass and Marianne Winslett, editors, *Proceedings of ACM SIGMOD 1994 International Conference on Management of Data*, pages 13–24, Minneapolis, MN, May 25-27 1994.

[HT85] Susan Horwitz and Tim Teitelbaum. Relations and Attributes: A Symbiotic Basis for Editing Environments,. In *ACM SIGPLAN 85 Symposium on Language Issues in Programming Environments*, pages 93–106, July 1985.

[HT86] Susan Horwitz and Tim Teitelbaum, "Generating Editing Environments Based on Relations and Attributes," *ACM Transactions on Programming Languages and Systems 8, 4* (October 1986), 577-608.

[HW92] Eric Hanson and Jennifer Widom. An overview of production rules in database systems. Technical report rj 9023 (80483), IBM Almaden Research Cente, October 1992.

[HZ96] Richard Hull and Gang Zhou. A framework for supporting data integration using the materialized and virtual approaches. In Hosagrahar V. Jagadish and Inderpal Singh Mumick, editors, *Proceedings of ACM SIGMOD 1996 International Conference on Management of Data*, pages 481–492, Montreal, Canada, June 1996.

[IK83] Toshihide Ibaraki and Naoki Katoh. On-line computation of transitive closure of graphs. *IPL*, 16:95–97, 1983.

[IK90] Yannis E. Ioannidis and Younkyung Cha Kang. Randomized Algorithms for Optimizing Large Join Queries. In Hector Garcia-Molina and Hosagrahar V. Jagadish, editors, *Proceedings of ACM SIGMOD 1990 International Conference on Management of Data*, pages 312–321, Atlantic City, NJ, May 23-25 1990.

[IK93] W.H. Inmon and C. Kelley. *Rdb/VMS: Developing the Data Warehouse*. QED Publishing Group, Boston, London, Toronto, 1993.

[IN88] Tomasz Imielinski and Shamim Naqvi. Explicit control of logic programs through rule algebra. In *Proceedings of the Seventh Symposium on Principles of Database Systems (PODS)*, pages 103–116, Austin, TX, March 21-23 1988.

[INSS92] Yannis E. Ioannidis, Raymond T. Ng, Kyuseok Shim, and Timos K. Sellis. Parametric Query Optimization. In Li-Yan Yuan, editor, *Proceedings of the Eighteenth International Conference on Very Large Databases*, pages 103–114, Vancouver, Canada, August 23-27 1992.

[ISO90] ISO_ANSI. ISO-ANSI working draft: Database language SQL2 and SQL3; x3h2; iso/iec jtc1/sc21/wg3, 1990.

[ISO92] ISO. Database language sql. Technical report, Document ISO/IEC 9075:199, 1992.

[Ita86] Giuseppe F. Italiano. Amortized efficiency of a path retrieval data structure. *Theoretical Computer Science*, 48:273–281, 1986.

[Jam96] James J. Lu and Anil Nerode and V. S. Subrahmanian. Hybrid Knowledge Bases. *IEEE Transactions on Knowledge and Data Engineering (TKDE)*, 8(5):773–785, 1996.

[JH91] Dean Jacobs and Richard Hull. Database Programming with Delayed Updates. In *International Workshop on Database Programming Languages*, pages 416–428, San Mateo, Calif., 1991.

[JL87] Joxan Jaffar and Jean-Louis Lassez. Constraint Logic Programming. In *Proceedings of Fourteenth Annual ACM Symposium on Principles of Programming Languages*, pages 111–119, New York, USA, 1987.

[JM93] Christian Jensen and Leo Mark. Differential query processing in transaction time databases. In *In [TCG+93]*, pages 457–491. The Benjamin/Cummings Publishing Company, Inc., 1993.

[JMR91] Christian Jensen, Leo Mark, and Nick Roussopoulos. Incremental implementation model for relational databases with transaction time. *IEEE Transactions on Knowledge and Data Engineering (TKDE)*, 3(4):461–473, December 1991.

[JMS95] Hosagrahar V. Jagadish, Inderpal Singh Mumick, and Avi Silberschatz. View maintenance issues in the chronicle data model. In *Proceedings of the Fourteenth Symposium on Principles of Database Systems (PODS)*, pages 113–124, San Jose, CA, May 22-24 1995.

[JS96] Theodore Johnson and Dennis Shasha. Hierarchically split cube forests for decision support: description and tuned design. Unpublished manuscript, 1996.

[JVdB91] Jan Paredaens Jan Van den Bussche. The Expressive Power of Structured Values in Pure OODB's. In *Proceedings of the Tenth Symposium on Principles of Database Systems (PODS)*, pages 291–299, Denver, CO, CA, May 29-31 1991.

[KAAK93] William Kent, Rafi Ahmed, Joseph Albert, and Mohammad Ketabchi. Object identification in multidatabase systems. In D. Hsiao, E. Neuhold, and R. Sacks-Davis, editors, *Interoperable Database Systems (DS-5) (A-25)*. Elsevier Science Publishers B. V. (North-Holland), 1993.

[Kan91] Younkyung Cha Kang. *Randomized Algorithms for Query Optimization*. PhD thesis, University of Wisconsin, Madison, May 1991, May 1991.

[KB94] Arthur M. Keller and Julie Basu. A predicate-based caching scheme for client-server database architectures. In *Proceedings of PDIS-94*, pages 229–238, 1994.

[KKS88] Hyoung-Joo Kim, Hank Korth, and Avi Silberschatz. (1988). PICASSO: A Graphical Query Language, Software—Practice and Experience. 18, 169–203.

[KDM88] Angelika M. Kotz, Klaus R. Dittrich, and Jutta A. M lle. Supporting Semantic Rules by a Generalized Event/Trigger Mechanism. In *Proceedings of the First International Conference on Extending Database Technology (EDBT)*, pages 76–91, Venice, Italy, March 14-18 1988.

[Kel86] Arthur M. Keller, The Role of Semantics in Translating View Updates, *IEEE Computer* 19:1(January 1986). pp. 63–73.

[KG85] Aviel Klausner and Nathan Goodman. Multirelations - Semantice and Languages. In Alain Pirotte and Yannis Vassiliou, editors, *Proceedings of the Eleventh International Conference on Very Large Databases (VLDB)*, pages 251–258, Stockholm, Sweden, August 21-23 1985.

[KH87] P. Kachhwaha and R. Hogan. An object-oriented Data Model for the research laboratory. In *Spring DECUS U.S. Symposium (Refereed Papers Journal)*, pages 43–55, Nashville, TN, April 1987.

[Kim82] Won Kim. On optimizing an SQL-like nested query. *ACM Transactions on Database Systems (TODS)*, 7(3):443–469, September 1982.

[Kim96] Ralph Kimball. *The Data Warehouse Toolkit*. John Wiley, 1996.

[KKM94] Alfons Kemper, Christoph Kilger, and Guido Moerkotte. Function Materialization in Object Bases: Design, Realization, and Evaluation. *IEEE Transactions on Knowledge and Data Engineering (TKDE)*, 6(4):587–608, 1994.

[KKR90] Paris C. Kanellakis, Gabriel M. Kuper, and Peter Z. Revesz. Constraint query languages. In *Proceedings of the Ninth Symposium on Principles of Database Systems (PODS)*, pages 299–313, Nashville, TN, April 2-4 1990.

[KLM+97] Akira Kawaguchi, Daniel Lieuwen, Inderpal Singh Mumick, Dallan Quass, and Kenneth A. Ross. Concurrency control theory for deferred materialized views. In Foto N. Afrati and Phokion Kolaitis, editors, *Proceedings of the Sixth International Conference on Database Theory (ICDT '97)*, pages 306–320, Delphi, Greece, January 8-10 1997.

[Klu80] Anthony Klug. On inequality tableaux. Technical report, Un.Wisconsin, Madison, CSD, TR.403., November 1980.

[Klu82] Anthony Klug. Equivalence of relational algebra and relational calculus query languages having aggregate functions. *Journal of the ACM (JACM)*, 29(3):699–717, July 1982.

[Klu88] Anthony C. Klug. On Conjunctive Queries Containing Inequalities. *Journal of the ACM (JACM)*, 35(1):146–160, 1988.

[Knu73] Donald Ervin Knuth. *Sorting and Searching*, volume 3 of *The Art of Computer Programming*. Addison-Wesley, Reading, Massachusetts, USA, 1973.

[Kor91] Robert R. Korfhage. (1991). To See, or Not to See—Is That the Query? in Proc. SIGIR '91 ACM Press, 134–141.

[KP81] Shaye Koenig and Robert Paige. A transformational framework for the automatic control of derived data. In *Proceedings of the Conference on Very Large Databases, Morgan Kaufman pubs. (Los Altos CA) 7, Zaniolo and Delobel(eds).*, pages 306–319, Cannes, France, September 1981.

[KR87] Bo. Kähler and Oddvar Risnes. Extended logging for database snapshots. In Peter M. Stocker and William Kent, editors, *Proceedings of the Thirteenth International Conference on Very Large Databases*, pages 389–398, Brighton, England, September 1-4 1987.

[KSS87] Robert A. Kowalski, Fariba Sadri, and Paul Soper. Integrity checking in deductive databases. In Peter M. Stocker and William Kent, editors, *Proceedings of the Thirteenth International Conference on Very Large Databases*, pages 61–69, Brighton, England, September 1-4 1987.

[Kuc91] Volker Kuchenhoff. On the Efficient Computation of the Difference Between Consecutive Database States. In Claude Delobel, Michael Kifer, and Yoshifumi Masunaga, editors, *Second International Conference on Deductive and Object-Oriented Databases, LNCS 566*, pages 478–502, Munich, Germany, December 16-18 1991.

[Lau89] Laurent Vieille. Recursive Query Processing: The Power of Logic. *TCS*, 69(1):1–53, 1989.

[Lar86] James A. Larsson. (1986). A Visual Approach to Browsing in a Database Environment. IEEE Computer, 19, 62–71.

[Lef92] Alexandre Lefebvre. Towards an Efficient Evaluation of Recursive Aggregates in Deductive Databases. In *Proceedings of the International Conference on Fifth Generation Computer Systems (FGCS)*, pages 915–925, Tokyo, Japan, June 1992. A revised version appears in New Generation Computing, 12, 1994, pages 131-160.

[Lev93] Alon Levy. *Irrelevance reasoning in knowledge based systems*. PhD thesis, Stanford University, 1993.

[LHM+86] Bruce Lindsay, Laura Haas, C. Mohan, Hamid Pirahesh, and Paul Wilms. A snapshot differential refresh algorithm. In Carlo Zaniolo, editor, *Proceedings of ACM SIGMOD 1986 International Conference on Management of Data*, pages 53–60, Washington, D.C., May 28-30 1986.

[LKM+85] Raymond A. Lorie, Won Kim, Dan McNabb, Wil Plouffe, and Andreas Meier. Supporting Complex Objects in a Relational System for Engineering Databases. *Query Processing in Database System*, pages 145–155, 1985.

[LMSS93] Alon Y. Levy, Inderpal Singh Mumick, Yehoshua Sagiv, and Oded Shmueli. Equivalence, query-reachability, and satisfiability in datalog extensions. In *Proceedings of the Twelfth Symposium on Principles of Database Systems (PODS)*, pages 109–122, Washington, DC, May 25-27 1993.

[LMSS95a] Alon Y. Levy, Alberto O. Mendelzon, Yehoshua Sagiv, and Divesh Srivastava. Answering queries using views. In *Proceedings of the Fourteenth Symposium on Principles of Database Systems (PODS)*, pages 95–104, San Jose, CA, May 22-24 1995.

[LMSS95b] James Lu, Guido Moerkotte, Joachim Schue, and Venkatramanan Siva Subrahmanian. Efficient maintenance of materialized mediated views. In Michael Carey and Donovan Schneider, editors, *Proceedings of ACM SIGMOD 1995 International Conference on Management of Data*, pages 340–351, San Jose, CA, May 23-25 1995.

[LS91] John W. Lloyd and John C. Shepherdson. Partial evaluation in logic programming. *Journal of Logic Programming, 11:217–242, 1991*, 11:217–242, 1991.

[LS92] Alon Y. Levy and Yehoshua Sagiv. Constraints and redundancy in datalog. In *Proceedings of the Eleventh Symposium on Principles of Database Systems (PODS)*, pages 67–80, San Diego, CA, June 2-4 1992.

[LS93] Alon Y. Levy and Yehoshua Sagiv. Queries independent of updates. In Rakesh Agrawal, Sean Baker, and David Bell, editors, *Proceedings of the Nineteenth International Conference on Very Large Databases*, pages 171–181, Dublin, Ireland, August 24-27 1993.

568 REFERENCES

[LSK95] Alon Y. Levy, Divesh Srivastava, and Thomas Kirk. Data Model and Query Evaluation in Global Information Systems. *JIIS*, 5(2):121–143, 1995.

[LST87] John W. Lloyd, Liz Sonenberg, and Rodney W. Topor. Integrity Constraint Checking in Stratified Databases. *Journal of Logic Programming (JLP)*, 4(4):331–343, 1987.

[LT84] John W. Lloyd and Rodney W. Topor. Making Prolog more Expressive. *Journal of Logic Programming (JLP)*, 1(3):225–240, 1984.

[LV89] Alexandre Lefebvre and Laurent Vieille. On deductive query evaluation in the dedgin* system. In *Int. Conf. on Deductive and Object-Oriented Databases 89, Kyoto.*, pages 123–144, December 1989.

[LW93a] Leonid Libkin and Limsoon Wong. Aggregate Functions, Conservative Extensions, and Linear Orders. In Catriel Beeri, A. Ohori, and Dennis Shasha, editors, *Proceedings of the Fourth International Workshop on Database Programming Languages*, pages 282–294, New York, NY, August 30-September 1 1993.

[LW93b] Leonid Libkin and Limsoon Wong. Some Properties of Query Languages for Bags. In Catriel Beeri, A. Ohori, and Dennis Shasha, editors, *Proceedings of the Fourth International Workshop on Database Programming Languages*, pages 97–114, New York, NY, August 30-September 1 1993.

[LW94a] Leonid Libkin and Limsoon Wong. Conservativity of Nested Relational Calculi with Internal Generic Functions. *IPL*, 49(6):273–280, 1994.

[LW94b] Leonid Libkin and Limsoon Wong. New techniques for studying set languages, bag languages and aggregate functions. In Inderpal Singh Mumick, editor, *Proceedings of the Thirteenth Symposium on Principles of Database Systems (PODS)*, pages 155–166, Minneapolis, MN, May 24-26 1994.

[LW94c] Leonid Libkin and Limsoon Wong. Some properties of query languages for bags. In *Proceedings of Database Programming Languages*, pages 97–114. Springer Verlag, 1994.

[LY85] Per-Ake Larson and H. Z. Yang. Computing queries from derived relations. In *Proceedings of the 11th International VLDB Conference*, pages 259–269, 1985.

[Mai83] David Maier. *The Theory of Relational Databases*. Computer Science Press, Rockville, Md., 1983.

[Mar81] Mario Schkolnick and Paul G. Sorenson . The effects of denormalization on database performance. Technical report, IBM San Jose Research Center, 650 Harry Road, San Jose, CA 95120, 1981.

[MB88] Bern Martens and Maurice Bruynooghe. Integrity Constraint Checking in Deductive Databases Using a Rule/Goal Graph. In *Proceedings from the Second International Conference on Expert Database Systems*, pages 567–601, Virginia, USA, April 1988.

[MD89] Dennis R. McCarthy and Umeshwar Dayal. The architecture of an active database management system. In *Proceedings of the 1989 ACM SIGMOD International Conference on Mangement of Data*, pages 215–224. Association for Computing Machinery, June 1989.

[ME93] James G. Mullen and Ahmed K. Elmagarmid. InterSQL: A Multidatabase Transaction Programming Language. In Catriel Beeri, A. Ohori, and Dennis Shasha, editors, *Proceedings of the Fourth International Workshop on Database Programming Languages*, pages 399–416, New York, NY, August 30-September 1 1993.

[Mic90] Zbiniew Michalewicz. Proceedings of the Fifth International Conference on Statistical and Scientific Database Management. In *Proceedings of the Fifth International Conference on Statistical and Scientific Database Management*, Charlotte, N.C., April 3-5 1990. Lecture Notes in Computer Science, Vol. 420, Springer-Verlag Inc.

[Mor83] Matthew Morgenstern. Active Databases as a Paradigm for Enhanced Computing Environments. In Mario Schkolnick and Costantino Thanos, editors, *Proceedings of the Ninth International Conference on Very Large Databases (VLDB)*, pages 34–42, Florence, Italy, October 31 - November 2 1983.

[MP90] Claudia Bauzer Medeiros and Patrick Pfeffer. A mechanism for managing rules in an object-oriented database. Technical report, Altair, 1990.

[MPP+93] Bernhard Mitschang, Hamid Pirahesh, Peter Pistor, Bruce G. Lindsay, and Norbert S dkamp. SQL/XNF - Processing Composite Objects as Abstractions over Relational Data. In *Proceedings of the Ninth IEEE International Conference on Data Engineering (ICDE)*, pages 272–282, Vienna, Austria, April 19-23 1993.

[MPR90] Inderpal Singh Mumick, Hamid Pirahesh, and Raghu Ramakrishnan. The magic of duplicates and aggregates. In Dennis McLeod, Ron Sacks-Davis, and Hans Schek, editors, *Proceedings of the Sixteenth International Conference on Very Large Databases*, pages 264–277, Brisbane, Australia, August 13-16 1990.

[MQM97] Inderpal Singh Mumick, Dallan Quass, and Barinderpal Singh Mumick. Maintenance of summary tables in a warehouse. In Patrick Valduriez and Joan Peckham, editors, *Proceedings of ACM SIGMOD 1997 International Conference on Management of Data*, Tucson, AZ, May 1997.

[MS93a] Jim Melton and A. Simon. *Understanding the New SQL: A Complete Guide*. Morgan Kaufmann, 1993.

[MS93b] Inderpal Singh Mumick and Oded Shmueli. Finiteness properties of database queries. In Maria E. Orlowska and Michael Papazoglou, editors, *Advances in Database Research: Proceedings of the Fourth Australian Database Conference (ADC)*, pages 274–288, Brisbane, Australia, February 1-2 1993. World Scientific Publishing Co.,PO Box 128, Farrer Road, Singapore 9128.

[MS94] Inderpal Singh Mumick and Oded Shmueli. Universal finiteness and satisfiability. In Inderpal Singh Mumick, editor, *Proceedings of the Thirteenth Symposium on Principles of Database Systems (PODS)*, pages 190–200, Minneapolis, MN, May 24-26 1994.

[MSVT94] Peter Bro Miltersen, Sairam Subramanian, Jeffrey Scott Vitter, and Roberto Tamassia. Complexity Models for Incremental Computation. *TCS*, 130(1):203–236, 1994.

[MU83] David Maier and Jeffrey D. Ullman. Fragments of Relations. In David J. DeWitt and Georges Gardarin, editors, *Proceedings of ACM SIGMOD 1983 International Conference on Management of Data*, pages 15–22, San Jose, CA, May 23-26 1983.

[Mum91] Inderpal Singh Mumick. *Query Optimization in Deductive and Relational Databases*. PhD thesis, Stanford University, Stanford, CA 94305, USA, December 1991. Technical Report No. STAN-CS-91-1400. Also available from University Microfilms International, 300 N. Zeeb Road, Ann Arbor, MI 48106. (313)761-4700.

[Mum95] Inderpal Singh Mumick. The Rejuvenation of Materialized Views. In *Proceedings of the Sixth International Conference on Information Systems and Management of Data (CISMOD)*, Bombay, India, November 15-17 1995.

[Nic82] Jean-Marie Nicolas. Logic for Improving Integrity Checking in Relational Data Bases. *Acta Informatica*, 18(3):227–253, 1982.

[NY83] Jean-Marie Nicolas and Kioumars Yazdanian. An Outline of BDGEN: A Deductive DBMS. In *Information Processing*, pages 705–717, 1983.

[Nor88] Donald A. Norman. (1988). The Psychology of Everyday Things. Basic Books, Inc., New York.

[OG95] Patrick O'Neill and Goetz Graefe. Multi-table joins through bitmapped join indexes. In *SIGMOD Record*, pages 8–11, 1995.

[Oli91] Antoni Olive. Integrity Constraints Checking In Deductive Databases. In Guy M. Lohman, Amilcar Sernadas, and Rafael Camps, editors, *Proceedings of the Seventeenth International Conference on Very Large Databases*, pages 513–523, Barcelona, Spain, September 3-6 1991.

[Ore90] Jack Orenstein. A comparison of spatial query processing techniques for native and parameter spaces. In *ACM SIGMOD Conf. on the Management of Data 90, Atlantic City.*, pages 343–x352, May 1990.

[Pai84] Robert Paige. Applications of finite differencing to database integrity control and query/transaction optimization. In H. Gallaire, J. Minker, and J. Nicolas, editors, *Advances in Database Theory*, pages 170–209, New York, 1984. Plenum Press.

[PI94] Sushant Patnaik and Neil Immerman. Dyn-fo: A parallel, dynamic complexity class. In Inderpal Singh Mumick, editor, *Proceedings of the Thirteenth Symposium on Principles of Database Systems (PODS)*, pages 210–221, Minneapolis, MN, May 24-26 1994.

[Poe96] Vidette Poe. *Building a Data Warehouse for Decision Support*. Prentice Hall, 1996.

[PS82] Christos H. Papadimitriou and Kenneth Steiglitz. *Combinatorial Optimization: Algorithms and Complexity*. Prentice Hall, 1982.

[QGMW96] Dallan Quass, Ashish Gupta, Inderpal Singh Mumick, and Jennifer Widom. Making views self-maintainable for data warehousing. In *Proceedings of the Fourth International Conference on Parallel and Distributed Information Systems (PDIS)*, Miami Beach, FL, December 18-20 1996.

[Qia88] X. Qian. An effective method for integrity constraint simplification. In *Proceedings of the IEEE 4th International Conference on Data Engineering*, pages 338–345, 1988.

[Qia90] Xiaolei Qian. An Axiom System for Database Transactions. *IPL*, 36(4):183–189, 1990.

[Qua96] Dallan Quass. Maintenance expressions for views with aggregation. In Ashish Gupta and Inderpal Singh Mumick, editors, *Proceedings of the International Workshop on Materialized Views: Techniques and Applications*, pages 110–118, Montreal, Canada, June 7 1996.

[Qua97] Dallan Quass. *Materialized Views in Data Warehouses*. PhD thesis, Stanford University, Stanford, CA, 1997.

[QW91] Xiaolei Qian and Gio Wiederhold. Incremental recomputation of active relational expressions. *IEEE Transactions on Knowledge and Data Engineering (TKDE)*, 3(3):337–341, 1991.

[QW97] Dallan Quass and Jennifer Widom. On-line warehouse view maintenance. In Patrick Valduriez and Joan Peckham, editors, *Proceedings of ACM SIGMOD 1997 International Conference on Management of Data*, Tucson, AZ, May 1997.

[Raa95] F. Raab, editor. *TPC Benchmark(TM) D (Decision Support), Proposed Revision 1.0.* Transaction Processing Performance Council, San Jose, CA 95112, April 4 1995.

[Rad95] A. Radding. Support Decision Makers With a Data Warehouse. In *Datamation*, March 15 1995.

[RAL91] Roberta Cochrane Rakesh Agrawal and Bruce Lindsay. On maintaining priorities in a production rule system. In Guy M. Lohman, Amilcar Sernadas, and Rafael Camps, editors, *Proceedings of the Seventeenth International Conference on Very Large Databases*, pages 479–487, Barcelona, Spain, September 3-6 1991.

[RCBB89] Arnon Rosenthal, Upen S. Chakravarthy, Barbara Blaustein, and Jose Blakely. Situation monitoring for active databases. In *Proceedings of the Conference on Very Large Databases, Morgan Kaufman pubs. (Los Altos CA) 15, Amsterdam.*, August 1989.

[RCK+95] Nick Roussopoulos, Chungmin Melvin Chen, Stephen Kelley, Alexis Delis, and Yannis Papakonstantinou. The ADMS Project: View R Us. *IEEE Data Engineering Bulletin, Special Issue on Materialized Views and Data Warehousing*, 18(2):19–28, June 1995.

[RFS88] Nick Roussopoulos, Christos Faloutsos, and Timos Sellis, An Efficient Pictorial Database System for PSQL, *IEEE Transactions on Software Engineering,* 14(5): 639–650, 1988.

[RH80] Daniel J. Rosenkrantz and Harry B. Hunt III. Processing Conjunctive Predicates and Queries. In *Proceedings of the sixth International Conference on Very Large Databases*, pages 64–72, Montreal, Canada, October 1-3 1980.

[RK86a] Nick Roussopoulos and Hyunchul Kang. Preliminary Design of ADMS+/-: A Workstation-Mainframe Integrated Architecture for Database Management Systems. In Wesley W. Chu, Georges Gardarin, Setsuo Ohsuga, and Yahiko Kambayashi, editors, *Proceedings of the Twelfth International Conference on Very Large Databases (VLDB)*, pages 355–364, Kyoto, Japan, August 25-28 1986.

[RK86b] Nick Roussopoulos and Hyunchul Kang. Principles and techniques in the design of ADMS±. *IEEE Computer*, 19:19–25, December 1986.

[RK89] Nick Roussopoulos and Hyun Soon Kim. ROOST: A Relational Object-Oriented System. In *Proceedings of the Third International Conference on Foundations of Data Organization and Algorithms (FODO)*, Paris, France, June 1989, pp. 404–420.

[Rou82] Nick Roussopoulos. View indexing in relational databases. Technical Report 2, ACM Transactions on Database Systems, 7(2):258–290, June 1982.

[Rou82b] Nick Roussopoulos, The Logical Access Path Schema of a Database, *IEEE Trans. on Software Engineering.* TSE 8(6):563–573, 1982.

[Rou87] Nick Roussopoulos, Overview of ADMS: A High Performance Database Management System, *Proc. Fall Joint Computer Conference*, (October 25–29, 1987).

[Rou91] Nick Roussopoulos. The incremental access method of view cache: Concept, algorithms, and cost analysis. *ACM Transactions on Database Systems (TODS)*, 16(3):535–563, September 1991.

[RRSS94] Raghu Ramakrishnan, Kenneth A. Ross, Divesh Srivastava, and S. Sudarshan. Efficient incremental evaluation of queries with aggregation. In *International Logic Programming Symposium*, pages 204–218, 1994.

[RS93] Tore Risch and Martin Sköld. Active rules based on object-oriented queries. *IEEE Transactions on Knowledge and Data Engineering (TKDE)*, 1993.

[RSU95] Anand Rajaraman, Yehoshua Sagiv, and Jeffrey D. Ullman. Answering queries using templates with binding patterns. In *Proceedings of the Fourteenth Symposium on Principles of Database Systems (PODS)*, pages 105–112, San Jose, CA, May 22-24 1995.

[RSUV89] Raghu Ramakrishnan, Yehoshua Sagiv, Jeffrey D. Ullman, and Moshe Vardi. Proof-tree transformation theorems and their applications. In *Proceedings of the Eighth Symposium on Principles of Database Systems (PODS)*, pages 172–181, Philadelphia, PA, March 29-31 1989.

[Tow85] Rowe, L.A. (1985). Fill-in-the-Form Programming. in Proc. 11th International on Very Large Databases. ACM Press, 394–403.

[Rut92] Chris Rutkowski. (1982). An Introduction to the Human Applications Standard Computer Interface. Byte. 7, 291–310.

[Sal83] Gerard Salton. (1983). Introduction to Modern Information Retrieval. McGraw-Hill, New York.

[Shn83] Ben Shneiderman. (1983). Direct Manipulation: A step beyond programming languages, IEEE Computer, 16, 57–69.

[SAB$^+$94] Venkatramanan Siva Subrahmanian, Sibel Adali, Anne Brink, Ross Emery, Adil Rajput, Timothy J. Rogers, Robert Ross, and Charlie Ward. HERMES: A Heterogeneous Reasoning and Mediator System. Unpublished Manuscript, 1994.

[Sag88] Yehoshua Sagiv. Optimizing datalog programs. In J. Minker, editor, *Foundations of Deductive Databases and Logic Programming*, pages 659–698, Washington D.C., 1988. Morgan Kaufmann.

[SAG96] Sunita Sarawagi, Rakesh Agrawal, and Ashish Gupta. On computing the data cube. Research report rj 10026, IBM Almaden Research Center, San Jose, California, 1996.

[SAH85] Michael Stonebraker, J. Anton, and Eric Hanson. Extending a database system with procedures. *UCBERL memo M8559.*, 1985.

[SALP79] Patricia G. Selinger, Donald D. Astrahan, Morton M. Chamberlin, Raymond A. Lorie, and Thomas G. Price. Access path selection in a relational database management system. In Philip A. Bernstein, editor, *Proceedings of ACM SIGMOD 1979 International Conference on Management of Data*, pages 23–34, Boston, MA, May 30 - June 1 1979.

[SB75] Hans Albrecht Schmid and Philip A. Bernstein. A Multi-Level Architecture for Relational Data Base Systems. In Douglas S. Kerr, editor, *Proceedings of the First International Conference on Very Large Databases (VLDB)*, pages 202–226, Framingham, MA, September 22-24 1975.

[SBG$^+$81] J. M. Smith, Philip A. Bernstein, Nathan Goodman, Umeshwar Dayal, T. A. Landers, K. W. T. Lin, and Eugene Wong. Multibase – Integrating heterogenous distributed database systems. In *National Computer Conference*, pages 487–499, 1981.

[SC288] IBM Form Number SC26-4348-1. IBM Systems Application Architecture, Common Programming Interface: Database Reference. Technical report, IBM, October 1988.

[Sch95] Joachim Schu. *Updates and Query-Processing in a Mediator Architecture*. PhD thesis, University of Karlsruhe, Institute for Algorithms and Cognitive Systems, October 1995.

[SDJL96] Divesh Srivastava, Shaul Dar, Hosagrahar V. Jagadish, and Alon Y. Levy. Answering Queries with Aggregation Using Views. In T. M. Vijayaraman, C. Mohan, and Alexander Buchman, editors, *Proceedings of the 22nd International Conference on Very Large Databases*, pages 318–329, Mumbai, India, September 3-6 1996.

[SdM88] Eric Simon and Christophe de Maindreville. Deciding whether a production rule is relational computable. In Marc Gyssens, Jan Paredaens, and Dirk Van Gucht, editors, *Proceedings of the Second International Conference on Database Theory (ICDT '88)*, pages 205–222, Bruges, Belgium, August 31 - September 2 1988.

[Sel86] Timos K. Sellis. "Global Query Optimization," *Proceedings of the 1986 ACM-SIGMOD International Conference on Management of Data 15*, 2 (June 1986), 191–205.

[Sel88] Timos K. Sellis. Intelligent caching and indexing techniques for relational database systems. *Information Systems*, 13(2):175–185, 1988.

[SF90] Arie Segev and Weiping Fang. Currency-based updates to distributed materialized views. In *Proceedings of the Sixth IEEE International Conference on Data Engineering (ICDE)*, pages 512–520, Los Angeles, CA, February 5-9 1990.

[SF91] Arie Segev and Weiping Fang. Optimal update policies for distributed materialized views. *Management Science*, 37(7):851–70, July 1991.

[Sha86] Leonard D. Shapiro. Join processing in database systems with large main memories. *ACM Transactions on Database Systems .*, 11(3):239–264, October 1986.

[Shi93] Kyuseok Shim. *Advanced Query Optimization Techniques for Relational Database Systems*. PhD thesis, University of Maryland, College Park, MD, June 1993.

[Shm87] Oded Shmueli. Decidability and Expressiveness of Logic Queries. In *Proceedings of the Sixth Symposium on Principles of Database Systems (PODS)*, pages 237–249, San Diego, CA, March 23-25 1987.

[Sho82] Arie Shoshani. Statistical Databases: Characteristics, Problems, and some Solutions. In *Proceedings of the Eighth International Conference on Very Large Databases (VLDB)*, pages 208–222, Mexico City, Mexico, September 8-10 1982.

[SI84] Oded Shmueli and Alon Itai. Maintenance of Views. In *Proceedings of ACM SIGMOD 1984 International Conference on Management of Data*, pages 240–255, 1984.

[SJGP90] Michael Stonebraker, Anant Jhingran, Jeffrey Goh, and Spyros Potamianos. On Rules, Procedures, Caching and Views in Data Base Systems. In Hector Garcia-Molina and Hosagrahar V. Jagadish, editors, *Proceedings of ACM SIGMOD 1990 International Conference on Management of Data*, pages 281–290, Atlantic City, NJ, May 23-25 1990.

[SK88] Fariba Sadri and Robert A. Kowalski. A Theorem-Proving Approach to Database Integrity. In J. Minker, editor, *Foundations of Deductive Databases and Logic Programming*, pages 313–362, Washington D.C., 1988. Morgan Kaufmann.

[SL76] Dennis G. Severance and Guy Lohman. Differential files: Their application to the maintenance of large databases. *ACM Transactions on Database Systems (TODS)*, 1(3):256–267, September 1976.

[SL90] Amit P. Sheth and James A. Larson. Federated Database Systems for Managing Distributed, Heterogeneous, and Autonomous Databases. *ACM Computing Surveys*, 22(3):183–236, September 1990.

[SLR94] Praveen Seshadri, Miron Livny, and Raghu Ramakrishnan. Sequence query processing. In Richard Snodgrass and Marianne Winslett, editors, *Proceedings of ACM SIGMOD 1994 International Conference on Management of Data*, pages 430–441, Minneapolis, MN, May 25-27 1994.

[Smi95] G. Smith. Oracle7 Symmetric Replication. Oracle white paper, part #a33128, Oracle Corporation, Redwood Shores, CA, April 1995.

[SN95] Ambuj Shatdal and Jeffrey F. Naughton. Adaptive Parallel Aggregation Algorithms. In Michael Carey and Donovan Schneider, editors, *Proceedings of ACM SIGMOD 1995 International Conference on Management of Data*, pages 104–114, San Jose, CA, May 23-25 1995.

[Sof] Arbor Software. Multidimensional analysis: converting corporate data into strategic information. Unpublished white paper at http://www.arborsoft.com/papers/multiTOC.html.

[SP89a] Arie Segev and Jooseok Park. Maintaining Materialized Views in Distributed Databases. In *Proceedings of the Fifth International Conference on Data Engineering (ICDE)*, pages 262–270, Los Angeles, CA, February 6-10 1989.

[SP89b] Arie Segev and Jooseok Park. Updating distributed materialized views. *IEEE Transactions on Knowledge and Data Engineering (TKDE)*, 1(2):173–184, June 1989.

[SPAM91] Ulf Schreier, Hamid Pirahesh, Rakesh Agrawal, and C. Mohan. Alert: An architecture for transforming a passive dbms into an active dbms. In Guy M. Lohman, Amilcar Sernadas, and Rafael Camps, editors, *Proceedings of the Seventeenth International Conference on Very Large Databases*, pages 469–478, Barcelona, Spain, September 3-6 1991.

[SR86] Michael Stonebraker and Lawrence A. Rowe. The Design of Postgres. In Carlo Zaniolo, editor, *Proceedings of ACM SIGMOD 1986 International Conference on Management of Data*, pages 340–355, Washington, D.C., May 28-30 1986.

[SR88] Jaideep Srivastava and Doron Rotem. Analytical modeling of materialized view maintenance. In *Proceedings of the Seventh Symposium on Principles of Database Systems (PODS)*, pages 126–134, Austin, TX, March 21-23 1988.

[SR96] Betty Salzberg and Andreas Reuter. Indexing for aggregation. Working Paper, 1996.

[SRF87] Timos K. Sellis, Nick Roussopoulos, and Christos Faloutsos, The R^+-Tree: A Dynamic Index for Multi-Dimensional Objects, *Proc. 13th International Conference on VLDB*, pp. 507–518 (Sept. 1987).

[SRK92] Amit P. Sheth, Marek Rusinkiewicz, and George Karabatis. Using Polytransactions to Manage Interdependent Data. In Ahmed K. Elmagarmid, editor, *Transaction Models*, pages 555–581, 1992.

[SS92] Michael D. Soo and Richard Snodgrass. Mixed calendar query language support for temporal constants. Technical Report 29, Computer Science Department, University of Arizona, Tucson, Arizona, May 1992.

[SSH86] Michael R. Stonebraker, Timos K. Sellis and Eric Hanson, "An Analysis of Rule Indexing Implementations in Data Base Systems" Proceedings *of the Annual Conference on Expert Database Systems*, Charleston, SC, April 1986.

[SSMR96] Ken Smith, Len Seligman, Dave Mattox, and Arnie Rosenthal. Distributed situation monitoring using replication. In Ashish Gupta and Inderpal Singh Mumick, editors, *Proceedings of the International Workshop on Materialized Views: Techniques and Applications*, Montreal, Canada, June 7 1996.

[STL89] Jaideep Srivastava, Jack S. Eddy Tan, and Vincent Y. Lum. TBSAM: An Access Method for Efficient Processing of Statistical Queries. *IEEE Transactions on Knowledge and Data Engineering (TKDE)*, 1(4):414–423, 1989.

[Sto75] Michael R. Stonebraker. Implementation of integrity constraints and views by query modification. In W. Frank King, editor, *Proceedings of ACM SIGMOD 1975 International Conference on Management of Data*, pages 65–78, San Jose, CA, May 14-16 1975.

[Sto92] Michael R. Stonebraker. The Integration of Rule Systems and Database Systems. *IEEE Transactions on Knowledge and Data Engineering (TKDE)*, 4(5):415–423, 1992.

[Sub94a] Venkatramanan Siva Subrahmanian. Amalgamating Knowledge Bases. *ACM Transactions on Database Systems (TODS)*, 19(2):291–331, 1994.

[Sub94b] Venkatramanan Siva Subrahmanian. *Hybrid Knowledge Bases for Integrating Symbolic, Numeric and Image Data*. In *Proceedings of the 1994 International Workshop on Applied Imagery and Pattern Recognition*, Washington, DC, October 1994. SPIE Press.

[SY80] Yehoshua Sagiv and Mihalis Yannakakis. Equivalences Among Relational Expressions with the Union and Difference Operators. *Journal of the ACM (JACM)*, 27(4):633–655, 1980.

[TB88] Frank Wm. Tompa and José A. Blakeley. Maintaining materialized views without accessing base data. *Information Systems*, 13(4):393–406, 1988.

[TCG+93] Abdullah Uz Tansel, James Clifford, Shashi Gadia, Sushil Jajodia, Arie Segev, and Richard Snodgrass. *Temporal Databases: Theory, Design, and Implementation*. The Benjamin/Cummings Publishing Company, Inc., 1993.

[Tim94] New York Times. Bug in chemical bank's ATM software, February 18 1994. Front page article.

[Tra87] Query Transformation. *Updating Derived Relations*. PhD thesis, Department of Computer Science, University of Waterloo, 1987.

[TSI94] Odysseas G. Tsatalos, Marvin H. Solomon, and Yannis E. Ioannidis. The gmap: A versatile tool for physical data independence. In Jorge Bocca, Matthias Jarke, and Carlo Zaniolo, editors, *Proceedings of the 20th International Conference on Very Large Databases*, pages 367–378, Santiago, Chile, September 12-15 1994.

[Ull82] Jeffrey D. Ullman, *Principles of Database Systems,* Computer Science Press (1982).

[Ull89] Jeffrey D. Ullman. *Principles of Database and Knowledge-Base Systems, Volumes 1 and 2*. Computer Science Press, 1989.

[UO92] Toni Urpi and Antoni Olive. A Method for Change Computation in Deductive Databases. In Li-Yan Yuan, editor, *Proceedings of the Eighteenth International Conference on Very Large Databases*, pages 225–237, Vancouver, Canada, August 23-27 1992.

[Val87] Patrick Valduriez. Join Indices. *ACM Transactions on Database Systems (TODS)*, 12(2):218–246, 1987.

[VBK91] Laurent Vieille, Petra Bayer, and Volker Küchenhoff. Integrity checking and materialized views handling by update propagation in the EKS-V1 system. Technical report, CERMICS - Ecole Nationale Des Ponts Et Chaussees, France, June 1991. Rapport de Recherche, CERMICS 91.1.

[VBKL90] Laurent Vieille, Petra Bayer, Volker Küchenhoff, and Alexandre Lefebvre. EKS-V1, a short overview. In *AAAI-90 Workshop on Knowledge Base Management Systems*, 1990.

[vdM92] Ron van der Meyden. The Complexity of Querying Indefinite Data about Linearly Ordered Domains. In *Proceedings of the Eleventh Symposium on Principles of Database Systems (PODS)*, pages 331–345, San Diego, CA, June 2-4 1992.

[vEK76] Maarten H. van Emden and Robert A. Kowalski. The Semantics of Predicate Logic as a Programming Language. *Journal of the ACM (JACM)*, 23(4):733–742, 1976.

[WC96] Jennifer Widom and Stefano Ceri, editors. *Active Database Systems: Triggers and Rules For Advanced Database Processing*. Morgan Kaufmann, Washington D.C., 1996.

[WCL91] Jennifer Widom, Roberta Jo Cochrane, and Bruce Lindsay. Implementing set-oriented production rules as an extension to starburst. In Guy M. Lohman, Amilcar Sernadas, and Rafael Camps, editors, *Proceedings of the Seventeenth International Conference on Very Large Databases*, pages 275–285, Barcelona, Spain, September 3-6 1991.

[Wil84] W. Williams. (1984). What makes RABBIT run? Int J. Man–Machine Studies, 21, 333-352.

[WDSY91] Ouri Wolfson, Hasanat M. Dewan, Salvatore J. Stolofo, and Yechiam Yemini. Incremental Evaluation of Rules and its Relationship to Parallelism. In James Clifford and Roger King, editors, *Proceedings of ACM SIGMOD 1991 International Conference on Management of Data*, pages 78–87, Denver, CO, May 29-31 1991.

[Wel95] Jay-Louise Weldon. Managing Multidimensional Data: Harnessing the Power. Unpublished manuscript, 1995.

[WF90] Jennifer Widom and Sheldon J. Finkelstein. Set-oriented production rules in a relational database system. In Hector Garcia-Molina and Hosagrahar V. Jagadish, editors, *Proceedings of ACM SIGMOD 1990 International Conference on Management of Data*, pages 259–270, Atlantic City, NJ, May 23-25 1990.

[WHW89] Surjatini Widjojo, Richard Hull, and Dave Wile. Distributed Information Sharing using World-Base. *IEEE Office Knowledge Engineering*, 3(2):17–26, August 1989.

[WHW90] Surjatini Widjojo, Richard Hull, and Dave Wile. A Specificational Approach to Merging Persistent Object Bases. In Alan Dearle, Gail M. Shaw, and Stanley B. Zdonik, editors, *Proceedings of the Fourth International Workshop on Persistent Objects (POS)*, pages 267–278, Martha's Vineyard, MA, sep 1990.

[Wid91] Jennifer Widom. Deduction in the Starburst production rule system. Technical Report RJ 8135, IBM Almaden Research Center, San Jose, CA, May 1991.

[Wie86] Gio Wiederhold, Views, Objects, and Databases, *IEEE Computer* 19:12(December 1986). pp. 37–44.

[Wie92] Gio Wiederhold. Mediators in the architecture of future information systems. *IEEE Computer*, pages 38–49, March 1992.

[Wie93] Gio Wiederhold. Intelligent integration of information. In *ACM-SIGMOD 93, Washington DC.*, pages 434–437, May 1993.

[WS83] John Woodfill and Michael R. Stonebraker. An implementation of hypothetical relations. In Mario Schkolnick and Costantino Thanos, editors, *Proceedings of the Ninth International Conference on Very Large Databases (VLDB)*, pages 157–166, Florence, Italy, October 31 - November 2 1983.

[WS92] Christopher Williamson and Ben Shneiderman. The Dynamic HomeFinder: Evaluating Dynamic Queries in a Real-Estate Information Exploration System. In Nicholas J. Belkin, Peter Ingwersen, and Annelise Mark Pejtersen, editors, *Proceedings of the 15th Annual International ACM SIGIR Conference on Research and Development in Information Retrieval*, pages 338–346, Copenhagen, Denmark, June 21-24 1992.

[WTB92] David L. Wells, Craig W. Thompson, and José A. Blakeley. DARPA open object-oriented database system. In *In Proceedings of the DARPA Software Technology Conference*, Los Angeles, CA, April 22-30 1992.

[WY76] Eugene Wong and Karel Youssefi. Decomposition - A Strategy for Query Processing (Abstract). In James B. Rothnie, editor, *Proceedings of ACM SIGMOD 1976 International Conference on Management of Data*, page 155, Washington, D.C., June 2-4 1976.

[Yan90] Mihalis Yannakakis. Graph-theoretic methods in database theory. In *Proceedings of the Ninth Symposium on Principles of Database Systems (PODS)*, pages 230–242, Nashville, TN, April 2-4 1990.

[Yao77] S. Bing Yao. Approximating the Number of Accesses in Database Organizations. *Communications of the ACM (CACM)*, 20(4):260–261, 1977.

[Yao79] S. Bing Yao. Optimization of query evaluation algorithms. *Transactions of Database Systems*. 4,2 (June 1979), 133–155.

[YL87] H. Z. Yang and Per-Ake Larson. Query transformation for PSJ-queries. In Peter M. Stocker and William Kent, editors, *Proceedings of the Thirteenth International Conference on Very Large Databases*, pages 245–254, Brighton, England, September 1-4 1987.

[YL95] Weipeng P. Yan and Paul Larson. Eager aggregation and lazy aggregation. In Umeshwar Dayal, Peter M.D. Gray, and Shojiro Nishio, editors, *Proceedings of the 21st International Conference on Very Large Databases*, pages 345–357, Zurich, Switzerland, September 11-15 1995.

[ZGMHW94] Yue Zhuge, Hector Garcia-Molina, Joachim Hammer, and Jennifer Widom. View maintenance in a warehousing environment. Technical Report, Stanford University, October 1994. Available via anonymous ftp from host `db.stanford.edu`.

[ZGMHW95] Yue Zhuge, Hector Garcia-Molina, Joachim Hammer, and Jennifer Widom. View maintenance in a warehousing environment. In Michael Carey and Donovan Schneider, editors, *Proceedings of ACM SIGMOD 1995 International Conference on Management of Data*, pages 316–327, San Jose, CA, May 23-25 1995.

[ZH90] Yuli Zhou and Meichun Hsu. A Theory for Rule Triggering Systems. In *Proceedings of the Second International Conference on Extending Database Technology*, pages 407–421, Venice, Italy, March 1990.

[ZHK96] Gang Zhou, Richard Hull, and Roger King. Generating Data Integration Mediators that Use Materialization. *JIIS*, 6(2):199–221, 1996.

[ZHKF95] Gang Zhou, Richard Hull, Roger King, and Jean-Claude Franchitti. Using object matching and materialization to integrate heterogeneous databases. In *Proc. of 3rd International Conference on Cooperative Information Systems*, pages 4–18, 1995.

[Zlo75] Moshe Zloof. Query-by-Example. (1975). National Computer Conference. AFIPS Press, 431–437.

[OOM87] Gultekin Ozsoyoglu, Z. Meral Ozsoyoglu, and Victor Matos. Extending Relational Algebra and Relational Calculus with Set-Valued Attributes and Aggregate Functions. *ACM Transactions on Database Systems (TODS)*, 12(4):566–592, 1987.

Source Notes

Several of the chapters in this book are reprints or extensions of papers that have appeared previously in conferences or journals. The list of the papers from which the chapters are drawn appears below, sorted by chapter.

Chapters 1–4 are new, written specifically for this book. However, an invited talk given at CISMOD 95 [Mum95] formed the basis of these chapters.

Chapter 5, "Data Integration Using Self-Maintainable Views," appeared in *EDBT 1996*. [GJM96]

Chapter 6, "Using Object Matching and Materialization to Integrate Heterogeneous Databases," appeared in *Proceedings of the 3rd International Conference on Cooperative Information Systems*, pp. 4–18. © 1995 IEEE. Reprinted with permission. [ZHKF95]

Chapter 7, "Query Optimization in the Presence of Materialized Views," appeared in *Proceedings of the 11th International Conference on Data Engineering (ICDE)*, pp. 190–200. © 1995 IEEE. Reprinted with permission. [CKPS95]

Chapter 8, "Answering Queries Using Views," appeared in *Proceedings of the 14th ACM SIGACT-SIGMOD-SIGART Symposium on Principles of Database Systems*, pp. 95–104. © 1995 Association for Computing Machinery, Inc. Reprinted by permission. [LMSS95a]

Chapter 9, "Adapting Materialized Views after Redefinitions," appeared in *SIGMOD 1995*, pp. 211–222. © 1995 Association for Computing Machinery, Inc. Reprinted by permission. [GMR95a]

Chapter 10, "The Dynamic HomeFinder: Evaluating Dynamic Queries in a Real-Estate Information Exploration System," appeared in *Proceedings of ACM SIGIR*. © 1992 Association for Computing Machinery, Inc. Reprinted by permission. This is a digitized copy derived from an ACM copyrighted work. ACM did not prepare this copy and does not guarantee that it is an accurate copy of the author's original work. [WS92]

Chapter 11, "Maintenance of Materialized Views: Problems, Techniques, and Applications," appeared in IEEE Data Engineering Bulletin, Special Issue on Materialized Views and Data Warehousing, June 1995.

Chapter 12, "Incremental Maintenance of Recursive Views: A Survey," is new, written specifically for this book.

Chapter 13, "Efficiently Updating Materialized Views," appeared in *Proceedings of the ACM SIGMOD International Conference on Management of Data*, pp. 61–71, 1986. ©1986 Association for Computing Machinery, Inc. Reprinted by permission. [BLT96]

Chapter 14, "Maintaining Views Incrementally," appeared in *SIGMOD 1993*, pp. 157–167. © 1993 Association for Computing Machinery, Inc. Reprinted by permission. [GMS93]

Chapter 15, "Incremental Maintenance of Views with Duplicates," appeared in *Proceedings of the 1995 ACM SIGMOD International Conference on Management of Data*, pp. 328–339. © 1995 Association for Computing Machinery, Inc. Reprinted by permission. [GL95]

Chapter 16, "Algorithms for Deferred View Maintenance," appeared in *Proceedings of the 1996 ACM SIGMOD International Conference on Management of Data*. ©1996 Association for Computing Machinery, Inc. Reprinted by permission. [CGL+96]

Chapter 17, "Incremental Evaluation of Datalog Queries," appeared in *Proceedings of the 1992 International Conference on Database Theory*, pp. 282–296. © 1992 Springer-Verlag, Berlin-Heidelberg. [DT92]

Chapter 18, "View Maintenance Issues in the Chronicle Data Model," appeared in *Proceedings of the 14th ACM SIGACT-SIGMOD-SIGART Symposium on Principles of Database Systems*, pp. 113–124. © 1995 Association for Computing Machinery, Inc. Reprinted by permission. [JMS95]

Chapter 19, "View Maintenance in a Warehousing Environment," appeared in *SIGMOD 1995*, pp. 316–327. © 1995 Association for Computing Machinery, Inc. Reprinted by permission. [ZGMHW95]

Chapter 20, "Efficient Maintenance of Materialized Mediated Views," appeared in *SIGMOD 1995*, pp. 340–351. © 1995 Association for Computing Machinery, Inc. Reprinted by permission. [LMSS95b]

Chapter 21, "Updating Derived Relations: Detecting Irrelevant and Autonomously Computable Updates," appeared in *ACM Transactions on Database Systems,* 14(3): 369–400. © 1989 Association for Computing Machinery, Inc. Reprinted by permission. [BCL89]

Chapter 22, "Queries Independent of Updates," appeared in *Proceedings of the 19th Conference on Very Large Databases*, pp. 171–181, 1993. Reprinted with permission from the VLDB Endowment. [LS93]

Chapter 23, "Implementing Data Cubes Efficiently," appeared in *SIGMOD 1996.* © 1996 Association for Computing Machinery, Inc. Reprinted by permission. [HRU96]

Chapter 24, "On the Computation of Multidimensional Aggregates," appeared in *Proceedings of the 22nd Conference on Very Large Databases,* 1996. [AAD+96a]

Chapter 25, "Maintenance of Summary Tables in a Warehouse," appeared in *SIGMOD 1997.* [MQM97]

Chapter 26, "ORACLES Snapshots," is new, written specifically for this book. All written material reproduced herein are © 1996 Oracle. All rights reserved.

Chapter 27, "Checking Integrity and Materializing Views by Update Propagation in the EKS System," is new, though the material has been taken from a previously unpublished technical report at ECRC.

Chapter 28, "Deriving Production Rules for Incremental View Maintenance," appeared in *Proceedings of the 17th Conference on Very Large Databases,* pp. 565–576, 1991. Reprinted with permission from the VLDB Endowment. [CW91]

Chapter 29, "The Heraclitus DBPL with Application to Active Databases and Data Integration," is based on material that appeared in *Proceedings of the 19th Conference on Very Large Databases,* 1993. [GHJ+93]

Chapter 30, "The Incremental Access Method of View Cache: Concept, Algorithms, and Cost Analysis," appeared in *ACM Transactions on Database Systems,* 16(3): 535–563. © 1991 Association for Computing Machinery, Inc. Reprinted by permission. This is a digitized copy derived from an ACM copyrighted work. ACM did not prepare this copy and does not guarantee that it is an accurate copy of the author's original work. [Rou91]

Chapter 31, "A Performance Analysis of View Materialization Strategies," appeared in *SIGMOD 1987*, pp. 440–453. © 1987 Association for Computing Machinery, Inc. Reprinted by permission. This is a digitized copy derived from an ACM copyrighted work. ACM did not prepare this copy and does not guarantee that it is an accurate copy of the author's original work. [Han87]

Chapter 32, "Join Index, Materialized View, and Hybrid-Hash Join: A Performance Analysis," appeared in *Proceedings of the 6th IEEE International Conference on Data Engineering (ICDE)*, pp. 256–263. © 1990 IEEE. Reprinted by permission. [BM90b]

Contributors

Sameet Agarwal
Microsoft Corporation
1/1060, One Microsoft Way
Redmond, WA 98052
sameeta@microsoft.com
Phone: (206)703-5764
Fax: (206)936-7329

Rakesh Agrawal
IBM Almaden Research Center
K55/B1
650 Harry Road
San Jose CA 95120
ragrawal@almaden.ibm.com
Phone: (408)927-1734
Fax: (408)927-3215
http://www.almaden.ibm.com/people/ragrawal.html

Petra Bayer
ECRC GmbH
Arabellastrasse 17
81925 Munich
Germany
petra@ecrc.de
Phone: +49(89)92699163
Fax: +49(89)92699170
http://www.ecrc.de/research/aim/tdb.html

Jose A. Blakeley
Microsoft Corporation
One Microsoft Way
Redmond, WA 98052-6399, USA.
joseb@microsoft.com
Phone: (206)936-5477
Fax: (206)936 7329

Stefano Ceri
Politecnico di Milano
Dip. di Elettronica e Informazione
Piazza Leonardo da Vinci, 32
I-20133 Milano, ITALY
ceri@elet.polimi.it
Phone: +39-2-2399-3532
Fax: +39-2-2399-3411
http://www.elet.polimi.it/people/ceri

Surajit Chaudhuri
Microsoft Research
One Microsoft Way
Redmond, WA 98052
surajitc@microsoft.com
Phone: (206)703-1938
Fax: (206)936-7329
http://www.research.microsoft.com/
/research/db/surajitc

Neil Coburn
Information Technology Consultant
3186 Heddle Road
Nelson, B.C.
V1L 5P4
CANADA
ncoburn@netidea.com
Phone: (250)825-2243
Fax: (250)825-2243

Latha Colby
Redbrick Systems
485 Alberto Way
Los Gatos, CA 95032
colby@redbrick.com
Phone: (408)399-7213
Fax: (408)399-3277

Prasad M. Deshpande
Computer Sciences Department
University of Wisconsin-Madison
1210 W. Dayton St.
Madison, WI-53706
pmd@cs.wisc.edu
Phone: (608)262-6624
Fax: (608)262-9777
http://www.cs.wisc.edu/~pmd/pmd.html

Guozhu Dong
221 Bouverie Street
Computer Science Department
University of Melbourne
Carlton, Vic 3053
Australia
dong@cs.mu.oz.au
Phone: +61-3-287-9167
Fax: +61-3-348-1184
http://www.cs.mu.oz.au/~dong/

Alan Downing
MS 959712
500 Oracle Parkway
Redwood Shores
CA 94065
Phone: (415)506-6916
Fax: (415)506-7228
adowning@us.oracle.com

Jean-Claude Franchitti
University of Colorado at Boulder
Department of Computer Science
Campus Box 430
Boulder, CO 80309-0430
Phone: (303)492-5964
Fax: (303)492-2844

Hector Garcia-Molina
Dept. of Computer Science
Stanford University
Gates Hall 4A, Room 434
Stanford, CA 94305-9040, USA
hector@cs.stanford.edu
Phone: (415)723-0685
Fax: (415)725-2588
http://db.stanford.edu

Shahram Ghandeharizadeh
Computer Science Department
University of Southern California
Los Angeles, California 90089
shahram@perspolis.usc.edu
Phone: (213)740-4781
http://perspolis.usc.edu/~shahram/

Timothy Griffin
Bell Laboratories
600 Mountain View, Room 2C-219
Murray Hill, NJ 07974
griffin@research.bell-labs.com

Ashish Gupta
amazon.com
2515 Fourth Avenue, #603
Seattle, WA 98121
482 Cuesta Drive
Los Altos, CA 94024
agupta@amazon.com
Phone: (206)441-0571
http://www.amazon.com

Joachim Hammer
Dept. of Computer & Information Science & Engineering
University of Florida
Gainesville, FL 32611-6125
Phone: (352)392-2687
jhammer@cise.ufl.edu

Eric N. Hanson
301 CSE
P.O. Box 116120
Univ. of Florida
Gainesville, FL 32611-6120
hanson@cise.ufl.edu
Phone: (352)392-2691
Fax: (352)392-1220
http://www.cise.ufl.edu/~hanson

Richard Hull
Bell Laboratories
600 Mountain View
Murray Hill, NJ 07974, USA.
hull@lucent.com

H. V. Jagadish
AT&T Laboratories
180 Park Ave, Bldg 103
Florham Park, NJ 07932
U. S. A.
Phone: (201)443-8750
http://www.research.att.com/~jag

Roger King
University of Colorado at Boulder
Department of Computer Science
Campus Box 430
Boulder, CO 80309-0430
roger@cs.colorado.edu
phone: (303)492-7398
Fax: (303)492-2844
http://www.cs.colorado.edu/homes/
          /roger/public_html/Home.html

Volker Kuechenhoff
BMG Entertainment International
Germany/Switzerland/Austria Holding GmbH
Steinhauser Str. 1-3
D 81667 Munich
Germany
volker.kuechenhoff@bertelsmann.de
Phone: +49-89-4136-543
Fax: +49-89-4136-193

Per-Ake (Paul) Larson
Microsoft Corporation
One Microsoft Way
Redmond, WA 98052-6399
palarson@microsoft.com
Phone: (206)703-6260
Fax: (206)936-7329
http://www.research.microsoft.com/~palarson

Alexandre Lefebvre
Bull
Rue Jean-Jaures
F 78340 Les Clayes-sous-bois
France
A.Lefebvre@frcl.bull.fr
Phone: +33-1-30 80 34 14
Fax: +33-1-30 80 69 52

Alon Levy
University of Washington
Department of Computer Science and Engineering
Sieg Hall
Seattle, WA 98195
alon@cs.washington.edu
Phone: (206)543-8099
Fax: (206)543-2969
http://www.cs.washington.edu/homes/alon

Leonid Libkin
Bell Laboratories
600 Mountain View
Murray Hill, NJ 07974, USA.
libkin@bell-labs.com
Phone: (908)582-7647
http://cm.bell-labs.com/who/libkin

James J. Lu
Department of Computer Science
Bucknell University
Lewisburg, PA 17837, USA
jameslu@bucknell.edu
Phone: (717)524-1162
Fax: (717)524-1822
http://www.bucknell.edu/~jameslu

Alberto O. Mendelzon
CSRI, 5 King's College Road
University of Toronto
Toronto, Canada M5S 3H5
mendel@db.toronto.edu
Phone: (416)978-2952
Fax: (416)978-4765
http://www.cs.toronto.edu/~mendel

Guido Moerkotte
Lehrstuhl für Informatik III
Seminargebäude A5
Universität Mannheim
68131 Mannheim
Germany
moer@pi3.informatik.uni-mannheim.de
Phone: +49-621-292-5403
http://pi3.informatik.uni-mannheim.de

Inderpal Singh Mumick
Savera Systems Incorporated
79 Maple Street, The Atrium
Summit, NJ 07901
Phone: (908)273-0724
Fax: (908)273-0831
mumick@savera.com

Barinderpal Singh Mumick
Lucent Technologies
475 South Street, Room #1W063
Morristown, NJ 07960.
bmumick@lucent.com
Phone: (201)606-2859

Jeffrey F. Naughton
Computer Sciences Department
University of Wisconsin-Madison
1210 W. Dayton St.
Madison, WI-53706
naughton@cs.wisc.edu
Phone: (608)262-8737
Fax: (608)262-9777
http://www.cs.wisc.edu/~naughton/naughton.html

Dallan Quass
Brigham Young University
519 TNRB
Provo, UT 84602
quass@byu.edu
Phone: (801)378-5036
Fax: (801)378-5933
http://db.byu.edu

Raghu Ramakrishnan
Computer Sciences Department
University of Wisconsin-Madison
1210 W. Dayton St.
Madison, WI-53706
raghu@cs.wisc.edu
Phone: (608)262-9759
Fax: (608)262-9777
http://www.cs.wisc.edu/~raghu/raghu.html

Nick Roussopoulos
Dept. of Computer Science
University of Maryland
College Park, MD 20742
nick@cs.umd.edu
Phone: (301)405-2687
Fax: (301)405-6707
http://www.cs.umd.edu/users/nick

Yehoshua Sagiv
Dept. of Computer Science
Hebrew University
Givat Ram 91904
Jerusalem, ISRAEL
sagiv@cs.huji.ac.il
Phone: +972-2-6585265
Fax: +972-2-6585439

Sunita Sarawagi
IBM Almaden Research Center
K55/B1-232
650 Harry Road
San Jose, CA 95120
sunita@almaden.ibm.com
Phone: (408)927-2853
Fax: (408)927-3215

Joachim Schue
University of Karlsruhe
Department of Computer Science
Institute for Algorithms and
    Cognitive Systems
Am Fasanengarten 5
76128 Karlsruhe
schue@ira.uka.de
Phone: +49-(0)721-608-4328
Fax: +49-(0)721-608-6116
http://iaks-www.ira.uka.de/iaks-calmet/
    /joachim/joachim.html

Avi Silberschatz
Bell Laboratories, MH 2T-210
700 Mountain Ave.
Murray Hill, NJ 07974
avi@bell-labs.com
Phone: (908)582-4623
FAX: (908)582-5809
http://cm.bell-labs.com/is/who/avi

Ben Shneiderman
Dept. of Computer Science
University of Maryland
College Park, MD 20742
ben@cs.umd.edu
Phone: (301)405-2680
Fax: (301)405-6707
http://www.cs.umd.edu/projects/hcil

Divesh Srivastava
AT&T Research
600 Mountain View
Murray Hill, NJ 07974.
divesh@research.att.com

V.S. Subrahmanian
Department of Computer Science
University of Maryland
College Park, MD 20742
vs@mimsy.umd.edu
Phone: (301)405-2711
Fax: (301)405-6707
http://www.cs.umd.edu/users/vs

Harry Sun
MS 959712
500 Oracle Parkway
Redwood Shores
CA 94065
hasun@us.oracle.com
Phone: (415)506-5195
Fax: (415)506-7228

Frank W. Tompa
Department of Computer Science
University of Waterloo
Waterloo, Ontario N2L 3G1
Canada
fwtompa@uwaterloo.ca
Phone: (519)888-4567
Fax: (519)885-1208
http://daisy.uwaterloo.ca/~fwtompa/

Rodney Topor
School of Computing and
    Information Technology
Griffith University
Nathan Queensland 4111 Australia
rwt@cit.gu.edu.au
Phone: +61-7-3875-5042
Fax: +61-7-3875-5051
http://www.cit.gu.edu.au/~rwt/

Howard Trickey
Bell Laboratories
700 Mountain Ave.
Murray Hill, NJ 07094
trickey@bell-labs.com
Phone: (908)582-6831
http://cm.bell-labs.com/cs/who/howard

Jeffrey D. Ullman
Computer Science Department
Stanford University
Stanford, CA 94305
ullman@cs.stanford.edu
Phone: (650)725-4802
Fax: (650)725-2588

Laurent Vieille
Bull
Rue Jean-Jaures
F 78340 Les Clayes-sous-bois
France
L.Vieille@frcl.bull.fr
Phone: +33-1-30 80 69 27
Fax: +33-1-30 80 69 52

Jennifer Widom
Dept. of Computer Science
Stanford University
Stanford, CA 94305
widom@cs.stanford.edu
Phone: (415)723-7690
Fax: (415)725-2588
http://www-db.stanford.edu/~widom

Christopher Williamson
610 Parthenon Court
Lafayette, CO 80026-8805
chrisw@dq.com
Phone: (303)665-0615
Fax: (303)665-0614
http://www.dq.com

Gang Zhou
University of Colorado at Boulder
Department of Computer Science
Campus Box 430
Boulder, CO 80309-0430
gzhou@cs.colorado.edu
Phone: (303)492-5964
Fax: (303) 492-2844
http://www.cs.colorado.edu/~gzhou/Home.html

Yue Zhuge
Stanford University
P.O. Box 8823
Stanford, CA 94305-9040
zhuge@cs.stanford.edu
Phone: (415)723-6805
Fax: (415)725-2588
http://www-db.stanford.edu/~zhuge/

Index